Giorgio Baruchello, Ársæll Már Arnarsson
Humour and Cruelty, Vol. 2

De Gruyter Studies in Philosophy of Humor

Edited by
Lydia Amir

Editorial Advisory Board
Noël Carroll, CUNY, New York, NY, USA; Simon Critchley, The New School, New York, NY, USA; Daniel Dennett, Tufts University, Medford, MA, USA; Stephen Halliwell, St. Andrews University, St. Andrews, UK; Kathleen Higgins, University of Texas, Austin, TX, USA; John Lippitt, University of Notre Dame, Sydney, NSW, Australia; John Morreall, The College of William and Mary, Williamsburg, VA, USA; Robert C. Roberts, Baylor University, Waco, TX, USA; Quentin Skinner, Queen Mary University of London, UK.

Volume 2

Giorgio Baruchello, Ársæll Már Arnarsson

Humour and Cruelty

Volume 2: Dangerous Liaisons

DE GRUYTER

ISBN 978-3-11-221399-5
e-ISBN (PDF) 978-3-11-075984-6
e-ISBN (EPUB) 978-3-11-076000-2
ISSN 2699-3481

Library of Congress Control Number: 2023937749

Bibliographic information published by the Deutsche Nationalbibliothek
The Deutsche Nationalbibliothek lists this publication in the Deutsche Nationalbibliografie;
detailed bibliographic data are available on the internet at http://dnb.dnb.de.

© 2025 Walter de Gruyter GmbH, Berlin/Boston
This volume is text- and page-identical with the hardback published in 2023.
Printing and binding: CPI books GmbH, Leck

www.degruyter.com

To our ancestors, whose unrecorded sufferings are unforgotten

Acknowledgments

This is our second volume devoted to the study of the concepts of 'humour' and 'cruelty', and we have already committed to writing a third. Inevitably, we have had ample opportunity to brood over the notion that the two of us, as authors, have set ourselves up for a very cruel joke. Perhaps no one will be remotely interested in this colossal undertaking which has taken years of our lives and a decent portion of our already-fragile sanity. Imagine two expectant middle-aged academics pouring over a text for months on end, hoping that their book will make an impact, only to have it collect dust in some library, or worse, inside a warehouse. Is it all for nothing? Just some frantic wriggling of two occasionally sentient hominids soon to be dead and forgotten? A cruel joke, indeed.

Cruel humour makes light of both our suffering and meaning in life. Given that the former is inescapable and the latter elusive, humour may serve as an important coping strategy in helping us navigate the adversity as well as the absurdity inherent in the human condition. But then submitting meekly to suffering or giving up on existential meaning is by no means an obvious and flawless recipe for a good life. Thus, we have come to the conclusion that hope and faith are, as it happens, the only credible ways forward. Promisingly, in this respect, many valuable souls have already demonstrated their faith in our project. Therefore, let us make proper use of these brief acknowledgments and display in print our most sincere gratitude and appreciation.

Lydia Amir should be recognised as the muse of our three volumes. She has shown exceptional generosity and fortitude throughout the sometimes-bumpy writing process. We are also deeply indebted to Christoph Schirmer, a philosopher himself and the Senior Acquisitions Editor for Philosophy at De Gruyter's. Not only has he been extremely patient and exemplarily professional, but he also made our endeavour an even crueller joke by transforming the original project from a single monograph into three distinct volumes. In addition, we want to extend our thanks to Ray Snider, who so ably assisted us with the proofreading and editing of the tome. We must also mention Ken Dorter, Professor Emeritus at the University of Guelph in Canada, who gave us much valuable feedback, especially with regard to the feminist and ethical studies conducted by the late Jean Harvey.

Very special thanks go to the noted French cartoonist Thibaut Soulcié, who provided us with an English-language version of a clever creation of his. As the reader will hopefully be able to gather at a later point in this book, his depiction of a bittersweet clown confronted with a cruelly impossible humorous task is the iconic rendition of several important themes running throughout this volume. Lastly, we must express our gratitude in the most emphatic manner to our spouses and families who put up with the inexorable exhaustion, tension, and disruption that our prolonged and painstaking scholarly venture brought into our lives. They were instrumental in keeping us and our project going—through their love, encouragement, selective indifference, tolerance, and … humour.

Iceland, January 2023   Giorgio Baruchello and Ársæll Már Arnarsson

Contents

Acknowledgments —— IX

Preliminary Remarks —— 1

1 A Tale of Two Concepts —— 37
1.1 Humour —— 37
1.2 Cruelty —— 89
1.3 Family Resemblances —— 148

2 Humorous Cruelty —— 157
2.1 A Fistful of Examples —— 161
2.2 Commonplace Humour —— 168
2.3 True Humour —— 237
2.4 Hermeneutics —— 241
2.5 Performances —— 248

3 Cruel Humour —— 301
3.1 The Elusiveness of Cruel Humour —— 301
3.2 More Views on Cruel Humour —— 312
3.3 Cruel Humour and the Self —— 328
3.4 Humorous Oppression —— 341
3.5 Humour's Cruelty —— 372

4 Dangerous Liaisons —— 374
4.1 A Doubt —— 374
4.2 A Dance —— 378
4.3 A Tetralogy —— 382
4.4 A Taxonomy —— 391
4.5 A Theory —— 397
4.6 A Dictum —— 404
4.7 A Dilemma —— 407
4.8 A Debasement —— 411
4.9 A Dichotomy —— 424

Bibliography —— 433

Index —— 481

Preliminary Remarks

> So the debate is unresolved, as it really is, for these questions are fiercely complicated. 'Moses' and 'Aron' are both right. And any serious argument about culture—which has to be, finally, an argument about truth—must honor that complexity.
> —Susan Sontag[1]

Humour is a universal feature of human communication.[2] Cruelty, for its part, is a universal characteristic of human societies.[3] At first sight, the two might be thought to belong at the opposite ends of the axiological spectrum. Humour being benign and cruelty evil; one loved and the other feared. A closer examination will reveal, instead, that the two are intimately related. In this volume, we will argue that humour is habitually, if not always and inherently, cruel. And, perhaps more depressing, we will also encounter and corroborate the perplexing notion that, for a joke or a jest to be effectively seen as funny, it usually requires a dash or two of cruelty.

Careful reflection on the concepts of 'humour' and 'cruelty', in other words, shall lead us to the unsettling yet reasonable questioning of a good few cherished intuitions about their alleged value, as well as about their mutual relationship, which their elaborate semantic and hermeneutical vicissitudes make even more daunting to approach. This being the case philosophically as much as psychologi-

---

1 Boyers, Bernstein, and Sontag (2015–2016), 262. The famous US journalist, feminist, and essayist Susan Sontag was referring here to Arnold Schönberg's unfinished 1932 opera *Moses und Aron*, in which the two Biblical patriarchs, who are supposedly cooperating in bringing God's Word to the Israelites, keep interpreting the same ideas and experiences in ever-divergent yet equally persuasive ways. Sontag's acceptance of their alternative, parallel viewpoints is a suitable vehicle wherein to express concisely our own embrace of the linguistic polysemy of both "humour" and "cruelty". In addition, the strange plight of the two Biblical heroes is an inspired representation of the challenges inherent to the co-authoring process, insofar as we ourselves were *not* always in mutual agreement while writing the present book, i.e., a large tome that further reflects the opera's duality in our methodological reliance on the main text *and* a large body of *footnotes* which *are not a secondary component, but an important integration of the main text.*
2 See, e.g., Ruch *et al.* (2019) and Cowan *et al.* (2016), 97.
3 We are not implying that "cruelty" proper cannot be a feature of human communication. See, e.g., "the public display of violence and the use of the mutilated, abject body as a means of communication" in Latin America at large and in Mexico in particular, where the attendant "*narconovela*" has been blossoming as a novel literary genre since the 1990s, mixing "cruelty and humour" (Adriaensen 2015, 65 and 76). More on communicative cruelty is discussed in our third volume vis-à-vis the 2015 *Charlie Hebdo* case.

cally.⁴ Clear and crisp definitions of these two terms are not available, in fact, unless artificially postulated and/or expediently presupposed.⁵

(1) Lexical definitions can give us pictures of what people mean, but these pictures are also nothing but time-specific still frames inside an ongoing, flowing, and ever-mutating reality.⁶
(2) Etymological ones can give us a sense of the roots whence the subsequent depictions have evolved, but they reveal as patently the distance separating the roots from the trunk, branches, and leaves.⁷
(3) Working definitions can simplify things most cleverly by removing *ab ovo* all sorts of unwanted complications and counterexamples, but they also compromise the candour and comprehensiveness of a serious scholarly account wishing to be true to history.⁸
(4) Operational ones, and other expert stipulations, perform the same clever trick, and they can even come across as much more impressively technical and argute than 'mere' working definitions.⁹
(5) Appeals to intuition and common sense are often reasonable and rhetorically recommendable, but, across the centuries, that which is taken as obvious and/or worthy of consideration has mutated more than once, while there have persisted discordant views across individuals and communities as to what must count as obvious and/or worthy of consideration.¹⁰
(6) Expert accounts, or Aristotelian 'noble opinions' (Gr. *endoxa*), can be insightful and inspiring, yet they are also most diverse and even contradictory, as

---

4 *Humour and Cruelty 1* (hereafter *H&C1*) offered a more-than-ample account of numerous such vicissitudes. As concerns the two cited disciplines, they are the academic designations with which we are professionally affiliated.
5 As shown in our first volume, such presuppositions and postulates have been far from rare.
6 We tackled in detail the issue of definitional impossibility in the final chapter of our first tome. Here, i.e., in the paragraph above, we are merely offering few broad strokes so as to help our readers to gauge *what* is at issue.
7 As noted in our first book, "humour" as something funny is a recent invention, unlike primeval "cruelty".
8 This sort of extensive expert account being the aim of *H&C1*.
9 Not to mention the bad habit of making all kinds of self-limiting and self-reflexive methodological qualifications in the beginning, only to forget about them along the course of one's own essay or book, and then start passing categorical and/or uncompromising judgements on all sorts of thorny issues calling for considerable nuance and, at times, sceptical *epoché*, not Moses-like assertiveness. Albeit often witty in his polemics, the noted Italian economist and sociologist Vilfredo Pareto (1935) was particularly notorious under this respect (see Mornati 2020).
10 In short, intuition and common sense vary both diachronically and synchronically.

our own expert account amply demonstrates.[11] Aristotle himself adopted such opinions with due attention and only upon cautious deliberation.[12]

"Careful reflection" means as well the conscious consideration and reconsideration of established theories, representative analyses, historical roots and developments, and usual as well as unusual approaches, with all the necessary eagerness and willingness to look at the same 'old things' from a different perspective, especially those that one believes to know *already*. Little is more inimical to thoughtful meditation, whether philosophical or religious, than thinking of possessing adequate knowledge of a thing, so that the activities of going back to it and looking at it afresh become culpable indulgences, undesirable nuisances, futile 'academic' endeavours, unwelcome burdens, or practical impossibilities—for only novelty and forward-looking progress can then be of genuine relevance to the informed, inquiring mind.[13] And yet, quite ironically, should even a person be ever so fortunate as to actually possess already adequate knowledge of a thing, still her understanding of it could be wanting.[14] After all, philosophy is supposed to be the love of wisdom—at the very least from an etymological perspective—, i.e., not of knowledgeability as such.[15]

Let us agree, for the moment, on the basic notion that both 'humour' and 'cruelty' are, if anything, complex cluster concepts, i.e., conceivably without well-defined sets of sufficient and necessary criteria, hence analogously to 'happiness',

---

11 We primarily mean *H&C1*, but the same is true of our other two volumes, i.e., hereafter, *H&C2* and *H&C3*.
12 See Frede (2012). We preach and practice humility and caution, *not* scepticism and relativism. At least, not intentionally. As to what exactly the reader will gain from our book, if anything at all, we cannot predict it, even if we may wish to facilitate it to some extent. *Books, once they are 'out there', lead a life of their own.*
13 See, e.g., the Wittgenstein-inspired essay by Carolyn Black (1983, 373) on how "obvious knowledge", such as "knowledge ... of one's own pains", is still worthy of philosophical reflection.
14 As done in our first tome, we use only the feminine pronouns and possessives when writing about "persons".
15 In keeping with this approach, we made an extensive use of rather 'classic' theories and thinkers, here as well as in the other volumes about our titular *concepts* (hence our use of *single quotation marks*, which also apply to non-literal usages of words). As regards our understanding of "wisdom" proper, we addressed it in our first tome, basing it upon P. Skúlason (2006), to which we must refer the reader (and as the *double quotation marks* indicate, linguistic *terms* as such are so distinguished from concepts, as are also longer quotes from other authors. Whenever no special emphasis on or distinction between concepts and words is needed, then no quotation marks appear).

'liberalism', 'justice', 'art', 'beauty', etc.[16] Part of their constitutive intricacy is that, in our daily life and conversations, we socialised humans think that we can grasp the gist of "humour" and "cruelty" without noticeable difficulty and, moreover, that we can use these two terms meaningfully and frequently, if not comfortably and unreflectively, when expressing ourselves. Nevertheless, under these prosaic circumstances, we still have made no conscious effort to get to their essence—if any such thing exists, of course.[17]

Better thinkers than us have tried, incidentally, and with some degree of success.[18] Yet, they have equally displayed conspicuous margins for patent theoretical disagreement and substantial interpretative plurality.[19] Conscientious and professional, these better thinkers have really sought to get to the bottom of all

---

[16] As regards the cited examples, we are to encounter here and, even more pronouncedly, in our third volume, the many varieties of *liberalism*, which can style right- as well as left-wing stances, whilst also agreeing on a few key values, such as individualism, entrepreneurship, private property, and liberty, i.e., more hazy concepts.

[17] What hides underneath the definitional issues of terms such as "humour" and "cruelty" is the ancient metaphysical question of the Same and the Different or, alternatively, of the One and the Many, i.e., whether and/or how our generalising abstractions (e.g., 'humour' and 'cruelty') apply to many entities and/or events, each of which is actually unique (e.g., no two tokens of *Panthera leo* are factually identical in any and every anatomical respect). As is discussed in Sections 1.1 and 4.3, Chesterton and Deleuze regarded "humour" proper as a veritable 'window' on precisely such a longstanding metaphysical landscape, which has engendered plenty of puzzles, whether amusing or not (e.g., Zeno of Elea's paradoxes). And as was discussed in our first tome, Polanyi's (1962c) *from-to* phenomenology offers a solution to, or at the very least, a thorough elucidation of, the ways in which we accommodate the tension between the Same and the Different (or the One and the Many). Respectively, these two poles can also be understood as the *nomothetic* and *idiographic* dimensions of "knowing" or "knowledge", which entails a fundamental tension between *erklären* (i.e., explaining by subsumption under principles or laws) and *verstehen* (i.e., understanding by case-specific depictions). On these epistemic distinctions, which are standard fare in history and the social sciences, see also Bakker (1995) and Nardin (2001), especially 102–110.

[18] We do not discuss here the many reasonable criteria whereby thinkers can be mutually compared and valued.

[19] 'Humour' and 'cruelty' are, in this respect, like all those contested concepts and expert terms that have long attracted the attention of philosophers, psychologists and other scholars. Instructively, and somewhat amusingly, McKee *et al.* (2020, 1085) reported about an entire "interdisciplinary … Delphi panel of 38 leading pornography researchers from a wide range of disciplines" that failed to agree on a single, shared definition of their own main research topic and concluded, most pragmatically, that practicing "researchers" should "choose" one definition that seems to work vis-à-vis "the needs of the[ir] project, so long as they make it explicit and justify their decision", i.e., "in a self-reflexive way". Our first book, in this connection, constituted an extensive instance of such a self-reflexive conceptual characterisation of 'humour' and 'cruelty', even if it did not produce expedient definitions.

these thorny matters.[20] Despite their efforts and occasional demonstrations of nothing short of speculative genius, with which the authors of the present book are regrettably unlikely to be gifted, there are to date no settled definitions that are embraced universally and unequivocally among Western humanists and/or the world's social and medical scientists.[21] The same, in truth, has also been the case with regard to a great number of central concepts of our culture, its scholarship, and even its socio-political life.[22] Wherever one looks intently, even when pivotal constitutional principles and basic moral notions are concerned, a multitude of possible and plausible conceptions continues to exist and prosper.[23]

---

[20] Thorny matters can be made even thornier by coining and/or employing clever technical terms, e.g., "pluralistic metasemantics" (Gamester 2017, title *et passim*). As far as the present book is concerned, even if its authors are unrepentant members of academia's menagerie, *we tried to limit any major feat of linguistic inventiveness and/or finesse*. We all have suffered enough already. Yet, to make things worse, we are also likely to have failed in our attempt at self-restraint, and on more than one occasion. Enough is not the end of our suffering.

[21] Not even when empirical scientists agree on given sets of working definitions concerning "aggression/cruelty and humour" do matters become straightforward and/or conclusive (Samson *et al.* 2016, 828). For one, "there is no stimulus library that provides humour researchers, or affective scientists in general, with a stimulus set that reliably induces positive, negative and mixed emotional states" (Samson *et al.* 2016, 828). And when a team of keen scientists try to establish such a stimulus set by choosing film clips, the whole operation becomes, admittedly, very artificial, e.g., "includ[ing] a rather small and homogenous sample" of female test subjects "sp[eaking] English as a first language" and "characteris[ing] the film clips" by way of "a very narrow range of emotion ratings", when it is known that "[a] broader range of emotions would better characterise" them (Samson *et al.* 2016, 832). *Humour research*, whether its champions are genuinely aware of it or not, *is littered with cruel ironies*.

[22] A noted 20th-century British 'liberal', William Beveridge (1945), who is regarded as the 'father' of the welfare state, could thus joke pithily about an equally famous 'liberal', Friedrich A. Hayek, who is still well-known for his *laissez-faire* approach: "Hayek's vogue with the opponents of doing anything is notable". For a concise yet comprehensive account of the multi-faceted history of "liberalism", its European and US-based varieties, and their often-neglected commonalities, see Rosenblatt (2018). We thus apply "liberal" to thinkers that most contemporary American readers would describe as "conservative". As to those readers who may find this Eurocentric usage odd or baffling, let us note that it should serve as a reminder of *the fundamental conventionality of language*. Also, while we all cling to established meanings for valid practical reasons, we must realise as well that "[t]erminological conservatism could hamper the cause of conceptual improvement". (Gasparri *et al.* 2022, 14) So, to make a long story short, let us keep an open mind and, at times, allow for some diversity and flexibility. What is more, even if we may disapprove of semantic and/or pragmatic variation and change, they are bound to happen anyhow at some point in the fluid history of language, of which our first tome bears ample and perhaps ponderous witness.

[23] *H&C1* developed an argument defending such plural existence and pluralistic prosperity, which apply to the humanities and social sciences in even broader terms, e.g., all the well-researched, erudite, and intelligent disagreements on how to interpret 'society', 'truth', and 'progress', or

As regards 'humour' and 'cruelty', Western philosophers in general have fared better than contemporary scientists, who have typically tended to shy away from such generally value-laden concepts and, instead, preferred to stick to what is easily observed, straightforwardly operationalised, conveniently formalised, and carefully measured.[24] Earlier scientists like Darwin, Spencer, and Freud, to name three noted cases in point, made extensive efforts to tackle 'humour' and 'cruelty', at least in some recognisable, cognate verbal forms, e.g., "laughter" and "algolagnia".[25] They were, typically, more open-minded in their choice of conceivable study subjects, and somewhat more imaginative in their methodologies and/or approaches than their contemporary successors have generally become. Protocols and precision are somewhat inimical to creativity and speculation.[26] As in all

---

the books by Nietzsche, Dworkin, McMurtry, or Habermas. Entire university faculties and book series would disappear, should studied reality possess only *one* facet and *one* attendant suitable hermeneutical framework. The world would also probably become more boring.

24 *H&C1* bore witness to how a few scientists, psychologists *in primis*, have nonetheless tried their best. In development economics, two contemporary World Bank's experts, Engle and Hallegatte (2018), warned their colleagues that *operationalised measurability is not always possible, required and/or useful*. Searching exclusively and/or too eagerly for it can even lead to neglecting and/or misrepresenting important dimensions of social life, e.g., resilience, which is the focus of their work. Every so often, scientists themselves must reflect on the limitations inherent to the ideal of fully quantified, empirical, explicit knowledge. Following Polanyi (1962c), who had had ample opportunity to consider the matter as a chemist, we could add many more such dimensions: reasonability, plausibility, genius, creativity, wisdom, courage, amiability, and funniness. Nevertheless, in the academic world that we inhabit, the misguided and often myopic search for such a quantifiability and, relatedly, for bureaucratic standardisation, is rife in all areas. Yet, sadly, *the apotheosis of "bean counting" means*, more often than not, *the euthanasia of that which really counts* (S. Skúlason 2022). Caution, then, should be advocated in this regard.

25 All three thinkers were duly referenced, in much more detail than here, in *H&C1*.

26 Without rehashing our first book, let us merely recall how Polanyi (1969a, 42) decried the "[s]cientific obscurantism" of the modern age, i.e., the narrow-minded self-mutilation of post-Galilean Western culture, inasmuch as all that is not adequately measurable or quantifiable is deemed unscientific and therefore irrational, subjective, and ultimately unworthy of serious reflection, e.g., drama, ethics, poetry, psychoanalysis, religion. Those who resist this self-inflicted intellectual cruelty have often been marginalised or even mocked. See, e.g., the scornful reviews of Hillman (1962) penned by Gifford (1962) and Lough (1962), whose assessments reflected the narrowly empiricist and largely behaviourist climate of their day's Anglophone social sciences. An eminent chemist, Polanyi (1962c) knew well that *empirical science can provide definite, measurable knowledge of only few, select aspects of reality*, i.e., those features that Galileo himself had described as "some affections" of the extant "natural substances" to be studied by his new science (as cited in Martinez 1994, 66 note 94). The rest, as Polanyi (1962c and 1969a) gathered, must be approached by means of *other* disciplines that employ different approaches, which may be better suited to the explored aspects. These other disciplines are *additional* forms of investigation that Western culture has produced and provided in its long history, so as to allow for *their* valuable share of human under-human endeavours, something has got to give, if anything viable is to happen at all.[27]

What is more, scientific knowledge reaches its sell-by date quickly.[28] Consequently, it needs vigorous maintenance and revision if it is not to end up, sometimes almost immediately, in the landfill of history.[29] Accordingly, even though Freud wrote both insightfully and systematically about humour and cruelty, the current sidelining of his work from mainstream academic psychology, especially

---

standing and self-understanding. Many modern intellectuals, however, seem to have forgotten about the inherent limits of empirical science, hence reducing the universe to those "affections" that can be treated 'scientifically', hence leaving everything else in the undifferentiated scrapheap of the 'irrational' and/or the 'subjective', and pretending that it has no epistemic relevance whatsoever, or that it does not even exist. See, e.g., Castoriadis (2005, 345), especially essays 3–4 and 10–12, on the wilful blindness of much Western academia to the imaginative, therapeutic and political value of depth psychology: "I define psychoanalysis as a practicopoietical activity... Psychoanalysis, like pedagogy and like politics, is the activity of one autonomy upon another ... and their aim is the creation of these new forms: autonomous persons and an autonomous society".

27 A *cruel irony* is afoot in this stately context. Namely, many good reasons, and especially *primafacie* ones, can foster the prompt and 'proper' closure of the professional mind: methodological concerns, the experts' general consensus at the given time, insufficient data, procedural precautions, the intellectual trends supported by citation numbers, etc. *Once a mind is closed on such laudable grounds, it can be very hard to open it again.* In our first tome, we recalled how Polanyi (1962c, 160) discussed the convoluted processes of "persuasion" required for any eventual "conversion" in the formal and natural sciences. The Aristotelians who contrasted Galileo's new theories were not the fierce dogmatists that Brecht (1939) satirised, but the reputable professionals of their day.

28 Many thick tomes have been written on what constitutes "scientific knowledge" and/or sheer "knowledge" as such. Perhaps it is a philosophical malaise of sorts or a bad intellectual habit. As none less than Carl Gustav Jung (1958b) was recorded quipping: "Only philosophers don't know what knowledge is. Psychologists do".

29 Many *cruel ironies* affect science at large, despite its hard-won and well-deserved status as one of the few socio-cultural tools which truly strive to honestly rely on humankind's rational, observational, and collaborative faculties. The quick supersession of most scientists' painstaking efforts is just *one* of them. Another, to which the US philosopher Richard Rorty (2001) was particularly attuned, is the fact that *science can tell us a lot about means, but very little about ends.* This is true on a large scale, e.g., scientific knowledge can help us split the atom, but it cannot advise whether to use this knowledge to make nuclear reactors or nuclear bombs. The same is true on a small scale too. In the 21st century AD as well as in the 12th century BC, many important decisions in actual persons' daily lives have kept being based upon religion, passion, common sense, ideology, aesthetic preference, intuition, and much else, but certainly *not* upon scientific premises and/or methods, e.g., whom to marry or befriend, whether or not to have children, which social order to fight for, whether to focus on the earthly joys or the otherworldly ones, to which scientific discipline or art to devote oneself wholeheartedly and unselfishly, whether to strive to be a good person or not, and what being 'good' demands. Scientists, too, must face these quandaries.

in the Anglophone world, means that we mostly catch measly glimpses of his Viennese ghost. Still skulking about, it has been left floating around in today's learned papers, essays, and monographs, yet only timidly and episodically.[30]

As we showed in a fulsome way in the first volume (hereafter *H&C1*) of our *trilogy* for De Gruyter's book series on the philosophy of humour (hence *H&C2* and *H&C3*), a hefty number of philosophical writings and scientific studies, including psychosocial and medical ones, are seemingly devoted to "humour" proper and/or "cruelty" as such. Some of them have been able to provide valuable insight into these two phenomena.[31] Here again, however, we regularly lack unequivocal and universal definitions of either term *qua* explicitly and/or expressly spelled-out topics for contemporary research.[32] The evasiveness of these two words causes in fact a multitude of problems for anyone trying to study either concept systematically, or—even harder—simultaneously. Recent social science, in particular, finds "cruelty" more challenging than "humour" itself.[33]

Prima facie, there have been plenty of scholars looking into relevant psychological and/or social aspects of cruelty. Most notably, we can cite those inspired by the atrocities of World War II or other recent conflicts, e.g., the sanguinary civil wars and the alleged "peace-keeping" operations taking place in countries such as former Yugoslavia, Iraq or Sierra Leone.[34] In contemporary science, "cruelty" proper, if and when it is addressed as such, is typically explained by extreme or

---

[30] Albeit commonly acknowledged in modern histories of medicine and psychology, Freud's main concerns and methods no longer enjoy much credit, especially among his empirically-minded descendants in the social sciences. At the same time, it is also true that Freud's chief claims, which caused so much scandal and debate when they were first published, have long become part of Western *common sense* and are no longer recognised as Freud's special contributions, e.g., the centrality of sexuality in our psychological life and development, the potency and presence of unconscious motives, the pressure and painfulness of long-interiorised hence 'invisible' heteronomous diktats, or the very simple fact that psychotherapy can be of help to restore people's wellbeing.
[31] The same warning applies here as in *H&C1*: *reader, beware of our quaint sense of humour, when attempted.* To which we must add: *reader, beware of our crude terms and horrible imagery, for our research must include them.*
[32] If any reader is under the impression that humour is not a serious research topic, then s/he is hereby invited to think of whether or not s/he would be happy to live in a world devoid of any humour whatsoever. As this rather simple thought experiment should lead most readers to conclude, *humour is an important feature of our lived reality*. It can be crucial *vis-à-vis* good workplace relations and lasting marriages. And as highlighted in our volumes, humour's frequent combination with cruelty makes reflecting on the former notion even more important a task.
[33] Once again, a more detailed and painstakingly referenced account of these vicissitudes can be found in *H&C1*.
[34] The long *durée* inherent to intellectual history leads to a different sense of "recent" than in personal life.

unusual "situational" factors, untreated "pathologies" and/or biological "abnormalities", i.e., as though it were triggered by any number of deviations from the proverbial norm, which is assumed *ipso dicto* to be kind and peaceable. "Cruelty" *per se*, apparently, does not command among today's social scientists the same troubled and troubling attention that it has commanded in Western philosophy and the humanities at large.[35]

The adherents to Socrates' and Plato's ancient discipline have repeatedly retrieved "cruelty" proper, or at least traces thereof, in the day-to-day existence of human beings, the hidden crevices and neglected interstices of their very souls, and/or many of their seemingly prosaic circumstances.[36] Ostensibly, it may not take anything eventful for some people to become cruelly resentful. Wars, illnesses, and aberrations might just be the most blatant and obvious forms that a far more mundane and pervasive proclivity of humankind can parade. Not to mention the peculiar case of the zealots and the self-righteous who merely require the perception of the most minute wrongs around themselves as justification for embarking onto brave campaigns of totalitarian ill-doing for the sake of goodness and, perhaps, in total good conscience.[37]

Be that as it may, in one of the numerous *ironies* that the fused study of 'humour' and 'cruelty' has inexorably led us into, it can be said that the two most famous experiments in the history of psychology did tackle the latter titular concept, and demonstrably so, even if both experiments were focussing on different issues.[38]

---

[35] As we remarked repeatedly in *H&C1*, studies characterising phenomena as "cruel" abound, but the in-depth investigation of what "cruelty" consists in is indeed a rare occurrence, especially in the social sciences. Such rare occurrences, of course, were duly highlighted and discussed in *H&C1*, and some of them are rehashed here too. Equally, we neither imply that philosophy is alone, in the liberal arts, in addressing "cruelty" proper. Exemplarily, the Paris-based art historian Iveta Slavkova (2022, par. 2) recalled how the French "abhumanist" avantgarde developed out of "the rawness and cruelty of recent history" and proceeded to accuse "lyrical humanism in art" of being "merely fallacious". Whether fortunate or not, very little philosophy can be 'accused' of being "lyrical".

[36] More on evil deeds arising from good intentions is discussed in Chapter 2 in connection with Philip Hallie's oeuvre. Also, as we discuss in *H&C3* in connection with Jungian psychology, individuals who ignore their own dark side are likely to *project* it onto other people and then persecute them as dangerous, depraved, dirty, etc.

[37] Many such cases were presented in *H&C1*, and a few more are discussed in detail in *H&C3*.

[38] The reader should not be surprised by encountering psychology and the social sciences so often in this book. As we explained in *H&C1*, *multi- and interdisciplinarity are both of great importance to us qua scholars*.

(1) The 1961 Milgram Experiment sought to explain how people, by obeying supposedly legitimate orders, are capable of hurting others in a heinous manner.[39] The experimenters recruited unknowing participants to supposedly study the effects of punishment on learning and memory. Their role was to control the administration of electric shocks to another pseudo-participant, who was an accomplice of the experimenters and received no actual shock. The quasi-shock generator had voltage levels ranging from "Slight Shock" to "Danger: Severe Shock".[40] The scientists were able to convince all of the participants to administer what the latter thought were 300 volts, to which the mock "learner" responded by kicking a wall, and were provided no more answers to the "task".[41] A sizeable majority proceeded to giving the most intense electrocution that the generator could supply, marked "Danger: Severe Shock".[42]

(2) The 1971 Stanford Prison Experiment (hereafter SPE) involved young male volunteers, who were randomly allotted the role of prisoner or guard in a pretend prison. Once again, obedience was the main declared theme of the experiment which, however, is remembered today for its unquestionable display of people's partiality for cruelty.[43] In a matter of days, in fact, the guards began repressing the prisoners. The former group's cruelty quickly escalated until, after only six days, the study was aborted for safety reasons.[44]

In this book's first chapter, we are to review some of the many conceptions of 'humour' and 'cruelty' that can be found in Western thought, focussing on few select

---

39 See Milgram (1963).
40 Milgram (1963), 372.
41 Milgram (1963), 375.
42 Milgram (1963), 375.
43 SPE has been so in/famous as to inspire movies, e.g., *Das Experiment* (2001) and its 2010 US remake. Please note that films, TV series, songs, operas *et similia* are *not* listed in the closing bibliography.
44 See Haslam *et al.* (2019), 809–812. Ironically, an often-underrated implication of these notorious experiments is the revelation of how generally effective are the constricting yet civilising structures at work in our societies, insofar as cruel behaviours as those so promptly displayed by the participants are *not* an ordinary feature of our lives, i.e., when these lives are led under the peaceful and peace-keeping conditions known to the inhabitants of most nations (e.g., the rule of law). Perhaps, *the civilising structures' associated neuroses and psychoses may be a cruel price worth paying*—until it becomes too high. Whether, when, how, and for whom this economy of cruelty goes into the red are just some of the many paradoxical dilemmas afflicting human existence, both individually and collectively (see our account of Hallie 1969 in this book and in *H&C1*). More on civilising neuroses and their civil management is said in *H&C3*.

'classics' of the established canons in the humanities and social sciences.[45] In particular, in our selection of representative sources from the history of our culture, we show how remarkably diverse and, at times, how contradictory these conceptions have been.[46] Rather than penning some tentative, convenient definition of the titular terms, which have exhibited so much semantic variability in their history, we content ourselves with two lists of their recurrent connotations.[47] Throughout this initial exercise, moreover, we illustrate implicitly how these hermeneutical divergencies, however puzzling or even frustrating they may be, are the price to be paid for our languages to function, produce insights and information, and be pragmatically suitable to their users, who are ultimately and ineludibly responsible for their contingent interpretations and applications.[48]

On the basis of Chapter 1's intentionally concise and inevitably selective survey, as well as of the attendant characterisations of the two titular concepts, we address in Chapter 2 the many forms of cruelty that can elicit humorous responses or routine laughter *in primis*. As we do so, we outline and discuss some significant contemporary approaches to "humour" proper in Western philosophy and thereby tackle the thorny notion according to which the familiar phenomenon of humour is but a token of just such an unkind species of cruelty, even in the former's most

---

[45] We acknowledge the thorny historico-political issues regarding canonicality, but we cannot address them here.

[46] As done much more extensively in *H&C1*, *we remain keen on the study of history*, both of psychology as such and more in general. The past is a treasure trove of knowledge and insight, as well as of errors and horrors. While a community's past history cannot be undone, at least it can be used to gain a better grasp of the present and, consequently, prepare for the future. Moreover, knowing the past means also realising why certain institutional arrangements were established, e.g., post-1929 State regulation of banks and high finance, or the constitutional protection of free speech. Hence, also why dismantling those arrangements may restart old troubles, e.g., increased likelihood of bankruptcies and rampant speculation, or the return of censorship (both systemic cruelties are discussed in *H&C3*). As a consequence, it is disconcerting for us to keep witnessing the slow demise of historical education in Western academia as allegedly "stuffy", "unimportant", or "useless", especially in the social sciences (e.g., the shelving of economic history and history of psychology in undergraduate programmes). Far too many scholars seem to have forgotten one of Martin Luther King Jr.'s most famous pearls of wisdom: "We are not makers of history; we are made by history" (as cited in Dunner 2018, par. 7).

[47] As we explain later, these characterisations are "family resemblances" *à la* Wittgenstein (1953, par. 67).

[48] A full-fledged, explicit argument in favour of polysemy was developed in the concluding chapter of *H&C1*. Let us note here that, in order for responsible interpretations and applications to occur, persons must, *inter alia:* enjoy sufficient mental and physical health; be adequately socialised; be capable of reflection; and be sufficiently free from dire need, crushing despair and/or stifling oppression—whether the last one is exercised by violent means or subtler ones, e.g., media bamboozlement and omni-pervasive social opinion, which we tackle in *H&C3*.

sophisticated and socially admired manifestations. By this we mean the so-called "true humour" that a handful of Western thinkers distinguished from commonplace humour and ascribed to gifted, profound, sublime, and/or especially humane souls who are believed to live in our midst.[49] The works of Joseph Addison, Arthur Schopenhauer, Luigi Pirandello, and Stephen Leacock are duly recalled, so as to outline and explore this "true humour".[50]

Chapter 2, in this way, constitutes the *theoretical* heart of the present project. In it, the reader can retrieve a set of arguments buttressing the thesis asserting that *humour entails cruelty*. All of this, we should add, notwithstanding the enormous diversity of philosophical and socio-scientific conceptions of these two titular notions that Chapter 1 briefly surveys and that *H&C1*, far more thoroughly, established *qua* comprehensive exercise in *Begriffsgeschichte*.[51]

In Chapter 3, we review some of the countless ways in which commonplace humour has been utilised as a cruel means, whether for cruel ends or not.[52] Con-

---

[49] Naturally, a clearer explanation of the difference between commonplace and 'true' humour will emerge here. Mentions of and brief musings on "true" or "real humo(u)r" abound, although *only few thinkers have ever pursued this subject in earnest.* (Ironically, it may be a sign that it is not a topic worth pursuing.) It should also be highlighted that the adjective "true" (or "real") has regularly been used in this context as a *commendatory* term with which 'deeper' epistemic and ontological properties are associated, in line with both the overt and the tacit objectivist metaphysics of most Western culture (see Rorty 1984 and 2001). *That which we like very much, in a philosophically significant twist of irony, becomes that which is and/or ought to be.* Whether then "true" is weakened or strengthened *qua* useful term because of its "ambiguity" and "plurality", for it can be applied to as blatantly diverse items as "trees, cruelty, and humour", it is a matter of philosophical debate that we cannot address here and that, to a significant extent, our in-depth discussion of Polanyi's (1962c) phenomenology-*cum*-epistemology in *H&C1* can help scholars to resolve (Sainsbury as cited in Dell'Utri 2016, 13).

[50] Carlyle (1835), K. Weber (1840), Cipolla (1988) and Critchley (2002a and b) should also be recalled as supporters of the notion of *true humour*, which they believed to be either notedly *compassionate* (Carlyle, K. Weber and Cipolla) or *progressive* (Critchley). Whilst detailing no "true humour" as such, Kierkegaard (2009) and Chesterton (1929–1973, par. 2) similarly stressed the *humility* of 'mere' "humour". Also, the introductory remarks in Cipolla (1988) are his sole direct theoretical reflections on "humour" proper—and they remind us of the fact that we must warn our readers that, *when needed, we cite and/or translate sources that were not available to us in English*. They are a miniscule fraction among the hundreds of cited titles in our book, which makes extensive use of sources available electronically, hence in keeping with Umberto Eco's pioneering embrace of digital archives and internet-based cultural dissemination. Indeed, and ironically, his former student Giovanna Cosenza (2016, par. 3) called the Mediaevalist Eco a "techno-enthusiast".

[51] This German term usually translates as "conceptual history", but "history of ideas" could do as well. These too are family-resemblance terms, probably.

[52] Whether the dis/value of the end determines inexorably the dis/value of the means is a problem we do not tackle.

sequently, we address studies about instances of humorous conduct that are palpably indifferent to the pain that they cause, take delight in causing such a pain, and/or display a penchant for morbid, horrid, gory, tragic, melancholic, and/or sorrowful topics. Put differently, we tackle studies dealing with instances of commonplace humour that have variously been called "aggressive", "oppressive", "violent", "offensive", "denigrating", "disparaging", "derisive", "sick", "black", etc. Or, more to the point, "cruel".[53] Psychology and the social sciences are our chief sources of information and insight in this regard, which simply ignores any aesthetic and/or ethical idea (or ideal) of a 'truer' and/or more 'real' type of "humour" proper.

This axiological or hierarchical indifference is no blameworthy fault staining someone's reputation or the cause of any particular surprise, at least as far as the present authors are concerned. Being constitutively descriptive rather than normative, psychology and the social sciences focus primarily on that which can be observed, recorded, analysed, and quantified, not on the sort of ends that we, thinking human beings, should, or even ought to, pursue in our existence, whether individual or collective.[54] Scientists are supposed to tell us mostly what happens, happened, or may happen in and around human life, not how to lead it.[55] Discern-

---

[53] To some extent, *we also talk from experience*. The authors of this book, in the course of their lives, have each been the object of ridicule on many occasions, some of which persistently, and for a great variety of alleged faults and/or negative characteristics such as birthplace (e.g., the Genoese are reputed to be avaricious), nationality (e.g., Icelanders are presumed to be heavy drinkers), residence status ("foreigner"), putative ancestry ("Jew"), physique (e.g., "fatso"), impaired vision ("four eyes"), political leanings ("commie"), religious beliefs ("Papist carpet-muncher", in a rhetorically creative case) or, during a recent conversation, being a "middle-class, middle-aged, white man". We suspect that many of our readers are familiar with this sort of mockery, whether as targets, initiators, participants, or witnesses. Episodic uses of it can be amusing, albeit hurtful, and *vice versa*. Regular, insistent uses, as we discuss in Chapter 2 in connection with Harvey (1999), can also establish and/or reinforce oppressive social relations and be disguised as, say, progressive challenges to the status quo, conservative defences of the very same or, quite often, 'mere' humour, i.e., something inherently innocent and light-hearted (see Section 3.3.4 in this book). Without forgetting, of course, the innumerable times when the received ridicule was deserved.

[54] We wrote "primarily" because a host of *normative elements are* indeed *at play*; subsidiarily *or secondarily*, in the sciences too, whether explicitly or tacitly, e.g., professional integrity, personal ideals, technological aspirations, practical applicability, future profitability, political acceptability, bioethical permissibility, public visibility, careerism, pride, petty vindictiveness, and melioristic aims (see, e.g., Polanyi 1962c, especially chap. 10 on the centrality of personal "commitment" in the formal and natural sciences). Scientists are, after all, human beings. As to "we humans", it is a common *hyperbole* suggesting broad generality or near-universality that we use in our books, like "we all" or "all of us". Nearly always, however, there exist exceptions, outliers and extraordinary cases.

[55] Again, we qualified our statement by writing "mostly". Medical science, pharmacology, much sociology, economics, therapy-aimed psychology, and climate science are clearly and frequently

ing yet wide-ranging, and consistent with the inductive logic inherent to standard socio-scientific inquiry, the wealth of expert references thus accrued in Chapter 3 aims, in any case, at corroborating empirically the notion whereby humour and cruelty can be said to be each other's best friend.[56]

Methodologically, Chapter 3's close attention to a substantial number of empirical studies aims *ipso facto* at complementing, or even countering a little, an age-old characteristic of the Western humanities, philosophy in particular.[57] We are referring to the trained tendency to rely upon established authority alone, like the well-meaning 17th-century Aristotelians who opposed Galileo—albeit not nearly so dramatically, in our case.[58] Similarly, Chapter 3's chosen focus aims also at circumventing the powerful yet oft-unseen axiomatic-deductive propensity affecting much Western thought and social science since at least Descartes' day and age—orthodox economics *in primis*.[59]

---

committed to giving precise and persuasive advice to individuals, groups, societies, governments, corporate boards, and even humankind at large. Still, it is chiefly in the humanities that we find intellectuals devoted to instructing us on *how to live*, which is the telling title of Sarah Bakewell's (2010) biography of Michel de Montaigne, i.e., one of the greatest and earliest philosophers of "cruelty" proper (see Section 1.2.3 and, of course, *H&C1*).

56 By devoting Chapter 2 to philosophical sources and Chapter 3 to socio-scientific ones, we aim at offering a sufficiently comprehensive account of recurrent themes and lines of study in the history of Western scholarship.

57 According to common sense, not to mention chaos theory, *a small difference at one level can make a big one at another*, e.g., the thin veneer of neurosis- and psychosis-inducing emotional self-restraint making a person 'civil' and a society 'civilised', or the slight unscrewing of these structures of psychic repression so as to allow for some healthy relief (we discuss this issue in detail in *H&C3*). The scientifically-minded reader, on his/her part, may wish to consider the minor yet non-trivial genetic differences between chimps and humans (see, e.g., Glazko et al 2005).

58 See, e.g., Turvey (2021, 29) rejecting the notion that visual comedy is interpretable by way of rhetorical categories.

59 The potentially funny pseudo-anthropology and general outlandishness of standard economics are tackled further in *H&C3*, e.g., presumed rationality, unlimited growth, tendency to equilibrium, fair competition, identity of 'needs' and 'wants', and professional forecasting of future events. For the moment, let us just recall how the noted California-based economists Smith and Wilson (2019, xiii) stated that, when trying to understand moral behaviour like the Scottish philosopher Adam Smith did in the 18th century, their 21st-century orthodox "economic education and modelling tradition handicapped [them] from the start". Their discipline, in essence, had to be *unlearnt* for them to become capable of beginning to grasp how real people actually behave (see also Silvestri and Walraevens 2022). Despite its enormous political clout and continuous claims of pivotal importance with respect to real-world affairs, standard economics is largely aimless, if not utterly detrimental (see, e.g., Veblen 1899, Pareto 1935, Keen 2001, Galbraith 2004, Castoriadis 2005, Keynes 2008 and Schlefer 2012). This dismal truth has been known since the 19th century, but orthodox economists' role as 'scientific' legitimisers of the status quo and, above all, of the powers-that-are, makes their academic and social standing both personally desirable and institutionally unassailable (see, e.g.,

We mean by this the well-trodden, top-down approach whereby a set of pristine definitions are provided *ab initio*, whence pristine conclusions are reached by force of crystal-clear rational reflection, but without having to peer intently at all, or at any, of the extant experiential data.[60] As the 20th-century Italian economist and philosopher Piero Mini quipped, both humorously and cruelly, on this frequently taken-for-granted methodological point:

> Following the Cartesian method, economics was able to proceed through the social universe with lightning speed. But it also absorbed the weaknesses and contradictions of Cartesianism, the most important of which was its aspiration to explain the whole of reality without even looking at it. Paradoxically, Descartes' rationalism became the irrationalism of "cast my eyes away that I may see better".[61]

Häring and Douglas 2012). In this way, their standing is akin to that of Christian clergymen in the Middle Ages (see Tolstoy 1900, chap. 12, par. 2). Given though this disciplinary and theoretical state of affairs' nefarious consequences for the world's ecosystems and human wellbeing at large, we must point it out as a striking instance of *cruel irony* (see also McMurtry 1998, 1999, 2002, 2011 and 2013b; Earle, Moran, and Ward-Perkins 2016; and Orrell 2017).

60 These axioms can come in very different guises and, at times, in disguises. Some are patently abstract and akin to geometrical postulates or to physics' fundamental definitions, e.g., the chief propositions in Spinoza (1985) and Wittgenstein (1989). Others are not so formalistic but are nearly as abstract, e.g., Descartes' "*dieu trompeur*" and "evil genius" (Faye 2001, 61), the select starting assumptions of all those economists affected by the so-called "Ricardian vice" (Kurz 2008, 241), or John Rawls' 20th-century version of social-contract theory based upon the thought experiment of the "original position" (D'Agostino 2008, par. 1). Many more have operated by identifying, intensifying, universalising, and/or hypostasising a seemingly observable given that, however, is never truly tested against and/or keenly qualified by means of thorough empirical investigation. Looking too intently at experiential and/or socio-historical reality, in fact, would make the intellectual picture considerably muddier and/or even contradict the basic axioms themselves, which are then revealed to be, *au fond*, veritable dogmas of pseudo-biology, pseudo-psychology, pseudo-history, pseudo-anthropology, pseudo-ethnography, etc. Noted examples include: certain people's rudimental aptitudes for commerce (e.g., A. Smith 1904, book I, chap. 2, par. 1); lupine aggressiveness (e.g., Hobbes' n.d.a. [1651]); sheepish fearfulness and malleability (e.g., Montesquieu 2001, book 1; Rousseau 1997, parts 1 and 2); selfishness (e.g., Sade 2010); sexual lust leading to procreation (e.g., Malthus and, later, scores of Darwinians in all human and social sciences; see, e.g., Žmolek 2019); desire for material acquisitions (e.g., J.S. Mill and Marshall, as discussed in Fairfield 2000 and Mini 1974) or for experiencing pleasure and avoiding pain (e.g., Bentham and J. Mill, as discussed in Fairfield 2000); and the standard yet misleading construct of *homo economicus* (see any Western undergraduate textbook in economics).

61 Mini (1974), 59. We discuss in further detail the grave limits of standard economic thinking in *H&C3*. For now, let us merely highlight how paradoxicality has often been predicated of "humour" as well as of "cruelty" proper, and that Mini (1974) retrieved this Cartesian penchant in as diverse thinkers as Hobbes, Montesquieu, Adam Smith, Ricardo, Malthus, Marshall, and Schumpeter, to whom he opposed a parallel epistemological tradition comprising Vico, Hegel, Marx, Schopenhauer, Kierkegaard, Nietzsche, and Keynes (though not the so-called "Keynesians").

Preferring a bottom-up approach, and yet operating within the standard confines of a philosophical study, we decided to follow a different path.[62]

(1) To produce no initial, expedient, working definition of either "humour" or "cruelty" whence the rest of our considerations about these terms and associated phenomena would then unfold logically, cogently and/or persuasively.[63]

(2) To include and discuss in Chapters 1 and 2 a great many established authorities—in the plural—even if mutually discordant and/or plainly inconsistent with each other.

(3) To tackle, in Chapter 3, said ample spectrum of socio-scientific studies, which also bring forth discordant and inconsistent conceptions of 'humour' and 'cruelty', inasmuch as the common-sense origin and nature of these two concepts do often result too shifty or too intractable for the protocol-bound experts.

If Chapter 2 is the theoretical heart of the project, then Chapter 3 is its *empirical* counterpart, at least insofar as it provides an up-to-date account of the socio-scientific studies of cruel humour, which exemplifies the intimate relationship between the two titular concepts and corroborates the claim that they cannot be truly separated *in toto*.[64] (And yes, if you wonder, this book has got *two* hearts, like the BBC's Tardis-equipped galivanting Doctor.)

In Chapter 4, we offer a set of concluding reflections on the *dangerous liaisons* that have been unearthed in our own research, stressing further the central idea that *a modicum of cruelty is inescapable whenever engaging in effective humorous conduct*, at least interpersonally.[65] Schematically, as the combined resources of the preceding three chapters are intended to exemplify and substantiate, Chapter 4 is

---

[62] We remark on "the standard confines of a philosophical study" because our approach remains somewhat abstract, as typical of *Begriffsgeschichte*, hence devoid of the idiographic precision characterising historical biographies and autobiographies, or the artful recreations of lived reality in which novelists and dramatists specialise and, at times, excel. On occasion, the Cartesian circularity mocked by Mini (1974) can be found in empirical scientific studies too, comically compressed into the experimental confirmation of the proverbial "bleeding obvious".

[63] Despite all previous failures, the desire to define "humour" proper is alive and kicking, as acknowledged, e. g., by Lazebna *et al.* (2022), who also offered therein an extremely concise overview of the main theories of humour circulating in today's academia and of the vast plethora of scholarly approaches to its linguistic aspects. Curiously, while its authors are Ukrainian and the publishing journal Brazilian, the main empirical tokens of humour discussed in the article are German jokes. There goes into the rubbish bin the trite stereotype of humourless Teutons.

[64] *H&C3* discusses how humour and cruelty may mutually conflict, yet without denying the main thesis of this book. In short, *for humour to be able to fight cruelty, the former must contain some of the latter.*

[65] Intrapersonal cruelties *via* humour, e. g., self-mockery, are also duly addressed in this book.

going to explore some more, elucidate further, express more vividly, and elaborate upon, the seven critical points listed below (though not each and every one of them to the same extent).[66]

(1) Humour can be intentionally cruel
(1a) in either an open or
(1b) a variously veiled manner, i.e., someone can and will use it in order to belittle, humiliate, exclude, berate, etc.[67]
(1c) an/other/s, or
(1d) even him-/herself, and/or
(1e) the group with which s/he identifies or
(1f) is identified by (a) context-relevant other/s.
(2) Humour can be somehow unintentionally cruel, i.e., it can attain the same harmful outcomes, merely by the fact that someone feels belittled, humiliated, excluded, berated, etc.[68]
(3) This type of unintended consequences can happen not only, or not even especially, because of
(3a) the conceptual-linguistic contents of a jest or joke, but also and/or simply because
(3b) their formulation may be somewhat too clever, too original, too immediate, based on inside knowledge, requiring particular linguistic competences, and so forth. Someone, to put it in another way, will not be 'in' the joke or fail to 'get' it, and therefore experience pain of some kind as a result, inasmuch as
(3c) s/he may realise that s/he is not so competent as the clever initiator/s and/or
(3d) some, many or, perhaps, most other participants in the social game at issue, or
(3e) fear as much, or
(3f) be confirmed in
(3fα) one,
(3fβ) some, or

---

[66] Such a schema conveniently underplays the semantic knots explored in *H&C1*. The reader must then take this schema with a pinch of salt, and avoid *reducing H&C2* to any exhaustive and exclusive argumentative 'skeleton' such as the present one, which is only meant to help the reader to grasp the main contours of our study.

[67] Determining the openness of this act, whether categorically or relatively, is fraught with difficulties.

[68] Writing "somehow" points in the direction of the difficulties related to determining this *un*intentionality.

(3fγ)   all of his/her additional attendant fears (i.e., doubts, anxieties, insecurities, etc.),
(3g)   which may centre on
(3gα)   him-/herself alone or
(3gβ)   a person and/or group thereof about whom s/he cares—whether
(3hα)   in earnest or
(3hβ)   not.[69]
(4)   The initiator/s of the joke or jest may even be aware of the possibility of producing some such unintended consequences and go ahead with the joke or jest anyhow, whether
(4a)   in good conscience (for, say, it is all just 'a bit of fun', after all) or
(4b)   not (for, say, making an/other/s merry is more important anyway, i.e., a lesser evil than abandoning the plan and possibility of being jovial).[70]
(5)   By producing some such harmful results, whether
(5a)   minor (e.g., mild embarrassment) or
(5b)   major (e.g., an identity crisis), and whether
(5c)   bald-faced or
(5d)   elusive,
(5e)   humour can thus contribute as well to
(5eα)   establishing,
(5eβ)   reinforcing, and/or
(5eγ)   perpetuating cruel socio-cultural institutions discriminating against, or otherwise originating hurt to, certain groups and/or individuals.[71]
(6)   Further cruelty can then ensue if any such groups and/or individuals respond to the perceived and/or personally suffered pain by cruel means, e.g., by way of privately-expressed dissent, vocal public condemnation, life-disabling social ostracism, daunting legal prosecution, open threats of reprisal, violent physical assault, outright murder, etc.[72]
(7)   A deeper and dejectedly ironic cruelty arises from this dismal landscape of often-amiable and amusing quotidian interactions, i.e., the non-negligible

---

[69] An individual may care more about being perceived by others as caring about some person/s and/or group/s than truly caring about any of them. To be seen as 'good' may matter more to him/her than being so.
[70] As we discuss in this book, measuring how 'full' and/or 'good' a conscience is might lie beyond anyone's skill.
[71] As we also remark upon later, determining whether any and/or minor/major harm ensues is not easy at all.
[72] The use of cruelty against humour is one of the crucial themes of *H&C3*.

crucible of each person's responsible choice about whether she ought to opt for humorous conduct or not. In other words,

(7a) whether or not to risk causing cruelty by engaging in jests or jokes, or

(7b) whether or not staying put within a sombre, ethically considered, yet humourless or less humorous social game, which is then deprived of a well-known instrument for consolation and resilience against prolonged existential ennui, continued psychic repression, recurrent personal frustration, persistent physical discomfort, or even grinding political oppression, i.e., humour.[73]

Whichever option one may prefer, the inherently delicate and potentially unnerving exercise of *personal* responsibility will inexorably be called for under specific and unique sets of lived circumstances, if the person at issue genuinely reflects on her actions.[74] In broader and more abstract terms, such a potentially cruel yet humorous conduct can then be thought of as being moral and/or advisable if and only if it is comprehensively life-enabling and, basically, if it works *qua* lesser evil in concrete socio-cultural, existential, and, *au fond*, personal settings.[75]

---

[73] The use of humour against cruelty is one of the crucial themes of *H&C3*.

[74] As regards the person's ultimate role and irreducible centrality in all evaluations, see Bengsson (2006), Polanyi (1962c) and Walsh (2020). Given how much use is made of Polanyi (1962c) in our research, it should be patent that we do not understand said "person" as meaning the sole abstract personhood that is to be found in, say, civil codes or commercial contracts (see *H&C1*). Rather, we grasp it as a term resting upon a much "thicker" and concrete set of interrelated notions, including "forms of recognition such as esteem, love, or solidarity", and denoting each and every human individual whom we may encounter in real life (Laitinen 2017, 172). To use a trendy concept in today's expert literature, *each person is the active ontological site of 'intersectionality'*. Each person is the nexus where the socio-cultural forces studied by so many humanists and social scientists converge, enmesh, fight against one another, and whence all of these forces pour out into the world as effectual agency. As to who exactly these persons are, it is clear that we are thinking of human beings. We do not address the issue of whether and how this 'thicker' personhood can apply to non-human creatures, e.g., dolphins and gorillas (see, e.g., DeGrazia 1997).

[75] As was the case with *H&C1*, so does *life-value onto-axiology* (LVOA) lie in the background of this book too as our implicit theory of value and, in truth, of our overall research (on LVOA, see Baruchello 2018a and b). Very succinctly, *all that which is compossible and comprehensively life-enabling is good. That which is comprehensively life-disabling, instead, is bad.* Standard dichotomies are, under this perspective, secondary, and they often cause people's minds and affects to get stuck in unproductive dualisms, e.g., liberalism vs. socialism, conservatism vs. progressivism, paternalism vs. autonomy, left vs. right, atheism vs. theism, modern vs. classic, etc. *That which is paramount is thorough life-enablement.* See J. Noonan (2022, 13, note 3) for a consistent and recent example of LVOA-based existentialism, which "work[s] from a materialist ethical interpretation of" LVOA. Unlike Noonan, we are open to a spiritual/religious one too, if thoroughly life-enabling.

"Dangerous", in this context, meaning "liaisons" with cruelty that can be construed as being humorous yet also harmful to:
(1) physical wellbeing (e.g., walking blind men into lampposts);
(2) psychological or spiritual wellbeing (e.g., the self-loathing and depression arising in persons who are exposed to relentless humiliation by means of repeated mockery and/or merciless teasing; or the illbeing of individuals who fail to grasp and/or appreciate the jests and/or jokes with which they are faced in a given social setting); and/or
(3) thinking and understanding (e.g., pupils who stop attending school because they fear being ridiculed by their teachers and/or classmates).[76]

Our overall aim is to give our readers something to think about, i.e., to clear avenues for reflection on 'humour' and 'cruelty', especially as regards the ways in which these concepts assist each other and play out jointly in the world of lived experience. Our conclusions, accordingly, aim at opening thought, not at closing it.[77] Primarily, we aim at inducing reflection, not at imparting instruction. Rather than *maîtres à penser*, we should probably be thought of as *médiateurs à penser*.

Our paradigm is egalitarian participation in reasoned conversation, not enthusiastic proselytising for radical conversion.[78] Besides, even the most eager activists, who want to change radically the world in which we live, must—at some point and at the very least—stop and think about what they are doing; i.e., not solely think and stop others from doing that particular thing which is supposedly hurting the

---

[76] These three criteria correspond to LOVA's three fundamental planes of being along which value and disvalue can unfold, i.e., biological motility (or action), felt being, and thought (see, again, Baruchello 2018a and b).

[77] As also explained in *H&C1*, our trenchant and definitive statements are few and infrequent, for the historical plurality and semantic instability of both "humour" and "cruelty" warrant *considerable epistemic humility* on our part. It is only *when blatant comprehensive life-disablement is at issue* that *we dare become more assertive*, consistently with our embrace of LVOA. When no such dramatic scenarios are the case, we acknowledge and respect the great diversity of intelligent views arising from the best exertions of our gifted colleagues.

[78] We discussed in the concluding chapter of *H&C1* how reasoned conversation can lead to gradual changes of view or even paradigm shifts, in line with Polanyi (1962c). As to how exactly we understand such a reasoned "conversation", we largely adhere to the philosophical conception of it provided by the 20th-century British philosopher Michael Oakeshott (2004, 187–199), to which we must refer our readers. We cannot discuss it in detail here. Rather, let us recall how he jokingly remarked on the fact that we "descended from a race of monkeys who sat in talk so long and so late that they wore out their tails" (Oakeshott 2004, 198).

world in some cruel manner and making the activists so eager to change it for the better.[79]

At times, in order to identify hidden cruelties and/or reveal humorous aspects that could easily go undetected, we ourselves must nonetheless endorse interpretative perspectives and entertain conceptual frameworks with which the reader may not be entirely familiar or even comfortable. We sincerely apologise hereby for any such potential discomfort, whether it counts as genuinely cruel or not.[80] Nevertheless, we do regard this intentionally bewildering approach to be a necessary means of 'dislodgment' of, *inter alia*, received views, commonplaces, cognitive hysteresis, trained incapacity, wilful blindness, methodological monism, groupthink, unquestioned common sense, or even sheer habit-driven logico-conceptual, affective, spiritual and/or imaginative inertia.[81]

Every so often, the human imagination needs a few nudges to really kick in. This must be done, even if the nudged party may feel troubled, even cruelly so,

---

[79] Reflections on violent revolutions are offered in *H&C3*, which is also the most 'activist' book in our trilogy.

[80] Some discomfort is perhaps inevitable, given that this book deals not simply with humour, but cruelty too. Also, make sure you don't drop it on your toes.

[81] Presumptions and preconceptions are a well-known and common obstacle, especially when heavily *cathected*. The motives for such an affective investment can be the most varied, and they certainly include financial ones. Perhaps, in yet another *cruel irony* for practicing academics such as ourselves, we are simply wasting our time trying to challenge obstacles of this kind and magnitude. Writing ponderous books may be a masochistic form of puttering away. After all, as the US congressman William Jennings Bryan of Nebraska is reported to have stated back in 1893: "*It is useless to argue with a man whose opinion is based upon a personal or pecuniary interest*" ("It Is Difficult" 2017, par. 5; emphasis added). Such notorious limitations of people's willingness to listen, hermeneutical elasticity and/or reasoning skills can also be at work among highly educated individuals who may have spent decades specialising in one particular interpretative perspective and/or set of fundamental concepts that are deemed essential for a certain type of expert study and/or important productive activity. Thus, they lost the aptitude for entertaining *in earnest* differing renditions of the same phenomena, alternative forms of explanation, novel conceptualisations, and/or divergent lines of understanding and self-understanding. See, e.g., Veblen (1918, chap. 7), focussing on capitalist businessmen's tunnel vision, and Hillman and Ventura (1992), focussing on the plight of psychologists, psychiatrists, and their patients. Based on our professional experience, we could add a good few ministerial representatives and academic managers, who sometimes cannot understand that public universities are meant to educate people rather than making a profit or paying out dividends, i.e., who cannot comprehend why, how and for what aim the institutions for which they work have come into existence and strive to operate. Instead of facilitating public universities' life and life-enabling functions, these administrators toil *de facto* against them—another *cruel irony*. And one that, as we suspect, many of our readers do know about.

because of the unexpected change of scenery.⁸² We could call it, in a not-so-subtle pun on a famous comic sketch by the British troupe Monty Python, a process of "nudge nudge, think think".⁸³

Imagining new 'things' means, in fact, acquiring the ability for 'seeing' these new things around and/or within oneself.⁸⁴ The 'hard' sciences themselves exemplify it, as studied in the 20th century by the noted French chemist and philosopher Gaston Bachelard, who discussed how matter, fire, water, air (and movement), space and time have variously been imagined in the history of Western research and, *a fortiori*, have come to be studied by empirical scientists.⁸⁵ Perchance, this imaginative ability can even make the difference between a worthy personal existence and an unworthy one.⁸⁶ This is, at least, the daring point made by the great 19th-century German thinker Arthur Schopenhauer, who brazenly stated:

---

82 On this paradoxical cruelty, see Section 1.2.5. As to how far can our imagination reach, there have been many hypotheses and theories. Castoriadis (1997) was open-ended. Vico (1948) and Jung (1960–1990, vols. 12–15) instead maintained that recurrent structuring patterns can be found across cultures, ages, and individuals, e.g., the former's *universali fantastici* [fantasy's universals] and the latter's *archetypes*, which we tackle in our third book.

83 The 1971 sketch at issue being known as "Nudge nudge, wink wink".

84 Concerning the significance of the imagination *qua* foundational human faculty whence all other cognitive endeavours develop, both individually and collectively, see Castoriadis (1997) and Jung (1960–1990, vol. 6), who preferred using the term "phantasy". Without imaginings, which are the proper objects of our imagination (i.e., not just 'images'), there would be no intimations, no insights, no concepts, no words, no theories, no theorems, no technologies, no theatres, no TV, and very little fun. *Imagination furnishes our world, for we are symbolic animals* (see also Cassirer 1980 and Jung 1958a). This is true at the personal level as well as at the socio-cultural one. We do not further pursue and complexify the issue of what 'symbols' are, e.g., as something more or else than a 'sign' or 'signifier'. We should have written another tome to properly address such nuances. Allow us to drop it.

85 See, respectively, Bachelard 1933, 1948, 1972 and 1982; 1961, 1972, 1982 and 1992; 1972, 1982 and 1983; 1972 and 1990; 1937; 1963 and 2013 (see also Bachelard 1965, conclusion, sec. 6). As the contemporary Polish philosopher Przemyslaw Bursztyka (2019, 1–2) also observed while writing about "culture and its irreducible plurality": "If culture arises out of symbolic formation of raw, meaningless physical stimuli or purely biological determinations; it lives in the acts of transformation and reconfiguration of [an] already established cultural inventory. That is to say, of situating past achievements in new horizons of meaning, values, or more broadly, human concerns. These creative efforts are not necessarily reflective or thematized. Usually they first take on different forms of pre-reflective experience of ourselves and of the world we live in; forms governed and expressed by collective imaginaries, symbols, archetypes, narratives, shared emotions, common practices and last but not least common forms of sensitivity or *sensus communis*."

86 See, e.g., the intriguing musings by the psychologists Hillman and Ventura (1992) on how people's perception and conception of their own inner life can vary, depending on whether they utilise materialistic terms (e.g., "brain", "genes") or spiritual ones (e.g., "soul", "passions"). Imagination is crucial *vis-à-vis* making up the fundamental categories, concepts, metaphors and/or rhetorical fig-

> [W]here every one is thrown upon his own resources, what a man has in himself comes to light; the fool in fine raiment groans under the burden of his miserable personality, a burden which he can never throw off, whilst the man of talent peoples the waste places with his animating thoughts. Seneca declares that folly is its own burden,—*omnis stultitia laborat fastidio sui*,—a very true saying, with which may be compared the words of Jesus, the son of Sirach, *The life of a fool is worse than death.*[87]

Unquestionably, Schopenhauer thought of himself as precisely such a "man of talent".[88] The authors of the present book are not as self-assured as he was. Mostly, they are just trying their best, which is not much. It may well be the case that they belong to the vast mass of fools, whom the noted Romantic and Orientalist philosopher ridiculed repeatedly in his works. Not least those about the academic environment that this book's authors have been inhabiting for decades.[89]

In any case, our potentially cruel nudging takes place without any guarantee whatsoever of winning the day, whether at all or at any rate. No dislodgment is ever granted, whether minor or major. No nudge is ever certain to cause prejudices, preconceptions or presuppositions to budge. Not even slightly.[90] Indeed, all kinds of unexpected accidents can happen in the course of such an intellectual endeavour.[91] Sadly, one can tinker most earnestly with his/her cherished yet lopsided world, trying wholeheartedly to give it a better balance, and make things worse in

---

ures by which we end up living *qua* symbolic animals. It is perhaps a *cruel irony*, but our fantasy is one of the crucial factors in determining our lived reality. Even the "facts" that we are said to come across in our life, including "brute" ones, are likely to depend on it, for "bruteness" itself can be conceived of, i.e., imagined, differently (Mulligan and Correia 2021, pars. 1.5–1.5.1).

87 Schopenhauer (2004), chap. 2, par. 12; emphases in the original.
88 The passages in his work displaying such a hubris are very far from sparse.
89 See especially Schopenhauer (1974), vol. 1, essay 2.
90 This cognitive and affective resistance is present in lowbrow contexts as well as in educated ones. See, e.g., Snelson (1993, 44) on the resistance to the germ theory in medicine, such that he wrote of an "ideological immune system" countering new explanations and interpretations (see also Campanario 2010). *En passant*, Snelson remarked on the etymology of "indolence", i.e., the Latin for "not painful". *Changing ideas*, or even just going through the effort of considering the reasons for and against doing so, *is a pain*—whether in the back, neck, head or elsewhere. *Coming across new or challenging notions can be experienced as cruel.* It might then be this fear of suffering that explains, as Galbraith (1991, 2) caustically noted, why "change in economics has been reluctant and reluctantly accepted" for the most part; hence not just the academic, social and/or economic self-interest whereby "[t]hose who benefit from the *status quo* resist change, as do economists who have a vested interest in what has always been taught and believed". (More on economic matters is discussed in *H&C3*.)
91 We discuss in Chapters 2 and 4 how even humorous nudges can go askew.

the process.⁹² And this is only *one* of the many cruel ironies that our readers shall encounter in this book.⁹³

Nota Bene

One supplementary short set of self-reflexive considerations is *de rigueur* here, before launching into the "tale of two concepts" that Chapter 1 is meant to provide to our readers, *per* its heading. Specifically, we must address the fact that, unescapably and understandably, H&C1 lies in the background of the present volume, whereas H&C3 lies ahead of the same. **The present book**, however, **can be read and enjoyed on its own**, i.e., without any prior knowledge of our earlier, hefty tome about humour and cruelty. Nor does it require reading H&C3 to reach some satisfactory conclusion, for H&C2 contains its own chief thesis and attendant set of reasoned arguments, evidence-based considerations, and thought-provoking expert authorities about the mutual assistance that the two titular terms provide to each other. **This book is**, in other words, **a self-contained and self-standing undertaking** within a larger multi-volume intellectual endeavour. While certain themes and sources do surface repeatedly in all three volumes or, at least, in two of them, *the books' intended main emphases and principal theses are specific to each volume.*⁹⁴

As a consequence, anyone wanting a far more extensive, detailed, informative, context-aware, and in-depth discussion of the intellectual history of the two titular terms should find *H&C1* a noticeably more fitting start, given its Lucullan banquet of direct quotes, critical notations, and scholarly references from both venerable sources and more contemporary researchers. Not to mention the extensive argument deployed therein in favour of conceptual-linguistic polysemy, upon the basis of Michael Polanyi's phenomenology-*cum*-epistemology, which is not rehashed here.⁹⁵ Hence, as regards those brave souls who have already read *H&C1*,

---

92 In consonance with Cipolla's (2011) tongue-in-cheek essay on stupidity, it might even be the case that about three quarters of humankind, at any point in time, are behaving in ways that are harmful to others and/or themselves.
93 *Cruel ironies* are clear instances of combination of cruelty and humour. That is why we highlight them repeatedly.
94 Many footnotes highlight by way of cross-references that which is central and that which is not in each of our three volumes, hence clarifying further which specific themes and theses each of them possesses and addresses.
95 A mere handful of footnotes clarify in *H&C2* certain basic Polanyian notions that can be useful in this context.

the present "tale of two concepts" (Chapter 1) might serve mostly, or even solely, as a concise summary of a few crucial ideas that were debated in our first tome. The members of this well-read group may then prefer to simply *skip Chapter 1 and move on to Chapter 2*.

In this case, they should be mindful of the fact that Chapter 1, as cruelly selective as it had to be, comprises nonetheless a few learned sources about the titular concepts that were peripheral or occasionally absent in *H&C1*. This means, primarily, Alexander Kozintsev with regard to humour and John Kekes with regard to cruelty. Secondarily, it means the inclusion of additional recent sources in the substantial apparatus of footnotes accompanying *H&C2*. We decided to have here these supplementary or expanded references in order to further integrate *H&C1*'s thorough historical and cultural map. Likewise, the same ideal map is to be further enriched by our third volume about humour and cruelty, which is devoted to their mutual conflicts.

Ratio Decidendi

Still, *no map should ever be as detailed as the landscape that it represents*, lest it ceases to be useful.[96] Thus, *cum grano salis*, an even more trenchant selection of relevant sources was made with regard to the present volume, based also on the four guiding criteria listed below.[97]

(1) We emphasised references that are *not* the very latest publications available in humour studies, preferring instead to highlight sources on which the dust has already settled.

(1a) This choice of emphasis is no mere antiquarian inclination, which certainly exists in the ivory towers inhabited by university professors in affluent Western countries.[98] On the contrary, said layer of dust is a good sign, for it confirms *ipso facto* that these sources possess some intellectual value or, at least, that their recep-

---

[96] This point was made, back in his day by Polanyi (1962c), whose work we discussed in detail in *H&C1*.
[97] We write "also" because additional criteria guided our choice, e.g., being multidisciplinary and apropos. Moreover, a *selection was the sole viable avenue in practical terms*, given the gargantuan number of humour studies that have been accumulating over the years in all kinds of disciplinary areas (see, e.g., Nissan 2012).
[98] In poorer institutional settings, stately professors may not be allowed to indulge in such a penchant. In any case, *plenty of recent sources are duly cited too*, as the reader can easily gauge by perusing the concluding bibliography.

tion by contemporary experts, especially in today's Anglophone academia, is by now a dependable datum.[99]

(1b) Moreover, as we explained and exemplified abundantly in *H&C1*, claims of ground-breaking originality are likely to make good sales pitches, but they are hardly tenable in light of the many recurrent themes in the intellectual history of both 'humour' and 'cruelty' *qua* meaningful ideas for philosophers, theologians, playwrights, historians, psychologists, and social scientists at large. This is, by the way, no attempt at badmouthing. Instead, it is a reminder of two simple facts.

(1bi) On the one hand, we often ignore or forget what was stated in the past. As a result, we embrace as novelties actual reformulations of old insights.[100]

(1bii) On the other hand, we are still the same breed of *homo sapiens* that inhabited Seneca's Rome, Montaigne's Bordeaux, and Sade's Paris.[101] Insofar as

---

99 We write "Anglophone academia" because this is the likeliest audience for our book, which is written in English by two Iceland-based academics—a philosopher and a biopsychologist, to be precise.

100 Not all types of personal *Bildung*—nor all psychological types *tout court*, for that matter—allow educated people to become as comfortable with plural hermeneutical frameworks and multiple historically-informed approaches as Polanyi was. Some types, *au contraire*, lead people straight into monism, reductionism, scientism, cultural imperialism, and other '-isms' favouring the elimination of most or all co-occurring cultural pathways *qua* undesirable 'competitors', and/or *qua* misguided or dangerous 'deviations' from an uncompromising superior 'norm' (see, e.g., Hereniko 2000, title *et passim*, defending "Indigenous knowledge" from "academic imperialism"). Or, more naïvely, some such types of *Bildung* may cause some students to presume that past Western intellectuals were somehow incapable of producing brilliant scholarship and/or attaining profound insights, simply because their methodology was not 'scientific' or 'modern' enough. And yet, those readers who have read Plato, Augustine, Dante, Goethe, Kierkegaard, Freud, or Polanyi himself are likely to deem such a conceit pathetically myopic, if not painfully mistaken, and patently mutilating (think, e.g., of how much wisdom becomes inaccessible by eliminating the study of 'dead' and/ or 'foreign' languages from educational curricula). As to those few who may have not reached this conclusion, we pity them, and we dread them too (see, e.g., Piaia 2011 on Malebranche's and Quine's high-handed dismissal of the history of philosophy *qua* subject worth studying).

101 We do not tackle here the vexed question of whether *homo sapiens sapiens* should be used instead. Rather, we insist on the *continuity across time* of the human make-up, both biological and psychological, for this continuity does help to explain the enduring appeal of conceptual insights into 'cruelty' and/or 'humour' that are as old, on occasion, as Seneca and Galen, and that can be easily corroborated in all kinds of socio-cultural domains, throughout human history, and at many different levels of scholarly qualification. *This is true also of their mutual criss-crossing.* Thus, while tackling "the sense of the ridiculous and the absurd" in Max Ernst's visual art, which was partially inspired by "the Marquis de Sade's macabre obscenities", Baquie (2013, 3 and 55) argued in her PhD thesis that the "dualism of humour and cruelty, of sadism in a process of change and transition between ruthlessness and satire", may be a veritable "Janus" motif, i.e., an "archetypal" configuration of our psyche. (Much more on Jungian psychology is said in *H&C3*.)

all these 'classics' observed the same kind of animal that contemporary scholars observe today, many of their intuitions and conclusions are bound to be analogous.[102]

(1c) We can also consider a powerful statement made by the late Paolo Villaggio, who was possibly Italy's most successful comedian of his generation and a well-published satirist, chansonnier, public intellectual, left-wing activist, and outspoken chastiser of public mores:

> Over the past 2,000 years, from Plautus to the present day, *humour has never changed its fundamental mechanisms. The fundamental mechanisms are always the same.* Desecrating a grave, pompous circumstance. The gentleman sporting a top hat slipping on a banana peel will invariably get a laugh. Instead, in the same situation, the downtrodden person, let's say with a limp as well, who slips, presents us with a dramatic situation, not a comic one. Or the swapping of two persons. Or the transformation of a real setting into a surreal one. These are the eternal mechanics of humour. That which changes, rather, is the specific humorous theme that is used as a vehicle to make people laugh... Mark Twain, at the end of the 19th century, said that one such theme could last up to 20 years. Today, with the mass media that we have at our disposal, it can last up to five years, in my opinion... Humour's themes, its characters, are consumed over a shorter period of time.[103]

Independently of how fast humour's vehicles consume themselves, the fact that an experienced and well-established professional in cinematic, theatrical, and written humour so forcefully observed its constitutive historical continuity gives us ample reason to take him seriously and ponder the matter to which he brought attention. Perhaps, in keeping with his example, allowing oneself to also look backwards and/

In a conference paper, Midgley (2011, 1) observed the same mixture of "cruelty and humour" in the visual art of "Goya, Otto Dix, Daumier, and Hogarth"—and André Breton found it in the paintings by Frida Kahlo (as cited in Zimbaldi 2012, 37). In an MA thesis, Van Overveldt (2020, 38) retrieved "the interaction of humour and cruelty" in children's literature, notably Roald Dahl's 1964 *Charlie and the Chocolate Factory.*

102 "Analogous" meaning, among other things, that the technical jargon and attendant details may well change considerably, and yet the fundamental insights and central ideas remain the same. This is not to suggest that scholarly research is futile or that everything has already been said. Rather, insofar as the researched topics are inherently interesting, *each generation of academics is bound to approach them with their own intellectual tools at hand.* Inevitably, these tools exhibit the jargon and the technical details characterising each person's time- and place-specific disciplinary background, expert lexicon, privileged methodology, etc. This too is a facet of Polanyi's (1962c, title *et passim*) "personal knowledge". The problem being, at times, that such background, lexicon and methodology facilitate the "scientific obscurantism" that he faced, feared and fought against (Polanyi 1969a, 42).

103 Villaggio (2018), emphasis added. (Villaggio died in 2017.) The main notions mentioned in this passage are dealt with in the remainder of this book, especially the dualities or incongruities of humour's said "mechanisms".

or acknowledge the wisdom of some older 'classics' is/are not a bad way to go about understanding humour *vis-à-vis* both its present state and its future one.[104]

(1d) And should the thoughtful, Anglophone academic reader find an Italian comedian's remarks on the bi-millenary continuity of humorous mechanics too amateurish to be worthy of scientific consideration, then s/he may want to meditate on the following piece of advice given by the far statelier Swiss psychiatrist and psychologist, Carl Gustav Jung, who wrote: "Open the ancient books and learn what will come to you in solitude. Everything will be given to you and you will be spared nothing, the mercy and the torment."[105]

(2) With the noted exception of Lydia Amir's research, we neither focussed particularly upon, nor endeavoured to gather as many references as possible about, the writings published by fellow members of the *International Association for the Philosophy of Humor* (IAPH), or those authored by the contributors to the Association's noteworthy *Yearbook*.[106]

---

[104] As the reader can gauge from the cited references, we did not *only* look backwards in this book. It is a matter of relative emphasis.

[105] Jung (2009), 241 note 110. We hope that the reader grasped the *humorous* character of the juxtaposition of Villaggio and Jung, especially insofar as the latter's very serious quote points also in the direction of the idea of 'cruelty' by talking of "mercy" and "torment". If the reader did not grasp it, then *we apologise for being too light-handed* in our veiled mockery of the *neophilia* characterising so much scholarship, which frequently assumes that the latest research is always the best and forgets as often about the enormous wealth of insights contained in the older one. In any case, *as of this point forward, our use of humour is going to grow in these preliminary remarks.* Beware!

[106] These prosaic details must be mentioned in order to properly contextualise the genesis and history of our work. Also, Amir is the first of many female voices to be encountered by the reader in our book. Hers and the late Jean Harvey's are going to be pivotal *vis-à-vis* the chief arguments developed in the present book. More in general, and as far as possible and sensible, *the authors of this book endeavoured to include expert views arising from historically marginalised and/or minoritarian groups*, whether in the main text or in the many, wide-ranging and detailed footnotes, which the reader is advised to peruse with care and consideration. Not all minorities could be included. And such a limitation should only be expected. The Routledge encyclopaedia of the world's recognised minorities, edited by Carl Skutsch (2005), consists of three thick volumes comprising over 560 entries, for a total count of more than 1,500 pages. Moreover, as students of humour and cruelty, we cannot ignore the *cruel irony* whereby someone can be, at one level, a member of a historically and/or presently oppressed minority and, at another, a member of a historically and/or presently oppressive majority (or, at times, simply a nasty individual). See, e.g., the Scottish-Icelandic legal scholar Rachael L. Johnstone (2022, par. 10) mentioning the heated debates occurring in today's Greenland about the dismal phenomenon of "'internal colonisation' by elites in Nuuk [i.e., Western Greenlanders] of the Inughuit [i.e., Northern Greenlanders] and East Greenlanders".

(2a) First of all, *H&C1* took care already of this task, to a significant extent.¹⁰⁷

(2b) Secondly, these esteemed fellow scholars are by now much more than familiar with one another's works, qualities, quirks, quests, and viewpoints, including our own.¹⁰⁸

(2c) Thirdly, in a book such as this one, our attention to 'humour' must be weighed against an equal attention to 'cruelty', which is as important a concept in the overall theses, grounding and structure of the book.¹⁰⁹

(2d) Fourthly, as a result of our decision, this book may be able to fill, or start filling, scholarly gaps in the extant Anglophone literature about "humour" proper that some of our readers might not even be aware of.¹¹⁰

(2e) Fifthly, because of the previous four considerations, *H&C2* can appeal to a broader audience than just the eager and enthusiastic cohort of today's Anglophone philosophers of humour, to which we are happy to belong ourselves, if they will have us—and with whom, as it was stated before, we are hereby engaging in an implicit and sustained philosophical dialogue that has actually been going on for many years through several other avenues.¹¹¹

(3) Whenever possible and palatable, we tried to refer to books, essays, and/or articles authored by humourists who were prone to muse theoretically on 'humour' and/or 'cruelty', or by professional theoreticians who reflected on such concepts and, at the same time, succeeded in becoming well-published humourists.¹¹² Accordingly, in the pages to come—whether in the main text of our tome or in its many detailed footnotes—the reader will encounter the names and/or words of Western intellectuals such as Karl Julius Weber, Thorstein Veblen, G.K. Chesterton, Stephen Leacock, Luigi Pirandello, Carlo M. Cipolla, Flavio Baroncelli, and Umberto

---

107 A keen perusing of that book's lengthy bibliography can easily prove this claim to be true.
108 Indirectly, *H&C2* and its underlying research would not exist without the inspiration and the interactions that we have been enjoying with our fellow members and *their* ongoing scholarly discussions and activities. As far as the present book is concerned, the matter at issue is one of *emphasis*, not of exclusion. Hence, as noted before, the reader will find many recent references here too, including to works by scholars affiliated with said Association.
109 While we are less strict here than in *H&C1* on our prioritising sources dealing explicitly and emphatically with "humour" and "cruelty" proper, we do *not* stray far from that original philological and methodological directive.
110 We mean no disrespect. As explained in *H&C1*'s introduction, we are most aware of *our own* ignorance and fallibility.
111 Lydia Amir being responsible for getting the present authors involved in the activities of the IAPH.
112 We write "well-published" because, as explained in *H&C1*, written sources are our privileged domain of study.

Eco.[113] While some of these thinkers will be easily recognised by most readers, others are likely to be unknown quantities.[114] However renowned they became in specific disciplines and/or cultural contexts, these thinkers' fame may have never reached others, or may have dissolved over the course of time. *Sic transit gloria mundi.*[115]

(4) Given our own personal and professional cultural backgrounds, and with the noted exception of the American philosopher John Morreall, we included a number of learned voices originating from outside today's hegemon of world culture, i.e., the United States of America.[116] Albeit indirectly, the names of the philosopher-humourists listed in the previous paragraph reveal already our geo-cultural decision. Its rationale is purely intellectual—subconscious motives aside, of course.[117] This deliberate inclusion is not a proud act of Icelandic or Italian chauvinism, a desperate cry for help by unappreciated minorities, or a valiant (or fool-

---

[113] A person's very name can unleash humorous strategies in an academic context. For one, upon commencing to teach economic history at Berkley in the 1950s, Cipolla started signing himself as "Carlo *M.* Cipolla", although he had never had a middle name. Cipolla never explained the motives for choosing this letter. Eventually, his election of "M." led to all sorts of speculations about his person, background, aims and writings, trying to reveal the mystery behind Cipolla's chosen initial. These speculations continue today (see, e.g., Lodi 2019, par. 4).

[114] In line with our previous tome, we must ask our reader to be open-minded, tolerant, and willing to entertain instances, imagery, ideas, values, arguments, and/or stances that s/he may have never encountered before and/or that may clash radically with his/her own conscious beliefs, public aims, and/or moral principles. The same attitude should be displayed towards controversial terms, themes, and authors that, given the scope of our research, we decided to address. It is also—if not primarily—in this affectively demanding way that philosophical understanding gains its depth and breadth. As Mark Twain is said to have quipped: "*An open mind leaves a chance for someone to drop a worthwhile thought in it.*" (We were unable to retrieve the original source for this well-known adagio.) Closing one's ears and mind because of a word (e.g., "communism", "Friedman", "fuck", "Catholic", "Marx") or strings thereof (e.g., quotes and/or arguments by 'camps' or experts with which we do not identify) is something that we advise against. It has been our experience that *something of value can be learnt even from texts in which many or most words and/or attendant thoughts are uncomfortable and/or unconvincing.*

[115] Used in papal coronation ceremonies until 1963, this motto reminded the new pope that earthly glory is transient.

[116] We write "world culture" rather than "Western" because the US' influence has reached all inhabited continents.

[117] The theme of people's unconscious drives returns several times in this book on a more serious note than here. Let us just remark, for the moment, that psychological behaviourism, despite being the methodological equivalent of scotoma, got one thing right: *observable conduct is much easier to investigate than its underlying motives.*

ish) feat of anti-imperialist defiance.[118] Much more simply, and quite amicably, our hope is to fill, or start filling, scholarly gaps in the Anglophone literature about "humour" proper that some of our readers might not even be aware of.[119]

Obiter Dicta

Despite the methodological rationale just explained, issue can still be taken with any act of exclusion (e.g., why is *x* not tackled? Is the author against *x*?) and/or inclusion (e.g., how does the author dare talk about *y*? Why is the author talking so little/much about *y*?). Whatever the actual deeper psychological motives for taking issue with largely warranted philosophical remarks may be, passable reasons for intellectual criticism can be retrieved without much effort, plausibly on any topic, stance, aim, and/or bookish activity that academics such as the two of us may happen to entertain, engage in, or display. There is really no rest for the wicked.[120]

(1) The situation is curiously akin to the joke of the two ties that the Bulgarian-born Yiddish playwright, musician, and scholar Moni Ovadia told his audiences at a number of theatrical performances, which we had the good fortune of attending in person in the 1990s. As we recall it from those shows, about 30 years later, the joke goes more or less like this:

> A proud Jewish mother buys two beautiful new ties, one red and one blue, for her son who has finally become a grown man. From now on, when he comes home from his boarding school to visit her, he must be dressed appropriately. Moreover, as soon as her son approaches the landing, sporting a nice jacket and, as is only to be hoped, a fancy red tie, the mother can ask him briskly: "why aren't you wearing the blue one?"[121]

Either tie can, must, and will be donned. But not both of them at once. Some pertinent references, regrettably yet reasonably, were—and will have to be—disregarded.[122] The reader finds in our books the sources that *we* chose to include, not

---

118 As we also noted in *H&C1*, the Francophones Deleuze and Guattari (1983, 13) went so far as to argue that truly original ideas spring exclusively from cultural "minorities" resisting the hegemon's "powerful signs that massacre desire", insofar as these signs reinforce the "perspectives ... of the [majoritarian] culture they inhabit".
119 Again, we mean *no* disrespect, especially since we are aware of our own ignorance of countless subjects and aptitude for making mistakes.
120 The reader can decide whether only the critics are wicked or the authors too, if not exclusively the latter.
121 There exist many variations on this joke, which Ovadia himself tinkered with in his shows. Here, we relied on our own memory of his theatrical performances.
122 We write "will have" because we are thinking of *H&C3*.

those that *s/he* would have liked to see cited, had s/he undertaken the ambitious and arduous task of writing three large tomes about humour and cruelty.[123] An author's duty is sometimes the author's privilege.

(2) Nevertheless, based on our past experiences, we can foresee that some readers will be pained to see a specific title or a certain name not being mentioned—not even in this book's many long footnotes or its extensive closing bibliography. Others, instead, will be disheartened by the presence of titles that they really dislike, or the authors of which the reader resents on philosophical, professional, political, partisan, poetic, prosodic, and/or personal grounds.[124] The same disconsolate, dichotomous, and dichromatic considerations apply to our choice of key themes and central topics pertaining to 'humour' and 'cruelty', these two concepts' mutual interplay, and the level of analytical detailing to which they are subjected.[125]

Choices had to be made. Sore ones too. Not least the fact that, in Chapter 1, we had to rely on the preposterously contrived yet prevalent convention whereby a thinker's arguments and insights can be adequately rendered by means of, say, an apt quote and a pair of stately paragraphs.[126] If the reader, while perusing the following pages, should then happen to be thinking of some stimulating connections and/or perceptive citations that could have been inserted and/or discussed but that were not, then s/he should reflect on the fact that we may well have written about them in our other two volumes—or at least *thought* about them at some point. (Let us hope that our reader will at least be able to spot

---

[123] The keen reader can refer to *H&C1* and, when available, *H&C3*, to get a fuller picture.

[124] In our experience, cruel enmities are most varied and based on all sorts of conscious and unconscious motives. In the aloof world of philosophy, for one, a firm rhetorical reliance on alliteration may cause unease or resentment.

[125] The necessary choice of emphasis implies, and applies to, both the depth and the width of each specific account that the reader finds herein. All tackled issues, in fact, can be complexified, almost *ad libitum*, if not *ad infinitum*, or even *ad nauseam* (see, e.g., the many meanings of "meaning" in Deleuze's philosophy, which is discussed in Chapter 1). Insofar as our accounts must play specific roles in the larger contexts of this book and of the book series to which it belongs, our accounts must limit the amount of digging and comprehensiveness that they pursue. Furthermore, as we explained in *H&C1*, too emphatic a detailing of a concept leads to destroying *both* the concept itself, which is then replaced by some subset of constituent details, *and* its epistemic utility *qua* such a concept. In our three volumes, we want to study 'humour' and 'cruelty' and their many manifestations in human life, not, say, six pragmatic modifiers in humorous communication, or 13 hormonal imbalances that were registered in a sample of violent offenders. (These two examples are hypothetical and somewhat hyperbolic, but they should do the explanatory job required of them.)

[126] Fortunately for us, then, *H&C1* is 'out there' to prove that we know a little better than that.

those passages where we indulged in our odd sense of humour. Moni Ovadia is not the only scholar capable of making a joke or two.)[127]

(3) Some words of caution should also be proffered with regard to our watchful, careful, painstaking, historically-informed, stitch-by-stitch approach, which does not open with few brazen statements, a clever abstract definition, and then provide a terse set of slender arguments constituting the bulk of the book. This is certainly one dependable and, at times, fruitful way of doing philosophy in many an academic quarter. We ourselves pursued it in a few previous works of ours. But not here. For two main reasons:

(3a) In philosophy, there exist a great many ways of engaging the reader and unleashing reason. It should be enough to put side-by-side and candidly compare the works left to us by Plato, Lucretius, Augustine, Aquinas, Montaigne, Suárez, Pascal, Vico, Kant, Nietzsche, Spengler, Wittgenstein, Camus, Gadamer, and Irigaray to realise the veracity and validity of this point and, considering the wealth of insights derivable from the aforementioned authors, accept it as permissible and productive, if not preferable.[128]

(3b) As we found ourselves exploring 'humour' and 'cruelty' with a keen scholarly eye, we came to the realisation that, if we wanted to be honest about the breadth and depth of these two concepts *as well as* the intricacies of their mutual interplay, our role-models, in terms of textual organisation and theoretical presentation, had to be eclectic, edifying, expansive thinkers such as, say, Adam Smith, Pareto, Jung, Cassirer, Weischedel, or Hadot.[129]

(4) Then again, Western philosophical approaches and their attendant formal methods and tastes can differ starkly. Some of our readers may have never truly encountered or textually engaged with any of the 'masters' whom we have just cited and, above all, whose scholarly work has been so inspirational to us. Established schools and sub-schools of thought within contemporary Western academia have their own contingent yet conditioning canons, which can sometimes vary

---

127 Given the central themes and topics of our book, we must leave the reader to ponder whether we are being cruelly humorous *via* the non-falsifiable omniscient claim made above, or we are highlighting a humorous cruelty characterising scholarly endeavours such as ours. Perhaps, we are doing both things at once.

128 We assume our academic readers to have come across most of the cited thinkers, at least in translation.

129 We are not suggesting that this realisation is the sole one that can emerge from such a scholarly enterprise, but it is certainly the one to which *we* arrived, armed with our inevitable "personal coefficient" (Polanyi 1962c, 17 et passim).

markedly across countries and continents, and they are undoubtedly capable of water-tight procedural and communicative self-compartmentalisation.[130]

Combined with individual habit and ingrained expectation, too stark of a departure from the assumed institutional norm can be too much to bear. As we are going to mention in Chapter 1, the unexpected may be funny, at times; but it can also be baffling, irksome, daunting, if not cruelly terrifying. Some disciplined minds may honestly be unable to positively cope with philosophical works that are sufficiently unlike anything else that they have stumbled across before in their respected and self-respecting professional life. Our present book, thusly, may turn into an instrument for hurt, displeasure and aggravation, however intellectually mediated, emotionally mild, fundamentally episodic, and/or academically misconstrued.[131]

(5) This last point refers to the simple yet significant circumstance whereby, having been published after surviving the most thorough processes of anonymous peer-review and non-anonymous editorial assessment, H&C2 can be legitimately said to have cut the mustard. Yet, not everyone likes mustard to the same degree. Some people find it ghastly. They would rather have ketchup, which is itself a vegetable, according to some die-hard Reaganites.[132] Cruelty, in subtler ways than mustard and most other sauces, can then infiltrate the purportedly sheltered, secluded, serene and solitary precinct of academic writing.[133] This rather sad fact about written creations is true, incidentally, of the reader as well as of the writer.[134]

---

[130] The so-called "Analytic-Continental" divide is only the most notorious example. We operate *underneath* it.

[131] Even writing "thusly" can be perceived as a cruelty by some grammatically sensitive readers. In any case, the dissatisfied reader should *not* despair. Our next volume will be an even better one.

[132] Readers unfamiliar with the debates about ketchup's official status in 1980s American schools may not get the joke, which we do not wish to 'kill' by explaining it in detail.

[133] This precinct is one among many where the gap separating people's perceived self-importance and their real-life significance can reach the utmost width and the sharpest contrast. The vicious ways in which purely academic battles are fought, the puffed-up pride and vanity of soon-to-be-forgotten professors, and the ultimately contingent nature of fiercely-guarded disciplinary borders are among the many *cruel ironies* that the two authors of this book have observed in their professional life. To be honest, they would gladly do without having to witness them, but this sorry spectacle seems unlikely to end any time soon. The noted English writer David Lodge (1984) offered a bittersweet, parodic, and slightly grotesque reminder of the follies and foibles of academia, which can express them in very cruel forms too, as recently recorded and discussed by the American feminist thinker Laura Kipnis (2017). More on the latter's reminiscences of, and reflections on, panics and persecutions, is said in *H&C3*.

[134] Arguably, with any book, *the writer and the reader enter into a sadomasochistic relationship*. Some colleagues, e.g., may be familiar with the experience of not being duly acknowledged and/or

(5a) Think, for one, about the interminable and scrupulous formal requirements of academic writing. These are a mere taste, and yet a meaningful token too, of just such subtle, cruel infiltrations. In addition, the authors' human fallibility, personal foibles and many other fragilities can make them even worse.[135]

(5b) For another, we must candidly report about one of the most heart-breaking experiences that we have had in our career and that we do keep having, insofar as we unrepentantly go on writing and publishing weighty academic books such as the present one. It is something that happens regularly, almost inexorably, whenever an author is so arrogant, so careless, so stupid, and so unwise, as to pick up a copy of his/her own published books. In point of fact, it must be some kind of self-imposed masochism.[136]

Specifically, we mean the cruel phenomenon whereby a book's author, despite countless revisions of the original manuscript, at least as many typesetting- and editing sessions with the publisher's expert teams, and the same author's more-than-generous contributions to some professional proofreader's retirement plan, spots immediately a few misprints, the odd non-italicised term, some errors that had been deleted before and yet have mysteriously resurfaced, and many other small but truly humiliating, annoying and exasperating minutiae reminding the author of the futility of all human exertions, if not of human existence itself.[137]

In the old days, thin sheets of paper containing late-spotted errors—the so-called "E.C"., i.e., *errata corrige*—would regularly slip out of newly-purchased books. Regrettably, this last-minute editorial practice has long disappeared. Looking backward, we wonder whether those thin sheets of paper were some kind of desperate love letters penned by the book's author to an uncaring, cruel paramour. For sure, that is how they feel to us.[138]

In sum, despite our best efforts and, hopefully, our growing expertise, we know that we are bound to keep making mistakes and failing to spot them in time. That is to say, to compound errors in the most depressing ways and, sometimes, the silliest manners. What is worse, even paid professionals seem more

---

cited, even when it is clear and/or known that one's own research lies behind someone else's. There and then, petty cruelty meets silly pride.

135 Any reader familiar with the peer-review system of contemporary academic publishing has sampled this cruelty.

136 Masochism and sadism were discussed in detail in *H&C1* and are tackled further here and in *H&C3*.

137 We suspect that our published readers must have had the same dreadful experience at some point in their career.

138 The paragraph above is yet another such message to our prior books, as well as to our present and future ones.

than capable of doing the same. If then one adds a book's latent cohort of hasty readers, disappointed colleagues, acerbic reviewers, ill-advised sycophants, and bungling users, the overall picture becomes even more disheartening. Worst of all, there is no way to avoid it. *Imperfection*, alas, *cannot be escaped in human affairs.* Keep this sobering realisation in mind while reading the following pages. This book is not only about "humour" proper, in fact, but "cruelty" as well.[139]

---

[139] This topic gains prominence in Chapter 4 under the guise of cruel fallibility in people's humorous conduct.

1 A Tale of Two Concepts

1.1 Humour

> Fun is (like cant, like humour,) an exceptional, untranslatable word.
> —Victor Hugo[1]

Humour is, as the celebrated American psychologist Harry Harlow pointed out in the second half of the last century, difficult to define, but easily understood.[2] At a common-sense level, everyone comprehends its meaning and uses it. Scholars too, despite their qualms and limitations, have been trying to do the same. As the reader perusing these pages will realise, there exists in fact a large and somewhat chaotic body of expert studies about humour.[3] But, as pointed out by John Morreall, who was one of the founders of the *International Society for Humor Studies* (ISHS), this interest in humour and its cognates is a recent phenomenon.[4]

To be exact, many of the 'giants' of Western philosophy, including Plato, Aristotle, Aquinas, Descartes, Hobbes, Voltaire, and Kant, did write about humour, or rather, about kindred terms such as "laughter", "play", "comedy", and/or "sat-

---

[1] As, ironically, translated by and cited in Vasey (1877), 179.

[2] See Harlow (1969), 227.

[3] See, e.g., the all-encompassing understanding of "humour" proper provided by the Zurich-based psychologist Willibald Ruch, as discussed in Arab and Davis (2022, 2) who reviewed recent Anglophone studies of "humour" proper *qua* means of fellowship, which is pursued by *including some people while excluding others* (see, e.g., Marra 2022). Ironically, this 'game' of inclusion-*cum*-exclusion has a logical-linguistic counterpart in the endless debates about the 'proper' meaning of "humour" proper. In fact, in the absence of metaphysical definitions capturing reality *in se*, the best that can be done is to produce *stipulative definitions* of one kind or another, which *incorporate certain predicates and expunge others*. On occasion, these stipulations correspond *grosso modo* to plausible lexical definitions at a given point in the history of a certain linguistic group, who have already experienced semantic variations (e.g., Galen's meaning of "humour" *versus* the one that it has for today's IAPH) and may well exhibit more in the future (e.g., the meaning of "humour" in the year 2733 AD). Other times, whether openly cast as such or presented as technical, operational or 'working' definitions, these stipulations are endorsed enthusiastically by a community of one, i.e., the individual scholar or scientist who is trying to identify "humour" proper and, oftentimes, contrasting it with "irony", "comicality", "clownishness", etc., in ways that few other language users care much about or, later on, remember. *H&C1* contains a few instances of this sober and sobering phenomenon, which reminds us of Aesop's (2002, #520 of the Perry index) parodic fable about the mountain giving birth to a mouse. *We would not be entirely surprised if the same sad fate awaited our own trilogy.*

[4] See Morreall (2020a). On the parentage and history of ISHS, see also Nilsen and Nilsen (n.d.a).

ire".⁵ Yet that which they wrote was severely limited in both scope and length.⁶ Bergson's 1900 book on "laughter" [*le rire*] was actually the first substantial work ever penned by a prominent European philosopher that focussed explicitly and extensively on this subject. "Humour" proper had to wait even longer, as far as the philosophical profession is concerned, while having enjoyed some more traction only among a select group of European essayists or *literati* (e.g., Congreve, Richter, Hood, Snyder, Pirandello) and a few theory-prone Western minds, who also happened to be self-declared "humourists" (e.g., Weber, Kierkegaard, Chesterton, Leacock, Esar).⁷

This prolonged disinterest is, *inter alia,* a reminder of the rift that can occur between science and reality. Humour is a universal human experience and influences our personal lives and societies in profound ways. Yet throughout Western history, it was only dealt with rather lightly by the most influential thinkers, who appeared to find it an intractable topic. Again, this may be since "humour" is a notoriously difficult term to define, partly because we, i.e., all linguistically-competent persons, are constantly surrounded by it, and because we have deeply personal interpretations of its meaning—let alone highly negative and even censoring ones.⁸ Nonetheless, the protracted scholarly neglect of this concept is perplexing.⁹ Perhaps, scholars and scientists prefer avoiding certain issues, however common and/or crucial they may be, if these issues appear to be: methodologically challenging; overly subjective; too risky; too risqué; and/or beneath the researchers' dignity

---

5 See, e.g., Morreall (1987) and (2016), and *H&C1.*
6 See, e.g., Morreall (1987) and (2016).
7 *H&C1* offers a lengthy account of the history of "humour" proper *qua* explicit theme for philosophical study, including many relevant quotes from, and even more references to, the aforementioned thinkers, and much else. See also Figueroa-Dorrego and Larkin-Galiñanes (2009) for a useful anthology of many such sources.
8 See, e.g., Morreall (2016). We tackle in detail the issue of the stern condemnation and censorship of humour in *H&C3*. For the moment, let us merely recall the legal scholar Natalie Alkiviadou (2022), who contended that EU-based jurisprudence has become more and more restrictive in our century *vis-à-vis* people's freedom of humorous speech, preferring instead to grant more and more protection from possible offense. When in doubt, censorship is preferred to the risk of fostering humorous communication that could be interpreted, in the worst cases, as 'hate speech'.
9 *Seeking to be funny, or to be able to appreciate that something is funny, will have to suffice as humour's overall working definition, for now.* When addressing "humour" proper, in any case, we duly signal it. We are comforted in our attitude by the definition of "humour" proffered twice by IAPH's founding president, i.e., "humour is the contemporary umbrella term we use to refer to the comic and its cognates" (Amir 2014, 234; 2019, 73).

qua public intellectuals, men or women of good standing, or self-respecting academic specialists.[10]

1.1.1 Origins of the Term

The etymological and cultural roots of the word "humour" fit perfectly with what we have just written about the ever-changing character of the concept itself. Around the 5th century BC, this notion became an integral part of medicine as practiced by Hippocrates, the Greek philosopher who is credited with fathering the discipline itself.[11] The original meaning of "humour" was, however, largely unrelated to that upon which we focus in the present book, for it meant "liquid" or "fluid", especially of bodily origin.[12] This definition of humour, moreover, provided the theoretical groundwork for medical practice from ancient times to early-modern days.[13]

Erudite readers might still be able to recognise it as the theory of the four fundamental fluids controlling bodily functions: yellow bile, mucus, blood, and black bile. This theory is likely to come across as a tad primitive and simple to the contemporary eye, but it was quite ingenious. By observing variations in these fluids, Hippocrates and his followers could estimate: the flow of energy through the body (blood); the state of the immune system (mucus as well as blood); the health of the liver and digestive system (yellow bile); and the effects of age and nutrition (black bile). Besides, by looking at the sedimentation of blood, which is a method still current in hospitals and clinics, the ancient physicians may well have had access to much valuable information on their patients' physical condition. Thus, Hippocrates maintained that both health and disease could be explained by the balance among these four fluids.[14]

In the 2nd century AD, Hippocrates' most famous successor in ancient medicine, the Greek physician Galen, adopted the theories and methods of his predecessor and made them extremely popular across the Roman empire. What is more,

---

10 Emblematically, Baruchello (2010) stresses how Western philosophers neglected for centuries the fundamental vital needs of our species (e.g., breathing, defecation) *qua* worthy topics for extensive and explicit scholarly study.
11 See, e.g., Castiglioni (2019).
12 As noted in *H&C1*, a suggestive continuity can yet be found in the term's own fluid, unending semantic shifts.
13 See, e.g., Castiglioni (2019). This original meaning of "humour" still persists (see, e.g., Gül *et al.* 2022).
14 See, e.g., Castiglioni (2019).

Galen's views became a dominant intellectual force for over a millennium, well into the Renaissance studies that experts would call "the birth of modern science" in the West.[15] Galenic "humourism" (or "humouralism") grew into the 'gold standard' for medical practice throughout this long period, using Hippocrates' tetralogy of fundamental humours to explain the causes and the treatments of disease and illbeing.[16]

The interplay between physical and psychological symptoms led also to the belief that the balance in our humours influenced human thoughts, affects, and behaviours; hence, to the enduring linguistic expressions whereby the psychological state of a person is described in terms of "humour", e.g., being in a "good humour" or a "bad humour".[17] Over time, the same nominal "humour" became associated with more general states of mind, traits of personality, defining moods, noticeable temper, etc.[18] *Inter alia*, this association was an early instance of today's theories and classifications of psychological or personality types, which, like their ancient counterpart, are also liable to becoming part and parcel of everyday jargon, e.g., the notions of 'extrovert' and 'introvert'.[19]

This transition from medical concepts to everyday parlance is still in vogue. A technical expression like "attention deficit" was unheard of a few decades ago, but is now used haphazardly among the non-clinical public to indicate any lapse in focus. We can find many examples of bastardisation of medical concepts by the public. The concept of 'schizophrenia' provides a good one.[20] The public should not be blamed, though, since the Greek etymon of this term literally refers

---

15 See, e.g., Jouanna (2012).
16 See Jouanna (2012).
17 See, e.g., Freschi (1843). "Umorale" is still used in Italian to refer to persons exhibiting major mood swings.
18 See, e.g., Kiblansky, Panofsky, and Saxl (1964).
19 The latest attempt at devising a psychological theory of types or, in his specific case, "temperaments"—hence directly recalling the implicit wisdom of ancient humouralism—was made by the late American psychologist David Keirsey (and Bates 1984), (1998) and (2010), who was born, incidentally, the same year as C.G. Jung's seminal book *Psychological Types* was published in the original German, i.e., 1921. Trait theories, which are sometimes cast bombastically as an entirely alternative psychometric approach, are a historical filiation of the earlier type theories and they too are indirectly rooted in ancient humouralism, whether their practitioners know it or not (see, e.g., Musek 2017).
20 The Belgian feminist thinker, linguist, and psychoanalyst Luce Irigaray (2002, 33–34) offered another good reason, though somewhat a more indirect one, for mentioning "schizophrenia" in a book about cruelty: schizophrenic patients are more likely to describe events and experiences as "cruel" than 'healthy' ones.

to a 'split head', even though this is not an accurate description of the actual psychiatric condition. Today, in ordinary parlance, people use it even to explain being ambivalent about certain options or opinions. This is nobody's fault or crime, in our view, but a mere fact of life. Language users are, ultimately, its owners too.[21]

1.1.2 A Particularly British Thing

Pinpointing the specific person/s and/or the exact moment/s in time of each developmental step in an etymological itinerary is, however, a fool's errand. We cannot say exactly how and when the concept of 'humour' expanded and/or evolved into its modern and contemporary forms. We know that the English playwright Ben Jonson wrote a comical satire in 1598 entitled *Every Man in His Humour*, and followed it up one year later with, *Every Man out of His Humour*.[22] Basically, Jonson equated "comedy" with "humour" proper, and understood it primarily as a matter of good mood and merriment, although it can also be seen from his writings that this was a rather novel usage of the term, the Galenic meanings of which continued to be employed too.[23] (A separate question could also be whether the modern form has even existed in a single comprehensible form at any point.)

At the close of the 20th century, the humour specialist Brenda Goldberg emphasised the special role of social class in this etymological development, and claimed that the British polite society of the 1600s and 1700s sought most intently to detach themselves from the cruder and often warlike entertainments of the 'great unwashed'.[24] The dichotomy between high- and low brow was, in her perspective, a fundamental socio-cultural issue of that age, which presented it under various guises, not least in that which one finds funny and how s/he may express merriment in public.[25] Then, the elite would have asserted their higher status by feasting on sophisticated new forms of "humour" proper, hence snubbing the roars of laughter of the 'inferior' classes, who were left to enjoy a simpler and

---

21 As we note later in this book, some philosophers have resented most vocally the unpredictable and uncontrolled way in which ordinary people make use of their language and change its semantics, or part thereof, in the process.
22 See Redwine, Jr. (1961), 316.
23 As cited in Redwine, Jr. (1961), 317 and 333.
24 See Goldberg (1999), 59–63.
25 See Goldberg (1999), 59–63.

rougher fare, the long-lived roots of which can be still be grasped in the surviving carnivalesque literature and folk traditions of many nations.[26]

The first Western thinker to author a whole essay dedicated to the de-medicalised, modern usage of "humour" proper was the 3rd Earl of Shaftesbury. Obviously, he was an aristocrat, and he is remembered as one of John Locke's intellectual *protégés* and partners.[27] Shaftesbury did not provide an exact definition of "humour" proper, but he clearly viewed it as a benign component of debates between free, educated, and well-meaning gentlemen.[28] According to his original essay on this topic, conversational humour can sharpen the wit of all participants, test the strength of reasoning, discover truth and falsity, and reveal hidden intolerance or bigotry.[29] It is a capable and captivating weapon, which only proficient debaters devoted to the worthy causes of free speech and refinement can and should make full use of, even when they may be opposed and challenged by the enemies of liberty: "the natural free spirits of ingenious men, if imprison'd and controul'd, will find out other ways of motion to relieve themselves in their constraint".[30] As Shaftesbury stated, even satirical "irony" and nonsensical "buffoonery" can and should be employed, if necessary: "[t]he greater the weight is, the bitterer will be the satir. The higher the slavery, the more exquisite the buffoonery."[31]

Shaftesbury's vision of "humour", as exercised "to ridicule folly, and recommend wisdom and virtue … in a way of pleasantry and mirth", is so tantalising that it is almost unbearable to have to sideline it, for it bears little resemblance to today's prevalent views—or even to what "humour" proper may have meant

---

[26] See Goldberg (1999), 63–64. Bakhtin (1976) and (2014) are representative studies on these folk traditions, which we addressed, to some extent, in *H&C1*. As stated therein, Bakhtin focussed on "laughter", not "humour" proper. At any rate, Bakhtin's works are a reminder of the extant ethico-aesthetic standards in humorous matters that are not those of *the middle and upper classes, whence most Western scholars still originate, hence also their tacit presuppositions* about decency, propriety, taste, etc. (More on these matters is discussed in *H&C3*.)

[27] We explained in greater detail their relationship in *H&C1*.

[28] See Shaftesbury (1732), part I, secs. 1, par. 2, 3, par. 1, and 5, par. 3. (*When using old, digitised editions or electronic versions, if possible and practical, we indicate chapters, sections and/or paragraphs.*)

[29] See Shaftesbury (1732), part I, secs. 3, pars. 1–2, and 5, pars. 1–2. In the 19th century, Dostoyevsky (2014, part 3, chap. 1, sec. 2, par. 5; emphasis added) echoed in part this approach to humour *qua* test of truth and stated: "I only understand that *laughter is the surest test of the heart*. Look at a baby—some children know how to laugh to perfection; a crying baby is disgusting to me, but a laughing, merry one is a sunbeam from paradise, it is a revelation from the future, when man will become at last as pure and simple-hearted as a child."

[30] Shaftesbury (1732), part 1, sec. 4, par. 6.

[31] Shaftesbury (1732), part 1, sec. 4, pars. 7–8.

to most of his English contemporaries.³² The evolving meaning of the term itself has mostly been attributed to the early-modern users of the English language, not to its most self-declaredly refined aristocratic users, to such an extent that this socio-linguistic aptitude was even considered by some to be a quintessentially British, if not exclusively English, attribute.³³

Such a cultural, ethnic element has consistently permeated the topic and the learned debates about it.³⁴ Even today's common sense reflects it, at least in many parts of the world.³⁵ Some nationalities are considered humorous, while others are decidedly not so. These are widespread stereotypes, of course. And they can still be very pervasive, especially when one wishes to be hilarious. The old joke goes something like this: "Hell is a place where the French greet you at the door, the Germans provide the entertainment, the British do the cooking, and the Italians keep everything organised."³⁶

Aristocrats such as Shaftesbury and high society at large may well have had their own self-gratifying ideas on the refined and clever meaning of "humour" proper in early-modern Britain. For such refined elitists, *fiat "umor" nobilis, et pereat vulgus.*³⁷ But as the Roman educator and rhetorician Quintilian had already realised in the 1ˢᵗ century AD, humour will always have the last laugh.³⁸ Already in the 18ᵗʰ century it was obvious that what was considered humorous in Britain was

---

32 Shaftesbury (1732), parts III, sec. 1, note to par. 3, and IV, sec. 2, par. 1.
33 See, e.g., Cazamian (1930), vol. 1, 4. Hierarchical positionings can also don jingoist attires, as signalled by the British complaints about the "Americanisation" of their native "humour" (Rolfe 2022, title *et passim*). Yet, in a further historical and definitional irony, "English humour" has not only been described as understated and refined, but also as marked by "the higher presence of cynicism and black humour", which make it "more cruel" than, say, Japanese humour (Martchev and Schnickel 2022, 46).
34 We ourselves have been busy writing three volumes about it.
35 Given the common-sense status of our two titular concepts, we integrated the many standard and stately academic references of our book (e.g., peer-reviewed journal articles) with occasional instances of presumedly lower-quality academic research (e.g., graduate theses) and 'popular' sources (e.g., TV series). With his typical wit, Baroncelli (2001, 23) doubted that "the work of professors may help at all, in the long run", and claimed that we can learn a lot about ourselves by taking into account sources at a "lower level" of academic status, such as "everyday conversations, newspapers, TV interviews, tics, manias, commonplaces". (The peer-reviewed journal article where he stated all this being humorously entitled: *The Four Indignities of Irresolute Liberals*.)
36 Icelanders are probably too few and too marginal to even deserve a well-known national stereotype.
37 This being a wordplay based on the famous motto of the Holy Roman Emperor Ferdinand I (*fiat iustitia, et pereat mundus*), which Kant made even more famous by using it to encapsulate his views on capital punishment.
38 See Quintilian (1920), book VI, chap. 3.

not necessarily refined and gentlemanly, but rather anything that could provoke a smile or a laugh. Cruel practical and published jokes, in which the victims are elderly, handicapped, hopeless, abused, bruised, raped, etc., were most common, and they enjoyed great popularity at all the levels of the British social hierarchy of that age.[39]

1.1.3 A Particularly Tricky Balance, or Two

If we consider the very first explicit, 'technical' definition of "humour" proper in its modern English sense—i.e., William Congreve's "singular and unavoidable manner of doing or saying anything, peculiar and natural to one man only, by which his speech and actions are distinguished from those of other men"—there is nothing in it, *logically*, that prevents anyone from singling out rather base, or even debased, traits and idiosyncrasies.[40] This consideration applies also to the art of comedy, with which a playwright like Congreve himself was obviously concerned.[41]

The same can be said of the definition provided by James Beattie, the Enlightenment Scottish poet and philosopher who also tackled "humour" proper in an explicit, 'technical' way, not too long after Congreve. It reads: "the comic exhibition of singular characters, sentiments, and imagery".[42] Moreover, less than one century after Congreve, the English philosopher, painter and essayist William Hazlitt was on the same wavelength with not just one, but two such definitions: "Humour is the describing of the ludicrous as it is in itself" and, less hermetically, "[h]umour, as it is shown in books, is an imitation of the natural and acquired absurdities of mankind, or of the ludicrous in accident, situation, and character".[43]

However worried about propriety and politeness as these British gentlemen could be—and indeed they all were—their definitions, *per se*, imply that *humour is*, basically, *that which we find funny*. And yet matters of balance, measure, degree, equipoise, or equilibrium kept being mentioned with regard to "humour" as such

---

[39] See Dickie (2003), 2–6. More on these 18th-century misdeeds follows in Chapters 2 and 3.
[40] As cited in Figueroa-Dorrego and Larkin-Galiñanes (2009), 362–367, in which we also read that Congreve believed "humour" to be impossible "to define" because it is "of infinite variety".
[41] See Figueroa-Dorrego and Larkin-Galiñanes (2009), 362–367.
[42] Beattie (1778), essay 2, 325.
[43] Hazlitt (1845), 13. *H&C1* offers a lengthier and more detailed account of these three British thinkers.

in its 'young', perchance unique, British sense.⁴⁴ Somehow, being funny was not the whole matter or, perhaps, it ought not to be, despite unrestrained common usage, as these gentlemen's recurrent expressions of social apprehension and moral reprehension inevitably suggest.⁴⁵

Characteristically, the influential 18th-century playwright and essayist Joseph Addison claimed that it is more than possible "to miscarry in Works of Humour", producing such aberrations as "extravagant Conceptions", "wild irregular Fancies", "unnatural Distortions of Thought", and "absurd, inconsistent Ideas" that their own creators would not be able to read "over to themselves without laughing".⁴⁶ When gone askew, the end result is "Nonsense", not "Humour", which "should always lye under the Check of Reason" and "requires the Direction of the nicest Judgment, by so more as it indulges itself in the most boundless Freedoms".⁴⁷

Another tricky balancing act is the one to be found between comical and sympathetic elements. As Beattie wrote, a capable writer could well grasp "comic singularities of a good man" and yet portray them "in circumstances of real distress", such that this "species of humour", should it manage to "force a smile" in its reader or audience, "will draw forth a tear at the same time", as exemplified by "Epic or Dramatic Comedy".⁴⁸ For his part, Hazlitt argued that capable comedians who engaged in feats of "humour" should focus primarily upon "the immediate oddity of the circumstances, and the absurdity or unaccountableness of a foolish action", so that "the ludicrous prevails over the pathetic" and "we receive pleasure instead of pain from the farce of life which is played before us", i. e., so that "comedy" does not slip into "tragedy".⁴⁹

At the close of the 19th century, the famous Spanish-American philosopher and essayist George Santayana echoed the former English author by reflecting on how "humour" calls inherently for a tricky balance between:

---

44 As we explained in *H&C1*, all these authors contrasted "humour" proper with either "wit" or "irony".
45 Again, we must refer our readers to the lengthier account provided in *H&C1*.
46 Addison (1711), editorial 35 (the volume comprising all editorials from *The Spectator* dates from 1891 and is listed as such in the closing bibliography; however, in our footnotes, we indicate the specific author, year of publication and editorial number). K. Weber (1840, part 4, 46–48) derived his own understanding of "true humour" from Addison's one, whose reflections on this subject we tackled extensively in *H&C1* and do not repeat here but partly.
47 Addison (1711), editorial 35.
48 Beattie (1778), essay 2, 325.
49 Hazlitt (1845), 1–2.

(1) the "agreeable" yet clearly unsympathetic depiction of irrational and/or odd behaviours (i.e., "the satirical" component, which "is closely akin to *cruelty*"), and,
(2) "the luxury of imaginative sympathy" (i.e., "the expansion into another life", which we, sufficiently healthy human beings, normally experience as rewarding, despite its being inevitably "painful" to some extent).[50]

Interestingly, Santayana took this nominal "cruelty" to be a given, which needed no debate or justification. Yet, s/he who decides what is to be called "cruel" is not a simple role to ascribe, whether in humorous matters or others. Is it the self-declared victim, the initiator him-/herself, or a third party? Perpetrators rarely claim that they are being cruel.[51]

Representatively, as we discuss in Chapter 2, the late Canadian ethicist Jean Harvey aimed explicitly at looking at "humour" from the neglected "perspective of the socially powerless" that spend their lives in "nonpeer relationships".[52] "Perspective" being the pivotal term here.[53] And as we are going to discuss in Chapter 3 with regard to cruel humour, extant empirical research indicates that the initiators and the recipients of unpleasant jokes and jests have often a diametrically opposed

---

50 Santayana (1896), par. 63; emphasis added. The thin veil separating comedy from tragedy was investigated in a recent essay collection edited by Oppliger and Shouse (2019), presenting 16 different tales on the personal and/or professional shadow-elements of stand-up comedy, e.g., aggressiveness, rebelliousness, depression, addiction, callousness, and bigotry. Hazlitt's very use of the term "farce" in the quoted passage suggests something profoundly painful, notwithstanding the concomitant ridiculous character. As observed *en passant* by the Canadian English scholar J. Coplen Rose (2013, 21; emphasis added), *"farce … produces both humour and cruelty"*. Whether then each artist combines the two in a tense mixture (e.g., Luigi Pirandello) or alternates between them (e.g., Oscar Wilde and Alfred Hitchcock, at least according to Mogg 2005), it remains a creative, aesthetic, *personal* decision.
51 See also Baruchello and Hamblet (2004). As the German-Austrian cultural theorist Wolfgang Müller-Funk (2022, 321; emphasis added) wrote: *"Our Self is a potential tyrant that tends not to acknowledge this fact."* His book is a fascinating philosophical exploration of "cruelty" proper in its own right, though far less concerned than ours with respect to staying close to sources making explicit use of this term alone and pursuing comprehensiveness.
52 Harvey (1999), 6–10.
53 We mean "perspective" *qua* particular viewpoint. Understood instead *qua* long-time and/or future prospect, a cruel *paradox of victimhood* emerges. If, on top of a claim of suffered victimisation, too cherished an identity is built upon it, the victimised person, group, and/or national culture are at risk of nailing themselves to the cross of that past trauma, i.e., leaving themselves without the option of resolving the trauma by overcoming it (e.g., by way of truth-and-reconciliation commissions) and/or condemning it to oblivion (e.g., by way of forgiveness or convenient forgetfulness, as noted by Ernest Renan 1992, 3–4 on the cruel process of nation-building). See, e.g., the study by the Bavarian historian Markus Meckl (2016) on Latvia's post-heroic, post-communist identity.

perception of the same social circumstances, as well as of their attendant levity and/or gravity.[54]

1.1.4 Enter the Germans

Known as the leading pessimist philosopher of the Western canon, Arthur Schopenhauer's masterpiece, *Die Welt als Wille und Vorstellung* [*The World as Will and Representation* or *Idea*], contains a chapter devoted entirely to "the ludicrous".[55] In this brief chapter, Schopenhauer articulated a theory of humour and laughter based on "the opposition ... between perceptible and abstract ideas".[56] This opposition, according to Schopenhauer, is able to engender "paradoxical, and therefore unexpected, subsumption[s] of an object under a conception which in other respects is different from it, and accordingly the phenomenon of laughter always signifies the sudden apprehension of an incongruity between such a conception and the real object thought under it".[57]

Generously, "[i]n order to come to the assistance of the mental inertness of those readers who prefer always to remain in a passive condition", Schopenhauer

---

[54] We have already remarked on the fact that the semantic instability of "humour" and "cruelty" has taught us much *epistemic humility*. Their perspectival character further counsels this attitude, insofar as it is very difficult to gain any solid certainty in the murky social domains that they colour, especially when they are combined into cruel humour (see Chapter 3). While it is obvious that chopping off someone else's limb is a cruel aggression, determining unquestionably whether or not a witty remark was a cruel aggression is far more debatable (see also Plester, Bentley, and Brewer 2022). Harvey (1999) emphasised glaring cases of social subordination related to race, gender, caste and class. Her insights are, however, arguably applicable to the subtler, pervasive, countless forms of stratification and subordination observable in seemingly egalitarian social milieus such as offices, schools and families, e.g., amidst petty bureaucrats, classmates, siblings, and married couples (see Chapters 2–3 and *H&C1*).

[55] Schopenhauer (1909), vol. 2, chap. 8. As to philosophical "pessimism" in general, the present authors take it *seriously* as a plausible interpretation of the human condition, i.e., not as an oddity, hyperbole, or pathology. Some readers may be so constitutively cheerful and full of life as to find this attitude strange and unwarranted. Others, instead, are likely to find it perfectly understandable.

[56] Schopenhauer (1909), vol. 2, chap. 8, 265. A really minor theme in Schopenhauer's oeuvre, P. Lewis (2005, 36) claimed nonetheless that the former's treatment of laughter "illuminate[s] the human predicament".

[57] Schopenhauer (1909), vol. 2, chap. 8, 265. Figueroa-Dorrego and Larkin-Galiñanes (2009, 327) claimed that Schopenhauer's understanding of humour, which pivots around linguistic-conceptual incongruity, anticipates "modern semantic theories of humour and more specifically Victor Raskin's", whom we tackle too.

listed "in this third [and final] edition" of his *magnum opus* numerous "examples", which aim at proving his point and at showing the great many ways in which ludicrous phenomena result from combining sufficiently peripheral particular tokens with the abstract concept under which these tokens can be reasonably categorised, e.g., juxtaposing a tiny dwarf and a professional basketball player *qua* equally valid examples of *homo sapiens*.[58]

During his adult life, Schopenhauer was reputed an excruciating colleague to work with, as well as an insufferably irritable neighbour. Yet, in his main philosophical work, he also exhibited true talent for gathering funny combinations instantiating the modalities in which the general principle of the ludicrous and incongruity can materialise in lived life.[59] While selecting and presenting all such modalities, Schopenhauer rehashed some of the typical notions concerning "humour" proper that Shaftesbury and other British thinkers had already written about, e.g., surprise as an essential psychological factor, satire as a time-honoured case, and "Don Quixote" as a magnificent literary expression of it.[60]

These repetitions also embraced the relationship between the ludicrous and sexuality, which was, for the German philosopher, the most serious matter of all. The gravity of sex is the case because, in Schopenhauer's metaphysics, animal life is said to depend, ultimately and inevitably, upon sex. And, *a fortiori*, so does all the suffering that animal life necessarily entails—not least our own *qua* frail, fallible, mortal human beings. Anticipating the relatively recent speculations on the existence of a 'selfish gene' within all animal creatures, Schopenhauer argued that the species tricks nearly all living individuals into having sufficiently strong sexual longings and, as far as human beings are concerned, into thinking of the satisfaction of such longings as a source of joy, which is so powerful as to covertly facilitate, in one way or another, the eventual perpetuation of the species and, with it, human suffering.[61]

The profound social and personal gravity, existential importance, and effective universality of sexuality in all known cultures can convert this theme into an ob-

---

58 Schopenhauer (1909), vol. 2, chap., 266. (*No quotation mark marks our examples as ours.*) As to the use of "dwarf", we hope not to have been offensive. The ever-changing standards of political correctness make knowing which terms to employ and which to avoid a very taxing matter. Yet another face of life's cruelty. In any case, we were comforted in our use of this term by the recent example of the English disability-studies specialist Erin Pritchard (2022), who explored the ways in which humour can work either against or in favour of dwarfs' respectful inclusion and personal dignity.
59 On Schopenhauer's ill humour and notoriety, see, e.g., Cartwright (2010).
60 (1909), vol. 2, chap. 8, 242. As regards prior British thinkers, Addison, Hartley, Beattie and Hazlitt stand out in particular, all of whom were discussed in detail in *H&C1*.
61 See, e.g., L. Wright (2008).

vious basis for ludicrous incongruities. Nothing is as easy a target for our jocularity as the most serious contexts and sombre issues. Think, for instance, of the countless comedies that pivot around love affairs, the regular comicality of lewd innuendos, the pathetic panting and mechanical pounding of actual copulation or, in another setting where gravity turns easily into levity, the ease with which an unpredicted occurrence at a funeral can lead the participants to smile, giggle or even laugh out loud.[62] Schopenhauer, like possibly only Hazlitt before him and certainly Freud after him, could not avoid noticing how much of people's ordinary humour orbits around sexual themes, behind which lurk the most dramatic issues for both the individual and the species, i.e., life and death.[63]

A piercing and taxing witness of all-too-human burdens and fragilities, Schopenhauer also revealed some of the evil that, in his view, conceals itself within all such ludicrous settings and events.[64] In particular, according to Schopenhauer, the clearest demonstration of the presence of this ingrained evil is the obvious "scorn" that is associated with "the predicate[s] 'ludicrous' or 'absurd'", which

---

62 See Schopenhauer (1909), vol. 2, chap. 8, 275.
63 We deal later with Freud's considerations. As far as Hazlitt (1845, 12) is concerned, the following quoted words must suffice: "comic humour" abounds in "the adventures, difficulties, demurs, hearbreadth 'scapes, disguises, deceptions, blunders, disappointments, successes, excuses, all the dexterous manoeuvres, artful innuendoes, assignations, billets-doux, double entendres, sly allusions, and elegant flattery" aimed at "the obtaining of those 'favours secret, sweet, and precious'" that poets and playwrights do not depict bluntly, but leave "to the imagination" of the audience to reconstruct. (Obviously, Hazlitt was not thinking of his day's pornography.)
64 Schopenhauer (1909) did not address a subtler cruelty implied by the process of subsumption of concrete particulars under abstract generalities, i.e., the logico-conceptual process upon which all ludicrous phenomena were said by him to ultimately rest. This process, in fact, involves *the marginalisation of individual uniqueness in favour of general commonalities*. As we discuss in *H&C3* in connection with the oeuvre of the US psychologist James Hillman (1995), this is a rather standard and methodologically mandated *modus operandi* in the social sciences, whereby actual persons are turned into tokens of sets, classes, categories *et similia*, which are themselves the result of *mathematical averages and/or statistical abstractions from the concrete individual cases* that were recorded experimentally. The actually existing entities of the social world are thereby replaced by the fictional ones created by our mathematical and logical ingenuity, which frequently forgets about this crucial step and leads all kinds of experts to address living people solely as instances of general notions (e.g., 'foreigner') rather than particular persons *in primis* (see, e.g., Gadamer 1996 on the 'vanishing' of the patient in the medical setting, where s/he is 'replaced' by data sets and clinical notions). As Jung (1958a, 9) wrote: "The statistical method shows the facts in the light of the ideal average but does not give us a picture of their empirical reality. While reflecting an indisputable aspect of reality, it can falsify the actual truth in a most misleading way." Long before him, Henri Bergson (1960) had made a similar point on the difference between the abstract time constructed for the sake of scientific knowledge and the concrete time experienced by each living person.

can so effortlessly become "insulting" rather than entertaining, given even a minor, subtle, yet sufficiently adroit alteration of the tone of voice, facial expression, phrasing, and/or circumstances.[65] Above all, Schopenhauer remarked on how we humans laugh most easily at other people's follies and foibles, but not at our own; nor, for that matter, at those of individuals with whom we identify deeply and/or about whom we truly care.[66]

In addition, Schopenhauer offered a crisp definition of "humour" proper, which, like some prior Western thinkers, he contrasted explicitly and starkly with "irony": "if ... the joke is concealed behind seriousness, then we have irony ... The converse of irony is accordingly seriousness concealed behind a joke, and this is humour. It might be called the double counterpoint of irony".[67] Humour, in short, is gravity feigning levity. (Curiously, Addison had famously characterised "True Humour" as exactly the opposite, i.e., levity feigning gravity, for "Ridicule is never more strong, than when it is concealed in Gravity".)[68]

Stressing further the mutual contrast between these two concepts, Schopenhauer stated: "Irony is objective, that is, intended for another", whether it is the audience or the adversary, so that they may eventually learn something.[69] "Humour", instead, "is subjective, that is, it primarily exists only for one's own self", who is "in a serious and sublime mood", but also surrounded by an inevitable and inevitably puerile and/or loathsome "external world ... to which [the self] will not give itself up", and therefore respond to by casting something profound and melancholy by means of a seemingly superficial and light-spirited "joke".[70] Whereas "[i]rony begins with a serious air and ends with a smile", the exact opposite occurs with "humour".[71]

---

65 Schopenhauer (1909), vol. 2, chap. 8, 275.
66 See Schopenhauer (1909), vol. 2, chap. 8. As we discuss later, Hazlitt (1845, 6) had made this point before Schopenhauer, and God knows how many other keen observers of humanity before them both. See, e.g., Lev-Ari and McKay (2022) on the minor phonetic changes that can turn innocent words into profanities.
67 Schopenhauer (1909), vol. 2, chap. 8, 276. *H&C1* covers in much more extensive detail many such prior thinkers.
68 Anonymous (most likely Addison) (1714), editorial 616. In the 20th century, Cipolla (1988, 6) defined 'true' humour as "a subtle and firmly joyful mental disposition of the human mind that is based upon a psychological foundation embracing both balance and well-being", i.e., not "vulgar, facile, offensive and prefabricated" jests.
69 Schopenhauer (1909), vol. 2, chap. 8, 276.
70 Schopenhauer (1909), vol. 2, chap. 8, 277.
71 Schopenhauer (1909), vol. 2, chap. 8, 277. Funnily enough, Cipolla (1988, 7) dissented from this sombre characterisation of "humour", which he too opposed to "irony": "When one is being ironic, he laughs *at* others. When one is being humorous, he laughs *with* the others. Irony produces tensions and conflicts. Humour, when it is utilised in the right measure and at the right moment ... is

The hidden, sublime gravity of "humour" and the astute intellectual work operated by the "true humourist" were said to be rooted in the etymon of the word itself, for "humour depends on a special kind of mood or temper (German *Laune*, probably from *Luna*) through which conception in all its modifications, a decided predominance of the subjective over the objective in the apprehension of the external world is thought".[72] Yet, in spite of his acute and fine conceptual distinctions, Schopenhauer grumbled that "at the present day the word humorous is generally used in German literature in the sense of comical", so that even silly jokes and uncouth comedies are attributed "a more distinguished name than belongs to them".[73] As he wrote: "humour is borrowed from the English to denote a quite peculiar species of the ludicrous", i.e., one that "is related to the sublime, and which was first remarked by them".[74] Such a serious and sublime humour is its "true" form; hence, "humour" proper "is not intended to be used as the title for all kinds of jokes and buffoonery, as is now universally the case in Germany, without opposition from men of letters and scholars".[75]

1.1.5 Many Mean Theories about Humour

Serious sublimity has remained, to date, a primarily German and Romantic *idée fixe*.[76] Despite Schopenhauer's protestations, the generally plainer and open-ended view of humour, which was already visible in the works of many British *literati* and publicists since at least Shaftesbury's day, has been far more influential, though perhaps not in its more uncouth and palpably unpleasant manifestations. As the contemporary Canadian psychologists Kuiper and Martin highlighted, nearly all of today's scientific assessments of "humour" proper, particularly in connection with psychological and physical wellbeing, either underemphasise or disregard altogether "the more common forms of humor based on punning, witty rep-

---

the best remedy to dissipate tensions, resolve situations that could easily become painful, and facilitate the mending of human relations".

72 Schopenhauer (1909), vol. 2, chap. 8, 277. In his writings about "temperament", K. Weber (1840, part 4, 26–34) equated "humour" with "the Britons' spleen" and contrasted it with "the *belle humeur* of the French" who speak, like the Italians, of being in *"belle, bonne, ou mouvaise humeur"* or "moods (*lunes*)", i.e., "moons".

73 Schopenhauer (1909), vol. 2, chap. 8, 278.

74 Schopenhauer (1909), vol. 2, chap. 8, 278.

75 Schopenhauer (1909), vol. 2, chap. 8, 278.

76 See Figueroa-Dorrego and Larkin-Galiñanes (2009) for an account of those few German Romantics espousing this sublime 'humour', which reveals deep truths by juxtaposing infinity and finitude, or the 'big' and the 'small'.

artee, and jokes that express aggressive and sexual themes", taking almost for granted that people's "sense of humor" is—or at least should be presumed to be—adequately refined.[77]

Some scholars, however, did investigate the shadier facets of "humour" proper, or at least those of its most common cognates, e.g., laughter, ridicule, wit, irony, comedy, parody, and satire.[78] Already in the 19th century, for instance, Hazlitt observed that:

(1) There exist frequent uses and, probably, abuses of "humour" itself *qua* intellectual "warfare" by "the meanest weapons".[79]
(2) Such "meanest weapons" being regularly deployed to dismiss serious issues, pooh-pooh the best of art, and turn any- and everything into a silly "parody" of itself.[80]
(3) Whereas "serious and impassioned" endeavours call for much effort, "humour" is a friend to "our indolence, our vanity, our weakness, and insensibility", for almost "[a]nything is sufficient to heap contempt upon an object" and cause it to look "ridiculous".[81]
(4) The same "meanest weapons" are thus employed also to vent "[s]pleen" at innocent and/or worthier people than the jester him-/herself.[82]
(5) Finally, Hazlitt noted that we all "only laugh at those misfortunes in which we are spectators, not sharers".[83]

Additionally, as was already noted, the first book about "laughter" ever published by a prominent Western philosopher, i.e., *Le rire*, was penned by the French Nobel-laureate Henri Bergson, who addressed this phenomenon as a stinging

---

[77] Kuiper and Martin (1998), 159. Such a trend may also be a sign of class origin among academics and/or of their readiness to *censor* (e.g., *qua* editors) and/or *self-censor* (e.g., to avoid 'scandals' jeopardising status or careers).

[78] *We are not implying that these cognates are any easier to pin-point and/or define than "humour" proper.* Polysemy, proteanism and scholarly disagreements abound about them too. See, e.g., Athanasiadou and Colston (2020) on the many expert views about "irony". Or read Murodova's (2022, 735) exemplary long list of diverse and partially overlapping rhetorical figures characterising the age-old literary genre of "satire", i.e., "exaggeration, hyperbole, irony, parody, burlesque, juxtaposition, comparison, analogy". Similarly, consider Dutta's (2010, 169) subtly shifting qualifications of Chinua Achebe's distinctive "humour and irony", i.e., "low key", "pure" and "satirical".

[79] Hazlitt (1845), 23.

[80] Hazlitt (1845), 24. Even serious terms such as "academic" and "professor" can be turned into mocking slurs.

[81] Hazlitt (1845), 23–24.

[82] Hazlitt (1845), 23.

[83] Hazlitt (1845), 6.

means of social control—an instrument of downright cruelty that society can unleash onto eccentric and/or lazy individuals. (We address Bergson's work in another section of this chapter.)

Today, scholars and scientists can therefore be said to possess well-established resources to pursue critical studies of humour, *if they wanted to*. Similarly, awareness of at least some of the cruel elements of humour emerge from the extant expert literature, given how many works circulate that are directed against misogyny, racism, body shaming, ageism, transphobia, etc. Many of these works, if not even most of them, claim that all such negative societal biases find regular expression in comic TV shows, comedies and/or stand-up theatrical performances.[84] (This line of criticism is addressed in Chapter 3)

Nevertheless, we must agree with the US psychologist Harry Harlow on the overarching notion that "humour" proper, especially in its commonplace manifestations, is generally taken to be a good thing.[85] In particular, it is normally believed to be a positive indicator for people's social acceptability, personal maturity, and overall wellbeing.[86] (We address in closer detail Harlow's views about "humour" proper in Chapter 3.) Simply put, it is still much more desirable to have a so-called "sense of humour", however imperfect or biased it may be, than being accused of having none at all.[87] Tellingly, when comparing today's "illiberal left" and "regressive right", the Italian political pundit Beppe Severgnini accused them both of possessing "no sense of humour", i.e., of taking seriously things that should be taken lightly (in this specific instance, debating angrily over an advertisement depicting the great composer Giuseppe Verdi dressed in women's clothing, as being either "sexist" or "unpatriotic").[88]

While censoring people's laughter or their failed attempts at humour are far from unheard of, praising something or someone for lacking any "sense of humour" is rare indeed an occurrence.[89] In truth, we can only cite, once more, Piero

---

[84] We have not conducted a statistical sampling; hence we do not know whether "many" becomes "most".

[85] See, e.g., how the editors of *Veterinaria Italiana* (2012, 343) commended the "humour" of the late Zimbabwean veterinary "Stuart Kenneth Hargreaves" alongside his "honesty, loyalty and sincerity", i.e., as a personal *virtue* in the traditional, technical, Aristotelian-Thomist sense of the term (see Carr, Arthur and Kristjánsson 2017).

[86] See Harlow (1969), 227.

[87] Naturally, this simple fact of associated life begs other important questions: What does it mean to have a sense of humour? Does it necessitate a knack for saying funny things, or is it enough to be able to grasp that something is funny? Or both? Some of these questions are addressed in the present book. Others are in *H&C1* and *H&C3*.

[88] Severgnini (2021), title.

[89] We tackle extensively the issue of censoring laughter and failed humour in *H&C3*.

Mini, who, while discussing Marx's contributions to Western economics and political thought, stated:

> If we wish to understand the phenomenon of the origins of the ideas of Marx the man, the well-known bromide that the Germans have no sense of humor goes further than determinism. Marx took Hebrew-Christian ideals and the ideals of 1789 seriously. He searched for them in life and did not find them. What he found were charlatans like J. Townsend, a priest of the Church of England, from whose works Marx quotes at length... [i]n his attack on society's hypocrisy.[90]

Albeit German, it is not much of a germane defence of the virtues of lacking a sense of humour; is it?[91]

Another issue that further muddles the study of humour is that it takes on many forms, even if we limit ourselves to those that can be operationalised and investigated empirically. Reiterating a structured joke is different from conversational joking, which involves spontaneous play with that which has already been said in a given setting, if not even some highly specific 'in-group' knowledge of prior issues and/or events.[92] As many among us have only learned the hard way, i.e., after trying in vain to repeat something funny from a previous verbal exchange, conversational humour typically requires 'being there' so as to be able to 'get it'. Theatre, cinema, and TV, emblematically, regularly pursue comical effects by recreating situations recalling or replicating real ones, so that the spectators may feel as though they can actually 'be there' and, as a result, enjoy the humorous utterings.[93]

Our present inquiry has thus been hindered thoroughly and repeatedly, since it is not always clear what our expert sources mean when discussing "humour" proper, to say nothing of its numerous cognates.[94] Among such cognates, jokes have been a favourite topic for contemporary psychologists and social scientists in the growing field of humour studies, probably because jokes have a sufficiently manifest and empirically approachable verbal structure, which contains regular components, such as a build-up and a final punchline. Jokes are also obviously in-

---

90 Mini (1974), 180.
91 We assume the question to be rhetorical.
92 We surveyed several representative studies on structured jokes in *H&C1*.
93 Occasionally, however, comedy makes use of unrealistic, Pythonesque circumstances to pursue the same ends.
94 The outstanding plurality of conceptions of 'humour' is testified empirically by our vast exploration in *H&C1*.

tended for humorous purposes—and there exists a genuine profusion of convenient examples from which to choose.⁹⁵

All these considerations notwithstanding, as most of us can confirm, jokes make up only a small share of what we would call "humour" in our daily lives. A relatively recent study showed that less than 20 percent of conversational laughter is elicited by structured linguistic-conceptual forms such as jokes or funny stories.⁹⁶ Most of the recorded laughter ensues instead from fairly banal remarks uttered at the 'right' point in time among the 'right' kind of people, e.g., "Look, it's Andre", or "Are you sure?"⁹⁷

"Laughter" itself seems much more related to mutual playfulness and positive feelings, or to the main emotional tone within a group, than to apt linguistic meanings or clever manipulations of words and thoughts.⁹⁸ So-called "canned humour" regularly exploits our propensity to laugh when others around us happen to laugh, whatever is being laughed at. Jokes, moreover, are also influenced by non-linguistic social factors to a decisive extent and, perhaps incredibly for some of our readers, jokes are not found in some human cultures.⁹⁹

Another conspicuous limitation to humour studies in today's Western humanities and social sciences is that these studies' focus is often set firmly upon the delivery of the message, rather than its reception. Laughter itself, despite being an easily measured behaviour in terms of empirical features such as volume, pitch, duration, pace, and rhythm, is only lightly and episodically scrutinised.¹⁰⁰ It is true that laughter carries with it a strong subjective *quid*, insofar as it can be interpreted in a great variety of ways, e.g., as being jolly, sarcastic, friendly, wicked, arrogant, embarrassed, mocking, nervous, etc. However, these hermeneutical options do not disqualify the more observable aspects that the empirical scientists can inspect, measure and/or assess. Indeed, these diverse interpretative avenues may even open additional ones for nitty-gritty experimental investigation. (We cover several such studies in Chapter 3.)

---

95 See, e.g., Kuipers (2008), 391.
96 See Provine (1996), 41. Sover's (2018) collection is as rare as it is commendable in its emphasis on non-verbal forms of "humour", which in this book comprise "caricatures and cartoons" (part 2), and "slapstick and physical comedy" (part 3). Perhaps humour scholars should slip on banana peels more often than they normally do.
97 Provine (1996), 41.
98 See Provine (1996), 41. We do not need to draw here subtler distinctions between "emotion" and its cognates.
99 See, e.g., Davis (1993).
100 See Eagleton (2019), 2 f.

There exist, of course, noteworthy exceptions to these skewed research emphases, particularly in recent anthropological, ethnographic, and business studies.[101] To further complicate matters, however, we must consider the deeply socio-cultural nature of most instances of laughter and, in fact, of smiles themselves (again, we cover some pertinent studies in Chapter 3). The unconscious and involuntary convulsions and changes in breathing patterns that are basic to laughter are not entirely devoid of cognitive elements, as one would expect, at least *prima facie*. A good example, which is likely to resonate with our readers' lived experiences, is a study showing that people are about *30* times more likely to laugh in a social context than when they are alone.[102]

1.1.6 Three Main Theoretical Frameworks

Given the lack of clear definitions and the plethora of methodological and conceptual issues accompanying such a spotty landscape, a motley crew of theories have been produced by Western scholars and scientists over the last two or three centuries. Nonetheless, there are at least three main frameworks that pop up repeatedly, sometimes in an obvious way, and other times under more indirect a guise or in highly creative, eclectic combinations.[103] These frameworks are commonly known as *superiority, incongruity,* and *relief.*[104]

(1) The superiority theory regards humour as an expression of personal and/or social triumph over other people and/or creatures. By making the so-called "butt of the joke" look and/or feel inferior, mistaken, and/or overpowered, the joker receives a boost to his/her self-confidence. The mechanism at play implies as well that the most frequently targeted persons, groups, or beings are frequently the less fortunate ones, the weakest, or those who happen to deviate patently and vulnerably from the proverbial norm.[105] Many scholars and scientists have subscribed

---

[101] Several examples of such exceptions were presented and discussed in *H&C1*.
[102] See Provine (1996), 41.
[103] *There exists no explicit rule as to determining what is obvious,* even within select fields of human agency. Each reasoning individual, when determining explicitly what is so and what is not so, is required to make a *personal* call, in line with the wisdom of Polanyi (1962c). As attested by daily experience, different conclusions can ensue.
[104] A thorough discussion of examples of all three frameworks, and combinations thereof, is available in *H&C1*.
[105] See Buijzen and Valkenburg (2004), 149.

to this point of view, which has been traced all the way back to Plato and, to a lesser extent, to his most famous pupil, Aristotle.[106]

The latter 'giant' of classical thought, assuredly, described comedy in rather harsh terms, i.e., as being a comic representation of inferior people, who are not utterly bad as such, but somewhat laughable, due to some mild vileness and/or bearable unpleasantness.[107] Funny rascals and odd types abound in comedies, whilst absolute monsters and pitiable clinical cases are not nearly as common in them.[108] In the late Renaissance, Hobbes was a firm believer in superiority as the very core of all laughing matters, writing of the "grimaces called laughter".[109] Later noted scientists, such as Freud in Austria and Harlow in America, were deeply influenced by the superiority theory.[110]

The wisdom of this dismal theory is not hard to grasp.[111] We all can easily recognise that humour, very often, is used as a weapon, i.e., in order to attack and wound all sorts of people, including effeminate males, homosexuals, immigrants, the disabled, southern Italians, Jews, younger siblings, bespeckled individuals, bespectacled ones, white cis-gender able-bodied men, elderly women, the hunchbacks, crooked politicians, the very fat, and the very thin.[112] Nobody is safe by default.[113] Everyone has his/her weaknesses and is, at some crucial point, vulnerable,

---

106 See, e.g., Morreall (1987).
107 See Aristotle (1933), vol. 23.
108 We address further this point when discussing the Benign Violation Theory of humour.
109 Hobbes (1985), part 1, chap. 6, sec. 8.
110 See Billig (2005), 38f.
111 Chapters 2 and 3 discuss the cases mentioned in this early section of our book.
112 A *cruel irony* lies behind the lines and is intentionally inserted in the list above, which contains two non-obvious tokens of vulnerability. In the paragraph above, we wrote "vulnerable" only, not "more vulnerable", "systemically vulnerable", "historically vulnerable", "especially vulnerable", etc. (LVOA can help establish depth and range of the life-disablement at issue.) *Vulnerability is a matter of context.* Thus, a seemingly privileged individual can find him-/herself under very unfavourable circumstances that make him/her the easiest target for stinging jibes or merciless snickering—a point made by the Victorian novelist W.M. Thackeray (as cited in Figueroa-Dorrego and Larkin-Galiñanes 2009, 503–506). In an often-neglected reiteration of Hobbes' (n.d.a. and 1985) dismal wisdom about the radical and inescapable defencelessness of all individuals, *there is no human being that, at some point in his/her life and/or under some respect, is immune from humorous attacks, including viciously cruel ones.*
113 *The listed categories can be mixed, varied and toyed with* at will. In recent years, we have personally witnessed how misogynist and ageist types of humour have frequently been blended with scorching political satire, so as to target prominent US Democrats such as Nancy Pelosi and Joe Biden. On the other side of the American barricade, Republican voters have often been targeted from the left and the left-of-centre of the ideological spectrum by way of scathing classist and misandrist jibes. Establishing which side has predominated and/or 'excelled' in such tokens of cruel humour is a quantitative and qualitative exercise that we do *not* perform here. For one, America's

even to the extreme. What is more, bullying in families, schools and workplaces has an attendant humorous undercurrent. Defeating an opponent in a competition, moreover, will also often be accompanied by a triumphant fit of laughter, or at least by some gratified snickering.[114] As attested by all kinds of theatrical and cinematic productions, we, as spectators, often laugh at the misfortunes of others. The same, not unfrequently, happens in real life.[115]

Fundamentally, here is at play one of the most potent psycho-social drivers ever attested in our culture, and not just in our own: *feeling superior to others*. Some individuals may parade their physical strength, fitness, or beauty. Others their youth, rank, or good taste. Some people race with horses. Others on high horses. Academics will fight battles of wits, titles, awards, and citations. The list is potentially endless, and it probably comprises many readers who feel superior to the present authors in keenness of insight, breadth of erudition, or beauty of style. Humour, in this perspective, is just one of the many available channels to cultivate such a feeling.

As Harlow pointed out in his psychological studies about "humour" proper, the comparative nature of our social relations and, in particular, of our status within the group, means that if we can put down someone else, then our own status improves, at least relatively to these unfortunate targets.[116] Therefore, we, human animals, are frequently on the attack. Or, at least, we are ever ready to seize the moment, not least by means of purported "humour", which Harlow believed to be constitutively, from a psycho-social perspective, a matter of disparagement and aggression, even in its most sophisticated expressions (e.g., satires, comedies, parodies, etc.).[117]

---

so-called "culture wars" are so heated and rancorous as to advise a modicum of critical distance on our part, not least for the sake of honest scholarship. For another, *our evaluative basis is rooted in LVOA*, not in the polarising dichotomies of today's American politics.

114 Roman arenas and the Circus Maximus loom large in our research as special places devoted to the combination of cruelty and humour (see *H&C3*). Yet, the same combination can be retrieved in the *circus minimus* of people's ordinary relationships, e.g., in their dealings with pathetic suitors, petty spouses, senile parents, and pranking siblings. Countless books, dramas and films have depicted such dealings in excruciating detail in the past. Many more will probably do the same in the future. In any case, we assume our readers to have come across an ample supply of telling instances of such cases, whether fictional or real. If they have not, then we envy them.

115 We presume that all readers who are parents have found themselves stopping their offspring from making fun of an individual that suffered some misfortune, trying thus to teach their child/ren the difficult and ever-changing art of knowing when and how to laugh, poke fun at, and make light of.

116 See Harlow (1969), 226.

117 See Harlow (1969), of which we give a more thorough account in Chapter 3.

Significantly, as evolutionary psychologists have repeatedly commented, the facial expressions that we utilise to show humour and aggression are eerily similar, i.e., baring of our teeth, grinning, and making barking noises.[118] Both humour and aggression are regularly said to have their roots in our primordial, 'wild' animal nature, rather than in some aloof, uniquely 'human' quality. True enough, animals do not display anything akin to our complex languages, which are the conduit through which much humour and attendant cruelty are expressed. Instead, animals reveal simpler and more basic forms of playfulness, which have been inherited by today's humankind, in all likelihood, for we all descend from mammalian ancestry, one capable of social interaction and self-organisation.[119]

Play among young animals, as among young humans, involves fighting, which is, in evolutionary terms, a crucial means to train the offspring in the skilful use of their in-born violent instincts and, as far as carnivores are concerned, their killer instincts. Thus, writing in the turbulent 1970s, the American literary scholar Leonard Feinberg described "humor" as a matter of out-and-out "aggression", either "obvious" or "playful", and aimed at all kinds of possible targets: "hypocrisy" (e.g., "unexpected truth"); "inhibitions" (e.g., "sexual humor"); "propriety" (e.g., "scatological humor"); "the design of the universe" (e.g., "cosmic humor"); "everything" (e.g., "black humor"); "logic and order" (e.g., "nonsense humor"); and "conformity" (e.g., "word play").[120] "Cruel/ty" proper, instead, was reserved by him, primarily, to the puppet "Punch", most "practical jokes" (i.e., pranks), and the vast repertoire of "sick jokes".[121]

(2) The incongruity theory, which we encountered in this book when discussing Schopenhauer, claims that we laugh at things that we find unfamiliar, surprising, baffling, puzzling, astonishing, etc. This stance has been a favourite of many contemporary social scientists, who are primarily interested in the way in which the human mind works when processing information.[122] Accordingly, humour is something that materialises when we start interpreting and categorising our perceptions and/or thoughts, only to have them take a somewhat startling turn from

---

[118] We discussed at length the contributions of evolutionary psychology to humour studies in *H&C1*.
[119] See, e.g., Morreall (1987).
[120] Feinberg (1978), 9, 27 and 75–183.
[121] Feinberg (1978), 40–42 and 166–167. More on pranks and cruel jokes follows in the next two chapters.
[122] The published volumes of De Gruyter's *Philosophy of Humor Yearbook* would confirm this point, but also indicate that ethical concerns about the ab/uses of "humour" proper are central to today's debates too.

what is customarily their cognitive route. When things are then put into a sufficiently different context than what we are used to—hence leading us into territory that is puzzling yet does not cause fear or major discomfort—surprise, fun, and satisfaction can occur.[123]

A few years ago, the American philosopher Noël Carroll posited that this theory had become the most important one among humour scholars, at least in the Anglophone world.[124] Its combination of linguistic, cognitive, and epistemic emphases is hard to resist for today's laboratory experts and university professors. Indeed, the UK literary critic Terry Eagleton recently affirmed that all the 'fashionable' new theories circulating in today's Anglophone academia are variations on the fundamental theme of incongruity: "the play theory, the conflict theory, the ambivalence theory, the dispositional theory, the mastery theory, the Gestalt theory, the Piagetian theory and the configurational theory".[125]

This great plurality of sub-theories is neither surprising nor discomforting, as far as we, the authors of this book, are concerned. Rather, it is the foreseeable result of the *Gestalt* switch that the scholars perform, whether conscious of it or not, when they stop attending *from* incongruity as a tacit premise for approaching humour in some particular forms (e.g., verbal jokes among colleagues, the visual gags of slapstick comedy) and start attending *to* incongruity itself in its many, possibly infinite, constitutive subsidiary details.[126] Insofar as each scholar comes armed with his/her own presuppositions, aims, interests, past experiences, technical categories, etc., s/he is bound to re/conceptualise the incongruity at issue in some variously original and ultimately *personal* way, i.e., not merely subjective, but believed by the individual scholar to possess universal significance, i.e., objectivity.[127]

This re/conceptualisation, in turn, leads to an equally variously novel perspective on humour too, albeit one-step, several-steps, or even many-steps removed from the actual matters that get meticulously analysed, detailed, measured, and/or construed in each specific study (e.g., pragmatic modifiers, literary devices, so-

---

[123] See, e.g., Krikmann (2006), 27. As was amply discussed in *H&C1*, these considerations have ancient roots.
[124] See Carroll (2014), 1–2.
[125] Eagleton (2019), 67. We should add to this list the "Dismissal Theory of Humor" discussed in Olin (2020, 61 f).
[126] See our account of this psychological and phenomenological "switch" in *H&C1*.
[127] See, again, *H&C1*, concluding chapter. Let us just note here that the re/conceptualisations can vary enormously from one another in both depth and breadth, from small increments to paradigm shifts. All the while, more water is being poured out of the tacitly presupposed well of our common-sense ideas of 'humour' and 'incongruity'.

ciological implications, neurophysiological responses). And inasmuch as each new research pathway is also a potential rabbit-hole filled with new questions and new challenges, there can easily derive new incongruities as well, i.e., the inevitable distances, discrepancies, and dissonances that all these different sub-theories provide on, allegedly, one and the same fundamental theme: humour.[128]

(3) The third main theory centres upon the notion of 'relief' or 'release', i.e., the idea according to which all normal reactions to humour help us to expel some pent-up psychic energy. This theme can be traced back to early Western intellectuals such as Shaftesbury or Spencer, but is perhaps most commonly associated with Freud and, in particular, his interest in how the culturally-supressed sexual and aggressive drives that are vital for each individual can find indirect ways to be expressed in allegedly 'civilised' settings.[129]

Freud's theories are no longer in vogue among contemporary psychologists, but his writings on terms such as "jokes", "wit", "laughter", and "humour" remain relevant.[130] This is true, at the very least, in historical terms, for no serious account of modern psychology can ignore Freud's seminal contributions. Besides, our own quotidian experiences would justify a Freudian focus, for humour studies centring upon sexuality (e.g., lewd jokes among female friends who can relax in one another's company) and aggressiveness (e.g., competitive conduct among male humour scholars themselves) are patently more than justified, given people's observable conduct.[131] Yet, however popular this theory may have been in Freud's day and age, and no matter how sensible we ourselves find it to be, no contemporary thinker would claim that relief, albeit important for our wellbeing, explains all aspects of humour.[132]

We should also mention that, when engaging in a commonplace humorous interaction, e.g., telling a joke, the joker and the listener enter into an unspoken pact, whereby it is presumed that the joker is no longer affirming the truth, and that the listener reciprocates by letting go of moral/ising and/or critical thinking.[133] In this way, the participants can be united in their temporary enjoyment of, say, rude,

---

128 See Chesterton's remarks in Section 2.4 on the wide crevasse separating the reductionistic psychological and physiological accounts of laughter from the complex humorous creations of comedians and other artists.
129 See Buijzen and Valkenburg (2004), 148–149, and Hurley et al. (2011), 74.
130 As we discussed extensively in H&C1, McDougall (1926) took Freud very seriously and argued that humour provides relief in the face of life's cruelty, which would otherwise be unbearable.
131 We also assume our readers to have had direct experience of the relieving benefits of humour and laughter.
132 See Kuipers (2008), 366.
133 See Perlmutter (2002), 158–159. The claims following in the same paragraph are based on the same text.

randy, ethnic, sexist, and/or sick jokes, knowing full well that what is being uttered may seem offensive, belligerent, and/or flatly cruel to some people.[134] Such an elaborate and voluntary suspension of common standards of morality and etiquette probably indicate a deep-seated need for humorous relief.[135] Smiling and laughing, after all, are often a sign of tension and, *inter alia*, are means of coping with uncomfortable situations.[136]

These three theories do not constitute three separate, well-defined schools of thought, but should be seen as each having its own focal point so that any given humorous phenomenon can be plausibly explained in at least three ways by means of pertinent aetiological elements, i.e., in a non-exclusive manner. In particular, it is reasonable to relate:
(1) relief theory to the psychophysiology of our emotional responses to such phenomena;
(2) the superiority theory to the inter- and intra-personal hierarchies that may be at play therein; and
(3) incongruity to the cognitive side and/or components of the same phenomena.[137]

All humour, even absurd jokes *à la* Groucho Marx or Woody Allen, has some logical structure, takes place within a socio-personal milieu, and demands a build-up of psychic tension that is then resolved in the surprised grasping or rethinking of the premise/s at play.[138] Therefore, while each theory may be capable of highlighting a necessary aspect of much, or perhaps all, humour, no single theory can be taken *per se* as being sufficient, exclusive, and all-encompassing, at least in our reasoned opinion.[139]

---

134 *Our* own referring to means of offense is not intended to be offensive. Readers that should feel offended by our non-offensive use of potentially offensive language or ideas must then consider *their* own personal affective contribution to the offensive interpretation of commonly offensive notions that are not being used offensively in the present uncommon setting, i.e., an academic study. See our account of Polanyi (1962c) in Chapter 2 and *H&C1*.
135 Further considerations on this point follow in *H&C3*.
136 See Hurley *et al.* (2011), 74–75.
137 This claim can be found in Buijzen and Valkenburg (2004), 148.
138 See, e.g., Swabey (1961).
139 We discussed in more detail in *H&C1* how these three theories can interact with, and effectively interpret, one another. Given today's prevalent emphasis by scholars and students on the incongruity theory and/or some astute filiation thereof, the present book may be seen as a rediscovery of the wisdom inherent to the superiority theory. In a similar vein, *H&C3* can serve as a rediscovery of the wisdom inherent to the relief theory.

Another theoretical construct that is significant for today's humour studies is the dichotomy between *structuralism* and *functionalism*. Scientists involved in the former have been more interested in *what* makes something funny, i.e., which 'bits' or 'ingredients' can be said to be at work. Whereas those who operate in the latter camp have cared more about *why* something is funny, i.e., what the purpose of humour is or may be.

However, an analogous proviso must be kept in mind with respect to this dichotomy as was already the case regarding the previous three general theories of "humour" proper. Most scholars in the field cannot be categorised exclusively into either camp and no given humorous phenomenon can be fully studied by means of either of them only. Nonetheless, as Weberian ideal types, such neat distinctions can prove helpful *vis-à-vis* grasping pivotal conceptual and/or methodological aspects of humour and, as such, they are drawn early in this first chapter.[140]

1.1.7 Charles Darwin and His Descendants

The functionalists of the 20th- and 21st- centuries are the direct ideological descendants of Charles Darwin. The great British scientist pondered extensively upon laughter—and cruelty—in his foundational research, especially the influential 1872 book, *The Expression of the Emotions in Man and Animals*.[141] In it, Darwin extended further his then-radical idea that human conduct and cognition are biological features and can therefore be inherited *via* the same mechanisms that are applicable to other biological features, e.g., the colour of our eyes or hair.

This means essentially that human conduct and cognitive patterns that have served our ancestors' survival are likely to be an integral part of our current structural and functional repertoire—whether each or any of us then openly acknowledges, utilises, and/or likes such a repertoire or not. In this way, Darwin set up a fundamental premise for all the scientists who have come after him: given that commonplace humour is an inborn and quasi-universal feature of humankind, it must have served an evolutionary purpose at some point in the history of our species. It likely enabled the survival of those who determined the species' path. The same must also be true of cruelty.[142]

---

[140] "Weberian ideal types" are, *in nuce*, convenient simplifying abstractions from messier empirical observations. However, such types are not absolute by any stretch whatsoever of the human imagination. See, e.g., Israel, Konieczny, and Ferstl (2022) on the relief-inducing psychophysiological responses to incongruity in jokes.
[141] See Darwin (1872), 33–86.
[142] This premise and its resulting lines of study are discussed further in Chapters 2 and 3.

Many Darwinians have thus been busy trying to explicate the remote origins and the evolutionary functions of commonplace humour, mainly in terms of sexual selection.[143] According to this thesis, whenever we engage in humorous conduct, we are not trying to be funny just for the sake of it. On the contrary, we do so because such conduct gives us a competitive advantage in building social capital and, potentially, mating.[144] These scientists have frequently paired possessing a sense of humour with brains; i.e., that intelligence predicts humour skills, and that humour, fundamentally, predicts mating success.[145] The aetiological paths that these scientists' explanations follow in each case can be convoluted, but the inherent causal logic is simple and consistent with Darwin's basic premise.

Characteristically, the 21st-century evolutionary psychologist Geoffrey Miller claimed that humour *per se* would have been of no evolutionary value among the early hominids living in the African savannas of paleoethological lore.[146] Instead, he suggested that some features leading to commonplace humour must have evolved *via* mechanisms of sexual selection; i.e., because of such features' function *qua* indicators of other, more valuable individual traits, e.g., intelligence.[147] Or, people's humour has become attractive for it signals deeper, more basic skills, and that is why it was passed on across generations, in the long history of our species.[148]

Other researchers have found scant empirical evidence for claims of this kind. There have been studies showing that the wittiness of suitors, partners and/or husbands has no significant correlation with the spouse's marital satisfaction, and is furthermore an extremely poor predictor of reproductive success.[149] Other studies find positive correlation between various sorts of creativity tests and measured levels of commonplace humour, whether produced or appreciated.[150] Yet, several studies found no such correlation.[151]

True enough, in daily life, we have all experienced unrestrained giggling and much laughter, especially throughout puberty. Still, it is hard to reconcile

---

[143] See an overview of such studies in Greengross and Miller (2011), 188.
[144] See, e.g., Hurley *et al.* (2011), 21. Evolutionary psychology tends to overestimate its own capabilities by attempting to explain literally *all* human behaviour along its characteristic lines of sexual selection and/or adaptation to environmental circumstances, while at the same time being singularly bad at predicting it.
[145] See, e.g., Greengross and Miller (2011), 188.
[146] G. Miller (2000).
[147] See G. Miller (2000), 415–416.
[148] See G. Miller (2000), 415–416.
[149] See, e.g., Storey (2003), 320.
[150] See the review of such studies in Storey (2003), 320–323.
[151] See Storey (2003), 320–323.

this inclination towards laughing with "humour" proper, whether ordinary or refined. All this juvenile ebullience is far more likely to have something to do with the sheer nervous energy associated with those formative years—hence recalling the wisdom of relief theory.

As far as juvenile ebullience and the need for release may go, it was already remarked that the playful aggression of mock fights is an integral part in the process of maturation among many mammalian species and in establishing a clear pecking order within a given group.[152] Evolutionary psychologists have often associated the laughter or laughter-like responses observable in primate play with nominal "humour".[153] For primates and hominids, this type of laughter would signal that the play in which the individual animals are engaged is pleasurable and, moreover, that they would like to continue.[154]

Stanford psychology professor William F. Fry theorised that such a type of play is dependent, like many jokes, upon a paradoxical principle: "This is an attack that is not really an attack".[155] Ostensibly, aggression and humour use nearly the same physiological mechanisms for visible and audible expression. This also corresponds with some of our own lived experiences, e. g., when highly emotional responses are accompanied by unwanted stupid grins or nervous laughing.[156] What the deeper meaning of all this is, and whether there is any deeper meaning to it, are matters of considerable debate.[157]

1.1.8 Henri Bergson

The English ghost of Darwin has been present in nearly all subsequent scientific work about humour. Nevertheless, some other scholars have had unique and highly original approaches. Bergson, for one, was interested in the links between human beings and their animal ancestry, the importance of emotions for laughter, and laughter's social qualities and functions. He developed an inimitable viewpoint, which still influences scholars and social scientists today.[158]

---

[152] See Storey (2003), 320.
[153] See Storey (2003), 323–324.
[154] See Storey (2003), 323–324.
[155] As cited in Storey (2003), 321.
[156] We expect that our readers have experienced such discordant occurrences or are able to fathom them. Apparently, they are already observable among primary-school pupils, whose laughter can be a sign of contentment as easily as of disquiet (Nugent 2022).
[157] Even a cursory look at the pertinent literature would reveal the plurality of views available.
[158] We remarked repeatedly on Bergson's enduring influence in *H&C1*.

Bergson maintained that human activities alone can be legitimately considered ludicrous and people find animals to be funny only when their behaviour resembles that of humans. According to him, the human being is not only "an animal which laughs", as many philosophers had already claimed, but rather "an animal which is laughed at".[159] Concomitantly, emotions were not the most important aspect of ludicrous phenomena; rather, their conspicuous absence was, as "laughter has no greater foe than emotion".[160]

In *Le rire*, Bergson is clearly channelling emotions such as pity, sympathy, amiability, or friendliness. Laughter, in his opinion, is rooted in a remarkable and marked absence of empathy.[161] That is why "the comical" was famously said by him to call for "a momentary anaesthesia of the heart".[162] Without temporarily shutting down our empathetic feelings, we, *human* animals, would not be able to laugh. Humour, under this perspective, would therefore appear to be tickling chiefly our rational side, as though the persons whom we laugh at behave irrationally. In the process, we also suspend our sympathetic affects, at least temporarily, so as to be able to truly enjoy these people's errors and misfortunes.[163]

Bergson's emphasis on the social significance of laughter is, on the other hand, unadulterated Darwinism. According to Bergson, laughter has at all times a social implication: "Our laughter is always the laughter of a group".[164] Equally important for him was the notion that, if we are not among those who are laughing, we become easily and almost immediately uncomfortable. Why is that? As Bergson suggested, the first idea that pops into our minds is that the group may be laughing at us.[165] The social element of laughter was pivotal, according to Bergson, who saw commonplace humour as a tool for effective and enforced socialisation. Laughter

---

[159] Bergson (1911), loc 48. As Amir (2013, 6–8) noted, far more philosophers remarked on the human being's supposedly unique ability to laugh than on our inherent ridiculousness. See also Amir (2019), xi.
[160] Bergson (1911), loc 52.
[161] This point is rehearsed in Chapter 2. *Cultural differences are often a major obstacle to mutual empathy*, free-flowing fun, cooperation, solidarity and many other respects. As even fictionally exemplified and humorously parodied in *Star Trek: Deep Space Nine*, "nobody can understand the Klingons but, as O'Brien says, that's the way they like it". (Star Trek 1999, 274)
[162] Bergson (1911), loc 61. A complete emotional shutdown would make humour unlikely, if not impossible. As noted by Shaftesbury et al., our 'animal spirits' and, in particular, the emotion of surprise, remain pivotal. What Bergson was emphasising in his work, then, is the suspension of rapport between the jokester and the laughee.
[163] See Bergson (1911), loc 43–58.
[164] Bergson (1911), loc 66.
[165] See Bergson (1911), loc 66.

serves to make people more socially mindful, more adaptable and, perhaps unsurprisingly, more pliable and obedient.[166]

Despite the overall dynamic nature of human society, its members can sometimes exhibit inelasticity in character, mind, and/or body. This functional failure reflects potentially harmful deviation from the expected norms, including undue lack of action.[167] The vulnerable and ever-tenuous unity of the group, in Darwinian terms, needs the people inside it to display repeatedly and reliably that they are, at least to some meaningful degree, marching in the same direction. Laughter is, therefore, a plausible, practical and, quite often, potent corrective tool, which some members initiate on behalf of society in response to human conduct that is not necessarily menacing, but that generates unease. As Bergson quipped: "Rigidity is the comic, and laughter is its corrective".[168]

1.1.9 Luigi Pirandello

The 1908 book entitled *L'umorismo* [*Humour*], written by the Italian Nobel-laureate playwright, novelist, and essayist Luigi Pirandello, focussed on "humour" proper, rather than on "laughter" or "the comical", as was the case in Bergson's earlier seminal work.[169] Pirandello devoted a considerable part of this book to going over the notorious definitional knottiness of "humour" proper. Like previous thinkers who had tried to get to grips with this thorny term, Pirandello concluded by acknowledging its patent polysemy and recognising that it is much easier to say what humour is not, rather than what it is.[170]

Pirandello concluded here that "humour" is neither "an exclusively modern phenomenon", nor "a prerogative of Anglo-Germanic nations".[171] He also distinguished between "humour", as is commonly understood in daily speech, and a particular aesthetic or artistic sense of it—"true humour".[172] This more authentic version of the term "humour" was not, in Pirandello's view, limited to either modern

---

166 See Bergson (1911), loc 93–101.
167 See Bergson (1911), loc 174–176.
168 Bergson (1911), loc 185.
169 Pirandello (1920). An eloquent English translation is available, i.e., Pirandello (1974), which is however not close enough to the original from a philological point of view, as is needed by our study of "humour" proper.
170 As we discussed in detail in *H&C1*, the semantic plurality of nominal "humour" started being acknowledged as soon as its modern meaning became prevalent, e.g., in Addison's 18th-century editorials for *The Spectator* (1891).
171 Pirandello (1920), 115.
172 Pirandello (1920), 115.

or Anglo-Germanic literature, especially that from the Romantic age. He claimed that it can be found already in the ancient and medieval literature of nearly every country, albeit in only few, artistically exceptional instances.[173] Pirandello's rare "true humour" was already exemplified in "Socrates attending *The Clouds* at the theatre and laughing with the audience at how [Aristophanes] ridicules him".[174]

"Humour" was then similarly distinguished by Pirandello from "art in general, as this was taught by rhetoric", insofar as the former is an "intimate, inaccurate, essential process that, inevitably, de-structures, dis-orders, dis-accords".[175] Equally, "true humour" is not "irony", as Pirandello wrote, given that the latter "is almost always comical yet without pathos".[176] Instead, quoting *verbatim* the Italian literary critic Momigliano, Pirandello emphasised how "humourists" poke fun at their own "melancholy", thus exhibiting a "painful dualism", which is "the true consolation of desperate people".[177]

Once again, *Don Quixote* was celebrated by Pirandello as an astounding case of "humour's laughter", such that, "the comical is overcome, not by the tragic, but through the comical itself".[178] When reading Cervantes, we "commiserate while laughing, or laugh while commiserating".[179] "True humour", therefore, could be said to consist in "the feeling of the contrary", i.e., sensing how every ludicrous event is immediately followed by sadness or bitterness, just like our shadows follow the body's every movement.[180] Pirandello's "feeling of the contrary" is, in other words, induced by reflecting immediately upon a prior feeling, without hiding it from view, and eventually merging the resulting new feeling with that prior one, even if such an act means a striking combination of two opposites, i.e., a "contradiction".[181]

According to Pirandello, who was himself famous for his comedies and humorous writings, this crucial "feeling of the contrary" could be elicited in all sorts of creative ways. For example, Pirandello listed the following methods and manners of "contradiction" (i.e., incongruity): "melancholy and forgiveness"; "melancholy and resentment"; "ridiculousness and seriousness"; "illusion and reality"; "morali-

---

173 See Pirandello (1920), 115–116.
174 Pirandello (1920), 37.
175 Pirandello (1920), 47.
176 Pirandello (1920), 56.
177 Pirandello (1920), 74.
178 Pirandello (1920), 107.
179 Pirandello (1920), 107–108.
180 Pirandello (1920), 113 and 115.
181 See Pirandello (1920), 180.

ty and calculation"; "intimate feeling and social convenience"; "habit and logic"; "consciousness and substratum" (i.e., the unconscious); "justice and injustice"; "hope and fear"; "our past selves and our present selves"; "busy daily life and life's emptiness or meaninglessness"; and "genius and insignificance".[182]

The first step in generating "true humour" arises when observing a person's "alertness to the contrary", e.g., when meeting an elderly lady covered in "make-up" and "youthful clothes" in the vain attempt to look much younger.[183] Such a sight is ridiculous, and is the quintessence of "the comical".[184] The second step takes place when the same person starts reflecting—promptly, instinctively, and however briefly—upon the reasons why the comical elderly lady is doing that, e.g., "to pitifully convince herself that she may be able to get her much younger husband to keep loving her".[185] At that point, the person at issue steps beyond the original comical awareness, and into "the feeling of the contrary".[186] That is where "the humorous" resides in its "true" form, according to Pirandello.[187]

Artistically, "reflection" seems to play a fundamental role in "humorously" breaking, or interfering with, the "spontaneous" imaginative inertia and compositional "harmony" of the fictional creations, e.g., by way of "intrusion" or "variations and digressions", but only as long as this "reflection" is as "spontaneous" and organic to the fictional creations as were the original inertia and harmony.[188] Humorous creations cannot be forced, lest they become stale, spurious, and unconvincing. As Pirandello asserted, "genuine humour" cannot arise from "mere verbal contradiction", "rhetorical decoy", or cold conceptual "contrast between ideality and reality", for it requires instead an "immediate doubling" of any "feeling" or "thought ... into its contrary", as though the feeling or thought instantly and organically reflected onto itself, to trace in its own opposite its very point of origin.[189]

Pirandello claimed that this crucial "doubling" of feeling and/or thought does not occur in "the comical, the ironic, the satirical", unlike in the creations of "humourists", who are sensitive artists embracing this bittersweet duplicity, which allows them to create, essentially, "that which looks like them".[190] Unlike "comics and satirists", "humourists" are not cold or stern judges, even in the face of "theft"

---

[182] Pirandello (1920), 134–136, 164–169 and 171.
[183] Pirandello (1920), 141.
[184] Pirandello (1920).
[185] Pirandello (1920), 141.
[186] Pirandello (1920), 141–142.
[187] Pirandello (1920), 142.
[188] Pirandello (1920), 148–150.
[189] Pirandello (1920), 156 and 163.
[190] Pirandello (1920), 113 and 163.

and "murder".[191] Unlike "sociologists", they grasp objectively the sad and troubling truths about living people, but also empathise with them.[192] Unlike "epic or tragic poets", these compassionate "humourists" do not depict "heroes" facing bravely life's "contrary and repugnant elements".[193] "[H]umourists" may well "dislike reality", experience the existential contradictoriness of "Being" and the meaninglessness of "the naked life", and perhaps naughtily enjoy "unmasking" human lies and inconsistencies; but they are not "angered" by any of this, about which they say, humbly yet captivatingly: "that's life!"[194]

1.1.10 Sigmund Freud

Another Western intellectual 'giant' who wrote extensively on humour and was influenced by Darwin, was Sigmund Freud. Although he shared some of Bergson's complexifying thoughts on the socially corrective nature of humour and the ruthlessness that it sometimes reveals, Freud saw commonplace humour, first and foremost, as possessing a psychic-hedonic purpose. In tandem with the rest of his work, humour was thus linked with the machineries of the two dominant forces that he believed to be at work within the human psyche: *sexuality* and *aggression*. Hence humour became for Freud, as most of our behaviours and thoughts, an instrument to either release or supress these feelings in the never-ending tug-of-war between the inevitably mutating and unstable crucial components of our psyche, through which the forces of sexuality and aggression are experienced and coped with by each person, i.e., our *ego*, the *super-ego*, and the *id*.[195]

As Freud observed, an innocent joke may provide moderate pleasure, but to be truly funny, it has to be tendentious.[196] Freud argued that the joke has to be either hostile (e.g., aggressive, satirical, offensive-defensive) or obscene (e.g., exposure), even if this means hurting other people's feelings in the process.[197] In his extensive characterisation of wit, upon which jokes are said to rely, the ingredients for cruelty can thus be readily identified, i.e., the willingness to forego concerns for other

---

[191] Pirandello (1920), 163 and 170.
[192] Pirandello (1920), 167.
[193] Pirandello (1920), 177–178.
[194] Pirandello (1920), 163, 166, 174 and 178–179.
[195] We discussed at length the central tenets of Freud's psychology in *H&C1*.
[196] See Freud (1960), loc 1518, 1527, 1537 and 1543.
[197] See Freud (1960), loc 1553–1554 and 1562–1563. *H&C1* offers a detailed accounts of all these strategies.

people's emotional wellbeing in the pursuit of one's own hedonic goals.[198] Bergson's anaesthesia of the heart finds thus a glaring echo in Freud's work.[199]

Unlike Bergson, Freud's chief attention was set upon the inner workings of the individual psyche. Nevertheless, Freud's theories included a complex interplay of social factors. Granted, his work must be read with wary consideration of the *Zeitgeist*, but it can still provide interesting insights today. For example, when it comes to smut, Freud maintained that lewd humour is directed towards a particular person whom the joker finds sexually arousing and/or expects to become aroused as well.[200] The targeted person may, however, experience embarrassment, both in reaction to the excitement and in the admission of it.[201]

A male child of his sexist age, Freud thought that smut is typically directed by men towards women as a form of seduction.[202] When men share smut in the company of other men, instead, it is because the desired libidinous situation cannot happen due to social inhibitions and/or prohibitions, and it has therefore to be imagined. In Freud's words: "A person who laughs at smut that he hears is laughing as though he were the spectator of an act of sexual aggression."[203]

In his writings about smut, Freud unwrapped the inner workings of not only the human psyche with respect to ordinary humour, but also his own psyche and the society that formed him. His discussion of smut reveals particularly well the gender- and class-based reality of his times and of his own circumstances.[204] Women were thus taken to be the passive targets of smut, and, amongst commoners, their physical presence was said to be required for men to start engaging in it.

In the higher echelons of society, on the contrary, smut stops once a woman enters the premises.[205] In 'refined' society, moreover, the quality of a joke depends on the discrepancy between what is said and what it causes the listener to imagine.

---

198 Freud (1957), 128.
199 A thorough discussion of Freud's works was offered in *H&C1*, especially as regards the difference between the callousness required for joking ("cruelty" proper) and the enjoyment of other people's discomfort ("sadism").
200 See Freud (1960), loc 1562.
201 See Freud (1960), loc 1562.
202 See Freud (1960), loc 1562.
203 See Freud (1960), loc 1568.
204 Among the many bio-socio-cultural factors that can be conceived of and investigated, gender remains a pivotal element with regard to producing and appreciating humour in general, as amply reported by contemporary empirical psychologists. See, e.g., Tosun, Faghihi, and Vaid (2018), who also remarked repeatedly on "hostility" and "sarcasm" as common features of humorous exchanges among people in the US and Turkey.
205 See Freud (1960), loc 1598–1603.

The greater the difference, the better the joke.[206] According to Freud, members of the social elite are not permitted to laugh at the same coarse smuttiness as the 'great unwashed'. Therefore, tendentious jokes are used to satisfy lustful and aggressive thoughts that would otherwise remain unbearably repressed.

This inherent emotional quality makes it impossible to distinguish with certainty whether people are really enjoying the technical aspect of the joke or just revelling in the crude obscenity of it. Given that such jokes, especially outside refined circles, frequently produce great roars of laughter while lacking any significant structural sophistication, Freud inferred that the latter element was central for humour to hit the mark.[207]

Smut also reveals another feature of Freud's psychoanalytic theories, i.e., the fundamental mixture of the sexual and the aggressive. A tendentious joke usually needs a minimum of three people: the joker, the target of the joke, and, as a minimum, one listener.[208] It is normally not the joker who gets the pleasure of hearing himself tell the funny story, but the inactive listener.[209]

According to Freud, smut puts these people into an emotionally intense and aggressive mutual relationship.[210] Typically, the joker's libidinal impulses are not welcomed by the female. Therefore, the male becomes hostile towards her and uses the inactive listener as his ally.[211] Smut exposes the woman in the mind of the listener, who in turn gets effortless sexual gratification.[212]

Freud identified several other types of tendentious jokes, including cynical, hostile, and sceptical ones.[213] All involve overcoming external or internal psychic obstacles, although it should be said that the latter sort is merely the internalised version of the former.[214] External obstacles refer to the possibility that an ill-considered joke might put our societal status in jeopardy.[215] Our internal obstacles, for their part, result from internalising the norms imparted to us by our parents and/or society.[216] Tendentious jokes provide us with an opportunity to circumvent

---

206 See Freud (1960), loc 1598–1603.
207 See Freud (1960), loc 1616, 1619, 1625 and 1644.
208 See Freud (1960), loc 1606–1612.
209 See Freud (1960), loc 1606–1612.
210 See Freud (1960), loc 1606–1612.
211 See Freud (1960), loc 1606–1612.
212 See Freud (1960), loc 1606–1612.
213 See Freud (1960), loc 1881.
214 See Freud (1960), loc 1905–1918.
215 See Freud (1960), loc 1905–1918.
216 See Freud (1960), loc 1921.

these obstacles, with noticeably more pleasure to be had from overcoming the internal obstacles than the external ones.[217]

This outlet for human emotions is, however, unevenly distributed. Some mortals have it in buckets, while others struggle in vain to be funny. The gift of "wit" proper is not related to intelligence, imagination, and memory, according to Freud, but to a personality-neurotic illness and a need to exhibit one's own cleverness in public.[218] This urge can be seen as a form of sexual exhibitionism. Perhaps stand-up comedians are comicality's unashamed flashers. After all, in the Freudian perspective, since jokes have to be potentially offensive in order to be genuinely funny, telling them to other people is almost as risky and risqué a business as flirting in a public place.[219]

Both Bergson and Freud signalled the importance of comparisons with other people's movements, behaviours, and manners of speech when it comes to commonplace humour.[220] Their conclusions are, unsurprisingly, very similar. If a person uses more-than-reasonable movements and/or less-than-reasonable thinking, we find them hilarious.[221]

True to character, Freud extended such a finding to include developmental aspects of the psyche, maintaining that when we laugh at someone, we actually laugh at the difference in psychic expenditure between that person and ourselves, i.e., we are essentially rediscovering that person's inner child.[222] Whether we laugh at ourselves or at others, it is always a recognition of immaturity. When we tell funny stories, then, we are constantly comparing the person that was with the person that is.[223]

---

[217] See Freud (1960), loc 1918.
[218] Freud (1960), loc 2293.
[219] See Freud (1960), loc 2257, 2259, 2293, 2297, 2310, 2317 and 2324.
[220] As with many authors writing about humour, both Bergson and Freud focussed on "laughter". This is partly unavoidable. As highlighted throughout our books, these facets, although closely related, do not always sync. Yet when it comes to important thinkers such as these two, it becomes necessary to also give "laughter" free rein.
[221] See Freud (1960), loc 3130–3137.
[222] See Freud (1960), loc 3628–3653, which applies to the rest of the paragraph above.
[223] While acknowledging the economising mechanism of psychic expenditure involved in these comparisons, the American philosopher Beau Shaw (2015, 31) argued that we substitute thereby the horrible pangs of "guilt" with the somewhat less severe pains of "humiliation". Either way, and whether the comparisons at play are about others or us (the latter case being Shaw's focus), "masochism" is claimed to remain a key ingredient of "humor" and, with it, so is "suffering" (Shaw 2015, 31). This substitution is also described as the principal reason for "the often-noted aspect of cruelty in humor" that "has given rise to many moral concerns about humor" (Shaw 2015, 44).

Freud's categorisation of "humour" proper was quite different from what is now commonly the case. Today's ordinary understanding of it echoes the snappy description provided by a contemporary of Freud's, the Canadian economist, essayist, and humourist Stephen Leacock, who wrote in a fictional dialogue: "what one would call a humorous nature" is anything "that would raise a smile, or even a laugh".[224] *Au contraire*, "humour" proper is not the overarching or umbrella-concept in Freud's theories. Rather, it is a specific presentation of the comical, which, in this case, economises on pent-up negative emotions such as pity, anger, pain, and tenderness.[225] (The same subordination to the idea of 'comicality' is true as well of Bergson's use of "humour" proper, which he defined as talking fastidiously about extant reality as though it were exactly how things should be, when they are not.)[226]

Freud's technical usage of "humour" proper indicates that it serves the same general psychic need as comicality at large. In essence, it is set in motion in order to provide emotional relief.[227] Besides, as was discussed before Freud by a few Western thinkers, for something to be humorous, this 'thing' needs to verge on the uncomfortable. Yet as soon as the discomfort outweighs the pleasure, the same 'thing' stops being funny.[228]

"Humour" proper, according to Freud, gives us an opportunity to find pleasure without giving heed to negative emotions. As such, it does not even require an audience, for we can enjoy it on our own, i.e., *in foro interno*.[229] Consequently, according to Freud, humour is the most easily satisfied type of the comic.[230]

With a few theoretical twists and turns along the way, such easily-satisfied humour became a part of what Freud considered to be the defensive mechanisms of

---

[224] Leacock (1913), 176. At the same time, Leacock (1938, chap. 1, sec. 5, par. 18) pursued "true humour" explicitly, like Addison, Schopenhauer, Pirandello, and very few other Western thinkers, i.e., mild "humour" that he deemed capable of "moving from lower to higher forms, from cruelty to horseplay, from horseplay to wit, from wit to the higher 'humor of character' (independent of the single phrase) and beyond that to its highest stage as the humor of life itself. Here tears and laughter are joined, and our little life, incongruous and vain, is rounded with a smile".
[225] Freud (1960), loc 3772.
[226] Predictably, we must refer the reader to *H&C1* for a detailed discussion of Bergson's use of "humour" proper.
[227] A professional academician and a noted humourist, Leacock's views cannot be ignored or easily dismissed.
[228] See Freud (1960), loc 3715. As seen in *H&C1*, Beattie, Hazlitt and Santayana were emphatic on this point.
[229] See Freud (1960), loc 3719 and 3727.
[230] See Freud (1960), loc 3726.

the psyche.²³¹ Others of the same sort include well-known cases such as repression, regression, and projection, all of which are part and parcel of the conceptual toolkit of contemporary psychotherapists. These mechanisms serve as our internal flight reflexes and block excessive discomfort. They are unconscious and, even though preventive, often lead to detrimental thoughts and behaviours.²³² In psychoanalytical treatment, the main objective is typically to bring these issues into consciousness for adequate assessment and deliberation.²³³

The defence mechanisms individuated by Freud are normally formed by the *super-ego*, specifically *via* early relations with parents and/or parent-like figures. Thus, the humourist can be seen as adopting the role of a parent in relation to his/her childlike audience, making fun of naïve worries and superficial suffering.²³⁴ Concomitantly, when demonstrating superiority towards others, the humourist is also dealing with his/her own childlike anxieties and limitations. Thus, in the context of commonplace humour, with the *super-ego* as the vessel for parental agency, it impacts the *ego* as a parent— or more Freudianly, a father—would treat his child.

The involvement of the *super-ego* in "humour" proper distinguishes this particular form of the comic from the lowly jokes that are more likely to affect the primal *id* and submit to basic urges.²³⁵ Basically, both jokes and humour serve to liberate and please the psyche, but only the latter does so by way of grandeur and elevation. This aggrandisement is due to the refusal of the *ego* to accept its own limitations and vulnerabilities. With "humour" proper, the *ego* narcissistically spurns being bogged down by the trauma and the sufferings of real life and, in a temporary show of defiance, makes fun of these occurrences.

However silly, superficial and ultimately inconsequential, Freud described humour as a brief and sometimes last hurray before the *de profundis* starts being sung for us or, less dramatically yet more unforgivingly, *restarts*.²³⁶ A prisoner fac-

---

231 See Freud (1928), 3.
232 Contemporary Anglophone philosophers and psychologists have largely abandoned Freud's approach. In our professional experience, they often exhibit a marked impatience regarding the very notion of unconscious drives and motives. Yet, as the South Tyrolean neuroscientist Yvonne Höller stated in a professional verbal exchange with us: "We may not be able to study the unconscious scientifically, but it is there nevertheless."
233 See Freud (1960), loc 3792–3795.
234 See Freud (1928), 3, which applies to the rest of the paragraph above.
235 See Freud (1928), 2, which applies to the rest of the paragraph above.
236 Numerous Jewish and Christian liturgies have included this Biblical psalm especially but not exclusively in funerary services. Also, through the centuries, this psalm has often been set to music, e.g., by Charpentier, Purcell, Mendelssohn, Vangelis and Pärt. As to writing "restarts", it is an indication of the fact that *humour gives us normally only a short respite from the cruel trib-*

ing his/her execution can make a joke about his/her last meal; a patient on the verge of undergoing life-threatening surgery can ridicule the way in which his/her stretcher is being handled; or a soldier bound to lose a limb can muse funnily on his/her future preferences regarding sport activities.[237] As Freud wrote: "Humour is not resigned; it is rebellious. It signifies not only the triumph of the ego but also of the pleasure-principle, which is able here to assert itself against the unkindness of real circumstances."[238]

Lastly, Freud emphasised the incongruity inherent in the appreciation of jokes, albeit with a distinct twist of his own. The fundamental part, in his view, was jokes having two simultaneous viewpoints. One being placed on the superficiality of what is being said; the other one tracking it instead into the individual's unconscious. The effectiveness of the joke was thus said to be dependent upon the difference between these two viewpoints.[239]

"Humour" proper, in contrast, did not have to possess these two different viewpoints, according to Freud.[240] Rather, it is fundamentally characterised by avoiding unpleasant emotions. It is jokes, instead, that depend upon releasing inhibitions and their attendant emotional contents by means of apt incongruities.[241]

1.1.11 Arthur Koestler

We find another essential contribution to the study of humour in the works of the Hungarian polymath Arthur Koestler, a declared admirer of Freud's psychoanalysis that gave "humour" proper considerable prominence in his own work. Specifically, Koestler defined it as one of the three foundations of human creativity, the other two being no less than science and art. All three creative processes involve what Koestler called "bisociation", i.e., a two-planed apprehension whereby the mind oscillates between starkly different frames of reference.[242]

---

ulations of existence. As laconically stated by Oscar Wilde (1913, par. 42) in his own *De Profundis*: "the secret of life is suffering. It is what is hidden behind everything."
237 The first example is based on Freud's own writings. The others are ours.
238 Freud (1928), 2. See also Critchley (2000), 31.
239 See Freud (1960), loc 3804–3815.
240 See Freud (1960), loc 3818.
241 See Freud (1960), loc 3824–3830.
242 See Koestler (1964), 35–36. A "state of oscillation" of body and mind had already been noted, with reference to "laughter" [*das Lachen*], by Immanuel Kant (as cited in Figueroa-Dorrego and Larkin-Galiñanes 2009, 330).

In humour, the bisociation at play involves linguistic-conceptual meanings, whereas in the sciences, it concerns objective analogy, and in the arts, the production of thought-images.[243] Accordingly, there are three types of creators in our midst: the jester, the sage, and the artist.[244] In parallel, there are also three main emotional states: aggressive in the case of humour; neutral objectivity in that of discovery; and sympathetic, admiring, or tragic in the case of art.[245] Indeed, the manner in which Koestler linked the emotional state of aggressiveness to nominal "humour" is particularly interesting. It seemed crystal clear to him that humour is, essentially, *aggressive* in nature.[246]

According to Koestler, we humans have only two ways to escape the more or less automated patterns of our thinking: our highly irrational dreams (a direct reference to Freud's studies on the subject), and our spontaneous flashes of insight, i.e., when we see things, ideas, or events from a fresh perspective.[247] This happens when we are "creative", which means when we experience "bisociation", i.e., when two coherent but mutually exclusive frames of references "vibrate simultaneously on two different wavelengths".[248] In contrast to routine thinking, which involves only a single plane or frame of reference, creative thinking, including "humour" proper, takes at least two.[249] In a punchline joke, the vibration happens at a very distinct moment, whereas in humorous poems or longer narratives the vibration is felt over a longer period and, often, varies in experienced intensity.[250]

All creative activities in the sciences, arts, and in "humour" proper, involve systematic training in looking for possibilities that are simultaneously impossible and yet perfectly logical.[251] This seemingly paradoxical function of our creative faculties is realised through the use of a logical process that is not usually applied to that particular type of situation, which Koestler called a "bisociation pattern", i.e., a method for exploring and inventing multiple perspectives (two, more often than not) that tend to be unexpected, absurd, baffling, or even seemingly out of control.[252] Importantly, in the case of "humour" proper, these patterns need to be ap-

---

243 See Koestler (1964).
244 See Koestler (1964), 27.
245 See Koestler (1964), 27. See also Krikmann (2006), 28.
246 As already noted, Feinberg (1978, 9) agreed emphatically on this characterisation of "humour" proper, which he found exemplified, *inter alia*, "in the tasteless cruelty of Don Rickles".
247 See Koestler (1964), 45.
248 Koestler (1964), 35.
249 See Koestler (1964), 35–36.
250 See Koestler (1964), 37–38.
251 Koestler (1964), 35. See also Sclavi (2008), 158–159.
252 Koestler (1964), 35.

plicable to real-life situations and require not only the involvement of the joker, but also the audience's venturing into the realm of non-conventional thinking.[253]

1.1.12 Deleuze and Kozintsev

Insofar as this project revolves around the concepts of 'humour' and 'cruelty', and their manifestations in interpersonal as well as intrapersonal life, it is prudent to call upon the 20th-century French philosopher Gilles Deleuze, who wrote a fair amount about both topics. Moreover, in a patent echo of another important Frenchman that we have cited, Deleuze published a book entitled *Bergsonism*.[254] Deleuze was also familiar with the nooks and crannies of Freudian psychoanalysis, and he collaborated for many years with an original and practicing psychotherapist, Félix Guattari.[255] Dropping his name seems very much apropos. Perchance, it is an acceptable exception to the regular *bon ton*.[256]

Most of Deleuze's ruminations on "humour" proper come from his complex ontological and epistemological studies about the limits of language and understanding, i.e., the point at which the linguistic articulation of thought falls apart in the face of existing reality.[257] According to contemporary formal logic, any given term can be said to *mean* the entity or entities to which it refers (i.e., its *denotation*, e.g., "Venus" means the planet Venus) or, alternatively, the list of characteristics whereby an entity or entities can be referred to by means of that particular term (i.e., its *sense* or, following Deleuze, its "signification"), e.g., "Venus"

---

[253] Koestler (1964), 35.
[254] Deleuze (1988), in which, to be frank, Deleuze made a most creative use of Bergson's insights.
[255] See Schuster (2016) for an interesting account of Deleuze's appropriation of psychoanalysis.
[256] This little joke recalls another shifty and polysemic term of our lexicon that keeps philosophers busy: "taste".
[257] Humour is *one* case in which the presumed connection between language and reality falls apart, especially in paradoxes revealing the conventionality of the words that we utilise. Many other cases can be encountered in our life, whether highbrow or lowbrow, e.g., finding the 'right' words to convey grief or love. As Polanyi (1962c) insisted, there can be tacit knowledge that we *cannot* make explicit, or only at a very partial rate, i.e., suggesting it or pointing in its direction, as *per* poetry, dogmas, myth, maxims, and expert jargon that only people who are trained into a discipline or specialised activity can make sense of. What is more, even when made explicit, important components of the original tacit knowledge can get lost and/or transformed into something altogether different. Compare, e.g., watching a football game and reading about it (see *H&C1*).

being the second celestial body from the star called "Sun" that is describable as a planet, revolves around the Sun, is observable from Earth, etc.[258]

According to Deleuze, there are two 'humorous' problems with this standard view.[259]

(1) The planet Venus, right now, is not the same entity as it was just a moment ago, or as it will be in the next moment. The same is true of pencils, computer monitors, plants, bookshelves, courage, protons, pebbles, and anything else that any of us can conceive of as being an identifiable entity of any kind. This issue applies to people too, whether present or not, hence reiterating the Buddhist stance whereby there exists no such thing as a personal 'I'.[260] Were we to seriously accept the vanishing of such an 'I', however, it would imply the annihilation of most, if not all, meaningful instances and expressions of human knowledge and agency.[261]

(2) In the history of Western philosophy, as well as in logic and mathematics at large, "paradoxes" have repeatedly shown us the ultimate confines of "signification", which is purely conventional (e.g., "if you say 'chariot', a chariot passes through your lips").[262] *Prima facie*, ordinary jokes would not seem to be as scholarly dignified as paradoxes but, as far as Deleuze was concerned, they too

---

[258] See Deleuze (1990), 135. Whether such lists are finite or infinite, it is a matter of philosophical contention.

[259] We do not tackle other dimensions of meaning, e.g., tone and force. Sense and denotation suffice here. Deleuze (1990) added himself a third 'meaning' of "meaning", i.e., "manifestation", which is the *affective* significance of the language-user's utterings. Thus his whole account can be said to comprise relations between words and objects (*denotation*), words and words (*signification*), and words and feelings (*manifestation*). These are also the three fundamental forms of symbolic meaning that were researched by Cassirer (1980), i.e., *representative*, *significative* and *expressive*, which also echo *grosso modo* to the three standard areas of linguistic studies, i.e., semantics, syntax, and pragmatics. The same three dimensions of meaning can be argued to be present as well in the work of the father of modern logic, Gottlob Frege (1892, 31 and 34); albeit stressing "sense" (signification) and "reference" (denotation), he also acknowledged "force" (e.g., ordering, inquiring, acting) and "tone" (or "colouring", as he wrote in German), i.e., the subtler rhetorical implications of our chosen terminology. As students of humour and cruelty, we know how important such subtleties can be to fulfil people's pragmatic aims, and how their misunderstanding can produce unintended offence, successful yet mistaken accusations, and so much pain.

[260] See, e.g., Conze (1980).

[261] See Deleuze (1990), 135. According to Bergson (1960, 209): "things considered apart from our perception do not seem to endure", for only an "endur[ing]" person, i.e., an "I" endowed with psychological "duration", can establish the persistence of these "things" in time. The *modern* Bergson was not the *postmodern* Deleuze.

[262] Deleuze (1990), 8.

test more than capably the limits of signification. Think, for instance, of "Venus" signifying 'the goddess of love who orbits around the Sun'.²⁶³

This perplexing yet clever collapse of logical and linguistic mechanisms of denotation and/or connotation was, for Deleuze, the "adventure of humor", or the "twofold dismissal of height and depth to the advantage of the surface", i.e., the "descent" from the established structures of graspable perception, coherent thought, and linguistic articulation into the original chaos whence all of them emerged in the first place.²⁶⁴ According to Deleuze, humour operates by plunging from our meaningful conceptual-linguistic units of abstract sense-giving and sense-making into the inherently meaningless pulverising plurality of reality.²⁶⁵ Thus understood, humour crushes any term aimed at grasping all the possible instances of a given phenomenon that, once the unifying and seemingly solid boundaries of that concept have disintegrated, explodes into innumerable, independent, and different spatiotemporal events or phenomena, both ontologically and epistemically.²⁶⁶

This disintegration, however, is not a misunderstanding of the original term, but a new understanding, at least *in potentia*.²⁶⁷ The plethora of singularities or "object-events" upon which any and every possible structure of human meaning ultimately rests discloses a blank, thin, firm, underlying field, or possibly a Spinozistic 'substance' of sorts, without which no connotation or denotation, however imperfect, could ever begin to be possible.²⁶⁸ There, arguably, the mind encounters a purely mathematical surface or a tropological strip, i.e., a plane devoid of any

---

263 The joke is ours, as silly as it may sound.
264 Deleuze (1990), 136.
265 In an ironic reversal, Hillman (1999, chap. 1, sec. 4, par. 3) stated: "The soul is only an abstraction until we meet its courageous will to live or its judicious decision or its humor". *Ipso dicto*, such a nominal "humour" signals: (1) valuable existential meaningfulness; and (2) an ontological solidity of the highest order, for *we realise that we possess a soul also thanks to its humour*, e.g., when an inner Socratic daemon instructs us not to take too seriously ourselves, our academic pursuits and/or our political values (narcissists and zealots may be incapable of this feat of self-deflation, however). Depending on the circumstances, this daemon can express any one of the three pivotal experiences highlighted by Hillman (1999), when not two or three of them together. As to the understanding of "soul" in this context, the reader should refer to the literature produced by Jung and the post/Jungians, who have generally depicted the soul as an active and unifying functional complex of the psyche, i.e., not a pre- and well-defined normative standard aimed at forcing people into given socio-cultural pigeonholes (see, e.g., Butler 1994).
266 See Deleuze (1990), 139.
267 See Deleuze (1990), 139.
268 Spinoza, like Bergson and Leibniz, influenced deeply Deleuze. See, in particular, Deleuze (1970).

physical thickness, one side of which faces the expressed and the expressible, and the other side which faces the unexpressed and the inexpressible. Playing around the edges of this unqualified totality, its infinite fabric of "object-events" and their abstraction into meaningful units of a higher order, Deleuze's nominal "humour" is said to be able to exploit the laws of human thought and communication, to reveal the fountainhead of all thought and communication, which neither, however, can truly grasp and hold, once and for all.[269]

Every law has exemptions and loopholes, every model anomalies, every concept incongruities, every norm exceptions: "The art of the aesthetic is humour, a physical art of signals and signs determining the partial solutions or cases of solution."[270] Epistemically speaking, with Deleuze's philosophical treatment of "humour" proper, we are tackling something that is very different from everyday humour and/or the convenient scholarly definitions of it *qua* "the attempt to stimulate amusement" that is signalled by "the pan-human emotion responsive to 'funny' or 'comical' objects" *via* "[l]aughter" *qua* "its visible and more or less faithful expression".[271]

The implications of Deleuze's postmodern and largely unamusing "humour" are inherently and inevitably sceptical.[272] *Pace* the attractive straightforwardness of formal logic, our ideas or concepts cannot be reduced to words, according to him, for words face eventually the unsolvable problem of having to capture and convey the potentially infinite conceivable attributes of such ideas or concepts— signification is doomed (e.g., the variety of conceptions and definitions of "humour" proper). Bodies, for their part, cannot be reduced to words either, for words cannot truly portray the ever-changing properties of any of them—denotation is doomed too (e.g., the funny contradiction between our past and present selves, as noted long ago, among others, by Pascal and Pirandello).[273]

In the 21st century, and through his own independent philosophical inquiries into the theories of laughter developed by Freud and Bergson, a Russian senior researcher at the Museum of Anthropology and Ethnography of Saint Petersburg, Alexander Kozintsev, reached strikingly analogous conclusions as to the unique

---

269 See Deleuze (1994), 5.
270 Deleuze (1994), 245.
271 Jauregui (1998), 329.
272 Deleuze's use of "humour" proper probed so far into the fields of ontology and metaphysics as to be idiomatically far out. Concomitantly, it added *yet another scholarly meaning of the term*, which is likely to have contained this connotation tacitly for a very long time. See, e.g., Chesterton (1958, 26), whom we tackle in Chapter 4.
273 Both instances were duly referenced in greater detail in *H&C1*.

ability of "humour" proper to collapse all structures of logical sense and linguistic representation.[274]

For one, the openly nihilistic Kozintsev stated:

> The basic hypothesis is this: the cause of the gelotic euphoria is neither the triumph of justice nor schadenfreude nor the rise in social status nor the "removal of censorship" nor the "economy in the expenditure of affect" (at least, not only that), but first and foremost *the eruption of a latent protest of human (or rather primate) nature against symbolization*, which is unconsciously perceived as a burden. Humor is a short-lived playful rebellion against symbolization, nature's temporary revenge in its rivalry with culture. By "defunctionalizing" language, that is, by freeing it from the referential function, humor frees us from language. Nothing else can adequately explain pleasure from humor, and only the intensity of this pleasure shows how burdensome for us, primates, is the symbolic communication to which we have grown so accustomed in the course of evolution. Only laughter shows that language, which we are used to regarding as something like our skin, is in fact mere clothing, which is quite possible to take off. Of course, only for a while and only at play.[275]

For another, Kozintsev added:

> [O]ne can speak of semantics only if one perceives the object seriously. To study what we call the "semantics of humor", we need to view comic texts as serious ones, that is, to forget about their rationale. And, *vice versa, to laugh, we must temporarily forget all thoughts, emotions, and judgments that we could associate with the given characters, situations, or events if we were to take them seriously.*[276]

It is then no surprise to often read erudite statements claiming that humour cannot be defined. In and by itself, as Kozintsev intimated, humour is inimical to the signifier-signified relationship that is at the very basis of all sensible semantics, if not even of all generally viable pragmatics.[277] All sense-giving and all sense-making can be destroyed by way of such a nominal "humour", the movement of which was conceived of by Kozintsev as a descent, i.e., as it was also suggested by Deleuze:

---

[274] See Kozintsev (2010), whom Morreall (2013, 195f) praised as being both sophisticated and thought-provoking.
[275] Kozintsev (2010), 161; emphasis added. The term "semiotic" could be used instead of "symbolic", i.e., the possibility of communicating something (e.g., an emotion, an order, a hypothesis) by means of something else (e.g., a word, a painting, a poem), according to a group's variously consistent set of shared conventions. "Symbols", though, can have more specific technical meanings, e.g., in Jungian psychology (see Brodersen and Glock 2017).
[276] Kozintsev (2010), 32; emphasis added.
[277] The point about pragmatics relates to the frequently-heard claim that "humour" proper is somewhat exceptional, i.e., that there is something about it that contradicts, or deviates from, people's more prosaic linguistic interactions.

> The path of humor is always degradation, sliding downward, an imaginary regression to an earlier stage of development (individual, historical, evolutionary) and the acquisition of the capacity of looking at one stage of development from another. This instantaneous temporary descent has become possible only thanks to the long and difficult path upwards, the path taken both by the individual him-/herself during his/her life and by the entire human species during ist biological and cultural history.[278]

As was also the case with Deleuze's own possibly 'Spinozistic' realisations about "humour" proper, an inarticulable reality might be revealed, however fleetingly and incomprehensibly, by such seemingly silly descents into nonsense, for it exists beneath all possible categorisations, including those concerning the individual him-/herself and the human species to which s/he belongs. As Kozintsev wrote:

> The sole object of laughter is the subject himself in his present and past, his own and that of his species. The subject's non-identity with himself, the perception of this non-identity, self-repudiation – this is the entirely subjective dialectic on which humor is based[, encompassing b]oth mutually negating views – "top down" (that of one's own stupidity from the standpoint of one's own cleverness) and "bottom up" (that of one's own wisdom from the standpoint of one's own folly).[279]

Ontologically speaking, Deleuze claimed reality to be, *in se*, nothing but "difference", i.e., a multitude of indistinguishable singularities occurring in space-time that we, as thinking and talking human beings, try to coerce within cogent structures of "repetition", e.g., the mundane concepts of ordinary languages and the sophisticated ones of technical jargon.[280] Humour, somewhat cruelly, exploits the laws of thought and of our languages to lead us into paradoxes. This reveals, however briefly, the plane of being whence human thought and languages emerged—a plane of being which neither thought nor language can grasp, epistemically, in a truly firm and adequate manner.[281]

"Humour" proper, in this 'Deleuzian' and, more broadly, postmodern or nihilistic perspective, is no longer an entertaining instrument for inter- and intrapersonal agency. On the contrary, it becomes a serious metaphysical instrument. Thanks

---

[278] Kozintsev (2010), 56.
[279] Kozintsev (2010), 55–56.
[280] See Deleuze (1994), 207–214. Ours being just one of many possible interpretations of these two Deleuzian key terms.
[281] Whether or not we can intuit partially this fundamental plane of being, if at all existent, is something that Deleuze's followers still debate, perhaps unsurprisingly, given the murky depths in which it seems to be located.

to it, the totality of being can be somewhat glimpsed in its constitutive multiplicity and, concomitantly, in its even deeper undifferentiation.[282]

Interestingly, the late Austrian-American sociologist Peter L. Berger similarly derived important ontological, epistemological, and even mystical insights from humorous matters, e.g., the common assertion of Freud and Bergson that the comic is "discrepancy, incongruity, incommensurability".[283] Therein, Berger retrieved "the discrepancy between man and universe", which reflects "the imprisonment of the human spirit in the world" and, crucially, "provides another signal of transcendence" to us mortals, i.e., an 'opening' of sort on a 'higher' or 'deeper' plane of being, which Berger himself argued to make religious belief possible and plausible.[284] Deleuze did not pursue this spiritual path. Neither did Kozintsev.[285]

Quite the opposite, Deleuze tackled "humour" proper in relation to a far less sacred and ostensibly different phenomenon, i.e., the psychiatric and psychoanalytic issue of "masochism".[286] According to Deleuze, such a humour is at work *qua* means of disjointedness and disintegration: "We can see this [humor] in demonstration by absurdity and working to rule, but also in some forms of masochistic behavior which mock by submission."[287] Deleuze saw masochism as a clever tool

---

[282] Ironically, while presenting a similar ontological dialectic depicting unique singularities ("instants") as the basis of continuous reality, Bachelard (2013, 7) used a tragic illustration, rather than a humorous one: "the cruelest mourning is the awareness of a future betrayed. When that shattering instant arrives as the eyes of a cherished being close forever, we immediately feel the hostile novelty of the next instant that comes to pierce the heart."

[283] Berger (1969), 86.

[284] Berger (1969), 87–88; see also Mascall (1971), appendix 2.

[285] In our century, Marmysz (2003, 152–153) reiterated this postmodern, declaredly "nihilistic" path in a way that makes "humour" a partial solution, insofar as it is said to "allow us to confront incongruities and, instead of being overwhelmed by them, to understand them in an unusual and original fashion", hence fostering "the capacity to make incongruities unthreatening and to interpret them in a manner that produces amusement". Somehow, Marmysz (2003, 85) thought that the conflict between "the real" and "the ideal" may be laughed at, or away. Considerably more sober was the interpretation offered by the US gender theorist Judith Butler (1994, 168 note 12; emphasis added), who regarded Foucault's oeuvre as teaching us that "[t]aken as a normative/normalizing ideal, the 'soul' functions as the formative and regulatory principle of this material body, the proximate instrumentality of its subordination. The soul renders the body uniform; disciplinary regimes train the body through a sustained repetition of *rituals of cruelty* that produce over time the gestural stylistics of the imprisoned body."

[286] The Freudian US psychoanalyst Tarachow (1949, 224) claimed all "comic" actions, especially in "comedies", to result from "a sadomasochistic impulse in which the aggression and the guilt are of about equal strength ... discharging the[ir mutual] tensions ... without the burden of resolving the ambivalence". As to Freud's clinical understanding of masochism, we addressed it in detail in *H&C1*.

[287] Deleuze (1994), 5.

for the *ego*'s deceptive self-affirmation, insofar as the masochist effectively persuades, stipulates a contract with, and indirectly steers the *super-ego* itself, which is in principle meant to rule over the masochist and, when required, punish him/her for his/her transgressions.[288]

The masochist's open act of submission is, in Deleuze's view, an astute expedient whereby the masochist's *ego* manages to attain that which the *super-ego* actually forbids: sexual pleasure; i.e., the actual release of the *id*'s instinctual drives and the attendant hedonic self-realisation.[289] As Deleuze wrote: "The masochist is insolent in his obsequiousness, rebellious in his submission; in short, he is a humorist, a logician of consequences."[290]

Humour's *modus operandi* becomes clearer when it is contrasted with the one characterising "irony" proper. As Deleuze stated: "Humor is the art of the surface, which is opposed to the old irony, the art of depths and heights."[291] The former defies the constricting laws or principles by leading them into a "paradox".[292] The latter, instead, challenges them head-on by way of patent contradiction.[293]

For the sake of illustration, Deleuze discussed two Biblical patriarchs, Job and Abraham, whom he took as being Western paradigms of the terms "irony" and "humour".[294]

(1) The 'ironic' Job questions directly God's supposed goodness by asking: "why are you doing this to me?"[295]

(2) The 'humorous' Abraham submits willingly to God's command to sacrifice to His glory his son Isaac, thus forcing God to recant, for so cruel a deed should

---

[288] See Deleuze (1989). According to some scholars, "suffering" may actually mean much more than sheer "pain" because of the conceptually and existentially thicker contours of the former, which however presupposes the latter in order to arise (Portmann 2000, 48–52). As to distinguishing between bad and good pain in a principled manner, under every circumstance, see McMurtry (2011), vol. 1, 44–85.
[289] See, once again, Deleuze (1989).
[290] Deleuze (1989), 89. Hence, 'masochistic' might be the lifestyle of those indigenous prostitutes interviewed by Corrinne T. Sullivan (2021, title *et passim*), who inferred their condition not to be one of subjection, as many well-meaning feminists and Christian missionaries believe, but of cunning self-affirmation by means of "pussy power". These women would seemingly submit themselves to patriarchy, yet to get what they want, in the end.
[291] Deleuze (1990), 9.
[292] Deleuze (1990), 9. Humour works like a *reductio ad absurdum* in mathematics (see, e.g., Daniel Smith 2006).
[293] See Deleuze (1990), 5–9.
[294] See Deleuze (1994), 7.
[295] Jacob, who struggles physically with God, could also be seen as a case of Biblical irony *à la* Deleuze.

never be made in His name—and also because God had granted Abraham his son Isaac *qua* token of His appreciation and special blessing.²⁹⁶

A cunning masochist, Abraham respects *de iure* the binding principle at issue, i.e., faithful obedience, but carries it to indefensible consequences, i.e., he pursues successfully *de facto* disobedience.²⁹⁷ Here lies, according to Deleuze, Abraham's alleged humour.²⁹⁸

1.1.13 The Linguistic Study of Humour

Given that the main objective of this book is to examine the mutually supportive relationship between 'humour' and 'cruelty' as well as the ways in which these concepts jointly reveal themselves in the world of lived experience, any examination of the purely structural elements of the former, e.g., the composition of a joke, is of limited relevance. It is, however, interesting to note that the polysemy exhibited by the scholarly approach to "humour" proper is the very foundation of humour, including humour of the cruel kind, at least according to the structuralist perspective. Let us consider just one case in point.

The pioneering Soviet-born linguist and humour specialist Victor Raskin claimed that our lives are full of instances, including humorous ones, where we must navigate the immense polysemy of our language, inferring meanings from words and sentences based upon our partial knowledge of the world and the limited lexicon available to us.²⁹⁹ Unless ill or seriously neglected, the human mind, through its maturation, becomes filled with cognitive structures (or "scripts") that make up a sort of common sense way of representing coherently what usually happens in situations that, *in se*, are ontologically unique and factually unrepeatable.³⁰⁰

What we speakers say about them, however, is insufficient to relay the full intended or thought meanings of our communication. But we do get away with it in most instances; i.e., no misunderstanding ensues.³⁰¹ Listeners can normally fill in

---

296 See also Cotte (2018).
297 See also Eco (1983) casting the difference between "humour" and "the comical" in nearly identical terms.
298 As explained in *H&C1*, Deleuze's idea of 'humour' is *not* something that is patently amusing.
299 See Raskin (1979).
300 Raskin (1979), 329.
301 Raskin (1979), 329.

the gaps by using their own partial knowledge and limited lexicon.[302] Thus, say, the sentence "Mary saw a black cat and immediately went home" is not readily digested, unless you know that black cats are a bad omen in some cultures.[303]

The human vocabulary is incomplete and unspecific, insofar as many words may have the same or similar meanings. And even with vast, subtle, and profound resources, nobody can truly make use of all the terms available in his/her language, nor can s/he expect his/her peers to be fluent in them all. Ignorance about most things, however diverse in each individual, is also the norm among all human beings.[304] To complicate matters further, words can mean different things, depending on the situation as well as on who is involved. As Polanyi pointed out regarding modern science itself, figuring out *any* meaning whatsoever requires, always and necessarily, *context*.[305] Without it, we are lost.

In this connection, Raskin offered an excellent example of a sentence possessing multiple meanings (25, to be precise): "The paralyzed bachelor hit the colourful ball."[306] Apart from the definite article, all the words in this sentence can have multiple meanings.[307] Besides, the deeper one analyses them, the more and more implications come to the surface.[308] Thus, "paralyzed" could refer to either disease or morality; "bachelor" to marriage, academia, warfare, or zoology; and so forth.[309]

Not all combinations would make equal sense to most people, but our brain is typically fast and able to sort out the likeliest meanings, including incongruous yet relatable ones.[310] This gives us an insight into how jokes work, according to Raskin: "The main hypothesis is that this humorous element is the result of a partial overlap of two (or more) different and in a sense opposite scripts which are all compatible (fully or partially) with the text carrying this element."[311]

A typical joke, in other words, presents us with two scripts. The humorous effect is created when the trigger or punchline causes us to suddenly change our understanding from the primary and, generally, more obvious script, to the second-

---

302 Raskin (1979), 329.
303 Raskin (1979), 329.
304 This sobering point applies to the two authors of this book and probably, their better colleagues too, notwithstanding their formal titles, awards, awe-inspiring airs, quasi-baronial powers, and/or latest impact factors.
305 See *H&C1*, in which we developed an extensive argument, based on Polanyi's views, concerning the pragmatic inevitability and value of polysemy in human language and thought.
306 Raskin (1979), 330.
307 See Raskin (1979), 330.
308 See Raskin (1979), 330.
309 Raskin (1979), 330.
310 See Raskin (1979), 325.
311 Raskin (1979), 325.

ary, incongruous, even opposing script. Simple and bad jokes render themselves freely to such a line of analysis, e.g., "What's the difference between a hippo and a Zippo? One is really heavy, and the other is a little lighter."[312]

The play on the words employed in the joke involves the variable meanings of the last word and, consequently, the possibility for two distinct elementary scripts to mutually overlap. In better and/or more complicated jokes, several overlaps can happen simultaneously. Koestler's older concept of 'bisociation' is thus further exemplified and, to a certain extent, complexified.[313]

"Overlap" was, according to Raskin, a necessary but not a sufficient condition for "humour" proper to occur.[314] Overlapping any two scripts whatsoever will not automatically sound funny to most people. Additional ingredients are needed if we want to make them smile and/or laugh. A common way for producing humorous effect is, therefore, to include in the second script sexual references, elements of surprise, well-tested clichés, glaring abnormalities, silly banalities, or outright obscenities.[315]

Yet again, the more sophisticated the joke is meant to be, the less elementary are the utilised scripts. Many such jokes, then, will rely upon subtler strategies or "implicature", i.e., they imply a meaning that goes well beyond the literal sense of what we say.[316] For instance, we may look at a painting and say: "The frame is nice"; hence implying that the painting is, in and for itself, pretentious rubbish.[317]

1.1.14 Summing Up, Summing Down

To conclude this summary overview of representative 'classics' in the Western humanities and social sciences, we can confidently state that commonplace humour can be studied from many angles, using different approaches. The same is true of "humour" proper too, whether ordinary or sophisticated. We mean, of course, the so-called "true humour", which we tackle in detail in Chapter 2.

Following the Darwinian tradition, humour can be seen as having had, or perhaps as still possessing, some function that is relevant to our survival as a species. As suggested by an array of Western philosophers, moreover, it can be said that, by

---

[312] The example is ours.
[313] Albeit recognising multiple hermeneutical planes, the term "bisociation" clearly suggests two such planes.
[314] Raskin (1979), 333.
[315] See Raskin (1979), 333.
[316] Raskin (1979), 327.
[317] The example is ours.

studying humour, we may be able to reveal important truths about the way human beings think. The two standard approaches dubbed "superiority" and "relief" can thus be seen as belonging primarily to the functionalist camp, whereas the so-called "incongruity" framework, which was already exemplified by Schopenhauer in the 19th century, has generally been keener on structural aspects.

Nevertheless, it is pivotal to notice that the exploration of humour does not allow us to place individual scholars or their theories into starkly demarcated ideological and/or methodological silos. Normally, as we have repeatedly stressed in our own research, a bit of everything—superiority, relief, incongruity, functionalism, structuralism—has been by far the norm among most interested scientists and scholars. Furthermore, the selective overview provided above is in no way a complete appraisal of all the interesting perspectives on humour that have been produced in Western culture.

For a fuller study, the reader should go back to *H&C1,* but even that first extensive exploration of ours was not exhaustive. No scholarly endeavour alone can accomplish such a feat, for there is simply too much material, plus all that which is not recorded, accessible, and ... known. More prosaically, no publisher would ever accept such a *Begriffsgeschichte* as a viable project. Therefore, let us save words and move on to "cruelty" proper.

1.2 Cruelty

> By the way, a Bulgarian I met lately in Moscow, Ivan went on, seeming not to hear his brother's words, told me about the crimes committed by Turks and Circassians in all parts of Bulgaria through fear of a general rising of the Slavs. They burn villages, murder, outrage women and children, they nail their prisoners by the ears to the fences, leave them so till morning, and in the morning they hang them—all sorts of things you can't imagine. People talk sometimes of bestial cruelty, but that's a great injustice and insult to the beasts; a beast can never be so cruel as a man, so artistically cruel. The tiger only tears and gnaws, that's all he can do. He would never think of nailing people by the ears, even if he were able to do it. These Turks took a pleasure in torturing children,—too; cutting the unborn child from the mother's womb, and tossing babies up in the air and catching them on the points of their bayonets before their mothers' eyes. Doing it before the mothers' eyes was what gave zest to the amusement. Here is another scene that I thought very interesting. Imagine a trembling mother with her baby in her arms, a circle of invading Turks around her. They've planned a diversion: they pet the baby, laugh to make it laugh. They succeed, the baby laughs. At that moment a Turk points a pistol four inches from the baby's face. The baby laughs with glee, holds out its little hands to the pistol, and he pulls the trigger in the baby's face and blows out its brains. Artis-

tic, wasn't it? By the way, Turks are particularly fond of sweet things, they say.
— Fyodor M. Dostoyevsky[318]

1.2.1 A Sorry Example from Your Childhood

Throughout this volume, we provide multiple examples of extraordinary cruelty to illustrate our reflections. The same was true of *H&C1* and, unsurprisingly, so it will be with *H&C3*. However, it is also important to include examples that are so commonplace and ordinary that we, run-of-the mill human beings, hardly recognise them as being cruel.[319] In this regard, "normative cruelties" is an excellent binomial, for it suggests both the ordinariness and the expectation of such deeds.[320]

Bullying in the schoolyard provides us perhaps with some of the most intuitive and representative cases of these daily and even expected cruelties. Despite multiple studies showing the detrimental effects of bullying on both physical and mental health, it is still seen as an unavoidable part of going to school and interacting with other children.[321] And while some level of conflict cannot be avoided in any sustained human relation, it is intriguing that most of us, according to the extant studies at least, deem it inevitable that certain children will be scarred for life due to these experiences, which are commonly avoidable yet unavoidably common.[322] In some cases, the inflicted cruelties are so profound that they can drive their victims to suicide.[323]

People frequently labour under the misconception that are verbalised in common expressions such as "girls are just mean", "boys will be boys", and "some kids are just asking for it". In other words, a dose of cruelty is taken to be a normal, necessary, even desirable, part of growing up. Despite the consequences staring us in the eye, and as documented by one of this book's authors, the most common fallacy is that the immaturity of a child might somehow make them less susceptible to bullying's aftereffects. The truth is quite the contrary. As adults, most of us

---

[318] Dostoyevsky (2018), 269.
[319] Dealing primarily with clinical issues arising from physical and psychological violence within couples and families, the late French neuropsychiatrist Yves Prigent (2003, title page *et passim*) wrote of "ordinary cruelty". Those among us who experienced child, spousal or parental abuse are likely to find *this* binomial sadly apt.
[320] Ringrose and Renold (2010), 573. As we will explain, Hallie (1969) had already studied these cruelties.
[321] See e.g., Arnarsson *et al.* (2015) and (2020), and Arnarsson and Bjarnason (2018).
[322] See Arnarsson *et al.* (2015) and (2020).
[323] See Arnarsson *et al.* (2015).

are much more likely to be able to ascertain the meaning of a run-in with a bully than a ten-year-old is, thanks to our more developed personal and social tools.[324]

The socio-cultural dimensions of gender, power, class, and identity are all-pervasive when it comes to bullying.[325] Blustering is, for one, heavily influenced by gender in the way we, as adequately socialised people, normalise behaviour, e.g., physically 'tough' boys *versus* verbally 'mean' girls.[326] What tends to be identified conceptually as 'school bullying' is thus behaviour that transgresses the gender-related norms.[327] Class-related norms matter too. As pointed out by the contemporary social scientists Ringrose and Renold, female bullies are often portrayed as both unfeminine and lower-class because of their physical aggressiveness.[328] This skewed logic applies to the bullies as well as to their victims. Meaningfully, the two cited authors go themselves so far as to frame some schoolgirls and schoolboys as "gender deviants", i.e., "bullies" and "victims" transgressing the established social norms of femininity and masculinity.[329]

When faced with bullying at school, people also tend to expect different behaviours from children, based on their gender. Boys are expected to "stand up for themselves", as the common phrase goes, whereas girls should "be friends" and make peace. In the scientific literature, it is frequently asserted that boys bully others in a more physical and direct manner, whereas girls resort to more indirect, conversational, and/or relational methods.[330] Similarly, female victims are thought

---

[324] See Arnarsson *et al.* (2015) and (2020).
[325] Of all these socio-cultural dimensions, "power" is probably the most polysemic and puzzling term, as we discuss further in this chapter and in the next, especially Section 2.2.3.6. Tellingly, the German founder of modern sociology, Max Weber, had already identified three main types of power, i.e., "economic (class), social (status) and political (party)"—the second one in this classic triptych being as mutable and as diverse in time and place as human cultures themselves can be (Gane 2005, 212). It is somehow an open secret of today's scientific community that we can talk about "power" and pretend that we understand one another at conferences or in academic books, even if no two scholars agree on what it actually means. In Italy, people would dub it a "Pulcinella secret".
[326] See Arnarsson *et al.* (2015) and (2020).
[327] See Ringrose and Renold (2010), 575.
[328] See Ringrose and Renold (2010), 574. Ironically, Karl Groos (1913, 219–220), the noted German pioneer of evolutionary child psychology, highlighted *female* cases of physical cruelty in childhood. Perhaps he did so because of their 'shock value', given the *fin-de-siècle* stereotype of young girls as 'angelic' persons, which still echoed sufficiently in the following centuries as to engender the artistic trope of "evil children" in horror tales (Renner 2013, title *et passim*). There can be very scary versions of the prosaic 'horrible children' that many parents have had to contend with in their life. Some, in the world of fiction, become veritable monsters.
[329] Ringrose and Renold (2010), 575.
[330] See Ringrose and Renold (2010), 575.

to react with helplessness and nonchalance, while males are seen as more likely to reciprocate with physical and/or verbal violence, i.e., insults and taunts.[331]

For a boy to be seen as a passive victim is to mark him out as a feminine, sexually ambivalent, abject failure. This position *qua* passive male victim is therefore abhorred by children—and adults—and is to be rectified at all costs.[332] Most parents and siblings do not want to have a 'sissy' in their midst. For all the alleged "progress" of the so-called "modern world", while female gender roles appear to have diversified considerably, male ones still echo the warrior ethos of ancient societies. This means that, as far as boys are concerned, school-bullying can thrive unnoticed under the mundane and repetitive guise of normative gender behaviour.[333]

School-bullying is also influenced by class, for it highlights the now-commonplace and quasi-universal (neo-)liberal idioms of "winners" and "losers", both of which also recall the principles of Darwinian competition. It thus becomes yet another pitfall of the school experience that a bullied child must navigate around the socially disparaging labels of "abject failure" and his/her demonisation by the others who may not share his/her background and use the fact against him/her.[334] Hierarchies are important, and the status of the child and of the child's family have a role in the game that is so cruelly played out in schools, sports clubs, and playgrounds all over the world.[335]

The Swedish-Norwegian psychologist Dan Olweus tersely defined "bullying" as follows: "a subset of aggressive behaviour characterised by repetition and an imbalance of power".[336] However, as pointed out by Ringrose and Renold, this polymorphous power has become more and more commonly associated with the psychological characteristics of the individual; this is clearly demonstrated by the standard emphasis of the scientific community on finding causal relations with the personality of the bully and/or of the victim.[337] The behaviour of the individual gets pathologised, while less attention is paid to the socio-cultural dimensions of power, such as those pertaining to class, race, gender, and sexuality.[338]

Several studies indicate that boys, reared in traditional masculine cultures, are quite physical, often violent, but there are stark limits to their ferocity. Anyone

---

[331] See Ringrose and Renold (2010), 575.
[332] See Ringrose and Renold (2010), 582.
[333] See Ringrose and Renold (2010), 576. See also Farrell (1993).
[334] Ringrose and Renold (2010), 575.
[335] Ringrose and Renold (2010), 575.
[336] Olweus (1999), 10.
[337] See Ringrose and Renold (2010), 576.
[338] See Ringrose and Renold (2010), 576.

transgressing those boundaries will be ostracised from the group and seen as an *outright* bully. There is measure in all things, apparently, including violence. To be plainly seen as such a violent bully is "neither desirable nor powerful for boys, in fact, the very opposite. The 'bully' label could function in multiple ways, including as a marker of weakness, pathology, sexual deviation, and class-based irrationality".[339]

The same studies suggest that boys who are physically violent against girls are considered and conceptualised as 'deviant'.[340] This is not surprising. Throughout history, too-frequent male-on-female violence has been openly condemned in most cultures. This condemnation is probably an offshoot of the traditional notion, be it evolutionary or cultural, of the heroic male who protects those that are close to him, especially female siblings and daughters, and never uses violence against weaker individuals, women *in primis*.[341] This ancient law apparently dominates today's schoolyards. But when one considers how remarkably common male-on-female domestic violence is, we are also reminded of the fragile barriers that keep our cruel nature at bay, as well as of the consequences of challenging the broader hierarchical context in which this ancient law is tacitly inscribed.[342]

Furthermore, we all are simultaneously repelled and drawn towards cruelty to a varying degree. We are offended and sickened by the TV news reporting on the gruesome barbarism that still exists in the world. Nevertheless, five minutes later, we have clicked on some so-called "true crime" series on *Netflix*, or participate in re-enactments of famous battles and wars, whether online or outdoors.[343] Most of us would never view ourselves as cruel persons, yet we may be oblivious to displays of our ugly side, peppering our lives in hopefully small doses.[344] We might excuse these occurrences by saying that we are being "cruel to be kind", or that we

---

339 Ringrose and Renold (2010), 582.
340 See Ringrose and Renold (2010), 582.
341 We distinguish "evolutionary" from "cultural" because the former term refers to significant changes to the genetic make-up of a population, whereas the latter does not; only the population's symbolic system mutates.
342 We do not mean to trivialise cruelty. Rather, we suggest that many a type and degree of "cruelty" proper exist. Some of them, unsurprisingly, are related to the patriarchal hierarchies of many a society.
343 On an analogous wavelength, Wilson *et al.* (2017, title page) discuss the case of ongoing "prison tourism".
344 We speak here of 'ugliness' in moral terms, but we cannot ignore the *aesthetic* component of this concept, which has had many patent reverberations in connection with both 'humour' (e.g., comic gargoyles and grotesque mascarons in architecture) and, as implied, 'cruelty' (see also Shklar 1984). In short, *there may exist a shared affective, evaluative, and conceptual ground beneath people's ethics and aesthetics*, whether individually or collectively.

are showing "tough love", or that we were dealing with the "competition", or that it was "just a bit of fun" (hence implying that the accuser is somehow overreacting).³⁴⁵

But when all is said and done, cruelty appears to be a potent, persistent, and perhaps, permanent fixture within the human psyche and its social manifestations, school bullying included. Our tentative justifications, moreover, may even indicate that, to be a fully functioning person, a bit of cruelty is actually a good thing —it's a cruel world out there, isn't it? So, you'd better be prepared to face it.³⁴⁶ As eloquently put by the Latvian-born political theorist Judith Shklar, the 'mother' of "liberalism of fear" in the late 20ᵗʰ century: "[C]ruelty is baffling because we can live neither with nor without it."³⁴⁷

1.2.2 Ancient Cruelty

Given that most noteworthy concepts in Western medicine, philosophy, and science can be traced to the ancient Greeks, whose myths and stories contained unparalleled cruelties, it may come as some surprise that their greatest thinkers gave it relatively little attention.³⁴⁸ Indeed, the first extensive and explicit reflections on "cruelty" proper are to be found in the work of a Roman rhetor, dramatist, politician, and Stoic philosopher, Lucius Annaeus Seneca.³⁴⁹

Seneca was the tutor and a senior advisor to the notorious Roman emperor Nero, and he later came to influence the work of countless following humanists and jurists, literally for centuries with his speculations about *crudelitas* [cruelty].³⁵⁰ Curiously, Seneca is noteworthy also in the history of the philosophy of laughter, insofar as he is recorded discussing, in *De constantia sapientis*, the importance of self-mockery as a tool to defend oneself from insults.³⁵¹ An instructive con-

---

345 More detailed considerations on these defensive strategies are developed in Chapter 2.
346 LVOA may help determine in principle which cruelties ought to be avoided and which cultivated.
347 Shklar (1984), 3. We discuss in some more detail the many available conceptions of 'liberalism' in *H&C3*. For the moment, let us just note how *her* conception of this portentous and contentious doctrine has kept finding scholarly applications, not least with regard to contemporary China (Luo 2021).
348 See, e.g., Calder (2011), Wiedemann (2005), and Woodard (2009).
349 See, e.g., Bartsch and Schiesaro (2015).
350 See, e.g., Grotius' (2005) references to Seneca and the former's repeated written use of "cruelty/cruel" *vis-à-vis tyrants*.
351 See Haugh (2017), 204–205.

sideration, given the subject of our book, as well as the deep and frequent affective overlap of jeers, jests, and cruelty, even when self-directed.[352]

Seneca interpreted cruelty as "hardness" or "harshness in exacting punishments", "intemperance of the soul in exacting punishments", or "the inclination of the soul towards more severity".[353] According to him, cruelty is a vice of *excess*, displayed by "those who have a reason for punishing, but no moderation in it".[354] Cruel people are therefore more than capable of determining the proper path of action but, misguided by a propensity towards sternness rather than lenience, they go one step too far. It is like they made a wrong calculation.

Seneca claimed that cruel individuals are not affected by "bestiality", which is the vice exhibited by those "who find pleasure in violence", i.e., a perverse and irrational inclination akin to "madness".[355] This is an important point insofar as it draws a neat distinction between those who are cruel, and those who, in modern parlance, we would call "sadistic". Twelve centuries later, Seneca's views were still being echoed, almost *verbatim*, by the most influential Aristotelian theologian of the Christian Middle Ages and Catholic saint—one Thomas Aquinas, who considered cruelty a form of greatly sinful "human wickedness" precisely because it includes an element of thoughtful deliberation.[356] Cruelty does not need any major excitability or loss of rationality to emerge, according to Aquinas. On the contrary, it can actually be very cold and extremely lucid.[357]

1.2.3 Montaigne and the Enlightenment

It was not until the 16th century that a major Western thinker decided to steer away from the Senecan and Scholastic view of cruelty, seeing it instead as a vicious trait

---

[352] We tackle self-mockery in Chapters 2 and 3. More on the affective substratum of jeers, jests, and cruelty is said in *H&C3*.
[353] Seneca (1900), book II, chap. 4, pars. 1 and 3. Many plausible translations are possible for the Latin's seemingly simple expression *"atrocitas animi in exigendis poenis"*, as well as for several other key-terms employed by Seneca, though not *crudelitas* itself (see, e.g., Malaspina 2022). A *cruel irony* applies to translating dead languages into living ones, which get farther and farther removed from the former.
[354] Seneca (1900), book II, chap. 4, par. 2.
[355] Seneca (1900), book II, chap. 4, par. 2.
[356] Aquinas (1920), part II of part II, question 159, art. 2.
[357] Both Seneca and Aquinas, as well as some relevant instances of their long-lived influence, were discussed in detail in *H&C1*. In this book, they are dispatched instead with a sheer subsection.

of human personality that is centred upon unmitigated passions.³⁵⁸ This Western thinker being the celebrated French essayist Michel de Montaigne who, unprecedented in the history of modern Western thought, devoted two whole chapters in his *Essais* to shedding light on this specific topic, which he also mentioned in many other essays (or, as written, "chapters").³⁵⁹

According to Montaigne, "cruelty" proper belongs to a long list of personal "vices" plaguing humans. He identified the root cause of this particular type of debasement: "cowardice is the mother of cruelty".³⁶⁰ Today's reader might want to swap "cowardice" for "fear", as it would harmonise better with the view that instances of cruelty related to racism or misogyny often seem to be fuelled by a sense of impotence or overbearing threat. Thus, cruelty can arise from xeno*phobia*, homo*phobia*, Islamo*phobia*, etc.

Indeed, the famous 20ᵗʰ-century Viennese psychoanalyst Alfred Adler wrote: "No act of cruelty has ever been done which has not been based upon a secret weakness."³⁶¹ The same view, moreover, can be found in the works of Francis Hutcheson, the father of the Scottish Enlightenment, who also authored an essay on "laughter" proper, stressing its springing out of incongruity and its capacity for leading people towards conviviality rather than animosity.³⁶² Whether we con-

---

358 This step away from the Senecan and Scholastic conception was *in se* no great innovation, for the effort with which Seneca and Aquinas connoted "cruelty" proper as distinct from "bestiality" and "madness" indicates by itself that the common understanding of the term at issue implied the vicious, sadistic quality that Montaigne discussed.

359 See Montaigne (1877). Philologically edited, the original can be consulted freely online (Montaigne 2018). Again, a more detailed account of his views was developed in *H&C1*. Here, we are being intentionally concise.

360 Montaigne (1877), book II, chap. 27, pars. 1 and 10.

361 Adler (1930), 105. Adler's focus was set on children's behaviour and upbringing. Still, we cannot but wonder on the plausibility of the seemingly 'heroic' and 'superhuman' assumptions made by Sade, Nietzsche, and Rand, or by social Darwinism, whereby many cruel acts have been explained as affirmations of people's predatory instincts. See also Adler (1921) for further claims of association between "cruelty" proper, neuroticism, and a misunderstood idea of 'masculinity' that today's callow parlance would probably describe as "toxic". His 1921 book comprises two chapters devoted, *inter alia*, to "cruelty" proper (i.e., part 2, chap. 1 and 5). Overall, Adler emphasised the role of culture over that of nature, which was central to Freud's approach, leading to a shift of focus that can be observed also in the writings of Jung, Horney, Klein, Reich, and Fromm. At the close of the 20ᵗʰ century, in light of the ecological collapse of our planet, a renewed emphasis on nature can be noticed, e.g., in Kristeva's and Irigaray's feminist approaches to psychoanalysis. This time, though, there is no glorification of Tennyson's (1850, 80, canto 55, 4ᵗʰ stanza, verse 3, and 1ˢᵗ stanza, verse 3) "Nature, red in tooth and claw", but rather the unnerving awareness that humankind could soon be among the "thousand types" that "are gone" forever.

362 See Hutcheson (2007) and (1973), which is about "laughter" proper.

sider Montaigne's or Hutcheson's case, their idea of 'cruelty' does not depict a cold or lucid path of deliberation, but a powerful and disorderly reaction to some profoundly disturbing affect.[363]

Doubtlessly, Montaigne's works may contain a faint whiff (and some quotes) of Seneca and Aquinas, but gone is the neat distinction between "cruelty" proper and, say, "bestiality".[364] There is no rational contemplation and/or deliberation at play in Montaigne's understanding of "cruelty" proper either; rather, there is a perverted loss of rationality turning humans into beasts.[365] Even his own rejection of cruelty was rooted in powerful emotion:

> Amongst other vices, I mortally hate cruelty, both by nature and judgment, as the very extreme of all vices: nay, with so much tenderness that I cannot see a chicken's neck pulled off without trouble, and cannot without impatience endure the cry of a hare in my dog's teeth, though the chase be a violent pleasure.[366]

Civilisation and education may have a role in preventing the progression of cruelty —or enhance it. Montaigne penned several remarks on this matter, and he was later echoed by John Locke, the father of the English Enlightenment.[367] It is true that some of the social reforms that Locke suggested in his writings sound decidedly cruel to the contemporary ear, such as "the separation of mothers from infants so that both can earn their daily bread, the whipping of children above the age of two who fail to earn their subsistence, the mutilation of the idle able bodied, and the flogging of cripples who refuse to work".[368] However, despite such inclinations towards what would be considered in the present era obvious cruelty, Locke was adamant, at least in words, in trying to prevent "cruelty" proper from spreading among the populace.[369]

In this connection, Montaigne and his later Enlightenment heirs, Locke included, believed that education played a critical role to that end; as also trying and limiting warfare, blood sports, gory entertainments, and public displays of torture, as

---

[363] We write "affect", but "passion", "emotion", "feeling", "sentiment" or "drive" could also be utilised.
[364] See, e.g., Montaigne (1877), book II, chap. 11, par. 20.
[365] See Montaigne (1877), book II, chap. 11, par. 24.
[366] Montaigne (1877), book II, chap. 11, par. 13. We need not distinguish "emotion" from "affect" *et similia*. As we explained in *H&C1*, too emphatic a detailing of a concept leads to destroying it and its epistemic utility. *Sometimes, in order to get the full picture, one must focus* off *the details, not* on *them.*
[367] See Locke (1824), par. 117.
[368] Andrew (1995), 35.
[369] See, e.g., Locke (1824), pars. 112–118.

well as the very popular form of public punishment and entertainment known as capital executions.[370] A true daughter of this tradition, the 'grandmother' of modern feminism, Mary Wollstonecraft, echoed Montaigne's intuitions and the Enlightenment spirit of his British successors, as she addressed the issue of male cruelty:

> [C]ruelty is first caught at school, where it is one of the rare sports of the boys to torment the miserable brutes that fall in their way. The transition, as they grow up, from barbarity to brutes to domestic tyranny over wives, children, and servants, is very easy. Justice, or even benevolence, will not be a powerful spring of action unless it extends to the whole creation; nay, I believe that it may be delivered as an axiom, that those who can see pain, unmoved, will soon learn to inflict it.[371]

Whether we focus on male or female behaviours, without due corrective planning and careful intervention, cruelty is bound to continue, if not metastasise. Representatively, in the 1950s, the Martinican poet and Marxist politician Aimé Césaire observed that the "force, brutality, cruelty, sadism, conflict, and … parody of education" characterising Western colonialism brutalises not only the colonised people, but also the colonisers, and especially those who profit the most from the exploitation of the former: "cruelty, mendacity, baseness, and corruption have sunk deep into the soul of the European bourgeoisie".[372] Therefore, if we really aim at keeping cruelty at bay, human feelings, attendant thoughts, and related institutions ought to be tinkered with and tweaked intelligently, for they are part and parcel of a socio-economic and ethico-cultural loop whereby collective structures influence individual behaviours and *vice versa*.[373]

Exploiting such keen psychological bases, the celebrated 18th-centuty penal reformer Cesare Beccaria, and many of his later liberal fellow-reformers, have stressed the importance of restrained and calculated deterrence in the legislative, judicial, and carceral spheres. Jeremy Bentham, the father of British Utilitarianism, wrote on these matters:

> [E]very act of cruelty produced by a passion, the principle of which exists in every heart, and from which everybody is exposed to suffer, creates an alarm, which will continue until the punishment of the culprit has transferred the danger to the side of injustice, and of cruel enmity. This alarm is a suffering common to all; and there is another suffering resulting from it,

---

370 See, e.g., Hutcheson (2007).
371 Wollstonecraft (1988), 172.
372 Césaire (1972), 42 and 48.
373 Quite obviously, in Césaire's case, that meant the end of the cruel colonial system, as also vocally pursued by his most famous student, i.e., the psychiatrist and philosopher Frantz Fanon.

which we ought not to forget, that pain of sympathy felt by generous hearts at the sight of such aggressions.[374]

It should be added that there were thinkers who did not believe that pure, unconditional cruelty, i.e., unmotivated and spontaneous, could exist. Surprisingly, given his grim pessimism in many other spheres, Thomas Hobbes was one of them.[375] Similarly inclined was the 18th-century Scottish philosopher David Hume. Despite his cynicism in many contexts of associated life, not least the controversial ones of theology and religion, he wrote: "Absolute, unprovoked, disinterested malice has never, perhaps, had place in any human breast."[376] Not even "the cruelty of Nero be allowed entirely voluntary, and not rather the effect of constant fear and resentment".[377]

Another Enlightenment thinker, the Neapolitan political economist Antonio Genovesi, stated in this respect: "No man is absolutely cruel; only relatively so."[378] Alternatively said, cruelty *per se* does not exist, and when people behave cruelly, there is a reason or a somewhat comprehensible motive for it, whether we can easily spot it or not. In Milan, Beccaria claimed himself that "man is only cruel in proportion to his interest to be so, to his hatred or to his fear".[379]

This 'denial' of sadistic cruelty as a feature of the human psyche was propagated into the works of successive scholars, many of whom have viewed cruelty as a sickness that can be healed. Instead of "cruelty" proper, we then encounter "sadism", a term which earlier thinkers like Seneca and Aquinas would have equated with "bestiality" or "savagery".[380] If sadism is a disease or disability, then there may well exist the possibility of a cure—or at least of some preventive interven-

---

374 Bentham (1864), 57.
375 See Hobbes (1985), part I, chap. 6, sec. 8.
376 As cited in Raphael (1991), vol. 2, 72.
377 As cited in Raphael (1991), vol. 2, 72. As Panzacchi (1897, 522) countered: "many of Nero's cruelties were caused by his aesthetic effervescence and artistic obsessions, unconstrained within natural boundaries". In any case, Nero's callousness and sadism have been so notorious in Western history that a 17th-century Austrian diplomat styled the Ottoman rulers' capricious and vindictive conduct in many of their domains as *"Neronische grausamkeit"* [Neronian cruelty] (Rayss Metzger as cited in Huemer 2022, 333, note 103).
378 Genovesi (1824), 15, unnumbered footnote.
379 Beccaria (1880), 140–141. On Beccaria's influence, see, e.g., Todaro and Miller (2014), A–K, 43–45.
380 The actual words "sadism" and, in parallel, "masochism", are the brainchildren of Richard von Kraft-Ebing (1892), whose 1886 *Psychopathia Sexualis* included many terms that have become standard. The latter term owes its name to the 1870 novel *Venus in Furs* by von Sacher-Masoch (1989). The former, to Sade, whom we discuss here.

tions. Cruelty, in this perspective, is not someone's moral failure, at any rate not first and foremost, but a systemic issue, which is to be countered or contained by apt measures of prophylaxis, as done with regard to, say, the plague, leprosy, or Covid-19.

Notably representative of the modern West's committed reformers, Bentham used "cruel" and "cruelty" as pejorative terms applicable to multiple phenomena, events, institutions, and/or praxes that he loathed or wanted to see changed. They included: exclusively human "anticipations of the future" (i.e., preoccupations and uncertainties); Dutch colonists' routine mishandling of "their cattle and their slaves" and people's "caprices" causing the suffering of living animals; political "[d]espotism" in all nations and varieties; "wars", their attendant spoils, and any lawful seizure of someone else's property "without indemnity"; unrealistic or inapplicable laws; "the English common law" in matters of "wills" and "succession", "divorce", spousal abuses and forced marriages; "dangerous character[s]" prone to "gratuitous cruelty" or "cruelty out of a mere motive of curiosity, imitation, or amusement", their cowardly ganging up against an isolated victim, or the many nasty "habits" that these unsavoury characters develop in time; formal confessions of dishonourable conduct in trials; public affronts and shaming as well as many "tortures"; extending indefinitely "the father's responsibility" towards "his children"; punishing innocent relatives and/or friends of the actual culprit; "expos[ing ...] the guilty to useless sufferings" or "leav[ing] the innocent to suffer" by using "too mild" penalties; "branding", "mutilations" and other "revolting cruelties" that "tend to barbarize the people which inflicts them"; and the institutional use of lawful "pardon without motive", i.e., excessive or unmotivated leniency.[381]

This growing therapeutic or corrective framework was, historically speaking, part of a much wider move towards secularisation in the Western world, which was thought capable of almost endless progress.[382] Gone were the medieval Chris-

---

[381] Bentham (1864), 66, 73, 109, 138, 144, 155, 183, 223, 229, 232, 259–260, 265, 294, 296–297, 315, 329–332, 345, 347, and 356. Bentham (1864, 259) touched on outright bloodlust, which he also listed *qua* "cruelty" among the pejoratives or "dyslogistic" terms commonly used to style "abstract moral qualities" applicable to human beings' "motives", i.e., "springs of actions" corresponding to "interests" pertaining to the "pleasures and pains" that are obtainable by way of "antipathy" or "ill will", i.e., "the irascible appetite" of our psyche (Bentham, 1817, table; in which "cruelty" appears alongside "spleen, ill-nature, waspishness, maliciousness, malignity, malignancy, venomousness ... barbarity, savageness, brutality, ferocity, vindictiveness, vengefulness, obduracy, obdurateness, implacability, callousness and unjust, improper, &c—asperity, harshness, rigour, severity, antipathy, &c".)

[382] Later events revealed cruel regress instead. E.g., Leacock (1942, chap. 1, par. 4) wrote: "Yet in spite of this lapse towards forgetfulness, till just a short time ago this almost world-wide freedom seemed to be a permanent achievement and advance of humanity. Then came the war. The shadow of force and tyranny has fallen over a great part of Europe. Liberty is here derided, there trampled

tian worries of personal sin and otherworldly salvation, which were replaced by those of this-worldly curative prevention and ingenious reform.[383] This centrality of apposite socio-institutional alterations, including educating and/or training people, to counter "cruelty" proper, was later highlighted by the Irish historian, liberal politician, and essayist William Edward Hartpole Lecky, notedly in his gargantuan 1869 *History of European Morals, from Augustus to Charlemagne*.[384]

Left to nature, which has created a plethora of merciless animals, human beings are unlikely to progress out of "cruelty" proper.[385] Lecky maintained that, however, it is possible to improve people through the use of humane establishments and enlightened art, so that they may learn how to "realise" empathically, i.e., to approach one another sympathetically and take into consideration the effects that they have on one another's lives, especially when these may be conducted in alien, strange, or even *prima-facie* obscene ways.[386]

Lecky noted that the reverse is also true, i.e., people can be trained in the opposite direction too—as Montaigne and several other philosophers and moralists had already observed before Lecky.[387] Like the great Frenchman, the Irish thinker took the notorious example of the Romans, who even at the height of their glorious empire, organised spectacles of carnage for the sake of mass entertainment.[388] No doubt Lecky would have a thing or two to say about today's enduring enthrallment with on-screen violence.[389]

1.2.4 Liberals and Their Critics

Some contemporary liberal scholars, like the aforementioned Shklar, were heavily influenced by the Enlightenment and the progressive approach of thinkers such as Lecky. As Shklar wrote: "the first right is to be protected against the fear of cruelty. People have rights as a shield against this greatest of human vices. This is the evil, the threat to be avoided at all costs. Justice itself is only a web of legal arrange-

---

underfoot, and everywhere in danger. Human kindliness is replaced by cruelties unknown for centuries". As we write this line, Russian troops invade Ukraine.
383 See, e.g., Baraz (2003).
384 See Lecky (1890), vol. 1. For an introduction to Lecky's life and works, see McCartney (1994).
385 Lecky (1890), vol. 1, 83.
386 Lecky (1890), vol. 1, 138 note 143, and 231.
387 See *H&C1*.
388 See Lecky (1890), vol. 1, 274.
389 The dis/continuity between the Roman games and today's ones are discussed in Chapter 2 and in *H&C3*.

ments required to keep cruelty in check."[390] A simple but important point. Sensible constitutional provisions, laws, and political arrangements can limit the amount and the degree of human (and animal) suffering within our societies.[391] Shklar's so-called "liberalism of fear" means a liberation *from* fear.

Shklar also came up with two sharp definitions of "cruelty" proper.
(1) "Cruelty is … the wilful inflicting of physical pain on a weaker being in order to cause anguish and fear … [it is] horr[ible] … [it] repels instantly because it is 'ugly' … [and] disfigures human character".[392]
(2) "Cruelty is the deliberate infliction of physical, and secondarily emotional, pain upon a weaker person or group by stronger ones in order to achieve some end, tangible or intangible, of the latter".[393]

A declared follower of Shklar's political programme, the pragmatist American philosopher Richard Rorty, reiterated her point by emphasising how "liberals … think that cruelty is the worst thing we do".[394] Echoing Lecky, Rorty argued that, in order to be less cruel, people should read interesting novels, watch good movies, and attend inspiring theatrical performances. The arts, in their myriad varieties and creative avenues, can spur the imagination and lead people to fantasise, conceive of, identify, and, hopefully, sympathise with the many ways in which we can be human, well beyond the confines of each personal existence, a specific personality type, the few lifepaths that we can witness directly, or the fewer ones that we can experiment with, during the variously brief duration of such a personal existence.[395] Having your heart touched by some of the world's most gifted artists would quite possibly serve as an antidote to cruelty, seeing that their greatness

---

390 Shklar (1984), 237.
391 As also discussed in Bülte (2018).
392 Shklar (1984), 8–9.
393 Shklar (1989), 29.
394 Rorty (1989), xv and 74.
395 The old notion of using the aptly called "humanities" to 'broaden the mind' and make people more 'humane', or the equally well-named "liberal arts" to 'liberate' people from their inflexible mental habits and/or noxious natural inclinations, was corroborated by Jung (1960–1990, vol. 3, par. 158; emphasis added), who observed how "[l]ack of consideration, narrow-mindedness, and inaccessibility to persuasion … in normal and psychological subjects" alike, frequently suffice in "mak[ing] a man … ruthless, and *cruel*". ("Man" being used here in a universalistic sense; i.e., the same consideration applies to women too.) As to which 'arts' Rorty (1989) had in mind, he did highlight novels and poetry, but he never stated that only these creative genres were the viable ones.

lies in their "fear of being, or having been, cruel ... not having noticed the suffering of someone with whom one had been in contact".[396]

Rorty maintained that the arts alone could contribute, more than any other celebrated discipline of Western culture, to "the creation of a world in which tenderness and kindness are the human norm".[397] Arguably, the arts are much closer to the felt side of being and/or to the lived experiences of human beings. These are comparative dimensions that the natural and social sciences may not adequately grasp. As Mini stated:

> The inability to deal with certain aspects of reality on the part of any discipline that prizes systematization (form) is well known. The most brilliant explorations of "states of mind", for instance, are not to be found in psychology texts but in novels. The reason is obvious. Psychology tries to explain taxonomically what is not amenable to be so explained. The novelist is free from such a delusion.[398]

At the same time, however methodologically-correct he may have been, Rorty was not optimistic about eliminating *in toto* selfish intra- and interpersonal cruelties—even though he did dream of a world where "love" will one day guide all human relations.[399] If anything, Rorty's works remind us of the disheartening fact that, in the pursuit of happiness in their private lives, most men and most women are likely to cause other people to suffer in a variety of ways, even if the collective institutions to which they subscribe may be officially devoted to the eradication of cruelty from the public sphere.[400] Liberalism, then, would be a social tool by which *at least* the public domain can be purified from the nefarious presence of cruelty. Or is it not?[401]

---

[396] Rorty (1989), 157.
[397] Rorty (1989), 160.
[398] Mini (1974), 152.
[399] Rorty (2000), 158 *et passim*.
[400] Rorty's work is, among other things, a reminder of how cruelty prospers in the most prosaic settings.
[401] *This is no rhetorical question.* The matter at issue is a *personal* determination, based upon which arguments and interpretations each reader finds the most persuasive. For one, *contra* the Enlightenment-fed Western conviction that secularisation is inexorably progressive and obviously beneficial, Hillman (1975, 96) stated: "[R]eligion, its odd minor sects especially, is an enormous treasury retaining and effectively organizing delusional systems, stereotypical behaviors, overvalued ideas, erotic obsessions, and sado-masochistic cruelties. The less religion, the more psychopathology spills out in the open and requires secular care." Ironically, humankind's old demons did not die at all with the demise of our cultures' alleged 'superstitions' and, as these demons resurface, they call for novel exorcisms, which may come now dressed in white coats rather than black robes, and make use of pills instead of prayers (LVOA might help us to establish which approach is preferable in each concrete case).

A 20th-century American moral philosopher and well-published Montaigne scholar, John Kekes, was vocally critical of "liberalism of fear", claiming that, in reality, "the pursuit of universal benevolence has often led to great cruelty, and is routinely justified by the belief that it has prevented even greater cruelties".[402] Kekes speculated that Shklar's and Rorty's projects were yet another example of good intentions paving the way to the proverbial hell.[403] He offered three chief arguments aimed at showing how defining "liberalism" itself as an inherent opposition to "cruelty" was wrong.[404]

(1) First of all, Kekes took issue with Rorty's claim that cruelty is truly "the worst thing we do".[405] He pointed out that genocide, terrorism, betrayal, exploitation, humiliation, brutalisation, tyranny, and so forth, can be considered to be worse—plausibly, if not plainly.[406] Instructively, as we discussed in *H&C1*, the great British humourist and essayist, G.K. Chesterton, had already pointed out how grand-scale life-destruction might well be *beyond* "cruel".[407]

(2) Shklar's and Rorty's definition of liberalism as opposition to cruelty entails surreptitiously that non-liberals are less averse to cruelty than liberals, and that by opposing cruelty, one has automatically become a liberal of sorts.[408] However, it should be obvious that non-liberals frequently oppose cruelty. As the American ethicist John Portmann pointed out just a few years after the publication of Kekes' critique of the liberal and thoroughly secular Richard

---

402 Kekes (1996), 841–842. See also Hunt (1999). For an overview of Kekes' philosophy, see Kazeem (2009) and, more narrowly yet also more apropos in our book's context, Simon's (1999) review of Kekes (1997).

403 Kekes (1996), 835 f. Slave trade and 'civilising' colonialism stand out in the litany of 'efficient' and/or 'well-meaning' liberal horrors, which even a committed, enthusiastic, and unrepentant 'free-market' thinker such as the historian of finance William Goetzmann (2017) acknowledged and criticised in our century. However, we could easily add: a few murderous revolutions fought in the name of "liberty"; some notorious examples of destructive urban planning (e. g., Genoa's 19th-century train stations); or the racial eugenics championed by the British botanist, birth-control campaigner, and feminist reformer Marie Stopes (1920). More on liberalism's paradoxical cruelties is said in *H&C3*. Also, as stated as well in *H&C3*, we do not imply that other socio-economic orders are incapable of dreadful cruelties. Rather, *we focus on liberal cruelties* because: (a) since the end of the Cold War, we have been living in a chiefly liberal world, especially in the economic sphere; (b) we address the staunchly cruelty-averse "liberalism of fear" of Shklar and Rorty; and (c) we discuss liberals claiming that no other order is as beneficial.

404 Kekes (1996), 835.

405 Kekes (1996), 835.

406 See Kekes (1996), 835.

407 Chesterton (1997), chap. 7, par. 14.

408 See Kekes (1996), 835.

Rorty: "[R]eligious writers have devoted much more energy to exploring human suffering than have philosophical ones".[409]

(3) Kekes' third argument was that, by giving more liberty to more people, liberal institutions give them *ipso facto* more opportunity to act cruelly.[410] Freed from external coercion and condign power, the men and the women of liberal societies have more choices to pursue to try and enjoy some happiness—surely, not all of them will be kind choices.[411] People may be, say, too selfish, too sadistic, too superficial, too sentimental, too supercilious, or simply too stupid, to make a truly constructive, life-enabling use of their personal freedom and constitutional rights.[412]

In the end, Kekes himself could not resist the temptation to upgrade Shklar's definition of "cruelty" proper, hence writing: "cruelty is the disposition of human agents to take delight in or be indifferent to the serious and unjustified suffering their actions cause to victims".[413]

The late Tom Regan, who enjoyed considerable fame as a liberal American ethicist and animal-rights activist, provided an interesting taxonomy of cruelty in the 1980s. Although utilised in his advocacy for animal rights, it can be extrapolated onto humans, both in broad institutional contexts and in prosaic small-scale ones.[414]

Regan stated that people can be judged as being cruel either for what they do or do not do, or for what they feel or do not feel.[415] The absolute crux of cruelty, according to Regan, is for people to take pleasure in someone else's suffering, which the former gleefully bring about and impose onto the latter. Some of us, however, may be forced to cause others pain, including significant discomfort, e. g., dentists and doctors, but such agents do not enjoy it. Therefore, according to Regan, they are not sadists.[416]

---

409 Portmann (2000), 6.
410 See Kekes (1996), 836.
411 See Kekes (1996), 836.
412 Good laws, good education, and good social monitoring may be effective against *some* of these shortcomings, but not all of them, especially the last one. As Cipolla's (2011, 59) fifth law of human stupidity states: "A stupid person is the most dangerous type of person", i. e., more dangerous than "bandits", whose behaviour can, at least, be rationally predicted. Stupid people, instead, will somehow find a surprising way to harm others *and* themselves.
413 Kekes (1996), 843, and (1997), 186.
414 See Regan (1983), 197–198. For an introduction to Regan's philosophy, see Lengauer (2020).
415 See Regan (1983), 197–198. Kekes (1996) insisted on this point too.
416 Regan (1983), 198. Kekes (1996) insisted on this point too.

In parallel, there are cruel people who feel no pleasure in making others suffer. Indeed, they seem to feel nothing at all. Their cruelty is characterised by a lack of appropriate feeling, e.g., they show no compassion, sympathy, or mercy.[417] Regan calls this sort of indifferent cruelty "brutal". He sets up four possible ideal types of cruelty, depending on whether people actively seek that which causes cruel suffering ("active") or merely let it happen ("passive").[418] They are:

(1) Active sadistic (e.g., a woman's prolonged and delighted toying with a hopeless suitor at a small dinner party to which both persons were invited along with some friends);

(2) Passive sadistic (e.g., some friends' enjoyment and encouragement of the woman's malicious conduct);

(3) Active brutal (e.g., the aloof host of the small dinner party facilitating the cruel act by inviting the two individuals at issue while knowing very well what could happen, given their personal history in the shared social circle to which all of them belong); and

(4) Passive brutal (e.g., some jaded friends, who are clearly seeing what is going on before their eyes, and yet saying and doing nothing about it).[419]

Making use of Regan's well-reasoned and well-organised approach is fraught with challenges. As Regan acknowledged, the dividing line between cruelty and non-cruelty can be uncertain for both the active and the passive forms.[420] For example, a woman is not considered cruel although she may fail to feed her pets every now and then. She is, however, cruel, if she fails to do so most of the time. But there is no exact number of times or fixed percentage that can determine the crossing-over.

Equally difficult is to ascertain the true inner motives that we, human beings, may have for causing suffering to others like us or to animal creatures. Regan assumes that it is because we either derive pleasure from it, or that we do not possess the mental faculties to empathise, or lastly, because we cannot avoid it, e.g., a doctor readjusting a broken limb. It is simply impossible to correctly identify all the pertinent causal mechanisms for our thoughts and actions, many of which are unconscious, i.e., such that they may become clear to the agent, if they ever do, only *ex post*—or after years of keen psychotherapeutic self-discovery.

---

417 See Regan (1983), 198.
418 Regan (1983), 198. As explained in *H&C1*, Bodin (1955) was the first to draw this distinction, in the 1500s.
419 See Regan (1983), 197–198. Accordingly, a person who were to strike a child or a non-threatening pet would be *actively* cruel, whereas one who, through negligence, should fail to feed a child or a pet to the point where its health deteriorates, would be *passively* cruel.
420 See Regan (1983), 198, which applies to the rest of the paragraph above.

The presence and influence of unconscious motives in human life should never be underestimated. If all that mattered in the ethical and political realms were the conscious will of people, the world's many people of good will would have already resolved most of their problems—merely by *willing* their resolution in a conscious manner. However, as shown more than amply by the prosaic experiences of addiction, our momentary lapses of self-restraint, the torturing obsessiveness of our *idées fixes*, and/or our countless as well as hopeless new year's resolutions, willing something in a conscious manner does not easily and/or necessarily translate into getting it, doing it, and/or even just striving for it in earnest.[421]

As another 20th-century American liberal ethicist, Philip Paul Hallie, remarked: "immorality" entails enormous motivational "complexities", akin to "a mass of intricately intertwined pipes", including "the ferocious ugliness" exhibited by cruel behaviours.[422] Awareness of such a limitation causes problems for the study of the human mind, but *per* Regan's definition, it depends on having knowledge of these inner workings, and is therefore bound to be severely hindered in the practical realm.[423]

For example, it is conceivable that your self-assured and caring dentist really enjoys the pain that s/he causes you, but sublimates his/her feelings, so that s/he does not have to come face-to-face with his/her real cruel self. Perhaps the brute does get some pleasure out of watching someone agonising, but his/her *ego* puts up defences of apparent ignorance in order to survive. Moreover, even an inveterate sadist can have mixed emotions, hidden within his/her breast, to which the external observer has no access.

To put it briefly, 'insight' is a wonderful concept, but notoriously over-rated when it comes to its relevance in psychology. Most of us, far more often than we wish to admit, have in fact no clue as to why we think and act the way we do. How many times have we done things that we did not want to do, e.g., smoking yet another cigarette? And how many times have we failed to do things that we wanted to do, e.g., phoning our elderly aunt? Perhaps we might just be better at reading others—or so many of us think, more often than not, in spite of much contrary evidence and direct experience.[424]

---

421 See, e.g., Jung (1960–1990), vol. 9.1, 20, par. 44.
422 Hallie (1985c), 42.
423 We probe this point in our Chapter 2.
424 Given this intricate reality, *we avoid trenchant statements and comforting simplifications on people's motives.*

1.2.5 Hallie in Particular

An even more detailed taxonomy of "cruelty" proper was put forth by the aforementioned Hallie. By himself, Hallie contributed more to the study of this notion than perhaps any other Western intellectual. As such, his work inspires our own to a significant extent.[425]

To begin with, Hallie defined the term "cruelty" in three non-identical yet converging ways:
(1) "the infliction of ruin, whatever the motives";[426]
(2) "the activity of hurting sentient beings";[427] and
(3) "the slow crushing and grinding of a human being by other human beings".[428]

Building upon these broad, different, yet largely coextensive definitions, Hallie produced a remarkable classification of "cruelty" proper.[429] For brevity's sake, it can be diagrammed as follows:
(1) "[C]ruelty upon humans" subdivides into (1a) "fatal cruelties", caused by nature, and (1b) "human violent cruelty", caused by people.[430]
(2) "[H]uman violent cruelty" can be (2a) "explicit", aka "direct" (i.e., caused by a patent "intention to hurt"), or (2b) "implicit", aka "indirect" (i.e., caused by "indifference or distraction") and capable of mutating from merely "episodic" into (2c) "institutionalized cruelty" by prolonged usage and habituation, i.e., such that it goes unnoticed *qua* cruelty in the eyes of both victims and perpetrators.[431]
(3) Lastly, "human violent cruelty" can be divided also into (3a) "sadistic" and (3b) "practical": whereas the latter refers to forms of instrumental cruelty, the for-

---

[425] We cannot measure exactly the level of this 'Halliean' inspiration, but we certainly refer to his definitions and taxonomies many times, and we largely base our own non-exclusive understanding of "cruelty" proper on them.
[426] Hallie, (1969), 14. Additional ones could be extrapolated from Hallie (1969), but this one is the first, most explicit and overarching definition.
[427] Hallie (1992), 229.
[428] Hallie (1985b), 2.
[429] Largely ignored and/or forgotten, only a few commentators have discussed and/or proposed explicit revisions of Hallie's definitions, the importance of which, whenever tackled, is not denied (see, e.g., Singer 2004).
[430] Hallie (1969), 5–6.
[431] Hallie (1969), 13–14, 29–31, 98 *et passim*. See also Hallie (1985a), 11.

mer is "self-gratifying".⁴³² (In essence, this is an anticipation of the distinction made by Regan between "sadistic" and "brutal" cruelties.)⁴³³

Perplexingly, Hallie came to realise that not all types of cruelty ought to be avoided and that their disappearance might be more harmful than their persistence.⁴³⁴ This realisation may be hard to accept. Probably, it was hard for him too. Hallie was a war veteran, committed humanist, long-time Jewish philosophy teacher at a Christian institution, serious Montaigne scholar, and charitable person with strong moral fibre.⁴³⁵ His recognition that cruelty may be necessary or even desirable at times should therefore not be misinterpreted as a light-hearted endorsement. Rather, Hallie saw cruelty as an integral part of the painful processes of personal growth and maturation, as well as of the artistic disclosure of sorrowful truths and multiple intense sensual elations.⁴³⁶ Our lives would be poorer were all these types of cruelty to vanish.⁴³⁷

And "cruelty" they all are, according to Hallie. They are *not* some milder-worded phenomenon, or some misunderstood form of apparent evil.⁴³⁸ Hallie's life-

---

432 Hallie (1969), 22–24 *et passim*. See Faris and Tucker (2022, 120 *et passim*) for a contemporary sociological study of "instrumental cruelty" in the context of bullying that echoes some of Hallie's earlier considerations.
433 While acknowledging that cruelty can vary in type and degree, Hallie never tried to establish a clear hierarchy of institutionalised victimisation. Historical horrors are horrible enough without having to say which one should horrify us more than another. Confronted with utter inhumanity, comparisons become preposterous. Was Hitler crueller than Stalin? Bocassa than Idi Amin? Axayacatl than Ahuitzotl? Nero than Caligula? Yet, as studied by the Belgian sociologist Jean-Michel Chaumont (2000, 167), such a competitive approach has existed and even led, in a *cruel irony*, victims and/or their representatives to fight among themselves over recognition and/or resources, claiming their "unique" sufferings to have been quantitatively and/or qualitatively greater than their competitors'. Solidarity is thus sacrificed upon the altar of scales of relative un/worthiness in the face of suffered cruelty.
434 See Hallie (1969). Slavery and the Holocaust loom large in Hallie's writings, and it should not be difficult to understand why. Yet institutional cruelty can occur under less dramatic circumstances, such as standard wage relations in liberal economies or hierarchical disparities within large organisations and organised social bodies, e. g., as regards accessing, addressing and/or allocating financial resources (see, e. g., Utz 1994, chap. 5 and 7).
435 See Hallie (1966) and (1977).
436 See especially Hallie (1969).
437 See, again, Hallie (1969).
438 *Clear definitions and orderly classifications are conventional theoretical constructs* facilitating the study of select phenomena. As such, they can and do vary a lot. The Spanish philosopher Antonio Campillo (2017, 86–87; emphases removed), for one, distinguished among: (1) the "violence" that "is caused by physical phenomena" as "force"; (2) the "violence" that "is caused by animals in general" as "aggressiveness"; and (3) the "violence" that "is caused exclusively by humans" as "cru-

long charitable volunteering and many of his academic works sought to contribute to the abatement of "cruelty" proper, as he believed that this term possessed a truly personal, tangible, "empirical" connotation—unlike "evil" alone and/or many of ist cognates, which were addressed, instead, in the bulk of the philosophical literature of his day, e.g., "oppression", "patriarchy", "aggression", "violence", "alienation", etc.[439]

This concern is especially clear as regards "institutionalized cruelty" (aka "institutional cruelty"), to which Hallie directed his readers' attention again and again, insofar as he regarded it as the most insidious type of cruelty in complex, modern societies.[440] This was the case because repeated, expected, routinely cruel behaviours, albeit capable of causing enormous suffering, can become so normal as to be taken to be a sheer, ordinary facet of the sadly and inevitably imperfect natural and/or human universe that both the victims and the perpetrators inhabit.[441] As Mini himself observed with regard to both Hegel's philosophy in Prussia and orthodox economics in the modern West, one may even go as far as to proceed with "the identification of the apparent cruelties, stupidities, and evil of the world with the work of Reason", in such a way as to "please those in power" and receive applause, consideration and/or pecuniary reward.[442]

Having said that, Hallie recognised that cruelty may be a necessary evil in dispensing, for example, penal justice.[443] No well-ordered society, in his view, could ever truly function without some organised system of reprisal for people's worst misdeeds and abuses, which no progressive campaign of religious moralisation, socio-cultural reformation, poverty relief, and/or emancipatory revolt has ever succeeded in eradicating.[444] As anomalous as this recognition may sound, cruelty

---

elty" proper, insofar as (3a) this third type of "violence" adds a "moral" dimension to the "harm" that all forms of violence produce onto their victims, whether (3ai) "inert" or (3aii) "living", and (3b) it extends said harm to the perpetrator him-/herself, who is somehow spoiled or made worse by his/her cruelty. In Australian English, the cruel perpetrator could thus be said to have *cruelled* his/her chances at being a good person, or a better one.

439 See Hallie (1988), 119 f.
440 Hallie (1970), 295.
441 The most astounding example is slavery, a sombre yet common institution in ancient and modern times (see, respectively, Ateneo 1990 and Vajda 2009). Hallie (1971) addresses it emphatically.
442 Mini (1974), 154.
443 See especially Hallie (1969). As we discussed in *H&C1*, Cesare Beccaria and Adam Smith were also keen on this point, as well as on calling penal remedies "cruel" rather than merely "evil", "painful" or something else.
444 Penal regimes can still be marked by "cruelty" to the utmost degree (see, e.g., Tofighian *et al.* 2022, par. 11).

was able to find, even in Hallie's own concerned humanism and deep ethical reflections, several justifications whereby it may, can, and ought to endure in individual as well as collective life.[445]

Apart from initiating the philosophical debates about the important topic of "institutional cruelty", Hallie identified this puzzling feature at the heart of cruelty and called it a "paradox".[446] Hallie recognised five typologies of this paradox:[447]

(1) Cruelty that is brought about without any open "intention to hurt", but in the name of altruism, happiness, justice, benevolence, equality, etc. As Hallie writes, "substantial maiming" can spring from "wanting the best and doing the worst".[448]

(2) Cruelty that is caused by an open "intention to hurt" which is, however, aimed at educating and therefore avoiding worse cruelties, e. g., "*in terrorem*" literary techniques.[449]

(3) "[T]he *fascinosum*" of "cruelty" proper, i.e., the strange lure that gruesome and sadistic thrills appear to have on many people, inducing among them various enjoyments and/or benefits, such as: "erotic stimulation"; "awareness"; wider sensual "imagination"; and the "pleasure" of "masochism".[450]

(4) Cruelty that is implied by the "growth" or maturing of the person, who must go through painful processes and gruelling experiences for the sakes of "individualis[ation]" and authentic human "subjectivity".[451]

(5) Cruelty that is "responsive", i.e., enacted in retaliation to "provocative" cruelty.[452] This situation is commonly exemplified by penal reprimands about which we have already written in this book, but equally by well-grounded social revolts, patriotic struggles, justified rebellions, and just wars—although Hallie was very cautious about all such life-destructive avenues and recom-

---

445 We discuss further this matter in the ensuing chapters of our book.
446 Hallie (1969), title page *et passim*.
447 Interestingly, as seen in the previous section, paradoxes are frequently associated with "humour" proper.
448 Hallie (1969), 14–20. This paradoxical process can be self-imposed too, as exemplified by Berlant's (2010, title *et passim*) psychoanalysis-inspired "cruel optimism" whereby people, say, pursue eagerly and even effectively a certain noble goal, which is actually detrimental to their long-term wellbeing and overall life-enablement.
449 Hallie (1969), 20–22.
450 Hallie (1969), 41–75. As also Susan Sontag stated: "Everyone has felt (at least in fantasy) the erotic glamour of physical cruelty and an erotic lure in things that are vile" (as cited in Maes and Levinson, 2012, 218).
451 Hallie (1969), 55–58 and 60–62.
452 Hallie (1969), 80 *et passim*.

mended avoiding cruelties that would "escalate" hence "creating new victims".[453]

Hallie's understanding of the paradoxical nature of cruelty, i.e., that it may be a necessary evil at times, is well-argued and more comprehensive than anything pursued before or after him, but not wholly original. Albeit rare, there have been Western thinkers who even went *beyond* the paradoxical view itself and claimed that cruelty can, in truth, be good. Most such thinkers argued that cruelty possesses no intrinsic disvalue, i.e., it is not bad *per se.* Rather, it possesses instrumental value alone, or chiefly so. Cruelty can therefore become acceptable if and when it is employed to pursue perceived positive aims. This is most obvious, once again, within the penal system, where cruelty can be seen as a sorry tool to serve society. Far fewer thinkers dared to argue that cruelty is inherently valuable.

In the following three subsections, we discuss representative voices from both these camps.[454]

1.2.6 Cruelty as a Positive

The notorious Italian political theorist Niccolò Machiavelli must be recognised as the first Western thinker who adopted the instrumental conception of "cruelty" proper, vocally and unapologetically. In his controversial 16th-century treatise *Il principe* [*The Prince*], the Florentine thinker distinguished between "cruelties being badly or properly used".[455] Among the latter stand out the victors described by ancient history, i.e., "heroes" that were praised by him precisely for their "cruel" yet decisive actions in war.[456] Given the circumstances, their cruelty was a "virtue", just like justice, honesty, or sobriety would be in times of peace.[457]

Cruelty is not an end in itself, then, but a context-sensitive instrument. Machiavelli certainly wished that every prince would want to purse clemency and

---

453 Hallie (1969), 79–82 and 166. The socio-political dimension hinted at above also implies the likely inevitability of cruelty. As the late American sociologist Barrington Moore, Jr. (1969, 67–68) wrote with regard to "the huge masses of cruelty that are everywhere around us", each person, being "[b]orn into a world we did not make", is bound to have "to take a stand for or against" them, i.e., to either allow for their continuation or "fight to establish the ultimate premises of [a] society", which, in his judgement, ought to strive to minimise the "suffering that is unavoidable" to its members, but also be ready to cause suffering, at times, for societal betterment's sake.
454 A fuller account was provided in *H&C1.*
455 Machiavelli (1908), chap. 8, par. 7.
456 Machiavelli (1908), chap. 17, par. 4.
457 Machiavelli (1908), chap. 17, par. 4.

be considered clement rather than cruel. Nevertheless, Machiavelli also argued that the same prince should be very careful not to misuse this clemency and recognise that, sometimes, nothing short of "cruelty" proper is needed to bring peace and harmony to the princedom.[458]

Other scholars have been more preoccupied with the *existential* value of cruelty, rather than the *political* one. In his 1988 book, *Le principe de cruauté* [lit. "the cruelty principle"], the French philosopher Clément Rosset rejected the commonplace identification of "cruelty" proper with sadism and made claims about the positive instrumental value of the former for each living and thinking person.[459] Eerily if not curiously, Rosset's claims sounded analogous to Machiavelli's ones, although the former was discussing the private sphere, not the public one and, moreover, Rosset's own definition of the term reads radically different from any other that we have encountered until now: "Cruelty [is] not ... pleasure in cultivating suffering but ... a refusal of complacency towards an object, whatever it may be".[460]

Rosset was a renowned Schopenhauer scholar and he echoed in many of his writings the latter's philosophical pessimism.[461] At the heart of Rosset's reasoning lies the dismal awareness of the fact that we mortals are condemned to live in a reality that is inexorably painful, tragic, disappointing, and, ultimately, nothing short of "cruel".[462] The human being, however, is never fully prepared to face this sorry realisation.[463]

This is unfortunate, according to Rosset, since if we want to be able to derive any satisfaction from and within the earthly condition in which we are cast, we must realise and accept that our life will always entail great suffering. Any and every "joy" that we may experience is, *a fortiori*, necessarily "cruel".[464] As also Oscar Wilde had written: "perhaps in nearly every joy, as certainly in every pleasure, cruelty has its place".[465] One must then find within him-/herself the heart to

---

[458] See Machiavelli (1908), chap. 17, par. 1. Whether Machiavelli was giving general advice on the art of statesmanship or had a much more specific aim in mind is a dilemma that has been debated since the Renaissance, not least by some of the most argute and committed revolutionaries and political thinkers in Italian history, e.g., Antonio Gramsci (1977, vol. 3, 1926–1929, Q17, par. 27).
[459] For an introduction to Rosset's work, see Lejeune (2012), 47–70. Rosset's title could also be translated as "the principle of cruelty", thus suggesting a dual reading, i.e., cruelty's conceptual-axiological foundation *and* cruelty's temporal-aetiological commencement.
[460] Rosset (1993), 18.
[461] See, e.g., Rosset (1968).
[462] Rosset (1993), 76 f.
[463] See, e.g., Téllez and Rosset (1999), 131.
[464] Rosset (1993), 17 f.
[465] Wilde (1994), chap. 11, par. 2.

stomach this sorry order of things, gulping down large amounts of agony and distress in order to be able to enjoy a modicum of joyfulness.[466]

Nothing positive escapes this dismal realisation, according to Rosset, not even romantic love. After all, as it was observed by the 20th-century Romanian existentialist thinker Emil Cioran: "Passion is also cruelty toward others and toward oneself, for one cannot experience it without torturing, without torturing oneself."[467] And as Jung stated in his *Red Book*, while considering the broader ramifications of "love" proper in the psychological, cultural, and spiritual spheres of human existence: "You are afraid to open the door? I too was afraid, since we had forgotten that God is terrible. Christ taught: God is love. But you should know that love is also terrible."[468]

Albeit cruel, reality can be enthralling and comical, according to Rosset, since its contradictions can be seen as enjoyably ridiculous, not just as tearfully tragic.[469] Rosset was thereby in agreement with Santayana's much older statement reciting: "Everything in nature is lyrical in its ideal essence, tragic in its fate and comic in ist existence."[470] Nonetheless, Rosset emphasised in his oeuvre the tragic side of things, not the comic one. He claimed that life's cruelty is in fact *double*. Not only is everything ultimately meaningless, but for us to live a worthwhile life, we must acknowledge this meaninglessness.[471] There exists, in the end, a cruel "alliance" between "life and the tragedy of life" that we cannot really escape from.[472]

Earlier in the 20th century, the French dramatist Antonin Artaud took a similar existentialist stance in his aesthetic ruminations on the so-called "theatre of cruelty".[473] As Artaud wrote: "Death is cruelty, resurrection is cruelty, transfiguration

---

[466] Some readers and pessimist thinkers have certainly thought of this bargain as not worth the price.
[467] Cioran (1970), 137. Cioran's enduring fame and profound pessimism do not mean that humour is unknown in Romania. Quite the opposite. See, e.g., the comprehensive collection of essays edited by Constantinescu *et al.* (2020), which indirectly confirmed the irreducible polysemy of "humour" proper and the immense plurality of its manifestations. The same can be said of other entries in the same book series whence the book on Romania derived, whether focussing on specific Central/Eastern-European nations (see Brzozowska and Chłopicki 2012 on Poland and Litovkina *et al.* 2012 on Hungary) or on linguistic "humour" more in general (see Litovkina, Daczi, and Barta 2010).
[468] Jung (2009), 235. Anyone familiar with the pangs of his/her conscience is likely to know that they can be cruel, whether justified or not. Anyone entirely devoid of them, instead, is probably either a saint or a sociopath.
[469] See Rosset (1991).
[470] Santayana (1922), 142. We addressed extensively Santayana's understanding of "humour" proper in *H&C1*.
[471] This is the main theme of Rosset's (1993) aptly titled book, *Joyful Cruelty.*
[472] As cited in Lejeune (2012), 249–250.
[473] Artaud (1958), 89.

is cruelty... Everything that acts is a cruelty."⁴⁷⁴ Insofar as art is nothing but a subcategory of human activity, drama itself has to obey the same cosmic logic of cruelty, which feeds the deepest and hidden forces of the human psyche.⁴⁷⁵

An Artaud scholar discussed this realisation many years later, highlighting how even silly clowns can be seen as Sisyphean characters, dramatically entangled within a veritable "circus of cruelty".⁴⁷⁶ The clowns' seemingly ludicrous plight and superficially amusing mock fights hide a much darker truth about our sad existential and psychological state. They are a bittersweet reminder of the human condition, which is anything but amusing. (The reader may then want to take another good look at Soulcié's cartoon in the opening pages of this book.)

As was the case for Rosset's unusual definition of "cruelty", Artaud's one also departed considerably from all previous ones: "Cruelty is not just a matter of either sadism or bloodshed, at least not in any exclusive way... [It] must be taken in a broad sense, and not in the rapacious physical sense that is customarily given to it."⁴⁷⁷

1.2.6.1 The Marquis de Sade and Captain Samuel Bellamy

Artaud's definition remains intriguing, albeit somewhat vague. Moreover, the term "sadism" has many good reasons to be mentioned in connection with "cruelty" proper.

For one, some Western thinkers have speculated about the questionable yet conceivable benefits of cruelty in its extremes, claiming that it can be instrumentally and even intrinsically valuable for at least some participants—the exact dividing line between these two forms of value being very uncertain and ethically untethered, at times. For example, the noted German social psychologist Erich Fromm observed that "an essential motivation" can be found even in "the depth

---

474 Artaud (1958), 85 and 101–103.
475 Ironically, Artaud's (1958) declared intention was to usher a new and truly 'modern' drama, but he may well have been rediscovering the 'gutsy' and 'gory' drama of medieval Europe, at least if Enders' (1999) scholarly depiction of the latter was correct. Interestingly, Hand (2005, 18) retrieved a similar continuity between traditional Japanese drama and modern horror films, i.e., a sophisticated "aesthetics of cruelty". Contemporary claims suggesting that "[o]ur era marks the end of traditional aesthetics" are probably as old as the Graeco-Roman world itself and, *in nuce*, exaggerated, bombastic, misinformed, if not utterly false (Chouliaraki 2006 in Vosmer 2022, 19). Plausibly, the only major difference from all previous eras is today's truly global dimension of the "commercial aspect" of such gruesome spectacles and crowd-pleasing "[a]nti-humanism" (Vosmer 2022, 18).
476 Ottinger (2004), title *et passim*.
477 Artaud (1958), 101 81–103.

of cruelty and destructiveness" characterising the seemingly self-gratifying phenomenon of "sadism", i.e., "the wish to know the secret of things and of life", as though the victim's extreme suffering and/or the perpetrator's extreme supremacy were capable of disclosing the metaphysical fountainhead of all being, as also envisioned by Artaud's experimental theatre.[478] Perhaps, *in extremis veritas*—not just *in vino*.[479]

For another, the joys of outright bloodshed have been praised by some rare voices in the West's philosophical and literary canon. Chief among these has been, unsurprisingly, the infamous Marquis de Sade, whence the very term "sadism" originated and who is better known today, at least among the general public, as a pornographer rather than as a philosopher.[480] Sade argued that humans should cast away the shackles of civilisation and return to a more natural state of being. For him, this meant a return to "cruelty" proper, as visible in animals, children, and "savages", inasmuch as "cruelty … is an expression of the laws of Nature but not of depravity", i.e., it is pure and unadulterated life energy.[481] As Sade noted, when ordinary people are left to pursue their natural instincts, they prey upon one another whenever the right opportunity arises.[482]

The rebellious and scandalous aristocratic Sade did not only see cruelty as a healthy regression to our natural state. In addition, he hinted at the possibility that there could be in it an element of cultivation and refinement, *pace* Shaftesbury's English gentlemen and their polished, yet far more moderate confrontation-

---

[478] Fromm (1972), 25.
[479] It is probably a *cruel irony* that Artaud, according to the Spanish literary expert Inés Ferrero Cándenas (2007), sought existentially important epiphanies in his aesthetic embrace of "cruelty" proper, while utter futility and human insignificance may actually be the exhilarating 'truths' disclosed by it, as exemplified in the literary oeuvre of the 20th-century Mexican writer Francisco Tario.
[480] The two professions are not mutually exclusive, but they rarely meet. Also, as explained in *H&C1*, we take "Sade" to primarily mean the mind behind the loose philosophical system that can be reconstructed from his novels, whether or not it corresponds to that of Sade-the-everyday-man as well. In doing so, we follow Georges Bataille's (1962, 188) example, though it should be noted that Bataille's (1962, 78–80) chief use of "cruel" and "cruelty" proper occurs in his discussions of human warfare, thus echoing Montaigne's older French musings.
[481] Sade (2010), 74.
[482] Leopardi (n.d.a.[1898], 1999, 2338, 2354 *et passim*) made analogous statements too. His argument was simple. The closer to nature we are, the weaker we are; the weaker we are, the more egoistical we become; the more egoistical we are, the likelier we become to be cruel to those who are weaker than us. However, Leopardi (n.d.a. [1898], 2360) did not embrace cruelty, but regarded it as a natural propensity of humankind, adding scorn to our well-established misery, for cruelty manages to subsist even at later stages of individual maturity and collective civilisation.

al "humour" to be developed among upper-class peers. Specifically, Sade distinguished between two types of cruelty.
(1) One was said to originate from stupidity and, involving no reason or analysis, made the cruel individual similar to a wild beast.[483] This condition, albeit natural, does not provide any major pleasure, according to Sade.[484]
(2) The other type was said to be the result of the sensitivity of the organs and to be reachable only by extremely delicate beings who must then cultivate it as a veritable art form.[485] They are Sade's notorious libertines who make calculated use of cruelty in order to awaken it, keep it going, and feed it.[486]

Like Hutcheson and Beccaria, Sade was stimulated by the spirit of the Enlightenment, and he sought to demystify human existence by exorcising from it the cruel domination of established religion, revered monarchs, and hypocritical ideals of 'civilisation'. As Sade wrote: "Lycurgus, Numa, Moses, Jesus Christ, Mohammed" are "rogues", who have been operating as "despots over our ideas" for aeons, and against whom the truly free spirits of his age had finally begun to rebel.[487]

Sade's conclusion was, however, an uncommon open advocacy of boundless hedonistic egoism and tough mutual competition such that the mighty could legitimately exploit the weak, and the weak legitimately revolt against the mighty, i.e., as much as they wished and could, as Nature had intended for them to do from the very start.[488] This amoral Nature had to be left free, according to Sade, however chaotically and cruelly so, in order to avoid its degeneration and, with it, the eventual loss of our species' vital instincts and survival skills, all of which are grounded

---

483 See Sade (2010), 75.
484 See Sade (2010), 75.
485 See Sade (2010), 75.
486 See Sade (2010), 75.
487 Sade (2010), 120.
488 See Sade (1999), part I, chap. 19. Unrecognised, his views echo today in evolutionary psychology. Yet this tense relationship between the State and the individual can also be found depicted by Schopenhauer (1903, 146, 157 and 208; emphases added), who compared the former's awesome "power" to a tight "leash that restrains the limitless egoism of nearly every one, the malice of many, the *cruelty* of not a few"; the third vice being defined as *"nothing but malicious joy put into practice"*, i.e., sadism, or *"the exact opposite of Compassion"*. The same characterisation of "cruelty" proper can be found in Schopenhauer (1957), first essay. Albeit brief and sketchy in comparison with, say, Seneca's or Montaigne's reflections on "cruelty" proper, it is in these essays that we can find Schopenhauer's more in-depth thoughts on *Grausamkeit* as such (if the translator is to be trusted, of course).

in the savage beast that we, allegedly 'superior' human beings, can still so promptly turn into, given the right circumstances, e.g., wars and revolutions.[489]

Sade's depiction of human life as struggle, oppression, rebellion, theft, and counter-theft sounds uncannily akin to that of some rarely sung protagonists of the early 18th century, i.e., the privateers and buccaneers of the New World. Let us cite here one of their few known speeches, which was delivered by a notorious pirate, Samuel Bellamy, who so addressed the captain of a captured ship:

> I am sorry they won't let you have your Sloop again, for I scorn to do any one a Mischief, when it is not for my Advantage; damn the Sloop, we must sink her, and she might be of Use to you. Tho', damn ye, you are a sneaking Puppy, and so are all those who will submit to be governed by Laws which rich men have made for their own Security, for the cowardly Whelps have not the Courage otherwise to defend what they get by their Knavery; but damn ye altogether: Damn them for a Pack of crafty Rascals, and you, who serve them, for a Parcel of hen-hearted Numskuls. They vilify us, the Scoundrels do, when there is only this Difference, they rob the Poor under the Cover of Law, forsooth, and we plunder the Rich under the Protection of our own Courage; had you not better make One of us, than sneak after the A—s of those Villains for Employment?[490]

Far from the Caribbean, Sade wanted to be admired in France as a truly mechanistic and naturalistic *philosophe*, arguing for the demise of all things Christian and 'superstitious', especially by demonstrating the logical impossibility of condemning "the wicked person" as being either immoral or unnatural.[491] Piracy, under this respect, would have been a fully justified human endeavour, however fiercely opposed it was at that time by the official governments of the 'civilised' nations that Sade and his more moderate fellow Enlightenment thinkers aimed at changing, at least initially, with their plays, speeches, pamphlets, essays, and books.[492]

According to Sade, the modern natural sciences demonstrated that the universe is nothing but ever-changing matter and energy, utterly indifferent to the suffering of its individual creatures, whose chief goals in life are as basic as they are patent: self-preservation and self-affirmation.[493] As Sade inventively inferred from the works of, say, Newton, Lavoisier, and Buffon, selfish libertinage was simply the logical result of the application of modern scientific rationality to human affairs,

---

489 See Sade (2010), 74.
490 As cited in Arvanitakis, Fredriksson, and Schillings (2017), 269.
491 Airaksinen (1995), 45–51. Needless to say, calling something "superstition" is an act of vituperation.
492 We ignore whether Sade was familiar with the piracy making headlines the early decades of the 18th century.
493 See Airaksinen (1995), 45–51.

the natural substratum of which was then made patent, even if it meant condoning the rape of innocent virgins, torture of servants, dismemberment of kidnapped victims, or incestuous brutalisation of family members.[494] As his novels' proudly anticlerical and vocally unchristian characters keep reminding the reader, we were not created in God's image. We are ferocious, carnal, egotistical beasts.[495]

As obnoxious as Sade's fictional dialogues and indecent as his pornographic shenanigans may appear to the contemporary reader, especially to the polite and politically correct academic, they nonetheless offer conclusions that are not altogether different from those reached in some later, non-pornographic, influential works by other, less randy Western thinkers.[496] Some might take offense at Sade's openly and intentionally extreme libertine position. However, we, the authors of this book, must remind the offended reader that, for one, the Russian-born, 20th-century libertarian icon Ayn Rand herself extolled our allegedly natural selfishness, the gratified rejection of civilised mores, violent sexual misconduct, and even outright homicide.[497] She did so when she explicitly selected and commended the "boastful and self-confident" egomaniac, sociopathic 1920s paedophiliac murderer "[William Edward] Hickman" as the true "model" for a new literary male hero of hers—her declared incarnation of the "Superman", who ignores and supersedes all ethical codes and social conventions by sheer strength of individual will.[498]

---

[494] Sade's cruel and selfish naturalisation of human affairs has been read as a prophecy of the profit-seeking, conflict-prone, individualistic, and socio-Darwinist modernity to come (see, e.g., Shapiro 1993).
[495] We are also animals capable of humour. Not only did Sade write comedies, but also his novels are rife with "black" humour (see, e.g., J. Phillips 2014, 530), if not "perverse humour", as stated by Mazières (2015, title page).
[496] In many of his novels, Dostoyevsky concerned himself with the notion of crime as natural and even rational for a genuine atheist. We should also add that the varieties of ideas about humankind's 'nature' developed by 17th- and 18th-century thinkers such as Sade were built on the flimsiest historical and anthropological evidence, to which they prioritised instead deductive system-building upon few abstract assumptions operating like axioms whence it was possible to reach useful conclusions about the 'right' society to be promoted. Thus, while some thinkers started from 'clear and distinct' premises whereby our species' nature can be said to be inherently "a brutal, cruel one", others preferred instead "to imagine original man to be a timid, frightened creature" (Mini 1974, 32).
[497] Sade's libertines and Rand's supermen may well exemplify that nihilistic type of "atheist" who "says with his voice, 'Change your mind to think there is no God and no evil either'", and "then ... turns a blind eye to the full reality of the hopeless suffering of other humans" (Shook 2022, par. 6).
[498] Rand (1997), 22–27. More on her work follows in Chapter 2.

1.2.6.2 Friedrich Nietzsche

Mentioning the term "Superman" segues perfectly into our next scholar, the 19th-century German philosopher, composer, and classicist Friedrich Nietzsche, who is arguably among the greatest Western thinkers of all times.[499] "Cruelty" proper is central to his philosophy, and he described it as belonging to one of the oldest and deepest substrata of human culture.[500] Modern civilisation was not at all the expression of "the voice of God in man", according to him, but the historical result of the unfulfilled vital "instinct of cruelty" turned back upon itself, i.e., after it could no longer discharge itself freely and fully in the outside world, as it did instead in prehistoric times or in the early stages of civilised existence.[501] (Not much later, Freud would pursue similar manoeuvres in his writings on psychological defence mechanisms.)

In Nietzsche's assessment, almost everything that we, the educated people, believe to be 'higher culture' is based on the spiritualisation and the psychic burrowing of our primordial instinct for cruelty, which must find alternative avenues for release.[502] The wild animal within us has not been killed off, but forced to pursue more indirect paths.[503] Some of our ancestors, as Machiavelli also admitted and exemplified himself, saw and celebrated "cruelty" proper as a "virtue", not a vice.[504] *Au contraire*, in the 'civilised' era of our species, this drive has been hidden from plain view and turned shameful, sick, and sinful.[505] Furthermore, as the persistent human appetite for gruesome entertainment bears witness, cruelty is still among us, within us, and can still be one of the great joys of humankind.[506] This constant craving feeds into another important characteristic of human nature, i.e., the lust

---

[499] It is a *cruel irony* that the famed 20th-century Italian pedagogist Maria Montessori (1971, 21) argued that Nietzsche's "superman" was merely a "glimpse" into the better human being that can arise from a well-reformed system of education focussing on young children's needs *qua* young children, their spontaneous creative individuality, and their innate abilities for self-motivation and self-organisation. Echoing scores of hopeful educational reformers since at least Montaigne's day, "cruelty and violence" would eventually vanish, and, with them, "criminality" too (Montessori 2009, 120–121). Better children make better adults who, in turn, make better societies, such that children are given "means of existence" to flourish on, rather than being cast into that "struggle for existence" which has been so dear to the social Darwinists (Montessori 2009, 117; emphases removed).
[500] Nietzsche (2004), "Genealogy of Morals–A Polemic", 81.
[501] Nietzsche (2004), "Genealogy of Morals – A Polemic", 81.
[502] See Nietzsche (2002), par. 229.
[503] See Nietzsche (2002), par. 229.
[504] Nietzsche (1997), par. 30.
[505] See Nietzsche (2002), par. 229.
[506] See Nietzsche (1997), par. 18.

for power, which, according to Nietzsche, is a fundamental energy pervading all things.[507]

Like Sade before him, Nietzsche drew our attention to the inherently cruel nature of Mother Nature, with her devastating catastrophes and mass extinctions. Nature is indifferent, merciless, and cares not for justice, which is, in their view, a mere human construct.[508] However, as one of her creations, humans are part of this pitiless natural world. There is therefore no good reason to take the lofty morality of humans so seriously. Rather, Nietzsche argued that we should investigate what lies behind our race's moral acts and ethical ideals.[509]

The answer is, according to him, our secret wish to make others suffer, i.e., cruelty. As Nietzsche wrote, in trying to "do our best", we are actually trying "to make the sight of us painful to another and to awaken in him the feeling of envy and of his own impotence and degradation".[510] Even our purported religious humility is yet another method of torturing our fellow human beings, if not even ourselves too, for internalised cruelty can also produce such unhealthy results, in his view.[511]

Nietzsche wanted us to accept human nature for what he understood it to be like, i.e., as ferociously cruel and unashamedly lustful. Its animal roots were openly acknowledged and advocated by him: "Do I counsel you to slay your instincts? I counsel you the innocence in your instincts."[512] In Nietzsche's view, modern 'progressive' political ideologies were nothing but secular forms of suffocating Christianity and, if left unchallenged, they were bound to bring about a universal flattening of all aesthetic values.[513] The solution to humankind's woes was not in

---

[507] See Nietzsche (1997), par. 18. This being a possible interpretation of his mysterious "Will to Power", which Wladimir Russalkow (1894, 11) retrieved already in Schopenhauer's depiction of the human being as "surpassing even the tiger and the hyena in cruelty". While Schopenhauer and Russalkow stressed the inextricable intertwining of cruelty and sexuality, Nietzsche's approach identified the sexual element as something distinct. Cruelty, in his perspective, does not need to be fuelled by lust. We can then understand Hillman's (1999, chap. 1, sec. 6, par. 1) much later psychological point when writing: "Sadistic cruelty may become ever more tyrannical as years eliminate other avenues of pleasure, and ambition does not necessarily moderate in later life."
[508] See Nietzsche (2002), par. 9.
[509] See Nietzsche (1997), par. 30.
[510] Nietzsche (1997), par. 30.
[511] See Nietzsche (1997), par. 30. If correct, humour, which many have seen as characterised by compassionate humility (e.g., Weber, Chesterton, Cipolla), would be a tool to aggrieve other people while feigning amiability.
[512] Nietzsche (1911b), part 1, par. 13.
[513] See Nietzsche (1911a), 7. Preserving the autonomy of the aesthetic realm from the encroachment of ethical, political or religious values was not only a core theme of Nietzsche's philosophy,

additional layers of duplicitous 'civilisation', but in a healthy recovery and rediscovery of our primeval energies, however dangerous this path may turn out to be at a collective level.[514]

If anything, it is difficult for us today to read Nietzsche and not to think of the horrors for which the Nazis were responsible, before and during World War II—however aetiologically unrelated Nietzsche and Nazism may be to a trained eye.[515] Somehow the Nazi's ideological appropriation of parts of his work and their mutual association *via* his sister and her anti-Semite husband make us connect the dots separating Nietzsche and Nazism in time, tones, and themes. It may be exegetically unfair, but it is also historically facile and, to a limited extent, theoretically plausible.[516]

Emblematically, even a charitable and humanising reading of Nietzsche's use of "cruelty" proper, such as the one recently pursued by the Lisbon-based philosopher Luís Aguiar de Sousa, must reinterpret creatively the attendant notion of 'conscience' in order to attain its goals.[517] Somehow, there is enough in Nietzsche's writings to make an honest reader suspect that he may have been close to the likes of Sade or the social Darwinists of his day.[518] Perhaps appropriately for Nietzsche's staunchly atheistic yet biblically aphoristic style of writing, the enduring exegetical conundrums involving his commentators are a patent and ironic case of *mixed blessing*.

---

but is also a sporadic phenomenon these days in Western philosophy, especially with regard to "humour" proper. Tackled in Chapter 2, Harvey's (1999) work can be seen as a representative case of the contemporary mainstream in most academic thought, which is generally keen on policing how we make fun of one another. If we interpret him correctly, Gimbel (2017) is then a rare case of recognition of humour's aesthetic autonomy, at least in abstract principle.

514 Scholars disagree on how much actual violence Nietzsche's paeans for war, conquering heroes and unrelenting self-affirmation involve and justify, but such praise abounds in his writings.

515 E.g., their regular use, especially against resistance movements, of collective punishment, which echoes as a disciplinary method in today's much more moderate contexts of schools and sports teams.

516 On Nietzsche's complex legacy in Germany, Nazism included, see Aschheim (1994). While Nietzsche can be reasonably characterised as an elitist thinker and a social Darwinist, he certainly did not share the later Nazi's penchant for blind nationalism and murderous anti-Semitism. These two horrors were not advocated by him.

517 Aguiar de Sousa (2022).

518 We discussed this issue in finer detail in *H&C1*.

1.2.7 Polanyian Thoughts

> The simple is cruel, it does not unite with the manifold.
> —Carl Gustav Jung[519]

Themes such as the enduring lure of cruelty, the tragedies of World War II, and the questionable achievements of the scientific rationality promoted by the outwardly well-meaning European Enlightenment, lead us to the last 'classic' about whom we reflect here: Michael Polanyi.[520]

Polanyi's analyses of the totalitarian cruelties of the 20th century, Nazism, and Stalinism *in primis*, offer a clear overview of the development of the relevant ideologies, and cast light on the interplay between the Enlightenment's dream of pursuing 'objective' science in all spheres of human action while turning traditional Western humanistic culture and morality, especially Christianity, into an irrational and deeply 'subjective' affair.[521] Although the ideals behind this dream had long fermented in educated circles, the defining set of circumstances for its subsequent and decisive growth was, in this perspective, the French Revolution of 1789.

According to Polanyi, this was a crucial event that "led the world towards a revolutionary consummation inherent in a post-Christian rationalism".[522] True enough, to blame the whole thing on "rationalism" may not be accurate, inasmuch as Polanyi also recognised the decisive influence of Romantic *ir*rationalism, especially in its Byronesque forms and fads.[523] However, the beautiful ideals and the bloody deeds of the French Revolution loom large in the cultural shift at issue, which even deified and worshipped personified Reason as a new pagan goddess.[524]

---

[519] Jung (2009), 355.
[520] We do not imply that Polanyi's sombre reflections about World War II are the only, best, or most relevant of all. Brecht's "humour and cruelty ... in his *Anti-War Book*" could be appropriate too (Marinho Oliveira 2021, 46). However, given how central Polanyi's philosophical work is to our own overall approach, we deem it sensible and useful to keep relying on his insights and arguments. See also *H&C1* for a fuller explanation of Polanyi's pivotal role in our cross-disciplinary research into humour and cruelty.
[521] Polanyi belongs to that anti-Cartesian line of Western philosophy which has long recognised the value but also the limits of 'objective' or 'scientific' reason, the absolutisation of which leaves aside many important 'irrational' dimensions of life and self-understanding, e.g., love, eroticism, play, creativity, sports, drama, poetry, the fine arts, music, comradery, cordiality, religion, existential mystery, etc. Pascal, Vico, Schiller, Kierkegaard, Dostoyevsky, Nietzsche, Veblen, Jung, Bataille and Marcel can all be listed among the members of this anti-Cartesian current.
[522] Polanyi (1969a), 13.
[523] See Polanyi (1969a), 13.
[524] This being a famous incident during the Jacobin's radicalisation of the French revolution under Robespierre.

Polanyi's complex historical-cultural argument can be summarised as stating that the revolutionary project was based on an underlying *critical* assumption, adopted chiefly from *philosophes* such as Voltaire and Jean-Jacques Rousseau, but expanded upon and exploited by later thinkers too, e.g., Marx, Lenin, and Nietzsche.[525] The critical assumption was that the pillars of Western society had *not* been created by a series of benevolent divine interventions, as the masses had been led to believe by self-serving monarchic and ecclesiastic authorities for many centuries.[526] Instead, they had been established by a greedy, ruthless, oppressive, cynical, and selfish elite.

There was literally *nothing* good or sacred in these pillars which, as contingent as they were in actuality, Polanyi believed instead to have contributed to the survival and, on more than one occasion, to the successes of Western civilisation—warts and all (e.g., the so-called "scientific revolution" of Galileo and Newton). But that was not the attitude of the revolutionaries. According to their simplistic yet convincing reconstruction, it had become the responsibility of any rational man to create a totally new and better society and morph themselves into new and better persons too. All of this had to be accomplished without the assistance of the prior ethical criteria of Western culture and the influence of the old Christian paradigms of virtue, i.e., in theory, as each revolutionary saw fit or, in actual practice, as the most persuasive ideologues of the day could make them see fit.[527]

It was generally believed and, psychologically speaking, *felt* that this momentous change had to happen without delay and by any means necessary.[528] The ruling classes would not give up their privileged lives without a fight. The only way forward was bloody revolution. All previous institution had to be demolished,

---

525 We must not forget that behind Polanyi's own line of criticism lie the experiences of Nazism and Stalinism.
526 See especially Polanyi (1969a), 13–18, which applies to the entire paragraph above.
527 Compare the revolutionaries' blank-slate rationalistic approach with, e.g., the ethics of responsibility advocated by the Jewish 'father' of 20th-century bioethics and environmentalism, i.e., Hans Jonas (1984, 130), who argued that there has always existed a "timeless archetype of all responsibility, the parental for the child", such that the "ontological ... chasm between 'is' and 'ought'" is "factual[ly] ... bridged" by "an ontic paradigm in which the plain ... 'is' evidently coincides with an 'ought'", i.e., the new-born's call for parental care. It is certainly a *cruel irony* that Jonas was a student of Martin Heidegger's, i.e., a declared supporter of the murderous Nazi regime, but also the 'father' of the ontological-ontic distinction used by Jonas (1984) in the latter's union of Natural-Law morality and Kantian ethics. *Good ideas can hide in the works of evil masters.* As regards the coincidence of 'is' and 'ought', that is also the deeper normative import of "onto-axiology", as *per* LVOA, or "ontoaxiology", as written by the contemporary Venezuelan IT educationist Nathaly Serrano de Barrios (2020, 170 *et passim*).
528 Again, see especially Polanyi (1969a), 13–18.

no matter the costs. Determination and willingness to sacrifice anyone and everything, in the name of a greater good, became ingrained in the revolutionary doctrine. And as in all revolutions of the modern age, any opposition to the glorious cause had to be dealt with swiftly and without mercy.[529] In other words, in a large-scale exemplification of Hallie's first paradox of cruelty, a perfect playground for cruel agency had been created, aimed at the attainment of humankind's eventual happiness.[530]

Armed with alleged enlightened and enlightening 'reason' alone, hence having no respect for any older moral-metaphysical tradition and/or religious intuition of the heart, the self-anointed prophets of the new age, new humankind, and/or new race combined eventually the worst of both worlds:
(1) the lack of any ultimate ethical foundation that could constrain their agency; and
(2) the unrecognised secular articulation of the murderous mystical frenzies and cruel fanaticisms that had been rightfully derided by scores of Enlightenment thinkers, e.g., the great Voltaire.[531]

As Polanyi pointed out, this logic came first into full and ferocious fruition with hell-bent Jacobins such as Robespierre and Saint-Just, and it continued to operate well into the 20th century *via* the self-perceiving great visionaries and revolutionaries, whether left- or right-wing in the extant political spectrum, e.g., Mussolini, Stalin, Hitler, and Mao.[532]

There also appeared a gradual progression and habituation into more and more violent praxes, "which transforms Messianic violence from a means to an end into an aim in itself".[533] These revolutionary leaders convinced their followers that their life-destructive actions were based purely on rational, objective science (e.g., racial anthropology and Marxist 'science'), and that everything which they did was therefore inevitable and unquestionable, for it was done upon 'objective' bases in the pursuit of a new, better society and a new, better humankind (e.g.,

---

529 See Polanyi (1969a), 13.
530 Paradoxical 'playgrounds' come in all shapes and sizes, including psychological ones. See, e.g., Ofshe and Watters (1994, 223) on the "the cruelty of recovered memory therapy", which is known to have facilitated, in a number of cases, the 'recollection' of past traumas that had not happened in real life, i.e., their outright *fabrication*.
531 See Voltaire (1912) and (1918).
532 Once more, see Polanyi (1969a), 13–18, which applies to the rest of the paragraph above but the cited passage.
533 Polanyi (1969a), 14.

"the new socialist man" boasted by the Russian Bolsheviks and Chinese Communists).

This "everything" signifying also the most gruesome mass reprisals and most callous comprehensive policies that Western civilisation likely had ever witnessed. All of them, ironically, being pursued under the supposed aegis of science's rational value-neutrality and intelligently applied instrumental thinking.[534] The Hungarian-born Polanyi took Stalin's murderous actions as an example:

> [T]here was yet some theoretical support needed. It was supplied by a new scientific sociology claiming to have proved three things: namely (1) that the total destruction of the existing society was the only method for achieving an essential improvement of society; (2) that nothing beyond this act of violence was required, or even to be considered, since it was unscientific to make any plans for the new society; and (3) that no moral restraints must be observed in the revolutionary seizure of power, since (a) this process was historically inevitable, and so beyond human control, and (b) morality, truth, etc., were mere epiphenomena of class-interest which science had proved to be ascendant.[535]

Despite being the diametrical opposites in geo-political terms, both 20th-century fascism and communism espoused utopian ideals, claimed to base their theories on science, and were ready to sacrifice millions in their pursuit of the greater good.[536] The strength of their adherents' conviction and commitment was real, as can be seen in the final days of the Third Reich, when the Nazis and their allies ramped up the annihilation of the Jewish people instead of using them as slave labour in the war effort.[537] And it was the same aggressive passion for moral sac-

---

534 As argued by Litz et al. (2022, par. 1), the mere witnessing of "acts" entailing "cruelty" can be a cause of significant "moral injury", which these researchers endeavoured to quantify. Psychiatrists, psychotherapists, but also lawyers, judges, juries, and insurers may conceivably benefit from such a quantification, if attainable.
535 Polanyi (1969a), 15–16. Müller-Funk (2022, 245; emphasis added) stated pithily: *"Cruelty is the substance of Stalinism* and not an accidental by-product."
536 It may be unfair to speak of "communism" *tout court*. The Soviet experience was long and internally diverse. As Fromm (1961, 22–23) wrote: "It is fortunate that the Russian regime has changed from cruel terrorism to the methods of a conservative police state. It also shows a lack of sincerity in those lovers of freedom who are most vocal in their hatred of the Soviet Union that they seem hardly to be aware of the considerable change that has occurred", as well as of the fact that the "inhuman, cruel, and revolting … terror" characterising "Stalinist" Russia was "no more so than the terror in a number of countries that we call free—no more so, for instance, than was the terror of Trujillo or Batista" (see also Marcuse 1972, 1, on Latin-America's "fascist and military dictatorships" and normalisation of "[t]orture").
537 Many scholars have debated this tragic yet peculiar event, e. g., Arendt (1985).

rifice to a higher goal, whether Romantic, racial or political, that filled the ranks of Hitler's *Schutzstaffel* and Stalin's most effective *apparatchiks*.[538] As Polanyi noted:

> People often speak of Communism or Nazism as a "secular religion". But not all fanaticism is religious. The passions of the total revolutions and total wars which have devastated our age were not religious but moral. Their morality was inverted and became immanent in brute force because a naturalistic view of man forced them into this manifestation. Once they are immanent, moral motives no longer speak in their own voice and are no longer accessible to moral arguments; such is the structure of modern nihilistic fanaticism.[539]

Whether any such inverted morality is still at work today in some quarters, it is a disquieting thought that we leave our readers to ponder upon.[540]

1.2.8 Our Own Relationship with Cruelty

> Jesus was nailed to the cross by a pack of sick, cruel, murderous *homines normales*.
> —Wilhelm Reich[541]

We all, at least in public, tend to frown upon the apparent barbarity of our ancestors and their enjoyment of ferocity and brutality; just recall the cruel shows in the Romans' games at the Colosseum, the Vikings' seasonal raping and pillaging, the Aztecs' ritual human sacrifices, etc.[542] A closer view of history seems, however, to reveal that the main change in the ferocity and brutality of humans has been in form rather than content.

1.2.8.1 Big Stories

It has only been a few decades since the slaughter of human beings of all ages and sexes took place on an industrial scale in almost every corner of the world. True, there was no Colosseum in Auschwitz, and no discernible fun was involved in Stalin's purges or in the continent-wide Operation Condor. Rather, it seems as though the ancient spirit of sadistic entertainment was replaced by callous bureaucratic

---

538 See Polanyi (1969a), 17.
539 Polanyi (1969a), 17–18. We discuss further several revolutionary atrocities in *H&C3*.
540 Armed with massive amounts of socio-economic and medical-environmental data, McMurtry (1999 and 2013a) argued that (neo)liberalism achieved analogous murderous results, buttressed by orthodox economic 'science'. More on this matter is said in *H&C3*.
541 Reich (1976), 549.
542 We write "seasonal" because, as the *Sagas* show, pillaging and raping required good weather and much light.

sombreness and technological efficiency.[543] Still, "cruelty" was patently the name of the game.[544]

Even today, masses of ordinary people will watch horror movies, gruesome documentaries, and grisly TV programmes, including those showing animal predators savaging their preys or horrific serial killers mutilating their victims.[545] All this, apparently, as recreation. Yes, the violence is vicarious and, most of the time, make-believe.[546] Then again, the way it stimulates our nervous system is like the real thing.[547] Thus also real footage of a gory decapitation is sure to go viral on the internet.[548]

At a broader cultural level, mass murderers and cruel warmongers are still revered and studied with no lack of admiration. It is they who, more often than not, established new states, larger kingdoms, or vast empires. These men (and very few women) are the heroes whom Nietzsche and the Nietzscheans could celebrate. Just to name a few: Alexander the Great, Julius Caesar, Tamerlane, Pachacuti, Ivan the Terrible, Toyotomo Hideyoshi, or Shaka Zulu.[549]

The remarkable evolutionary success that humanity has enjoyed thus far is grounded on its ability to work together. Humans are not the strongest, biggest, most poisonous, or fastest animals, but they have a unique capability to communicate. This is what sets them apart from other herds. As a consequence, the concept of 'communication' has, in today's world, an aura of benevolence about it. All problems would supposedly be solved, it is often heard, if only people were to "communicate" more.

Such is the conventional wisdom. Which conveniently forgets that almost all problems are created by means of communication too. Not least those requiring mass mobilisations and complex organisational deeds. The Holocaust and the gu-

---

[543] See, on this aspect of modern cruelty, Fromm (1961), 198–199.
[544] Largely premeditated, Nazi and Stalinist cruelties were closer to Seneca's conception than the Roman games.
[545] See Stannard (2004). These issues are discussed further and deepened in the following two chapters.
[546] Some noticeably sadomasochistic TV shows walked intentionally the grey line separating severe discomfort and mild torture, mixing psychological humiliation and physical excruciation, e.g., Japan's *Za Gaman* (1980–1986) and *Susunu! Denpa Shōnen* (1998–2002), or the long-lived US *Jackass* series (2000–2022), which is openly meant to be seen as humorous or 'fun' (see also Graham 2017 for a broader discussion of so-called "reality TV").
[547] See Stannard (2004).
[548] See Stannard (2004).
[549] Even in today's peaceful liberal societies, *odd champions of excess still command public attention*. The great satirist of *belle-époque* extravaganza and gilded emulation, Thorstein Veblen (1924), would probably still feel very much at home in today's West.

lags witnessed and loathed by Polanyi come to mind once more. When dealing with "cruelty" proper, it is difficult not to think of them.[550]

1.2.8.2 Small Stories

We do not have to think of major massacres alone, however, or of the most nefarious protagonists of our past, e.g., Genghis Khan, King Leopold, Talaat Pasha, Stalin, or Hitler.[551] As the noted US psychologist James Hillman remarked at the close of the last century, it may be enough to look at contemporary Western societies, their prosaic working structures, and several phony 'welfare' solutions:

> By looking closely at Hitler, we may miss the demon closer to home. Faceless corporate boards and political administrators make decisions that wreck communities, ruin families, and despoil nature. The successful psychopath pleases the crowds and wins elections… Public programs are being proposed to test schoolchildren for their "genetic predispositions", to uncover potentials for crime and violence in terms of character traits and personality, "weeding out" those who show such factors as "early irritability and uncooperativeness". These traits indicate not mainly crime, but that genial exceptionality on which a whole society depends for leadership, invention, and culture. Besides, once sorted out, on what compost heap would the weeds be thrown? Or would they merely be "improved" and rendered compliant by drugs to which you may not say no, or kept in privately owned, for-profit penitentiaries exempt from labor laws and minimum-wage scales?[552]

Human social cognition is highly developed and enables us to read deeply into the meaning of speech and gestures. It is, however, fallible and we all have often drawn erroneous conclusions. Not to mention how easily disrupted it is. Bad breath, missing teeth, hyperhidrosis, weak bowels, hot flushes, rheumatisms, toothaches, conspicuous ugliness, or equally conspicuous attractiveness can all

---

550 Such immediate mental associations are obviously a result of our own upbringing and cultural milieu.
551 A contemporary of Polanyi, Oakeshott (2004, 108) argued that "the intellect, and indeed our whole physical nature, can enable us to distinguish between our own inclinations and that inner voice of God speaking in the heart", i.e., our moral conscience. Unfortunately, when the inclinations coincide with the alleged voice of secular and scientific reason itself (e.g., the Nazi's racial anthropology and Stalin's Marxist science), fanaticism can find the new atheistic avenues for cruel expression studied by Polanyi. Then, perhaps, our "physical nature" may be a better aid, e.g., the heart's natural sweetness praised by Aquinas and Montaigne (see Chapter 1 and *H&C1*). However, as signalled by cases such as the Marquis de Sade and Ayn Rand, not all human beings come equipped with the same degree of such a sweetness, if they have any at all to start with. *Hic sunt dracones*, really.
552 Hillman (1996), chap. 10, secs. 1 and 6, 214–247. On the last point, see also the Norwegian criminologist Nils Christie (2017, title page) tackling "crime control as industry", i.e., "gulags, Western style". More on penal cruelties is said in *H&C3*.

quickly and easily destroy the required mental concentration. And the same goes for annoying accents, poor grammar, non-idiomatic terminology, odd phrases, unusual sentence construction, and Oxford commas.[553]

Our intelligence also provides us with the ability to reflect on our own feelings, actions and thought, although, again, this mechanism is also liable to error. When it comes to self-reflection, it is perhaps our self-serving nature that is the cause of most blunders. Yet again, being self-serving is a key to survival as well. It is often so for the individual.

When it comes to the survival of the species, instead, we all have within us many other inherited mechanisms. Among them there is the capacity to put yourself into someone else's shoes, i.e., to sympathise with their plight or "realise", as Lecky would say.[554] These are not just 'nice-to-have' qualities, but important survival skills. In essence, they can prove decisive for the species' own prolonged existence.[555]

At the same time, humans have a palpable cruel side too.[556] Cruelty is, moreover, found in cognate species as well. It is our ability to practice it at industrial levels that makes us unique.[557] It would be tempting to link this cruel side to our self-serving individualistic nature. In fact, some of the most atrocious behaviours shown by human groups have been pursued with rather selfless motives in mind, or in view of the greater good. Even Hitler, Stalin, and Pinochet may

---

[553] We hope the reader to have grasped the joke, which targets a cruelly mistreated aspect of written language.

[554] See Cerniglia *et al.* (2019).

[555] In the end, a species endures if and only if enough of its individual members survive and reproduce.

[556] The American anthropologist Melvin Konner (2022, abstract *et passim*) argued that "cruelty" proper has been an integral component of humankind's successful evolutionary history (i.e., our species has not died out yet), especially among its sexually exploitative dominant males—no matter where in the world we go looking. At the same time, the example of contraceptive practices, which are acknowledged in the same article, suggests that human ingenuity can 'play around' our powerful genetically-inherited libidinal urges and, in the process, make them less controversial (e.g., vast harems of captive concubines are no longer the norm in any country). In *H&C3*, we discuss how "humour" proper, alongside several other socio-culturally cultivated channels, has been used to 'purge' *libido* and aggressiveness in ways reducing actual bloodshed and carnage, i.e., conspicuous cruelty.

[557] "[I]ndustrialized cruelty" is mentioned in Gilyazova *et al.* (2020, 20) with regard to the Holocaust, which, intriguingly enough, produced quite a lot of humour, not only in its aftermath (see, e.g., Slucki, Finder, and Patt 2020), but also while taking place (see, e.g., Grzybowski 2020, parts 2 and 3). More on humour and genocide is said in *H&C3*.

have thought of being the agents of positive change in the world that they inhabited, no matter the painful means that they elected to employ.[558]

1.2.8.3 Common Stories

For most people, the thought of cruelty being such an obvious part of our psyche is probably an uneasy one. Seeing it as something innate is likely to be beyond the pale for many, for that would mean that 'innocent' children too could have a streak of cruelty.[559] Thomas Hobbes himself, with his exceptionally sinister view of the human condition, found it difficult to imagine that any person could take pleasure in the suffering of others without any ulterior motive. Many of us would agree with him, seeing cruelty as a 'sick' or 'mad' deviation from human nature, rather than part of its natural, healthy make-up.[560]

Cruelty is not an either-or phenomenon, however. People are not either cruel or kind. Most of us possess both qualities and have been so all our lives.[561] There are, of course, endless examples of horrendous cruelties from the world's many theatres of war. Yet most cruelties take place, far less murderously, in the mundanity of our daily lives, e.g., gossiping, mocking, ostracising, embarrassing, pranking, bullying, ignoring or minimising negative consequences, failing to do the right thing, betraying trust, being selfish, etc.[562]

We have all been cruel towards those we claim to care most about, i.e., our families. We are not only cruel towards our siblings and peers in our youth, but also in our relationships to spouses, even our own children. The violence and the harm may be generally and/or seemingly negligible, but the sting of cruelty is nonetheless real. Moreover, it is easily revealed under such prosaic circumstances, i.e., whenever we are on the receiving side of this ilk of social 'games'.[563]

When we are on the 'giving' side, instead, cruelty is almost invariably a very effective way of controlling other people's emotions and asserting our dominance over them, albeit we would rarely call such lines of conduct "cruel". Rather, we

---

558 Since we cannot peruse either soul, we are left with sheer speculation about their inner motives.
559 In Western culture, the doctrine of the Original Sin has long implied as much, as also mentioned in *H&C1*.
560 See Mayes (2009), 22.
561 See, e.g., C. Miller (2018).
562 Some such cases are discussed in Chapters 2 and 3, for they fall under the umbrella of ordinary humour.
563 As seen, this condition was already identified in ordinary humour by Hazlitt and Schopenhauer: we may easily laugh at others for certain shortcomings, but we do not laugh as easily at ourselves for the same ones.

would produce some convenient self-exculpatory strategy. Under such a cover, few of us could resist the temptation of being cruel. As Rorty himself admitted, our private plans for self-realisation may be dependent upon minor yet repeated cruel actions in interpersonal relationships, e. g., breaking up with blameless, well-meaning, virtuous, and loving partners, whom we no longer find sufficiently attractive and/or inspiring, whether physically, spiritually, or both.[564]

1.2.9 "Cruelty", Really?

If the reader agrees that we are all capable of cruelty—and that we all, or nearly all, have exhibited it in our lives—the next question must be whether the nature or brain processes of a child who picks on his/her schoolmates and, say, a sadistic killer, are different. Can it really be the same psychological feature that underlies both persons, just more amplified and out of control in the latter case? Is it all "cruelty" proper?

As seen, no single, clear, agreed-upon definition of the term "cruelty" exists.[565] Still, there are a few assertions that we can readily make here too, based primarily on the extant literature surveyed succinctly in this volume's first chapter, which we integrate further hereby. The result being, however, a reiteration of the term's vast polysemy, which we have met again and again.[566]

(1) As stated by 20th-century philosophers such as Shklar and Hallie, cruelty can cause physical, psychological and/or material harm to another person.
(1a) In the most severe cases, it can lead to severe deprivation and/or death.[567]

---

564 The example is ours.
565 This issue was highlighted in lengthy detail in *H&C1*.
566 The polysemy, if not the occasional vagueness, of the titular concepts is discussed further in Chapters 2 and 3, but tackled most extensively in *H&C1*. In parallel, Hillman (1962, title page *et passim*) offered a comprehensive account of the therapeutically valuable lexical ambiguity of "emotion", which he argued to be *all* the different things that philosophers, theologians, *literati*, and psychologists have been studying for centuries, i.e., the many legitimate aspects of an inexhaustible phenomenon—as also Polanyi (1962c) would concede with regard to the polysemic, useful, 'thick' concepts of our ordinary languages (see Ryle 1971 and Geertz 1973 on distinguishing between 'thick' and 'thin'; the former author being rather keen on the humorous aspects of the human experience).
567 All these scholars assumed dejection, deprivation and death to be obviously bad. They were neither inveterate pessimists preferring non-being to being, nor mystics, theologians, or philosophers adhering to the "remedial approach", as the contemporary Nigerian philosopher Ikechuwuku Anthony Kanu defined it—according to which "God allows suffering and evil to test our moral and spiritual strength and stamina, and to purify us as we go through life. So, suffering and evil are a kind of moral and spiritual medicines for us humans" (Kanu 2017, 68).

(1b) In others, to injury, physical and/or mental pain, or serious injustice.
(1c) In most instances, the effects are both physical and mental, and they also tend to have far-reaching consequences, which can then self-perpetuate across generations.[568]
(2) Cruelty must involve some volitional act on the part of the perpetrator.
(2a) However, intentionality is a complicated creature, insofar as the real motives of any living individual are often unconscious.[569]
(2b) In addition, it usually seems that most people have few problems in justifying their cruel actions.
(2c) Regret is regrettably not as common as we may wish to assume. The sky is the limit when it comes to convenient self-justifications.[570]
(3) Cognate concepts, e.g., 'violence' and 'evil', are not easily distinguishable from 'cruelty'.
(3a) Any and every cruel act would appear to involve physical and/or mental violence of some kind, even when an impersonal or super-personal agency is being deemed cruel (e.g., Destiny or Mother Nature), or when the suffered harm is best described in medical terms as a pathology, a genetic error, or a birth defect.
(3b) Are not our intentions in cruel acts obviously evil in their nature? In his 1999 nominal research on "evil" proper, the Hungarian-born psychologist Ervin Staub grappled with the definition of the term and how it differs from "violence", while also offering a plethora of insights that can be easily transposed into the semantic field of "cruelty" itself.[571]
(3bi) Using genocide as an example, Staub pointed to the intricate planning and decision-making processes that must be involved in determining to destroy a whole population or subset thereof. Although the progression from a single individual voicing one's antipathy towards a given group to a community engaging in a systematic extermination of a minority is violently explicit, Staub noted that the real motivation is often implicit and unconscious, and that the collective dimensions of the murderous act add extra layers of aetiological complexity.[572]
(3bii) There is also an issue of scale. Staub originally referred to the term "evil" solely in cases of genocide and mass killings. Later, he extended it to include

---

[568] See Staub (1999), 180.
[569] See, e.g., Kiernan (2007).
[570] See, e.g., Kiernan (2007).
[571] See Staub (1999).
[572] See Staub (1999). See also Kiernan (2007), 179.

harm in all forms of intentional agency capable of causing pain, suffering, death, or loss of human potential, in a patent echo of Hallie's earlier definitions of "cruelty" proper.[573]

(3biii) Another element defining 'evil' as a concept became, in Staub's later works, the willingness of individuals to engage in extremely harmful behaviour without any provocation or instigation, i.e., in sadistic, aka "self-gratifying", cruelty (our reference to Hallie, again).[574] That Staub saw as being different from the commonly termed "violence" which most people can show when they happen to be under attack or burdened with severe frustration of basic needs.[575] This realisation, in his theory at least, can then be used to differentiate between the words "violence" and "cruelty".[576]

(3biv) The fourth element at play is the persistence of greatly harmful behaviour, which can evolve in some individuals, groups, and/or societies, and persist through time.[577] This being a reiteration of Hallie's original and coherent linguistic use of "institutionalized" or "institutional cruelty".[578]

(4) Taking together all these connotations, Staub's definition of "evil" follows as "persistent, unprovoked, and intensely harmful behaviours".[579] So, how does "cruelty" proper fit into this? Is there a qualitative or merely a quantitative difference between the ideas of 'evil', 'violence', and 'cruelty'?

(4a) Grabbing the bull by the horns, the South-African neuropsychologist Victor Nell defined "cruelty" as *"the deliberate infliction of physical or psychological pain on other living creatures, sometimes indifferently, but often with delight"*.[580]

(4b) For the moment, given its semantic convergence with the definitions offered some years before him by Anglophone scholars such as Shklar, Hallie, and Regan—whose work Nell does not appear to be aware of—his definition will have to do, even if it could be taken to be a definition of "violence" instead.[581]

---

573 See Staub (1999). See also Kiernan (2007), 179.
574 See Staub (1999). See also Kiernan (2007), 179.
575 See Staub (1999). See also Kiernan (2007), 179.
576 See Staub (1999). See also Kiernan (2007), 179.
577 See Staub (1999). See also Kiernan (2007), 179.
578 We discussed in detail in *H&C1* how the concept of 'institutional cruelty' has been rediscovered by later thinkers.
579 As cited in Kiernan (2007), 180.
580 Nell (2006), 211, emphasis added.
581 See Nell (2006).

(4c) In our century, for instance, the World Health Organization put forth a definition of "violence" as "the intentional use of physical force or power, threatened or actual, against oneself, another person, or against a group or community, which either results in or has a high likelihood of resulting in injury, death, psychological harm, maldevelopment, or deprivation".[582]

(5) Also in our century, the New Zealand-based suicidologist Keren Skegg argued for a simpler definition of "violence", which is seen as a harsh reaction to provocation, i.e., counteractions to verbal threat or physical danger with the goal of eliminating it.[583] As Hallie would dub it, it is a case of "responsive cruelty", which implies a "provocative cruelty" as its cause, if not even as its justification.[584]

(5a) The threat or danger at issue, incidentally, can be real or imaginary, and it can be directed towards physical risk or just expose a psychological vulnerability of the agent.[585]

(5ai) Thus, the violent reaction to others can appear as completely over-the-top, irrational, insane, and/or involve actions directed at someone much weaker than the threatened individual.[586]

(5aii) When the violence is directed towards the self, instead, it is usually intended to get rid of excruciating emotional pain, either temporarily or once and for all.[587]

(5b) In the case of cruelty, the behaviour may not be much different, from an external point of view, but the psychological motivations are no longer the same, according to Skegg.[588] When we act cruelly, the physical or psychological pain that we are about to inflict is no longer a means to an end, but rather an end in itself.

(5c) In violence, then, we seek to dominate the situation and our own experiences, whereas in cruelty we seek to dominate the inner workings of another person.[589] Therefore, even though we can be violent to ourselves, and engage in self-harm or even self-destruction, we cannot be cruel to ourselves

---

582 World Health Organization (2014), 2.
583 Skegg (2005), 1480.
584 As noted, Hallie (1969) advised moderation in the application of responsive cruelty, which can easily escalate.
585 See Skegg (2005), 1480.
586 See Skegg (2005), 1480.
587 See Skegg (2005), 1480.
588 See Skegg (2005), 1480.
589 See Skegg (2005), 1480.

under this perspective, which is clearly incognizant of Hallie's extensive research and, to some extent, detached from much common sense.[590]

(5d) In the case of "evil" proper, Staub argues that two main motivations exist.[591]

(5di) One is simply to harm others.

(5dii) The latter is the misconception whereby performing such actions is seen as serving higher ideals or entailing benefits. "Violence" can, in this view, evolve further, and individuals or groups thereof can move up (or down) along an ideal axis of malice and engage in better (or worse) acts, the worst among which can be dubbed "cruel".

(5e) Staub notes also that it is important to observe that, while in theory we may all be capable of cruel acts, the best predictor of future practice is past practice.[592] A person or a group that has already shown cruelty is more likely to repeat it than those who have not yet engaged in such life-disabling behaviours.[593]

What causes us two to choose "cruelty" proper over other cognate terms that are so frequently used in the extant literature, e.g., "violence", "evil" or "sadism"?

(1) In our view, "violence" is, primarily, too physical in its main connotations and fails to describe crucial psychological aspects of the horrible yet mundane phenomena that we are discussing in this book, e.g., a person's delight in causing another's sorrows.[594]

(2) "Evil" is, in today's linguistic usage, an abstract ethical and theological idea, while "sadism", for its part, has become too clinical.[595] Describing someone as

---

590 See Skegg (2005), 1480.
591 Staub (1999), 180–181, which applies to point 5d in its entirety.
592 See Staub (1999), 181.
593 See Staub (1999), 181.
594 We write "in our view", *as it applies at the time of writing.* One of academic publishing's many ironies is that the author's views may actually change between the time of writing and that of publication, circulation, scholarly reception, and/or public debate. *Books and articles are syntheses and conclusions as much as they are experiments and forays.* This is also the reason why *we relied mostly on the works of dead authorities rather than living ones.* Unlike the living ones, dead authors are hardly likely to change their views—or to let us know about it. And should we ever to be accused of changing our own mind on the basis of new evidence, better arguments or deeper insight, we can reply in the same way as Bertrand Russell (1965, i) did long ago: "I have been accused of a habit of changing my opinions in philosophy. I am not myself in any degree ashamed of having changed my opinions... I claim only, at best, that the opinion expressed was a sensible one to hold at the time when it was expressed."
595 We are not implying that technical abstractions are worthless or misdirected. Quite the opposite, as amply shown by mathematics in engineering, they do have their rightful and useful place in the realm of human agency.

"evil" or "sadistic", moreover, is different than describing them as "cruel". The statement "we all have a cruel side" is probably more reasonable to most people than if we were to use words like "violent", "sadistic" or, to a lesser extent, "evil".[596]

(3) Similarly, we may deem particular behaviours to be "evil" or "sadistic", but that would carry with it inevitable references to the personality of the subject. Not so with "cruelty", insofar as we can expect a person to behave in a cruel fashion now and then, without it being a dominant characteristic of their personality—although it can be, and markedly so.

(4) Above all, as Hallie noted, the term "cruelty" possesses an "empirical" quality, which makes concrete suffering and personal responsibility much more easily associated with it than its cognates. That is also why, in the end, we too adopt his ethical stance, conceptual approach, and lexical choice.[597]

1.2.10 Victor Nell

Apart from providing yet another plausible definition of "cruelty" proper, Nell argued that the reinforcement value of inflicting pain and causing carnage derives from *predatory* adaptations of our species, beginning in the Middle Cambrian period, i.e., around 500 million years ago.[598] Perhaps Sade and Nietzsche were not really off the mark when they recalled the animal roots of human drives and behaviours.[599]

Specifically, Nell put forth five hypotheses as to the nature and function of "cruelty" proper that can be summarised as follows:[600]
(1) Cruelty is a behavioural derivative of predation.
(2) Cruelty is driven by reinforcers that spring from this adaptation.
(3) Because cruelty presupposes the intention to inflict pain and is therefore exclusively a hominid behaviour, it dates to no earlier than *homo erectus*, about 1.5 million years ago.

---

[596] No empirical research seems to have been conducted on this point. Therefore, we generalise from experience.
[597] Whilst Hallie is our key inspiration regarding "cruelty" proper, Amir plays a similar role with regard to "humour".
[598] See Nell (2006), which we discussed in extensive detail in *H&C1*.
[599] Naturally, we can easily reply that "civilisation" means precisely the taming, however limited, of our 'inner beast'.
[600] The five notions in the list effectively summarise the entirety of Nell (2006).

(4) Cruelty has fitness benefits in solving problems of survival and reproduction in forager, pastoral, and urban societies.
(5) The enjoyment of cruelty is a culturally elaborated manifestation of the predatory adaptation.

1.2.11 Cruelty as a Matter of Personal Wellbeing

Cruelty can also be approached from another end, i.e., as a glaring *lack of empathy*, which is "the ability to understand and share in another's emotional state of context".[601] This definition highlights the dual nature of 'empathy', which relies both on cognitive processes and affective capacity. The former refers to the ability to understand another person's emotional state, whereas the latter refers to the capacity to share this emotional state.[602]

The terms "empathy" and "sympathy" were, in the beginning, used synonymously, but in recent decades many scholars found it important to distinguish between them.[603] Sympathy has come to be thought of as the affective component of empathy.[604] When we, as socially well-adapted people, encounter a distressed person, our empathetic response is approximately like the one exhibited by the distressed person, i.e., we put ourselves into their shoes. Our sympathetic response, on the other hand, reflects more our feelings of concern that emerge from considering consciously a person's plight. In daily practice, however, the two often go hand-in-hand.[605]

It is generally assumed that empathy promotes prosocial and/or altruistic behaviour.[606] Furthermore, it is believed that empathy inhibits antisocial or aggressive behaviour, insofar as those sorts of behaviours are externalised when individuals fail to appreciate the feelings of others.[607] Measuring empathy is a complicated matter. As most social sciences today rely on self-reported questionnaires, the

---

[601] Cohen and Strayer (1996), 988.
[602] See Blake and Gannon (2008), 45. Again, we do not yet need finer lexical distinctions between "affect" and "emotion".
[603] In *H&C1* we tackled older cognate notions of 'empathy' (e.g., 'natural sweetness') in the works of Seneca, Aquinas, and Montaigne.
[604] See, e.g., Marshall *et al.* (1995), 100–101, which applies to the rest of the paragraph above.
[605] The great 20th-century German thinker Max Scheler (1915, 110 note 1) further complexified the understanding of "compassion" or "sympathy" by excavating more basic tendencies to hatred and love that are prior to and distinct from them both, noticing as well how even our "lust for cruelty" may itself imply some sympathy.
[606] See, e.g., Miller and Eisenberg (1988), 324.
[607] See, e.g., Miller and Eisenberg (1988), 324.

field is riddled with problems of validity and reliability. However, some studies have convincingly shown that sex offenders, for example, have empathy deficits and/or exhibit lower levels of empathy than others.[608]

1.2.11.1 George Ainslie

Cruelty, in lived experience, seems obviously related to a lack of empathy. Seneca's speaking of "harshness" and Montaigne's immediate feelings of disgust and concern in his characteristically aristocratic hunting forays point glaringly in such a direction.[609] But what if we take a mischievous U-turn and suggest that this cruel lack of empathy and/or sympathy might sometimes be necessary, if not desirable and, ultimately, even good? This is what the contemporary American psychiatrist, psychologist, and behavioural economist George Ainslie has dared and done.[610]

In recent years, Ainslie developed an interesting way of framing cruelty as a self-control device against sympathy (also kown as empathy).[611] In his reasoned assessment, it is a form of *self-protection*. Since sympathy as a mental response gets quickly rewarded by emotion, it is inherently difficult to bring under voluntary control. Sympathy might be a universally beneficial and admired trait of character, but there are obvious and serious pitfalls associated with it, insofar as it can be exploited to our detriment. There are people in this world who would have no qualms in abusing our sympathies, and it is therefore a vital question how to deal with them. In short, Ainslie argued that when other options are unavailable, "cruelty" proper might be the most convenient method of resisting such persons.[612]

1.2.11.2 C.G. Jung

The idea that a dose of real unpleasantness, however disguised or misapprehended by the individual and/or his/her community, is necessary to be a fully functioning human being is not new. In the realm of popular fiction, even Captain J.T. Kirk

---

608 See, e.g., Brown *et al.* (2012), 412. We discussed such studies in detail in *H&C1*.
609 The US law professor W.I. Miller (1997, 24) regarded ideas such as 'cruelty', 'indignation' and 'disgust' as belonging to the same ethically significant conceptual network, i.e., "neighbors" in a rather dismal neck of the woods.
610 See Ainslie (2006).
611 See Ainslie (2006), 225, which applies to the entire paragraph above.
612 Ainslie did not consider another troubling aspect of empathy, i.e., its pivotal role in bringing about "collective possession", mass hysteria, village mentality, and other forms of life-disabling "psychic contagion" (Contrera and Torres 2017, 11). We discuss some phenomena of this ilk in Chapter 4 and in *H&C3*.

knew that our 'dark' side, not least our deepest and most "secret pain", is an essential component of our self, which could not work well, or at all, without it.[613]

Most prominently and much more seriously, this dreary wisdom was defended in the 20th century by Jung in the stately and sombre realm of clinical work, where he coined the technical notion called "the shadow".[614] As he wrote: "The shadow is a tight passage, a narrow door, whose painful constriction no one is spared who goes down to the deep well. But one must learn to know oneself in order to know who one is."[615] A fundamental component of our psychic make-up, this "shadow" stands between our conscious self and the unconscious, which is both personal and collective, according to Jung.[616]

In this interstitial umbra of our psyche, suppressed and half-forgotten, the *ego* is said to deposit its shames, terrors, embarrassments, traumas, horrors, humiliations, wrongs, despicable attitudes, shameful actions, perceived sexual filth, seething resentment, unforgiven emotional slights, wanton capriciousness, and all that cumbersome emotional 'garbage' that, if not brought to consciousness and expressed in some way, will then act upon us through unconscious mechanisms of release, e.g., continual forgetfulness, obsessions, nightmares, compulsions, slips of the tongue, paranoia, clinical neuroses, schizophrenia, and other full-blown psychoses.[617]

If you don't do anything about your shadow, then—as the old saw has long been warning us all—the devil will.[618] In order for a person to be mentally healthy,

---

613 We are referring to a monologue by the iconic sci-fi character in the 1989 movie *Star Trek: The Final Frontier*.
614 By discussing Jung's work both here and, above all, in H&C3, we implicitly agree with the noted Australian writer and literary scholar David Tacey (2011, 14), who argued "that we cannot bracket out Jungian studies from the university curricula on the grounds that the clinicians have exclusive ownership of this knowledge". While we do not forget Jung's insistence on not reducing his therapy-aimed theoretical constructs to an aloof conceptual or metaphysical system, we nevertheless regard his constructs to be useful to approach psychological phenomena.
615 Jung (1960–1990), vol. 9.1, 21, par. 45.
616 The collective side of the unconscious being probably Jung's most famous departure from Freud's conception. It is also one of the most controversial. Yet, it continues to inspire insights, reflections, and speculations in many learned areas across the world's humanities. For one, the contemporary American poet and writer Richard Hague (2019–2020, 29–31) discussed his lived instances of "racial memory", i.e., past "experiences" that may be stored "somewhere in [our] DNA, or in the collective unconscious" and that resurface in an individual's psyche as dreams, visions, "déjà vu" and other "odd psychological phenomen[a]".
617 See Jung (1960–1990), vol. 9.1, 21, pars. 44–45.
618 We do not mean that Satan itself intervenes, though we cannot exclude it *a priori*. Rather, we mean that a neurotic complex or subsidiary personality takes over and causes a person to utter

she must consciously let her shadow's contents find at least *some* concrete paths for outward expression.[619] As Jung wrote: "The shadow is a living part of the personality and therefore wants to live with it in some form. It cannot be argued out of existence or rationalized into harmlessness."[620]

1.2.11.3 F.M. Dostoyevsky

Psychodynamics aside, many thinkers have speculated along these lines, long before Jung's analytical psychology and Ainslie's behavioural economics had come into existence.[621] Sade and Nietzsche took this idea to its conceivable maximum. More moderately, and inspired by the age-old legacy of Orthodox Christianity, the 19th-century Russian literary giant Fyodor Mikhailovich Dostoyevsky pursued a similar line of assessment.[622]

Arguably, no other writer has ever delved more surgically into the human psyche and explored the nature of evil more intricately and deeply than he did. Dostoyevsky has thus been called the "cruel talent", the "apostle of the religion of human suffering", an "epileptic monster whose genius has led us astray", the "imp of the perverse", and much else.[623] In particular, in one of his most famous novels, *The Idiot*, Dostoyevsky addressed the inner conflict of the main character, the Christ-like epileptic Prince Myshkin, whose personal struggle can be read, psy-

---

something she did not intend to utter, eat some food she had promised herself not to eat, sleep with someone whom she claimed to dislike, etc.
619 We saw in *H&C1* how Anita Phillips (1998, 50–51) argued that ritualised erotic "[m]asochism is part of the feminist shadow", which, in Jungian terms, "contain[s] within it the images and longings that feminism has discarded but that remain strongly and necessarily present in women's lives", e.g., "menstruat[ing], giv[ing]birth to babies, breastfeed[ing]", i.e., the "other side of life" that "feminism", by "promot[ing] female assertion and achievement ... unavoidably denies... [O]nce one's chosen attitudes [are] in place, there [is] a kind of coalescence of all the rejected elements, a shadow personality that act[s] in a compensatory way to the conscious side."
620 Jung (1960–1990), vol. 9.1, 20, par. 44.
621 So-called "psychodynamics" is largely based on Jung's "analytical psychology", aka "archetypal psychology".
622 Throughout our trilogy, the sources cited have been mostly works of philosophers and social scientists. An even more comprehensive inclusion of the usage of the titular "cruelty" and "humour" in all of the arts would have been a worthwhile exercise. But this would have produced at least three more volumes, and, most importantly, surpassed our sadly limited expertise. Imprecision and imperfection, then, would have cruelly grown further.
623 Šajkovic (1962), 142.

chologically, as a tug-of-war between the *super-ego* and the *ego* that is gone askew.[624]

Myshkin suffers from the most adorable of weaknesses: an overabundance of goodness. His underdeveloped *ego* causes him to have a flimsy sense of reality, which not only prevents him from achieving truly good results but, in the end, causes defeats and destruction for himself and those around him. As Dostoyevsky seemed to know, an unconstrained *super-ego* can be just as damaging as the *id*, which should never be repressed *in toto*. As *per* the title of the novel, Myshkin is said to be an "idiot". He may be morally superior, spiritually wise, and philosophically inquisitive. Yet his lack of insight into the evil that may still reside in himself and, above all, into that which agitates those who live around him, is idiocy indeed.

This realisation is likely to leave the reader disturbed:

> We balk at perceiving Myshkin's "idiocy" because his intellectual weaknesses are weaknesses we admire. We are aware of our own malice and envy, our tendency to do less than justice to the qualities if almost all other human beings – all, indeed, but a handful whose accomplishments in some curious way feed our own narcissism. How then can we despise a man who suffers from an excess of generosity, who "sees the good" in everyone and everything? Or, hating ourselves for our concessions to expediency, how can we despise a man who is invariably honest and candid? We face the same difficulty in taking a critical view of Myshkin's actions. We know our own timidity and cowardice. How can we despise a man who acts spontaneously and, though frail, even rashly, manifesting no fear? We know how incapable we are of accepting the words of Jesus about the lilies in the field; an anxious, wizened old man possesses our soul and keeps even our charities within bounds.[625]

Dostoevsky wanted us to see Myshkin's goodness as the driver of the tragedy that unfolds in the novel.[626] With one eye on reality, the reader knows that unbridled goodness and generosity are naïve, may even be considered immoral and, yes, cruel. A mistaken picture of humankind can only produce errors and tragedy. Jung's own admonishments about acknowledging and accepting our 'dark' side were certainly a warning about such a risk.

---

624 See Lesser (1958), which applies to the whole paragraph above. We consider his interpretation insightful and relevant, although we doubt that Dostoyevsky would have agreed with him, citing instead the theological and religious implications of Myshkin's 'idiocy', i.e., the sinful *quid* of human nature and the need for God's grace. Still, Dostoyevsky himself provided a much more complex Christ-time character in *The Brother Karamazov*, i.e., the young monk Alyosha, who is instructed by his mentor to leave the safety of the monastery and live in the world, thus getting to know sin, not least the one hiding within his own soul, hence learning true self-/forgiveness.
625 Lesser (1958), 212.
626 See Lesser (1958), 212, which applies to the whole paragraph above.

Besides, it is idiotic to accept lovingly and unconditionally everyone and everything. The appropriate response to something cruel is, perhaps, more cruelty. We all need to keep our distance from people who might harm us physically, emotionally, and/or socially. This is, at least, what Ainslie's reflections on the subject would advise.

1.2.12 Cruel Humour as a Matter of Paradoxical Wellbeing

From a psychological perspective, our 'shadow' needs to breathe too, so to say.[627] Our instinctual impulses, if uncontrolled, can certainly lead us astray, but they are also the driving forces behind most of our life-affirming actions. Complete restraint of basic emotions such as hunger, anger, and *libido* might turn occasional individuals into exceptional sages and saints, but will also cause many more people to become troublingly unbalanced. Revealingly, in *The Idiot*, Prince Myshkin is masochistically drawn to the sadistic Rogozhin, and *vice versa*.[628]

The Christ-like paragon of virtue, in other words, would appear to require a demonic counterpart for its own wellbeing, and so would the latter appear to require the former. This is certainly a twisted cruel irony.[629] It is also the first of several more such ironies, which we briefly outline below, as an appropriate conclusion to the present section and an intimation of themes that are developed to a fuller extent in Chapters 2 and 4.[630]

(1) Cruelty in general, and cruel humour in particular, may be pathways that, albeit frequently inordinate or immoral, possess a deeper *raison d'être* in the general equilibrium of our psychic life and of its interaction with the 'outer' world, in which we all find ourselves living, laughing, crying, and hurting.[631] Undisciplined and unpleasant, cruel humour may be, in other words, a better alternative to other

---

[627] We borrow this expression from a statement made by a Jungian psychologist, G.R. Buccola, during an informal conversation. A more thorough assessment of this theme is offered in *H&C3*, where we argue that humour may be needed, even if it is cruel, if not especially because of its cruel ingredient.
[628] See Lesser (1958), 213–214.
[629] It is also a theme of Jung's analytical psychology and ancient Gnosticism, but we cannot address it here.
[630] One of these themes plays also a major role in *H&C3*.
[631] Further considerations on cruel humour's positive psychic import are developed in *H&C3*. We retain this short sub-subsection and its cursory acknowledgment of this point in case our reader is not to peruse that volume.

forms of cruelty, if not even a dramatic, biting, yet necessary outlet for our aggressive tendencies.

Sometimes, in the face of incorrigible but all-too-human imperfections, we must settle for the lesser evil. As Freud and Jung argued, insofar as modern societies repress our natural aggressiveness and our *libido* to a psycho-pathogenic extent, it may be healthy and wise to opt for a little evil every once in a while. As the latter stated, we may have "to inflict defeat on [our] virtues", which are exceedingly internalised, turned into our very 'flesh', and often pursued well past the advisable points of well-balanced mental health and applicable practical wisdom.[632]

In the 1930s, the renowned British economist John Maynard Keynes made an analogous point with regard to capitalism and, very much *à propos*, "cruelty" proper. As he wrote:

> dangerous human proclivities can be canalised into comparatively harmless channels by the existence of opportunities for money-making and private wealth, which, if they cannot be satisfied in this way, may find their outlet in cruelty, the reckless pursuit of personal power and authority, and other forms of self-aggrandisement.[633]

We do not only have to worry about our vices which, left unchecked, can grow into the brutal heartlessness decried by Seneca and Aquinas, or the vicious bloodlust witnessed by Montaigne in times of warfare and by Locke in the behaviour of puzzlingly sadistic children. Paradoxically, we must also worry about our virtues, which may turn troublesome when pursued too eagerly and/or blindly, i.e., without keeping a watchful eye on their associated costs or, in Jungian terms, the shadow that these virtues inevitably cast.[634] Sometimes the good can be sought by us too ardently for our own good.[635]

The seemingly praiseworthy goal of perfection may not be one that is suited for thoroughly imperfect creatures such as ourselves. Perhaps this is actually the deeper wisdom of the Latin proverb stating *commune naufragium, omnibus sola-*

---

[632] Jung (1960–1990), vol. 9.2, 25, par. 47, in which he also adds that such a line of conduct does not mean immorality, but "making a moral effort in a different direction". We explore this topic in more detail in *H&C3*.
[633] Keynes (2008), chap. 24, part 1, par. 5.
[634] Jung (cited in Becker 2001, 147) wondered: "But what if I should discover that the least among them all, the poorest of all beggars, the most impudent of all offenders, yea the very fiend himself – that these are within me, and that I myself stand in need of my own kindness, that I myself am the enemy who must be loved – what then?"
[635] LVOA can be of use in determining when the critical threshold has been crossed.

*cium.*⁶³⁶ In essence, we ought to settle for an intelligent and life-enabling standard of common imperfection.⁶³⁷

(2) Yet another cruel irony would ensue from the virtuist scenario that Prince Myshkin embodies and exemplifies. One that is most apropos in the context of the present book. Specifically, humour itself would be one of the first fatalities in a perfect human world. Not only because plenteous virtue would prevent us from engaging in most types of humour, if not even in all of them, since they are extremely likely to contain a cruel ingredient, whether callous, sadistic, or both (we discuss this point much more thoroughly in the next chapter). Also, plenteous virtue would mean the absence of vice, which is a standard target, if not the prime one, for all kinds of humorous attacks.

What could a stand-up comedian ever joke about should there no longer be, say, moral failure, political corruption, the rages of old age, or the silliness of youth?⁶³⁸ And what comedies could ever be written, should there be no more fraudsters, egotists, gluttons, creeps, philanderers, stutterers, bigots, floozies, hooligans, fanatics, outcasts, butterballs, dotards, weirdos, queens, tenderfoots, or tenderfeet? How to have fun, should there be around only considerate people, who would read all of the hereby-listed common comic types—or, at least, some of them—and interpret them immediately, and hence condemn them most severely, as horrible stereotypes, despicable means of insult, and/or indirect forms of cruel discrimination, i.e., without grasping, acknowledging, and/or considering their ludicrous facets too, which talented artists may yet reinvent in a successful manner?⁶³⁹

(3) These rhetorical questions could also be cast in a slightly different way: what sort of mirth could be enjoyed in Paradise, Shangri-La, and/or under conditions of total human perfection? Perhaps, humour and laughter would still be present, though in a highly singular form. Representatively, while writing on the sort of laughter exhibited by the Buddha himself, the Thai philosopher and religious scholar Soraj Hongladarom wrote:

---

636 Literally, "a common shipwreck, a solace to all"; i.e., an ancestor of "misery loves company".
637 We discuss in more detail in *H&C3* some of the cruelties arising from virtuist pursuits, e.g., Puritanism. As to "virtuism" and "virtuist", we use these terms in line with Vilfredo Pareto's (1914) classic study on the subject.
638 "Vice" is hereby interpreted in the sense of a *personal defect*, which can be moral, aesthetic, behavioural, or sexual. Current English parlance still accommodates all of them. Things might change in the future, of course.
639 More is said in this book's concluding chapter on the cruel ethical, aesthetic, and/or existential tensions arising from having to choose between humour and dourness, doing so, and/or failing in so doing.

> The Buddha ... "laughs the loudest laugh" and "most vigorously like the lion-king", and emits "rays of light which shone flaming like the fire taking place at the end of a kalpa"... The Buddha's laughter ... is not the kind that could lead him to the door of defilements. The Buddha is utterly pure and is utterly free from such lowly possibilities. His laugh is a resplendent, confident one, the laughter of one who has completely destroyed all possibilities of even the slightest and most subtle of the defilements. It is the expression of one who is full of compassion and love, a reflection of pure, transcendent happiness.[640]

Buddha's laughter, in short, is the hyperbolic version of the one exhibited by the innocent child and/or the guiltless simpleton whose mirth flows out of an overabundance of *joie de vivre*, i.e., the utmost 'good humour', as *per* the psychological application of the Hippocratic-Galenic medical theory of bodily health. Apparently, Dostoyevsky may have been correct in dubbing Prince Myshkin "the idiot".[641]

(4) The ambiguous status of much commonplace humour, and especially of the cruel sort that both threatens and liberates, is a point that was not lost on Kozintsev, who liked exploring the paradoxical aspects of this phenomenon as well as of its cognate notions, laughter *in primis*.[642] Among other things, Kozintsev's approach offers a plausible defence of our frequent use of abrasive humour, while also suggesting that the theory of relief may be, albeit limited, the most insightful of the three standard ones:

> In our prehuman ancestors, the "recoding" signaled by laughter had an extremely narrow meaning: "I'm pretending to bite you, but it's just play". In humans, the meaning was extended to the extreme: "I'm pretending to violate all cultural norms and taboos, but it's just play". Despite this extension, the basic meaning of the signal has remained the same. Peals of laughter caused by trifling and primitive stimuli as well as the contagiousness of laughter as such do not accord with the cognitivist theories of humor, but are easy to understand given *the need for an occasional collective liberation from the burden of basic human capacities – language and culture*.[643]

---

640 Hongladarom (2013), 243.
641 We assume our readers to grasp tacitly the implied equivalence of "the guiltless simpleton" and "the idiot", though no offence is meant by this. Such an individual, as seen, could actually be God incarnate, or akin to it.
642 Ambiguity does not need to be an unresolved problem that, if duly tackled, must then vanish once and for all. In line with Polanyi (1962b), we can understand it as a legitimate feature of our lived reality, which entails vague, unaccountable and/or indeterminate aspects too, some of which being crucial in the exact and natural sciences, e.g., coming up with a problem to be investigated and turned into a testable hypothesis, or deciding that what is being observed is not mere noise but a yet-to-be-established phenomenon or part thereof. Also, insofar as the same reality can be approached from different personal standpoints, ambiguity may simply be the recognition of this difference when attended *to* rather than just *from* (see Chapter 2 and *H&CI*'s concluding chapter).
643 Kozintsev (2010), 107; emphasis added.

Armed with this psychically liberating understanding of "humour" proper, Kozintsev himself took a stab at the all-too-good Prince Myshkin, whom he judged to be the proverbial 'white fly' in the much-muddier human context that many of our readers are probably familiar with:

> There is nothing "objectively funny" in the person we consider the object of our laughter, nor can there be; for he temporarily ceases to be for us a real object, the subject of a serious relation, and what we call a "nonserious relation" is no relation at all. What then does he become? For the laugher – a comic actor, a participant in an imaginary carnival, a distorting mirror in which the laugher sees himself. The problem is that the "object" is not ready to join in the game. This nonconcurrence engenders innumerable dramas. The laugher, who has fallen captive to the "illusion of intent", experiences pleasure so unlike all other kinds of pleasure – that caused by the liberation from seriousness. Unlike him, the person who has furnished the pretext for laughter – if he is not similar to those rare near-saints like the hero of Dostoevskii's novel *The Idiot* – feels bitterness and anger because he supposes that playing the imitation of inferior people is beneath his dignity (a deceived lover is at times capable of laughing at his fate, but is it easy to tolerate someone else's laughter?).[644]

We do not know how many of our readers are themselves akin to Prince Myshkin. Given our lived experience, though, we must assert that people like him have been hard to come by.[645]

(5) Under all the "nonserious" humorous relations and opportunities for temporary relief studied by Kozintsev hides an additional, deeper, and subtler ironic cruelty, which Dostoyevsky's novels explored almost obsessively, yet without making any explicit theoretical analysis of it. We mean the peculiar fact that, by having occasional moments of mirth and relaxation frequently fuelled by laughing water and festive carnivals of sort, life appears once again to be benign, enjoyable, welcoming and friendly. As a result, the momentarily relieved person is eventually enticed into throwing herself back into the thick of it, where more suffering and more disappointment inevitably await her. Humour, and cruel humour too, by making cruel things a little more bearable and/or even awfully amusing when perpetrated by us at someone else's expense, serve therefore as *de facto* guarantors of

---

[644] Kozintsev (2010), 144. Behind Dostoyevsky's work lies the Orthodox tradition of God's "fools" (see Dumas 2020): being mentally deranged yet morally innocent, the idiots remind us of the gulf between us and our Creator, whose love we must seek, emulate, trust in, and rely upon, if we wish to save ourselves from eternal damnation.

[645] Perhaps, we have just been the victims of bad luck; or we cannot spot a saint when we meet one.

these things' persistence in time and of their continued influence in human interactions.[646]

1.3 Family Resemblances

> [O]lder cultures ... have a better sense of th[e] enigmatic force in human life than does our contemporary psychology, which tends to narrow understanding of complex phenomena to single-meaning definitions. We should not be afraid of ... big nouns; they are not hollow. They have merely been deserted and need rehabilitation. These many words and names do not tell us what 'it' is, but they do confirm that it is. They also point to its mysteriousness. We cannot know what exactly we are referring to because its nature remains shadowy, revealing itself mainly in hints, intuitions, whispers, and the sudden urges and oddities that disturb your life and that we continue to call symptoms.
> —James Hillman[647]

Given the many extant conceptions of 'humour' and 'cruelty', the study of these concepts is fraught with difficulties. Most of these difficulties are common to all scholarly and scientific studies; others plague the humanities and/or select social sciences in particular; and a few of them are specific to the chosen topics. Let us mention three such difficulties in particular.

(1) First and foremost, there is a glaring lack of common definitions for both concepts. As a result, different authors have miscellaneous basic premises to begin with, resulting in divergent conceptions of the same concept.

(2) On top of that, it is exceedingly difficult to group all these authors into precise schools of thought, as most of them are not constricted by any such framework.

(3) Lastly, there is no consensus about the functional aspects of these two notions and even less on the structural ones.

---

646 This dismal and somewhat paradoxical relation between humour and cruelty is consistent with Rosset's existentialist philosophy, which we duly outlined in this chapter and, in more detail, in *H&C1*.

647 Hillman (1996), chap. 1, sec. 2, pars. 11–12, 10. As amply discussed in *H&C1*, analytical defining and detailing allow for greater conceptual precision as well as for the increased accuracy of empirical testing, but they also reduce the overall scope and ordinary salience of what is being studied. Hence, the farther removed we become from *the original lived experiences* of actual persons, whence the overarching common-sense notion of 'humour' arose.

In other words, we find ourselves squarely set within the realm of the "pre-paradigm", as the American philosopher Thomas Kuhn explained in his famous 1962 book, *The Structure of Scientific Revolutions*.[648]

For scholars in the humanities and the social sciences, however unsettling such a condition may be, this is not an uncommon situation. Thus, even though there is a palpable dearth of shared definitions, fundamental premises, and no single, universal *modus operandi*, many such scholars and scientists have not been deterred from tackling these subjects. And to do so—as also the many representative cases outlined in the previous subsections indicate—most scholars and scientists have relied, ultimately and perhaps inevitably, upon ordinary language, which is a useful yet extremely complex instrument. As the contemporary Indian philosopher Arindam Chakrabarti eloquently expounded on this point:

> Words are sometimes said to clothe our thoughts and beliefs. But, like some clothes, they usually reveal more than they conceal, often imposing shapes on our ideas which they might have lacked in their naked state. Beliefs put on the dress of language not only when they are exhibited but also when they travel from one person to another. Perhaps this whole sartorial imagery is wrongheaded. The very notion of beliefs or awareness episodes in their pre-linguistic nudity may be a myth.[649]

Consistent with this self-reflexive and epistemically prudent line of thinking, we conclude this chapter with two short lists of "family resemblances" *à la* Wittgenstein, i.e., connotations that, as the 20th-century Austrian engineer and philosopher wrote, "overlap and criss-cross" one another—in this case, across the immense semantic field subtending to the many instances of the two concepts that we have encountered.[650]

---

648 Kuhn (1970), 187. See also Arnarsson (2016), Parker (2015), and Zagaria, Andò, and Zennaro (2020) on the enduring plurality of psychological paradigms. This plurality endures even if individual scientists, professional associations and/or academic units may sometimes act as though only their own approach existed and/or were to be taken seriously. This wilful blindness (or trained incapacity) has been present, to an even greater degree, among 'orthodox' economists, whether 'saltwater' or 'freshwater' ones, whose disciplinary field includes Marxist, evolutionary, post-Keynesian, Austrian, ecological, and other 'heterodox' schools of thought (see, e.g., Galbraith 2009). More on the curious, humorous and, not unfrequently, cruel world of economics is discussed in *H&C3*.
649 Chakrabarti (1992), 421.
650 Wittgenstein (1953), par. 67. *H&C1* offers an even broader variety of diverging conceptions, whence the two lists, longer than here, emerge *qua* concluding result of our extensive philosophical and psychological exploration, which is the necessarily bulky and fastidious precondition for any tenable conclusion based on inductive reasoning.

We doubt that a single definition of each titular concept, however clever and conveniently abstract, could successfully cover all of these logically acceptable instances, which have been in use for extended periods of time and/or adequately buttressed by way of:
(1) argute theoretical reflections;
(2) insightful remodulations of the pre-existing semantic field; and/or
(3) plausible empirical inquiries into human cultures, beliefs, personalities, and behaviours.[651]

At the very least, *we* have been unable to concoct any such clever and conveniently abstract definitions in this book. Better thinkers may yet be successful. Or they may be more cautious than we ourselves decided to be. According to the Slovenian thinker Peter Klepec, for one, even our mere searching for "common denominators" of "cruelty" proper at the conceptual level "is proving to be a Pandora's box from which everything alive falls out".[652]

We do appreciate and, to a degree, sympathise with his criticism. The more general abstract thought we utilise, the more specific lived immediacy we euthanise. Having said that, we do consider the laborious mental steps of excavating, abstracting, and highlighting select conceptual connotations from the veritable historical maze of divergent perspectives on "cruelty" (and "humour") proper to be a 'necessary evil' of the intellect. Our mind, we contend, requires such steps, however judiciously contained, as well as the restrained modicum of critical aloofness that these steps entail for the sakes of, on the one hand, facilitating interpersonal communication about "cruelty" (or "humour") proper and, on the other hand, achieving a better—albeit never complete—intrapersonal grasp of the notion(s) at issue.[653]

---

[651] As noted, *H&C1* developed a theoretical defence of our concepts' polysemy, based on Polanyi (1962c).

[652] Klepec (2021), 191, whose criticism was directed at Baruchello (2017), which lies behind this book's section 1.2. We thank our colleague both for his appreciation of our research, which is described as "rare" in its theoretical and historical depth, and for his feedback on our hereby-used English translation of his work (Klepec 2021, 190).

[653] Dismally yet appropriately, Klepec (2021) is a reminder of the fact that in philosophy, just like in economic matters, there is no such thing as a free lunch.

1.3.1 Humour

As regards the concept of 'humour', the chosen family resemblances are as follows.

(1) *Laughability:* Most commonly, albeit not always, 'humour' has been related to laughter. Humour should cause people to laugh by snickering, chortling, chuckling, guffawing, roaring, etc. Yet, it is certainly true that laughter can be, at times, divorced from humour, e.g., gelotic pathological seizures and gas-induced laughing fits.[654]. Conversely, humour can be infused with so much elegiac or sublime sentiment, so subtle and cerebral, or even taken to be a philosophical tool for gaining insight into deep and/or obscure ontological or epistemic matters that laughter falls out of the equation.[655] At times, even smiling may be unwarranted.[656]

(2) *Medietas:* Ideas relating to good measure arise persistently in connection with 'humour'. Thus, we are often told that we should avoid doing "too little" (e.g., being too meek, too tactful, too empathic, too undifferentiated, too ordinary, etc.) or "too much" (e.g., being too assertive, too coarse, too buffoonish, too acerbic, too brainy, etc.). In comedy or satire, but also in daily razzing or persiflage, we can be said to go "too far" or play it "too safe". Different types of humour, not least between low- and high-brow, or commonplace and 'true' ones, have thus been predicated upon the chosen emphasis on some crucial 'ingredient' or another, which shifts the overall balance in a given direction, e.g., eroticism, poignancy, subtlety, sympathy, etc.

(3) *Role-centredness:* The jokester and the so-called "butt of the joke" are rarely one and the same person or group. In any case, the two roles are very different from each other—even when the former may happen to be sympathetic to the latter, or *vice versa*.[657] As sadomasochistic relations exemplify, the master/mistress and the slave have distinct parts to play, even when taking turns, and notwithstanding their need for each other.[658] A single individual can play the two roles, e.g., letting his/her *super-ego* maltreat the *ego via* merciless self-mockery.[659] However, children may exhibit 'good humour' without any such roles playing a part in their smiling and laughing exuberance, or *joie de vivre*.[660]

---

[654] See, e.g., Borloz (2017).
[655] As seen, Deleuze's definition of "humour" proper fits the bill with regard to the third example.
[656] Once again, this could be Deleuze's case.
[657] See, e.g., McCann, Plummer, and Minichiello (2010), 505.
[658] We assume our readers to know enough about such erotic practices, whether they engage in them or not.
[659] More on self-mockery follows in Chapter 2.
[660] We reiterate this case in Chapter 2.

(4) *Surprise:* Surprise has been recognised as crucial for centuries and in multiple instances, and is understood recurrently in similar ways: a stimulus, a shock, a novelty, a change of scenery, etc.[661] Other important factors have also been frequently associated with surprise: expectations, temperament, alcohol-consumption levels, general frame of mind, etc. Depending on them, in fact, something becomes likelier to be grasped as surprising—or not. Not all surprises come forth as humorous, though, whether to the so-called "butt of the joke", the jokester, or the witness of a potentially humorous event. Only those who excel in 'reading' the context correctly have a good chance at being surprising in a way that is received as humorous rather than offensive, stupid, threatening, etc.[662]

(5) *Sociality:* Without social beings, contexts, and institutions, no humour could exist, absent the basis for its: onto-logical presence (i.e., a community of adequately evolved symbolic creatures, who breathe, feel, and speak); pragmatic production (i.e., the community's symbolic conventions that allows instances of humour to occur, more or less successfully); and permissible purposes (e.g., amusing people, abusing people, determining relative social status, and romantic or reproductive appeal). As to the solitary instances of humour that we are all likely to have engaged in before a mirror or at home, they should be seen as originally interpersonal activities that were internalised and made intrapersonal.[663] At that point, however, the social element clearly loses its centrality, even if it does not disappear *in toto*. As to more extreme exceptions, we can mention mentally deranged individuals, who cannot be socialised in any significant manner and yet smile, laugh, and generally manifest 'good humour' aplenty.

(6) *Malevolence:* Various types of evil have often been said to be part of humour, e.g., vulgarity, humiliation, mercilessness, sadism, weakness, indifference, nihilism, elitism, spite, oppression, envy, laziness, resentment, anger, etc. As the following two chapters illustrate unequivocally, there is much available corroborating evidence for this dismal point. At any rate, it is also patent that "humour" proper has been repeatedly characterised as a pleasant and positive component of human life and, philosophically, of "the good life" itself.[664] Indeed, in Chapter 2, we discuss two contemporary philosophers aiming at pro-

---

[661] See, e.g., K. Kenny (2009) in the context of so-called "docu-parodies".
[662] A major economic historian and a talented humourist, Cipolla (1988, 6) spoke of "the instinctive grasp of when and where humour can be voiced", which only some elect individuals possess. He aspired to be such a person.
[663] See Fernyhough (2017) on soliloquy, including funny cases thereof.
[664] See Amir (2014), title *et passim*.

moting humour as the best avenue for self-acceptance and self-realisation in our imperfect and cruel world.
(7) *Duality:* Incongruous combinations of differing elements, typically in pairs, have regularly been mentioned regarding "humour" proper. Hence, here, we use "duality".[665] Paradoxes, contradictions, bisociations, discrepancies, uncertainties, intrusions, interruptions, ambiguities, etc., have been cited *ad nauseam* in the works of scholars and scientists studying humour.[666] Yet, all these paradoxes *et similia* are not funny *per se*.[667] As was the case for the family resemblance of surprise, so does duality call for more 'ingredients' in order to engender humour, whether in its prosaic rude forms or in more 'refined' artistic ones.[668]

1.3.2 Cruelty

As regards the notion of 'cruelty', the chosen family resemblances are as follows.
(1) *Painfulness:* Typically, cruelty is said to imply pain—bodily, mental, severe, small, defensible, unpardonable, imagined, actual, cathartic, catastrophic, character-building, soul-crushing, expiatory, gratuitous, etc. The kind varies, but pain it is in any case. And yet, morality and the accusations of "cruelty" proper have sometimes extended to forms of evil-doing that have not caused, or may not cause, any discernible pain whatsoever. In other words, there may be plausible instances of painless cruelty.[669] This notion may sound odd, but we can mention here: corpse-defiling necrophilia in a private morgue; malicious gossip about a departed person that was left without relatives or friends; and the wanton destruction of a wasp nest or an anthill, a beautiful work art

---

[665] See also G. Noonan (1988, 913f), who explains humour at large in terms of "duality" proper.
[666] See also Krikmann (2006) for a synoptic overview of all such dualities.
[667] As laconically yet, in our view, correctly stated by the contemporary British artist and art historian Paul Clements (2022, 1), "humour" is truly an "ambiguous phenomenon that is highly contextual and relative to time and place". It is ambiguous because of its polysemy. But it also ambiguous in its entailing dualities that, at times, are funny and, other times, are not. Moreover, whether funny or not, some such dualities can even be cruel.
[668] It can be argued that the greatest comedians are those who can find unerringly such ingredients.
[669] Mixing humour twice, a cruel cook spits into some food to be served to an unaware, loathed patron, who will never know of the incident. Curiously, the same act, or similar ones, can also be performed on libidinous grounds. They may even be self-directed, as in a case of happy coprophagy reported by von Kraft-Ebing (see G. Scott 1996, 179).

that is unknown to everyone but its destroyer, or some other inanimate object, such as a common chair.[670]

(2) *Excessiveness:* Whatever the context, claims concerning "cruelty" proper frequently indicate that someone has crossed a meaningful threshold. The crucial boundary may involve, *inter alia*, politeness, uprightness, respect, graciousness, fairness, or even survival. Moreover, the crossing of this boundary must be 'unmasked' and/or denounced by someone else as a blameable act. Normally, the one who does so is either the victim of the alleged "cruelty" or some witness. Far more rarely, yet not illogically, it may be the perpetrator, who realises that s/he had erred in some form/s of thinking, feeling, and/or, above all, behaving.[671]

(3) *Role-centredness:* Usually, "cruelty" proper requires victims and perpetrators, even if the latter may be obscure, e.g., God, Mother Nature, Fate, etc. The two roles are distinct, but there may be occasions when they are one and the same, i.e., a self-abusing agent, whose *super-ego* or *id* acts as the *ego*'s cruel master.[672]

(4) *Power:* The two roles of victim and perpetrator call for enough power differential to allow for "cruelty" proper to materialise in some form. The differential may be as little as the opportunity for an ancient slave to mock the senseless, head-in-the-clouds, but also free and well-off Thales of Miletus, who fell into a well while taking a stroll and, depending on the version of this ancient tale, pondering upon a philosophical problem or gazing at the stars.[673] Or it may be the differential in physical allure and erotic self-confidence that allows the nubile young maid to tease and tempt the older pious priest.[674] As long as some sting can be inflicted, or a momentary sense of superiority achieved, anyone can be cruel. As Chesterton quipped: "Christianity ... says that [we] are all fools. This doctrine is sometimes called the doctrine of original

---

[670] Robinson (2019), title *et passim*. As A. Taylor (1932, series I, lecture 8, par. 25) stated on attributions of the adjective "cruel": "it is the cruel man, rather than the suffering he causes, who is the direct object of our loathing". Their perpetrator-based conception, then, contradicts H. Lewis' (1982, 3–4) one, which is victim-centred: "we speak of cruelty to animals but not to pieces of wood or stone", which lack "an 'inner' experience".
[671] We include thoughts and feelings because someone may connote them linguistically as "cruel".
[672] Given our references to Freud's psychoanalysis, we use examples based on its subdivision of the psyche. A Jungian approach, which further subdivides our psyche, would allow for even more instances of inner conflict.
[673] The famous anecdote is also reported in Amir (2013), 7.
[674] For recent reiterations of this trite trope, see the 2013 comedy and BBC's 2016–2019 dramedy *Fleabag*.

sin. It may also be described as the doctrine of the equality of men... All men can be criminals, if tempted."[675]

(5) *Culpability:* Frequently, "cruelty" proper is associated with a *mens rea* of sorts.[676] Notably, Nell argues that there are two "preconditions for cruelty", i.e., "an action, which is the deliberate infliction of physical or psychological pain on another living creature or on the self" and, suitably, "a mental state, namely the intention to inflict pain, which in turn presupposes a theory of mind".[677] Most approaches in the social sciences, ethics, jurisprudence and theology, have shared this accusatory outlook.[678] However, there have also been social and/or medical studies tackling impairments, whether physical or psychical, that would exclude, reduce, or cancel this *mens rea*.[679] Additionally, the recurrent understanding of cruelty as brutality (or callousness) reminds us that a person's intention to cause pain may be secondary and result from ulterior aims, which can be regarded as being so supreme, holy, honourable, impartial, lucrative, valuable, and/or cogent, as to make the chosen path of agency a positive one.[680] Hence, "cruelty" has been sometimes dubbed "good", whether instrumentally (e.g., Ainslie) or intrinsically (e.g., Nietzsche). One could then be proud of being "guilty as charged".[681]

(6) *Malevolence:* Well-argued yet episodic instances such as those of Ainslie and Nietzsche do not refute the fact that, almost archetypally, "cruelty" proper is

---

[675] Chesterton (1919), chap. 12, par. 14 (who also adds: "all men can be heroes, if inspired").

[676] Determining whether and how much a person is responsible for a cruel act is up to judges and priests.

[677] Nell (2006), 212.

[678] See, e.g., Lévitt (1922–1923) and Ćorović (2022, 47f), whose lengthy English-language abstract outlines the ongoing reformation of Serbia's penal code with regard to addressing "cruelty" proper *qua* judicially significant aggravating factor, plus its attendant forensic and conceptual complexities.

[679] See, e.g., Hallevy (2015), exploring the complexities of psychiatric diagnoses and penal implications thereof.

[680] This callousness can be so prosaic and so practical as to become invisible and routinised to nearly all persons, i.e., "institutionalized" *à la* Hallie (see *H&C1* for a richer account of his views). Ponder on, e.g., how no moral thought whatsoever is given to the invertebrates and small vertebrates that are destroyed by the thousands whenever erecting a new building or a new road on their life habitat. Only some ethically and/or religiously motivated 'eccentrics' would openly and duly consider their fate. Perhaps, suitable candidates could be "the contemporary philosopher-ethologist Dominique Lestel" or the Tunisian writer "Yamen Manaï", given their special focus on the importance of human-animal relationships for human flourishing (Moser 2022, par. 1).

[681] We expect the reader to be familiar with this expression, which comes from the judicial domain.

deemed to be an evil, even when only a lesser or a necessary one. We leave each reader to pass judgement on this matter, as s/he confronts thorny cases of possible, and possibly good, cruelty. Such judgements must be passed in the face of specific circumstances that escape, inevitably, any convenient general abstraction.[682] In fair tribunals, after all, each case is tried on its own merits and demerits, even if the laws are general and the constitutional principles universal.

(7) *Paradoxicality:* In those rare circumstances when cruelty's inevitable or desirable character has been pinpointed, such a peculiar character has often been deemed paradoxical, rather than good.[683] Somehow, few intellectuals have been willing to go so far as Sade or Nietzsche. 'Paradox' offers a convenient middle ground, if shaky and perplexing, given that cruelty's acknowledged paradoxes frequently comprise the nastiest of known evils, exemplifying surprising dualities that, normally, are not humorous to most observers.[684]

It is on the basis of the understanding of the concepts of 'humour' and 'cruelty' which all such family resemblances allow for, that we proceed to address and assess the issues of humorous cruelty and cruel humour in the next two respective chapters.

---

[682] As we argued in *H&C1*, talking of "cruelty" opens the door to considerations of personal responsibility.
[683] See, in particular, Hallie (1969).
[684] As we observed, duality may be a necessary condition of humour, but it is not sufficient on its own.

2 Humorous Cruelty

E mentre il sangue lento usciva
E ormai cambiava il suo colore,
La vanità fredda gioiva:
Un uomo s'era ucciso per il suo amore.
— Fabrizio De André[1]

Cruelty can be hilarious.[2] Albeit undoubtedly grisly, a hanging that turns unexpectedly into a beheading or the sudden loss of a limb on the battlefield are reputed to have led to laughing fits.[3] Over countless generations, public torture and executions have attracted large crowds.[4] What is more, the convened multitudes participated by cheering, hooting, laughing, and/or singing during the event.[5] It was as though they were attending a carnival.[6] Let us also recall here Harlow, who retrieved repeated historical instances of "humour" proper in "[m]assacres, mutilations, torments and tortures".[7] As to the gruesome yet ecstatic thrills of outright sadists, whether taking place in some remote 18th-century French castle or in

---

1 *While the blood poured out slowly / and his face's colour began to change, / Vanity rejoiced coldly: / A man had killed himself out of love for her* ("La ballata dell'amore cieco" [The Ballad of Blind Love], 1966).
2 We adopt here Hallie's three roughly coextensive definitions of "cruelty" and attendant taxonomy, which are both reflected in many additional takes on the same subject, such as Collins (1974), Lecky (1890), Nell (2006), Regan (1983), and Shklar (1984) and (1989). These non-identical yet largely convergent interpretations of cruelty embrace all cases of direct and indirect causation of suffering that is enjoyed (sadism) or ignored (brutality), ranging from a person's verbal abuse to a society's destruction by means of war, financial speculation, etc. As to "cruelty" proper being hilarious *per se*, Esar (1961, 230) mentioned "cruel duel" among token "two-word rhymes", such as "stupid Cupid" and "sound hound", that are meant to be clever rejoinders to "proposed ... [n]on-rhyming phrases like dumb cherub, ruthless combat, healthy dog", in "test[s]" of a person's "verbal ingenuity". Esar's account thus corroborates Gruner's (1997) argument, whereby humour is said to be rooted, at least genealogically, in tests of superiority.
3 The unplanned decapitation of Saddam Hussain's half-brother Barzan Ibrahim al-Tikriti occurred in 2007 because of the hangman's miscalculation of the ratio between body weight and rope diameter in a drop-down execution, as listed in Frater (2010). Concerning a soldier's sudden maiming on a battlefield, see Tritle (2015).
4 An enduring legacy of the adoption of Islam, public canings in Aceh, Indonesia, are still commonplace and attract large gatherings of "cheering" spectators (Ramadhan 2019, 29).
5 Linking executions to older religious practices, G. Scott (1996, 21) wrote: "The sacrifices, first of animals and then of humans, were applauded by the populace; the roasting of victims was accompanied with hoots of joy. So, too, the torturing of prisoners of war, the punishment of criminals."
6 See, e.g., Gatrell (1996), and E. Simpson (2008).
7 Harlow (1969), 230. Presented in Chapter 1, we discussed his work in detail in *H&C1*.

the very central Roman arenas of the ancient world, these grotesque displays are now beyond most people's direct acquaintance, daily anticipation, and deliberate ambition.[8]

Granted, some individuals who are very keen on sadistic thrills are known to seek vocations enabling them to access unsuspecting animals or vulnerable people, as well as settings where violence upon these living beings is expected. As the Austrian 20th-century liberal economist Ludwig von Mises noted quite tactlessly for today's conversational and moral standards: "fetishists, homosexuals, sadists and other perverts can sometimes find in their work an opportunity to satisfy their strange appetites. There are occupations which are especially attractive to such people. Cruelty and blood-thirstiness luxuriantly thrive under various occupational cloaks."[9] Back in the 18th century, and somewhat more politely, the French Enlightenment polymath Denis Diderot had already written: "A person does not become cruel because he is an executioner; but an executioner because he is cruel."[10]

Disinfestation, animal husbandry, abattoirs, police work, shelters, hospices, fight clubs, hunting, and the army are mentioned in the vast and growing socio-scientific literature on "the 'Dark Triad' of personality" (i.e., "subclinical psychopathy, subclinical narcissism, and Machiavellianism"), and on these sadistic individuals' "appetite for cruelty".[11] There may be times, however, when large groups of human beings have ample opportunity, and apparent license, to explore and pursue "the dark side of personality".[12]

As Seneca and Montaigne observed centuries ago, wars offer precisely such conditions.[13] Writing in the early years of the allegedly 'civilised' and 'progressive'

---

8 These geo-historical locations should suggest, however delicately, useful memories of Montaigne and Sade.
9 Von Mises (1998), 586–587.
10 Diderot (1883), 65. In this work, Diderot (1883, 75–76) also briefly acknowledged the "ridicule" and "cruel satire" characterising "actors and authors" that "keep a stage accent in private life", thus projecting a gravitas that does not truly belong to them, for they are far more prosaic than the grand characters to whom they give life in the theatre. We are thereby confronted with yet another *cruel irony*, this time arising from the thespian realm whence the prevalent modern linguistic usages of "humour" proper arose (see Chapter 1 and *H&C1*).
11 Buckels *et al.* (2013), 2201; their examples. Some authors add "sadism" proper, "direct" and/or "vicarious", and turn the sorry triad into a tetrad, e.g., Thomas and Egan (2022), 1–4.
12 See Zeigler-Hill and Marcus (2016). Testifying to the polysemic nature of "cruelty" proper, their book covers "narcissism", "callous personality", "psychopathy", "Machiavellianism", "sadism", "spite", "maladaptive risk taking", "destructiveness", "authoritarianism", and "negative affectivity"; and they focus on causes such as "fearless dominance", "sensations seeking", "distractability", "inability to ignore", "perfectionism", "overconfidence", "emotional lability", "anxiousness", "depressivity and anhedonia", and "high and low self-esteem".
13 See our extensive discussion of Seneca and Montaigne in *H&C1*. See also Tritle (2015).

20th century, the renowned Norwegian-American economist and humourist, Thorstein Veblen, noted the for-profit economic logic lurking behind the lethally efficient industrialised warfare of modern Western nations such as imperial Britain, republican France, the Kingdom of Italy, Wilhelmine Germany, and the proudly democratic United States of America.[14] With more than merely a pinch of sarcasm, Veblen affirmed:[15]

> Such debaucheries, extravagances of cruelty, and general superfluity of naughtiness as are nameless or impossible in civil life are blameless matters of course in the service. In the nature of the case they are inseparable from the service. The service commonly leaves the veterans physical, intellectual, and moral invalids (as witness the records of the Pension Office). But these less handsome concomitants of the service should scarcely be made a point of reproach to those brave men whose devotion to the flag and the business interests has led them by the paths of disease and depravity. Nor are the accumulated vices to be lightly condemned, since their weight also falls on the conservative side; being archaic and authenticated, their cultural bearing is, on the whole, salutary.[16]

Wars can be, *inter alia*, proxy, cross-cross border, civil, large-scale, small-scale, symmetrical, asymmetrical, conventional, irregular, just, unjust, liberation struggles, acts of conquest, conflicts of attrition, short, long, and longer than planned.[17] In all cases, the exceptional business of killing, maiming, and terrifying other human beings for the State, in the name of freedom, for the sake of progress and civilisation, or in view of a substantial paycheque, supplies and legitimises, at least *prima facie*, effectual conditions that facilitate the presence and the prospering of cruelty on a truly massive scale.[18] During wars, in fact, the snuffing, mutilating, torturing, raping, humiliating, breaking, and defying of living bodies and living minds—or even dead ones—can become concrete avenues for widespread personal agency.[19]

---

14 Depending on the country, language and, above all, the class-based axiological perspective, this period has been variously dubbed "the gilded age", "*la belle époque*", "the progressive era", and "the age of imperialism".
15 "Veblen is frequently described as an iconoclast, satirist, and social critic" (Waller and Robertson 1990, 1027).
16 Veblen (1904), chap. 10, note 8.
17 The noted 20th-century German-American sociologist Hans Speier (1941, 445–454) reduced all these types of warfare to three abstract forms, or 'ideal types' *à la* Max Weber, i.e., absolute, instrumental, and agonistic. Yet he did not consider the many metaphorical usages of this term, also in the academic context, e.g., the biologist Paul Seabright's (2012) book, *The War of the Sexes*. For the moment, we too discount these far-from-rare usages.
18 See, e.g., Baumeister (1996).
19 The cruelty of "corpse desecration" lies in the "great suffering" caused "to the surviving families of the deceased", the "widespread disgust" it elicits, and "other cultural norms which tradi-

The perpetrators of all these cruelties can be soldiers, partisans, rebels, State employees, private contractors, medics, gaolers, and many other individuals.[20] They can belong to the most disparate ethnic groups and be male as well as female.[21] In turn, these possibilities for cruel agency can lead to the discovery of new forms of elation involving living as well as dead victims.[22]

Some of these are capable of eliciting laughter and conspicuous merriment among the perpetrators.[23] Allegedly "cold" wars or even nominally "surgical" and "peacekeeping" military interventions have created such conditions and, *a fortiori*, facilitated such cruel, humorous behaviours.[24] Recent examples include:
(1) Argentina from 1976 to 1982;[25]
(2) Bosnia during the 1990s;[26] and
(3) Iraq in the early 2000s.[27]

In all these cases, gross human rights abuses and smiling jocularity found ways to emerge and unfold aplenty.[28] They involved blatant instances of State-sanctioned

---

tionally have been considered less subjective, such as requiring consent, protecting ownership of personal property, and protecting public health and safety" (Ochoa and Newman Jones 1997, 543). See Rolston, III (1982) on cruelty to the comatose.
20 See, e.g., Beaumont (1990) and Adams, Balfour, and Reed (2006).
21 See, e.g., Cohen (2013, 384 and 404), contradicting "conventional wisdom" and showing how "women are participating in the wartime rape of non-combatants", and "while some women committed the actual rape of victims (that is, by inserting objects into victims' bodies), other women were involved in gang rape by holding down the victim... [R]ape serves a bonding function... Many of the fighters reported that rape was an activity they viewed as 'fun' or 'entertainment' ... [as they] 'joke about some guys were not doing it correctly ... and ... the entire unit watches. Everyone laughs and is jubilating'".
22 Defiling corpses for fun does not require, always and necessarily, extreme circumstances. Sandström (2015, 18) reported of medical students "who were practising surgery on a cadaver [and] removed its ears and stitched to the ass cheeks of the body, apparently as a reference to some sort of humorous German saying".
23 See, e.g., United Nations (2010), 35–36 and 50. See also chap. 9 in Welch (2022, 141), writing of "cruelty fueled by sarcasm".
24 See, e.g., McCoy (2006).
25 See, e.g., Borisov (1986).
26 See, e.g., Sustersic (2015).
27 See, e.g., Philpott (2005) and Fine and Corte (2022, title *et passim*), who covered several other instances of "dark fun" among like-minded sadists and opened their article with an apt quote from Montaigne's *Essays*.
28 As regards "stripping people naked and degrading them", the well-known US private Lynndie England replied in a 13 August 2009 BBC interview: "if it helps get whatever information they might have, sure". Besides, as the interviewee went on to explain: "this happens at colleges in dorm rooms or whatever here in the U.S. all the time" ("US Woman Soldier Unrepentant").

torture and/or similarly merciless and legally dubious "interrogation techniques", which prompted laughter and grinning derision of the victims among the perpetrators. Conspicuously, both the Greek Army's torturers in the 1960s–1970s and the Sudanese ones in the 1980s–2000s referred to their torture sessions as "parties".[29] (As far as the Iraqi case is concerned, following the terrorist attacks on New York in 2001, countless Western academics found themselves suddenly busy trying to justify *de facto*, if not *de jure*, the use of torture, primarily by way of abstract 'lesser-evil' and 'ticking-bomb' scenarios.)[30] In the end, a new secular layer of gruesome imagery was added to the traditional religious one, in which the forgiving Jesus Christ has been depicted, again and again, while mocked by his torturers and/or a spiteful crowd.[31]

2.1 A Fistful of Examples

> One must have a heart of stone to read the death of Little Nell without laughing.
> —Oscar Wilde[32]

Wars and warlike circumstances aside, today most people are confined throughout their lives to considerably milder sadistic thrills.[33] As Portmann stated: "Gossip and laughter are the precarious chinks in the armour of disguise; they stand as the chief behavioural manifestations of pleasure in the suffering of others."[34] Such minor thrills can arise inside a number of quotidian contexts.[35] We can list, for instance:

(1) novel- and/or soap-opera-like romantic rivalries (e.g., stealing someone else's partner to humiliate that particular someone);[36]

---

29 Elgadi (2018), 29.
30 See, e.g., Moher (2003–2004).
31 See, e.g., A. Phillips (1998), 56–65 and 143–149, and Spivack (2002).
32 Wilde (1995), 138.
33 Concentration camps should be included among warlike circumstances, which allowed for countless sadistic jests by the guards towards the inmates and by the seasoned inmates towards the newcomers (see Levi 2018).
34 Portmann (2000), 200. Recently, none less than Pope Francis condemned "gossip", or "chatter" as "a plague more awful than Covid-19" (Watkins 2020, pars. 1 and 17). Yet again, ironically, such 'idle talk' may well have some redeeming properties and/or uses, as discussed, e.g., by Susan E. Phillips (2007) with regard to late-Medieval English literature and social history.
35 Some of the listed examples are discussed in more detail in *H&C3*.
36 See, e.g., Wilke and Cox (1999).

(2) the power imbalances and attendant abuses of work relations (e.g., mobbing);[37]
(3) youthful tomfooleries done, *prima facie*, just for kicks (e.g., nasty pranks to junior-year college students or new recruits, wanton acts of vandalism);[38]
(4) the ritual humiliation of aspiring and deceived romantic and/or erotic partners repeatedly celebrated by pop singers (e.g., Britney Spears' 2000 song "Oops!... I Did It Again");[39]
(5) the rather private titillations allowed by
(5a) pet ownership (e.g., driving a cat mad with a pointer's beam),
(5b) gastronomy (e.g., starving snails), and
(5c) cooking (e.g., lobsters being boiled alive);[40]
(6) unbarred daydreaming or solitary deviant fantasies;[41] and
(7) the audio-visual stimulations of
(7a) dubious internet sites,[42]
(7b) gruesome computer games,[43]

---

[37] See, e.g., Roscigno, Lopez, and Hodson (2009).
[38] See, e.g., Bochenek and Brown (2001).
[39] See, e.g., Fiske (2011). Curiously, 500 years ago, Bruno's (1985, 1013) definition of *crudeltà* dealt already with this merciless toying: "[W]e call cruel the person who does not allow herself to be enjoyed or enjoyed fully, hence being an object of desire rather than of possession; therefore, as regards the individual who does not possess, he cannot be in complete peace, for he desires, suffers and dies" (Bruno's original text leaves open the attribution of gender to the "person" and the "individual"). As scores of Romantic poets and teenage wannabe bards have exemplified in later centuries, and as surprisingly few philosophers have asserted, *unrequited love and/or sexual dissatisfaction are among the commonest and most excruciating pains that can be experienced in human life.* See, e.g., Schopenhauer (1909) and (1897, 202; emphasis in the original), where we read: "It is in truth no hyperbole on the part of a lover when he calls his beloved as coldness, or the joy of her vanity, which delights in his suffering, *cruelty.* For he has come under the influence of an impulse which, akin to the instinct of animals, compels him in spite of all reason to unconditionally pursue his end and discard every other; he cannot give it up." As also sung by pop stars and media starlets all over the world, *love is cruel* (e.g., Tori Deal and Jordan Wiseley).
[40] In a parody of Tolstoy's all-embracing empathetic pacifism and humanism, the Soviet writer Andrei Donatovich Sinyavsky, better known as Abram Tertz, made one of his characters speak of "the sadism of cooking", not only as concerns sentient animals, but living plants too, e.g., "wheat" (as cited in Clardy and Clardy, 1980, 156).
[41] Mees (1966, 317) reported of "unpleasant electric shocks" curing "sadistic fantasies".
[42] See, e.g., Rasmussen (2015) and Maddison (2013). We focus here on audio-video stimulation. However, for completeness' sake, printed media should also be mentioned, e.g., the so-called "Boy-Love" subgenre in the broader 1970s–1990s Japanese manga tradition. The subgenre at issue focussing on male-on-male "rape fantas[ies]" created by "predominantly female" artists for an "implied ... female" readership (Graves 2016, 2–3).
[43] See, e.g., Greitemeyer (2015).

(7c) mass-marketed TV programmes,[44] and
(7d) innumerable motion pictures.[45]

For large sectors of humankind, it is only in these plural, diverse, and comfortably plainer contexts that humorous amusement and sadistic cruelty can show up openly and mix together to very different levels of intensity.[46] Besides, more or less morbid displays and mixtures such as these occur eminently—though, once again, not exclusively—in vicarious forms.[47] This is not to say that they are utterly innocent. Albeit typically fictional, these seemingly harmless vicarious forms cater themselves to a real appetite for evil.[48] Countless philosophers, theologians, scientists, and scholars of all stripes have often claimed it to be rooted very deeply within us.[49]

Some students of cruelty and cognate phenomena have argued that this appetite for evil has existed since the very infancy of our animal species (i.e., phylogenetically), if not also from the infancy of each and every person (i.e., ontogenetically).[50] Who, as a child, has not, say, laughed at TV episodes in which Wile Coyote, Sylvester, Yosemite Sam, Tom, or Jerry, got flattened by a steamroller, crushed by boulders, blown up by homemade rockets, or were otherwise mutilated, electrocuted, incinerated, pulverised, squashed, flayed, exploded, beheaded, quartered, and martyrised in the most imaginative if cruel ways?[51] Who, as a teenager, has failed to perceive the funny side of over-the-top videogames such as *Doom* and *Mortal Combat*?[52] Or of horror comedies such as Roger Corman's *Raven* and Tim Burton's

---

[44] "It may well be that we moderns have no time to march off to the public square to watch a hanging; we are too busy watching violent films and videos" (Portmann 2000, 139).
[45] McIntosh *et al.* (2003) provided many examples of violent comedy in US movies and argue that their increased frequency reflects higher levels of socio-economic insecurity in the populace.
[46] The body-centred mixture of humour and crude imagery is also reflected in common English parlance by phrases such as "splitting one's sides", "laughing until it hurts", "to die laughing", "to bust a gut laughing", etc.
[47] Potter and Warren (1998) argued that humour is used to disguise and trivialise violence on television, which is an effective source of affective arousal for the viewers. The blood is fake, but the excitement is real.
[48] The case of so-called "reality TV" lies between reality and fiction, and it often includes sadistic laughter. See, e.g., episode #2 of the 2020 *Netflix* series *We Are the Champions*, in which hooting crowds watch contestants cause themselves major discomfort, if not harm, by ingesting inordinate amounts of hot chilli peppers.
[49] Quite simply, there is no field of study of human behaviour without such voices.
[50] See, e.g., Baumeister and Campbell (1999) and Jones (2013). Cruelty fascinates countless people.
[51] As Colman *et al.* (2014, 1) concluded: "Rather than being the innocuous form of entertainment they are assumed to be, children's animated films are rife with on-screen death and murder."
[52] Markedly darker games certainly exist too, especially in the Japanese tradition of "hentai manga", i.e., comics, visual novels, video games, and animated movies portraying sexual "perver-

Beetlejuice?[53] And who, as a young adult, has failed to grasp the magnetic intensity of the grinning archvillains of Sergio Leone's spaghetti Westerns?[54]

As vicarious and even as fictional as these minor, perchance childish, pleasures may be, they too reveal, nevertheless, the titillation that cruelty can elicit within our psyche.[55] This is an observation that has been made repeatedly, and extensively commented upon, notably by Nietzsche and Freud.[56] Not to mention their larger and larger cohorts of intellectual emanations, epigones, emulators, exegetes, and effective evolutions.[57]

True enough, Nietzsche and Freud may not have watched colour movies, *Looney Tunes*, or played computer games, but both were probably circus spectators.[58] Under the big tent, clowns have unswervingly been (among other indignities): spanked, clubbed, punched, kicked, hammered, thrown into tubs of water, squirted in the eyes, and splattered in the face with sods, pies, and buckets of different liq-

---

sion", which is the literal translation of the Japanese "hentai" (Klar 2013, 121 f). However, it has been argued that this Oriental artistic tradition is fundamentally "parodic" in its unrealistic drawings and storylines (Klar 2013, 121). (See also Pratama, Gunarti, and Akbar 2017.) Then, we are led to conclude that *humorous features and gruesome ones can join hands* together.
53 Carroll (1999, 145–146) acknowledged this film genre, noting also how the mixture of horror and comedy may be as old as Romantic gothic literature (Carroll 1990, 241, note 24). As to over-the-top videogames, they corroborate Beattie's (1778, essay 2, 366) older claims on hyperbole *qua* commonest humorous technique.
54 See, e.g., Cumbow (2008). A satisfied grin is likely to be on the viewers' faces when vengeance, these films' leitmotif, is finally accomplished. We expect our readers to be familiar with these cartoons, games and films.
55 As seen, Freud (1960) and (1928) claimed all pleasures to be, at root, childish, including those of humour.
56 Recalled briefly in Chapter 1, a more thorough account of their views was developed in *H&C1*.
57 The amusement derived from artistic depictions of cruelty has been corroborated by scholarship at all levels (see, e.g., Shipka 2007). Moreover, while vicarious cruelty's activation of the brain's pleasure centres has been empirically recorded, no such direct physiological corroboration exists for the hypothesis that it may also be conspicuously cathartic, i.e., conspicuously purgative of our violent proclivities (see, e.g., Gentile 2013). The catharsis at play may nevertheless be there, yet grasped in patently mediated socio-cultural terms rather than in seemingly immediate biophysical or biochemical ones (we write "seemingly" because biophysical and biochemical notions are themselves symbolic creations of our psyche; as noted by Jung 1960–1990, vol. 9.2, 237, par. 376, even "the most elementary building-stone in the [modern] architecture of matter, the atom ... is an intellectual model"). More on these emotionally emetic (or laxative?) matters is said in *H&C3*.
58 As Stoddart (2000, 4) remarks: "Friedrich Nietzsche turns to the circus to find a figure – the tight-rope walker – to allegorise man's precarious journey of development as a crossing over an 'abyss'".

uids. All this, of course, in order to make generations of people laugh out loud and share the merriment, particularly children.[59]

Freud, who died in 1939, must have watched his share of film comedies, especially slapstick ones.[60] Since the age of nickelodeons, amusing motion pictures of various lengths have depicted a fantastic quantity of mishaps, mortifications, misunderstandings, misfortunes, and mauling that would certainly ruin a person's day, if not her entire life.[61] They include: vehicle crashes, knocks on the head, long falls down stairways and hillsides, cheating partners, terrible bosses, ungrateful sons and daughters, horrible neighbours, fierce pet owners, domestic pets turned into wild beasts, abusive policemen, sadistic judges, brutal jail mates, dumb friends, greedy clients, and much else.[62]

In the real world of ordinary partnerships, kinships, and fellowships, people get teased, whether tactfully or not, because of their errors, personalities, occupations, hobbies, origins, accents, social status, quirks, physical attributes, earthly possessions—or lack thereof.[63] The amusements at play here are not merely or inevitably vicarious. Villainous enemies are superfluous too. The "aggressive and oppressive" humour that today's celebrated Canadian novelist Margaret Atwood denounced *vis-à-vis* "keep-'em-in-their-place sexist and racist jokes" is by no means an abnormal fare inside all-white and all-male white-collar banking offices, all-ethnic and all-female blue-collar *maquiladoras*, mixed educational institutions, upper- and working-class sports clubs, traditional families, or homosexual couples.[64]

The closeness and intimacy that provides us with love, companionship, comradery and meaningful relationships can easily turn into oppressive enclaves whence it is hard, or impossible, to escape.[65] Buddies, colleagues, close relatives, closer partners, and closest siblings poke fun pitilessly and even incessantly at one another, and sometimes far more at one than another, in a display of the shrewd art of knowing where to bite, how to sting, what to hit, whom to include,

---

59 See, e.g., Ottinger (2004).
60 The masters of slapstick comedy embodied Addison's "true humour" *qua* facetiousness feigning seriousness; especially Buster Keaton, nicknamed "the Great Stone Face" (Oldham 1996, 8).
61 Matt Meese's fictional sportsman Scott Sterling reiterates online the slapstick tradition on the silver screen.
62 Freud was invited to star in a documentary; he declined (Trahair 2005). Footage of a dying Nietzsche exists too.
63 The available evidence suggests that, to a significant extent, our ancestors poked fun at one another for the same things that we still find funny today (Halsall 2002). Certain forms of humour appeal to the audiences of all ages, apparently, e.g., Aristophanes' and Plautus' rambunctious plays.
64 Atwood (2006), 132 (more on such jokes ensues in the next chapter). On the last example, see McCann (2011).
65 Being the fundamental social unit, families are also an obvious place for cruelty to occur.

whom to ostracise, when to pounce, where, how, and which buttons to push in order to provoke from the butt of the joke (i.e., the so-called "laughingstock") an appropriate pained reaction.[66] Then, once the desired reaction has been obtained, the initiators of the joke may cherish it alone or share it with an audience.[67]

With regard to spectators, competitive sports can offer the largest audience imaginable. Major football tournaments and Olympic games attract billions of spectators, thanks especially to the explosive media developments over the past century. Before the greedy and excited eyes of countless watchers, an inferior adversary can be teased, toyed with, taunted, and trashed.[68] Typically, all this grinding activity brings forth a gloating smile on the victor's face and on their supporters' too, if not a roar of satisfied triumph and a more or less fleeting sense of superiority.[69] (Such derisory behaviours can also be observed in other competitions with few or no spectators. Sneering humiliation likes an audience, but does not necessitate one.)[70]

With regard to corridas, animal blood sports, and other forms of bestial combat, challenge, and entertainment, whether legal (e.g., bull-riding, coursing, fox hunting, camel wrestling, select circus shows) or illegal (e.g., dog- and cockfights, rat- and badger-baiting, bear dancing), they all remind us that most competitive sports emerged from our remotest social and cultural customs in ages when interaction between humans and animals was far more routine than today.[71] These customs include, among other things, religious sacrifices, ritual hunts, unforgiving rural practices, and the soldiery's time-honoured traditions and violent games.[72]

---

[66] Comedic renditions of such abuses are portrayed in John Cleese's 1968 TV show "How to Irritate People".

[67] The more unequal are the initiator's social status and the butt of the joke's one, the more likely is the latter's self-defence to descend from "retaliation response" to "constrained silence", or even "total nonresponse" (Harvey 1999, 61). Echoing such concerns, Billig (2005, especially chap. 8) highlighted the audience's further humiliation of the joke's butt by "unlaughter", i.e., indifference to the rejoinders and/or other attempts at humour by the joke's butt.

[68] Pre-existing socio-cultural tensions contribute too, as explained in Miguel, Saiegh, and Satyanath (2008).

[69] In the 2019 Swimming World Championship, the gold-medallist Sun Yang uttered at the silver-medallist Scott, with a smile: "You are a loser." Scott refused to shake Sun Yang's hand, believing the Chinese athlete used illicit doping substances. Scott's belief was later proved true ("Sun Yang" 2020).

[70] Similar reactions can occur in individuals who simply *imagine* being in that position of superiority.

[71] Albeit illegal, bear dancing is still practiced in parts of Asia (see, e.g., D'Cruze et al. 2011).

[72] We write "unforgiving" to distinguish the gruesome rural customs (e.g., slaughtering animals) from the peaceable ones. "[A]griculture" may well comprise the latter too, arguably to such a point that Genovesi (1825, 313) celebrated this domain as the best 'school' for cultivating people's gentler

In some cases, the ancient mixture of sport and religion endures ostensibly in our present day and age (see, e.g., the so-called "Palio" that has been held in Siena since the Middle Ages).[73]

Across the centuries, having been institutionalised and modified in many respects, i.e., from the perspective of the manifest cruelty that they entail and allow for, all of these socially codified activities have gradually become less lethal, less gory, less life-threatening, more selective, more symbolic, i.e., more 'humane' and, declaredly, more "civilised"—although sometimes only moderately so.[74] Mirroring insights provided by Leacock, these controversial sports and energetic distractions might be a sign of remarkable moral progress. Specifically, Leacock compared them with the changed spectacles of the Western circus:

> The Romans liked to see a chariot and its occupant smashed in the circus; we prefer to see a clown fall off a trapeze. Our clown, poor creature, is the living symbol of our redeemed humanity, uplifted from cruelty to make-believe. Humor thus grew to turn on a contrast between the thing as it is, or ought to be, and the thing smashed out of shape and as it ought not to be.[75]

American football, rodeos, and physical sports such as wrestling and boxing may well represent today the lawful frontier that this process of civilisation has reached.[76] Hooliganism and dog fights, unlawfully, remind us instead of its primeval roots.[77]

---

inclinations and perpetuating a time-honoured socio-cultural enemy "of treachery, of cruelty, of war". Make hay, not war!

73 See Tourneur (1927).
74 See, e.g., Jewell (2012), 11–26.
75 Leacock (1935), 11. More on this positive interpretation of vicarious cruelty can be found in H&C3.
76 As G. Scott (1996, 48–49) wrote: "[T]he witnessing of flagellation was looked upon as an entertainment, and as such was popular among the society ladies of the day [... who would] go and see the delinquents whipped, much as today they might go to see a boxing match." The frontier at issue is porous, as vividly depicted by the former Canadian footballer, and current philosopher, McMurtry (1971, 42 and 58), in "Kill'em! Crush'em! Eat'em Raw!". See also Fiske and Rai (2015), who portrayed American football's violence as a broad metaphor of violent conduct.
77 See, e.g., Avgerinou and Glakomatos (2011). "Hooliganism" includes as well playful wanton violence and/or murderous romps, especially as perpetrated by small bands of people, e.g., throwing stones at passing cars on motorways, pointing laser beams at airplane pilots, and beating or burning homeless persons. These cruel pranks have a well-established pedigree. See, e.g., Dickie (2003) and (2011) on 18th-century England.

2.2 Commonplace Humour

> When you get older, 45 plus, men stop fancying you. Or put it another way, the men I fancy don't fancy me. I want a young man. I love beauty. So what's new?
> —Susan Sontag[78]

The widespread understanding of purported "humour" as that-which-is-conducive-to-laughter, if not merely to-smiling, was deplored by both Schopenhauer and Pirandello.[79] *Pace* their protestations, it is still commonplace in contemporary parlance and, given what they both wrote, so it seems to have been in their own day. Even a sophisticated and compassionate humourist such as Leacock admitted that "what one would call a humorous nature" is, prosaically, something "that would raise a smile, or even a laugh".[80] Logically then, *whenever* any direct or indirect entertainment is labelled by someone as "cruel" and, at the same time, it leads to risible amusement or satisfied grins in some quarters, then it is possible to talk of "humorous cruelty".[81]

Albeit empirically plausible and, as we have just reiterated, textually corroborated by one of Canada's most famous humourists, this logical possibility may still be too unprincipled from an aesthetic and/or moral standpoint, and/or semantically too equivocal, especially for the academically specialised reader perusing these pages—whether joyfully and amiably so, or with sudden pangs of frustration and

---

[78] As cited in Mackenzie (2000), par. 22. Sontag's remark touches directly on three standard themes associated with humour as well as with cruelty: ageing, middle-/old age, and sexual frustration. Indirectly, it acknowledges the notion, which was already tackled in *H&C1*, whereby beauty and youth should be regarded as forms of power (see, e.g., of how much effort, time and money are spent every year by men and women around the world to approach and/or retain traces of youthful beauty, whether by means of clothing, make-up, physical exercise, ointments, or surgery). The quote concludes by indicating wittily that these issues are *timeless* concerns, which can have clear reverberations onto humorous matters (see, e.g., Pirandello 1920 on age-mismatches *qua* comic trope). If one wishes to accuse Pirandello or Sontag of 'ageism', it is possible (see Chapter 2). In any case, these 'ageist' scenarios, whether comedically rendered or not, have been central to Western culture for millennia, from Graeco-Roman religious cults to Oscar Wilde's (1894, stanza 85) reference to the Phrygian myth of "Atys with his blood-stained knife" in *The Sphinx*. How many fat satyrs have chased swift young nymphs? And how many revered immortal goddesses have fallen in love with handsome young shepherds? Surely Susan Sontag lacked no company, though probably not the kind that she was hoping for in her middle age, *per* the quoted quip.
[79] Addressed in Chapter 1, a more extensive account of their views was provided in *H&C1*.
[80] Leacock (1913), 176 (a fictional dialogue).
[81] Who decides what is to be called "cruel" is not simple. Perpetrators rarely claim that they are being cruel, as debated by Baruchello and Hamblet (2004). Tellingly, Harvey (1999, 6–8) aims specifically at looking at humour from the oft-underplayed "perspective of the socially powerless" inside "nonpeer relationships".

2.2 Commonplace Humour — 169

the occasional flush of odious resentment.[82] Hence, to be adequately technical and severe, we follow in this section Regan's lead and, above all, Hallie's ingenious taxonomies of cruelty.[83] On that basis, we can now identify various cases of humorous cruelty that, at the very least, fit their articulate, thorough, reasoned, and scholarly interpretations of "cruelty" proper.[84] Subsequently, we are going to narrow further our focus and address two much more specific conceptions of "humour" proper, or "true humour", as dubbed by Schopenhauer and Pirandello. On this narrower basis, we finally proceed to reasoning chiefly about salient features of the "sentiment of the contrary" that the latter thinker claimed to lie at the core of the phenomenon of humour.[85]

As we do all this, we also engage with few representative instances of contemporary philosophical scholarship about "humour" proper, notably the highly representative contributions by John Morreall, Lydia Amir, and Jean Harvey.[86] We thus tackle intriguing issues arising from their studies and combine them with insights provided by other thinkers.[87] The scope of our intellectual navigation is then enriched and our philosophical diving goes deeper, casting light on the dark, cruel cavities of "humour" proper.[88]

---

[82] Naturally, we hope and expect the former set of reactions, but the latter is also possible. Unfortunately, there is no account for people's touchiness and bad taste.
[83] Presented in Chapter 1, a more extensive account of their views was provided in *H&C1*.
[84] See the second footnote of this second chapter.
[85] Schopenhauer and Pirandello provide the clearest, most vocal, most extensive, and least embarrassed criticisms of the commonplace understanding of "humour" proper. That is why we select them for the continuation and the conceptual narrowing-down of our study in the present chapter. They are the master-advocates of "true humour".
[86] Morreall and Amir are still alive and active. Harvey died in 2014. (One of this book's authors had the honour of studying under her guidance at the University of Guelph, Ontario, in the early 2000's.) Morreall and Amir are known primarily today as humour scholars. Despite enjoying academic fame chiefly as a feminist thinker, Harvey's best-known book, *Civilized Oppression*, deals with "humour" as such to a great extent. Different contemporary thinkers could have been selected, but these three philosophers' emphases on ethics, religion, and the dilemmas of human existence make their works particularly interesting for us.
[87] As the reader will see, considerable space is given to thinkers who were also noted humourists in their lifetime.
[88] As we explained in *H&C1*, we conceive of our own research as a form of intellectual seafaring and attendant aquatic sports, in line with Polanyi's (1962a and c) ideal of scientific and scholarly communities *qua* "societ[ies] of explorers". Also, the oblique reference to dentistry in the context of cruelty is not entirely casual.

2.2.1 Fatal Cruelties

Regarding the fateful cruelties that our species must endure, we can state with confidence that natural cruelty, as awful as it is, is also capable of making people laugh, sometimes heartily.[89] Let us reflect on four particular cases:[90]

(1) One of the oldest examples of *Schadenfreude* is to be found in Lucretius' influential poem *De rerum natura*, in which the Epicurean poet savours watching a vessel at risk of shipwrecking from the safe vantage point of the coast.[91] We do not know whether Lucretius smiled or laughed, given the terrible circumstances that he described.[92] Somewhat bizarrely, but also very much apropos, the 20th-century French philosopher Georges Bataille distinguished between a ship's "dismasting", which is "cruel", and the same ship's "sinking", which can be met with "laughter" and "a joyful heart".[93]

Be that as it may, deriving amusement from the observation of natural catastrophes bringing havoc onto other people is not an unknown phenomenon.[94] It is not even particularly rare. Today, satellite and cable news, tabloids, clickbait, and sensational journalism offer many examples of this human propensity.[95] As to Lucretius' morally culpable enjoyment of other people's perilous maritime circumstances, sailors themselves, while facing terrible storms, have been known to erupt into cheerful singing and/or fits of screaming laughter. In some way, these vulnerable hardies felt inclined, and were arguably more than willing, to defy the dooming forces of nature in a potentially last act of desperate yet headstrong

---

[89] As noted in Chapter 1, what kind of laughter may be elicited by a causal agent varies considerably, e.g., smiling, chuckling, tittering, giggling, chortling, cackling, snickering, sniggering, galdering, rasping, squirking, etc.
[90] Additional settings are tackled in our Chapter 3 and in *H&C3*.
[91] By "Epicurean" we mean here a follower of the ancient philosopher Epicurus, not an immoderate *bon vivant*. Portmann (2000, 41) tried painstakingly to distinguish between *Schadenfreude*, which is morally correct when evil people get their comeuppance, and "malicious glee", which is immoral. The distinction is logically plausible and was hinted already by Aquinas in his *Summa*. Yet it is impossible for us to know which feelings occur in a person's breast and to distinguish between the two. Portmann's viewpoint, in short, is God's own one.
[92] Scholars have been debating the degree of Lucretius' possible *Schadenfreude* for centuries (see, e.g., Prosperi 2015).
[93] As translated and cited in Amir (forthcoming). Because her book was an unpublished manuscript at the time of writing, we could not provide more detailed bibliographic information.
[94] See, e.g., Watt Smith (2018).
[95] See, e.g., Taras (2015).

rebelliousness, or in an equally desperate attempt to sustain morale before an insurmountable foe.[96]

(2) The same mocking, if not mirthful, reaction emerges in the face of challenging medical conditions, poor health, infectious pathologies, physical injuries, and mental illnesses.[97] So-called "black" or "sick" humour has accompanied plagues and epidemics since Boccaccio's middle ages.[98] It still occurs regularly among, and frequently appeals to, health professionals, and paramedics, among others.[99] Entertaining remarks have often been made by suffering people themselves, who can be as prone to laugh at their own circumstances as they are to cry about them.[100] Not to mention being laughed at by other individuals, which is possibly the most common form of humour in recorded history.[101]

For centuries, people disfigured, deformed, or disabled by genetic anomalies, grinding ailments, or grave accidents, have provoked as much fun as they have been able to inspire great pity.[102] In Western culture—and in Anglophone countries, in this specific lexical case—the "cripple", the "lame", the "blind", the "deaf", the "dwarf", the "scrofulous", the "mongol", the "spastic", the "hunchback", the "cabbage", the "vegetable", the "lunatic", the "thick", the "freak", and the "retard" have been a prosaic source of much amusement, including among these individuals and within these groups.[103]

---

[96] The latter instance is depicted in Melville's *Moby Dick* (2008–2017, chap. 119). (The reader should recall that the novel is based on first-hand seafaring experiences.)

[97] Given that medical categories, especially when relating to a person's genetic make-up and mental illnesses, are at least in part a social construct, Hallie's distinction between nature's "fatal cruelties" and human-made "violent cruelties" entails a large grey area, which reverberates in our own selection and discussion of representative cases (see, e.g., Casado da Rocha 2005; Hacking 1999, chap. 4; and Bridges 2014).

[98] Curiously enough, our book was written during the Covid-19 pandemic. As to our comprehensive use of "cruel humour", we are echoing the open-ended synonymity embraced by numerous humour scholars such as Vosmer (2022, 7; emphasis added), who wrote: "black humor refers to humor that is grotesque, macabre, ironic, absurd, satirical, gallows, scatological, pornographic, cruel, paradoxical, bitter, sardonic and insensitive, *or any combination of these*".

[99] See, e.g., Healy (2001). *H&C3* discusses in detail this form of humour as a coping strategy.

[100] See, e.g., Granek-Catarivas *et al.* (2005).

[101] Our remark about self-directed humour comes before the one about other-directed humour to reflect a little-considered truth: talking to oneself constitutes most of our talking (see, e.g., Fernyhough 2017).

[102] See, e.g., Barnes (1991).

[103] Politically incorrect and insulting notions carry the painful yet meaningful memory of this long history of derision and are often chosen pointedly by historians (e.g., Dickie 2011) and the derided themselves (e.g., Mairs 1986). Therefore, they should be listed *explicitly* here too, as unpleas-

Many ill, suffering, and disabled individuals have also been targets of foul pranks. These supposedly merry games included, not least in 18th-century Britain, walking the blind into walls, tossing dwarves, shoving cripples into ditches, thumping the feeble and the infirm, hitting hunchbacks on the hump, tripping the one-legged, and teasing the deaf and the poor-sighted.[104] Occasionally, these pranks caused serious bodily harm to, or even the death of, the beleaguered laughingstock.[105] Chillingly, these particularly unlucky victims should be thought of as the collateral damage of a long-tolerated popular form of entertainment that, in actual practice, extended beyond sick and disabled individuals. Pranks targeting the poor have been just as common, in fact, finding new instantiations in contemporary mass media too.[106]

(3) As anticipated by Sontag's opening quip, laughter can also arise with ease and frequency in the overlapping contexts of people's aging and old age. Both have been made fun of in countless cases, such as the stereotypical buffoons of the *Commedia dell'Arte*, e.g., Pantalone.[107] Numerous comedic, operatic, cinematic, and/or literary equivalents have then emerged thereof, e.g., Gogol's Pljuškin.[108] Male and female, old persons' features and personae have been the fodder of low- as well as high-brow humour since classical times, if not even before.[109]

As it happens, middle-aged men and women can make fun themselves of their own white or vanishing hair, stiffer limbs, decreased *libido*, ungainly skin, increasing fat deposits, and poorer eyesight, or of the convenient myths about the wisdom of maturity that they might cunningly nurture in order to appeal to younger part-

---

ant as they may read at first. Concerning a recent example of comedy making fun of the mentally impaired, see the 2008 film *Tropic Thunder*.
104 See Dickie (2011).
105 See Dickie (2011). We are left to speculate about what impact these pranks have on the victims' mental health.
106 Making the poor fight against one another for food or money is a cruel lark that the well-off have been indulging in since Homer's *Odyssey*. The 2002–2006 *Bumfights* film series is a late descendent of this ilk of pranks.
107 To boot, Pantalone was often represented as avaricious, effeminate, and a hunchback (see, e.g., Ellis 2009, 7–8 and 120–121). As to the younger comic character Zani (aka "Zanni", "Gianni", or, in English, "Zany"), Bierce (2000, 244) regards it as *the* progenitor of the humourist: "A popular character in old Italian plays, who imitated with ludicrous incompetence the *buffone*, or clown, and was therefore the ape of an ape; for the clown himself imitated the serious characters of the play. The zany was progenitor to the specialist in humor, as we to-day have the unhappiness to know him. In the zany we see an example of creation; in the humorist, of transmission."
108 Pljuškin is a character from Gogol's 1842 *Dead Souls* that is now a literary icon of avarice and senile obsessions, like Molière's Harpagon, Dickens' Scrooge, Dostoyevsky's Prokharchin and Verga's Mazzarò.
109 See, e.g., Falkner and De Luce (1989).

ners.[110] The elderly may then continue this humorous trend by self-satirising their baggy and wrinkly bodies, utter impotence and infertility, and/or various physical and mental incapacities, which can make death itself seem like a well-earned repose from otherwise unceasing conditions of discomfort.[111]

How and when people joke varies considerably, and so it also seems to matter very much whether the aging and the aged start cracking jokes or not, with whom, and under which specific circumstances.[112] At times, as Harvey remarked, a person's "self-respect" may be at issue in a humorous, nonpeer social setting.[113] As also noted by Bergson, whenever humour occurs, structured social games are afoot, in which the stakeholders' perceptions of relative status play a major role.[114] One thing is to be the person making fun of an alleged condition of inferiority among perceived equally inferior people; another is to be made fun of by an allegedly superior person because of that very same assumed condition of inferiority, which the joke's initiator does not share (yet or visibly, at least).[115] What is meant as a pat, then, can be experienced as a slap.[116] And which one is the act causing offence is, once more, a highly contextual and personal matter.[117]

(4) Laughter can mushroom in the face of death itself.[118] We do not know whether the dead can laugh.[119] We do know, however, that the dying have been capable of it.[120] The prospect of one's own demise, as daunting and as sobering as it may be to most individuals, does not result always and only in trembling, shocked

---

110 See, e.g., Baroncelli (2009), 136–137. This book showcases Baroncelli's mix of humour and philosophy, and its title is itself a pun on one of Lina Wertmüller's most famous films, the 1984 dark comedy *Mi manda Picone*.
111 See, e.g., the popular 2018–2019 Netflix series *The Kominsky Method* and the long-lived BBC Scotland's TV series *Still Game*, produced and broadcast in 2002–2007, 2014 and 2018–2019.
112 More on this point is also discussed in our Chapter 3 regarding social-group jokes and disparaging humour.
113 Harvey (1999), 73.
114 Presented in Chapter 1, an extensive account of his views was offered in *H&C1*.
115 See, e.g., Douglas (1968), whose anthropological analyses are based on Bergson and Freud.
116 The Milanese actor Diego Abatantuono (Baldini and Abatantuono, 2021, par. 9) stated that, back in the 1970s, "nobody took offense if called *terrone* [a derogatory term for Italy's Southerners]. It was a term that, in that setting, was as affectionate as a pat on the cheek. The tone establishes the offence. Today it is the opposite: words are stones, often taken out of context." Apparently, the derided changed the prevailing hermeneutical framework.
117 While a slap may be felt as an honourable challenge by a peer, a pat can be experienced as a patronising gesture.
118 Concerning mushrooms and death, a Russian proverb states: "All mushrooms are edible; some only once."
119 Merry ghosts populate, e.g., Pushkin's (1916) 1830 story "The Coffin-Maker".
120 See, e.g., Kinsman Dean (2007) and Marinoff (2020).

numbness, gravity, contrite preparations for the afterlife, or remorseful tears.[121] Perhaps it should or even ought to do so from a religious perspective. But people can be silly and/or sinful at any and every point of their lives, even on their deathbeds.[122]

As to the living and reasonably healthy individuals, who may opportunely or temporarily neglect the fact that they too are dying, there is no shortage of reported experiences, funny anecdotes, stage comedies, and/or comic films making fun of death and its ambience.[123] Whether competently or weakly parodied, no place is safe, no time is sacred, no theme is spared, no gravestone is left unturned: church rites, memorials, burials, wakes, funeral transportations, the purchase of urns, the scattering of someone's ashes, morgues, autopsies, the clothing and preparation of corpses, the incineration of corpses, ancient and modern embalming, the cryogenic freezing of terminal patients, critical surgeries, organ donations, organ trafficking, homicides, attempted homicides, manslaughters, suicides, botched suicides, successful slaughters, mass exterminations, genocides, the annihilation of the entire human race, the end of life on Earth, the end of the universe, and all kinds of fatal accidents.[124]

In the vast realm of fiction, even the borderline case of the so-called "living dead" has proven a fertile ground for comedies.[125] In the real world, instead, readers who may have attended a few mournful events should know themselves how funerals and similar sad occasions can offer ample and, inevitably, recurrent opportunity for amused sniggering among the participants as soon as anything unex-

---

121 See, e.g., Tritle (2015).
122 In Pietro Germi's and Mario Monicelli's 1975 comedy-drama *My Friends*, the main character is shown dying and playing a last practical joke on his confessing priest, to whom the former mutters hilarious nonsense mixed with seemingly plausible words—one of the signature pranks in the film (see Canby 1976).
123 See, e.g., T. Scott (2007). Cruel humour is dealt extensively within the ensuing Chapter 3.
124 Since 1985, the bestowing of *Darwin Awards* to people who caused their own demise by feats of conspicuous stupidity or gross short-sightedness has been a global example of humour about death, which thereby continues the assumedly primitive cruel laughter directed at someone else's suffering or departure from life. This *post-mortem* mockery of stupidity goes on, despite the likely fact that no one is immune from committing some dangerously stupid action during his or her life, as is sarcastically yet perceptively discussed in Cipolla (2011), whose basic laws of human stupidity were recently formalised by Tettamanzi and da Costa Pereira (2014, 1) where we read: "One should not be misled by the humorous tone of Cipolla's essay into thinking his theory cannot be taken seriously. In fact, in most cultures, humor and jokes are a way to tell truths that hurt without breaking social norms or sounding irrespectful". Still, one irony looms large, given Cipolla's scepticism about aprioristic theoretical economic modelling and his preferential emphasis on empirico-historical research (see Boldizzoni 2011).
125 See, e.g., the 2004 horror comedy *Shaun of the Dead*.

pected takes place—albeit with the frequent exclusion of the dead person him-/herself and/or of his/her closest relatives and friends.[126]

2.2.2 Self-Mockery

Making fun of one's own genetic or medical condition has long been known to scholars and laypersons alike.[127] Recently, it has developed into a successful entertainment industry.[128] Notably, disabled comedians have been growing in number and in popularity in several Western countries.[129] In their affirmation as appreciated entertainers, they have been following the trail of other successful artists emerging from minority groups that had been traditionally the targets, rather than the initiators, of popular humour and offensive pranks, e.g., black comedians in the US, female comedians in Italy, Muslim comedians in France, gay comedians in Mexico, and Indian comedians in the UK.[130]

In this respect, we can only wonder about the lots of potentially great humourists that socio-economic inequalities prevented from blossoming. As noted a long time ago by the famous Italian pedagogist Maria Montessori:

> [T]here are [wo/]men of genius who are destined to feel their inborn intelligence suffocating under the cruel tyranny of existing economic conditions, which punish pauperism with obscurity and hold protection and favours at a distance. A thousand various conditions of our social environment hinder powerful innate activities from finding expression and attaining elevated social positions.[131]

What is more, on today's artistic scene, these traditional 'butts' of jokes have been allowed to make humorous remarks about themselves, one another, and 'normal' people at large that the other members of society are no longer making or are not

---

126 Many have argued that the closer to home a joke lands, the less funny it feels.
127 Self-mockery as a means of "self-consolation" for the historically downtrodden was discussed, representatively, in Sibony (2009), 31. Grignard (2009, 174) made analogous remarks about "camp ... humour" among gay men as a means of self-protection in contemporary homophobic communities marked by "hostility, cruelty, and sadness". Critchley (2000, 31) went as far as interpreting Freud's conception of 'humour' as being entirely based on a mechanism of "self-mockery" (i.e., the *ego* mocks the *super-ego*) and functioning as an "antidepressant".
128 As remarked already with regard to disease, the line separating natural and human cruelties is far from clear.
129 See, e.g., Lockyer (2015).
130 See, e.g., Gimbel, Chandra and Zhan (2020).
131 Montessori (1913), 252. Consistently with LVOA, poverty-reduction strategies are of paramount importance.

expected to make.¹³² This, at least, applies inside refined and cultured social circles.¹³³ Somehow, behind the assumption of equality, there lies a subtle inequality, which grants long-oppressed, long-ridiculed subjects the singular warrant to enjoy *de facto* greater freedom of speech in public spaces than their alleged right-thinking, polite peers do.¹³⁴

There are at least three possible explanations for this peculiar social generosity, which would appear to contradict, at least *prima facie*, the oft-voiced claims about a "dictatorship of political correctness" in contemporary Western societies.¹³⁵

(1) This greater freedom of speech, so subtly accorded by contemporary social custom to minority comedians, is an indirect and ingenious way to pay moral compensation.¹³⁶ Current societies, aiming at fostering peaceful coexistence, may well have to make amend for centuries of discrimination and ill-treatment.¹³⁷ As Harvey wrote in *Civilized Oppression*, "institutional apologies", collective "expressions of regret", and other public acts of contrite self-humiliation, especially if conveyed in full "sincerity" by the "privileged members of society", are truly meaningful, particularly to the victims of past abuses and to their heirs.¹³⁸

---

132 See, e.g., former US President Donald Trump, who caused an uproar during his 2016 presidential campaign by ridiculing a disabled reporter, Serge Kovaleski (see, e.g., Carmon, 2016). Matthews (2018, title) would probably argue, however, that Trump's "Triumph of Cruelty" should be found in the immigration policies that he promoted.
133 See, e.g., Garcia (2014).
134 This greater comedic freedom can be parodied itself, as discussed in Weaver (2011).
135 As stated, e.g., by the novelist and songwriter Francesco Guccini, interviewed by Laffranchi (2021). The former's concerns return in *H&C3* within a more detailed account on political correctness as such.
136 The likeliest legal criteria in this connection should probably be "satisfaction", "rehabilitation", and "guarantees of non-repetition", for neither "restitution" nor pecuniary "compensation" can apply to cases of legal remedy for damages of such magnitude and complexity (see Novic 2020, 642).
137 Albeit conceding the plurality of plausible and/or possible terminological definitions of "humour", Bouquet and Riffault (2010, 22) emphasised: "being able to laugh at oneself", "making life's tragedy more livable", "social correction", "social intelligence", and "a way to gaze upon the world". Three of these five recurring themes show clear potential for personal *and* collective empowerment or, at least, viable collective coexistence.
138 Harvey (1999), 131–139. See, e.g., Coetser (2020, 121–122) on the "land acknowledgment" that was made by "[t]he organiser, as well as a number of speakers" at the "[2018] Environmental Philosophy Conference at the University of Guelph", where Harvey taught for many years.

2.2 Commonplace Humour — 177

These symbolic actions are, *in nuce*, public acts of self-mortification.[139] As such, they are said to: lead to growth in the "moral awareness" of "institutions" and "the community at large"; facilitate reconnection "between the victims and their local community"; help prevent future repetitions of the past abuses; build "new and more appropriate relationship[s]" between estranged groups and individuals; enable "reconciliation"; re-establish the "proper status" of people that had been condemned, sometimes for centuries, to "third-rate membership in the moral community"; and validate these people's position "as honest and accurate recounters of events".[140]

(2) Insofar as conspicuous inequalities in wealth, status and power persist and grow within society, this greater freedom of speech is a disingenuous and/or blunt social construct. While inappropriate obscenities are being uttered freely inside a theatre, or on a TV screen, by seemingly empowered representatives of long-ostracised minorities, the members of the privileged majority can laugh *with* them *in foro externo*, while also laughing *at* them *in foro interno*. In this way, the members of the privileged majority keep alive, and may derive joy from, the memory, if not the full realisation, of the effective subordination of these specially enfranchised representatives and, *a fortiori*, of the groups of people that they represent.[141]

Accordingly, the self-restraining, right-thinking, and polite moneyed patrons belonging to the well-established majority can relish the prospect of feeling like the feudal lords and feudal ladies of old who allowed their jesters to utter all sorts of crude remarks, even about their own entertained and embarrassed—if not enraged—*seigneurs* and *seigneuresses*.[142] On the one hand, these patrons can enjoy the intrinsic fun provided by the jesters' wit and sense of humour—as the contemporary American philosopher Chris A. Kramer rightfully remarked, even "adversarial audiences" can appreciate "subversive humor" directed at

---

139 Forms "of self-torture" extending "into self-sacrifice" have long been known and associated with "purificatory" aims, "invest[ing] blood with a sacredness that may account for the origin of cooking" (Marett 1932, chap. 5, par. 1). Self-mockery itself, under this respect, may be yet another tool for aiming at deeper values, and a cunning tool to boot. As the Slovenian philosopher Slavoj Žižek (2012) noted, self-mockery can be a convenient signifier whereby to soften the seriousness of the underlying signified message and, by so doing, facilitate its being taken seriously rather than rejected, for whatever reason (e.g., being outmoded, overdemanding, melodramatic, etc.).
140 Harvey (1999), 131–139.
141 Humour's touchy social mores *vis-à-vis* ethnicity and gender were discussed in Lockyer and Pickering (2005).
142 Bayless (2020) showed that jesters were not alone in using humour to mock the elites in Medieval Christendom. As to "patron", its etymology is *pater*, i.e., the Latin term for the powerful person *par excellence:* the *pater familias*.

them.¹⁴³ On the other hand, the same lords and ladies can *ipso facto*, if not *ipso dicto*, display great magnanimity *vis-à-vis* the jesters' daring repartees.¹⁴⁴ As a consequence, the patrons can also feel very good about themselves and their socially visible generosity.¹⁴⁵

In the stately language of today's sociology, contemporary patrons of comedic acts, i.e., the contemporary analogues of feudal lords and ladies, can enjoy being "the culturally privileged [who] activate their cultural capital resources" in dedicated settings, such as "the Edinburgh Festival Fringe".¹⁴⁶ Still, especially but not solely in the medieval context, everyone involved remains aware that the witty and rude jesters come from an inferior social station and can be reminded of their low rank in an instant.¹⁴⁷ For all the tongue-lashing which the witty jester may employ, the noble matron has always held the leash and whip in her tight grip.¹⁴⁸ However empowering it may seem or be, there is always some degree of risk that is involved in speaking *in loco perdentis*.¹⁴⁹

(3) The greater freedom of speech at issue is part of the infinite variations of the many extant social games, which include "carnivals" whereby rules are loosened, so that the attendees may be free to relax and show traits that, normally, are kept under lock and key.¹⁵⁰ This possibility extends to all ranks.¹⁵¹ Freud's and the Freudians' interpretations of all humorous phenomena as socially permit-

---

143 Kramer (2020), 153.
144 See, e.g., Čapaitė (2003).
145 As seen in Chapter 1, Nietzsche was very keen on revealing the self-serving character of alleged moral agency.
146 Friedman (2011), 347.
147 On jesters' low status see Pietrini (2010). Albeit rewarded, sometimes lavishly, jesters knew well where they stood in the social hierarchy. Not even wealth could erase the mark of social inferiority, as exemplified today by the most successful "porntropreneurs" (Pezzuto 2019, 30f). Unless "legal" (aka "general" or "social") justice is in place, and in a very broad way, "commutative" justice cannot eliminate all prior disparities (Utz 1994, par. 5.2.6).
148 Overseeing domestic discipline, the alcoves of the Roman *dominae* were commonly adorned with whips, rods and other instruments of corporal punishment (see, e.g., G. Scott 1996, 61).
149 Without having to hereby kill the joke, the reader who is not familiar with Latin may wish to check the meaning of "perdens, perdentis" and that of the common-law expression "in loco parentis".
150 Even the pessimist Leopardi (n.d.a. [1898], 2528) stated: "All is foolish in this world but fooling around. All is worth laughing about but laughing about everything. All is vanity but beautiful illusions and pleasing frivolities." We discuss further these 'carnivals' and their psychic functions in the concluding chapter and, above all, in *H&C3*.
151 See, e.g., Waterman (1998). Bakhtin's works are the key references in all recent studies on the carnivalesque.

ted circumstances, in which ordinary self-control and self-repression are reduced and circumvented, point neatly in this direction.[152]

Theatres, cinemas, football stadiums, pub-crawling rituals on Friday and Saturday night, gay pride parades, street protests, bull sessions, and weed- or alcohol-fuelled parties among close friends and relatives may all be examples—large and small—of today's carnivals.[153] In these social contexts, expected conventions are suspended, at least to a noticeable extent, and are temporarily replaced by others, which unleash, to some degree, those 'animal spirits' that civility aims normally at repressing almost by etymological definition.[154] Repression cannot be total and incessant, lest we socialised humans harm ourselves to the point of most severe neuroses and psychoses. (Indeed, as seen in Chapter 1, Shaftesbury had already observed as much with regard to our inherent propensity for raillery.)[155]

Special societal occasions have been repeatedly created and maintained, sometimes across many centuries, allowing for animality or, in a less beastly tone, for uncivil conduct to come to the open and be discharged in ways that the community accepts. As the US-based contemporary philosopher Lauren Olin noted in a recent study of these phenomena: "sexual and hostile humor are … widely appreciated", insofar as they act as "representations of social relationships and norms … remain[ing] robust even in the face of evidence that the rules they prescribe are sometimes broken".[156] Under such socially-established propitious conditions, uncivil conduct can and may in fact be elicited, experienced, experimented with, enjoyed, encouraged, engineered, and exploited by the community in which it unfolds.[157]

For instance, in the Nordic and the Baltic countries of the late 20th and early 21st centuries, binge-drinking sessions on Friday and Saturday nights have been leading regularly and recurrently conspicuous scores of intoxicated, half-conscious, and, eventually, half-naked horny women and men into beds, sofas, public toilets,

---

152 Again, an extensive account of their views was provided in *H&C1*, in which we also addressed Cassirer's echoes of Bakhtin's popular, anti-authoritarian festivals of the Middle Ages and insolent Renaissance comedies.
153 See, e.g., Pearson (2012) and Saint John (2004).
154 See, e.g., Davetian (2009).
155 See Shaftesbury (1732) and (1999), which we tackled in detail in *H&C1*. Interestingly, Baier (1993, 454 and 457) noted how "Shaftesbury's and Hutcheson's" approach inspired David Hume's, such that "self-derision" was seen by him a means of *self*-correction, whereas "mock[ing] gently", instead, one of *other*-correction.
156 Olin (2020), 66.
157 See, e.g., Skey (2006).

and/or other convenient places.[158] After sufficient exertions and ejaculations, the eventual continuation of the species has thus been enabled, as haphazardly and as chaotically as the whole process may have been implemented by its unconscious, or barely conscious, participants.[159]

This alcohol-fuelled mating ritual has been kept alive among people who, under normal circumstances, would be too afraid of inappropriateness and attendant social frowning were they to seek romance by sober public courtship that could be deemed archaic, patriarchal, offensive, ridiculous, and/or embarrassing.[160] In one of the many curious and, in all probability, cruel ironies of Western cultural and social history, countries in which spirits and drunkenness had been regarded as the devil's instruments now allow their young inhabitants to be intoxicated and indulge in casual sex rather than being sober and, God forbid, démodé, if not even sexist.[161]

Under the third perspective, minority comedians and their colleagues, as free and as bad-mannered as they are allowed to be, can be creatively grasped as inhabiting yet another socially constructed "carnival" whereby special performative spaces are set in place to reassert the extant powers by permitting these powers' temporary derision.[162] In these peculiar social oases, privileged audiences can enjoy impropriety and, concurrently as well as harmlessly, can be chastised mildly for the terrible sins of their fathers and forefathers who cruelly oppressed the comedians' fathers and forefathers.[163] Both sadism and masochism, under a Freudian psychoanalytical perspective, could then be said to find room to subsist, advance, and be enjoyed, given the liberty for self-expression that comedians happen to have on such unique, empowering occasions.[164]

---

[158] See, e.g., Part et al. (2011). Other pre-festive evenings in the countries' official calendars should be added. Also, many other countries in the world display similar trends and traditions, e.g., Scotland.
[159] This sort of behaviour is not being implicitly recommended hereby.
[160] See, e.g., Abrahamson (2004). More on these matters is said in *H&C3*.
[161] We write "young" because these are the inhabitants who stand a reproductive chance. Alcohol-fuelled escapades can be observed among older people too.
[162] The time-honoured existence of carnivals does not always protect their participants. Higher powers can intervene and operate reprisals, whether arbitrarily, episodically or predictably.
[163] See, e.g., Seizer (2011).
[164] Four comedian-audience sadomasochistic relationships were explored in Tarachow (1949, 215–216), using the matrix of comedian and audience, on the one hand, and victim and perpetrator, on the other, i.e., "the masochistic comedian", "the story-teller", "the practical joker", and "the sadistic comedian".

Whichever of the three explanations outlined in the preceding subsection may best apply to the case of disabled and minority comedians, insofar as risible mocking takes place, then humorous cruelty occurs, sometimes multi-fold.[165]

2.2.3 Human Cruelties

Mockery, whether cast as "wit, humour" or even "self-irony", is part of a "shame morality" that aims at securing social "peace and cooperation" by embarrassing people in public.[166] Mocking, at a deeper level, is an act whereby people find delight in someone else's painful misfortunes, or even in their own.[167] As pleasant and as conducive to laughter as this experience may be, mocking is, among other things, a malicious deed, and it has been recognised as such since Plato's day.[168]

Albeit favouring the more humane and progressive "true humour", which many of his own writings aimed at exemplifying, Leacock himself wrote, *qua* true child of his politically incorrect age:

> The Red Indian exulting and jibing over his tortured victim ... the scoffers that stood and "mocked" around the Cross; the taunts of the hanging judges; the sneer of the infidel; the brutality of the critic—all these are mockery, a thing debased and degraded from what it might have been. Too much of the humor of all ages, and far too much of our own, partakes of it.[169]

Characteristically, in the penal sphere, mockery has been indispensable for the implementation of various types of punitive forms of "public shaming", such as the "stocks and pillory" of old, which have reappeared today in novel and creative var-

---

[165] As seen, Hallie's (1969) taxonomy distinguished between the "fatal cruelties" of nature and the "violent" ones that humans inflict on each other. That is why we entitle the ensuing subsection "Human Cruelties".
[166] Baier (1993, 438 and 456): Kant's "guilt morality" is the private adjudication by one's own conscience.
[167] Dennett and Ronell took self-mockery as paradigmatic, also of the *modus operandi* of philosophy, as noted by Amir (2019, 82), as exemplified by Democritus, Seneca, Montaigne, Shaftesbury, Nietzsche, and Richter.
[168] *Pace* Plato's or Aristotle's concerns, the much larger realm of mockery has certainly made ample use of such misfortunes (see, e.g., Dundes and Hauschild 1988, on "Auschwitz Jokes").
[169] Leacock (1935), 11–12. In what is still the most extensive critical study of his work as a humourist, Lynch (1988, ix–x and 5) described its quintessence as the expression of a socially concerned "tory humanism" that tried to avoid radicalism while advocating reformism (i.e., the "Middle Way") without ever challenging the fundamental values of "tolerance", "social responsibility", and compassionate kindness.

iations, e.g., "perp walks" in front of TV cameras and paparazzi.[170] Not to mention the serialised and televised voyeuristic humiliations operated by means of so-called "true-crime documentaries".[171] Whether chiefly castigatory or primarily entertaining, these recent variations exemplify how mockery is just *one* of the many and largely avoidable cruelties with which humans afflict one another, and themselves—the most notorious ones being associated with sadism.[172]

2.2.3.1 Sadism

In terms of *active* sadistic cruelty, Sade's libertines embody one of the greatest feats of villainy that can be encountered in real life.[173] What can be worse than people deriving pleasure, oftentimes of a sexual nature, from their victims' imprisonment, enslavement, torture, rape, degradation, humiliation, mutilation, or murder? [174] Especially when the victim is innocent of any crime.[175]

In fictional depictions, sadists of this ilk are marked by the mad laughter of the evil foe. It is like the mark of truly satanic, unrepentant malice, and of the most chilling inhumanity.[176] In historical reality, a victim's wretched laughter may actually be the case. Consider, for one, the Han dynasty's favourite method of torture, whereby someone could be tickled, perhaps to the point of death.[177]

Causing and rejoicing in other people's suffering has normally been seen as utterly immoral, grossly indecent, and so perverse as to be almost unnatural. Significantly, in Western history, an analogous strong reproach has been directed at any mirth arising from making sentient animals suffer needlessly. This was exemplified in a well-covered historical "episode" concerning a band of "printer's apprentices in Paris during the 1730's", who

---

170 See, e.g., Kaiser (2002).
171 See, e.g., Stoneman and Packer (2020).
172 Self-mockery, especially if complicit, exemplifies "self-punishment and self-humiliation", which occur in all cultures around the world, as shown in chap. 10 of G. Scott (1996, 100).
173 Wishing to express all the violence, oppression and decadence of Mussolini's regime, Pasolini adapted Sade's *120 Days of Sodom* for the big screen in 1975 and portrayed the latter's libertines as inveterate fascists.
174 Some, e.g., G. Scott (1996, 163), have claimed sadism to be purely sexual in nature.
175 See, e.g., Rudorff (1968).
176 Mad it may be, but it is laughter nonetheless. Moreover, it can be widely appreciated. In the 20th century, the gifted US actor Vincent Price became world famous for his Mephistophelian laughing.
177 Institutionalised and routinised, torture may be a case of sheer brutal cruelty. Historically, though, considerable sadism accompanied its experience and application (see, e.g., Cobain 2012 and G. Scott 1996).

gleefully collected all of the cats ... [making noise] on the roof and howl [of the printing shop where the apprentices worked and slept] ... and proceeded to massacre them by placing them in sacks and smashing them with iron bars. They then gathered the cats, some still barely alive, and held a mock trial. The cats were pronounced guilty, given last holy rites, and hanged on a small gallows... During the following days, the apprentices joked about the event and reenacted the scene in mime at least twenty times. Years later one of the participants noted that it was the most hilarious event of his life.[178]

Such extreme forms of cruelty, albeit recorded in history, can be so shocking to the minds and so unbearable to the hearts of decent people that these very same forms end up being deemed nothing but abstract philosophical fictions without basis or symptoms of an underlying sickness that is unrecognised and misrepresented by sensation-seeking chroniclers and commentators. They are, in other words, strange intellectual 'ghosts', i.e., misconstructions of unfortunate behaviours awaiting acceptable scientific explanation and/or apt social resolution. No sane person can be really this wicked, can she?

Yes, maybe she can. If anything, it has repeatedly been argued by Darwinians and Darwinists of all stripes that the origins of laughter itself must be found in the primitive pleasures experienced by our oldest ancestors, triumphing over an adversary and sinking a club (or some other primeval yet effectual murderous implement) into the latter's thick but brittle skull.[179] A variation on this particularly unpleasant image was used by Leacock himself:

Our laughter originated ..., it would seem, long before our speech as a sort of natural physical expression, or outburst, of one's feeling suddenly good, suddenly victorious. It was a primitive shout of triumph. The savage who cracked his enemy over the head with a tomahawk and shouted "Ha! Ha!" was the first humorist. Here began, so to speak, "the merry ha! ha!", the oldest and most primitive form of humor. It seems odd to think that even today when we give our acquaintances the "merry ha! ha!" over their minor discomfitures, we are reproducing, true to type, the original form of humor. The Germans would call it *Ur-Humor*. But we don't need to; we can call it simply the archeocomical or if we like the paleoridiculous... The original humor was expressed by actions, not by words. It was, and is, represented by progressive gradations as victory, cruelty, teasing, horseplay, hazing, practical jokes and April Fool.[180]

---

178 Robert Darnton's 1984 *Great Cat Massacre and Other Episodes of French Cultural History*, as reported *verbatim* in Favazza (2011), 18. Additional points about sadistic humour can be found in Chapter 3.
179 See, e.g., Rapp (1951).
180 Leacock (1935), 12. Behind Leacock's remarks hid countless 'serious' studies of allegedly "primitive" humankind as prone to all kinds of cruel behaviours, as still reiterated in allegedly "modern" societies by criminals and, as the great Austrian writer Robert Musil seemed particularly intrigued by, children (see Gess 2022, chap. 3 and 8).

Fun, perchance surprisingly to some or our readers, could be a direct descendant of blood-soaked fangs.[181] This is certainly the conclusion that we are to reach if we pay heed to the many extant exercises in evolutionary elucidation of laughter, not just Leacock's reflections on the subject, and bring them to bear on numerous cases of cruel behaviour observed in rather ordinary settings and situations. In practice, gloating over a defeated rival in a confrontation allows us to pursue active sadistic cruelty in everyday life.[182]

As a sad yet telling fruit of direct experience and observation, corroborating remnants of the primordial satisfaction described by Leacock can be witnessed in the present day without too much effort.[183] These fruits occurring, moreover, under less ghastly circumstances than in our primitive past, e.g., whenever beating an opponent, whether in a physical confrontation (e.g., a bar fight) or in a verbal one (e.g., a public debate).[184] Prevailing and prevarication may well be, in other words, close cognates, and not just semantically. As such, they can also be the springboard for levity.[185]

Instead of avoiding a confrontation, confrontational individuals shall seek it consciously, perchance proactively, and they may conceivably enjoy the agonistic experience *per se*, as well as its positive outcome, if any is to be obtained.[186] Win-

---

[181] As Davenport (1976, 172) writes: "We laugh in cruelty when our enemies fall." Besides, "shrieking", "screaming", "roaring", and "shouting" are all synonyms of "laughing", and "fits" and "convulsions" are associated with it too. Commonplace humour, especially in its most uncouth forms, is a reminder of our predatory side.

[182] The pursuit of confrontations made McMurtry (2013a, 277) define the human being "homo contendens".

[183] Nietzsche's and, even more explicitly, Bataille's self-styled "philosophy of laughter" would confirm laughter's connection with this primordial element of our psyche, inasmuch as the senseless, selfless abandonment of laughter is deemed akin to the ecstasies of childish play, unashamed eroticism, and utter anguish. All of them: lie beyond full articulation in intersubjective language; point to the prelinguistic abilities that we share with 'lower' animals; and make the fundamental energies of the universe present and palpable to the subject—as masterfully discussed in Amir (forthcoming). Some scholars interpret Bataille's work as disclosing important features of humour (e.g., Newall 2012). However, neither 'classic' modern thinker wrote much of "humour" proper. Both spoke instead aplenty of "laughter" and, in the latter's case, also "parody" and behaving like a "clown" (Amir, forthcoming).

[184] See, e.g., Infante and Rancer (1982).

[185] Hazlitt (1845, 23) claimed spleen to be easily vented onto others by means of humour, which seemingly legitimises and aptly facilitates such evil actions by dressing them as playful and/or innocuous jests. The same spiteful operation can be performed in non-humorous ways, e.g., destructive attacks cast as constructive criticism, hateful aggression wrapped as pious correction, malevolence disguised as tough love, or pettiness sold as propriety.

[186] See, e.g., Burbank (1994).

ning the confrontation, in other words, crowns the whole risky effort with the sweet taste of victory.[187] At that point, smiling or laughing with satisfaction can be relished in an open and unobstructed manner, whether or not this glorious moment is then accompanied by the further shaming, abusing, punishing, degrading, and/or humiliating of the defeated rivals.[188]

Morally speaking, this potentially humorous and enduring type of active sadistic cruelty may come across as dubious, if not blatantly objectionable.[189] Hence, in order to avoid being accused of seeking out foes to fight, overcome, and gloat over, bellicose and argumentative individuals are likely to prefer couching their actions in terms of, say, constructive criticism, self-righteous payback, justified challenge, messianic revolution, emancipatory fighting, or even progressive satire.[190] Indeed, as regards the last item, the 20th-century literary critic Joseph Bentley had no qualms calling this social positioning "sadistic", suggesting that, *pace* all the moralistic public reasons for his or her mordant oeuvres, "the satirist" is "like the benevolent schoolmaster ... [who] gets more pleasure from the caning than from whatever virtue may result".[191]

As Sade's libertines, Nietzsche's blonde beasts and everyday sadism exemplify, self-interested rationalisations, if not even plain self-deception, can easily be at work whenever people wilfully explore, and purposefully engage in, activities causing others to suffer, including tomfooleries and pranks, both of which can be just 'a bit of fun'; can't they?[192] Caustic commonplace humour is no exception.[193] Nor are higher forms of humour, at least not necessarily.[194] In particular, as re-

---

[187] On this physiologically recorded taste, see Chambers, Bridge, and Jones (2009).
[188] See, e.g., Matsumoto and Willingham (2006).
[189] To pre-empt this kind of judgement, Burbank (1994, 1) opened her book by stating: "In these pages, I shall argue that women's overt aggression is, in some circumstances, a positive, enhancing act. I shall also argue that when we deny women their aggressive possibilities, we potentially diminish their being."
[190] See, e.g., Bentley (1967).
[191] Bentley (1967), 389 (the powerful icon of the caning schoolmaster is derived from Bertrand Russell's works). As S. Stein (2000, 26) added: "Satire is the most gratifyingly bellicose of the *belles lettres*."
[192] More on this matter is said in Chapter 3.
[193] Responsive cruelty and other forms of cruelty, including active sadistic cruelty, are not mutually exclusive. While pursuing a morally justifiable end, e.g., national liberation, a person may find opportunities to indulge in sadistic pleasures, insofar as the enemies are imprisoned and become utterly vulnerable to their freedom-fighting tormentors, who may then acknowledge the sadism at play or rationalise it away, e.g., *qua* deserved punishment.
[194] Faktorovich (2020, 149–151) wrote: "Fiction has the benefit of being a falsehood, so it is impossible to fully separate intentions from outcomes and from hidden meanings or if the opposite was

gards humorous cruelty, moulding their agency as virtuously retaliatory, i.e., as an instance of Hallie's "responsive cruelty", the very same people who seek out confrontations to be fought and, hopefully won, can also engage in the titillation of cruelty with a lighter heart, whether they are truly justified or not, at least in a moral sense.[195]

Bellicose, quarrelsome, and argumentative individuals may even lead themselves to believe wholeheartedly that they are doing good, letting virtue triumph over vice, promoting knowledge and understanding, or that they are fighting for a just and noble cause.[196] While meditating on his own professional experiences among analytic philosophers, the late Italian ethicist and humourist, Flavio Baroncelli, stated: "Toleration is the most widespread and deeply cherished value; that is why at scholarly conferences, rather than exchanging pleasantries and veiled criticisms, we show a propensity to hit each other in the spots where it hurts the most."[197]

A touch of sadism, under this humorous perspective, might turn out to be a fellow traveller of the many self-styled Good Samaritans of the world.[198] Or, for that matter, of those open-mindedly and open-heartedly "democratic ... analytic thinkers", who alone seem to know "what the meaning of a term should be, were common people not as stupid as they are".[199] Behind the witticism, a perplex-

---

intended... Satire, tragedy and misogyny might look about the same, and ... be distinguishable based on the reader's leanings."
195 Determining the criteria for, and the positive application of, such a justification, is *not* easy. Whether "political terrorism" should be deemed "irrational" or not, for instance, is discussed by Kirk (1983), 41.
196 Although such eagerness for fighting may take the form of satire, it can also become an enemy of humour, e.g., campaigns against 'sexist' comedians in the UK or 'immoral' ones in countries implementing Sharia law. We discuss such troubling cases in *H&C3*.
197 Baroncelli (2011), 18–19, where he also poked fun at the "priestly posturing" of "Continental philosophers".
198 Baroncelli (2011), 18. The Good Samaritans and the analytic philosophers so parodied, place themselves above the pitied individual/s, standing *de haut en bas*, like the ancient Roman satirists. Besides, as Margaret Thatcher in/famously observed, the parable of the Good Samaritan teaches us that owning wealth is a blessed thing. Had the Samaritan been poor, he could have not helped anyone at all. Pareto (1935, par. 1809) too had stated as much long before her: "If the Franciscans are to live by alms, there must be other people to provide the alms; and if they are not going to take thought for the morrow, there must be people to do that thinking for them. They can be improvident only if they have a society of providents to live in, otherwise they all starve and the game is up."
199 Baroncelli (2011), 18. Aware of this perplexing penchant among many of our colleagues, we prefer giving up on the tempting idea of producing sharp, learned, brilliant, universal linguistic definitions of "humour" and "cruelty".

ing yet intriguing 'Hallian' epiphany is possibly revealed.[200] Wherever there is cruelty, there appears to be ample room for paradox.[201]

2.2.3.2 Blurred Borders

At the close of the 20th century, Hallie commented many times on the frequent blindness of allegedly ethical agents with regard to their own cruel motives, which can be, in any case, inextricably intermixed with the openly acknowledged ones, hence making the full ethical appraisal of the situation extremely thorny—and so also any legal and/or political evaluation of the same situation.[202] For instance, as regards the US penal institutions of his day, Hallie wrote:

> A policeman, a judge, or a warden could justify a monstrous retaliation for a little violation by putting on his doctor's hat and uttering the vague epithet: "This is for your own good". With all this power and with these humane intentions, the criminal justice establishment could hide from themselves and from the public at large the shameful passions that were actually dictating their decisions, passions like fear and disgust with regard to blacks, Spanish-speaking people, the poor.[203]

Consistently with the first paradoxical manifestation of cruelty that Hallie categorised and we discussed in Chapter 1, his ethical investigations and reflections remind us that even the most well-meaning moral and social agents can end up causing avoidable, terrible pain, especially if they are totally unaware or proudly

---

200 In truth, several epiphanies might be contained in this witticism. For one, in *H&C1* and *H&C3*, this humorous remark of Baroncelli's is used to corroborate the notion that conceptual-linguistic polysemy may be inevitable.

201 One such cruel paradox affects also Baroncelli's (2011, 18–19) humorous take on his own colleagues, at whom he often poked fun for their frequent lack of humbling reflexivity. In our experience, though, it is among common people, not philosophers or intellectuals, that we retrieve the starkest examples of that widespread and deep-reaching superstition whereby men and women, whether young or old, *genuinely* believe that their particular understanding of reality is reality itself, i.e., the thorough neglect of the fact that they could be *wrong*.

202 Hallie (1985c), 42. Anscombe's (1963, 11, par. 6) intention-revealing question, "why are/were you doing that?", is seemingly obvious and easy to grasp, it reassures common sense, but, psychologically, it scratches the mere surface of our motives. Whether one subscribes or not to psychoanalysis, our psyche *is* a deep and vast domain.

203 Hallie (1972), 674. "[T]he monstruous" can easily turn into a source of mirth, for it shares with "the humorous" the tendency to challenge "human cognitive limits and limits of humanity itself" (Boryslawski 2020, 256).

unreflecting about their possible 'dark' inner urges and cruel proclivities.[204] Sometimes, this occurs on a massive scale, without the responsible agents ever questioning the actual goodness of their motives and/or the moral adequacy of the chosen means.[205]

As commendable and as recommendable as seeking to do good may be for each and every one of us, the possibility of grave error, including producing a mistaken assessment of one's own role and/or true intentions, remains an unsettling part of the picture.[206] Apart from humorous contexts, the aggressive yet well-intentioned commitment of freedom fighters, heralds of justice, and other committed activists have recurrently facilitated and, ultimately, led to cruel outcomes in the most diverse socio-historical settings.[207] Some of them, moreover, have been so peculiar as to be able to reveal strange, profound, ironic cruelties affecting the human condition. Let us consider here two such settings.[208]

2.2.3.2.1 Burning Out-Laws

The first one is that of Tomás de Torquemada and his much maligned Spanish Inquisition. Mentioning Torquemada in a book discussing laughter and humour might seem bizarre.[209] After all, nobody expects the Spanish Inquisition.[210] Howev-

---

[204] Ironically, a reverse version of it can also be identified, i.e., the possibility of positive goodness arising only in the context of evil-doing: "[W]hen there was no visible crisis, the lives of the people showed few signs of solidarity" (Hallie 1993, 8).
[205] Many serious pundits' justifications for NATO's wars in the 1990's and 2000's—e.g., redressing past injustices, emancipating women, and promoting human rights—constitute suitable examples of this psychological phenomenon, as well as another instantiation of the paradoxical character of cruelty studied by Hallie (1969). (See also Levene and Roberts 1999 for other example of well-meaning slaughters in our world's bloody history.)
[206] E.g., Hillman (1995, 56) on cruel "literalist" moralising, as discussed in *H&C3*.
[207] Several examples of sadism by self-styled freedom fighters, i.e., the Afghani mujahedeen, were reported by Gnad (2012, 91). This is a novel based on journalistic and other eye-witness reports collected in that country during the 1990's, when the Taliban seized power. One stands out, i.e., the so-called "Raqs-e-morda" or "dance of the dead", in which a platoon of armed men would stop a random car at a roadblock, seize the driver, behead him, pour boiling oil into his neck, play loud music, and enjoy the show of his decapitated body 'dancing' about while they clapped and laughed as well. This macabre "dance" was recorded also in Bitani (2014).
[208] Whereas Hallie's first paradox returns in *H&C3*, the two chosen settings are unique to *H&C2*.
[209] The grisly context of torture does not destroy completely the space for humour. As evoked by a graphic bas-relief on top of the main doorway into Genoa's Saint Lawrence cathedral, the martyred saint is said to have uttered to his torturers who were literally grilling him: "I'm well-done on this side, now. Turn me onto the other one."
[210] This Pythonesque statement hints at the secular mindset that we and our readers possess *qua* children of the 20th and 21st century. The Inquisition's premises, rationale, and aims are foreign, if

er, there is a simple reason behind it. Torquemada and his implacable torturers, according to the records available to us, were engaged in pursuing that which Hallie would dub "responsive cruelty".[211]

Torquemada and his fellow inquisitors saw themselves as responding, with the greatest zeal, to the most terrifying criminal *and* spiritual threat against the sole institution providing the one and only true path to eternal bliss, i.e., the Catholic Church.[212] In their era, the terrifying threat at issue was being posed by the misguided, possibly satanic—hence dreadfully dangerous and inherently powerful—cruelty of heretics, miscreants, and unredeemed or unredeemable heathens.[213] In a nutshell, the inquisitors embodied most patently Livy's famous sentence: "*crudelitatis odio in crudelitatem ruitis*" [you plunge into cruelty by hatred of cruelty].[214]

The inquisitors' practical aims and methods were, indisputably, different from those of many other, modern and possibly more fashionable self-styled heroes of that which is just and noble, including, logically, the confrontational individuals about whom we have written in the previous subsection. Similarly, the degree and the gravity of the responsive cruelty at play are also blatantly divergent. There is no doubt whatsoever that the 15th-century Spanish inquisitors stand out for their confident reliance on extreme severity. The blood and the suffering that they caused are the stuff of horror movies—and of black legends.[215]

This appalling ugliness is probably why any justification for the actions of Torquemada and his colleagues sounds implausible to today's secular readers. How can they not be ranked and reviled as a bunch of fanatical clerical sadists?[216]

---

not preposterous, to most of us. However, some religious zealots in certain regions of the world may not walk a too far-removed path even today.
211 See, e.g., the 'revisionist' Vélez (2020).
212 See Vélez (2020).
213 See Vélez (2020)
214 Livy (1898), book 3, chap. 53, sec. 7.
215 The Inquisition's infamies and their alleged culprits are often mythical. When researched—e.g., by Taparelli (1851, 614–615)—we read the victims of "the cruelty of the inquisition … instituted by Ferdinand of Aragona" in 1478 to be, five years later, "298", whose killing Pope "Sistus IV condemned … in his 29 January 1482 letter", instructing "Torquemada" to get "the severity and … the victims … reduced".
216 The moral standards "of the Middle Ages" were cruelly peculiar, as noted by the anticlerical Pareto (1902–1903, vol. 1, 237): "the cruelties of the Inquisition were in no way in disaccord with those of the rest of penal legislation … [and common] people were in agreement with the Inquisition". Besides, echoing Smith's utilitarian acceptance of vast historical "cruelties", the liberal Pareto (1914, 229–230) stated, e.g., on "the [Legatine] Inquisition's origins": "we must confess that the ills of [France] were considerably less severe … had it fallen under the Cathars' virtue-worshipping

As Chesterton commented apropos of animal cruelty, people must not lump together things that are clearly dissimilar:

> If the dog is loved he is loved as a dog; not as a fellow-citizen, or an idol, or a pet, or a product of evolution. The moment you are responsible for one respectable animal, that moment an abyss opens as wide as the world between cruelty and the necessary coercion of animals. There are some people who talk of what they call "Corporal Punishment", and class under that head the hideous torture inflicted on unfortunate citizens in our prisons and workhouses, and also the smack one gives to a silly boy or the whipping of an intolerable terrier. You might as well invent a phrase called "Reciprocal Concussion" and leave it to be understood that you included under this head kissing, kicking, the collision of boats at sea, the embracing of young Germans, and the meeting of comets in mid-air… [T]he moment you have an animal in your charge you soon discover what is really cruelty to animals, and what is only kindness to them.[217]

Pace the great Chesterton, our reference to Torquemada is not outlandish. Dog owners are not alone in being familiar with—and sometimes failing to recognise—the threshold separating the use of "necessary coercion" from "cruelty" proper. Jurors, insurers, masseurs, dentists, surgeons, parents and referees, among others, know this too, occasionally at the expense of their income, reputation, liberty and/or career.[218]

These moral agents also know that pain, whether physical or psychological, is sometimes necessary, and that mistakes can be made in its selection, application, and termination. They realise that harm ensues when someone is committed to an allegedly benevolent course of action, along which mistakes may be made—grave ones too. They also appreciate, or should know, that this possible harm admits of degrees, while remaining harmful in any case. Even so, they are willing to take the risk.[219] These people are, in essence and somewhat ironically, *responsible* persons who do not shirk from their ethical and/or professional duties. And as the Austrian

---

yoke". At the same time, ironically, Pareto (1935, vol. 4, par. 430, note 2) deemed Pufendorf "cruel to the poor animals" for "not let[ting] them have a natural law in common with man".

217 Chesterton (1958), 148–149.

218 Of course, there are also individuals who shirk from their duties for the sake of, say, income or success. See, e.g., Poutoglidou *et al.* (2022) on fraudulent, deceitful and even cruel conduct among medical researchers.

219 It may be a token of cruel humour, but the inquisitors were actually patient and quite thorough. As Reich (1953, 68) noted: "It took eight years to get Giordano Bruno to the stake; it takes only a few hours to put hundreds of innocent men and women to the wall today", i.e., in many parts of the world in the mid-20th century. Modern technology and modern administrative structures can truly work dark wonders.

Nobel-laureate economist Friedrich Hayek observantly conceded, under sinister conditions, "cruelty may become a duty".[220]

Occasionally, these actors might recognise that, now and again, the plausibly guilty agents—themselves too, hypothetically—may not be aware of the harm and/or of the degree thereof for which they are responsible and, therefore, they may disagree, whether mildly or wholeheartedly, with the accusers who state instead that harm has in fact occurred and/or that it is still occurring—these accusers being the agents' victims, more often than not. Entering and wallowing in a veritable can of worms, all manner of lawyers, psychiatrists, journalists, historians, and forensic experts have specialised in determining who is right and who is wrong in these contentions, or in trying to do so, or, in yet another cruel irony, in sounding veritably professional and most credible whenever talking or writing about it in a public forum.[221]

Whatever harm should be eventually detected or considered probable, under such diverse and variously nuanced circumstances, the original goodness of the motives of all these morally responsible agents can still be profoundly analogous in nature, if not identical, including the motives of the scary Dominican friars that were once busy burning heretics and witches at the stake.[222] Thus, in a striking passage on the proper penal discipline to be reserved to tried-and-sentenced witches, the 16th-century French polymath Jean Bodin, who has been celebrated for centuries as an early herald of religious and political tolerance, wrote candidly: "there is no penalty cruel enough to punish the evils of witches, since all their wickednesses, blasphemies, and all their designs rise up against the majesty of God to vex and offend Him".[223]

---

220 Hayek (2001), 154. In this case, Hayek was chiefly concerned with the systemic cruelty of his century's totalitarian regimes, and notably communist Russia and fascist Germany.
221 Our readers find themselves in the same position *vis-à-vis* the cases that we present in our book.
222 While the burning of heretics had been, albeit sporadic, among the Church's lawful punishments since the early Middle Ages, the burning of witches appeared *de facto* only as of the 15th century (see Kors and Peters 2001, 113–118). *De jure*, drawing on centuries of technicalities about forms of divination and sorcery inherited from Roman law, Pope Alexander IV issued in 1258 a decree addressing this issue and commanding the clerical inquisitors to pursue crimes of witchcraft if and only if it could be proved that they were conducive to heresy.
223 Bodin (2001), book 4, chap. 5, 205. Such a stance must sound bizarre to those of us who live in a thoroughly secular West, devoid of God as much as of angels, immortal souls, demons, and Satan. Whether the loss of all such traditional religious beliefs is a sure antidote against all cruelty is uncertain. Baudelaire (1988, poem 29) worryingly remarked: "Dear brothers, when you will hear someone boast the progress of the Enlightenment, do never forget that the finest trick by the devil is to persuade you that he does not exist."

2.2.3.2.2 Burning In-Laws

An arguably analogous paradoxical tension between presumable yet inscrutable good motives and intolerably bad actions across blatantly unequal specimens of "aggression and cruelty" ranging, say, from "from mothers-in-law burning their daughters-in-law because of dowry disagreements to women stealing each other's boyfriends", was retrieved in our century's America by Phyllis Chesler, who is a proud "feminist psychotherapist", the founder of the Association for Women in Psychology, and the author of *Woman's Inhumanity to Woman*.[224] No scary Catholic inquisitor of old, then; nor a pyromaniac witch-hunter.[225] As Chesler stated:

> It helps to understand that in these non-Western countries where you have mothers-in-law dousing daughters-in-law with kerosene for their dowries and we say "how shocking", we have a version here. You have here mothers who think their daughters have to be thin, their daughters have to be pretty and their daughters need to have plastic surgery and their daughters have to focus mainly on the outward appearance and not on inner strength or inner self. It's not genital mutilation but it's ultimately a concern with outward appearance for the sake of marriageability.[226]

What drives such a relentless motherly concern? Is it unadulterated "aggression and cruelty", or some misguided conception of the good? Which inhuman fallen angels hide inside those human, maternal bosoms? Alas, we have no answers. No univocal and absolutely certain conclusion can be ascertained in these matters, in our judgement. The range and character of human motives is opaque, if not fundamentally impenetrable. As observed by Edith Stein, the noted German Jewish philosopher, Carmelite nun, and martyred Catholic saint:

> As is well known, we civilized people must "control" ourselves and hold back the bodily expression of our feelings. We are similarly restricted in our activities and thus in our volitions. There is, of course, still the loophole of "airing" one's wishes. The employee who is allowed

---

[224] Chesler (2002a), pars. 1, 9 and 16.
[225] Chesterton (2008, par. 2) offered an alternative exculpation: "The Church did, in an evil hour, consent to imitate the commonwealth and employ cruelty. But if we open our eyes and take in the whole picture, if we look at the general shape and colour of the thing, the real difference between the Church and the State is huge and plain. The State, in all lands and ages, has created a machinery of punishment, more bloody and brutal in some places than others, but bloody and brutal everywhere. The Church is the only institution that ever attempted to create a machinery of pardon. The Church is the only thing that ever attempted by system to pursue and discover crimes, not in order to avenge, but in order to forgive them. The stake and rack were merely the weaknesses of the religion; its snobberies, its surrenders to the world. Its speciality—or, if you like, its oddity—was this merciless mercy; the unrelenting sleuthhound who seeks to save and not slay."
[226] Chesler (2002a), par. 17. See also Chesler (2002b).

neither to tell his superior by contemptuous looks he thinks him a scoundrel or a fool, nor decide to remove him, can still wish secretly that he would go to the devil.[227]

As Hallie himself wrote, "revolt" can be "mental, that is, internal".[228] But who is in the right position to gauge it and assess its moral and/or political value, and how? Whenever one is supposed to grasp what truly lies inside people's heart, it is probably the case that only an omnipotent God, or perhaps a more prosaic psychoanalyst, can figure it out with solid certitude.[229]

2.2.3.2.3 Burning Laughing-Stocks

A light heart accompanies another manifestation of the same cruel 'Hallian' paradox, which consists essentially in doing the worst by having the best intentions; or, less demandingly, in doing something bad by seeking something good. This time, though, we are back into the context of commonplace humour. Some burning continues here too.[230]

Specifically, we invite the reader to consider a well-meaning person who, at a social gathering, wishes to prove herself humorous and have the guests laughing in the aisles.[231] Steeped in a sexist, racist, or bigoted culture, she may be following a standard form of conduct, which is time-honoured and only occasionally challenged by variously named "radicals", "zealots", "boors", "pedants", "Bible thumpers", "Mackerel snappers", "PC fascists", and other "oddballs" living at the fringes of the social mainstream to which this person and most other party guests belong. This individual will therefore start making scorching jokes or blistering remarks directed at a certain person or group of persons.[232]

---

[227] E. Stein (1989), 52. In 1942, Edith Stein and her sister were gassed to death in Auschwitz by the Nazis (see Ruiz Scaperlanda 2017).
[228] Hallie (1954), 25.
[229] Saint Paul Apostle argued for the former (Rom 2.1–11). Westerink (2012, 117), citing Calvin, wrote that Lacan, if not Freud himself, argued for the latter—deeming our conscience, *en passant*, "the most cruel of all executioners". We can only speculate about human motives upon the basis of our experiences, *in primis*, and the fallible scholarly and discordant scientific sources accessible to us. No easy solution is at hand, in our view.
[230] Let us recall once more Leacock (1935, 11–12) listing together: "The Red Indian exulting and jibing over his tortured victim ... the scoffers that stood and 'mocked' around the Cross; the taunts of the hanging judges; the sneer of the infidel; the brutality of the critic—all these are mockery, a thing debased and degraded from what it might have been. Too much of the humor of all ages, and far too much of our own, partakes of it."
[231] Both authors of this book have witnessed such occasions and behaviours.
[232] Pranks, even when not so nasty as those listed in Dickie (2011), can be even more scathing, though they too can be animated by the same jolly motives, i.e., having "just a bit of fun",

Inevitably, the targeted person or group of persons will end up feeling bad—notwithstanding, in a patent cruel irony, all the joyful laughter that is now bursting around her/them, if not because of her/their feeling bad.[233] Furthermore, with her jokes or remarks, which the jest's initiator deems to be fundamentally innocuous, this well-meaning person might even be reinforcing, unconsciously and unintentionally, a prolonged and unjust intersubjective set-up whereby certain individuals or groups are the regular targets of just such jests and become, *a fortiori*, the pained victims of burdensome belittling.[234]

On the one hand, initiating and pursuing the mocking act suggests active *sadistic* cruelty. If the guests laugh hard, it is because the jokester is being competently tough on the chosen laughingstock. The former knows where, when, and how to strike the latter. On the other hand, insofar as the aim of the mocking act is general merriment and the means are deemed innocent by all who matter, the initiator of the mocking act might be guilty of active *brutal* cruelty instead. The hardness at play would then be a hardness of the heart, analogous—hence, not identical—to the way someone can be said to be hard of hearing.[235] Plausibly, the border between these two types of cruelty is blurred or "fuzzy", *per* Regan's taxonomy.[236]

When distinguishing between types of cruelty, in fact, Regan stated: "Passive behaviour includes acts of omission and negligence; active, acts of commission... Both active and passive cruelty have fuzzy borders... But ... once ... cruelty is present ... there are paradigms nonetheless".[237] Being able to distinguish between sadism and brutality in all cases would imply knowing with confidence, at the very least, whether the agent has a self-gratifying intention to hurt the victim (i.e., sad-

---

which large numbers of bystanders laughing at the victim's plight would only confirm to be so (Attenborough 2014, 138).

[233] "The presence of good motives alone cannot ensure that the actions or emotions of a person will be moral" (Portmann 2000, 172). As seen before, Kozintsev (2010) was also aware of this perspectival and affective mismatch.

[234] Quoting psychologist Naomi Weisstein, Harvey (1999, 12) referred to "caste, class, race, and sex inequalities". Analogously, Krebs' (2010, ii and 11) white, male, Anglophone interviewees claiming to use "disparagement humour in a purely sarcastic way" were said to maintain "colonial" oppression in Canada, or "the whitestream".

[235] Far from being an uncouth form of reasoning, analogical thinking is a useful intellectual tool in all sophisticated cognitive endeavours, including today's formal and empirical sciences (see, e.g., Helman 1988).

[236] Regan (1983), 197. Summarised in Chapter 1, a richer account of his views was offered in *H&C1*.

[237] Regan (1983), 197.

ism), as well as whether s/he is hurting the victim solely in pursuit of another goal (i.e., brutality), such as social order and law-abidingness.[238]

2.2.3.2.4 Behind All the Smoke

In the hypothetical case of the social gathering that was just discussed, such a goal would mean the visible gaiety of the vast majority of the guests at the party.[239] This knowledge of the initiator's intentions may not be accessible, perhaps even to the agent him-/herself, for s/he may be acting unreflexively, customarily, and/or be engulfed by self-deception.[240] The two forms of cruelty could also coexist and reinforce each other, e.g., active sadism fuelling the excitement of the mocking act *per se* and passive brutality making it possible for the jest's initiator to enjoy the amusement resulting from the accomplished mockery. Once again, God alone or a gifted psychoanalyst might be the only entities who could peer into a person's heart and measure her true motives with compelling exactitude.[241]

Grasping people's intentions and blaming culpable agents, as surprisingly commonplace as these two activities are—in daily conversations, on social media, in academic writings—are thorny domains, in all likelihood. There is a conceivable phenomenological explanation for this curious duality, which may count as yet another cruel irony of the human condition, including its humorous aspects.[242]

---

238 Similar fuzziness may arise in connection with distinguishing between 'active' and 'passive' sadism (e.g., a policeman cracking peaceful demonstrators' skulls for fun and an observer's enjoyment of the gruesome show) and/or between 'active' and 'passive' brutality (e.g., a policeman beating a peaceful demonstrator and most citizens' indifference to such a habit). We refer to police brutality (or sadism) as a token of cruel behaviour because of George Floyd's murder and related trials at the time of our writing these lines (see, e.g., Poulos 2021).

239 From a strictly utilitarian perspective, mocking successfully select individuals and/or minorities can be a moral act and rule, for it secures adequate pleasure to many, even across generational time, while paining marginally the few, e.g., Europe's Jews, America's Indigenous Peoples, the handicapped. As Rosen (1990) observed, John Stuart Mill himself was among the earliest critical voices expressing concerns about the possible justification for mistreating minorities under the premises of Benthamite utilitarian ethics.

240 See, e.g., Trivers (2000).

241 We insist on the non-transparent nature of motivation because, as noted in *H&C1*, it is far from obvious that we can determine with any certainty whether a person is purely in a "paratelic state" or not (A. Roberts 2019, 116).

242 Concisely, while empiricism focuses on *what* makes things dis/appear and/or what can be done with them (e.g., the biochemistry of recurring nightmares and their pharmacological suppression), phenomenology focuses on *how* things dis/appear and/or what we 'see' in them (e.g., dream amplification in archetypal psychology). Interestingly, subatomic physics and phenomenology have eventually converged on the notion that there is no sharp distinction between *subject* and *object*, insofar as the former, *inter alia*, establishes what can be a token of the latter and in which

While any of us attends *from* people's motives *qua* part of the countless subsidiary details at hand, in order to attend *to* their actions *qua* focal objects of our attention, the former set of psychological drivers is seemingly obvious.[243] When instead we shift our attention and try to grasp the actual motives themselves, these psychological drivers become far less transparent.[244]

(1) The mystery resulting from such a *Gestalt* shift is ordinarily shrugged off given, first of all, the ultimate inconsequentiality of most actions by most people under most circumstances.[245] Humorous conduct, moreover, is typically approached as something 'light' and of little importance, unlike, say, ponderous academic pursuits, commercial interests, bodily health, sexual satisfaction, socio-political justice, or positive family relations.[246]

(2) Secondly, little seems to have to be said, or thought of, *vis-à-vis* any individual's exact motives, intentions and/or reasons, as long as his/her behaviour adheres, in the broader context of prevailing social conduct, to the expected norms. That is to say, as long as most citizens respect the law, most players abide by the rules, most spouses stay faithful to each other, most children listen to the teacher, most soldiers obey their superiors, most employees stay productive and subservient, and/or most consumers buy enough of the advertised goods.[247]

---

form (e.g., 'light' as a wave or a particle), while the latter, even when it is conceived of as a mystery or an unknown agency (e.g., a yet-undiscovered efficient cause), limits that which the former can achieve (e.g., the inescapable vital needs for food and sleep) and affords the former opportunities and resources that we can make use of in an immediate, instinctive manner (e.g., fruits ripe for the picking; see Gibson 1986). Moreover, in a sort of parallel rendition of the layers of unconscious depth examined by Jungian psychology in the last century, the phenomenological tradition has kept alive the notion of different levels or modes of awareness, which contemporary neuropsychological research is laboriously rediscovering on its own (see, e.g., Budson *et al.* 2022).

243 See especially Polanyi's (1962c) *from-to* phenomenology, presented in detail in *H&C1*.
244 See *H&C1*. As far as humour is concerned, these shifts of focus can be used to obtain comic effects in at least two ways: (1) by 'zooming in' and catching an incongruous subsidiary detail (e.g., a person dressed as a dinosaur in what was grasped initially as a silent crowd waiting for a subway train); (2) and by 'zooming out' and placing the initial focal point in a surprising setting (e.g., the same person in a jungle where actual dinosaurs live).
245 We mean no disrespect. This inconsequentiality applies to us too.
246 Nothing prevents these serious domains from becoming objects of laughter, though, if someone is so inclined.
247 About the last example in the list above, see the pioneering work pursued by Galbraith (2007).

When conspicuous deviations occur, and/or other matters of genuine or alleged importance arise, the mystery is duly examined.[248] Depending on the specific case and on the ends being pursued, Catholic confessors, trained judges, Jungian psychotherapists, forensic consultants, motivational coaches, carefully selected juries of peers and/or seasoned legal experts, keen psychologists, and even deep-searching ethicists *à la* Hallie can be called upon at some point, and in some capacity, in order to determine the actual motives, intentions, and/or reasons that may have been playing out, as far and as plausibly as possible, and all in the name of some standards of 'normalcy' and/or tacit socio-cultural expectations.[249] The results that appear at the end of these analyses, and whether they are universally convincing or not, are empirical as well as theoretical issues that have been keeping multiple cohorts of experts and countless interested persons rather busy for centuries, including many philosophers.[250]

2.2.3.3 Blame

However light the heart of the mocking person, all cases of humorous mockery are instantiations of the superiority theory.[251] As criticisable and criticised as this theory may be, "superiority" is still a sensible umbrella-term under which a host of analogous behaviours pertaining to commonplace humour can be subsumed, such as putting down, teasing, satirising, mortifying, scoffing, dismissing, etc.[252] Those who don't get this point, or disagree with us, are therefore either ignorant fools or stupid asses. (In case you did not get it, this is a silly joke exemplifying the theory at issue.)

Whether taking place in actual or fictional conflicts, a domestic or even academic setting, and even in the absence of any open conflict whatsoever, all mock-

---

248 The influential 20th-century Marxist thinker Herbert Marcuse (1970, 213) did something of this kind when tackling the very Polanyian issue concerning the relationship between abstract concepts and particular experiences, as well as the broader theme of the inherently symbolic nature of the human animal (see *H&C1*). Interestingly, the word "cruelty" comes into play therein: "The substantive universal intends qualities which surpass all particular experience, but persist in the mind, not as a figment of imagination nor as more logical possibilities but as the 'stuff' of which our world consists. No snow is pure white, nor is any cruel beast or man all the cruelty man knows—knows as an almost inexhaustible force in history and imagination."
249 This thorny issue resurfaces in some of the modern socio-scientific studies examined in Chapter 3.
250 See, e.g., M. Smith (2017).
251 See, once again, Leacock's (1935, 12) vehement blasting at "mockery, a thing debased and degraded".
252 For a standard contemporary critique of this theory, see, e.g., Morreall's many essays and books.

ing behaviours establish, inevitably and necessarily, a hierarchical relationship. The ways in which this mocking can ensue are most diverse, and can be as simple and direct as an insult (see our silly joke above) or as subtle and indirect as an intellectual duel. As the renowned American philosopher Gerald Dworkin tellingly wrote: "I have been in philosophical arguments which reminded me of a Scrabble game. Words were placed on the table with no connection to those already out, no meaning appeared, and the sole purpose seemed to be to maximize points scored."[253]

Whether based on pre-existing hierarchies of another kind, or being an *ad hoc* and a very transient one, this hierarchy is such that the enjoyer of the specific humorous occurrence revels in looking *de haut en bas* at the joke's butt.[254] Generally, the 'laughee' is expected to suffer in some way and to some degree, even when s/he may not be present at the mocking scene.[255] In addition, if the butt of the joke complains and/or tries to counter the ongoing belittling, s/he is liable to be victimised further by means of, say, sarcasm, horselaugh, name-calling, and sardonic humour.[256] Alternatively, s/he can be openly ignored, disdainfully side-stepped or manipulatively gaslighted.[257]

This morally questionable feat of victimising victims by means of sarcasm, name-calling, ridicule *et similia* can occur at all levels and in all provinces of human agency and affairs. In the context of international financial relations, for instance, the contemporary British sociologist Dennis Smith commented on the intentional and prolonged

> [h]umiliation ... [in] the case of the reluctant bailouts requests made during the Eurozone crisis by the so-called "PIIGS"—hardly an innocent acronym—and the cuts in government spending forced on them by the European Union. Requests for help often followed several days of denial and were normally treated by the politicians who made them, or at least by

---

[253] Dworkin (2020), 240.
[254] "[T]reating others as inferiors" is always a form of "social cruelty", according to Andrea Sangiovanni, as quoted and discussed in Floris (2020, 408), who argued that there are circumstances in which hierarchical attitudes and conduct are justified because of genuine superiority/inferiority (e.g., parent-child relations, competitions).
[255] A satirist and an audience can gang up in attacking an absent third party (see, e.g., Tarachow 1949). The social status and the relations of the mocked person/s can be damaged also *in absentia*, as exemplified by malicious gossip, which seldom laughs in the victim's face. Harvey (1999, 54) addressed this harm as part of people's "communication mechanisms" that may not always translate into physical and/or psychological pain and yet cause harm by way of reduced opportunities for employment, mental growth, joy, romantic love, self-respect, etc.
[256] Harvey (1999), 54.
[257] Harvey (1999) confirms this consideration, which we base however on repeated direct experience.

their domestic parliamentary opponents, as admissions of weakness and failure. There was a strong implication in some foreign media comments, especially in North Europe, that the "PIIGS" had been exposed as unworthy ... reckless and irresponsible,

even if the 2008 crisis was not of these countries' making, but of the private banking sector's at large and, especially, of the world's biggest creditors.[258]

Dealing with the moral complexities of daily social interactions, Harvey listed six ways in which "blaming the victim" materialises.[259] All six of them can involve commonplace humour.[260] In some cases, they can also give rise to twisted, unsettling, and bitter ironies:[261]

(1) "There is in fact nonmoral harm, but then the victim is inappropriately 'blamed' for it"; e.g., making fun of male car-crash victims who drove so-called "small-penis" cars, without there being any "evidence of neglect or ... nonmoral failing on their part".[262] Namely, on the sheer basis of a negative stereotype about men driving powerful vehicles.[263]

(2) "There is in fact moral harm (harm involving a moral wrong), but then all accountability of the actual agent is dismissed by simply denying there is any harm at all"; e.g., men's claims of being the victim of sexual harassment or domestic violence being derided and dismissed as factually impossible and/or "making false accusations".[264]

(3) "There is in fact moral harm, but then all moral responsibility of the actual agent is dismissed by the claim that the harm is nonmoral (for example, a nat-

---

[258] Dennis Smith (2014), 84. A representative account of commonplace humour's uses and abuses in diplomacy and international relations can be found in a recent issue of *Global Society* (2021) devoted entirely to humour.

[259] Harvey (1999), 80.

[260] The reader must keep in mind our earlier warning regarding our looking at things from unusual and uncomfortable perspectives, so as to reveal instances of cruelty and/or humour that could easily go unnoticed.

[261] Platov (2012, 294 *et passim*) discussed a parallel bitter irony involving "cruelty", rather than humour, i.e., accusing an enemy of "cruelty" in order to launch into one's own (e.g., the 'civilising' duty of colonial warfare).

[262] Harvey (1999), 80 (the example is ours). Harvey's grasp of the damning and damaging powers of mockery extends beyond, or behind, physical and psychological pain alone, for the laughingstock can be harmed in their standing and/or opportunities while unaware of being mocked, whether temporarily or permanently (e.g., due to death, linguistic barriers, physical barriers, or mental barriers such as severe autism or humour-blinding acatamathesia).

[263] Blaming "the [n]ut behind the [w]heel" has been a tactic of car manufacturers in avoiding "blame for highway deaths" (Freese 2020, 67). "Blaming the victims" is profitable, its "immorality" aside (Freese 2020, 53 and 173). More on capitalist cruelties is said in *H&C3*.

[264] Harvey (1999), 81 (the example is ours). See, e.g., Gadd *et al.* (2002).

ural harm)"; e.g., employees having sensible reasons to complain are often scorned by bosses and/or colleagues as pathologically "'oversensitive', 'paranoid', 'thin-skinned'", or "whatever ... nonmoral defect" is said to be noticeable "in the victim[s]".[265]

(4) "There is in fact moral harm, but then it is claimed that in accounting for it, we must look at some crucial contribution from the victim".[266] For instance, the targeting of Canadian Catholics reported by anti-bigotry observers being underplayed by the same researchers because, say, the person responsible for the horrible 2017 Quebec City mosque shooting was a right-wing, trigger-happy, Islamophobic, solitary, white-supremacist, male citizen—of Catholic family background.[267]

(5) "There is in fact moral harm and the crucial responsibility of the actual agent is acknowledged ... , but then it is claimed that some contribution from the victim makes the harm more serious than it would otherwise have been, and that that contribution involves some moral or nonmoral fault of the victim".[268] For example, a murdered man is ridiculed as "silly" for having walked in a poor city district wearing expensive clothes or having talked too frankly to a stranger: "he should have known better than telling [his unsuspected murderer] about his wealth".[269]

(6) "There is some harm, and any responsibility for it by an agent is acknowledged ... , but once the harm has occurred, then it is claimed that something untoward in the victim's response makes the ultimate outcome worse ... and that ... involves some moral or nonmoral fault of the victim" such as "overreacting[,] ... failing to limit or reduce the harm ... [, or] protesting the harm in an inappropriate manner".[270] Say, in the case of male-on-male rape, the sniggering at men who "should have been able to defend" themselves from the assailant/s.[271]

---

[265] Harvey (1999), 81–82 (the example is ours; one of the authors having been an active trade unionist).
[266] Harvey (1999), 82.
[267] The example is based on an experience that one of the present authors had at a 2020 conference, where a report on sectarian violence in Canada was delivered which clearly recorded the victimisation of Catholic citizens, whose plight was however underplayed, as he was later explained, because of the presumed privileged social status of such citizens and their association with past cruel tragedies committed by other individuals that were variously linked with Catholic institutions. Yet another instance of Hallie's first paradox of cruelty, in all probability.
[268] Harvey (1999), 83.
[269] Changoiwala (2016), 273. Again, the example is ours.
[270] Harvey (1999), 84.
[271] Clarke, Moran-Ellis and Sleney (2002), 46 and 63. The example is ours.

With reference to commonplace humour, one of the most frequently heard formulae whereby complaining laughingstocks can be dismissed, marginalised, underplayed, ignored, and/or effectively victimised further is that they have no "sense of humour".[272] And as Lydia Amir wrote: "What is meant by 'sense of humor' is the aesthetic sensitivity to the stimuli that evoke the experience of the comical: It is the capacity to perceive the amusing aspects of a situation or to construe the situation as amusing."[273] Therefore, to many onlookers, these whining persons are nothing but boring and humourless grouches, while the occasioned margin for critical and self-critical reflection is nipped in the bud.[274] After all, who likes a party-pooper?[275]

2.2.3.4 Rome

Killjoys spoil not only the fun of the actively sadistic person, but also that of the *passively* sadistic one who would gladly witness someone else's humiliation and enjoy the show. As seen in Chapter 1, many thinkers and researchers have remarked repeatedly upon the quintessentially *social* character of humour. The humour derived from enjoying the spectacle of someone else being cruel to another is no exception.

We have already mentioned in this book that people can support a jest's initiator by laughing *at* the butt of a joke *with* its initiator and/or refusing to laugh at the rejoinders coming from the joke's butt.[276] People can also encourage a prankster's mischief, even if the pranks target individuals who are identical to the laughing crowd in social station, age, gender, disability, general misfortune,

---

[272] Harvey (1999), 2. It should be noted that the constitutive inner tension of "true humour" makes compassion easier to appear than in "commonplace" one, which can be utterly heartless.
[273] Amir (2019), 73.
[274] Well-meaning feminists can do it too, e.g., intellectuals complaining about the viral internet campaign mocking gender-specific male suffering by way of "memes with sentiments like 'I Drink Male Tears', and … embroidered hats and macramé 'misandry' crafts" get blamed for failing to appreciate "the humorous appropriation of male-bashing and misandry by prominent feminists" (Marwick and Caplan 2018, 553). As to internet memes in general *qua* means of cruel humour, see Marlin-Bennett and Jackson (2022).
[275] Sills (2020, 94) is one such well-meaning party-pooper: "we cannot deny that to observe only the craft of humor that perpetuates a culture of abuse is irresponsible scholarship". Responsible intellectuals *ought* to pass judgement. As to the term "party-pooper", albeit colloquial, it possesses a ridiculing *brevitas* explaining its use in our book. In the realm of showbusiness, for instance, actress Nichelle Nichols declared, regarding her colleague who played captain James Tiberius Kirk in *Star Trek:* ""Bill Shatner is a flatulent, selfish lard-a*** who would c*** on the last piece of pizza just so you wouldn't enjoy it" (as cited in Sheridan 2007, par. 34).
[276] See also Billig (2005, chap. 8) on "unlaughter", describing such a humiliating refusal.

etc.²⁷⁷ People can even compete fiercely for, attend eagerly, fund generously, and justify culturally, the cruel antics performed before them. Indeed, by so doing, they can confirm, *qua* paying spectators, Regan's aforementioned remarks about the fuzzy line separating active from passive sadism.

Ancient Rome supplies us with many examples of sadistic antics, active as well as passive.²⁷⁸ Gladiatorial combat may have turned into standard fare of Hollywood's sword-and-sandal movies, but the ancient Romans' imagination for cruel games was much more daring than that of any contemporary David Lynch or John Carpenter. For instance, the American art historian John R. Clarke wrote: "Imagine seeing a nude criminal fitted with wings made of wax and feathers hoisted high above the floor of the Colosseum and then dropped" in order to perform a "public execution" consisting in the "hilarious … comic reversal of the myth" of Icarus and Daedalus.²⁷⁹ Not only is a common criminal dressed like the mythical father instead of the mythical son. Also, people in the audience are induced to laugh because of "Daedalus's desperate attempt to fly with his fake wings, even though he knows well as the crowd that he has no chance of succeeding".²⁸⁰ And a whole crowd of people did laugh indeed.²⁸¹

Clarke continued: "Or imagine a woman playing Pasiphae, who lusted after a bull."²⁸² In a theatrically expanded version of the then-commonplace punishments by bestial rape and/or capital execution, "the criminal Pasiphae meets her death attempting to have sex with a real bull. The bull is the executioner as well in the literal enactment of the myth of Dirce, with the criminal tied to the animal and dragged to her death".²⁸³

Other instances of this Roman humorous cruelty include: "Nero's making human torches out of Christians for the entertainment of the populace"; "a criminal gotten up as Orpheus … initially successful in calming the beasts" but eventually "mauled and dispatched by … a hungry bear"; and Hercules' apotheosis "turned ridiculous when a condemned criminal/Hercules was made to mount a pyre set up in the arena or forced to don the *tunica molesta*, an inflammable gar-

---

277 Dickie's (2011) provides many examples of this complete lack of class solidarity.
278 As seen in Chapter 1 and, to a greater extent, in *H&C1*, Rome's cruel games are a paradigmatic case of cruelty.
279 Clarke (2007), 23.
280 Clarke (2007), 23.
281 This quantitative point matters *vis-à-vis* the optimistic claims about humour entailing 'benign' violations only.
282 Clarke (2007), 23.
283 Clarke (2007), 23.

ment smeared with pitch. Instead of the miracle of ascension to Olympus the crowd saw a man burned alive".[284]

Today's circuses and football stadiums, in Rome and elsewhere, can give us a far milder, very faint, almost parodic idea of what these ancient shows must have been like.[285] And so do most definitiely their partial yet prolonged continuation in the guise of public executions *qua* time-honoured means of popular entertainment. As the prolific 20th century British author George Ryley Scott wrote:

> [T]he Romans gleefully watched the slaughtering of girls and boys ... the English aristocracy feasted their eyes upon the dying struggles of fighting-cocks, bulls, bears and dogs... [W]hen executions were performed publicly, sadists revelled in the spectacle ... packed with gloating, gibbering, enthusiastic men and women ... on a par with the modern boxing contest or football match ... when social distinctions ... were, for the moment, totally forgotten. Peers and peasants mixed with each other ... [and] exchanged jests and jokes with the greatest of good humour.[286]

At contemporary arenas, obscene, offensive, obtuse, yet heartily amused jeering and uproarious taunts aimed at referees and players are performed weekly, almost ritually. They take place all around the globe and involve hundreds of thousands of individuals from all social classes who derive great pleasure in booing, whistling at, insulting and/or chanting at umpires, teams, managers and players, ridiculing them, their ancestors, mothers, fathers, sisters, wives, girlfriends, children, teammates, employers, fellow nationals and townspeople, and so forth.[287] As uncouth as these utterings may be, the more refined spectators and/or the social scientists who attend these collective acts of verbal aggression cannot but notice and be entertained by the unruly spirit of popular carnival that they embody and express *via* massive, coordinated soundwaves.[288]

2.2.3.5 Brutality

Leaving aside the ancient Romans' games and their furious thrills or even their milder counterparts inside modern football stadiums, there are certainly far

---

[284] Clarke (2007), 23–24.
[285] By "football" we mean the sport called "soccer" in North America, where "football" is played predominantly by hand and with an oval object.
[286] G. Scott (1996), 171–173. Scott wrote more than 40 books between the 1910s and the 1970s dealing with birth control, prostitution, sex, nudism, STDs, corporal and capital punishment, animal husbandry, and cockfighting.
[287] See, e.g., *Cori da stadio* (n.d.a.). More on these phenomena is said in *H&C3*.
[288] See, e.g., Pearson (2012), Armstrong and Young (2000), and Hoy (1994) on fandom as Bakhtinian carnivals.

more ordinary and far less contentious admixtures of ridiculous and sorrowful elements that can bring an amused smile on our faces or cause us to burst into a roaring laughter.[289]

2.2.3.5.1 Avoiding Tragedy

Whether any of us aims at making people titter in amusement at a clever witticism, smile in thoughtful appreciation of a funnily disguised pearl of wisdom, or guffaw energetically at a barefacedly comical scene, whatever degree of tension that there may be in the discursive items at play between the ridiculous component and the tragic component, this tension must be resolved in favour of the former.

This is a point of widespread agreement. No controversy arises in this respect. If anything, in *H&C1*, we detailed how many noted thinkers testify to this insight, e.g., Beattie, Hazlitt, and Santayana, whose views we also briefly summarised in Chapter 1. What is more, all these distinguished thinkers warn humourists not to over-play the heart-rending card. Doing so would critically compromise and eventually destroy the intended hilarity of their work and therefore dilute their artistic exercise into sheer commiseration.[290]

Bergson's "anaesthesia of the heart" is, plausibly, the most famous, if not the most insightful, explicit reformulation of this aesthetic and artistic axiom, extended to human psychology at large.

2.2.3.5.2 Avoiding Heartfulness

Bergson's 'cardiac slumber' relates as well to the recurrent connotation of maliciousness *qua* essential ingredient of humorous laughter. Tellingly, at the close of the 20th century, an American expert on speech and rhetoric, Charles R. Gruner, wrote that "innocent humor" is a "mirage".[291] A few years later, Buckley echoed him: "However innocent the laughter might seem" or wish to be, "a signal of supe-

---

[289] Scores of scholars and scientists have repeatedly remarked on the ambiguous character of humour, which mixes a laughter-centred element and a sorrowful one. The words vary, but the idea is the same. Hence, in this chapter, "comedic", "comical", "funny", etc. are used as synonyms, and so are "tragic", "pathetic", "sad", etc.

[290] The relative emphasis on the laughter-centred or on the sorrowful elements of a work of art creates an ideal continuum of genres ranging from, say, farce, on the one end, to tragedy, on the other. Tracy (2016) claimed that the medieval authors of the *Fabliaux* got the emphasis wrong and 'killed' the comedy that was meant by them.

[291] Gruner (1997), 147f.

riority may always be found".[292] In 2020, the Israeli mathematician and humour scholar Ron Ahroni observed how both Bergson's "anaesthesia of the heart" and superiority theory "are based on detachment of empathy, namely of identification", pointing out some possible affective roots of the malicious ingredient of humorous conduct.[293]

We ourselves, in *H&C1*, remarked on the notion that, taken in their pragmatic settings, all feats of humour, including those based on 'merely' logical or fanciful incongruities or dualities that pose no threat, are bound to entail an implicit hierarchy between the ingenious jokester and the unimaginative recipients.[294] Think, for instance, of any conceivable adversary in a game of wits that arises in a social setting upon the proffering of such incongruities or dualities, and/or of the awe-struck listeners, whose intellectual faculties may not be adequate to grasp them. Or think of those individuals among the latter who, failing to fully understand what is going on, are then terrified or unsettled by the prospect that someone may be poking fun at them and/or at something or someone that they care about, whether in good or bad faith.[295]

Translating this insight into the terminology of standard 20th-century British linguistic philosophy, even the most irreproachable jest may be so at the *locutionary* and *illocutionary* levels, i.e., in terms of abstract conceptual content and stated intention.[296] However, at the *perlocutionary* (aka "perlocutory" in some published academic works) level, which pertains to the social effects of our utterings, the jest cannot be sure to be innocent.[297] Specifically, there may always be someone who is belittled by ingenious phrases beyond his/her understanding and past his/her threshold for wounded pride, diminished self-worth, ignited anger, or emotional sensitivity.

2.2.3.5.3 Avoiding Inferiority

If we decide to utter or pursue the potentially hurtful jest anyhow, we are *ipso facto* precluding and/or downplaying the possibility that someone may get hurt. We are being *callous*, in short, even if the prevalent social mores may well allow for such a boorishness—or even promote it, e.g., by focussing on other aspects of humour, such as its jovial spirit, positive effects on people's physical

---

[292] Buckley (2003), 191.
[293] Ahroni (2020), 55.
[294] Gruner (1997) was decisive in leading us to this realisation.
[295] Under this respect, a clever jest of this sort can be irreproachable if executed only *in foro interno*.
[296] See Austin (1962), 99–101.
[297] See Austin (1962), 99–101.

health, function as a bonding mechanism, unique ability to convey messages in a rapid and succinct manner, inherent intellectual ingenuity or rhetorical creativity, etc. Those who are offended, to boot, can be regarded as oversensitive, odd, or eccentric, i.e., once again, *de haut en bas*.[298]

A hierarchy is established *every* time a jest is made in the public domain, however fleetingly or lightly we initiate it, or even whether or not the jester or jokester is fully aware of the perlocutionary consequences of his/her actions. Which is not surprising. This acceptance is likely a matter of habit in historically stratified communities.[299] As several scholars have observed, after all, duels in clever exchanges are a time-honoured and well-established form of socially-situated verbal, mental, and affective swordsmanship that

(1) the educated elites of the West have long cultivated (e.g., *à propos*, using foreign words to make witty remarks at a faculty meeting or signalling one's supposedly superior erudition), and
(2) the less educated ones have appropriated and applied in their own ways (e.g., inventing rude yet hilarious nicknames for one's pals at the local pub).[300]

As such, these duels must end up with a victor and, *a fortiori*, a loser. And as the standard Olympic podium indicates, the former stands a little higher than the latter.

---

[298] Quite obviously, this hierarchical positioning gives credit to the superiority theory of humour, but it also points towards the Bergsonian anaesthesia of the heart insofar as such a positioning requires the superior party to minimise or discount whichever tendency s/he may have to bring about an egalitarian equilibrium that could erase or ease the sense of humiliation, displeasure, discomfort, etc. that the inferior party is very likely to experience.

[299] In a cruel twist of irony, *seemingly obvious power hierarchies are not always and/or necessarily so*, for context and re-contextualisation can turn all kinds of established structures upside-down. Western comedies have made repeated use of this known fact, straying the *prima-facie* 'privileged' among the 'outcast', the 'educated' among the 'ignorant', the 'modern' ones among the 'primitives', the 'sane' among the 'insane, etc. Sometimes, this comic process has been instantiated by one and the same comedy in two different centuries, e.g., the film *Swept Away*, (1974 and 2002). In which direction are the punches flying then: up or down? Even the much maligned regime of "neoliberalism", which the British geographers Simon Springer and Levi Gahman (2016, title *et passim*) told bluntly to go "fuck" itself in an uproarious rant, can find experts willing to defend it openly and unashamedly insofar as they can claim it to be the best planet-wide institutional tool for the material improvement of entire societies, hence for that of their weakest members too (see, e.g., Bowman 2017, Casey 2016, and Shearmur 1992). *H&C3* offers our own assessment of neo/liberalism, its cruelties and, as odd as it may sound, its humour.

[300] See also Barthes (1970) on the class-based elements of Western rhetoric.

2.2.3.5.4 Avoiding Awareness

Consistently with these considerations, to which we must return later in both this chapter and the concluding one, Bergson's 'cardiological' approach can be argued to open the way for a richer understanding of the intimate relationship between humour and cruelty, along two foremost interpretative axes.

First, being cognizant of the reduced empathy involved in humorous behaviours, we can hypothesise that the theories of incongruity and play bring this detachment to the point that the agents no longer perceive the implied hierarchies of the socially-situated humorous games which they initiate and/or participate in, e.g., quick-witted *versus* slow-witted, lateral-thinking *versus* literal-thinking, creative innovator *versus* habit-bound inheritor, insider *versus* outsider. We all may become so used to making use of commonplace humour that we no longer notice and reflect upon the socially-based moral and/or psychological costs of such an activity, which is generally regarded as positive for all people who engage in it, or at least for those who start and steer successfully this particular social game.[301]

Secondly, given the regular and recurring conceptual distinction of 'cruelty' into either sadistic or brutal (see Chapter 1), we can further understand the role played by Bergson's metaphorical "anaesthesia of the heart" in connection with two additional aspects of the many contexts in which humorous conduct unfolds within groups and societies.[302]

2.2.3.5.5 Avoiding Bloodlessness

In a *maximal* sense, by operating on anaesthesia of the heart, we all may be letting a modicum of sadistic cruelty come into play under the guise of the aggressive, scathing, mordant, astringent, sharp, or aptly-named "satirical" element of commonplace humour. This is precisely how Santayana dubbed the corrosive ingredient of humour and, more importantly, what he suggested in his writings on the subject. We bite because we want to bite; and we want to bite because we want to witness the biting's effects. In short, we want to see blood.[303]

Such a candid opening to the possibility of sadism inhabiting humour is certainly more likely with regard to all those forms of commonplace humour

---

[301] These 'costs' are more apparent and controversial in the case of cruel humour, which we tackle in Chapter 3.
[302] See also *H&C1*.
[303] As seen in Chapter 1, many scholars and scientists stressed the predatory nature of our species.

where compassion and pathos are of no major concern whatsoever, if at all.[304] Among these forms of commonplace humour are also those acts of verbal swordsmanship requiring the creative use of acerbic witticisms, down-putting puns, uncommon insults, and clever retorts.[305] As in classic fencing, there's no better sign of victory than seeing one's opponent bleed. And this is not just fun. It is *fighting*.

As Chesterton remarked about puns and related comic matters:

> In the Bohemian half of the Early Victorian world wit reigned as a kind of institution. Wit was to these intellectual people something like what sport is to simpler people; it was a permanent open competition, free but yet formal lists in which young men could win their spurs. Wit ... is in this sense warlike.[306]

In a different context, Chesterton even admitted that "humour" itself could be weaponised: "Dickens ... was the English poor man, whose weapon is humour. He was always in a sense the comic servant mocking the solemn master, like Sancho Panza following Don Quixote."[307]

Later in the 20th century, the American classicist Albert Rapp confirmed this interpretation of wit and related it to laughter at large, as with Homer's heroes being "full of cruel and savage laughter"; or as with ancient youngsters amusing themselves by beating up "a cripple", since "the 'brainy' branch of the laughter family, 'wit', is so often cruel, aggressive, and 'rapier-like'" as to resemble its uncouth physical counterpart.[308] Psychologically, Rapp equated the sensuous enjoyment of wit and laughter with those arising from erotic physical frictions, i.e., in sexual acts, which are usually regarded as necessary and defining components of "sadism" proper in both psychology and criminology:

---

304 Echoing Pirandello's earlier musings and linguistic formulation, Leacock (1938, chap. 9, sec. 1, par. 2) wrote of "true humour", *contra* every other form of ridicule: "pathos keeps humor from breaking into guffaws and humor keeps pathos from subsiding into sobs. It is like the union of two metals, one too hard, the other too soft for use alone. *Sunt lachrymae rerum*; the world is full of weeping. But it would be a terrible place if there were nothing else. Nor can laughter stay alone except for the loon and the jackass."
305 Concerning "salutary" and "cathartic ... clever replies and retorts" and "witty comebacks", Esar (1954, 149–162) classified as the main types of "gag" or "[r]epartee ... [t]he insult ... the double insult ... [the] double-edged shaft ... [the r]eversible repartee ... [the p]arallel repartee ... the panhandle ... the hobo gag ... the hecklerism ... [the s]entry or sentinel dialogue ... the Who was that lady? gag ... the knock gag ... and ... the soup fly".
306 Chesterton (1958), 167.
307 Chesterton (1932), part 3, chap. 5, par. 2.
308 Rapp (1951), 92 and 177, note 10.

> Once the separation has been made between titillation in the sense of massaging or rubbing, and the laughter-provoking struggle of tickling, then we may still ask: Is there a connection between the latter and erotic stimulation? Clearly there is. The connection is to be found in the playful aggression or fighting which from time immemorial has been recognized as an important aid to erotic excitation; as in the case of playful biting, scratching, and striking. And, I might add, unplayful.[309]

Reflecting on "the erotic often obscene jocosity due to the sexual urge", the 20th-century American philosopher Marie Taylor Collins Swabey tried to segregate

(1)   "what is worth laughing at", i.e., clever comical incongruity, from
(2)   "what makes us laugh" *tout court*,
(2a) such as lowly "humor" induced by means of "superiority", which, at least "in principle",
(2b) can frequently be dubbed "sadism", insofar as
(2bi) this humour "appeal[s] to cruelty, brutality", and
(2bii) is commonly instantiated by "spiteful criticism and the infliction of pain with anaesthesia of the heart increasing proportionately", or
(2biii) by comic characters encountering "such fates as boiling in oil, drawing and quartering, impaling on spears, hammering to pulp, marinating in machinery, and tortures of all sorts".[310]
(2biv) Swabey retrieved a tinge of this sadism "[e]ven in Edward Lear, Lewis Carroll, and so-called non-sense humor", which is often taken to be a quintessential instantiation of clever comical incongruity, given that "a certain anaesthesia of the heart is clearly present" in their works too, e.g., "the shrill cry of the duchess 'Off with her head!' or ... gorgonlike visages of various eggheads and other droll characters in the illustrations of Tenniel and Lear".[311]

In our century, the Ukrainian engineer and humour scholar Igor Krichtafovitch came to similar conclusions, explaining the function of "humour" proper in Darwinian terms of evolutionary advantage over competitors: "humor is always used as an intellectual weapon in the fight for increasing one's social status; or as preparation for intellectual combat; training or a warm-up of sorts".[312] Its social analogues are "fencing ..., archery, and box[ing]".[313]

---

309 Rapp (1951), 131.
310 Swabey (1958), 819–832. Her article deals chiefly with "the comic", not "humor" proper.
311 Swabey (1958), 832.
312 Krichtafovitch (2006), 71. The objections to humour "punching down" rather than "up", as well-meaning as they may be, do not deny that "punching" is what goes on with humour, in line with Krichtafovitch's stance.

2.2.3.5.6 Avoiding Seriousness

In the glitzy world of Hollywood showbusiness, the noted comic actor, writer, producer, and filmmaker Mel Brooks reportedly said: "Tragedy is when I cut my finger. Comedy is when you fall into an open sewer and die."[314] We may interpret this statement, *prima facie*, as indicating sadism *tout court*. However, that is not necessarily the case. Callousness may be all that is required for the comedic effect of a lethal fall to succeed.

In a *minimal* sense, in fact, if there is commonplace humour going on, there must be, automatically, at least a modicum of brutal cruelty at play. Sadistic cruelty can also arise, of course. As we have just seen, it is probably not uncommon. Yet nothing so bloodthirsty must come into play *de rigueur*, at least logically, for humour as such to subsist.[315]

This latter line of argument is a less counterintuitive and possibly more crucial lesson to be derived from the recurring instructions telling all potential entertainers that they should underplay the pathetic element of humour for it not to turn into commiseration. Certain emotional dispositions are necessarily toned down, or quite simply switched off, insofar as humour, at least in its commonplace renditions, requires that *someone and/or something must not be taken seriously*, thus preventing, among other things, the target audiences from being outraged, offended, belittled, excluded, horrified, and/or staggered by the gag.[316]

It is in this sense, then, that humour can be said to entail or imply cruelty. Brutal cruelty is certainly less egregious than sadistic cruelty. However, it is also and nonetheless a widely acknowledged species of the idea of 'cruelty'.[317] Additionally, as far as commonplace humour is concerned, this realisation also cuts underneath Regan's as well as Hallie's distinction between 'sadism' *qua* delight in another's suffering, and 'brutality' or 'callousness' *qua* absence of adequate sympathy or compassion.[318] With closer scrutiny, it would seem that sadism builds upon brutal-

---

313 Krichtafovitch (2006), 72.
314 We were not able to retrieve the origin of this quote, which multiple sources report, e.g., *goodreads.com*.
315 Hidden in the bosom of each person, the line separating sadistic from brutal cruelty is impossible to gauge.
316 Humour, however, can miss the mark in low- as well as high-brow contexts. See, e.g., Oloskey Mills (1974).
317 The philosophers' longstanding indictment of laughter as malicious is thus further corroborated.
318 See Chapter 1.

ity, for it adds to the lack of compassion the delight in another's misfortune, whereas brutality can stand alone, i.e., without any delight.[319]

Though we may not be able or willing to relish the sadistic, satirical component of commonplace humour for its own sake, such banter would not take place *at all* without the partial—or at times complete (e.g., virulent satires, outlandish farces)—disengagement of the sympathetic propensities of our soul, i.e., without engaging, once again, into a thorough anaesthesia of the heart.[320] Commonplace humour, to function *qua* humour, demands *some* cruelty, and the brutal type is conceivably the least damned and least damnable one that human societies can allow for on a frequent or even regular basis.[321]

2.2.3.5.7 Avoiding Fun

The best proof available for our claims about the inextricable presence of cruelty within humour is thus provided by all those people who, when faced with a token of commonplace humour, focus exclusively or primarily on the pathetic component rather than the satirical one, hence failing to appreciate the risible aspect of the joke and find it pleasant, amusing, or worthy of laughter.[322] For instance, an individual who happens to find the falls of Charlie Chaplin, Buster Keaton, or Harpo Marx scary, unsettling, or a cause for worry is not going to laugh.[323] Similarly, a spectator who finds pitiable the endless bad luck and the repeated mortifications of downtrodden characters such as Donald Duck, Mr. Fantozzi, Pulcinella, or Harlequin will not appreciate their intended comicality.[324]

---

[319] As noted in Chapter 1, some compassion may yet be present in sadistic behaviour, for the sadist would not be able to enjoy another's suffering if the former were totally detached from the latter *in affectibus*.

[320] Hence the talk of "guilty pleasures" *vis-à-vis* watching "trash TV" (McCoy and Scarborough 2014). While the guilt is felt, it is reduced to a secondary status in comparison to the pleasure that is concomitantly felt as well.

[321] Even Krichtafovitch's (2006, 83–100), titular "formula" can accommodate this insight without paving the way to sadism, which he took instead as the genealogical key to humour *qua* means of individual self-affirmation in the evolution-driven competition for suitable mates. Concisely, the formula reads as follows: "EH = PE*C/Tp + BM" (i.e., "PE" is "Personal Empathy", "C" is the "complexity" of a joke's "riddle", "Tp" is the time for "its solution", "BM" is "the background mood" of the audience, and "EH" is "the effect of humor").

[322] Letting depressed, suicidal patients laugh is useful but hard (see, e.g., Richman 1995).

[323] See, e.g., Mireault and Reddy (2016), especially the chap. "When Humor Goes Missing".

[324] Max Horkheimer and Theodor W. Adorno (2002, 110) argued that comic characters like "Donald Duck in the cartoons" receive their beatings so that the spectators can accustom themselves to their own under capitalism. In times closer to us, the New Zealand-based postfeminist academic Kendra Marston (2018, 117) made an analogous claim about the tales of socio-economically privi-

Outside the realm of fiction, the same prevalence of the tragic over the comic can occur when people observe a person or a group of persons being teased or made fun of, with apparent success, by someone else.[325] Not all observers will participate gleefully in the teasing, or even allow the derision to go on unremarked, uncriticised, or unopposed, sometimes at risk of one's own rank, reputation, relationships, career, peace of mind, or personal safety.[326] Equally, tabloids and TV shows creating comedic situations out of poverty and ignorance may be too much to bear for some viewers and/or readers.[327]

Such sensitive individuals cannot stand the sight or even the notion of poor and ignorant people being mercilessly laughed at while also being treated mercilessly and, more often than not, being called names that further deepen the humiliation, e.g., "Waste people. Offscourings. Lubbers. Bogtrotters. Rascals. Rubbish. Squatters. Crackers. Clay-eaters. Tackies. Mudsills. Scalawags. Briar hoppers. Hillbillies. Low-downers. White n[*****]s. Degenerates… Rednecks. Trailer trash. Swamp people".[328]

Morally or socially committed persons, whose private and/or professional life pivots around a certain religious, ethical, or political creed, may also fail to appreciate much commonplace humour.[329] Faced with mundane humour, these persons would invariably find therein too much light-heartedness *via-à-vis* major and un-

---

leged, white women's melancholia, self-discovery travels, and thorny romances in Hollywood's 21st-century movies, which were said to turn "the cruelties of capitalism" into an inevitable fate to be accepted with a gender-specific sense of poetic *ennui*, i.e., rather than, say, revolution.

325 Insincere or "humourless laughter" could still be possible, though, whereby "[t]he ostensible gaiety of laughter masks emotions such as sadness, despair, anger, fear, regret", etc. (Brody 1950, 200)

326 See, e.g., "Marine Gets Beat Down" (2013).

327 See, e.g., 1990s and 2000s TV shows such as *Judge Judy* and *The Jerry Springer Show*. British sociologist Tracy Shildrick (2018, 132) spoke in this respect of "poverty propaganda" making use of televised 'poverty porn' that has "real effects and influence on the way that those experiencing poverty are treated, on how poverty as a condition is responded to and, ultimately, on how those experiencing poverty feel about their own lives". Dong (2022, 93) included such for-profit mediatic entertainments among the many tokens of "the neoliberal 'theatre of cruelty'" tragically available to 21st-century audiences, Western as well as Eastern.

328 Isenberg (2017), 320 (the original text includes the uncensored formulation of the cruel racist term). See also the 1997 book by the same title, and much similar content by Wray and Newitz.

329 As Portmann (2000, 112) noted: "it is possible for a compassionate person to be insensitive to the pleasures of others". These pleasures may well include the morally questionable joys of commonplace humour.

forgivable failures of individuals and/or communities.[330] Such serious matters ought not to be taken so lightly. No anaesthesia of the heart takes place then—or an insufficiently potent one.[331]

2.2.3.5.8 Avoiding Humour

These individual and/or collective failures include a potentially colossal congregation of despicable tokens of behaviour, patterns of thought, praxes for social interaction, and/or traits of character. They comprise: blasphemy, heresy, sin, immorality, bad manners, bad taste, superficiality, culpable haplessness, insufferable stupidity, paltriness, unpardonable ignorance, forgetfulness of social rank, lack of patriotic spirit, class oppression, cultural imperialism, cultural appropriation, racial prejudice, sexism, misogyny, misandry, misanthropy, insensitivity, disrespect, callousness itself, self-centredness, speciesism, ageism, ableism, mentalism, sanism, neuronormativism, heteronormativism, fattism, parochialism, narrow-mindedness, and ethnocentrism.[332] Not so long ago, a conservationist auteur was accused of nothing less than "wolfism".[333]

Complementarily, given the apparent overabundance of devotion to all kinds of just and noble causes and the concomitant paucity of intellectual finesse, declaring oneself openly to be in favour of anything means opening the doors to challengers and aggravations. Accordingly, as soon as one describes him-/herself in some way (e.g., a woman, Marxist, or Buddhist), s/he can be accused of not being "inclusive", i.e., of some 'exclusiv*ism*' of sorts.[334] It is, once again, a manifestation of the curious logic of Moni Ovadia's joke of the two ties.[335]

Such an ungainly and uncomfortable list of '-isms' could go on for several pages. It would name any high principle as much as any low prejudice that the human imagination can concoct, for as long as any actual person should happen to hold in grave contempt any one of these tokens, patterns, praxes and/or traits

---

[330] The case is analogous to that of Voltaire, who, being unable not to think of the brutal cruelty behind the castrati's condition, could not bring himself to enjoy their artistic performances (see Feldman 2015, 346–347, note 10).
[331] Given the ultimate privacy of the anaesthesia, it is impossible to quantify it.
[332] The list is intentionally long and cuts through facile left/right and progressive/conservative oversimplifications. "Ethnocentrism" has also found positive usages, however, e.g., Rorty (1989) in political philosophy and Tripković (2018) in constitutional theory. As such, it is a genuinely "controversial" notion (Llanera 2017, 135).
[333] Rocci (2021), par. 1. Though no intentional humour was involved in this particular case, the unintentional one of such a peculiar '-ism' should not escape our reader's grasp.
[334] See, e.g., R. Smith (2022).
[335] See this book's Preliminary Remarks.

in a socially viable context, i.e., in a linguistic community in which commonplace humour can be given form and expression.[336] (Logically, if humour cannot arise in any shape or form, its condemnation cannot follow.) Wherever and whenever something serious is detected and endorsed as such, i.e., by a community member, then social rejection can take place as a result of that person's critical agency among her fellows.[337]

If and when the critical agents' hectoring propaganda, heartfelt persuasion, and/or ethical proselytising prove successful, the socially-established conceptions of humorous phenomena can indeed mutate. Reform has, after all, been part and parcel of the recorded changes of most communities' socio-cultural appurtenances. This change may not embrace the whole of society and be confined to specific groups, particularly among the elites. As repeatedly seen in our research, especially *H&C1*, the quest for so-called "refinement" in Western humour has frequently been intertwined with a conscious effort aimed at establishing clear distinctions of rank within society, i.e., separating 'high' from 'low' culture, the 'proper' people and the 'great unwashed'.

Still, genuine bottom-up change can be enacted too. Although the targets of the now-loathsome forms of so-called "humour" may belong to quantitative and/or qualitative "minorities", the changes in Western etiquette and/or laws affecting humorous conduct indicate that, if duly organised and engaged, some minorities can actually exercise sufficient power over the rest of society.[338] Aristocrats and plutocrats are not the only small groups that can acquire significant clout. In a peculiar and intriguing reiteration of the Mediterranean-wide affirmation of the Christian religion that Sade and Nietzsche resented so much, even the provincial slaves' creed can become the global masters' creed.[339]

Provided, of course, that the bulk of these minorities are keen on such changes, rather than an even smaller yet highly effective revolutionary vanguard

---

[336] The successful US comedian Dave Chappelle realised that far too much racial and sexist prejudice, albeit personally unintended, was emerging in connection with his own televised gags and, being incapable of operating any longer an anaesthesia of the heart, he decided to quit and stay put for several years (as reported in Deen 2020). His work was also controversial for other people and, unsurprisingly, it has attracted the interest of US ethicists and philosophers, e.g., Ralkovski (2021). Chappelle's case is yet another reminder that humour's *duality* applies to the audience's reactions: there are those who laugh *at* and those who laugh *with* the character/s, e.g., Carroll O'Connor's in/famous Archie Bunker in two 1970's and 1980's CBS shows.
[337] Even "[t]he American Psychoanalytic Association banned ... [the satirical *Journal of Polymorphous Perversity*] at the group's annual convention, declaring that humor was 'inappropriate'" (Ellenbogen 1996, xiv).
[338] Baroncelli (1996), 68–69.
[339] See Chapter 1 and *H&C1*.

belonging to them and/or claiming to be speaking for them. That is to say, in a further possible cruel irony of human history, another miniscule guiding elite akin to the priests of old or the Russian Bolsheviks. As Baroncelli observed, such an elite might today comprise those "tolerant, open-minded and truth-loving liberals" that live on university campuses and aim at selecting the ways in which people may have fun.[340] It is they, then, not the people whom they say to love and serve, that are to decide whether and when an anaesthesia of the heart is justified or not.[341]

In any case, historically speaking, the socially established conceptions of 'humour', 'laughter' and 'fun' have patently mutated on more than one occasion, as testified by the mass of stock targets and permissible subjects of Western comedy. In today's refined societies, poking fun at an elderly man's impotence has become embarrassingly 'ageist'. Ridiculing an obese man's cumbersome way of walking is promptly and vocally rebuked as "fat-shaming".[342] Making witty remarks on a woman's sexual promiscuity instantiates a loathsome case of 'slut-shaming'.[343] The canons, criteria, and circumstances of humour, especially yet not exclusively in its commonplace forms, have notably transformed. In all probability, they will keep doing so.

2.2.3.5.9 Avoiding Words

If the cow is sacred, choosing it as one's laughingstock cannot but turn the jokester into a scurrilous swine, if not into a dangerous godless boor.[344] And if the expected moral, aesthetic, social, behavioural and/or linguistic norm is to dutifully respect each extant cow—which, as seen, can multiply into a humongous herd—the room for humour dissipates and, subsidiarily, so does the actual room for living persons' free speech. In yet another cruel irony emerging from our study of

---

340 Baroncelli (1996), 69.
341 More on these matters is said in *H&C3*.
342 Given the plump shape of this book's authors, this could be a touchy subject for them too. See Jenkins (2022) for a handy review of the extant literature on the representation of fat persons in today's US and UK TV, as well as for a token of the recurrent lexical association of "cruel" and "cruelty" with "humour" and "laughter" in this context.
343 More on sex-related matters follows in the last chapter of this book and in *H&C3*.
344 Perhaps, one day, the growing sensitivity towards the sorry plight of our fellow animals will make their metaphorical and paradigmatic rhetorical functions uncouth and undesirable (see, e.g., Széll 2022). Thus we apologise hereby to our descendants, should they happen to be affronted by our lack of manners and consideration. *We meant no offence.* We simply could not predict the future of ethics, etiquette and eloquence. Who can?

humour, people's chances for self-expression can be curtailed for the unimpeachable sake of goodness itself—one pious nod or genuflection at a time.³⁴⁵

In particular, sexual terms, subjects, and oblique references have known truly inconstant degrees of explicitness in Western literature, comedy, and public discourses. Often, they have found room for survival and/or full expression solely in special Bakhtinian carnivals, confined to singular social settings and, primarily, to lowly crowds. The same is true of many vulgar, impolite, uncouth yet popular terms, many of which have been used in humorous contexts—at least in the commonplace understanding of the key-term, e.g., mock aggressions, playful banter, daring boutades, acts of derision, open sarcasm. In an ironic twist on the early-modern educated Britons' search for 'refinement' discussed in Chapter 1 and, to a greater extent, in *H&C1*, it could be said to be a case of *fiat "umor" populi, et pereat Shaftesbury*.³⁴⁶

Even today, for all the *demo*cratic spirit of modernity, much of the *demos'* vernacular and commonplace humour has been opposed by the educated circles, who often see it as a prime and urgent mission of theirs to duly reform the ways in which common people speak, not least whenever engaging in something that these uneducated boors conceive of as 'humour'. What is more, the well-meaning members of these elites can still be easily disturbed by uncouth words *per se*, whether sexual or not, e.g., "fuck", "lame", "cunt", "greasehead", "midget", "cum", "retard", "Eskimo", or, as we discuss further in connection with A.J. Ayer's upsetting thoughts about cruel slights, "n[*****]" (i.e., Section 2.5.2).³⁴⁷

Such a cathectic immediacy,
(1) for one, further indicates the inexorable presence of an anaesthesia of the heart
(1a) in the ways in which the perceived 'great unwashed' horse about and,
(1b) at times, comedians themselves, who seem to take a perverse yet Freudianly sensible pleasure in exploring the grounds that are forbidden to all decent persons.³⁴⁸
(2) For another, it is also interestingly revealing of

---

345 More is said about the issues of humour's dissipation in the face of seriousness and free speech in *H&C3*.
346 Suspiciously, Lord Shaftesbury died in the year 1713. Did the yahoos win the battle?
347 Our censoring the last term in the list signals that there can be crueller domains than sexuality itself. As Montesquieu, Kant, Hallie and many others incessantly reported, *slavery is plausibly humankind's greatest crime*.
348 As discussed in Chapter 4, there arises at some point the cruel dilemma of siding with the 'refined' ones or with Bakhtin's common 'folk' instead.

(2a) the potentially hurtful (i.e., cruel) class reversals that such a rude commonplace humour can establish, however fleetingly;[349]
(2b) as well as of the deep-reaching and diffuse censoring forces of top-down social opinion, which is examined in detail in *H&C3*.[350]

For the moment, let us just note how some people's shock and shudder, whether genuine or mainly well-rehearsed, can be produced by the sheer *mention* of some of these disapproved-of, inappropriate, oft-insulting, yet sometimes humorously-intended terms, whether the humour is then also cruel or not.[351] This kind of blatantly negative affective reaction can happen even when the words at issue are clearly *not* being used in order to ridicule and/or insult anyone by any stretch of the imagination whatsoever—as in the present case, i.e., a stately scholarly study of humorous phenomena that, regrettably, may also be cruel, and sometimes horribly so.[352]

By inducing such strong emotional responses, these words represent a peculiar secular version of the profound unease that any open reference to Satan caused, and perhaps still causes, among the simple religious souls of Europe's Orthodox and Catholic countries.[353] This mere analogy is based on humble personal observations.[354] However, injunctions against ever uttering the devil's name are not rare, including in other monotheistic creeds, and they have been duly recorded. We can cite, for instance, a contemporary Turkish scholar, Günseli Gümüsel, who discussed the paradoxical case of the only known publicly "satanist" sect in today's Middle East, i.e., the Yezidis, who, even if "they worship Satan", "never say 'satan'" and "do not say ... words like 'lanet, nial, seretan, hitan, bostan ... bat, nat ...' which are derived from the word and rhythm of the word 'satan'", since "they are extremely afraid of it".[355]

---

349 We are not suggesting that the educated and the elites are incapable of crude expressions, including humorous ones. However, it is in working-class environments that this kind of popular rhetoric is more widespread, tangible and permissible, as artistically depicted, e.g., in Spike Lee's 1989 dramedy *Do the Right Thing*.
350 As we explain in *H&C3*, LVOA can help establish which trends are good and which are bad.
351 The studies cited in Chapter 3 cover thousands of cases of people taking offense at crude verbal utterances, and so do many more that are cited in *H&C1* and *H&C3*.
352 Even more such phenomena are tackled in *H&C3*. Our readers are thus forewarned.
353 Other Christian and Muslim confessional groups may be so disquieted, in addition.
354 Let us stress here the point that analogies are neither identities nor equivalences. Satan, for one, is supposed to be evil. The people ridiculed or taunted by means of rude terms, very often, are innocent victims.
355 Gümüsel (2019), 157.

Curiously, the contemporary China-based psychologist Theo A. Cope suggested that an eerily analogous "fear of Jung" may exist among our century's self-respecting 'scientific' psychologists.[356] These experts appear to dread being associated with the famed Swiss clinician whose openness to occult phenomena and creative take on theological and philosophical sources are frankly unsettling for such serious specialists, who are faithfully trained into the strictest adherence to standard operational protocols and sound empirical methodologies.[357] Worse still, Jung wrote extensively and repeatedly about "Satan", "the devil", and the many psychiatric, mythical, historical, and cultural incarnations of the accursed Other.[358] Perhaps—just like Lucifer or, a tad less supernaturally, the common man whose undignified humour Shaftesbury and many other gentlemen aimed at superseding —the 'eccentric' Jung should not be trusted either.[359]

2.2.3.6 Disparities

When laughing at someone else's alleged misfortunes, if something really serious has therein been detected and endorsed as such, the concerned person/s can be offended by its humorous treatment, even if the commonplace humour's declared and patent target/s cannot experience physical and/or psychological pain, or be directly harmed by it. Think, for example, of the extinct dodo being still a symbol of ridiculed stupidity, or of Queen Boadicea and her warriors being scorned for their doomed opposition to the Romans' vastly superior war machine.[360]

Insofar as these person/s can be said to experience suffering of some kind—on behalf of the absent and/or extinct target/s—the possibility of commonplace humour's continued connection with cruelty persists, notwithstanding that the intended or accidental harm is aimed elsewhere.[361] While an anaesthesia of the

---

356 Cope (2006), title *et passim*.
357 Cruelly, the parameters for seriousness and soundness have been known to vary from time to time.
358 Satan and his/her/its minions keep popping up in our books. This is no coincidence. Not only are devilish things notoriously cruel, but Lucifer and the demons have been frequently depicted while snickering or laughing.
359 *We* do discuss Jung here and, even more in detail, in *H&C3*. May God and serious psychologists forgive us.
360 Indubitably, *qua* matters of personal interpretation, additional subsidiary elements can be added or subtracted at will to turn the overall quality of these examples: the dodo becoming a Christ-like symbol of innocence *vis-à-vis* human cruelty and cunning; and Boadicea and her Britons being gallant patriots fighting for a lost cause.
361 The examples of the dodo and Boadicea indicate how paradoxical can be the outcomes of a genuine concern *vis-à-vis* the cruelty of commonplace humour. Shall we take seriously all the people who take something so seriously as to be pained by its ridiculing? Or shall we err on the side of

heart can facilitate humour, an extension of people's empathy, even towards beings or communities that no longer exist and that cannot experience any suffering or diminution, works in the opposite direction.[362]

2.2.3.6.1 The Art of Getting Wise

This contrast between laughability and empathy is true with regard to other people as well as to oneself. When laughing at one's own misfortunes, a suitable anaesthesia of the heart is required. How else could the affected individual/s find anything funny in their own disgrace, rather than shock, misery, sadness, or despair? Perhaps surprisingly, tragedy-struck persons have been capable of this feat, though maybe not on a regular basis. Laughing at oneself does not come as easy as laughing at others. As seen, both Schopenhauer and Hazlitt wrote that it is much trickier for human beings to have the emotional aloofness necessary to grasp something as amusing, when the source of this amusement is a person or an entity that we love dearly—our dear self *in primis*.[363]

We are not implying that such a self-directed cruelty should be avoided at all costs or in all cases.[364] On the contrary, it may be a paradoxical yet necessary step towards the acquisition of life-enabling philosophical wisdom. As Amir argued:

> Ridiculousness is sustained only by ignorance. Replacing ignorance with self-awareness, we not only transcend the tragic sense of life, but also transcend ourselves by achieving what is so foreign to our nature as explained by Nietzsche and Freud: self-acceptance. Humor ... becomes redemptive itself in encouraging self-acceptance to a degree that surpasses the limitations set by humanity, when defined only by tragedy and confusion. *The liberation humor brings forth rivals the highest ideals of religion and philosophy.*[365]

---

levity and joviality? Is it a matter of degree of painfulness (e.g., an animal lover shedding tears over the long-gone dodo), human dignity (e.g., no man or woman who died in battle ought to be ridiculed, no matter how long ago it may have happened), or sheer convention (e.g., we can laugh at ancient Britons, but not at the fallen of the Great War)? *We do not have clear-cut answers to this sort of questions. Clearly, before us lies only a risky and murky call for personal responsibility.*
362 See especially Santayana (1896).
363 See also Santayana (1896), as discussed extensively in *H&C1*.
364 Reflecting on rather humourless "regrets" and "remorse", Max Scheler (1921, 37) wrote of people's "cruelty to themselves" as signalling "secret vices or mental illnesses hiding under a semblance of virtue".
365 Amir (2019), 138; emphasis added. Interestingly, Du Toit and Whaley (2021, 96) identified both "spirituality" and "humour" among the "coping strategies" regularly utilised by people working in "trauma clean-up" teams in today's South Africa. More on humour *qua* coping mechanism on crime scenes is to be tackled in *H&C3*.

We all can reflect and attain a better, wiser understanding of ourselves, according to Amir; we can redescribe our condition, diminishing the merely ridiculous and gravely tragic components in favour of the truly humorous one.[366] Genuine humour, in Amir's sense, can and ought to be pursued and gained.[367] To do this, we must be stronger than our impulses to cry and despair. We must find a path towards an eventual smile, if not towards a merry chuckle. Brutal cruelty, *a fortiori*, can then be said to be a prerequisite of humour, above all at this thorny existential level, which comprises more than just humour about the many misfortunes that are brought upon us by nature.[368]

Likewise, it includes cases of humour about misfortunes that are caused by other people.[369] These misfortunes may have been brought about directly, indirectly, or even institutionally.[370] Gallows humour, even though morbid to some sensitive souls, is a well-known manifestation of this droll self-effacement.[371] Humour among conscripts, prison mates, even inmates in concentration camps, are instances of the same phenomenon.[372] Humour about 'horrible bosses' in the workplace is yet one more.[373] To which we can add humour regarding parents, parents-in-law, and people in positions of authority.[374]

---

[366] Amir's (2019) distinction between sheer ridiculousness and wiser humour becomes clearer later in this chapter.
[367] Further details and considerations on Amir's (2019) philosophy of humour follow in this chapter.
[368] How exactly we operate this anaesthesia is a mystery, but it is likely to be one of the will's many *tacit* abilities.
[369] Self-deprecation occurs here in the presence of a lower degree of inevitability than regarding the fatal cruelties of nature or fate. Thus, Harvey (1999, 65) warned about the deplorable moral "complicity" of the victim. The case of "masochists" is even more extreme, as A. Phillips (1998, 81) argued, for "cruelty may be positively welcomed" by them. However, as G. Scott (1996, 179) noted: "Masochistic phenomena" can be "unconnected with cruelty"; for instance, as reported by von Kraft-Ebing, "Marie Alacoque 'licked up' the excrement and sucked the festering of sores of sick persons … [and] Antoinette Bouvignon de la Porte mixed faeces with her food".
[370] *Pace* the implicit determinism of liberals' "market forces", social Darwinists' "natural selection" and Marxists' "historical materialism", we believe socio-political and economic arrangements to be human creations which truly autonomous collective bodies can call into question and reshape (see in particular Straume and Baruchello 2013).
[371] Humour can be a most effective coping mechanism under the worst circumstances, as discussed, e.g., in Sbattella and Molteni (2008). Hyperbolically, the pessimist Leopardi (n.d.a. [1898], 1894) argues that we laugh "chiefly about things that are effectively all but laughable, and often we do so precisely because they are not laughable".
[372] See, e.g., Oster (1998).
[373] See, e.g., the 2011–2017 *Horrible Bosses* comic film series.
[374] See, e.g., Powell and Paton (1988).

Humour about unemployment, economic insecurity, fear of destitution, and, broadly, all those largely avoidable conditions of socio-economic inferiority, passivity, and hazards, are variations on the same theme.[375] The dreadful context of war itself—normally the sad offspring of well-off bellicose leaders sending worse-off others to die in their name—establishes many, often surprising, opportunities for humour. Soldiers, for instance, have been known to challenge the enemy by laughing at them and/or charge into battle with roaring laughter.[376] Alternatively, they have been recorded, on occasion, to react to lethal wounds and impending demise by chortling rather than crying.[377]

2.2.3.6.2 The Art of Getting By

That which Amir depicts as wise and enlightened—i.e., laughing at one's own sorry condition, of which we are fully aware and for which we are not directly responsible—can then be interpreted as a far less philosophically praiseworthy achievement. At best, it can be characterised as a survival mechanism within or under cruel social settings.[378] Rebellion and indifference being likely to make things worse, laughing with those who laugh at us may then be the only sensible way to cope with, and go about, the dreadful business of living inside so cruel a society.[379] If we have an in-built instinctive drive to survive, if not even a moral duty to go on living for as long as we can, and either or both of them make a sig-

---

[375] Like slaves and serfs of old, many of today's workers reify the economic order into a natural one (e.g., "tsunamis", "bubbles", "overheating"), the cruelty of which is thus "institutionalized". Yet, behind it lie deregulated banks, CEOs, business-friendly politicians, and wilfully blind economists (see, e.g., Galbraith 2004). More on these matters, which can have humorous reverberations too, is said in *H&C3*.

[376] A hyperbolic fictional depiction of this phenomenon can be found in Stanley Kubrick's 1964 comedy *Dr Strangelove*, in which the character of Major T.J. "King" Kong, played by Slim Pickens, rides a nuclear warhead dropped onto a Soviet target, waving his cowboy hat, hooting with elation and cheering in screaming laughter.

[377] See Tritle (2015).

[378] See, e.g., Powell and Paton (1988). Al Gini and Abraham Singer (2020, 30) explain the long-standing tradition of Jewish humour *qua* remedy to a historical existence that has been "cruel ... always hard, a struggle". See Sover (2021) for a veritable cornucopia of tokens of and thoughts about Jewish humour, which rightfully looms large in the extant literature on humorous matters. More on Jewish humour is said in *H&C3*.

[379] Societies devoid of cruelty may not exist, and that might even be a good thing, as paradoxical as it sounds.

nificant difference, we may well have to engage in repeated self-effacing humour.[380]

Inevitably, life will call upon us to decide whether or not to rely on this kind of humour, in the face of inevitable cruelty, social as well as existential. Besides, if power imbalances continue to be present within a social context or community, then cruelty can most certainly find room and opportunity. As Hallie wrote: "[C]ruelty happens only when the victimizer has more power than the victim."[381] And where on earth, we wonder, is there no power imbalance? Where can genuine parity be found among the millions of unique individuals with their incredibly diverse mix of talents, quirks and imperfections?[382]

On this matter, Baroncelli once quipped: "I've never known of a diversity that – except in ethnological or social history textbooks – didn't bear a mark of superiority or inferiority."[383] Notwithstanding our many abstract and concrete equalities, which are nobly and noticeably enshrined in many a constitution, we all differ from one another as well. Personal identities and comparative senses of un/worth are thus built on such an omnipresent and rather obvious diversity, whether in the public sphere or in the private one. Sometimes, this diversity is celebrated, loudly and publicly. How many people have been publicly praised for being "unique", "special", "inimitable", "original", "irreplaceable", or "one of a kind"? Siblings, partners, friends, colleagues, and close associates play with such a feature all the time.[384]

The same is true, though, of our own enemies, competitors, and of all sorts of cruelly-minded individuals who may not get along with one another very well.[385] What is more, this diversity reflects also onto comic matters, whether conspicuously cruel or not, and it is all the stronger whenever the disparities at play are the most pronounced, e.g., in terms of political clout, financial means, special legal protections, or entrenched social pre-eminence. Sharp and deep hierarchies may

---

[380] While personal survival may seem at first an instinctual drive and an obvious fact of life, it can also be construed as a duty to oneself (e.g., the deontological opposition to suicide, as explained in Cholbi 2000) and others (e.g., as parents, spouses, fellow citizens). It can also be seen as the result of predominant social forces shaping and reshaping local cultures and the resulting sense of personhood with which the individual acquires and grapples (see, e.g., Pack 2018). However, for as long as a person is capable of lucid reasoning, the final word on whether to go on or not is left to each of us. If incapacitated, instead, different legal regimes assign this decision to spouses, children, etc. See, e.g., Wallace's (1976, 57) editorial, entitled "Pulling the Plug: Who Decides?".
[381] Hallie (1997), 234.
[382] We regard both questions as being rhetorical.
[383] As cited and translated in Veneziano (2008), par. 9.
[384] We presume our readers to have come across many such cases.
[385] The concluding subclause is a litotes, of course.

thus determine the openings for and the success of much commonplace humour. As Leacock jibed: "any hotel clerk with plastered hair is ready to laugh with the son of a multimillionaire. It's a certain sense of humour that they develop."[386]

People's inexorable and inherent diversity are likely to be part also of "the fundamental division between noble and ignoble [wo/]men" that Bataille's "General Economy" famously claimed to be at play in all unequal human *poleis:* "The cruel game of social life does not vary among the civilized countries, where the insulting splendour of the rich loses and degrades the human nature of the lower class."[387] Luxury being only *one* of the many forms that the "accursed share" of an economy's excessive production can take.[388] Other forms include the fine arts, public shows and entertainments, religious functions and perchance Freudianly, non-reproductive sex; but also nominally "cruel" activities such as human sacrifices, repressive State organisation, and the murderous warfare so deeply loathed by Montaigne.[389] In turn, all these differences and related hierarchies indirectly reflect the underpinning energy-surplus characterising the Sun's physical reactions and the Earth's bio-chemical systems, insofar as plurality, diversity, nonpeer statuses, and assorted imbalances are likely to be aetiologically rooted in the ontological make-up of our very universe—according to the noted French thinker, of course.[390]

More to the point, in the entertaining "Dialogo tra Andrea Dworkin e Nelson Mandela" penned by Baroncelli, the titular characters are said to have come to a secret agreement on power and inequality, which are claimed, once again, to pervade *all* types of social diversity. Specifically, in order to "combat their handicap", i.e., their ripe age, and keep "appealing to young women", wrinkly heterosexual old-timers like Mandela and obese middle-aged lesbians like Dworkin end up agreeing that they must go on relying upon and shamelessly spouting about convenient rhetorical "myths", such as "the wisdom and experience" of old age or the bizarre yet catchy radical theses proffered in preposterous academic "books

---

[386] Leacock (2001–2009), chap. 2, sec. 6, par. 21. The British TV comedy *The Windsors* (2018–2020) made frequent reference to this fact by letting Prince William believe that he was the greatest humourist who ever lived, given that everyone around him laughs at his jokes—for they all are beneath him in Britain's social hierarchy.
[387] Bataille (1997), 178. More on Bataille's use and understanding of "cruelty" proper is said in H&C3.
[388] Bataille (1967), title *et passim.*
[389] Bataille (1967).
[390] Bataille (1967), title *et passim.*

showing that Plato … justified and strengthened male power".[391] As the fictional Andrea Dworkin timidly admits in the conclusion of her hilarious imaginary dialogue with Nelson Mandela: "I realise that in a truly egalitarian world, without differences in wealth, prestige, intellectual charm, in short, power, beautiful people would go with beautiful people … old people into the dung-heap … the fat ones…".[392]

2.2.3.7 Duties

Having settled the unequal status of all, or nearly all, real people *vis-à-vis* one another, i.e., their being involved in "nonpeer" mutual relations, Harvey's *Civilized Oppression*—as well as its focus on the moral harms that disrespectful conduct can provoke—reminds us of the fact that it is still up to each and every one of us to decide:

(1) whether or not to (let people) laugh,
(2) what to (let people) laugh about,
(3) whom to (let people) laugh at, and/or
(4) whom to (let people) laugh with,
(5) up one's sleeve or not, or
(6) 'loudly' refuse to do so.[393]

This personal call is demanded even inside the most commonplace, routinised, and seemingly innocuous social settings, such as circles of close friends and families.[394]

Public, commonplace humour requires the full use of the deliberative mechanics of our conscience, i.e., *in foro interno*. As Harvey stated, while we enjoy the benefits of our being part of a moral community, we cannot avoid "the obliga-

---

[391] Baroncelli (2009), 136. It was reported to us that the fictional dialogue was based on exchanges between Baroncelli and Dworkin, who were both middle-aged and conspicuously overweight when they met in the US.
[392] Baroncelli (2009), 137. Humour's "inherent power" is attested also by the American anthropologist Donna M. Goldstein (2013, 275), especially in demarcating the border between insiders and "outsiders". In the same passage, Goldstein complained about "anthropologists" for failing to "have spent" sufficient "time exploring humor".
[393] Harvey (1999), 8 *et passim*. Harvey's analyses included also self-directed humour, as we have seen.
[394] Considering the differences in mental speed and emotional make-up among individuals, we cannot conceive of actual settings where full peer relations are the case, except for infancy and senile or pathological stupor.

tions that attach to membership in the moral community".[395] Therefore, before laughing anyone out of court, the court must be in session.

Following Harvey's logic, the ethical duty of treating people respectfully presents itself in the face of commonplace humour too, which is an intra- and interpersonal activity occurring within a moral community where all kinds of nonpeer relationships exist. What kind of respect and how much of it are owed to the relevant person/s under each specific set of humorous circumstances is impossible to determine *ex ante* and *in abstracto*. Harvey herself did not belabour this point. Perhaps, she intentionally avoided it.[396]

As a rule, and in all modesty, we hereby suggest following the concise wisdom of the contemporary Scottish-Icelandic legal scholar Rachael Lorna Johnstone, who, while discussing the work of the Italian political philosopher Anna Elisabetta Galeotti, affirmed that "recognition respect and appraisal respect are not of a different nature but rather shades of the same thing", hence endorsing

> a *presumption* of respect at level x for each person *qua* person, which amount can be increased on the basis of appraisal ($x + a$) or can be reduced on the basis of exceptionally immoral or anti-social behaviour ($x - b$). However, $x - b$ can never fall below a basic threshold (y), for example, to justify torture, non-consensual medical experimentation, or to treat human bodies as consumable economic resources. y is the level of equal minimum respect.[397]

In the context of commonplace humour, then, the responsible agent must consider, among other things: if and when s/he may wish to resort to humour; whether or not to do so; to what extent; about what; for how long; and with whom to do it.[398]

---

395 Harvey (1999), 142–143.
396 In the Aristotelian-Thomist tradition, the application of general, abstract moral principles to specific, concrete unique circumstances is the realm of practical wisdom (aka "phronesis"), which cannot be articulated fully in explicit words, for these operate at, again, a more general and abstract level (see, e.g., Noel 1999). Maxims, proverbs, rules, and laws can be formulated linguistically, but virtuous conduct can only be shown by factual agency, which attends *from* those linguistic inputs (and additional ones that are specific to the circumstances), so as to attend *to* the good deed to be performed, whether successfully or not. As we all know—sometimes in an embarrassing or troubling manner—there is no explicit rule regarding how we should follow even the simplest explicit rule. As such, moral behaviour further exemplifies Polanyi's (1962c) philosophy, upon which we rely.
397 Johnstone (2010, par. 14; emphasis in the original). This approach is a tad controversial, for it suggests that, although a modicum of respect is owed to all equally, some persons may nonetheless deserve more (e.g., on the grounds of their education, expertise and exploits), while some persons should receive less (e.g., due to ignorance, ineptitude and immorality).
398 This is a highly abstract rendition of the actual practical circumstances under which humour may occur or not, insofar as individuals have often no time to engage in any explicit, prolonged,

A fortiori, this sort of respectful deliberation, as recommended by Harvey, requires, at the very least: some ability to see things from another's perspective; the realisation of the degree and gravity of the non-parity at play; much tacit *savoir faire*; and the luck of not meeting a targeted laughingstock on a day when s/he/they has/ve no desire whatsoever to laugh or be laughed at, for whatever motive.[399]

For each morally competent person's humour to be "better aimed", attentive deliberation is called for, according to Harvey, unless some highly hypothetical "[m]orally alert humor" has somehow succeeded in becoming second nature to that person.[400] Until we, the adequately socialised language-users, reach such a positive, palatable, plausible, possible, purposeful, politically correct, and not-yet-present point in time, much remains uncertain, undefined, untethered, and unsettling. Thus, as a general heuristic, any facile hilarity ought to be avoided by the ethically responsible person, insofar as "[a]ccidental oversights and even a society-wide lack of awareness account for *far more* injustices and wrongs than do malice or indifference".[401]

Harvey's moral ideal necessitates plenty of time, good will, and committed effort. It is no joke at all. If anything, *it is the place where jokes come to die.* This is no grim exaggeration. As Harvey herself candidly acknowledged: "for an initial period when the relevant perceptual skills are being acquired, spontaneity may be hindered"; hence stopping "[h]umor" from being "sparkling, quick witted, born on the moment", and leading it to "become strained and dull", when not "tediously self-conscious and timid".[402] Rather than running the stupid and potentially cruel risk of dropping the bomb, the ethically responsible person should better keep quiet.[403] As also Carroll once stated: "sometimes silence is the best policy".[404]

---

and profound deliberation, but rather have to rely on habit, expectation, and, above all, "tacit integration" of countless details (Polanyi 1962c, 93).

399 Luck, albeit troubling, is a crucial factor in the realm of moral agency (see Levy 2011). Very few Western thinkers have rendered luck its due, focussing instead on agency that can be steered or determined by human will. Among these few, we can highlight Machiavelli (1908) who devoted a long chapter (nr. 25) to this peculiar factor long before Nagel (1979), Williams (1981), or even Adam Smith's *Theory of Moral Sentiments*, as examined under this respect by Garrett (2005).

400 Harvey (1999), 15. Harvey conveniently ignored the fact that ethical standards and social expectations can change subtly, suddenly and/or countless times during a person's life; self-monitoring and self-revision are *endless*.

401 Harvey (1999), 142; emphasis added.

402 Harvey (1999), 15. Spontaneity is a crucial component of effective humour under most circumstances, which are non-scripted, e.g., daily conversations and improvised theatre (see, e.g., Landert 2021).

403 Based on personal interactions, we can testify to Harvey's personal coherence in this regard. Kind and considered, she was always softly-spoken and somewhat reserved, and we cannot recall her ever initiating any jest.

2.2.3.8 Dozes

Faced with such a challenge, in daily life, the demanding moral duties implied by culturally widespread humorous attitudes and practices are repeatedly ignored, underplayed, forgotten, or even ridiculed themselves because, after all, it is all 'just a bit of fun'.[405] All of this happening, incidentally, in low- as well as high-brow contexts and circumstances.[406] If, adhering to Bergson's and many other thinkers' insights, we accept the notion that we have to operate an anaesthesia of our hearts for the sake of humorous merriment, the ethical duties that such merriment involves can be easily and seriously impaired by our less sympathetic attitude.[407]

Out hearts' sleepiness and the resulting brutality that this sleepiness involves in humorous contexts might well cause us to become less prone, likely to detect, and/or engage in concrete instances of moral consideration and moral agency.[408] *Sleeping is a basic life need*, though.[409] Without adequate rest and recuperation, as we all know, illness and death ensue. Therefore, it could be argued that

---

404 Carroll (2014), 117.
405 The ongoing concerns regarding political correctness are part of humour's ethical implications and their misrecognition, as discussed in Hughes (2010). At a deeper level, the widespread unwillingness to subject humour to moral constraints corroborates further the notion of its 'release' function, similarly to the erotic sphere, which too is often seen and lived as a special domain where people may "fulfil the aching need for perverse transgression" (A. Phillips 1998, 117). "[I]nsofar as, to be 'normal', we all need to be a little neurotic and a little psychotic, by the same token—and consequently—we are all in need of laughter, now and again" (Santoro-Brienza 2004, 84).
406 Raudino's (2003–2008, 7) extensive study of Umberto Eco *qua* Italy's famous humourist is very telling, in this respect, for it never considers the power relations, implicit hierarchies and resulting humiliations that allowed Eco to engage in the "virtuoso's pieces and linguistic games" for which his humour is still well-known today.
407 Actualised primarily by means of tacit abilities of self-direction, humour's required callousness indicates that the tweaking of sympathetic feelings at work inside it is analogous, but not identical, to the one taking place among, say, nurses, police agents, surgeons, and educators who must balance their propensity to care with the emotional aloofness necessary to perform their duties efficiently, e.g., without crying or screaming (see, e.g., Carmack 1997).
408 Commonplace exculpations such as "I didn't mean it" and "I was being silly" or "stupid" hint precisely at the careless *superficiality* of jokes and other remarks that are made in jest and nonetheless hurt someone's feelings.
409 For a clear-cut definition of "need"-*cum*-distinction-from "wants" or "preferences", and for a precise list of humankind's fundamental life needs, see McMurtry (2002, 156–157). The same distinction, derived from the tenets of LVOA, was tackled by J. Noonan (2006, 57–59), who emphasised the need for free time. The tension between needs and wants runs throughout McMurtry (2013b).

moral ineptitude, or incoherence itself, may not always be unwelcome, personally and/or socially speaking, at least insofar as commonplace humour is concerned.[410]

Interestingly, while tackling the issue of political correctness *vis-à-vis* the oeuvre of the celebrated 20th-century analytic philosopher A.J. Ayer, Baroncelli observed, *en passant*, that we should never underplay the beneficial social outcomes of our species' time-tested lack of moral virtue.[411] Indifference, nonchalance, superficiality, dispassion, if not even a modicum of inconstant hypocrisy, and a charitable—perhaps Freudianly sadomasochistic—acceptance of mutual offences can go a long way in creating room for humour and, more importantly, wellbeing.[412] Acting in perplexing yet providential unison, the same moral failures can prove equally useful in keeping the peace—which is, again, much more significant a result than humour itself.[413]

2.2.3.8.1 Interiority and Inconsistency

At an even deeper level of psychological assessment, such a lack of moral virtue can also be construed as a necessary channel whereby we, if sufficiently balanced, can give adequate space and opportunity for the many lower-order personalities inhabiting our psyche to find some healthy discharge, i.e., along a Jungian line of understanding of people's mental life. True enough, these personalities are, normally, hierarchically structured and experienced.[414] This is the case with nearly all healthy individuals, inside whom the conscious *ego* is formed during youth *qua* guiding centre of selfhood and personal "continuity".[415] At times, and most unhealthily, these personalities can be chaotically anarchic, as observable in schizophren-

---

410 "True humour", instead, may be cognizant of the moral tension at play and rely on it for its artistic ends.
411 See Baroncelli (1996), chap. 7. On Ayer's work and career see Macdonald (2005–2018) and Rogers (1999).
412 See Baroncelli (1996), chap. 7.
413 One of the authors of this book is an Italian who has lived on foreign soil for almost half his life. Had he been resentfully provoked every time someone made some tongue-in-cheek yet unsettling remark about the mafia or used "eyetie" and "goombah", he would have never been able to complete this book.
414 As we discuss in more detail in *H&C3* in connection with Jung's seminal insights, each individual living psyche can be depicted as a parliament of variously well-formed personalities or affectively-charged complexes.
415 Jung (1960–1990), vol. 9.1, 66, par. 135. As clinically studied, the *ego* may fail to duly acknowledge this intra-psychic plurality, and even reduce itself to those conscious aspects of the *ego* that work very well in public, i.e., the so-called *persona*. As Jung (1960–1990, vol. 9.1, 123, par. 221; emphasis added) quipped: *"the temptation to be what one seems to be is great, because the persona is usually rewarded in cash"*.

ic patients who can actually hear and/or speak *qua* all such different "little people".⁴¹⁶

Depending on the circumstances, as Jung argued, some of these inner people (aka "complexes") can take charge, however temporarily, in a life-enabling way, e.g., when "the Father" emerges within a young soldier and makes him stoical, sane, and alive on the battlefield; or when "the Mother" surges inside a young woman who thus becomes capable of withstanding unprecedented physical pain, enduring willingly prolonged strain, and eventually delivering a new life into this world.⁴¹⁷ How many times, upon reflection, can we say that we exhibited a different personality in our bosom or conduct, i.e., one that was not our usual "ego"?⁴¹⁸ Such deviations from the norm being facilitated, perhaps, by: the consumption of laughing water; the exceptional liberties of a socially permitted carnival; the pressing demands of unexpected circumstances; or the sublime feelings of romantic involvement, spiritual elation, and creative impulse.⁴¹⁹

Ralph Waldo Emerson most certainly had the last two situations in mind when quipping "consistency is the hobgoblin of little minds".⁴²⁰ Perhaps, the normally dominant conscious *ego*, upon which our moral integrity and behavioural consistency depend in daily life, should sometimes better go to sleep. As a matter of ultimate survival, the *ego* must actually do so. We all have to go to sleep every night, fall into unconsciousness and, feasibly, dream.⁴²¹ If we do not do so often and long

---

416 Jung (1960–1990), vol. 8, par. 209. Unlike Deleuze and Guattari, Jung was not welcoming schizophrenia as a new anthropological ideal, but the integrating awareness of our inner plurality. Harmony in diversity, in short.
417 Jung (1960–1990), vol. 9.2, 3, par. 1, and vol. 9.1, 214–215, par. 396. The examples are our own.
418 On a personal note, we can recount numerous occasions when someone uttered phrases like "the devil made me do it", "I wasn't really myself", or "that's not my usual self". Analytical psychology has many hypotheses on *which* 'self' it was or could have been. Yet Jung (1964, 88) was well aware of the fact that a person who has never lived through any such moments would be unable to grasp their affect-laden meaning: "if they are mere images whose numinosity you have never experienced, it will be as if you were talking in a dream".
419 We expect that most of our readers have had such experiences or are able to imagine them.
420 Emerson (1841), 7. Taken together, e.g., Plato's dialogues tackle different topics and end with contradictory claims.
421 We write "dream" to suggest images of oneiric activity, which depth psychology considers to have, *inter alia*, compensatory functions, i.e., the satisfactory experiencing of repressed sides of the psyche. As we are going to explain in *H&C3*, humour itself can play such a compensatory function. Indeed, *conscious activities such as humour may work better than nightdreams*, given at least the limited empirical corroboration of the latter's compensatory function recorded over the decades by a few researchers (see, e.g., Domino 1976 and Hotson 2000).

enough, in the end, we get sick and die—let us be pedagogically redundant on this medical point.[422]

2.2.3.8.2 Immorality and Indifference

Whether we follow *in toto* or at all such a Jungian line of understanding, there remains nonetheless the observant point that a community of lazy, casually inattentive, and consistently easy-going individuals, however ethically imperfect and philosophically disappointing they may be deemed to be, can better accommodate personal diversity and cultural plurality. Such attributes would also include humour in both good and bad taste.[423] In all probability, they would comprise Baroncelli's own scathing jokes about obtuse philosophers, hypocritical academics, dirty old men, and self-serving LGBTQ+ fat thinkers.[424]

Emerson and Baroncelli aside, few Western thinkers have been openly positive about our species' many imperfections, not least human hypocrisy or people's mercuriality.[425] Even so, while praising Montaigne's intellectual and personal honesty with regard to talking openly and frankly about his own frailties, sins, and inconstancies, the great Russian existentialist Leo Shestov noted: "Three-fourths of our education goes to teaching us most carefully to conceal within ourselves the changeableness of our moods and judgments" and feign to be "a stock, a statue, the qualities and defects of which are known to everybody", so as not to become objects of ridicule, "satires and humorous sketches".[426]

Also, such a morally imperfect and advantageously indifferent community could exhibit this kind of lazy yet effectual tolerance far more easily than one whose members pursue virtue, propriety, and correctness wholeheartedly, condemn vice most passionately, and display a keen vigilance *vis-à-vis* one another's

---

[422] Our most inimical critics are hereby invited to experiment with sleeplessness for a few weeks.
[423] *The real test of tolerance and pluralism occurs when we encounter stances and behaviours that we dislike or disagree with. Tolerating that which we like or agree with is not much of a test.* As to the thorny issue of separating between good and bad taste, see, e.g., Kuipers (2008).
[424] The coarseness of the chosen linguistic expressions is *intended* because it is relevant. Humourists, in general, seem to enjoy, if not require, scathing jokes and risky postures, unlike polite old aunts and quiet friars. Also, the negative reactions that certain readers may have, such as editors and reviewers, indicate a penchant for *self-censorship* affecting today's universities in allegedly liberal nations. This is an issue that we address in *H&C3*.
[425] In the 18th century, Mandeville's (1989) appraised virtue and vice in an 'immoral' way, i.e., by turning selfishness into a virtue. Smith's "invisible hand" and "own interest" have been so mis/interpreted too, for they point towards a doctrine of socially positive unintended consequences. Yet, Smith's "own interest" is far more complex a trait than Mandeville's outright egotism (see, e.g., Smith and Wilson 2019, chap. 2, 7 and 11).
[426] Shestov (1920), part 1, par. 100.

shortcomings—when not just *vis-à-vis* another's.[427] As Cioran so perceptively wrote whilst reflecting on the wisdom of Saint John Climacus: "'He who is inclined to lust is merciful and tender-hearted; those who are inclined to purity are not so'... It took a saint, neither more nor less, to denounce so distinctly and so vigorously not the lies but the very essence of Christian morality, and indeed of all morality."[428]

2.2.3.8.3 Inclinations, Interests, and an Ingratiation

Once we step outside of, say, stately Western books, progressive universities, and serious essays about ethics—or, for another, the committed strivings of the most conscientious Christians—being moral comes across as merely one among the many actual aims that real persons have, both when interacting with one another and with themselves.[429] Being witty, sounding smart, looking pretty, fitting in, impressing the boys or the ladies, making money, having a career, having fun, fulfilling a whim, making a splash, being admired, or remaining unnoticed are all possible concomitant aims that, more often than not, take precedence over eminently moral considerations, whether categorically or comparatively. Such shocking things have been rumoured to happen, from time to time, even among the allegedly judicious and assuredly judgemental members of Western academe.[430]

---

[427] See Baroncelli (1996), chap. 7. Undoubtedly, in our career, we have met a fair share of fellow academics who were very keen on denouncing all kinds of social injustices, structural inequalities and cultural harms, and yet steamrolled select colleagues in a callous manner and/or targeted others in sadistic ways. Ironically, they found it much easier to attack the devils that they saw so clearly around themselves than to see the ugly daemons swarming inside their own soul. Evil belongs to the *Other* alone, and it is often cast as an '-ism' of which this Other is guilty.

[428] Cioran (2011), 123.

[429] A witty Biblical passage (Matthew 7:3–5) on specks and logs (or motes and beams) alludes to the fact that many self-righteous individuals are far more prone to spot and criticise other people's shortcomings than to identify, reflect upon, and/or attempt to correct their own. (We assume our readers to have heard of this Biblical passage and, of course, to adhere wholeheartedly to its sobering wisdom as they read the present book.)

[430] See, e.g., Kaufmann (2021, 181) for a recent empirical investigation of partisanship and ideology in today's Anglophone academia, "find[ing] a) a strong left skew in the professoriate; b) significant political discrimination against conservatives; and c) chilling effects and self-censorship". Even if the present authors probably contribute to the "left skew" mentioned in the empirical study, we find these results rather disquieting. Anyway, more on liberalism, censoriousness, and self-censorship is discussed in *H&C3*.

Nor do epistemic goals and considerations fare any better, in all likelihood.[431] As Bertrand Russell wittily remarked:

> The first thing to realize, if you wish to become a philosopher, is that most people go through life with a whole world of beliefs that have no sort of rational justification, and that one man's world of beliefs is apt to be incompatible with another man's, so that they cannot both be right. People's opinions are mainly designed to make them feel comfortable; truth, for most people is a secondary consideration.[432]

Then adding and possibly teasing, or maybe trying to ingratiate himself with, his own audience: "You, dear readers, have of course no prejudices; but you will admit that in this you are different from most people."[433]

Who knows? Perhaps, we are hereby as lucky as Russell was, or pretended to be, in the unprejudiced attitude of our readership.[434] Or if not, in having readers who, at the very least, would like to think of themselves as unbiased and candidly open-minded, while they are actually not so, or hardly as much as they believe to be—and whether or not they so believe in genuine good faith or, as it may also happen to fallible and complex creatures such as ourselves, in self-deceiving bad faith.[435]

2.2.3.9 Dilemmas

Acting as counterpoint to Jungian psychology and Baroncelli's 'immoral' yet intriguing suggestions, which pivot around the notion of socially beneficial unintended

---

[431] We do not exclude *a priori* that there may be gifted individuals who are thoroughly moral and always right. Given our life experiences, however, we do not regard these hypothetical cases as the most common specimens.
[432] Russell (1968), 2.
[433] Russell (1968), 2.
[434] It may not be possible to remain candidly open-minded when some stances in moral or political life challenge radically our own "ethos ... emotional universe ... [and] all that [we] value in human experience and human achievement", as Russell (2016) himself wrote in a scathing 1962 letter directed to, and at, the British fascist leader, Sir Oswald Mosley (Russell was a vocal left-winger throughout his adult life).
[435] As repeatedly argued in our own trilogy, it may simply be impossible to be totally unbiased, or even unlimitedly open-minded. Not only do we need starting premises that are accepted upon faith, as discussed by Polanyi (1962c) in relation to modern science itself and Hazlitt (1912, 56–60) on "prejudices" *qua* presupposed structures of cognitive apprehension and agency. More prosaically, we may also be forced to accept other people's claims upon faith, however indirectly supported by circumstantial evidence and considerations, insofar as we do not have the time and/or talent required to acquire, assess, and informedly assent to their competences and conclusions, e.g., physicians, physicists, and car mechanics.

consequences and open room for the many uses (and abuses) of humour, Harvey's work reminds us of the fact, and reasserts with sincere commitment, that the intended discharge of our ethical duties does not cease to exist as such, even if the circumstances may work not in their favour. Quite the opposite, our ethical duties endure, even if we happen to live in a community that is happily blind to at least part of their own members' moral demands regarding one another.[436] Once we wake up from our moral torpor, in other words, we cannot avoid being confronted by the ethical implications of our conduct and of its consequences, humorous ones included, whether we like it or not. Ethical duties persist, even in the face of potential hurdles or paradoxically likable spill-overs of unethical distractions, at least for each morally competent individual in a sufficiently evolved community.[437]

As boring, uninspiring, demanding, 'Socratically' stinging and/or pragmatically troubling as a person's practical reason may be, this faculty of ours can still acknowledge its own duties in a lucid and candid manner.[438] That which ought to be done is purely so in the eye of our moral conscience, irrespective of any heart's anaesthesia, our overall psychic health, and/or the indirect social advantages of people's ethical lethargy and mutual inconsequence.[439] In the end, then, *we are cast between a rock and a hard place.*[440] Whenever being humorous is at issue,

---

[436] We are using here "moral" and "ethical" as synonyms.

[437] Mental impairment, psychiatric conditions, and educational failures can cause individuals to be morally incompetent (see, e.g., Dillard 2011–2012).

[438] Socrates compared himself to a gadfly, whose task was to sting a lazy horse into action, i.e., to spur the morally inept Athenians into an ethical path of self-improvement (see DiCarlo 2011, who elected Socrates his hero).

[439] The relationship between our rational faculties and our emotional dispositions with respect to moral deliberation and free agency is a notoriously contested issue in Western ethics. That they both play a role, however, is recognised by all philosophical traditions, whether they prioritise the former set of factors or the latter. We presuppose here, as also did Harvey (1999), that we can master the art of self-control and self-direction to a meaningful extent, *contra* the determinism of many modern intellectuals, including science-fiction writers like H.G. Wells, who was gently satirised for imagining that "our civilization will find itself in an interesting situation, not without humour; in which the citizen is still supposed to wield imperial powers over the ends of the earth, but has admittedly no power over his own body and soul at all" (Chesterton 2000, par. 7).

[440] This depressing conclusion may seem perplexing, given humour's social acceptance as lighthearted, cordial, playful, and relaxing. However, digging into this phenomenon can vindicate the conception of 'humour' developed by Deleuze (1989 and 1990). Insofar as humour operates as the destroyer of established meanings, much more than mere semantics are imperilled by its use, whether in its commonplace or nominally "true" forms. Aesthetic, ethical, economic, legal, social, political, religious, logical, psychological, epistemic, and *all* other values, which we can entertain and appraise if and only if they have a solid meaningful form, can be annihilated by humour. Laughter, in this perspective, is the potential ally of uncommitted nihilism, utter illogicality, and ultimate madness, which Deleuze arguably embraced himself as a possible rendition of the deep-

we are inescapably presented with having to make a seemingly prosaic, but actually difficult, complex, subtly cruel choice, i.e., whether to be, or not to be, funny. Or, to be more precise, whether to try, or not to try, to be funny, which means also exposing oneself and others to the cruel risk of cruel failure.[441]

Hopefully, as we take on this ordinary yet challenging challenge, we will not err in being either too boorish or too silly. Similarly, we should also hope that we will not err in being either too bland or too offensive, and/or in selecting our comic target/s, audience/s, and means of mirth in a sensible and sensitive manner. And yet, insofar as any choice, if not even each and every socially salient aspect of the composite act of choosing, is in itself tantamount to a hopeful personal *performance*, we can stay assured that we may still go belly up. And, as it happens, that we will indeed go belly up at some point—sometimes, unfortunately for us and for all affected parties, truly and miserably so.[442]

This dismal condition is, in essence, a likely case of *spes ultima rea*.[443] Life's cruelty thrives also in its trifling moments upon which we tend, perhaps conveniently or even healthily, not to reflect much on a daily basis.[444] Indeed, as regards humour-related choices, we may even decide to take a brave or foolish nap—morally speaking—for the sake of having fun and/or letting others have fun.[445] Too judgemental a disposition of the heart and mind cannot but reduce the probability of enjoying humour in many of its manifestations, which are typically anything but innocent, lest they come across as too 'proper', regimented, right-thinking, timorous and, worst of all, they are accused of being "boring".[446]

---

est, distinction-less reality of being in his declaredly "rhizomatic" and "schizoid" metaphysics (see Lopez 2004). Seemingly liberating, this criterion-less totality can be, when embraced subjectively, overwhelming and dramatic, as *per* the experiences of intoxication (Deleuze struggled with alcoholism, after all) and "mental illness" (e.g., Deleuze's doubts on the aims of "modern therapy", i.e., to restore or introduce a "unitary whole", "stability", "psychic integration", as explained by M. Roberts 2006, 191–192). *Staring reality in the face may be enthralling, but it can also be estranging.*
[441] More on humorous failures is said in *H&C3*.
[442] Successful performances are never assured. Even the best comedians fail. Moreover, as regards the import of Polanyi's (1962c) 'from-to' phenomenology, choices further exemplify it, insofar as they imply tacit integrations of multiple subsidiary details for the agent to be able to attend to the specific aim at issue, e.g., humour.
[443] This being a pun, not an instance of rhetorical barbarism.
[444] See, e.g., McDougall (1926), whose work we discussed in *H&C1*.
[445] These moral "naps" may be personal 'carnivals' of sorts, the beneficial and/or necessary occasions in which our psychic wellbeing is being taken care of by the daring individual who opts for risky laughter instead of cautious dourness, in line with Shaftesbury's seminal intuitions about humour as a means for relief (see *H&C1*).
[446] Lukošienė (2016), 163.

2.2.3.10 Decisions

Personal responsibility is inescapable.[447] Eventually, in all our intersubjective interactions, our context-dependent liberty-*cum*-responsibility is going to be put to the test. Whether, though, we are ready and/or competent or not is a major question mark, not least with regard to humour in all of its variations.[448] The cruel dilemma of whether or not to avoid humour, so that nobody is at risk of being offended, is a variation on a subtending troublesome theme of ethical life in general. This is a puzzle that cannot be solved, but only experienced and coped with as best as we can, swallowing the doubt and the pain that it may cause to us *qua* reflecting persons. Specifically, whenever we make a choice, which can be good or bad from a moral perspective, we put ourselves in a cruelly difficult position—if and when we come to realise it *and* think about it. In short, we must *make a decision*.[449]

Given the imperfect creatures that we are, decisions on humour are based on fallible faculties, vague maxims, incomplete information, obdurate biases, contingent guiding principles, selective memories, tentative heuristics, social traditions taken as obvious truths, knee-jerk reactions upheld as unshakeable insights, ingenious abstract fictions that we believe to be actual things, and shoddy habits that we may well mistake for sound strategies. Often and, arguably, to avoid the paralysing and stinging realisation of our sorry condition, we just act, relying on patterns of conduct, a large pinch of hopefulness, mutable standards of relevance, plausibility and evidence, the overall flow of social conduct, plenty of tacit inputs, and the 'white lie', according to which we know what we are doing.[450]

---

447 In Anglophone linguistic philosophy, the US thinker Stanley Cavell (2003, xiii) came close to this realisation when arguing that "Austin identifies speaking as giving one's word, as if an 'I promise' implicitly lines every act of speech, of intelligibility, as it were a condition of speech as such." As we discussed in *H&C1*, this was essentially Polanyi's (1962c, title *et passim*) claim about "personal knowledge" at large, and it also underpinned his moral interpretation of Frege's modern logic. Each person is ultimately *responsible* for her claims.
448 Additional considerations about the cruel choice between humour and humourlessness appear in *H&C3*.
449 This fundamental ethical problem impinges upon an even deeper epistemic issue, i.e., the necessarily faith-based preconditions for all knowledge, as explained in *H&C1* with regard to Polanyi (1962c) and Quine (1963).
450 We are not implying or advocating any moral relativism, as purported instead by liberal ordinalism, legal positivism, and much postmodernism. LVOA, human rights jurisprudence, and the Natural Law tradition remind us of the likely existence of universally valid determinations of good and bad, based upon sound appraisals of value. Yet even if we are keen on these ethically and axiologically substantive views, there remains the crucial fact that *each* responsible person must come to recognise and assent to such determinations in both theory and practice. Hence, as emphasised in Section 2.5, even if a person may follow this path, intellectual, emotional, moral,

At a deeper level, such Gordian knots can only be cut by way of a person's embrace of a fundamental, socially-bestowed onto-axiology, whether this leap of faith occurs consciously—hence responsibly—or not—hence irresponsibly—or somewhere in between these two 'decisive' poles.[451] As insightfully stated by the contemporary Canada-based political philosopher Charles Taylor while discussing Michael Polanyi's work: "You don't have ethical, moral, or, for that matter, religious views about the value of things unless you really *have them* as powerful intuitions" that inform your conduct and affect your behaviour.[452] The same logic of personal commitment applies to the "metaphysical views" underlying the sort of epistemology that we live by, for we all cannot live without one, no matter how poorly conceptualised it may be by the person clinging onto it, or merely applying it in an unreflective manner, like someone who never spent any time checking the ground on which s/he stands.[453]

If the former pole applies fully, a subtle cruelty still continues to lurk behind our responsible and very 'Alexandrine' piece of swordsmanship. Specifically, the more responsible we are, the more we are also aware that we have decided to embrace a certain set of psychic objects *as though* they were real and compelling—knowing all too well that they are constructed psychic objects first and foremost, i.e., if we are fully and truly honest with ourselves on an epistemological level.[454] What is more, in yet another example of life's cruel irony, we have no practical alternative path available. In a bittersweet way, we cannot but cast the fate of our whole life, both this- and otherworldly, upon such unnerving philosophical bases, which only unreflecting ignorance, habit-driven inertia, adamant dogmatism, intellectual dishonesty, expedient superficiality, and die-hard scepticism may be capable of avoiding for as long as they truly last in a person's existence.[455]

---

and practical *performances* are called for, meaning that the possibility of error persists at many levels.
451 See, again, Polanyi (1962c) and Quine (1963), as discussed at length in *H&C1*. See also Barden and Baruchello (2019, chap. 2–3 and 7), in which we explained how reason, intuition, and adherence to tradition can coexist and cooperate in sustaining a person's fiduciary embrace of ultimate beliefs that cannot be simply demonstrated.
452 C. Taylor (2017), 23; emphasis in the original.
453 C. Taylor (2017), 23.
454 See Vaihingen (1935) and Avaliani (2018).
455 Once philosophical reflection is started in real life, *we* find it impossible to opt for any of these alternatives.

2.3 True Humour

> It has sometimes been made a wonder that things so discordant should go together—that men of humour are often likewise men of sensibility. But the wonder should rather be to see them divided; to find true genial humour dwelling in a mind that was coarse or callous. The essence of humour is sensibility; warm, tender fellow-feeling with all forms of existence. Nay, we may say, that unless seasoned and purified by humour, sensibility is apt to run wild; will readily corrupt into disease, falsehood, or in one word, sentimentality.
> —Thomas Carlyle[456]

With reference to Schopenhauer's and Pirandello's narrower, literary, stereotypically British (or not), and elitist interpretation of "humour" proper, we can observe an analogous inherent 'Bergsonesque' logic of 'cardiac slumber'.[457] We have three chief reasons for this statement:

(1) Concerning both the fatal and the human-made cruelties of life, "true humour" can arise in the face of all kinds of accidents, fatalities, errors, and horrors. Indeed, the seriousness of these horrors is precisely that gloomy depth which feeds the sublime mood of the humourist and furnishes the pathos that, combined with superficial comicality, generates the duality required for "true humour" to

---

[456] Carlyle (1835), 454. To make a short story shorter, Carlyle (1835, 453–455) briefly addressed the issue of "true humour" in an obituary commemorating the German writer and humourist Jean Paul Friedrich Richter (aka "Jean Paul"), whereby "humour" was contrasted with "irony", and "[t]rue humour" was said to "spring not more from the head than from the heart; it is not contempt; its essence is love; it issues not in laughter, but in still smiles, which lie far deeper. It is a sort of inverse sublimity; exalting, as it were, into our affections what is below us, while sublimity draws down into our affections what is above us". According to Carlyle (1835, 453–454), only Cervantes could be put on a par with Richter as a towering 'true' humourist in the Western canon. And as seen in Chapter 1, Schopenhauer (1909) and Pirandello (1920) were to inherit and philosophically expand upon such a compassionate, subtly smiling, Romantic conception of "humour" proper. Given the extent of their disquisitions, the two later thinkers were tackled by us in much more detail than Carlyle, both here and in *H&C1*. Besides, Carlyle's (1853) advocacy of racism and slavery would make him a better choice *vis-à-vis* 'cruelty' than 'humour'.

[457] We write "stereotypically British" because, as Pirandello (1920) argued, "true humour" is found in all literary traditions, e.g., Cervantes' *Don Quixote*, which is a recurrent point of reference for humour scholars. Ironically, for all the attributions of "humour" or even "true humour" that the Spanish writer received, Nietzsche's *Nachlass* includes some brief comments on Cervantes' masterpiece in which his comedic style is associated with nothing short of "Grausamkeit" [cruelty], thus corroborating further the essential link between our titular concepts, even when "humour" proper is said to be compassionate, refined, humble, etc. (Slama 2022).

emerge.[458] Tellingly, one of Schopenhauer's chosen examples came from Shakespeare's *Hamlet* and dealt with death in one of its most terrible modalities, i.e., suicide, which the titular character is contemplating before a baffled Polonius: "You cannot, sir, take from me anything that I will more willingly part withal, except my life, except my life, except my life."[459] Pirandello's own chief exemplification of "true humour" referred to a desperately made-up and hopelessly attired old lady whose age conspires against her prospects of keeping her younger husband attracted to her.[460] How can anyone even smile in amusement, not to mention laugh, when confronted with such tragic aspects of the human condition?[461]

The answer is, once again, Bergson's emotional numbness; i.e., callousness, aka brutality. As Amir herself acknowledged: "By keeping desire in check, and reducing sadness, fear, anger, shame and disgust, humor puts into effect 'a momentary anesthesia of the heart'."[462] In the realm of fiction, the *active* brutal cruelty of the playwright, film-maker, or novelist consists precisely in creating adequate diversion by way of comical counterpoint which must facilitate the lowering of compassion or, if compassion needs no lowering, its keeping it well where it is.[463] The humourist is a pâtissier mixing different ingredients, aiming at producing an appetising new cake with a subtle contrast of flavours, but not an appetiser or a strange new dish that does not work as a dessert.[464]

Mistakes are possible, of course.[465] Undeniably, the subtler the intermingling of comedic and tragic elements becomes, the riskier the whole enterprise is.[466] The *passive* brutal cruelty of the spectator or reader consists in going along with the humourist's strategy and allowing a personal departure from or diminution

---

458 The term "duality" embraces all the oppositions, bisociations, incongruities, etc. that humour has been said to consist in, especially *qua* "true humour", which mixes in a strange tension satire and pathos (see Chapter 1).
459 Schopenhauer (1909), vol. 2, chap. 8, 277.
460 As noted, age-uneven matches have been another standard theme in film comedies, the roots of which can be found in ancient Greek comedy, e.g., Aristophanes' *Lysistrata* (see Henderson 1991, chap. 3–7).
461 *Hamlet* is a tragedy, and dramatic, age-uneven romances exist (see, e.g., Verga 1881).
462 Amir (2019), 105.
463 There may be cases where the compassionate element is heightened to approach "true humour", if not move past it, e.g., the normally farcical clown becoming a tragic hero in Leoncavallo's opera *Pagliacci*, or Hugo's (2002) Gwynplaine, the protagonist of *L'homme qui rit*, whose indelible smile is the result of cruel mutilation (see also Paul Leni's remarkable 1928 film adaptation of Hugo's melodrama, i.e., *The Man Who Laughs*).
464 Our readers are free to like their food in any form, order, or typology. *De gustibus non disputandum est.*
465 Poorly received film comedies aiming at sophisticated humour were discussed in Salmi (2011).
466 See, e.g., Oloskey Mills (1974).

of one's own sympathetic feelings in the face of cruelty and making someone else suffer.[467] The more sophisticated the humourist's operation, the trickier it can get for the spectator or reader to follow it to its desired climax.[468] As Pirandello noted, humourists walk the tightrope between the tragic and the comic—and some of them may fail in getting the level of this tension just right.[469]

(2) We should not forget that sadism remains part of the picture too. Insofar as the satirical component is actually pursued, even the most refined humourist is *actively* sadistic, to some degree, in line with the hereby-endorsed conceptual taxonomies by Hallie and Regan. Moreover, all humourists are *passively* sadistic, inasmuch as they find the satirical component funny. It is true that "true humour" stresses sympathetically the sorrowful plight of the humorous character or real person more than the corresponding 'false' humour, which is concerned with laughter alone and, consequently, does not have to perform the same sympathetic operation. However, while there may be much tension or ambiguity between comicality and tragedy, the latter element is never allowed to triumph, lest humour, especially *qua* "true humour", disintegrates. Hazlitt and Santayana were adamant on this point.[470]

(3) Although frequently associated with the incongruity theory of humour, "true humour" is an example of the *superiority* theory.

(3a) Schopenhauer's humourist was a quintessentially Romantic soul, a proud token of superiority. As *per* his Shakespearean example, Hamlet was a representative of Schopenhauer himself and his select spiritual peers, who alone are genuinely capable of experiencing and enduring sublime, profound, unsettling truths which the common people around them cannot even begin to fathom. It is only insofar as the superior types are forced to interact with the inferior ones that the serious truths grasped by the former come to be expressed in facetious words which the latter find strangely amusing or, as with Polonius in Shakespeare's tragedy, amusingly puzzling. "True humour" was, according to Schopenhauer, depressing seriousness dressed deceitfully in gleeful levity—*pace* Addison's claims to the opposite. The sublime spirit, by performing this duplicitous operation, is actively ridiculing the inferior ones, while the spectator or reader is invited to participate

---

[467] Those who enjoy "having the upper hand" in society, according to Harvey (1999, 37 and 57), often disagree with those who are "on the receiving end" on whether cruelty has occurred or not.
[468] See, again, Oloskey Mills (1974) and, in addition, Busch (1987).
[469] Outside the realm of fiction, these conditions apply to people's attempts at producing "true humour" by way of clever storytelling, refined joking, brilliant anecdote, subtle commentary, intelligent conversation, etc.
[470] See Chapter 1.

in the sophisticated act of clever denigration that is being performed, if s/he is capable of it.[471]

(3b) Declaredly humane and sensitive, Pirandello's "true humour" was also based upon a modulation of interpersonal superiority.[472] The Sicilian dramatist was not so uncompromisingly dismissive as Schopenhauer of all those souls who cannot experience the same complex mixtures of emotions and thoughts that the sensitive, cultured humourist is able to grasp.[473] Nevertheless, Pirandello's humourist and, in all likelihood, the readers and spectators who can follow the humourist's subtle art must necessarily understand the comical component at play, which requires recognising the obvious inferiority of the joke's butt, who is then pitied, in a further case of hierarchical positioning. Pirandello's "true humour" did not deny the hierarchy established by grasping the immediate comicality of another person. Quite the opposite, his conception of 'humour' required this hierarchy for its 'true' form to be credible. Plus, it added the implicit spiritual hierarchy whereby the same insightful person can also commiserate with the comical 'other', whose inferiority is, consequently, *twofold.*[474]

---

[471] It is quite ironic to read the following passage from Kozintsev (2010, 44), who found no genius or spiritual superiority whatsoever in humorous concoctions, but also only by underplaying the artistry that they may require: "The primary source of comedy lies not in the object, but in the fact that the subject ceases to take the object seriously and replaces it by a primitive likeness, a puppet, a pretext for laughter, arbitrarily invented by the subject, who suddenly becomes so primitive himself that he temporarily loses the ability to reason, judge, resent, sympathize, feel shame, etc. Besides the artistic skill necessary, indeed, only to prepare and arrange the collapse of seriousness, the subject maintains only a superficially grasping observation (even this, however, often proves unnecessary) and a capacity for very primitive associations, that is, qualities with which babies, mentally retarded or intoxicated people, and animals are endowed."
[472] See Chapter 1.
[473] Schopenhauer's celebration of the sublime Romantic genius persisted in Pirandello (1920, 134), who claimed true humourists to be naturally gifted with the undisguisable apprehension of the "sentiment of the contrary".
[474] Chesterton's (1929–1973, par. 2): "Humour" proper dissented by way of "humility", i.e., s/he who grasps the comical hence pitiable aspects of the Other grasps also the Other's being the mirror of one's own equally comical hence pitiable self. Amir's path towards wisdom performed an analogous operation which, by reducing a person's self-importance, should make all who are so diminished more likely to accept themselves in a charitable spirit.

2.4 Hermeneutics

[T]he truth is unhappily hardly ever amusing.
—Fyodor M. Dostoyevsky[475]

A middle-aged, corpulent man slips and falls on the ice before our eyes.[476] How are we going to interpret the event?[477] What are we going to do? How are we going to react? We can shout, cry, call for help, or say nothing. We can also smile, snort, chuckle, or laugh aloud. It can take a split-second, or a little longer.[478] Feasibly, it could be the first time that we witness anything like that. Or else, as is the case for many months in our Iceland, it is a habitual sight—and a seasonal fright.[479]

2.4.1 Attitudes

Not all people respond in the same manner. For some, "funny" might apply as an apt descriptor. For others, "dangerous", "unfortunate", or "sad" could be better options, whether uttered openly, pondered and hypothesised quietly, or inferred from observable behaviour.[480] Our age, personality, and previous experiences are likely to play a role in leading us towards certain hermeneutical options rather than others.[481] This is, after all, typical of human conduct possessing moral connotations

---

475 Dostoyevsky (1900), 779.
476 Our oft-cited humourists of note, Chesterton and Baroncelli, or this book's authors, alas, could be this man.
477 With "hermeneutics" we mean the study of interpretation, not a school of thought, e.g., Gadamer's.
478 Response times to humour have been studied for decades (see, e.g., Katz 1993).
479 One of the present authors worked in his youth as a warehouse clerk for an Icelandic publishing company and, while carrying a large box filled with philosophy books, slipped on the ice and fell violently onto the concrete stairway that he was walking on, hitting the edge of a step with the back of his head. There was silence; there was blood; and there was no laughter whatsoever. Above all, his love for philosophy books was undamaged.
480 Whether or not and, if so, how well we can infer people's thoughts from their visible behaviour are unresolved issues in psychology. At the same time, it is a daily activity *performed* by nearly all humans.
481 Given the icy subject, it may be worth recalling the iceberg-like nature of our reasoned deliberations, including ethical ones and, particularly, those about cruel humour. However consciously —and whatever conscious—*deliberation* may be at stake, this mental process is only the tip of the iceberg. Underneath it—or in its *Gestalt*-like background, if you prefer—there lie countless presuppositions that are hardly ever brought to the surface and examined. Such is the *modus operandi* of

and calling for a degree of deliberation, whether this deliberation occurs or not, and whether most of it is tacit rather than explicit.[482]

On the chance of such falls on the ice, or other slippery surfaces, Leacock stated:

> I admit that there is in all of us a certain vein of the old original demoniacal humour or joy in the misfortune of another which sticks to us like our original sin. It ought not to be funny to see a man, especially a fat and pompous man, slip suddenly on a banana skin. But it is. When a skater on a pond who is describing graceful circles, and showing off before the crowd, breaks through the ice and gets a ducking, everybody shouts with joy. To the original savage, the cream of the joke in such cases was found if the man who slipped broke his neck, or the man who went through the ice never came up again. I can imagine a group of prehistoric men standing round the ice-hole where he had disappeared and laughing till their sides split. If there had been such a thing as a prehistoric newspaper, the affair would have headed up: *"Amusing Incident. Unknown Gentleman Breaks Through Ice and Is Drowned"*. But our sense of humour under civilisation has been weakened. Much of the fun of this sort of thing has been lost on us. Children, however, still retain a large share of this primitive sense of enjoyment... [And so do] the Scotch.[483]

How we thinking humans respond to our environment, with which we try to cope also by way of humour, reflects the interpretative attitudes that we have acquired throughout our life, including at infancy. For instance, try to remember when our parents or care-givers showed us how to react to a mistake or a fall: essentially, by crying about it or by laughing at it.[484] In any case, we cannot predict with certainty how we ourselves or others will respond. With each new event, with each new slip, our response is open to variation, especially inasmuch as laughter is subject, according to contemporary neuroscience, to "minimal voluntary control".[485]

Interpreting an event as amusing or disturbing is part of our fluid, habit-sensitive, and painfully opaque set of tacit abilities, whereby we can lead the will in a variety of directions, making choices quickly, based upon internalised heuristics rather than careful and prolonged assessments of the situation.[486] These assess-

---

the human mind under *all* circumstances, as we discussed at length in *H&C1*, in keeping with Polanyi (1962c). Major problems arise when we become incapable of revising such necessary presuppositions on the bases of experience or remaining open to novelty, discovery, surprise, and inspiration. As Jung (2009, 311) poetically noted: "a wise man does not want to be a charioteer, for he knows that will and intention certainly attain goals but disturb the becoming of the future".

482 See, e.g., Allen (2014).
483 Leacock (2018), chap. 17, pars. 25–31. No anti-Scottish sentiment is implied by our use of this quote.
484 See Mireault and Reddy (2016).
485 Provine (2016), 1533.
486 See Allen (2014, 6): "the whole of life is potentially of moral significance and ... some aspects and moments are morally urgent, such that a responsible attitude is required throughout it, al-

ments come into play later, normally.[487] Yet even before we may be forced by the circumstances to review the situation with greater conscious care, our interpretative reaction is not an entirely automated and unsophisticated process either. People's voluntary control over laughter may be minimal, but it is not absent, as shown by their ability to resist the instinctual reaction to laugh if tickled or in a contagious social context.[488]

2.4.2 Attributes

As far as commonplace humour and, even more so, "true humour" are concerned, the gap between them and our species' instinctual, emotion-driven laughter is as broad and as wide as the gap between literate human beings and howling furry primates.[489] This gap, in other words, is quite large. In all probability, it signifies and signals the whole breadth and depth of civilisation itself—a vast crevice indeed.[490] As Chesterton wrote:

> The speculations on the nature of any reaction to the risible belong to the larger and more elementary subject of Laughter and are for the department of psychology; according to

---

though specifically moral concerns and considerations are likely often to be latent and implicit". Tellingly, in medical triage, M. Meyers (2004, 105) spoke openly of crucial "decisional skills" that are honed tacitly by way of repeated professional experiences.

487 Scholarship itself reflects this *ex-post* lucidity. See, e.g., Harakchiyska and Borisova (2020), who developed a concise and clear model of the many types of practical competence or skills required for a person to use humour effectively in foreign-language teaching and learning.

488 See Provine (2016).

489 Leacock (2018, chap. 17, par. 61) wrote: "really great humour which, once or twice in a generation at best, illuminates and elevates our literature", does exist, such that "humour is blended with pathos till the two are one, and represent, as they have in every age, the mingled heritage of tears and laughter that is our lot on earth".

490 Analogous disregard for the vast crevice separating our bio-physiological make-up from the complex socio-cultural behaviours that civilised humans can exhibit is exemplified by much socio-scientific and medical literature. For one, Konner (2022, abstract) suggested that cruelty-reducing "cooperation" occurs because of the presence of "oxytocin, which promotes parochial altruism", although the cited studies supporting this direct causal link are about chimps and bonobos. How many intermediate steps can there be between a hormone and, say, a parliament, a peace march in downtown Vienna, the idea of a merciful God, or a constitutional draft? And how many are there between said hormone and, for instance, complex conceptual constructs such as 'friendship', 'solidarity', 'love', or even 'hormone' itself? Far too often, in the positivistic milieus of our culture, biological, and physiological explanations come across as instances of *jumping the gun*, which would be humorous if they were not also cruel examples of "the crippling mutilations imposed by an objectivist framework" (Polanyi 1962c, 403).

some, almost for that of physiology. Whatever be their value touching the primitive function of laughter, they throw very little light on the highly civilized product of humour. It may well be questioned whether some of the explanations are not too crude even for the crudest origins; that they hardly apply even to the savage and certainly do not apply to the child. It has been suggested, for example, that all laughter had its origin in a sort of cruelty, in an exultation over the pain or ignominy of an enemy; but it is very hard even for the most imaginative psychologist to believe that, when a baby bursts out laughing at the image of the cow jumping over the moon, he is really finding pleasure in the probability of the cow breaking her leg when she comes down again. The truth is that all these primitive and prehistoric origins are largely unknown and possibly unknowable; and like all the unknown and unknowable are a field for furious wars of religion. Such primary human causes will always be interpreted differently according to different philosophies of human life. Another philosophy would say, for instance, that laughter is due not to an animal cruelty but to a purely human realization of the contrast between man's spiritual immensity within and his littleness and restriction without, for it is itself a joke that a house should be larger inside than out. According to such a view, the very incompatibility between the sense of human dignity and the perpetual possibility of incidental indignities, produces the primary or archetypal joke of the old gentleman sitting down suddenly on the ice. We do not laugh thus when a tree or a rock tumbles down; because we do not know the sense of self-esteem or serious importance within. But such speculations in psychology, especially in primitive psychology, have very little to do with the actual history of comedy as an artistic creation.[491]

In real life, cultured humour and creative comical phenomena cannot be reduced to the instinctive laughter of some hypothetical caveman.[492] Our cultural evolution, more than the natural one, explains why, whenever humour is at hand, hermeneutical alternatives are open to us and so are associated behaviours, implying

---

491 Chesterton (1929–1973), par. 3. The quotation is long but, given its relevance to the point being made, worth citing in full. As to Chesterton's importance in 20th-century intellectual history, see Hurley (2012). Recently, and without any apparent knowledge of Chesterton's advice, Goddard and Lambert (2022) reiterated similar concerns about the theoretical overreach of evolutionary hypotheses concerning the primeval origins of laughter and humour. In any case, it should be clear that Chesterton's acceptance of the superiority theory of laughter (and humour) was genealogical, and it was combined with a clear sense of the importance of incongruity. Fleming's (1966, 4) scathing criticism of Chesterton's stance as a sheer and full endorsement of the former standard theory was therefore off the mark. Rather, Fleming's (1966, 7; emphasis added) reflections should be highlighted here as anticipating Amir's own theories, which are discussed in detail in this book, especially when writing: *"Humour ... is an art of existence, an intellectual comforter and a profoundly civilising influence."*

492 In 1877, the British novelist George Meredith remarked on the cultural quintessence of laughing matters, but his "Essay on Comedy" was "soon overshadowed by Darwinian and Spencerian evolutionary explanations of laughter ... as an instinctive survival mechanism" (Niebylski 2004, 21).

a modicum of self-command.⁴⁹³ Or, as the contemporary Canadian humour specialist Jim Lyttle affirmed: "[H]umour does not involve any processes so automatic as to be immune from ethical censure."⁴⁹⁴ These hermeneutical alternatives include, among others: whether to cause laughter, in which form, whether to laugh, how much, in combination with passive observation or active assistance to the fallen man, in a mocking or empathic manner, with or without ulterior motive, and so on, with as many variations as there are actual living persons involved.⁴⁹⁵

As we discussed in *H&C1*, concepts can be said to function *qua* cognitive *Gestalten* organising potential information belonging to: the external world that we observe, i.e., the object of our cognition (e.g., the man fallen on the ice); its surroundings (e.g., the thickness of the ice, the presence of snow, the time of the day, etc.); and the internal world that we ourselves, if sufficiently healthy and properly socialised, have access to (e.g., our own bodily knowledge about falls on the ice, our memories of analogous events, our expectations regarding individuals of a certain age, etc.). In other words, there are:
(1) 'objective' details (e.g., the body parts impacting the ice), and
(2) 'intersubjective' ones (e.g., the medical notions accessible to us at our particular level of socially arranged acculturation); and there are
(3) 'subjective' ones (e.g., our unique perspective on the fallen man, our sight of it and our understanding of the associated medical risks, as well as our even more unique emotional, ethical, and aesthetic relationships with the fallen man on that occasion).⁴⁹⁶

All these details are combined in our initial appraisal of a given situation (e.g., "a fall on the ice"), which we grasp first holistically by "tacit integration" or organic "synthesis" of countless details.⁴⁹⁷ It is only *in secundis* that we may de-structure the situation into its particular components, i.e., by conscious analysis of some of

---

493 Chesterton's long quote is an important reminder of how the unique 'cultural evolution' of our species opened up a vast, creative, and eminently social playfield for our faculties that biological reductionism, neuropsychology, and evolutionary thinking in general either neglect or misrepresent. His awareness was echoed in recent years by the British philosopher Raymond Tallis (2011, title *et passim*) who coined the sarcastic term "Darwinitis" in order to ridicule these influential intellectual trends which regularly fail to acknowledge humankind's humanity.
494 Lyttle (2002), 8.
495 See, e.g., Carse (2005) and Olson (2015).
496 However cold and abstract our talking of concepts may seem, our *Gestalten* are always coloured with affect, including the seemingly aloof and 'objective' scientist's "intellectual passions" (Polanyi 1962c, 103 *et passim*).
497 Polanyi (1969a), 141.

the details at issue (e.g., the man's size, the ice's consistency, the kind of worn shoes, etc.).[498]

The number, plurality and heterogeneity of these details mean that, as there is a shared space of interpretation and understanding according to established categories of thought and behavioural patterns, so there is a space where personal variations and deviations can occur. These variations and deviations can be so many and so drastic, as to lead the Australia-based political scientist Wayne Cristaudo to assert that "people are inevitably participating in making very different worlds, which, nevertheless, exist side by side".[499]

Above all, such a hermeneutical space is also the context where our personal liberty and responsibility are challenged, even when it is a 'sheer' matter of humour.[500] And that is why, in the realm of fiction, artists tinker with elements that may increase the likelihood of generating a comic scenario rather than a tragic one.[501]

2.4.3 Artistry

The artists' artistry consists precisely in leading other people's hearts and wills in a planned direction, analogously to the tested principles of rhetoric, which the skilled orator and the advertising guru utilise in order to persuade their audiences to believe and behave as wished.[502] Falling on one's posterior, for instance, is far likelier to be interpreted as "funny" rather than "sad". Falling on one's head, instead,

---

[498] Tacit knowledge is hard to define. Yet many thinkers and scholars have tried to say something sensible about it. For instance, the psychophysical immediacy of laughter was central to Bataille's "philosophy of laughter", which is said to focus on "that which is incommunicable with respect to articulated discourse insofar as it involves an experience of consumptive contact whose intensity and violence rupture the discursive homogeneity of the discrete subject whose differential isolation (*qua* 'I') guards the possibility of the articulable acquisition and exchange of material and conceptual commodities" (D. Wright 2017, 8–9).
[499] Cristaudo (2021), 554.
[500] See Polanyi (1962c) and *H&C1*.
[501] With "artists" and "artistry", we refer to creative adroitness and capable workmanship in the artistic context, understood in a very broad sense, i.e., not just the select 'giants' celebrated in art history, museums, theatres, etc.
[502] As discussed in Barthes (1970, par. A.4.3), rhetorical agency is "subordinated to the public's 'psychology'".

has often the opposite effect, particularly if followed by a loud cry or, worse, by stillness.[503]

Some recipes are known to work better than others and are rehearsed incessantly (e.g., "canned humour"), but artists are frequently on the lookout for quality, originality, or novelty. These aesthetic dimensions, which are crucial in the work of humourists too, are not coextensive. The much-published and radio-broadcast humourist, G.K. Chesterton, sardonically noted on such matters:

> There is no clearer sign of the absence of originality among modern poets than their disposition to find new topics. Really original poets write poems about the spring. They are always fresh, just as the spring is always fresh. Men wholly without originality write poems about torture, or new religions, or some perversion of obscenity, hoping that the mere sting of the subject may speak for them. But we do not sufficiently realize that what is true of the classic ode is also true of the classic joke. A true poet writes about the spring being beautiful because (after a thousand springs) the spring really is beautiful. In the same way the true humorist writes about a man sitting down on his hat because the act of sitting down on one's own hat (however often and admirably performed) really is extremely funny. We must not dismiss a new poet because his poem is called "To a Skylark"; nor must we dismiss a humorist because his new farce is called "My Mother-in-Law". He may really have splendid and inspiring things to say upon an eternal problem. The whole question is whether he has.[504]

In the world of creative fiction, new approaches are still experimented with, failures encountered, fixes made. It is an endless process. Man plans; God laughs. New plans are made. It is a parallel two-way course of, on the one hand, innovation (or sophistication?) and, on the other hand, reduction to safer cues (i.e., so-called "dumbing-down"), which persists in literature, cinema, TV comedy, TikTok videos, etc.[505] Within it, the subjective components of the processes of tacit integration required for interpreting an event are not erased from view. The uncertainties of effective artistry persist as well, to a meaningful and sometimes cruel degree. Therefore, in our societies, we still reward successful humourists and scoff at unsuccessful ones, as did Addison in *The Spectator*, 300 years ago.[506]

---

[503] Hartley (1801) had already acknowledged that the shock or surprise making us laugh can equally lead us to cry, if duly intensified, and that some shocks or surprises are found funny by some individuals, but not others (see *H&C1*). See Granitsas (2020) for a contemporary reiteration of analogous insights and concerns.
[504] Chesterton (1911), 10–11.
[505] See, e.g., Steggle (2007).
[506] As to measuring success in general, there is no single metric (see, e.g., Schoonbaert and Roelants 1996).

2.5 Performances

> [E]ven a competent language user might slip in his or her performance, misjudging the hearers' acceptance of [a] type of humor or perceiving the situation as more casual than others do.
> —Nancy Bell[507]

How any of us interprets an event correctly, i.e., in an intersubjectively effective way, according to prevailing standards, remains a mystery, whether in real life or in the arts. Every day, amid countless cases of adequate performances, myriad errors also occur. To a large extent, however, these stumbles do not prevent social interactions from being successful. As mysterious as our fallible competence may be, then, the competence endures. When it comes to check on our sense of humour, we know that we can do most things that are required of us, but we cannot resolve or justify our proficiency.[508]

This commonplace explanatory restriction is not one of utter ignorance. We know, for example, how to swim, ride a bicycle, tie our shoelaces, and perceive an event, including humorous ones. What is more, we know that we know it. We realise that we can swim, cycle, tie our shoelaces, and grasp an event to the point of being able to teach it to others, such as our own or other children, or those with whom we share a joke. We can display this skill on multiple occasions. Few can explain it, though, in explicit terms, which in any case would help little with regard to performing the required actions (e.g., educating professional footballers about the physics of their playing, or teaching a comedian the physiology of laughter).[509]

Empirical psychologists and modern pedagogues can tell us what works more and less often, but not why. Their domain is limited both theoretically and methodologically to empirical surveys and statistical comparisons. Physicians and biologists can tell us what biophysical and/or neurological structures underlie that which works or prevents it from working, but not why and how the structures at play are experienced subjectively and intersubjectively as meanings.[510] As complex and as medically useful as their scientific accounts may be, physicians and biologists merely add new examples to the long-known list comprising blind per-

---

[507] Bell (2015), 13.
[508] Young and old age, genetic conditions, injury, and illness can change dramatically the level of proficiency.
[509] *Ditto*. When learning to tie our shoelaces, we are not given a book to read or even told exactly what to do. At some point, someone must have shown us how to do it and said: "Do like this."
[510] It is the "mystery of ... how meaning originates and occurs" (von Manen 2016, i).

sons who cannot read a written text and deaf people who cannot hear what is being said or the music that is being played. A gap is in place between what our embodied thought can produce, i.e., a skilful performance, and the abstract language in which we, as unique talking animals, may wish to express it.[511] It is a gap between know-how and know-that, or the so-called "performative" and "propositional" types of knowledge.[512]

Lexical distinctions do not solve the problem. They exemplify it further. "Knowing how" means knowing how to perceive and make sense of the graphic signs that we call "graphemes", "letters", "words", etc., as well as their mutual relations on the page. *Mutatis mutandis*, the same holds true for the spoken word, its technically-defined "phonemes", "tones", etc., which we not merely hear, but normally listen to and utter as we express our own thoughts, including humorous and cruel ones. As Michael Polanyi insightfully crystallised: "the use of language is a performance" too.[513]

All linguistic expressions, not just our humorous jokes or our cruel hecklings, must be interpreted by living persons. This is true even of the most universal and explicit pieces of human communication, such as the demonstrations of formal logic and the symbolic laws of quantum physics: "numbers do not of themselves point to events".[514] Again, a gap is in place between what our embodied thought can produce, i.e., "tacit knowing", and the abstract language of "explicit knowing" in which we may wish to cast the former, e.g., textbooks, manuals, scholarly articles, scientific papers, etc.[515] Polanyi codified this additional realisation in a famous short statement: "[W]e can know more than we can tell".[516]

All the explicit rules and information that are implicit in any adequately socialised person's conceptual abilities and spoken language are transmitted in ordi-

---

511 Our linguistic abilities are well beyond anything comparable that can be observed in other animal species.
512 Mingers (2008), 62.
513 Polanyi (1969a), 193. A fuller account of his views was given in *H&C1*.
514 Polanyi and Prosch (1975), 30.
515 Polanyi (2009), 4. In this book's acknowledgments, Polanyi (2009, vi) thanked "Professor Philip Hallie of Wesleyan ... who responded to my thoughts and enriched them." We do not know what their discussions focussed on but would surmise scepticism and degrees of awareness, for Hallie was an expert on both, not just cruelty. See, e.g., Hallie (1979), i.e., a review of Henry's *Philosophy and Phenomenology of the Body*.
516 Polanyi (2009), 4. When dealing with "tacit knowing", Polanyi (1962c, 142–143 and 194) was *not* talking chiefly of "unconscious" or "subconscious" information (e.g., Lazarus' and McCleary's "subliminal" knowledge, Eriksen's and Kuethe's "subception", or the phenomena of "learning" and "discovering without awareness").

nary adult-child interactions in the person's early years.[517] It is only after much schooling that some speakers become able to describe explicitly, i.e., to explain or explicate at least some of the information and the rules of their own mother tongue (e.g., case declensions), thought processes (e.g., syllogistic patterns), or read books about them—not to mention write one.[518]

Were we to produce all possible physical and chemical analyses of, say, a wristwatch, we would still be unable to tell the time by reference to these studies alone. We would have explicit information aplenty, but contextually pointless information—not *per se*, but *per* the aim that is being pursued. In other words, the "tacit dimension", for which Polanyi is credited and studied today, refers to knowledge that we certainly have but is difficult to describe explicitly or formally.[519] We can ride a bike and see it as a desirable skill, but the books about biking assume that we have mastered the skills of balancing and pedalling. Our bike-riding skills cannot be imparted to others by mere words.[520]

2.5.1 Institutionalisation

Different aims require different descriptions, different modes of experience, different disciplines or, as Polanyi wrote, different "comprehensive ... interpretative framework[s]" and "standards", which is what the many lines of study in human culture, from arithmetic *via* engineering to drama and religion, provide us with or, at least, those who acquire, use, and/or benefit from them to any significant extent or degree.[521] Inchoate and mutable, as well as oblique and filled with tacit ingredients, comedy is the "comprehensive interpretative framework" determining what is to be regarded as humorous in the arts.[522] The arts, however, are only one of the many social contexts where humour takes place, whether this is labelled "true", "false", "commonplace", or left indeterminate.[523] Daily conversations, the professions, comic books, or social media are as much the rightful place of hu-

---

517 Polanyi (1962c), part two ("The Tacit Component").
518 Polanyi (1962c), part two ("The Tacit Component").
519 Polanyi (2009), title page.
520 *Mutatis mutandis*, these considerations apply to the motor and cognitive skills needed to read our book.
521 Polanyi (1969b), 82–84. See also Polanyi (1962c).
522 Stott (2005) offered an inevitably selective but intelligently comprehensive account of Western comedy.
523 Pirandello (1920) admitted that it is difficult to determine whether a certain poet is a 'true' humourist or not.

mour as comedy *qua* socially-acknowledged artistic and theatrical discipline has been for millennia.[524]

There are, in other words, both *in*formal and formal humourists. Together, whether as the family's jokester or hopeful TV scriptwriters, all these variously capable humourists are the masters who maintain, tweak, and grow the conceptual and pragmatic domain of 'humour' for their cultures. As such, these individuals, whether they operate informally or formally, are those members of society that bring about and/or preserve, for the most part, the moral and aesthetic standards applicable for and to their human community, who may be as broad as a nation's literate masses or as restricted as a single cell-mate in a remote prison. All these unsuspecting masters of the comical signal to one another, and to everyone else around, with both their daring innovations and abysmal failures, the limits of what is acceptable to groups of people, under which conditions, in which venues, at what personal cost, etc.[525]

Taking stock of the considerations presented in the previous pages, it can be stated that all these informal and formal experts' regular derision of certain typical targets (e.g., bum-showing plumbers, loud tenors, crooked lawyers, dim-witted teenage boys, head-in-the-cloud professors) requires from the experts as many regular feats of active sadistic and/or brutal cruelty.[526] The experts' function is precisely to humiliate these people in funny ways, hence letting the amusement overpower whatever sympathy the degradation may elicit. For their part, audiences must share in a modicum of passive sadistic and/or brutal cruelty because failing to take delight in the discomfiture of the selected targets and/or sympathising too much with them would destroy the fun of the social act that is being performed.[527]

All these informal and formal experts are therefore the largely unaware, uncoordinated, and unintended masters of one of the most commonplace forms of

---

524 See, e.g., Bremmer and Roodenburg (1997).
525 Bremmer and Roodenburg (1997) tackled successful cases. Yet there may have been at least as many failures.
526 One of the authors of this book is a trained classical tenor, the father of two teenage boys, and a professor.
527 As discussed in Dickie (2011), the 18th century has repeatedly been said to have initiated a long process of cultivation of empathy whereby certain pranks became slowly unacceptable and certain targets for open humour less and less likely (e.g., the mentally challenged, raped women, the obese, the sight- and hearing-impaired). Yet, as Dickie's own research disclosed, this depiction is probably exaggerated and culpably selective, projecting a veneer of decency that the people who lived in those days did not possess to such a much lauded extent.

"institutionalized cruelty", as Hallie would dub it.[528] The socially absorbed and unconsciously accepted standards of humour determine whom we, as socialised persons, laugh at, how, when, where, and why, in such ways as to avoid negative societal sanction and even legal sanction or economic losses. Censors, religious leaders, moralists, judges, legislators, and other public officials play a role too in establishing the Polanyian "framework" of plausible humour. So do parents, educators, and many other voices that people encounter in their lives, but they do not set the chief public example.[529] Comedians of all stripes do.

Sometimes, by playing at the edges of institutionalised cruelty, comedians make mistakes, and so do more prosaic individuals who fail in being humorous in the accepted ways. Mistakes, at times, cost them dearly. One does not have to launch an internationally-renowned whistleblowing website in order to face serious trouble in the allegedly "liberal" nations of the West.[530] Apparent and alleged "bad taste" in one's own choice of humour, an employers' concern for corporate reputation and profitability, and/or the possibly well-meaning complaints of upset co-workers or internet users can create a truly explosive mix.[531] Even well-meaning disabled employees and famed intellectuals can happen to lose their jobs in an instant as a result of this cocktail.[532] Humour is often claimed to be "just a bit of fun", but if the *bit* at issue causes enough of a stir, one's life can be thrown into turmoil.[533]

The possible cruelties do not stop here. We have already addressed in this book the fact that, whenever the common standards of humour are widely accepted and/or standard humorous practices seem largely innocuous, the laughingstocks who dare complain can be easily dismissed as "whiners", "boors" or, as Harvey

---

528 Such social standards exemplify the notion of a self-adjusting "spontaneous order" (Polanyi 1948, title), later appropriated by Hayek and projected by the latter onto the whole socio-economic order (see Jacobs 1997–1998).
529 *H&C3* investigates many such cases.
530 We refer here to Julian Assange, founder of Wikileaks, currently imprisoned and possibly to be extradited to the US where he could face the death penalty. As to the international profile of Wikileaks, see Fox (2017).
531 Pirandello (1920, 11) claimed that "good taste" is as "ineffable" and as "hard to define" as "humour".
532 See Brian Leach, "who was sacked by Asda for sharing a Billy Connolly post which mentioned 'suicide bomber'" upsetting "an Asian female employee who worked for Head Office" (Sutcliffe, 2019, pars. 1–5), or "film critic David Edelstein, who made a stupid, quickly deleted, misfired 'joke' on his private Facebook page, regarding the death of … director Bernardo Bertolucci" (Kipnis, 2018, par. 1). More on these matters is said in *H&C3*.
533 See Ronson (2015).

writes, "trouble-maker[s]".⁵³⁴ Alternatively, the laughingstock may opt for laughing both *at* themselves and *with* the enjoyers of the socially permitted humour, for the standards are so ingrained as to make it inconceivable, implausible, embarrassing, or unwise to do otherwise.⁵³⁵ Refusing to participate in the social game would cause these targeted people to be stigmatised as "poor sports", "no fun", "too touchy to laugh at themselves", etc.⁵³⁶ As Harvey wrote, under these circumstances, "the victim is facing a 'lesser of the evils' kind of choice".⁵³⁷

Furthermore, routine and "institutionalized" cruelty, unlike exceptional cases, can become part and parcel of the fabric of reality such that both perpetrators and victims may become entirely blind to it *qua* cruelty (e.g., "cruel humour is not 'real' cruelty"), or simply accept it as one of the many cruelties that we humans must endure in our life (e.g., "life is tough and you better get used to it").⁵³⁸ This process of socio-cultural and often, politico-legal normalisation is particularly easy to occur in the context of humour insofar as this context is tacitly assumed to be 'just a bit of fun', namely something allegedly positive, socially recommended, and patently less significant than many other cruel physical and/or psychological experiences. Among such cruel experiences stand out especially those involving devastating physical pain rather than mere psychological suffering, however deep the latter may be. 'Real' cruelty entails real blood for some commentators.⁵³⁹

2.5.2 Insults

Writing about the social and cultural roots of cruel "intolerance" within modern communities, the famed 20ᵗʰ-century British analytic philosopher A.J. Ayer stated: "The treatment of words as insulting", such as "the word 'n[*****]' ... in the United

---

534 Harvey (1999), 59.
535 An intermediate option is to laugh with the participants at another laughingstock, thus changing the target.
536 Harvey (1999), 14.
537 Harvey (1999), 75.
538 "[I]n many places in the world a man in poverty who even mentions unsafe conditions or unfair procedures is immediately fired and blacklisted" (Harvey 1999, 59).
539 Writing about the American humourist James Thurber, Hutchens (1963, 2–4) stated that the former "loathes cruelty", while being both "a humorist and a satirist", who "is by nature a bitter man" and "a would-be misanthrope", but can also show "sympathy for the out-of-luck man" as much as "contempt for the pretentious and stupid one", preferring innocent children to adults, and finding the "life of dogs to be more rational than that of humans, and their courage and loyalty generally superior". Magically, Thurber's satirical humour is not cruel.

States" or "the impersonal use of 'he'", is grossly mistaken.[540] Ayer presented two main reasons for this claim.

(1) Insults are a matter of pragmatics, not semantics, i.e., it is not that which the word means that offends, but the intentional use of their meaning/s for the sake of offending someone else.[541] According to Ayer, it is an overreaction caused by well-meaning yet excessive irrational sensitivity to try to prevent people from using "'n[*****] brown'" when it is meant "as innocent[ly] as calling a colour 'off white'", or "that children should no longer have the chance to read about the adventures of *Little Black Sambo*", if and when no disparagement of any sort is intended.[542]

(2) "Cruelty" is undisputedly a matter of concrete violent actions, such as "reviling, oppressing, murdering and torturing", but it is hardly as intuitively a matter of locutions *per* or *in se*.[543] At the very least, some forms of crude bodily mutilation are obviously and universally deemed cruel, whereas the same human minds and cultures seem far less likely to reach so easily an agreement, if any at all, on the alleged cruelty of sheer linguistic expressions, if not even crude remarks.[544]

For Ayer, words as such "are not genuine slights", even if and when they come across as seriously "inappropriate", especially yet not exclusively "where it is

---

540 Ayer (1987), 94 (the original text includes the uncensored formulation of the racist term). Veblen (1918, *120–121, notes [sic] 1*) had already remarked on the relationship between, on the one hand, a "reasonable degree of 'humanity' and congenital tolerance" and, on the other hand, a reduced penchant for the "fatal extravagances of cruelty and sustained hatred between groups", and like Ayer, Veblen meant "animosities" compromising "group subsistence" and/or individual survival, not sheer verbal "disparagement".

541 Ayer (1987), 94. This point would seem to be confirmed by some socio-scientific studies (see Chapter 3).

542 Ayer (1987), 94. His work is a reminder of the difficulties that can be encountered in determining whether, where, when, and how demeaning and/or domineering demeanours can be deemed tantamount to nominal "cruelty", as long debated in jurisprudence with regard to the 18th-century concept of "mental cruelty" (see, e.g., Gagné 1970 and Griswold 1986), which in turn reiterates the definitional issues of "cruelty" itself (see, e.g., Mahapatra 2022). As the Indian legal scholar Mehak Mahapatra (2022, 324) wrote: "Mental cruelty has not been defined or mentioned clearly under any law. It is entirely subjective and depends totally upon the person, time, the facts and circumstances of the case."

543 Ayer (1987), 83.

544 The scholarly floor is, unsurprisingly, open to much debate. E.g., while not tackling "cruelty" proper, the Italian philosopher Andrea Borghini argued for the recognition of "verbal violence", which often ties into people's "exercise of humor", such as "politically incorrect jokes" and "mocking" (as cited in Ireland-Delfs 2020, 10).

clear that no insult is intended", *pace* the loud protestations of 20th-century "feminists" and other well-meaning agents of social change.[545] In Ayer's view, if we honestly aim at pursuing progressive ends, we should worry about that which some people do or strive to do while using certain words, not about the words as such.

Symptomatically, no locution is labelled "cruel" by Ayer in his text, even when it is said to be "pejorative", "[o]ffensive" or "derogatory", e.g., "Gooks ... yellow ... Wog, Babu, Froggy, Hun, Spick, or Dago".[546] Historically-laden linguistic expressions possessing much potential for derision and public humiliation—say, "Paki", "Darky", "Redskin", or "Chink"—may have cut bitterly at times, but they never cut deep enough to start talking about "cruelty", at least as far as Her Majesty's white, male, upper-class subject A.J. Ayer, was concerned.[547]

Then again, *we*, i.e., this book's authors, might be misguided. Perhaps, some tacit inverted snobbism or an ethnic, gender-based, and/or working-class prejudice may be at work here, leading us inadvertently into creating a convenient yet dishonest rhetorical escamotage. As far as we can tell, Ayer was neither evil nor superficial. Cruelly, there may be a measure of good sense in his stance to which we ourselves, i.e., the present authors, do not respond well at an immediate level. But which we are also willing to examine in some more depth.[548]

2.5.2.1 Potentialities

For one, we cannot avoid noticing that the socio-ethico-logico-linguistic matter at issue here is analogous to the one arising from the distinction that the German logician Gottlob Frege posited between the "content of a possible judgment" and the propositional "recognition" that a sentence is true, which is "manifest[ed]" in the formal assertion " $\vdash$.p", i.e., someone's commitment to its universal truthfulness (aka objectivity).[549] If genuine disparagement is to be the case, then

---

545 Ayer (1987), 94.
546 Ayer (1987), 93–97.
547 Many philosophers, humanists, and social scientists claim the opposite: words can cut deep enough to be cruel. Chesterton (1919, chap. 15, par. 12) distinguished between "positive cruelty", which manifests itself "in acts", and "negative cruelty", which does "so in words". On this basis, it can be argued that Ayer's stance would probably cause the jests' targets failure to take part in dubious humorous games to be liable of further victimisation because of their being "oversensitive", "paranoid", "thin-skinned", etc. (Harvey 1999, 81–82).
548 LVOA is our ultimate basis for value judgement, not gut feeling or conventional academic wisdom.
549 Frege (1956), 294, which was discussed in detail in *H&C1*. Note that we wrote "analogous", not "identical".

some specific breathing-and-talking person operating within a specific interpersonal context must intentionally make use of a term (or a longer string thereof) in order to disparage someone else—and under the former's personal responsibility.[550]

In se, the term (or string) itself is merely a *potential* mocking slur or hypothetical insult, which the receiver may honestly mistake for an actual mocking slur or insult, with all kinds of cruel consequences.[551] Misinterpretation is familiar enough a phenomenon in human life, but it can arise all the more easily whenever a message is capable of activating powerfully and instantaneously the recipient's affectivity. Thus, while a person may be genuinely trying to be funny or thought-provoking, she can end up digging a deep hole out of which she may never be able to climb, or her own grave. Other 'mistakes' can then occur in bad faith, i.e., dishonestly, in yet another instantiation of human cruelty, which would consist in putting words and attendant ideas into someone else's mouth and attached head.[552]

It is far from unthinkable that the potential mocking slur or hypothetical insult may *not* be *yet* a mocking slur or an insult. Logically as well as pragmatically, it is in fact a possible and sometimes probable item for lexical research, historical study, empowering reclamation, comedic wit, Freudian slip, pathological coprolalia, political creativity, poetic reinvention, inane repetition, and so forth.[553] Indeed, by the 'magic' virtues of stipulation, any given term can mean anything, if those who use it agree on such a reformulation of extant words and adhere to it.[554]

Without an interpersonal context in which people's intentions and interpretations can be played out, the complete meaning of a term cannot be credibly determined, for crucial "personal coefficient[s]" are still absent from the overall picture.[555] As Frege observed long ago, and as we noted before in this book, meanings reflect also eminently subjective elements, such as "force" (e.g., quoting an academic source is not the same as making a normative assertion) and, above

---

550 As anticipated in *H&C1*, the Polanyian theme of personal responsibility runs throughout our books.
551 Some of these nefarious consequences are discussed in great detail in *H&C3*.
552 We assume the reader to have come across such cases in his/her life.
553 Think, for one, of how a word disintegrates into sound when repeated numerous times on its own, as in a childish game or a comic sketch *à la* Lenny Bruce (more on Bruce is said in *H&C3*).
554 Children and spies, among others, have been known to make such stipulative uses of ordinary terms.
555 Polanyi (1962c), 329.

all, "colouring" or "tone", i.e., the register, aka the many subtler, nuanced and generally tacit implications of human communication, i.e., its "rhetorical motives".[556]

If we do not take these motives into account and, concomitantly, we do take seriously someone's claim that an actual offence came to pass, then we are favouring *ab initio* someone's interpretation over another's, in a flagrant violation of the equal moral status of all persons, which we typically presuppose in today's liberal societies. (Some readers may not share into such an egalitarian presupposition.) Somehow, by so favouring, we are neglecting numerous alternative explanations, e.g., error, truth-seeking, pathology, and humour itself. In the process, we are also at risk of letting our sympathetic feelings and/or good will lead us astray, for we may end up falling for, or perhaps committing ourselves, a logical fallacy *ad misericordiam*.[557] (A serious logician, Frege would be unlikely to ever approve of it.)

Ayer, for one, was certainly one such egalitarian thinker. And so was Baroncelli. Yet, they disagreed with each other on this thorny issue. The former denied that words as such could actually be cruel slights. The latter, in spite of his general Humean scepticism about all sorts of philosophical topics, objected.[558] The same egalitarianism applies to the authors of the present book, who are therefore strongly disinclined to making other people feel unequal by means of mocking slurs or insults. At the same time, and upon due reflection, the same authors are also rather uneasy with regard to taking all claims of offence and/or verbal cruelty at face value.[559]

2.5.2.2 Perplexities

At the time of writing, FIFA's president Gianni Infantino became prominent in the international press for offering a heartfelt yet ill-received rebuke of much criticism that had been directed at FIFA with respect to hosting the 2022 male football's World Cup in the Emirate of Qatar, which is notorious for poor labour practices and other human rights violations.[560] As Infantino argued, this criticism was West- and Euro-centric, superficial, and could be compared to hurtful discrimination, given that his own emotional reaction to it reminded him of the horrible time

---

556 Respectively, Frege (1892) and Burke (1969), xiii *et passim*. See also Penco (2017).
557 This fallacy is also known as an *appeal to pity*.
558 See especially Baroncelli (1996).
559 After all, don't we scrutinise people's faces in order to determine whether or not they should be trusted?
560 "On Eve of World Cup" (2022).

when, as a child, he was constantly "bullied" at school "for being Italian and for having red hair and freckles".[561]

Taking claims of offence and/or verbal cruelty at face value may well be a common and well-established social practice today, but the same can be said of daily customs that were later abandoned and that most of us now abhor, e.g., taunting Jews or homosexuals with impunity—or Italian émigrés in Switzerland, for that matter.[562] Saying that most people do certain things or react in a certain way is no normative justification. It is, at best, descriptive anthropology.

But we do not mean to trivialise the issue either. Quite the contrary. Pain is at hand here and ought not to be ignored. Prudential reasoning, if not ethical duty itself, demand that we pay immediate and honest heed to claims of suffered pain, including Mr. Infantino's, as a logical consequence. As we saw in Chapter 1, it may even be necessary to go searching for people's unreported pain at times because institutionalised cruelty à la Hallie may have made both the perpetrators and the victims deaf and/or blind to its incessant presence in their excruciatingly intertwined lives.[563]

While we do understand that genuine pain can be suffered—and we suffered it ourselves, on occasion, perchance like Mr. Infantino—we cannot underestimate the possibility of plain and simple misunderstanding either. Additionally, we are not entirely unaware of the Machiavellian strategy whereby someone may be 'playing the victim' so as to turn the table on the real victim/s, in yet another cruel form of twofold victim's victimisation that could be plausibly added to the ones identified and discussed by Harvey (see Section 2.2.3.3).[564] Sometimes, the one crying "wolf" is the wolf itself.

We, the authors of this book, have no sympathy for so-called "hate speech" and we do not court bad taste *per se*, even if we are willing to tolerate a good deal of it in the name of personal liberty and peaceful coexistence.[565] Neither are we blind to the many historically-known negative consequences that actively policing potentially offensive language over, say, learning to ignore it and/or cultivating ataraxia can unintentionally unleash for people's freedom of speech, expression of political

---

[561] "On Eve of World Cup" (2022), par. 6.
[562] See, e.g., the 1973 dark comedy *Bread and Chocolate*, dealing with the immigrants' quotidian humiliations.
[563] No offence is meant in any way whatsoever by the metaphorical use of words such as "deaf" and "blind".
[564] Less nefariously, "playing the victim" can be the result of "mental imbalance" (Myler 2017, abstract).
[565] In our case, LVOA determines the extent and limit of this tolerance. Our position is made clearer in *H&C3*.

criticism, deep-rooted need for artistic or aesthetic transgression, or relaxed use of humour.[566] Not to mention the countless abuses that State authorities, corporate businesses, and bosses at large can promptly make of such a policing, whether it is enforced legally or socially.[567]

Mental health itself may be in the balance. As a good few thinkers cited in Chapter 1 avowed, we live already under conditions of constant repression of our instincts. Shall we truly monitor proactively our linguistic usages, including humorous ones, and thereby add to the extant pressure and its attendant host of neuroses and psychoses? Or shall we risk offending someone else (or being offended ourselves), at least unintentionally, so that people may keep using their language freely in order to be humorous, without having to second-guess themselves all the time?[568]

This is yet *another* cruel dilemma emerging from our studies, especially in the context of humorous conduct. As stated by Freud and others, humour is one of the socially constructed tools that we all have at our disposal to obtain occasional relief from the system of psychic repression that is, in all likelihood, tragically required for civilised living.[569] Jokes are no joke. They are a time-honoured means of mental rebalancing. They are a much-needed breather. Yet they can swiftly become means of raw aggravation too.[570] Somehow, also in laughing matters, cruelty's presence seems to be inevitable, for any choice that we humans make is fraught with opportunity costs. And any worthy goal that we decide to pursue does cast a shadow of its own, however small or expediently ignored by the right-thinking person this shadow may be.[571]

2.5.2.3 Prosecutions and Prohibitions

At any rate, whenever humour tries to be innovative or merely plays around the borders of predominant social and/or legal acceptability, the laughingstock may have better luck in seeking redress than Mr. Infantino did with his seemingly

---

[566] LVOA can help establish and assess which consequences are negative and which are positive.
[567] More on these matters follows in *H&C3*, where we focus especially on social enforcement.
[568] The psychological underpinnings of this dilemma are discussed in greater detail in *H&C3*.
[569] See Chapter 1.
[570] The problem at issue persists even if we take seriously neurophysiological studies comparing insults with "mini-slaps in the face" because of the potent way in which derogatory terms grab people's attention (Struiksma *et al.* 2022, 1). Any such "mini-slaps in the face" can hurt, but they are neither normal nor major "slaps", and they do not make their victims bleed. Once again, the question arises: is 'real' cruelty a matter of spilling blood?
[571] More on these matters follows in *H&C3*.

heartfelt complaints to the world's gathered press.[572] Someway, their implicit and/or explicit accusations of "cruelty" appear less controversial and less implausible than Infantino's ones did, whatever contrary arguments Ayer or his devotees could be able to adduce.[573]

(1) Thus, shocked Italian Catholics succeeded in having Pier Paolo Pasolini face charges for blasphemy due to his 1962 short comedy *La ricotta*, in which the main character ends up ejaculating while tied to a cross on the set of a film about the life of Christ.[574]

(2) In 2012, the obviously offended Ben & Jerry corporation got all copies of the X-rated parody of their ice-cream flavours destroyed.[575]

(3) Welsh feminists had a Benny Hill-style fun run cancelled in 2017 because it was deemed "sexist" and "demeaning to women", even if the organisers' declared intention was "to simply have a bit of fun".[576]

(4) One year later, the Russian authorities banned the distribution of Antonio Iannucci's "black comedy", *The Death of Stalin*, deeming it "boring, repugnant and insulting".[577]

2.5.3 Hierarchies

Recurrent humour against social superiors, who may even allow it and be amused by it, can be institutionalised cruelty too. *Prima facie*, it would seem to be a form of responsive cruelty *à la* Hallie. However, an external-internal separation between in-group and out-group is enough inequality to allow the in-group to mock the

---

572 God alone knows what was in Mr. Infantino's heart when he made his ill-received statements.
573 At the time of our writing, the comic duo "Pio and Amedeo" caused an uproar on Italian TV by concluding their comedy show *Felicissima sera* [Happiest Evening] with a 20-minute monologue in which Amedeo asserted that they were "fed up with political correctness" and intentionally used offensive expressions and stereotypes about "women, Jews, blacks, and ... homosexuals", arguing, in a late echo of Ayer's stance, that "malice does not reside inside words or in the world, but in the brain: it is a matter of intention" ("Bufera su Pio" 2021, pars. 1 and 2). Their public stance was followed by angry criticisms from declared representatives of the targeted groups.
574 See Peretti and Reizen (2019). The short comedy was part of the 4-director film *Ro.Go.Pa.G.* On a sheer practical note, the libidinal feat suggested in the film is not an easy one to manage, in our view.
575 See "'Ben & Cherry's'" (2015).
576 "Frisky Benny Hill" (2017), pars. 1–3.
577 Bennets (2018), pars. 1 and 7; emphasis added.

out-group, who may however remain superior to the in-group in other ways.[578] As marginal as its import is, this distinction between groups involves enough power differential which the targeted out-group could easily prove to exist by preventing it, chastising it, or annihilating it.[579]

In "A Man's a Man for a' that", one of Robert Burns' most famous poems, Scotland's bard captures and, above all, instantiated himself *qua* local commoner of peasant pedigree this ephemeral yet effective hierarchical reversal:[580]

> Ye see yon birkie ca'd a lord,
>   Wha struts, an' stares, an' a' that,
> Tho' hundreds worship at his word,
>   He's but a coof for a' that.
> For a' that, an' a' that,
>   His ribband, star, an' a' that,
> The man o' independent mind,
>   He looks an' laughs at a' that.[581]

Taking some of this psychological pain with a smile can itself be a worthy display of the very social power that is being challenged and, momentarily, suspended or reversed. The relationship between king and jester in the Middle Ages or leading politician and newspaper cartoonist today can teach us something about institutionalised humour *qua* reliable flag for power imbalances in other areas of social life.[582] While the laugher enjoys at least a crumb of context-specific empowerment, the laughee exposes implicitly who has the authority to either distribute people's daily bread or lethally fail to do so.

This two-party social game discloses an underlying structure of unequal mutual advantage or, as the Romans described their own contractual relationship with the immortal gods, of *do ut des* [I give something to you so that you give some-

---

[578] In all contemporary academic literature, humour targeting so-called "privileged" groups is taken to be morally untroubling, if not praiseworthy. See, e.g., Rodrigues and Collinson (1995). Yet even the super-rich are people.
[579] Cruel responses to mockery are to be discussed in further detail in *H&C3*.
[580] We use "pedigree" sarcastically to suggest the socially 'proper' perception of Burns' status in his day.
[581] [*You see that fellow called 'a lord', / Who struts, and stares, and all that? / Though hundreds worship at his word / He is but an idiot for all that. / For all that, and all that, / His ribbon, star, and all that, / The man of independent mind, / He looks and laughs at all that.*] Burns (1993), 489–490, 3rd stanza. This poem and the peasant-turned-poet Burns' unashamed enthusiasm for the French Revolution caused him infamy in British polite circles. How truly radical his views really were, however, is uncertain (see, e.g., Baxter 1989).
[582] The contemporary analogue of so-called "roasting" sessions is discussed in the next chapter.

thing to me].⁵⁸³ Considerable historical evidence, for instance, suggests that pre-Reformation ecclesiastical authorities provided ample and magnanimous room for carnivalesque misrule, which was inclusive of open mockery of the Church at its highest levels, if not the Christian faith itself.⁵⁸⁴ It is only after the Reformation, while a weaker and shaken Holy See was busy trying to restore its control over Christendom, that these popular festivities came to be prohibited, and the most unruly of them were erased from the folklore of many European nations.⁵⁸⁵

2.5.3.1 Downward Comparison

In recent decades, with burgeoning studies of social comparison choices, it has been generally assumed that people use downward comparisons for self-evaluation (i.e., figuring out where they stand relative to other persons) or self-enhancement (i.e., building a favourable evaluation of the self).⁵⁸⁶ These studies have shown that people usually choose to compare themselves with someone who is better off. However, most of these studies compare choices in situations with rational evaluation under low stress. Altogether different results have been obtained when the subject's *ego* is under threat. In such conditions, people show a notable preference for self-enhancing comparison.⁵⁸⁷

One of the most consistent findings in the extant literature is the correlation between attitudes towards self and attitudes towards others. This means that people who have negative attitudes about themselves also evaluate other people negatively. This has been demonstrated across a number of different studies and does not seem to be caused by any methodological factors. Relevant to these findings are others that show that prejudicial attitudes among children are related to their parents' penchant for punitiveness and rejection, suggesting that this relationship is mediated by the effect of parental harshness on children's self-esteem.

---

583 See, e.g., Müth (1959).
584 See, e.g., Humphrey (2001), and Lederer (2006).
585 See, e.g., Verberckmoes (1999). Albeit prone to use carnivals as anti-papal farces, Protestant countries proceeded to an analogous process of elimination of unruly popular carnivals (see, e.g., Ehrstine 2000).
586 See Wills (1981), 249. All claims made in the subsection's first two paragraphs are based on this study.
587 The present sub-subsection could well belong to Chapter 3. Yet, insofar as it deepens some of the key issues tackled in the previous ones, we include it here. Also, ironically, this sub-subsection points to a subtle and somewhat silly logical consideration. Since cruel humour can be a cruelty, it is a cruel cruelty which, cast humorously, becomes humorous cruelty. *Chapters 2 and 3, in short, are variations on a single theme.*

"Disparagement humour" is normally defined as any amusement that denigrates or presents someone or something in a negative light.[588] It often leans on the use of negative stereotypes based on gender, ethnicity, employment, appearance, etc., in order to deliver its punchline and solve some apparent incongruity.[589] As is typical of much cruel humour, the disparaging joke is light in form but abusive in content.[590]

From a Freudian perspective, we humans are said to enjoy this type of humour because it gives us a much-needed and socially accepted cover for our repressed hostilities towards others. However, in the 20th-century, a noted social and developmental psychologist, Thomas Ashby Wills, suggested that disparagement humour also offers an opportunity for people to enhance their own subjective wellbeing by comparison with a less fortunate other. In particular, Wills' *Downward Comparison Principle* was a proposed solution to a paradox to be found in the social psychology of his day, which postulated that people in threatening situations preferred to affiliate with others who felt threatened rather than those who did not experience any threat.[591]

Another 20th-century study by Darley and Aronson had already showed that, given a choice, subjects selected an affiliation partner who is even more fearful, inasmuch as that option meant that they could gain an even more favourable comparison.[592] Following this line of study, the health scientist Jean-Paul Bell similarly observed subjects who were in either happy or depressed moods and gave them a choice of three potential affiliates (happy, neutral, or very unhappy).[593] The results showed that the depressed subjects preferred affiliation with the very unhappy target person.[594] The reason for this phenomenon is, most likely, that being around fellow-sufferers reduces stress.[595] Or, once again, that misery loves company.

Downward comparison theory predicts that threatened subjects will show a greater preference for affiliating with unfortunate persons, irrespective of whether the nature of the others' misfortune is the same as that of the subject.[596] Individuals in groups where rewards were equally distributed were less satisfied than people in groups that included one particularly unfortunate member. Specifically,

---

[588] See Janes and Olson (2000), 474.
[589] See Janes and Olson (2000), 474.
[590] See Janes and Olson (2000), 474.
[591] See Wills (1981), 245.
[592] See Darley and Aronson (1966).
[593] See Bell (1978).
[594] See Bell (1978).
[595] See Wills (1981), 248.
[596] See Wills (1981), 245. All claims made in the paragraph above are based on this study.

downward comparison was hypothesised to be useful in frustrating situations that people had difficulty rectifying. In such situations, people experienced decreased subjective wellbeing, and wanted it restored.

A prompt solution to this problem is therefore to compare oneself with another person who is worse off, insofar as the favourable comparison enables a person to feel better about his/her own situation. Normally, people dislike observing negative affect in others. When they themselves are experiencing negative affect, however, the opposite holds true.

Wills also noted that persons with low self-esteem were more likely to engage in downward comparison.[597] This is in line with an interesting psychological study by Fisher and Fisher, who found in the 1980s that professional humourists had typically experienced serious deprivation in childhood.[598] Most often, these individuals were born to mothers who were unable to show affection or warmth.[599] Humour, then, became a defence mechanism to compensate for the anger and the anxiety that they experienced.[600]

Earlier still, moreover, Freud himself pointed out that, although few people were endowed by the gift of "wit", this gift was not in any way related to prestigious attributes such as intelligence, imagination, and memory.[601] Instead, Freud claimed that there was a correlation between wit and personality-neurotic illness, and that successful jokers are often "not remarkable in other ways".[602] A psychoneurotic constitution might actually be a necessary condition for the construction of effective jokes.[603] If true, humourists and stand-up comedians would not be merely emotionally compromised individuals, but also far less intelligent persons that they are frequently taken to be because of their hilarious performances.[604]

Another important feature of Wills' downward comparison is that it tends to be directed at targets of lower status.[605] The range of potential targets is large for self-enhancing comparison, and Wills maintained that the selection of a target for downward comparison probably depends upon a combination of factors like so-

---

597 See Wills (1981), 246.
598 See Fisher and Fisher (1981).
599 See Fisher and Fisher (1981).
600 See Fisher and Fisher (1981).
601 See Freud (1960), loc 2257 and 2259.
602 Freud (1960), loc 2293.
603 See Freud (1960), loc 2252, 2256, 2289, 2293 and 2295.
604 Comedians-turned-politicians may thus not be an advisable or safe choice for the voters, e.g., Beppe Grillo in Italy and Jón Gnarr in Iceland. However, there is no lack of politicians-turned-clowns, or worse.
605 See Wills (1981), 246. All claims made in the paragraph above, plus the following two, are based on this study.

cially learned preferences, *Zeitgeist*, or personality variables opportunity. Thus, Wills included a specific *Target Principle* to his theory because the research indicated that people consistently selected safe targets, i.e., groups or persons whom the dominant culture considers acceptable to denigrate. In every study he reviewed, where subjects were given a choice between an equal-status and lower-status target, they chose the latter.

Lastly, Wills noted that people were ambivalent about downward comparison. In other words, people do not view downward comparisons with less fortunate others as wholly admirable. On the contrary, they seem to know that it is cruel. They approach such comparisons with mixed feelings, and yet they engage in them openly and frequently. It is not just that people necessarily revel in the misfortunes of others. Rather, when they have an opportunity for self-enhancement through favourable comparison, the evidence indicates that people will grab it. And the cruel world in which we live is rife with such opportunities, for there exists no dearth of threats to our own *ego* and relative social status. Humour, under such prosaic circumstances, becomes the weapon of choice.[606]

2.5.3.2 Broader Implications

According to Wills, the essential task in investigating humour is to distinguish between primary and secondary issues. For him, the primary issue for a theory of humour was the resolution of two apparently paradoxical facts:
(1) That humour depicts a person experiencing a negative situation; and yet
(2) that the audience responds to this depiction by positive affect.

The resolution proposed by the downward comparison principle is to view humour as another type of the broader process involving comparisons with less fortunate others. In other words, the essence of humour-creation is to present misfortune, whereas the essence of humour-appreciation is that the misfortune is occurring to someone else.[607] Angela Carter's phrase, "comedy is tragedy that happens to other people", captures this sentiment perfectly.[608] In point of fact, the 21st-century humour scholar Marina Riumina took this rumination even further and defined the comical as the situation where evil happens to other people while giving the audience the opportunity to safely enjoy the spectacle, i.e., as though they were untouchable gods.[609]

---

[606] Chapter 3 explores many such facilitating circumstances.
[607] See Wills (1981), 263.
[608] Carter (1991), 213.
[609] As cited in Kozintsev (2010), 2.

It should be noted that humour frequently involves something which the audience feels insecure about, e.g., boss-employee relations, marital dissatisfaction, job security, book reviews, or ridicule from others and, last but not least, sex. In terms of social comparison, humour gives the audience an opportunity to mollify their own insecurities through favourable comparison with another person's misfortune, frustration, foolishness, imperfection, blundering, embarrassment, posturing, or stupidity.[610] And as the popularity of humour reveals, people are eager to take advantage of such opportunities.[611]

Wills' approach supports chiefly the superiority theory of humour.[612] As regards the involvement of elements of duality or incongruity (e.g., exaggeration, surprise, subtlety, or cleverness), the downward comparison principle explains them in a very Freudian way as technical devices, one purpose of which is to obscure the real aim of the whole process that is afoot and successfully present another person's misfortune for the enjoyment of an audience. All the theories emphasising the incongruity-resolution aspects of humour are, *a fortiori*, fondling a secondary issue and ignoring the more important aspects of it.

According to Wills, humour is always at someone's expense. Sometimes, the safest solution for the joker is to use him- or herself as a target. Many known humourists have used this approach, whether occasionally or predominantly. The possible costs to their own wellbeing should not be ignored, though. And the comedians do not ignore it. Thus another very common alternative is to select a target that is known to be disliked by the audience.[613]

A fundamental problem for theorists in psychology, and social psychology in particular, has been to account for behaviour that seems to provide the agent with no discernible material reward.[614] Deriving pleasurable subjective sensations from the unpleasurable experiences of others would be one example of such a problem. Theorists in the field have tried to solve this by invoking drives that are then variously said to be "resolved", "relieved", or "catharted".[615] But drive the-

---

610 See Wills (1981), 263.
611 See Wills (1981), 263.
612 See Wills (1981), 264, which applies to the whole paragraph above.
613 Chapter 3 cites additional studies confirming this point.
614 See Wills (1981), 265, which applies to the whole paragraph above.
615 According to Steele (2021), one of them was the Canadian social theorist Erving Goffman, who would have thus reiterated in sociology, perhaps in an unaware manner, several older observations about laughing matters made by Aristotle, Aquinas, Shaftesbury, Cassirer *et al.* (see Chapter 1 and *H&C1*). In this context, we should stress the dubitative adverb "perhaps", for Goffman was not always open and/or honest with regard to giving due credit to his intellectual sources, e.g., Kenneth Burke (R. Kenny 2008). As noted before, Jacobs (1997–1998) made a similar point on Hayek's appropriation of Michael Polanyi's ideas about spontaneous order. Conceivably, such is the path that

ories and hydraulic models do not always work successfully for the empirical evidence at hand. According to Wills, many such theoretical conundrums can be resolved by framing them as self-enhancement processes and specifically, as comparison processes, even if the self-enhancement is not externally observable and can only be inferred indirectly—with more than a modicum of wishful thinking and some blind hope in the human race, given our empirically verifiable attributes.[616]

2.5.4 Switches

When it comes to "true humour", the perils of miserable failure grow further. Unlike less sophisticated buffoonery and crass comicality, "true humour" plays around the much-subtler "sentiment of the contrary" analysed by Pirandello.[617] Whichever formulation one may prefer, there appears to be in "true humour" an especially subtle tension at play between the element of "the satirical", which Santayana described as "closely akin to cruelty", and the element of "imaginative sympathy" whereby we all identify and, to some extent, suffer with the mocked, ridiculed, humiliated person and/or group.[618]

Different responses are therefore possible to truly humorous jests, jokes, comedies, comic films, and much else, which can even fail terribly whenever individuals and/or large audiences find the pathetic element at play more appealing than or prevalent over the comedic one.[619] Insofar as such a dual tension or ambiguity is central to humour, and especially "true humour", people can learn and operate intentionally a *Gestalt* shift, or switch, that allows them to grasp at will the pathetic element, or the comic one, as predominant.[620]

---

some people take, somewhat cruelly, in order to secure their academic success. They do not simply steal some other scholar's thunder; they actually rob the latter of his/her well-deserved place in the sun.
616 The limits of Wills' work are those of standard empirical psychology, which cannot peer into people's souls.
617 Addressed in Chapter 1, a detailed account of their views was offered in *H&C1*.
618 *Ditto*.
619 Humourists might be a special 'breed' of human beings, as also Pirandello (1920) suggested in his works. "We are all mistaken, except for the humourists. They alone have perceived how to amuse oneself with the inanity of all that is serious and, equally, of all that is frivolous" (Cioran as cited in Demont 2017, par. 32).
620 Wittgenstein (1953) discussed the case of the duck-rabbit optical illusion, which originates from an 1892 issue of the humoristic magazine *Fliegende Blätter*. What we see is not the simple result of what we are exposed to, but also of how we engage with it, armed with our concepts, expectations, memories, etc. Normally, our acquired perceptual habits drive the whole game. On

Performing this kind of switch can be a sufficiently straightforward conscious operation, e.g., in the case of real and fictional circumstances where the tension is veritably pronounced and the distance between the two registers is, so to speak, limited.[621] In the realm of European high culture, we can find several oft-discussed instances of this ilk, such as:
(1) Franz Kafka's and Samuel Beckett's works;[622]
(2) Fyodor M. Dostoyevsky's novels and short stories;[623]
(3) Bertolt Brecht's "epic theatre";[624] and
(4) the bittersweet Italian film comedies of the 1950s, 1960s and 1970s.[625]

Not knowing whether to laugh or cry, the reader/viewer can focus at will on the comedic side of things, hence laughing a bitter laughter, or on the tragic one, hence crying tragicomic tears. In all such cultured cases, the possibility of laughing out of the other side of one's mouth is built intentionally in the narrative fabric that has been skilfully woven by the artist/s.

This switching of focus is a mental operation analogous to our ability to perceive the corner of two walls and a ceiling as protruding towards or away from us.[626] Or, using another example, to resolve the perceptual instability of optical il-

---

other occasions, however, we are called by instability or novelty to make a much more deliberate choice: we *decide* what we see.

621 As studied by *Getsalt* psychology, too short a distance between two perceptual principles or instances thereof can cause ambiguity or instability, as also in the duck-rabbit optical illusion discussed by Wittgenstein (1953).

622 J. Meyers (2012, 760) entitled aptly his essay "Kafka's Dark Laughter". O'Neill (1983) claimed Kafka to be too dark, and compared his comic failures to Sade's ones, which are openly gory. As to Beckett's humour, Kennedy (1989, 45 *et passim*) used, very much *à propos* and repeatedly, the term "tragicomic". Today's cinephiles may have experienced similar aesthetics, or analogous failures, in the films by Peter Greenaway or Lars von Trier.

623 Funnily, Busch (1987) wrote a whole book in the attempt to highlight the generally unnoticed comedic side of Dostoyevsky's oeuvre. As Freeborn (1989, 123) noted in his review of the book: "The humour in Dostoevskii frequently comes too close to the morbid and sadistic for it to elicit a spontaneous laugh." Only an equally troubled and pained 'soulmate', such as the great Romanian existentialist Emil Cioran (1970, 153), could write as follows: "we have quite failed to understand Dostoevsky if we do not realize that humor is his chief quality".

624 Significantly, Brecht's *engagé* theatre made use of the comic techniques and insights of the great Weimar slapstick artist, Karl Valentin (see, e.g., Calandra 1974).

625 See D'Amico (2008).

626 "Trained" is the key term here, if it is true that "humor may be taught and learned" (Amir 2019, 113). Cipolla (1988), as seen, regarded our knack for being humorous a matter of instinct. Scholars, as usual, disagree.

lusions in the alternative ways available to us.⁶²⁷ As to switching specifically between pathetic and comical interpretations, being capable of hermeneutical shifts of this kind may require more effort than resolving optical illusions or rearranging our perceptions. This switch is taken as an important indicator of a heroic personality or great wisdom, if not of progress with respect to irregular mental conditions, sexual deviance, and other troublesome weaknesses and pathologies.⁶²⁸

In ordinary life, we can interpret an incident or event as something tragic, e.g., the loss of an irreplaceable household item having sentimental value, a major disruption of one's own routine and peace of mind, or an incurable illness announcing the end of life. However, we can also interpret the same incident or event as something comical, e.g., a silly mistake, a strange way to make new friends, or God's wicked way of letting us know that He is waiting for us.⁶²⁹ What is more, we can start with the former interpretation and then switch to the latter. The first example (i.e., the broken kitchen tool) is normally not greatly demanding in terms of our efforts for reinterpretation.⁶³⁰ *Au contraire*, the third one (i.e., the fatal illness) may require a long process of meditation, soul-searching, and self-revision.⁶³¹

The factors at play in such a process of reflection and self-redescription are likely to be multiple. Our natural dispositions, our habits of heart and mind, our level of acculturation, and the availability of alternative imaginative-conceptual frameworks through which to address the same event and experience it differently are all probable potent coefficients in this equation. This rich diversity and the switches that it allows for have enormous implications regarding the kind of life that we lead, may lead, believe to be leading, and/or choose to believe to be leading.

Which *Gestalt* switches are commonplace—and which are not—says a lot about the presupposed aspects of our lives. Thus, while scholars are prone to discuss the nature and functions of humour in the human and social sciences, hence placing 'seriousness' in the background, they never ask questions such as: What is seriousness? What is the function of seriousness? Why are we serious? Answering these questions is not necessary to determine what the default position is like, for

---

627 See, e.g., van Campen (1997).
628 See, e.g., Madigan (2013), Taels (2011), and Wilson and Cox (1983).
629 We use the masculine pronoun here to distract less from the central meaning of the sentence.
630 Even a dramatic case of breaking something, or something breaking, e.g., the "unsinkable" Titanic, can be seen as hilarious, according to Rosset and, apparently, several colleagues of his (as cited in Amir, forthcoming).
631 See, e.g., Amir (2019) and Rorty (1989).

this is already shown by the preferred point/s of emphasis, i.e., *via* implicit contrast.[632] Humour, in this specific case, is clearly the exception, not the norm.[633]

2.5.5 Self-Education

We all are deeply conditioned by our biology, society, culture, and early years of life.[634] Nonetheless, precious space may still exist "for philosophic self-education" in adulthood.[635] Realising the potential for existential enrichment that the ability to switch from a tragic view of life to a comic one can engender, two well-known contemporary humour scholars stressed hermeneutical *self*-training as a path to secular salvation.[636] They are John Morreall and Lydia Amir, whose published works we are now going to dissect and reflect upon.[637]

Morreall, to begin, juxtaposed the "comic and tragic visions of life" by way of numerous mutual oppositions which he claimed reduce the desirability of the latter and let the former come across as "reasonable and appealing".[638] The oppositions between "the tragic and comic visions" were said to be, respectively: "Mental rigidity versus mental flexibility"; "Low versus high tolerance for disorder"; "Pref-

---

[632] This logic is also exemplified by Amir's (2019, 108) humour-centred resolution of what she claimed to be the commonplace "shame and disgust" pertaining to "the body", its "animal or material" *quid*, male "semen", women's "menstruation, sex and [giving] birth", "physicality and the secretions of the body" and our "sticky mortal part", all of which goes to show how removed her expected readership is from, for one, Anita Philips' (1998) feminist masochistic alternative, embracing sex and odd sexual fetishes *qua* avenues to accept and, perchance, enjoy the body, its liquids and their eroticisation. See also João Florêncio (2020), which we tackle in more detail in *H&C3*.
[633] We do not cast any value judgement. Perhaps the prevalence of the serious over the humorous is a mere factual reflection of the prevalence in life of tragedy over comedy or of the psychological make-up of our species, such that a tragic interpretation has been 'wired' into us by evolution rather than a comic one. Etymologically, "humour" has pathological roots. Still within Jonson's plays, "humour" indicated an "unbalanced presentation of human qualities and moral infirmities outdoing reason and causing the loss of the self" (Takase 1983–1984, 9).
[634] We do not address the issue of the likely or exact length of these early years in people's infancy and childhood.
[635] Amir (2019), xi. Hard determinists would disagree with this stance, which clearly endorses free will.
[636] By "secular salvation" we mean "redemptive truth" *à la* Rorty, i.e., finding an answer to the existential question *par excellence:* what shall we do with our lives? (Rorty 2001, title page *et passim*).
[637] Amir (2019, 47–48) aimed at nothing less than "non-religious ... redemption", "liberation" or "emancipation".
[638] Morreall (1998), 333. This essay constitutes the bulk of chap. 2, 3, and 4 of Morreall (1999).

erence for the familiar versus seeking out the unfamiliar"; "Low versus high tolerance for ambiguity"; "Convergent versus divergent thinking"; "Uncritical versus critical thinking"; "Emotional engagement versus emotional disengagement"; "Stubbornness versus willingness to change one's mind"; "Idealism versus pragmatism"; "Finality versus a second chance"; "Spirit versus body"; "Seriousness versus playfulness"; "Heroism versus anti-heroism"; "Militarism versus pacifism"; "Vengeance versus forgiveness"; "Hierarchy versus equality"; "Less versus more sexual equality"; "Respect for versus questioning of authority and tradition"; "Rules versus situation ethics"; "Social isolation versus social integration".[639]

Amir, for her part, suggested that the tense alternative between the tragic and comic views of life can be dispensed with, first of all, by acknowledging the fact that, while enduring the many sorrows of our mortal existence, "[w]e are the butt of an anonymous joke".[640] As Amir notes, we may desire anything and everything and aim for all kinds of gratifications; however, all our faculties are limited; our knowledge is limited; and our life on this speck of earth in the boundless void of space is limited—we will never get all we want. Still, we can laugh, repeatedly, alone as well as together with others, and find some comfort in these experiences. Then we can move closer to the same acknowledgment by also "embrac[ing the] ridicule" lying at the very heart of this seemingly cruel "anonymous joke", which will come to be seen as connoted inherently, not just accidentally, by comic "levity" as well as by tragic "seriousness".[641]

Tragedy and comedy, or the tragic and comic views of life, are thus to be allowed to coexist in a state of "tension" which, according to Amir, we cannot resolve once and for all, unless we are willing to pay dire intellectual prices—at least from a rationalistic perspective—such as: missing important truths about reality; misrepresenting reality in one way or another; endorsing "unwarranted metaphysical assumptions" that philosophers have long unmasked and demolished; passing judgement when none is truly warranted; etc.[642] Let us stop trying to resolve this tension, counselled Amir.[643]

---

639 Morreall (1998), 339–352. Of these self-explanatory oppositions, only "Respect for versus questioning of authority and tradition" comes across as forced and implausible, especially in light of Sophocles' tragedies, which contain a forceful critique of the hubris of political power *vis-à-vis* deeper, or higher, principles of human conduct (e.g., parental love, familial duties). Similarly, 19th-century naturalism in European literature and drama, or Italian neorealism in cinema, are also tokens of anti-authoritarian tragedy (e.g., Zola's novels and De Sica's *Umberto D.*).
640 Amir (2019), 238. The joke's anonymity hints at Amir's agnostic, if not atheistic, background assumptions.
641 Amir (2019), 142 and 238.
642 Amir (2019), 13 and 236.

Consistently with Freud's and, more widely, Western psychoanalysis conclusions on this issue, Amir claimed that we cannot "overcome alienation" *in toto* in our life, but only reduce it, no matter how much we might desire to do so.[644] As unpleasant as they may be, conflicts are normal and "constitutive of the complex being that [we are] and of the complicated relations [we] entertain with a world [we] do not fully understand".[645] Aware of such insuperable limitations, Amir's sophisticated and accepting "self-knowledge" is meant to lead to self-improvement as well as to general improvement, for it should be capable of eliciting within us deeper feelings of "humanity" and "sympathy" in the face of our essential condition *qua* "ridiculous" human beings, which we share with all our fellow humans.[646]

Familiar with Kierkegaard's considerations on this matter, Amir believed humour to be warm, sympathetic, and, at least *in potentia*, able to foster the virtue of *humility* which pathetic beings like ourselves should better cultivate.[647] Specifically, as Amir understood and defined the human being, we are all taken to be examples of "*Homo risibilis*, or the ridiculous human being".[648] Essentially, then, our constitutive worthlessness is not definitively disproved; if anything, it is reinforced.[649] Rather, "humour" proper is preserved too, and it is recast as an existential lifeline, which Amir christens with an incisive oxymoron: "compassionate aggression".[650]

As Amir explicated this figure of speech, she wrote that "humour" is to be seen as "a form of intrapersonal communication" that can diminish "the tension between the factions of the self" and facilitate "further inner change" in the pursuit of inner peace and wellbeing.[651] By pursuing this path of wise "self-acceptance",

---

643 Because of this conscious ambiguity, Amir's stance can be read as less militantly dichotomous than Morreall's.
644 Amir (2019), 238.
645 Amir (2019), 238.
646 Amir (2019), 196 and 238.
647 See, e.g., Amir (1996). We discussed Kierkegaard in detail in *H&C1*, not here.
648 Amir (2019), xi. Many scholars have tackled humour as an inherently contradictory phenomenon, e.g., the psychiatrist William Fry's (2010) oxymoronically entitled book, *Sweet Madness*.
649 Ujhelyi, Almosdi, and Fodor (2022) recently added another element to the humiliating devaluation of *homo risibilis* insofar as they showed experimentally how a successful Turing test could be performed, granting an artificial intelligence the ability to mimic human "humour" proper, and therefore being mistaken for a human by a human.
650 Amir (2019), 113 and 142. Humour *qua* path to self-acceptance before unresolved and possibly insoluble existential puzzles was the conclusion reached also by Marmysz (2003), Heller (2005), and McDonald (2012).
651 Amir (2019), 87–88.

Amir's approach hinted as well at the dialectical one that Pirandello attributed to Cervantes (i.e., "overcome[ing] the comical ... through the comical itself") but did not pursue himself in *L'umorismo*, since the Sicilian dramatist preferred focussing instead on the unresolved coexistence of antithetical forces within humour (i.e., the "feeling of the contrary").[652]

Pushing a little further the notion of a possible comical overcoming of the painful experiences in life, Amir argued that the "tragic oppositions" explored by dramatists and philosophers alike (e.g., free will and fate, moral duty and social allegiance, marital fidelity and erotic love, personal commitment and existential meaninglessness) can be reconceptualised by a feat of trained creativity and come to be seen as "comical incongruities".[653] Interestingly, an analogous dialectical approach had already been suggested in the 1990s by an American religious thinker, historian, and Presbyterian minister, Conrad Hyers.

Working upon the basis of Bradley's and Hegel's prior reflections about tragedy and comedy, Hyers distinguished "three levels of humor", which we list below.[654]

(1) "Paradise" (e.g., childhood's "exuberance of life itself"; "horsing around" for its own sake; smiling and laughing uncontrollably out of sheer *joie de vivre*; being infused with 'good humour').[655]

(2) "Paradise lost" (e.g., adolescence's "comic reflection of ... conflict and anxiety, success and failure, faith and doubt"; the gleeful discovery of hidden ironies and embarrassing paradoxes; the pleasant unpleasantries of teasing and mocking).[656]

(3) "Paradise regained" (e.g., maturity's "acceptance, resolution, and larger harmonies ... generated ... by ... reconciliation"; the charitable reinterpretation

---

[652] Amir (2019), 88 and 107.
[653] Amir (2019), 73–76. The natural sciences can also lead to the potent realisation of such "tragic oppositions". Whether these oppositions can then be turned or not into "comic incongruities" is a *personal* feat that some noted scientists, such as Ludwig Boltzmann and his heir Paul Ehrenfest, were arguably incapable of doing. As known, both founders of thermodynamics committed suicide (see Reiter 2007 and Van Lunteren and Hollestelle 2013).
[654] Hyers (1996), 84–92, which applies to the numbered quotes as well.
[655] Childhood's laughter is a blatant confirmation of humour *qua* release of pent-up psychic energy. Pragmatically, it too contains an element of cruelty, inasmuch as observing adults are thereby reminded of the fleeting nature of youth, joyfulness, vitality, and life itself. Thus many elderly persons avoid contact with children.
[656] The dualities grasped as of adolescence support the incongruity theory of humour, but they are also accompanied by social hierarchies, e.g., between siblings—hence superiority.

of the ironies and paradoxes discovered in our youth; the smiling acceptance of life's complexity and finitude).[657]

Transformative feats of hermeneutical creativity such as Hyers' light-hearted 're-gaining of paradise' can be accomplished, in line with Amir's later study, if and only if we teach ourselves to laugh gently at such puzzles whose tragic character we do not entirely forget either.[658] Basically, we step from the level of "the immediately funny" to that of a more meditative, self-aware, self-critical, perchance melancholic, yet also potentially wise and enlightening "self-referential humour" about our own many limitations.[659]

High culture offers more than a few tools for such a project of interpretative reinvention, which Amir described as "egalitarian".[660] It is up to each and every person to make use of these cultural tools, or not.[661] If we intend to pursue this philosophical path for self-review, we must acquire the intellectual tools and the force of will for "keeping shame and disgust at bay" before life's tragic conflicts, so as to be capable of "living with the unresolved tension of our situation" and, in chorus, "preserv[ing] our humanity".[662] As Amir observed, it can be terribly easy to despair once we realise that our "human condition" consists in being bound to experience "conflicts … within [ourselves], in [our] relationships with others and with the world, together with [our] incapacity for self-acceptance".[663]

Amir judged a handful of Western thinkers, Montaigne and Nietzsche *in primis*, to have been capable of precisely this feat of creative transcendence.[664] As

---

[657] Clearly, Amir's philosophical project aims at achieving something akin to Hyers' re-entry into paradise.
[658] A truly encyclopaedic scholar, Amir (2019, 6 *et passim*) knew of Hyers and referred to his 1996 book *vis-à-vis* the notion of "the tragic paradigm", but she did not discuss his three levels or types of "humour" proper.
[659] Amir (2019), xi and 237.
[660] Significantly, Amir (2019, 113) contrasted critically her own approach with "Nussbaum consider[ing] the idea that most people may come to accept their incompleteness, powerlessness, and mortality as far too optimistic".
[661] Amir (2019), x. Implicit in Amir's project is the idea that a greater degree of acculturation offers greater options. As stated by Ortega y Gasset (1946, 43–44): "Culture is what saves human life from being a mere disaster; it is what enables man to live a life which is something above meaningless tragedy or inward disgrace."
[662] Amir (2019), xi and 113.
[663] Amir (2019), 237–238.
[664] *Au contraire*, Pirandello (1986, 13) suggested that human beings are prone to soften their apprehension of reality with comforting illusions. No taxing intellectual work is needed: "No matter how cruelly we try to get rid of nature's providential illusions, which are meant for our own good, we fail. Luckily, we get easily distracted."

such, they should be studied if we are to search committedly for guidance in this enlightening process of "philosophic self-education".[665] The 16th-century French essayist was thus commended repeatedly as a paragon of peaceful, tolerant, humble, Pyrrhonian, and "secular" wisdom in these murky yet important matters, i.e., how to live.[666] In her view, Montaigne exemplifies that which an educated and self-reflexive kind of humour, if taken seriously, can offer to us *qua* reasonable mirror of reality and, above all, *qua* valuable existential option.[667]

2.5.6 Apologetics

Both Morreall and Amir are eminent experts in humour studies.[668] In their published works, they delved into the extant literature with intelligence, competence, and eloquence. In the process, they made the best possible case for taking the comic view of life most seriously.[669] In the 1990s, Richard Rorty claimed that the philosophical works and thought experiments by John Rawls and Robert Nozick could be read as "intuition pumps" injecting, respectively, more "justice" and more "market" into the shared axiology of the cultural West.[670] Morreall's and Amir's philosophies serve an analogous pumping function, although this time with regard to "humour" proper.[671]

---

665 Amir (2019), xi.
666 Amir (2019), 224, citing Bloom. "Pyrrhonian" and "Pyrrhonism" come from "Pyrrho", father of scepticism.
667 Conceivably, it could be argued that the person exposed to "true humour" can still look, so to speak, to her right, where the tragic component lies, then to her left, where the merely comic is, and finally pick either, however informed that person may be about what the other side is like. "True humour" and its constitutive tension, in this way, could be de-structured and brought back to either basic component. Reaching a higher or deeper insight does not imply being able, or even willing, to hold on to it. Weakness, retreat, and refusal are *personal* options too.
668 By starting scholarly research about humour at a time when academia ignored this topic or treated it as philosophically secondary, if not beneath itself, and by establishing successful consultantships for businesses, organisations, and individuals, Morreall and Amir have been laughing all the way to the bank for decades.
669 Amir's (2019) subtitle reads *"Taking Ridicule Seriously"*, echoing Palmer (1994) and Morreall (1983).
670 As translated and cited in Mattio (2008), 235–236. Rorty's rendition of the so-called liberal "marketplace" of ideas was also amply recalled in this article, i.e., as a nominally oriental "bazar" of different lifestyles, ideals, etc.
671 "Intuition pumps" are thought experiments, i.e., parables or enthymemes eliciting intuitions, not explicit arguments producing demonstrations (see Dennett 1984 for a critical presentation, and 1991, for a more positive one). Perhaps, *we* are one such pump for tragedy.

In their committed, informed, and nuanced approach to the concept of 'humour', both Morreall and Amir operated in a way that, intriguingly, is subtly specular to Pirandello's earlier conception of it.[672] This fascinating game of mirrors takes place along two main theoretical lines.

(1) Like the famous Sicilian humourist, both Morreall and Amir tackled "humour" proper as a tense combination of mutually opposite feelings and/or thoughts. Yet, in their publications, the order in which these feelings and/or thoughts present themselves is inverted. While Pirandello described comicality turning into pity, so as to become "true humour", both Morreall and Amir invited their readers to take the tragic aspects of existence and turn them into something lighter and brighter, and thereby smile gently at the burdensome realities of life.[673]

(2) According to Amir, the transformation at play is meant to produce nothing less than a new form of compassionate "wisdom".[674] Nevertheless, Morreall's and Amir's comic understanding of the human condition sought no abyssal depths or celestial heights.[675] In line with Pirandello's own approach, and steeped in the post-metaphysical and post-religious ethos of much contemporary philosophy, it opened a path towards moderate relaxation and melancholic accept-

---

672 See our account of his views in *H&C1*.

673 Amir's use of an oxymoron in describing her own version of "true humour" implies superiority *vis-à-vis* mere comicality, thanks to her version's entailing a pronounced coefficient of humaneness or sympathy that is absent in mere comicality. Amir's transcendence is thus likely to be, rather than a Hegelian *Aufhebung*, a reformulation of Pirandello's distinction between commonplace humour and "true humour", not a synthesis of logical opposites producing a novel conceptual entity. After all, Amir's reply to the tension between the tragic and the comical views of life does not imply a genuine, categorical transcendence, but merely the wise acceptance of said tension.

674 See especially Amir (2019).

675 Amir's approach recalls Eco's (1985) one too, insofar as Eco's *third* level of humorous self-observation under tragic circumstances that others find comical (e.g., being a cuckold) is a feat of imagination requiring considerable self-detachment and self-reflexivity, insofar as it requires stepping above comicality (i.e., the first step) and the feeling of the contrary (i.e., Pirandello's second step). It must be added, however, that this sort of self-observation can multiply and pile up *ad infinitum*, insofar as the same self can then observe him-/herself observing humorously him-/herself under tragic circumstances that others find comical, hence adding to the tragedy, for s/he can now see how desperate s/he is to find a way out of his/her misery. Then, the same self can observe him-/herself observing him-/herself observing him-/herself ... and so on. Each time, a switch between the comic view of life and the tragic one occurs and becomes, as it were, available for existential self-understanding.

ance of human frailties and foibles, not a window into some hidden truth about the nature of being, or even just the human being."[676]

Scholarly details and minor differences aside, both Morreall and Amir provided an imaginative existentialist philosophy investigating the comedic potential of all the absurdities, mishaps, obstacles, paradoxes, and pains that we all are destined to encounter in our life and may be tempted to interpret under a far more mournful, dark, tragic perspective. In their work, the comic view of life finds the most lucid and most committed expression known in contemporary philosophy: "an *apologia* for laughter and humor".[677]

As creative, appealing and intelligent as it can be, the comic alternative depicted by the existentialist philosophies of Morreall and Amir is not *in se* a rebuttal of the tragic view of life. Their alternative is, rather, a rich illustration of an arguably merrier option which each person will then have to consider and elect in *lieu* of the tragic one—if she is willing to pursue it, capable of attaining it, and sufficiently justified by her specific circumstances. In other terms, the tragic view of life is not proved wrong *per se* by either Morreall or Amir. Instead, it is connoted negatively and, specifically, it is critiqued as marked harmfully by its hopeless striving for the sublime, as well as for its opening up the despairing pits of *Angst*.[678]

If anything, though, anxiety (aka "anguish") can easily arise from humour that *fails* to be read as humour.[679] This mismatch can occur even in Morreall's own ethologically and psycho-evolutionarily informed conception of this phenomenon, i.e., in the "play" that it is allegedly meant to be. As he wrote:

> The oldest play signals in humans are smiling and laughing. According to ethologists, these evolved from similar play signals in pre-human apes. The apes that evolved into *Homo sapi-*

---

[676] Unromantically, Morreall (1998, 354) claimed that "the comic view" of life "puts no stock in the sublime".
[677] Morreall (2020a), xiv.
[678] Discussing Heidegger's tragic existentialism, Amir (2019, 25) cited Schmidt's pointed choice of words to grasp its core elements: "'guilt' and 'the tragedy of appearance'". On our part, we understand *Angst* as existential anxiety and pursue no more nuanced connotation of it, as hinted, e.g., by Leacock (1914, 120), who wrote of "[a]nxiety deepen[ing] into dread, and ... dread [giving] way to the cruel certainty of despair".
[679] Pathologies may cause some people to become liable to gravely misread friendly aggressions, such as those of humorous banter and irony, e.g., paranoia and persecution complexes. However, such a line of misinterpretation does not require mental maladies to find a fertile soil from which it can germinate. First, all persons can make mistakes, including reading a situation as threatening when it is not meant to be so. Secondly, as anticipated with our mention of Sergio Leone's films, the most dangerous intentions can be hidden behind not so much as laughing, but sheer smiling itself and in a rather gentle way at times, i.e., without a hint of sardonicism.

ens split off from the apes that evolved into chimpanzees and gorillas about six million years ago. In chimps and gorillas, as in other mammals, play usually takes the form of mock-aggression such as chasing, wrestling, biting, and tickling. According to many ethologists, mock-aggression was the earliest form of play, from which all other play developed... In mock-aggressive play, it is critical that all participants are aware that the activity is not real aggression.[680]

As a species, we do appear to engage in, and enjoy enormously the kind of monkey play that Morreall described in connection with the phenomenon of humour.[681] The gloomy gorilla is an even rarer beast than the normal one has sadly become these days.[682] Morreall and Amir are therefore probably correct in assuming that the frustrated striving for the sublime and the despairing pits of existential anxiety are likely to make the tragic view unappealing to many, or even most, living persons.[683]

On the other hand, neither defect makes the tragic view of life logically impossible, empirically erroneous, and/or existentially implausible. Morreall and Amir did not demonstrate that such frustration and anxiety are inherently flawed. Instead, as a valuable existential alternative, they showed their readers how another path can be followed which relies on a humorous understanding of the conflicts and contradictions marring our life.[684] In other terms, in their writings, Morreall and Amir did not reduce the field of possible existence and exploration by chopping off one side. Quite the opposite. They increased it by casting light on another

---

[680] Morreall (2016), par. 5. In contemporary linguistics, Shilikhina (2017, 107) offered an ample study of "Metapragmatic Markers of the *Bona Fide* and *Non-bona Fide* Modes of Communication" that reveals the complex negotiations occurring empirically among people who engage in mutual dialogue, including of the humorous kind, hence alerting her readers to the very bumpy ride that we must face in real life when trying to communicate at all, *pace* the stock simplistic assumptions of smooth and habitual intersubjective discourse in her field of study.

[681] Tapley (2013) accused Morreall of failing to distinguish between this kind of "play" and actual "humour" which, once again, slips through the fingers of those who try to grasp its nature.

[682] This is not meant as a scientific statement for which a reference should be supplied. It is, instead, a token of creative and non-literal use of language.

[683] Humour's preferability is also the outcome of the four June 2000 Paris lectures about the two chief "paradigms" of "tragedy" and "comicality", i.e., philosophical and psychoanalytical, given by Critchley (2000). Negating negation, Critchley did sound far more Hegelian in his lectures than either Amir (2019) or Pirandello (1920).

[684] Morreall's description of the animal "play" of which humour was said to be an example is based on an incongruity, i.e., the mismatch between the apparent signal of harmful aggression and its proper interpretation as harmless interaction. Mistakes can occur in these performances, involving an emitter and a recipient of the signal at issue; hence fear, anxiety, dread, or cruel retaliation can ensue too. As Meyer (2000, 310) wrote, humour is a "double-edged sword". Our interpretation of Morreall's theory as being "actually a development of the Incongruity Theory" was shared by Bardon (2005, 472), who focussed himself on humour *qua* "cognitive flexibility".

side, while assuming that the lugubrious and disheartened tone of tragedy will make it too painful for the dark side to be preferable to the comic alternative that they embraced.[685]

2.5.7 Tragedies

A tacit prejudicial attitude towards pain, not just sublimity and anguish, colours both Morreall's and Amir's works.[686] Yet pain, as well as sublimity and anguish, may not need to be avoided at all, as Morreall and Amir regularly implied.[687] Pain, frustration, and anxiety might, instead, be part of the paradoxical cruelty that Hallie thought we all must continue to cherish for the sake of personal maturation and human authenticity, without having to "seek a way out of … the tragic sense of life".[688]

Let us consider three lines of critical reasoning in this regard:

(1) Morreall's clever oppositions, as insightful as they are, can be easily reconceptualised in such a way as to underplay his preference for a comic view of life and privilege the tragic one instead. Consider the following list: "Coherence versus hypocrisy"; "Low versus high tolerance for chaos"; "Preference for the safely tested versus seeking out the risky untested"; "Low versus high tolerance for equivocation"; "Consensus versus disagreement"; "Principled versus unprincipled thinking"; "Commitment versus indifference"; "Perseverance versus volatility"; "Aspiration versus unscrupulousness"; "Determination versus indeterminacy"; "Humanity versus animality"; "Responsibility versus irresponsibility"; "Courage versus cowardice"; "Devotion to a cause versus readiness to compromise"; "Justice versus licence"; "Excellence versus ignorance"; "More versus less division of labour"; "Respect for versus undermining of crucial values"; "Integrity versus opportunism"; "Distinction versus mediocrity".[689]

---

[685] Existential and metaphysical conundrums can make comedic fodder; see, e.g., Woody Allen (Kalman 2011).
[686] See, e.g., Amir's (forthcoming) appraisal of Bataille's "philosophy of laughter" whereby "laughter is an impulse by which anguish is dispelled", and her commending discussion of the "secular monks" who embraced "Epicureanism" and its ideals of "happiness" *qua* "peace of mind … health of the body and … *ataraxía*", i.e., paths to "liberate us from pain and terror" (Amir 2019, 50).
[687] As the Jungian psychoanalyst G.R. Buccola (2019, 12) reported, both "Angst" and "anguish" owe their etymology to the Greek "goddess of necessity", *Ananke*, who overpowers rationality and cannot but be suffered.
[688] Amir (2015), 97.
[689] Again, we assume the terms used in these oppositions to be sufficiently self-explanatory to the academic reader.

(2) As regards Amir's eloquent and erudite approach, transcending creatively the unresolved tension at the heart of "humour" proper may not require adopting a comic view of life. Significantly, the Danish Protestant mystic and self-declared "humourist" Søren Kierkegaard had suggested, in the 19th century, that "humour" proper, albeit theologically commendable, is only the *penultimate* step into faith.[690] Emphasising "the amusing aspect" of religious experience, "humour" is capable of providing some relief but, at some point, the intimidating acceptance or refusal of faith will have to be faced: "Humour is not faith but is prior to faith; it is not after faith or a development of faith."[691]

Humour's role, basically, would be to reduce our stress levels as we come to realise that religious belief—notably, of the Christian sort—is full of puzzling contradictions, e.g., the virgin birth, the crucified son of God, love as law, sin as death, death as life, etc.[692] Eventually, each person must decide whether to abandon him-/herself to the embrace of this logic-defying God or not. And this is no joke. Each person must determine whether to accept religion's awesome terrors of worthlessness before an Almighty God and the related dangers of eternal damnation, or the burdensome 'gifts' of unbelief, i.e., utter personal transience and existential meaninglessness. Neither final option is risible, whether *prima facie*, in a considered manner, or with any deeper scrutiny.[693]

When the penny drops, then, we should all get pensive. Amir's suggested solution, i.e., a Pyrrhonian suspension of judgment that is genuinely open to the rationally unsolvable knots of our constitutive tensions and existential ambiguities, is itself an option entailing significant consequences. Wisdom, even if humorous, comes always with a price tag. Think, for one, of what could happen to us in the afterlife, should we follow the sceptical trajectory and also be truly endowed with an immortal soul, as Kierkegaard and many other Western thinkers have repeatedly intimated.[694]

The human condition, which Amir herself described in her writings as serious and grave, may well have to be tackled that way too, in the end. Humour, as much

---

690 Kierkegaard was discussed at length in *H&C1*.
691 Kierkegaard (2009), 244. See also Evans (1987).
692 We do not need to delve any deeper here, as we did instead in *H&C1*. See however Marfo *et al.* (2022) for a representative study of humour *qua* stress-relief mechanism in the face of epidemic illness and increased likelihood of death in the context of today's Ghana.
693 The nihilistic tone of Nietzsche's "laughter", praised by Bataille and others, is tackled in Amir (forthcoming).
694 Amir (2019), 51. Her negative attitude towards religious beliefs is not tacit. Seeking a non-religious form of salvation, she sided with Malinowski, who dubbed religion "wishful thinking" (Amir 2019, 53).

as we may wish to enjoy the company of it throughout our lives, should better accompany us for only part of the journey. After making plenty of silly faces in front of the mirror, in all probability, we shall have to look our image in the eye and reflect on ourselves. Poking fun at our sorry condition, instead, or even approaching it in a more light-hearted way, plausibly armed with Amir's "compassionate aggression", could miss the crucial existential point.[695] Indeed, it may postpone, if not derail, a fundamental, deadly serious, *existential* decision about what to do with one's own earthly finitude and a notional otherworldly infinity.[696]

For instance, as amusing as Monty Python's 1983 comedy *The Meaning of Life* may be, its constant lampooning of the most significant events and/or processes in life (e.g., conception, birth, growth, adolescence, middle age, death) and derision of the human institutions that can help us in thinking about them and facing them (e.g., schools, the Christian religion, high culture) could be considered as symptoms of humour's inability to take the final step into faith.[697] Even worse, they could exemplify Hazlitt's notion of cynical humour laughing off grave matters and pooh-poohing the earnest efforts that have been made in trying to grapple with these grave matters, whilst also offering no concrete alternative solutions about the same predicaments.[698]

(3) Amir's admiration for Montaigne is misplaced in this specific existential and theological context. Like many contemporary academic commentators who read Montaigne's work through today's secular lenses, Amir too forgot about Montaigne's religious and specifically Catholic faith, which he practiced conscientiously throughout most of his life and, meaningfully, on his deathbed.[699]

---

[695] Kierkegaard (2009), 227, note 1. See our detailed account of his philosophy in *H&C1*.
[696] The secular viewpoint is predominant in the West today, especially in academia, but is historically marginal.
[697] Following Pascal's (1993, thoughts ##200–227 of the Chevalier edition) famous and, at times, humorous thoughts on humankind's penchant for diversion (e.g., playing cards, dancing and, tellingly, comedy), it could be argued that, however clever or refined, any humour targeting religion's deepest truth (i.e., our glorious divine origin) and paramount aim (i.e., returning to that divine glory) is an unwise attempt at downplaying them both, which are actually the most important matters of all under a Christian perspective (and not only a Christian one, for numerous religions and philosophies have argued that the fate of our immortal souls should be life's chief concern). It is one of humour's *cruel ironies* that it might make us blind to life's important matters.
[698] Whilst busy trying to 'shock the bourgeois', Nietzsche and his French 'laughing' heirs (i.e., Bataille, Deleuze, and Rosset) got stuck into this penultimate step, which Amir (forthcoming) favoured while seeking a secular way out by exploiting the collapse of meaning, e.g., in play, anguish, eroticism, paradox, and uncontrollable laughter.
[699] See Bakewell (2010).

Undoubtedly, the great French essayist displayed in his philosophical writings a remarkably placid acceptance of human contingency, as well as a famously Pyrrhonian attitude towards human reason and its frail determinations, which Montaigne claimed to be too liable to error to be capable of grasping the fundamental truths about our place in the universe. As Amir noted, Montaigne's sceptical, humble, self-centred approach "is a joyful affirmation of life in the face of contingency and despair that follows the failure of the philosophical act in its heroic forms. Hume calls it 'the gaiety of Montaigne'."[700]

Behind all of these commendable intellectual traits, however, there transpires Montaigne's wilful surrender to the ultimate comfort that 15 centuries of ecclesiastical tradition had preserved until his day *qua* sole means of salvation, which was taken to be beyond human powers, including the faculty of philosophical and/or scientific reason: Jesus Christ, the Holy Gospels, and the Sacraments of Mother Church.[701] With these implicit metaphysical and existential backings, Montaigne could certainly afford to be a relaxed, self-effacing, and humorous disciple of Pyrrhonism in the early-modern age.[702]

In comparison, instead, Amir's project is a renewal of the ancient pagan hope of attaining true happiness in this life by solely cultivating our contingent earthly virtues.[703] Notably, the virtue that she dubs, oxymoronically, "compassionate aggression". On the opposite metaphysical side, Montaigne's Catholic and, more broadly, Christian tradition teaches us that a complete *beatitudo* can be enjoyed

---

700 Amir (2019), 127.
701 Montaigne's Catholic Pyrrhonism, as most patent in both his "Apology for Raymond Sebond" and lifelong churchgoing, were discussed by Screech (2000), Maia Neto, Paganini, and Laursen (2009), and Hartle (2003).
702 Amir (2019, 144, note 8) sounds as though she was partially aware of her rather personal take on Montaigne's work: "Montaigne repeatedly comments on humanity's inanity yet voices an affirmative view of life akin to a theodicy. The absence of any explanation of how he reaches the final affirmative stage has bemused commentators. I can enlighten this significant issue with the argument that Montaigne anticipates part of the *Homo risibilis* worldview I present here, though I cannot be certain that I am not projecting my thesis onto his work." *We too may be at risk of projecting our own theses onto Morreall's and Amir's understanding of 'humour'*. Unfortunately, this is part of the many hermeneutical dangers and exegetical pitfalls awaiting anyone who writes a philosophy book and makes use of other voices too, i.e., not just his/her own. Is it wiser to ignore one's own colleagues, then?
703 Amir's (2019, 129) secularism led her to misread another deeply Christian thinker, i.e., Dostoyevsky, whose warnings against rationalism, which is personified by *Ivan* Karamazov, she failed to recognise as such, taking instead their literary expressions at face value: "Yet men, with all their indisputable intelligence, do take the farce of existence as something serious, and this is their tragedy." This is Satan's talk, though. From a Christian perspective, which *Alyosha* Karamazov personifies in the novel, life and our souls' salvation *are* a serious business.

in the afterlife alone, i.e., after cultivating duly and conscientiously our morally praiseworthy virtues in this life for as long as we mortals are given to spend—and suffer—on this earth, while benefitting from God's sustaining and saving grace.[704]

2.5.8 Ironies

Devoid of religious hopes and consolations, the fictional Tristan portrayed by the Italian Romantic poet and pessimist philosopher Giacomo Leopardi in his *Operette morali* [Short works on ethics] is probably a more candidly sceptical and a certainly more stoical alternative to the real Montaigne.[705] Tristan is said to be facing bravely the utter nothingness of human life, laughing bitterly at the full revelation of our meaninglessness: "to see, with stoical gratification, all of destiny's cruel and hidden cloaks being stripped off".[706] Here is, perhaps, the only consolation available to the strong minds and the strong hearts that, depriving themselves of any religious hope, dare to stare firmly at such an utter pointlessness. As Leopardi noted: "They who dare laugh are the masters of the world, almost like those who are ready to die."[707]

Nevertheless, even this line of conduct may have some unnerving implications for Morreall's and, above all, Amir's endorsement of "humour" proper *qua* path towards humankind's wise acceptance of its fate.

(1) In our century, the nihilistic Kozintsev challenged even this minimal, stoical, perhaps desperate yet openly laughing wisdom. He did so by identifying humour's highest redeeming quality in its ability to suspend, for a moment, the painfulness arising from the contrast between that which we find good (e.g., the ideal of a divine order to the universe in which we all live) and that which we find bad (e.g., the realisation that the universe is, in fact, a chaotic totality with neither a motive nor a purpose). Humour is an analgesic; a time-limited painkiller.

This is all the glorious bliss, deep insight, and unique magic that humour is capable of, according to him:

---

704 See, e.g., Utz's (1994, par. 1.2.6) neo-Thomist project in the closing decade of the 20th century.
705 See our detailed account of their views in *H&C1*.
706 Leopardi (n.d.a. [1835]), 227.
707 Leopardi (1982), par. 78. Leopardi (n.d.a. [1898], 121–122) brought together cruelty and smiling *vis-à-vis* suicide. Upon reaching the "utmost despair", the person seeking her own death displays "that malevolent, bitter and ironic smirk similar to the one exhibited by a cruel man effecting his vengeance after a long and irked longing".

Therefore both polar views on the relationship between laughter and the bad – the optimistic ("we destroy the bad by laughing") and the pessimistic ("laughter expresses pleasure in the bad") – prove equally illusory. Laughter has no designs against the bad; nor does it transform the bad into the good. It merely neutralizes the good/bad opposition, along with all other oppositions on which our worldview is based. That is why the themes of most jokes are so salient: hot issues are temporarily neutralized by humor. The more painful the topic, the more acute the pleasure from its neutralization. Hence the healing effect of humor.[708]

The liberating wisdom that humour can bring about is, in other words, short-lived:

> We are accustomed to viewing speech as more reliable, at least more important, than preverbal unconscious metacommunicative signs. Laughter, however, tries to convince us that we are wrong; it insists that it is the nearly forgotten preverbal language that tells the truth, whereas words mean nothing. The rebellion against language and culture cannot be long-lived. Laughter subsides, and everything returns to its proper place. The ultimate result of humor (apart from the pleasure of play and the ancient festive feeling of the renewed world) is precisely "nothing"... If this paradox is not enjoyed, if the meaning of this strange play is obscure, all that's left is to shun humor and deem it a dubious way of expressing dubious things.[709]

(2) In accordance with Leopardi's heroic and forbearing persona of Tristan, the roaringly stoical solution was replayed in Nietzsche's philosophy as well, albeit in aptly Wagnerian tones.[710] Nietzsche proclaimed a superhuman creature who affirms a warrior-like "yes" to life in the midst of endless natural carnage, pitiless human competition, and the profoundly sense-shattering notion of the eternal recurrence of the same, such that, in a universe where material combinations are finite and time infinite, all that has come to pass will eventually occur again and again, and again.[711]

Nietzsche's lyrical *alter ego*, Zarathustra, is frequently depicted as laughing bravely in the face of this "sorry scheme of things", as Nietzsche himself described

---

708 Kozintsev (2010), 41.
709 Kozintsev (2010), 113. Logically, *rebellion presupposes an established regime*. Humorous rebellion, then, can be said to be parasitic upon a well-established linguistic-conceptual and socio-psychological order. Tellingly, in Hungary, the tradition of "anti-proverbs" recorded by Litovkina et al. (2012, 285 et passim) presupposed a solid and enduring common lore of anecdotes, mottoes, and adagios, without which their intentional alteration would be comically ineffective. See also Litovkina (2015) for a more cosmopolitan account of the same phenomenon.
710 We write "aptly" because *Tristan und Isolde* is one of Wagner's finest operas, notwithstanding Nietzsche's and Wagner's ill-fated friendship (see Hollinrake 2015). As to Wagner's operas being *more* than fine, Esar (1954, 135) cited Rossini's "biogram": "Wagner is a composer who has beautiful moments but awful quarter hours."
711 See, e.g., Löwith (1997).

reality.⁷¹² Under this respect, Amir was correct in picking Nietzsche as a token of creative, humorous transcendence of the "tragic oppositions" of life and, above all, of acceptance of "living with the unresolved tension of our situation". Zarathustra did not resolve the tragic oppositions. Instead, he accepted them laughingly—while simultaneously rejecting the traditional otherworldly consolations of Platonic metaphysics and Judeo-Christian religion.⁷¹³

Whether Nietzsche's Zarathustra can aspire to fulfil Amir's aims without losing his putative "humanity" is, however, less probable. Zarathustra is the prophet of the so-called *Übermensch*, i. e., a "super-" or "beyond-man" who belongs to the future.⁷¹⁴ Humanity is exactly what must be overcome, in Nietzsche's view. Emblematically, in Nietzsche's philosophy, this prophesised overcoming called for establishing entirely new values, destroying all old metaphysical and religious beliefs, and pursuing a course of cultural or even biological transformation.⁷¹⁵ This path is open to "everyone and no-one", as the subtitle of Nietzsche's famous poem reads.⁷¹⁶

Amir's creative transcendence by way of her own "true humour" may well be consistent with this course of transformation. Yet far more so than she bargained for.⁷¹⁷ Her wise humourist could be exactly such a new version of the human being that is to pass.⁷¹⁸ In either case, it would not be humanity as it is and as we, present humans, know it.

(3) Furthermore, as the contemporary Australia -based ethicist John Lippitt noted, Zarathustra pursues an elitist "laughter of the heights" *contra* the "laughter of the herd".⁷¹⁹ The humorous path to "wisdom" that Nietzsche's *alter ego* repre-

---

712 Nietzsche (1911a), 8.
713 See, e.g., Wicks (2008).
714 The interpretations of the *Übermensch* are plethora, hence we do not dare push ours any farther than this.
715 We use "humanity" in an intentionally vague sense, for the 'humanity' that Nietzsche aimed at overcoming could be primarily the ethos of the Platonic-Christian tradition, the population of a future Earth, this population's genetic make-up, or all of these. Lemm (2009), besides, argued that Nietzsche's project aimed at making us reconnect with our inner animal being. We cannot say. On the verge of indecision, one may have to take a roundabout way.
716 Again, how to interpret Nietzsche's claims in a more detailed manner is something that we do not pursue here.
717 Possibly a mere slip of the tongue (or hand), Amir (2019, 195) calls her alternative a "creed".
718 Depending on how the details of Nietzsche's philosophy are interpreted, Amir's (2019) "humour" is going to be more or less consonant with it. We do not have any definitive interpretation of such details, however.
719 Lippitt (1992), 39. It is reasonable to assume that Zarathustra embodied intentionally the starkly hierarchical features characterising Nietzsche's select classical and modern philosophical mentors, especially Schopenhauer. The great pessimist was unashamed in splitting humankind into the

sents is, in other words, profoundly undemocratic.[720] The comic view of life praised by Morreall and Amir is liable to being out of reach for many human beings and, as Amir wrote, "egalitarian".[721]

All ancient schools, West and East, claimed to be interested in teaching men and, less frequently, women how to become sages, but none of them ever expected people at large to embrace and embody wisdom.[722] Even Christianity and Islam, both of which still claim to be open to all and offer universal salvation, admit conspicuously uneven degrees of perfection. In addition, they foresee some unrepentant sinners bound to suffer eternal damnation.[723]

Morreall's and Amir's emphasis on an existential switch to a comic view of our condition is, as a result, likely to be correspondingly selective, whether they like it or not.[724] The unintended irony of their case being that "true humour" proves itself to be, once again, beyond many people's reach, aspiration, and/or understanding.[725]

(4) Crucially, some individuals may be unwilling to value and choose the humorous, light-hearted, or comedic side of things, especially if it means accepting Amir's "egalitarian creed, based on our common ridicule", which wishes to "serve as a basis for an ethics of compassion", i.e., a bittersweet, smiling springboard for tolerant and peaceful coexistence.[726] Why should one choose "love", "empathy" or "compassion", rather than utter selfishness and merciless egotism (as with, e.g., Sade's libertines), if there are neither compelling reasons (e.g., those of Aristotelian-Thomistic philosophies) nor a final system of justice (e.g., as *per* the West's Christian religion or Kant's moral philosophy)?[727] Why be friendly

---

mutually opposite camps of "the average man" and "the genius", "who alone can laugh" and "glow with mirth" in the face of "sorrows" that the former type of person can only suffer in a "grave and dull" manner (Schopenhauer 1896, 115). Not only must people hurt, but if they fail to laugh at it, then they are gloomy plebs to be ridiculed by the select superior minds.

720 Amir (2019), 221.
721 Amir (2019), x. In the same page, she also described it as "open-ended" and "non-dogmatic".
722 See Morreall (1999).
723 This eschatological offer can be made cruelly: "The worst that can be said of the Moslems is, as the poet put it, they offered to man the choice of the Koran or the sword" (Chesterton 2004, chap. 3, par. 5).
724 Ancient philosophers could be inflexibly elitist. Many contemporary ones can be unwarrantedly democratic.
725 Two elitist thinkers, Schopenhauer and Pirandello, would not be surprised by this realisation.
726 Amir (2019), 205–206.
727 Amir (2019), 205.

furry little rodents or meek sheep, when we can be fierce tigers or—Nietzsche's favourite and symbolic high-flying predator—proud eagles?[728]

Life is bound to chew us all into a pulp, more or less slowly, yet certainly and inexorably. The great Romantic artist Francisco Goya gave our world a masterly allegorical depiction of this dismal reality.[729] Be they infants or elders, all men and women become, at last, cadavers. It may then be wise to do some biting, pecking, munching, triturating, and/or gnawing of our own while it is still possible. Before becoming time's prey, we might enjoy being ourselves predators, even if only for a short time. Whether we like it or not, our earthly existence is, *inter alia*, a plausible game of possible game.[730]

Amir may prefer and elect sages embodying "the ridiculous animal", but some other reasoning individuals may happily embrace Nietzsche's fierce conqueror and/or Sade's amoral libertine—notably in their youthful years, which are known to be few and extremely valuable, if this life is all that we have to live.[731] In the sceptical, post-religious, and post-metaphysical context assumed by Amir, moral concerns cannot hinder us too much, for they have no compelling basis to rely upon.

(5) But we should not worry too much. After all, in this widespread late-modern context, the pulverising meaninglessness of our utter insignificance in this chaotic universe, which produced us humans by blind mechanisms of fortuitous Darwinian selective mistakes in ever-changing environments, annihilates any deep axiological claim and/or reasoned existential stance.[732] Nothing makes real

---

[728] See, e.g., J. Miller (1990) and Thatcher (2016), 240. An intermediate position would be to respect and bestow right upon a select group of peers with whom principles of justice, equality, compassion, mutual assistance, and recognition are given plenty of room to exist and be enjoyed, as in the *Herrenvolk* democracies of Jacksonian America and *Apartheid* South Africa (see, e.g., Vickery 1974). These elite groups could be styled as lions or orcas.

[729] We are not-too-subtly referring to the messy mythical accounts of Cronos (aka Khronos, Cronus, and much else) *qua* ancient god of time, who was said to devour his own children.

[730] "Game" meaning 'play' or 'recreation', as well as 'kill', 'target', or 'feed'. As to the quality of our wordplay, the reader is free to smile with praise or shake his/her head in sorry disbelief.

[731] Amir (2019), 226.

[732] The utter meaninglessness of our condition defies even Pascal's (1993, thought # 264 of the Chevalier edition) consolatory metaphor of the human being *qua* "thinking reed", i.e., a weak and finite creature capable however of embracing in its mind the infinite, dark, cold, and complex universe in which it must live, suffer, and die (see also Shatner 2022, par. 20, for a recent reiteration of this insight). *Being a "thinking reed" is therefore a double cruel irony:* we are painfully powerless creatures whose most glorious faculty makes them painfully aware of precisely such a painful powerlessness. Moreover, insofar as our thinking can encompass everything that can be thought, *a third cruel irony ensues* as well: our most powerful faculty is bound to produce the many divergent interpretations and contradictions that are humanly conceivable.

sense, in the end because nothing possesses any real, inherent, metaphysically solid, and personally compelling meaning.[733] It's all a big and cruel "anonymous joke", isn't it?[734]

(6) For his part, while championing the comic view of life, Morreall himself kept writing disapprovingly of "rigidity", "linear, step-by-step thinking", intolerance, "convergent thinking", "stubbornness" and the "less intelligent ways" of the tragically inclined minds.[735] Some people, in other words, are excluded from attaining a comic view of life by Galenic humour, medieval character, ingrained habit, moral judgement, social aspiration, school diploma, or IQ level, if not by biological default.[736]

Albeit philosophically insightful, capably phrased, and cleverly unsettling, Morreall's choice of terms does not have to be taken uniquely. For instance, in yet another unintended irony, the individuals who are disinclined towards a comic view of life may simply be prone to empathise much, maybe too much, with human or other sorrows in order to dismiss them humorously, no matter how humble and profoundly sympathetic this humour may strain itself to become. "Charity", "empathy", "sense of relevance", "sense of urgency", and the "more compassionate ways" could be selected as the proper descriptors in *lieu* of Morreall's disparaging ones.

(7) Perhaps, in his brave campaign against the humourless Puritans, Morreall became too belligerent. Somehow, along the way, he lost sight of the wisdom of Nietzsche's most famous and, in our view, subtly humorous warning which the German thinker directed to all the keen intellects that happen to be engaged in fights at close quarters against religious dogma, mystical asceticism, entrenched superstition, or the "tyranny and unreason" of "morality['s] … long compulsion": "Whoever fights with monsters should see to it that he does not become one him-

---

733 Rosset's philosophy, which we summarised in Chapter 1 and discussed in *H&C1*, is representative of this nihilistic attitude, which is widespread among 20th- and 21st-century Western thinkers.
734 Amir (2019), 238. If metaphysical reasons (e.g., the Natural Law tradition) and religious beliefs (e.g., Christianity) are discarded as theoretically unsound and culturally *passé*, selfish hedonism and irresponsible anomia become two among many plausible existential options left for eventual individual evaluation and election. This is, at least, the picture emerging from Amir (forthcoming). We are thus reminded of Dostoyevsky's (1900, 717) preoccupation whereby, "[w]ithout God and immortal life … [a]ll things are lawful, then", and "a clever man can do what he likes". We cannot resolve this issue here, but we can alert the reader to its existence.
735 Morreall (1999), 22–27.
736 A regular clinical correlation has been identified between humourlessness and autism (see, e.g., Troncon 2017). Some patients display fear of being laughed at: "gelotophobia" (Forabosco, Ruch, and Nucera 2009, 233). We discuss this psychiatric disorder in further detail in Chapter 3.

self. And when you stare for a long time into an abyss, the abyss stares back into you."[737]

(8) The same tragically inclined hypothetical individuals may be suffering too horribly to believe that there is anything funny going on. Life is a real bitch, as far as these poor people are concerned. And the bitch can have terrible fangs too.[738] However we may fight against them and transform ourselves because of the fight, monsters do exist—also, if not especially, within our poor souls.[739]

This grand guignol that so many among us are so desperately stuck in is, seen from the right angle, a valley of tears too—if not precisely the latter metaphorical place above all else. It is a most frightful place, even if it is not a literal one. As poignantly written by a seasoned psychotherapist in the late 20th century:

> The study of lives and the care of souls means above all a prolonged encounter with what destroys and is destroyed, with what is broken and hurts—that is, with psychopathology. Between the lines of each biography and in the lines of each face we may read a struggle with alcohol, with suicidal despair, with dreadful anxiety, with lascivious sexual obsessions, cruelties at close quarters, secret hallucinations, or paranoid spiritualisms. Ageing brings loneliness of soul, moments of acute psychic pain, and haunting remembrances as memory disintegrates. The night world in which we dream shows the soul split into antagonisms; night after night we are fearful, aggressive, guilty, and failed.[740]

The depressed and the senile persons encountered by ordinary psychiatrists and nursing experts are, in all certainty, trite cases of such a deep despair, but they are not the only ones who are worth considering in this chapter.[741]

---

[737] Nietzsche (2002, pars. 146 and 188). We wrote "subtly humorous" because, while suggesting dreadful scenes of moral abjection and/or mental disintegration, Nietzsche's warning also exploits a comic reversal, i.e., one thing becoming its opposite. Jung's stately principle of enantiodromia comes to mind as well, in this respect.

[738] Once again, no offence is meant by the occasional use of strong metaphors, when rhetorically apt.

[739] We doubt that any of our readers has never experiences significant spiritual tumult in his/her life.

[740] Hillman (1975), 56. On top of being a seasoned psychotherapist and a well-published psychologist, Hillman was also an accomplished public speaker who was admired for his brilliant sense of humour. Perhaps he himself embodied and expressed the instrumental use of humour *qua* psycho-affective protection from too persistent and pronounced a daily encounter with cruelty that the psychologist McDougall (1926) highlighted almost 100 years ago and, *a fortiori*, that we discussed extensively in the concluding chapter of *H&C1*.

[741] See, e.g., Clark and Warren (2016), 32.

2.5.9 Grinds

> A myriad of men are born; they labor and sweat and struggle for bread; they squabble and scold and fight; they scramble for little mean advantages over each other. Age creeps upon them; infirmities follow; shames and humiliations bring down their prides and their vanities. Those they love are taken from them, and the joy of life is turned to aching grief. The burden of pain, care, misery, grows heavier year by year. At length ambition is dead; pride is dead; vanity is dead; longing for release is in their place. It comes at last—the only unpoisoned gift earth ever had for them—and they vanish from a world where they were of no consequence; where they achieved nothing; where they were a mistake and a failure and a foolishness; where they have left no sign that they have existed—a world which will lament them a day and forget them forever. Then another myriad takes their place, and copies all they did, and goes along the same profitless road, and vanishes as they vanished—to make room for another and another and a million other myriads to follow the same arid path through the same desert and accomplish what the first myriad, and all the myriads that came after it, accomplished—nothing!
> — Mark Twain[742]

The two canonical pessimists of Western thought, Leopardi and Schopenhauer, presented us with a depiction of the human condition that, with its incessant grinds, is anything but laughable.[743] Sade and Rosset, for their part, added one that is hardly cheerier, though not inherently pessimistic. Laughter in the face of the inevitable horrors of living, as filled as living is with ultimate insignificance and unending grief, is thus revealed to be yet another pained grimace akin to tears.[744]

2.5.9.1 Lacking Matters

Philosophical pessimism and its close existentialist relatives are, however, only a pedestrian token. As written, the socio-economic aetiology of depression can teach us important lessons too. With deeper scrutiny, it can explain not only the clinical phenomenon, but also the rationale for a tragic view of life *qua* thoroughly

---

[742] Twain (1924), vol. 2, 2 February 1906, par. 13.
[743] "Grinds" mean the dreary, slow, crushing effect of "the ill of living", as the Genoese Nobel-laureate poet Eugenio Montale (2012, 521, stanza 1, verse 1) described our seemingly aimless existence. Its verbal form, "to grind", is defined as "to afflict with cruelty", in American English, by the 2021 online edition of the *Collins Dictionary*.
[744] In yet another feat of philosophical pessimism and psychological acumen, Leopardi (n.d.a.[1898], 2687–2688) observed that, as we grow old, we "lose the faculty of crying", while we become "more inclined and used to laughter", for this is the result of "the human being becoming more and more familiar with pain".

sensible, realistic, and understandable response to a cruel life in a cruel society in a cruel world.[745]
(1) Dramatically and polemically, Harvey herself wrote that the "black South African ... trapped in permanent poverty" has plenty of good reasons for his or her "lack of self-esteem" and unwillingness to laugh at it.[746]
(2) Similarly, an honest, hardworking and responsible family man, who is battling against a deadly illness, all the while betrayed by the woman he loves and to whom he swore his undying fidelity while her behaviour causes him public humiliation, is an example of Job-like torments, for which even the subtlest 'true' humour is a no-go response.[747]

These are just two examples amongst millions. Cruelty is rarely a stranger in human life. Hellholes come in all kinds of shapes and sizes, so that all sorts of people may find a suitable one into which they can sink, suffer, and, eventually, succumb. These hellholes can be as vast as Siberia or Anatolia, or as claustrophobic as the Venetian ghetto or the Gaza strip.[748] They can be as murderously efficient as any short-lived extermination camp run by the SS during World War II. Or they can display over many decades the chilling and killing potential of the Third World's spiralling debt, crumbling infrastructures, corrupt leaderships, and general lack of fiscal and monetary resources, which foreign creditors, so-called "aid donors", and vulture funds have regularly made sure to seize for their own benefit.[749] They can be located within prison cells, hospital wards, and private flats. Or they can hide under Parisian bridges, inside Sardinian caves, and along Manhattan's skyscrapers where homeless people seek warmth, shelter, and a place to sleep, or, at last, to die in peace.[750] They can be as localised and as concentrated

---

[745] See, e.g., Fullilove (2002).
[746] Harvey (1999), 7–8. Ironically, the Cameroonian-born philologist Théophile Ambadiang (2018, 147–152) identified a "(black) African humorous *ethos*" pivoting around cruel experiences and expressions, e.g., "insulting monikers", "self-derision", and people "taking their tribulations and themselves as the butt of their jokes".
[747] The Coen brothers' unusually sombre 2009 film, *A Serious Man*, depicted dryly such a Job-inspired situation.
[748] "Siberia" and "Anatolia" are here metonymies for some of the worst atrocities of the 20th century.
[749] On the Third World's plight, see, e.g., Payer (1974), and McMurtry (1999) and (2013).
[750] While homelessness in Paris and New York is fairly well-known, the Sardinian case is probably far less familiar to our readers. Therefore, see Sardegna Sotterranea (2017).

as the aching body of an incurable patient, or be as scattered and as untouchable as the unravelling mind of a victim of Alzheimer's disease.[751]

Why should anyone teach him-/herself to look at his/her crushing reality as something risible, especially when it is clear that such an ordeal is the result of culpable agency by selfish, insensitive, unjust people and/or institutions which must be endured sometimes over entire lifetimes and/or several generations?[752] Sparing no critical blows, Harvey observed that such interpersonal and socio-economic lines of analysis are regularly neglected by contemporary humour experts in *lieu* of an "individual-based approach", which ends up making the lack of "a sense of humour" a "serious personal defect".[753]

In line with this widely assumed individualistic standpoint, none less than Leacock wrote in the 1920s:

> A peculiar interest always attaches to humour. There is no quality of the human mind about which its possessor is more sensitive than the sense of humour. A man will freely confess that he has no ear for music, or no taste for fiction, or even no interest in religion. But I have yet to see the man who announces that he has no sense of humour. In point of fact, every man is apt to think himself possessed of an exceptional gift in this direction, and that even if his humour does not express itself in the power either to make a joke or to laugh at one, it none the less consists in a peculiar insight or inner light superior to that of other people.[754]

Yet, as we all should know from the medical realm, there are no silver-bullet solutions for each and every ill. Laughter may therefore be *not* the best medicine, i.e., something inherently constructive that is advisable and applicable in all or most circumstances.[755]

---

751 We do *not* engage in the competitive struggles aimed at determining who suffered the most and/or most cruelly, as discussed in Chaumont (2000). Rather, we want to show *how familiar and how frequent cruelty can be*.
752 Harvey's black South African has an equally unfortunate counterpart on the other end of the continent, i.e., Egypt, where hope in a better future under perpetual neoliberal job insecurity is called "cruel" (Pettit 2019, 722).
753 Harvey (1999), 8. Morreall was the intended, and cited, target of Harvey's critique. We wonder what she would make of St. Clare (2018, 164, 167 and 172), who knew Harvey's work, criticised it for not being specific enough on "what counts as resistance", and made "happiness ... a manifestation of resistance", however "internal or subtle", to be included among "the duties of the oppressed".
754 Leacock (2009), chap. 10, par. 2.
755 Harvey (1999), 8. A late, indirect reply to this criticism was issued in a speech delivered by Morreall at the 6th Annual International Conference of the Centre for Phenomenology in Chintsa, South Africa, on 13–14th June 2019. Concisely, it advises not to play with serious matters. Analogous remarks appeared in Morreall (2020a and b).

2.5.9.2 Laughing Matters

As concerns the courageous idealists who wish to change the socio-economic order and make it impossible for a community to be able to throw anyone into the same "threatening ... conditions" experienced by Harvey's deprived Black South African, they too may be overly focussed on serious matters to be able to see the same matters from a humorous perspective.[756] An analogous point can be made about theologians, mystics, philosophers, and *literati* addressing the most important existential issues of all: the meaning of life, existence of God, leap into faith or atheism, desirability of suicide, dread of old age and its inevitable anguish, etc.[757] These are far too grave matters to justify wasting our time by treating them humorously, not to mention expecting others to take them lightly.[758]

Although it is always possible to turn any of these solemn matters into something funny, ridiculous, or even subtly humorous, doing so may lead people's minds and hearts away from the 'meat' of those issues and therefore fail to guide them in a truly constructive direction. This danger, as seen in Chapter 1, was amply noted by the likes of Addison and Hazlitt, among others, albeit with differing emphases and choices of lexicon. In the face of life's horrors and of its thorniest conundrums, it is either naïve or disingenuous to claim that we all must end up smiling or laughing, or that our doing so is the best and wisest route. Laugh all you like, even on your deathbed, and see whether the horrors disappear—or merely endure them under a blanket of noise and apparent cleverness. We, the authors of this book, regard the latter conclusion as the likelier.[759]

One does not need to be a "Puritan" or endorse the Puritans' values in order to comprehend the partial truth—but truth nonetheless—of "the traditional charges against laughter and humor", for which examples can be found without much effort.[760] A vocal adversary of "Puritan" gloom, Morreall collected, listed, and dismissed all these charges, favouring instead a "Franciscan" view of Christianity and of human life writ large.[761]

---

756 Harvey (1999), 8.
757 See, e.g., Ahmed and Bonis (2012). Contrarian as much as creative, the US philosopher and English specialist Drew Daniel (2022) collected and discussed with great gusto the comedic renderings and witty comments about self-harm and/or suicide peppering Britain's Renaissance literature (and beyond).
758 By casting it as religion-replacing wisdom, Amir (2019) did indicate that we ought to pursue a lighter path.
759 As seen, even the nihilist Kozintsev (2010, 113) suggested that humour provides only temporary relief.
760 Morreall (2008), 27.
761 Morreall (1999), 117–118 and (2008), 23. We discuss in more detail this stance in *H&C3*.

According to the latter, obviously inspired by the preaching of Saint Francis of Assisi, we all ought to give ample room to jests, comicality, enthusiasm, and cheerfulness, for they too are theologically legitimate and ethically permissible graces from a benevolent God.[762] This being the one and the same *fons vitae* that, at the end of the day, most Protestants and Catholics have been worshipping since the days of the great Christian schism, which, ironically, unleashed the terrible interreligious cruelties that were observed and denounced by Montaigne.[763]

As a matter of professed creed and personal inclination, we ourselves feel closer to the Franciscan conception, but we cannot dismiss the Puritan charges as easily and as trenchantly as Morreall did. Then let us list these charges below and, in parentheses, signal how their outright dismissal is, *au fond*, prejudicial and mistaken.

(1) "Humor is hostile" (yet, yes, it is; e. g., put-down jokes);[764]
(2) it "diminishes self-control" (e. g., bull sessions);
(3) it "is irresponsible" (e. g., the cynic's turning everything into a joke);[765]
(4) "insincere" (e. g., Tarachow's apt description of the "comic thrust" as "a weapon of revenge" whereby one can "transgress" and, in tandem, utter: "It is only a joke.");[766]
(5) "idle" (e. g., laughing at an argument defending an unusual stance, rather than thinking it through and determining its actual soundness);
(6) "foolish" (e. g., Hazlitt's words of caution on humour discussed in Chapter 1);[767]
(7) "hedonistic" (e. g., former Italian PM Silvio Berlusconi's characteristic joviality, notorious jokes, criminal behaviour, and eponymous *bunga-bunga versus* Mother Teresa's sombre tone, her vows of chastity, poverty and obedience, and the sedate Catholic rituals in which she participated);[768] and
(8) it "fosters sexual license" (*ditto*) and
(9) "anarchy" (*ditto*).[769]

---

762 Morreall (1999), 117–118 and (2008), 23–38. See also Eco (1980), 87, 137–140 and 481–482.
763 We cannot exclude *a priori* that some Protestants and Catholics may have believed exclusively in a *cruel* God.
764 The charges are in Morreall (2008), but the examples, unless otherwise noted, are ours, not Morreall's.
765 See, e. g., Hazlitt's (1845) remarks on the malice of humour.
766 Tarachow (1949), 225.
767 A more detailed account of his views was offered in *H&C1*.
768 Berlusconi was convicted of tax fraud in 2012 and the sentence confirmed in both successive degrees of adjudication (see Day 2015). In 2013, he was barred from public office for six years and condemned to community service at a home for the elderly with dementia. On Mother Teresa's very different lifestyle, see Spink (1997).
769 The examples of Berlusconi and Mother Teresa apply also to the last two "Puritan" charges.

2.5.10 Masks

Humour scholars, most readers, and we ourselves are prone to welcome commonplace humour, true humour, and mirth at large on as many occasions as it is humanly possible. Consistent with this disposition, we too may be tempted to treat moralising seriousness and religious gravity as passé. However, it may be wise to pause and ponder upon the perplexing fact that none less than the famous author of *The Virtue of Selfishness*, i.e., the 20th-century prophetess of individualistic libertarianism and ruthless capitalism, married cruelty and humour.[770]

As we signalled in Chapter 1, after selecting a disreputable child murderer as "[t]he model" for a new and equally murderous literary hero of hers incarnating Nietzsche's *Übermensch*, she equipped her "model" with a pronounced propensity for the facetious in all aspects of life but his own naked self-interest.[771] He is *homo economicus* on steroids, or on nitrous oxide. In either case, he is a queer fish that many of us would find baleful and suspect.[772] This is how Ayn Rand depicted her planned hero in her *Diaries:*

> He is perfectly cynical. Stone-hard. Monstrously cruel. Brazenly daring. No respect for anything or anyone... He has a brilliant sense of humor. Rather a cruel, sardonic kind of humor... [H]e can laugh at everything and approach all things lightly, with an attitude of superior disdain. His mind is brilliant enough to see the ridiculous side of everything. He gets immense enjoyment from shocking people, amusing them with his cynicism, (ridiculing) before their eyes the most sacred, venerated, established ideas... He does not understand, because he has no organ for understanding, the necessity, meaning, or importance of other peo-

---

770 Rand (1964) (her book being subtitled *A New Concept of Egoism*).
771 Rand (1997), 22. Her "model" had stated in court: "I am like the state: what is good for me is right" (Rand 1997, 43). Rand claimed that "[n]o matter what the man did", he presented "a daring challenge to society", for "he feels superior to all" and "really stands alone, in action and in soul" because of "his utter lack of anything that is considered a 'virtue'" and "his immense, explicit egoism ... and his cleverness" (Rand 1997, 37–38).
772 It is known that the aesthetically and aristocratically inclined Nietzsche loathed both the English Utilitarians' "pig philosophy" (Carlyle 1850, 268) and the liberals' *de facto* deification of shopkeeper mentality. However, in her influential works of fiction, Rand managed to tie together these different strands by depicting the self-maximising and self-pleased capitalist entrepreneur as a larger-than-life character standing beyond good and evil, in proud defiance of tradition and superstition. As to her concomitant brazen abandonment of age-old principles of morality, which Adam Smith (1904) could still take largely for granted in his 'backward' era, it is the logical consequence of making each individual the sovereign in all matters, ethical ones included, as some noted 20th-century liberal economists implicitly conceded. Robbins (1935, 24–25), for one, stated that "[e]conomics is entirely neutral between ends", be they "noble" or "base"; while von Mises (1960, 56) wrote: "Modern economics makes no distinction among ends, because it considers them all equally legitimate."

ple … he has the true, innate psychology of a Superman. He can never realize and feel "other people". […Only] himself … as Nietzsche said: "The noble soul has reverence for itself"… The boy has a marvelous, fascinating laugh… [A] clear, ringing laugh, the laugh of an unhesitating, unquestionable joy … the laugh of the real life itself … show[ing] more than anything else what the boy is.[773]

Somehow, we do not find this perplexing fact reassuring, especially as regards the seemingly obvious pairing of laughter and superhuman sadism.[774] But there is more.

Even though we are indebted to their research, we do not intend to follow the lead of Morreall and Amir to its end.[775] We do not wish to pit the tragic and the comic view of life against each other, or blend them into an uneasy tension and ask our readers to choose the latter view rather than the former. On the contrary, based on the reflections offered in the previous chapter and paragraphs, to say nothing of the even larger selection of literature examined in *H&C1*, we conclude that *two equally important existential options are on the table.* (Yes, ironically, another cruel dilemma.)

2.5.10.1 Films and Faiths

Tragedy and comedy are, fundamentally, open-ended. At the same time, they are also so experientially and empirically justified as to represent reasonable paths for people to follow under that great variety of unpredictable personal and socio-historical conditions that we call "life".[776] As Ludwig Wittgenstein poignantly stated in his celebrated *Tractatus*, "*Die Welt des Glücklichen ist eine andere als die des Unglücklichen*" [The world of the happy person is another than that of the unhappy person].[777] Depending on the circumstances under which concrete human

---

773 Rand (1997), 26–29.
774 Our rejection of Rand's approach is ultimately based upon LVOA.
775 Amir and Morreall are our key references here, but they are not the only humour experts to espouse this approach. Heller (2005, 29 et passim), for example, argued that the "paradox" of human existence, i.e., its being cast in an irresolvable tension between the natural and the socio-cultural dimensions, can only be laughed at, ultimately.
776 Even life's "bittersweet … joy", which we encounter in what "Philip Hallie" called "metaphorically and literally … the eye of a hurricane", may not be "worthwhile", overall (Tabensky 2009, 38–53, 44 and 48).
777 Wittgenstein (1989), 171, proposition 6.43. An almost identical formulation can be found in Wittgenstein's earlier *Notebooks* (1984, 77, 29.7.16), where it is followed by the question: "*Ist sehen eine Tätigkeit?*" [Is seeing an activity?]. This interrogative reminds us of the personal coefficient of all knowledge, hence the possibility that two persons, sharing the same culture and studying the same reality, may come to very different conclusions.

beings happen to live their lives and make their choices, either view of life can become more sensible and/or more meaningful than the other.[778]

Someone may look at the landscape at dusk and see a flowering countryside intriguingly enriched by a telling sign of human ingenuity: the thin, parallel, red-brown lines of a dreamy, silent railway, which disappears into the far-away horizon. Another may look at the same crepuscular landscape and see an old, rusty, deserted railway surrounded by the mangy weeds and melancholic bushes that often take root in and around industrial embarkments. A reminder of both nature's and civilisation's inherent frailty, liability to disease, and eventual transience. Depending on *who* does the observing and *which* aspect/s is/are grasped more forcefully, the combination of available stimuli into either depiction is as viable, plausible, and credible.

(1) This interplay between subject and object is, for one, the underlying perspectival and phenomenological lesson of the so-called "Kuleshov effect" in the art of cinema, whence so much humour has been created and where this powerful aesthetic effect is usually approached in connection with the film-maker's and, in particular, the editor's creativity and skill in engendering affective-conceptual responses in each specific targeted audience.[779]

(2) At an even deeper level of scrutiny and existential import, the 'father' of psychology in the US, William James, observed how a living person's different affective attitude towards fallibility can lead to very different decisions in matters of faith.[780]

(2a) On the one hand, if one is led by fear of error in observation-based claims, s/he will veer towards un- or disbelief, for the available scientific facts are inconclusive.

(2b) On the other hand, if one is led by hope in the cosmic order, then s/he will veer towards belief.

---

[778] On a parallel path, Heidegger argued, in the 20th century, that our predominant mood determines the ways in which we approach reality, which degree of self-awareness we can reach, and which facets of reality we eventually focus upon (see, e.g., Elpidorou 2015). *Angst*, in this respect, makes us strangers to ourselves and the world, causes us to stop taking ourselves for granted, and leads us to reflect on our mortality and the kind of meaningful existence that we may wish to pursue. As painful as it is, in short, angst makes us *wiser*.

[779] See, e.g., Prince and Hensley (1992). Unlike a landscape, the cinematic object presented to the subject is manipulated.

[780] See James (1912), 1–31.

In nuce, reality is, to a partial yet significant extent, in the eye of the beholder—and this significance is epistemic, aesthetic, ethical, and existential.[781]

2.5.10.2 Faces and Freedoms

Wisdom can have two legitimate faces. That which is graspable as risible can also be rendered tragically, not least as regards intuiting the deepest 'essence' of things, i.e., the possible metaphysical roots of all life, far beyond the reach of scientific knowledge and/or logical thought. As Jung noted in his most Nietzschean work, i.e., the *Red Book*:

> "The sum of life decides in laughter and in worship, not your judgment". I must also speak the ridiculous. You coming men! You will recognize the supreme meaning by the fact that he is laughter and worship, a bloody laughter and a bloody worship. A sacrificial blood binds the poles. Those who know this laugh and worship in the same breath.[782]

In their earthly existence, actual people may have to grapple with contradictions, oppositions, obstacles, and other events that can make comedy or tragedy more or less plausible, as though they were, *qua* hermeneutical frameworks of the human condition, inversely proportional to each other.[783] Given that comedy and tragedy were the two iconic masks of ancient theatre, we all can indeed end up wearing either of them, but not both at once, *pace* Amir's proposed accepting of all "tension". As Weber summarised the wisdom that he too, like Schopenhauer and other German Romantics, believed to be born of Albion: "The Briton's final words are called: 'Humor the only test of gravity, gravity of humor'."[784]

Even if we tried to wear both masks simultaneously, one mask would still be on top of the other. Which one we choose, alone or on top of the other, will be very much the outcome of the stage that we are on and of the play that is unfolding with us in it, not just our personal preferences and/or philosophic self-education, which is only one factor among many. Through either mask, whether it is the sole one that we wear or the one whose eye-slits determine our final gaze over the

---

[781] Stating that each person interprets things in her own way may seem obvious, but when one starts reflecting on what these 'things' may be, this 'obvious' consideration becomes deep, paramount, complex, and demanding.

[782] Jung (2009), 230.

[783] The very incongruity of ideality and reality is also the ground upon which tragedy sprouts. We can conceive of beauty, but we are surrounded by ugliness; we can think of justice but cannot but notice all the injustices taking place around us; and we can identify the moral law, but we face immorality every day.

[784] K. Weber (1840), part 4, 6.

world, we cannot but see the audience, the theatre, ourselves, and the very sky above us in a different shape.

Tragedy and comedy are distinct, legitimate existential apprehensions of the whole. Even the nihilistic Kozintsev who, as seen in Chapter 1, stressed the non-serious and nonsensical character of all "humour" proper, acknowledged the unsmiling ponderousness of that which lies behind—or perchance beneath, beside, before, or beyond—our comedic and comic efforts: "we can laugh only at something, or rather, use as a pretext for laughter only something that we have recently treated (and, probably, will again treat) seriously".[785]

Life may well be comical at times, perhaps "ontologically" so.[786] Yet it can likewise be profoundly and thoroughly tragic. Even farts and burps, which may seem always and infallibly comical in their puerile bodily immediacy, turn dreadful and disheartening when we witness them in an agonising person whom we love and care for.[787] As also Harvey's critical remarks on race and poverty in South Africa remind us, there may be good reasons why a gloomy philosophical tradition seeing human life as intrinsically painful, and sometimes cruelly painful, has been accompanying us since Lucretius' time, if not even before.[788]

Finding analogies, commonalities, secret passages, or even open passages between the comic and tragic views of the human condition is certainly possible, but it is not always so and, moreover, it does not have or ought to be so, no matter how desirable such opportunities might be according to some well-meaning and very capable thinkers.[789] When mired in prolonged chronic pain and pitiless crushing hopelessness, people can lose their capacity for seeing life's contradictions in any comic light whatsoever, and such an existential blindness can be epistemically reasonable, socially appropriate, and morally justifiable.[790] As we discuss in the next chapter, these suffering human beings may yet be capable of cruel humour, whether predominantly, exclusively, sporadically, or at best. Such an option,

---

[785] Kozintsev (2010), 34.
[786] Amir (2013), 7.
[787] This point is based on personal experiences with loved relatives as they were dying. As to burps and farts being a staple of commonplace humour, see Allen (2007) on the Middle Ages.
[788] Rosset (1991 and 1993) argued reality to be not only ontologically comical but also ontologically cruel. In this, Weidenbaum (2020, 125) echoed him: "Life does not just fill us with amusement; life *is*, from a certain angle, simply comical—as much as it is sad, disappointing, and much else."
[789] See, in addition to the thoroughly-discussed Morreall and Amir, Myrmasz (2003) and Heller (2005).
[790] The near-totality of the scholarly literature about "humour" proper regularly underplays those who go on living despite their own failing bodies, burdened souls, or both; hence, also the plausibility of a tragic worldview.

though, should be their free *personal* choice, not some sort of social requirement or, worse, a duty.[791]

---

[791] In line with Polanyi's (1962c) emphasis on the personal *quid* at play in all human contexts, Hillman (1996, chap. 9, sec. 3, pars. 14–15, 207) noted that the extant approaches in philosophy and psychology reflect the very different individual reactions that can follow the most terrible "accidents" in life, including the "repetitive, abusive cruelty" shared by soldiers or siblings: "Fatalism answers: Everything is in the hands of the gods. Teleological finalism says: It all has a hidden purpose and belongs to your growth. Heroism says: Integrate those shadows or slay them... [E]xisten[tialism] forc[es] speculations... What does it mean, why did it happen, what does it want? ... Developmental theory regards the accidents ... as ... trauma, which may be sublimated, transformed, and integrated through time." Unless personal freedom is denied in principle (e.g., Spinoza 1985) or in fact (e.g., MacKinnon 1993), *diverse personal responses and lifepaths can unfold after surviving one and the same socio-culturally recognised type of cruelty.*

3 Cruel Humour

> Among the Greenland Eskimo, contests of ridicule were once their only judicial procedure, even for such offenses as murder. Someone who had a complaint against another challenged him to a contest before the clan or tribe in which they took turns ridiculing each other. There was no distinction made between defensible accusations and mere slander; the parties were even allowed to snort in their opponent's face or tie him to a tent pole. All that counted was who got more laughs at his opponent's expense. That person was declared the winner by the assembly, and if the shame of the loser was great enough he and his family were ostracized from the community.
> —John Morreall[1]

3.1 The Elusiveness of Cruel Humour

Our readers might, by now, have some foreboding that delivering a definition of "cruel humour" is no easy feat. In fact, most scholars in the field refrain from offering a clear and concise description of it. Mostly, they assume that their readers share the same background and presuppositions.[2] Which is understandable, but only to a point, especially insofar as some of them maintain or imply that humour is intrinsically or predominantly cruel.[3] Some of them, moreover, have resorted to cruel humour in order to outline its essence:

> "Black humor is like food – not everyone gets it".
> "Black humor is like a pair of legs – not everyone has it".
> "Black humor is like a kid with cancer – never gets old". [4]

As Chapter 2 discusses, we agree that all humour, especially when it takes place in interpersonal contexts, carries with it some trace of cruelty, however residual or/

---

[1] Morreall (1983), 9. No offense is meant by quoting a scholar writing "Eskimo" in the 1980s. *The same applies to any other term that the reader may find politically incorrect and/or offensive.* Unfortunately, it is not easy to keep track of what exactly is deemed admissible, given the many geographical and social settings where English is used, the diversity of extant Anglophone macro- and sub-cultures whence our readers may come, these cultures' mutable and mutating trends, and the absence of an ultimate and immutable *arbiter elegantiarum*.
[2] Talking about "cruel humour", just think of how our personal perspectives and priorities could change were we to seriously give credit to those experts who argue that our universe is a computer simulation (run by aliens?) or a complex gigantic machine giving us the convenient illusion of free will (see, e.g., Zahedi 2015 and Yu 2020).
[3] See e.g., Harlow (1969).
[4] Gubanov, Gubanov, and Rokotyanskaya (2018), 379.

and unintended it may be. Concurrently, we acknowledge that there is abundant room for nuance and, moreover, that everyone has a noticeably different tipping point. Therefore, the cruel element in jokes may often cause us to experience not only enjoyment, but also a mixture of negative emotions, such as shock, revulsion, or shame. Jokes can be guilty pleasures.

Besides, these bad feelings can drown out the humorous element altogether. Or they can make it unlikely to be detected at all. Thus we no longer perceive a joke, however cruel or inappropriate it may be, but only an outright insult or provocation. In turn, such perceived insults and provocations can lead to cruel reprisals. Cruel humour eventually dissolves into outright cruelty for all involved parties.[5]

As the first two jokes cited above demonstrate, cruel humour in generous doses is not something that everyone can appreciate. Additionally, the use of cruelty in humour can go terribly wrong, and many of us approach it with apprehension. We need to 'read' the targeted person well before testing her boundaries with what could be otherwise construed as a wholly unsuitable joke. The same goes for the other participants. Therefore, cruel jokes frequently involve considerable intimacy between the joker and the audience to be attempted, and then to be successful at all or at any rate. After all, as a team of contemporary social scientists specialising in so-called "black humour" suggested, a regular wholesome humorous comment is an attempt to lift the communication to a more amicable level, whereas a cruel joke tries to expose someone's personality.[6]

The third joke above highlights that cruel humour can take on universal themes and timeless taboos such as death, diseases, deformities, and discrimination.[7] Therein lies some of the key differences between patently cruel humour and subtler forms thereof. We may laugh hysterically at someone falling into a pond, seeing that s/he gets out of it with hair and clothes soaking wet and dignity gone. For sure, there is a pointed hint of cruelty in our laughter. But what if someone goes into the water and dies? Making a joke about that or laughing at it is hu-

---

[5] This last sentence itself presumes that the readers share enough background and presuppositions with us two.

[6] See Gubanov, Gubanov, and Rokotyanskaya (2018), 379. The available 'chromatic' criteria vary a lot in the extant literature, depending on the scholars, their mother tongue, and/or their academic affiliation. E.g., in recent Colombian social sciences, Moya *et al.* (as cited in Pinto Guargati 2022, 63–64; emphases added) distinguished *"green* humour" (about "sexual conduct"), *"black* humour" (about "death"), and *"white* humour", which is all the humour that is neither of the preceding types, nor "political and labour-related", "religious", "sexist" (i.e., about "gender superiority", whether "machoistic" or "feminist") and/or *"cruel"* (i.e., reliant upon "discrimination because of race, disability or substance addiction").

[7] See Gubanov, Gubanov, and Rokotyanskaya (2018), 379.

morous cruelty taken to another level, for such a case of cruel humour contains a significant component of stark irreversibility which no amount of clever wit can change. The dead will remain lifeless; the terminally ill will remain uncured; and a severed limb will remain lost.[8]

As another team of contemporary humour scholars has recently intimated, in an unaware reminder of Hallie's reflections about "cruelty" proper, cruel humour can be interpreted as an inherent paradox, since it broadcasts simultaneously two conflicting messages.[9] Specifically,
(1) it launches an explicit belittling message directed at a chosen target, along with
(2) an implicit befriending message stating that this denigration can be enjoyed free from despicable motives and/or malevolent intentions.

While disparaging, cruel humour also says that it is "just a joke", which is meant to amuse and not to be taken seriously, or *too* seriously. Humour is thus the perfect cover story to maintain social acceptability even while expressing prejudice and/or malice. Humour allows us to avert the normal challenges, rebuttals, or hostile reactions that non-humorous cruelty would evoke. If anything, it can be a convenient smokescreen.[10]

Although displayed under the pretext of social acceptability, cruel humour often represents an expression of negative prejudice, varying in subtlety and conveying abrasive stereotypes or antagonistic attitudes towards certain persons and/or social groups. Moreover, in order to 'get' a cruel joke, one must usually share with the joker at least some knowledge concerning certain disapproving stereotypes and/or preconceptions.[11] As seen in Chapter 2 with respect to Harvey's ethical considerations, this sort of humour can therefore help to articulate and strengthen such collectively-shared demeaning notions and attendant attitudes among the audience.

Cruel humour can even delegitimise a social group by declaring them, openly and repeatedly, socially acceptable targets for deprecation, e.g., teenage boys, unmarried women, middle-aged men, Jehovah Witnesses, immigrants, oddballs, Mus-

---

8 See Gubanov, Gubanov, and Rokotyanskaya (2018), 379.
9 O'Connor *et al.* (2017). All claims made in the paragraph above and the ensuing ones are based on this work.
10 As we discussed in Chapter 2, it may even be used to cover up the intolerable cruelty of existence.
11 In any case, *'getting' a joke is always a cognitively complex skill requiring much acculturation and admitting of degrees.* See, e.g., Arróniz Parra and Padilla Cruz (2022).

lims, and Jews.[12] In addition, the humorous component undermines the seriousness of the cruel expression of negative prejudice and/or malice, making its/their circulation, if not its/their acceptance, easier to take place. Cruel humour, even when effectively harmful, can appear innocuous.[13]

3.1.1 What Have We Learned So Far about Cruel Humour?

Cruel humour is not for everyone. Nevertheless, it is a pervasive feature of life. One cannot help but speculate that it can have a special role in human interactions, or at least in some of them. Previous research, for one, has shown that people initiate and enjoy cruel humour because, *inter alia*, it reaffirms threatened social and/or individual identities. In line with the superiority theory, it distinguishes one's "in" group as superior to other relevant "out" groups.[14] For another, it has been recorded how humour is the key component of comedic entertainment, for it succeeds in creating social distance between the individual who initiates the joke or prank (or the group that the individual represents), and those who are the comic target of the joke or prank.[15]

(1) As we discussed in Chapter 1, the superiority theory assumes that the joker's intentions are to make his/her target look inferior, wrong, or defeated. Accordingly, this theory often frames laughter as an effective social corrective. Bergson's philosophy of the comical, as also seen in Chapter 1, argued as much. Laughing at socially undesirable behaviours not only heightens one's own sense of superiority, but it also encourages the target of the joke to correct the offending behaviour. The group being laughed at is "censored by laughter", while the group that laughs is unified by a feeling of dominance.[16]

(2) The incongruity theory, instead, stipulates that we laugh at things that are unexpected or surprising. Absurdity, nonsense, and shock are the quintessential elements of humour.[17] And they certainly are in a multitude of cases, whether commonplace or refined. In the case of cruel humour, however, an additional duality is likely to be at play, since the humorous cues are taken to also

---

12 Additional forms of social marginalisation can then make the suffering of cruel humour harder to bear.
13 See also Ford and Ferguson (2004), 85.
14 O'Connor *et al.* (2017), 567.
15 See Green and Linders (2016).
16 Green and Linders (2016), 244.
17 See Buijzen and Valkenburg (2004).

communicate that the perceived act of disparagement and/or violence is non-threatening, thereby turning the potential aggression into something playful.[18]

(3) The third major theoretical framework of humour, as seen, is relief theory, which claims that the reason why we laugh is, fundamentally, to rid ourselves of excessive nervous tension or, as postulated by Freud, repressed sexual and aggressive energies.[19] In this connection, Freud claimed that for aggressive humour to be received in a positive manner, it must distract the listener so that s/he becomes less aware of the content of what s/he is laughing at.[20] If, on the other hand, the listener manages to keep his/her full attention to the evidence that humour expresses aggressive impulses, the inhibitions are activated and s/he becomes less able and less likely to enjoy the occasion.[21]

A cleverly-designed 1960s study by the US-based psychologists Gollob and Levine provided considerable empirical support for Freud's claims.[22] In it, they had participants rate the humorousness of cartoons, some of which had aggressive content. Ten days later, the same participants were given the same cartoons, but they were also told to focus on their content before rating them. The same participants then rated the comicality of the same cartoons a second time. The results showed that the participants regularly rated the aggressive cartoons as funnier than the neutral cartoons on the first test, but as less funny than the neutral cartoons on the second one. Presumably, the instruction to focus on their content activated internalised socio-moral norms about violence or cruelty that prevented the participants from adopting a merely humour-based mindset which, by itself, would lead them to appreciate the aggressive cartoons as funnier than the neutral ones.[23]

---

[18] See Ford and Ferguson (2004). See also Feinberg (1978).
[19] See Buijzen and Valkenburg (2004), 148–149, and Hurley *et al.* (2011), 74. More on this follows in H&C3.
[20] See Gollob and Levine (1967).
[21] See Gollob and Levine (1967).
[22] See Gollob and Levine (1967), 368–370, which applies to the whole paragraph above.
[23] Occasionally, in this chapter, we highlight the methods utilised in the cited experiments, for they are the truly creative side of the work performed by social scientists and their main distinguishing feature from humanists.

3.1.2 Cruel Humour in Everyday Life

> We're just busy dead people, who confabulate that they're making a life for themselves.
> —Luigi Pirandello[24]

Some authors have maintained that cruel humour has become more and more popular in modern times.[25]

3.1.2.1 Mortality

Somehow, psychologically, cruel humour is said to serve as a compensatory mechanism for the disappearance of cruelty in our daily existence. Specifically, this process has been linked to three main factors:

(1) Global urbanisation and economic development have meant that we have been largely removed from actual death and the dying.[26] These, by and large, have been relocated from our family farms and homes into mechanised factories, hospitals, and a host of specialised institutions. Undoubtedly, we are reminded of death every so often (e.g., by the sounds of ambulances). However, we do not notice actual death very much as if we had it in front of our noses most days of the year.

(2) There has been an increased access to, and pervasive presence of, the mass media, first with the advent of newspapers and the radio, then television and the Internet. The daily news of the world that we absorb is "literally saturated with the theme of death, usually sensational and sudden".[27] Today, our senses are so bombarded with reports of vicarious murder and mayhem that to go through a day without encountering them would be inconceivable.[28] That would certainly not have been the case for our ancestors, who, for the most part, lived in rural communities and, also for the most part, were illiterate and had no access to any media.[29]

(3) The tremendous advances that have been accomplished in medicine, public hygiene, pharmacology, and plastic surgery have made us almost nonchalant about mortality.[30] We spend much of our lives as though we should never

---

24 Pirandello (1987), 330.
25 See e.g., Gubanov, Gubanov, and Rokotyanskaya (2018), 381.
26 See Gubanov, Gubanov, and Rokotyanskaya (2018), 382, which applies to the whole numbered list above.
27 Gubanov, Gubanov, and Rokotyanskaya (2018), 381–382.
28 See Gubanov, Gubanov, and Rokotyanskaya (2018), 382.
29 See Gubanov, Gubanov, and Rokotyanskaya (2018), 382.
30 See Gubanov, Gubanov, and Rokotyanskaya (2018), 382.

die, protracting juvenile habits and adolescent expectations well into adulthood, as externally signalled by the continued use of youthful attires, forms of courtship and lifestyles, well past the traditional 'age of reason' and, perhaps, of aesthetic or even ethical appropriateness.[31]

The combination of these three factors might explain our modern-day appetite for cruel humour.[32] Natural and human cruelty, according to this line of socio-scientific research, has become a constant but also a more abstract feature of modern life.[33] Cruel humour, in this perspective, works as a means whereby to regain a correct sense of reality.[34]

3.1.2.2 Teasing

But for all that, we could state as easily that our sense of reality is steeped *ab ovo* in lived instances of cruel humour, which then extends in later years as well. Teasing, for example, is not only patently associated with childhood, but it has also been found to be ubiquitous in adulthood, and arises across a wide range of different interactional settings in all studied cultures.[35] This phenomenon is of particular interest to those undertaking research about cruel humour because teasing is multi-layered, and it mixes invariably elements of provocation with elements of non-seriousness. This mixture is what lends teasing to being interpreted and evaluated in different ways by the participants, depending on their age, gender, acculturation, and where they stand in the social game.

However, teasing not only combines provocation with various modes of non-seriousness, but also involves itself a vast range of very different practices which have made it a fertile ground for empirical study across a wide range of disciplines. The results of the extant socio-scientific inquiries about teasing are not particularly surprising, at least for those who are familiar with the older philosophical literature that we discussed in Chapter 1. Cooperation and conflict often go hand-in-hand when it comes to joking and humorous activities at large.[36] In the scientific literature, teasing is frequently interpreted as a viable means of socialisation involving playfulness and levity, particularly among children, and also as a nonviolent means of social control, at least at a physical level.[37]

---

31 Each reader may freely reflect and pass judgement on this aesthetic and moral consideration.
32 See Gubanov, Gubanov, and Rokotyanskaya (2018), 382.
33 See Gubanov, Gubanov, and Rokotyanskaya (2018), 382.
34 See Gubanov, Gubanov, and Rokotyanskaya (2018), 382.
35 Haugh (2017), 204–218, which applies to the whole paragraph above.
36 See, e.g., Kotthoff (2006), 15.
37 See Boxer and Cortés-Conde (1997).

As it was lucidly outlined by two contemporary experts in pragmatics, Diana Boxer and Florencia Cortés-Conde:

> Teasing requires that the conversational joking be directed at someone present. This person is either the addressee or a hearer and becomes the center of an interaction in which a humorous frame has been set up. Teasing runs along a continuum of bonding to nipping to biting. Because this is a continuum, these constructs are not mutually exclusive, and the boundaries are not always clear. As with all talk, much depends on the identification of context, and indeed the exact message cannot be interpreted without encoding/decoding the metamessage.[38]

The metamessage can then be made apparent, either by a disclaimer or by using more contextualised cues, such as exaggerated intonation, laughs, or winks.[39]

Above all, teasing is a cruel means of shaming, by which one tries to inhibit and/or change the actions of their target/s by imposition of noticeable pain. It also conveys a particularly effective message about the relationship of the involved individuals, including family, one's peers, one's romantic suitors, or even the larger community.[40] There is in it an interesting mix of bonding and biting, inclusion and exclusion. People can joke at the expense of others (exclusion) and thereby assure themselves of the existence of shared values and perspectives (inclusion).[41]

As stated, teasing also plays a noticeable role in the formation of gender roles and romantic relations.[42] It is, for example, widespread among adolescent girls, where it serves a variety of purposes. A verbal allusion to sex may offer girls a playful way of distancing themselves from traditional gender roles, but it may also strengthen adherence to well-established norms of alleged beauty and accepted femininity. Girls may use teasing to experiment with new models of behaviour and renegotiate traditional standards, but also to further enshrine them in their worldviews.

As boys typically become important in the adolescent culture of ten- to 14-year-old heterosexual girls, humorous yet scathing provocations are used as a means of experimentation and exchange with boys. As with all teasing, the content of the comments is generally negative and hostile, but the tacit contextualisation cues, which the targeted boys have often a very hard time grasping and grappling with, indicate that they should be understood as playful too. Romantic and/or sexual interest can thus be conveyed without having to expose one's true feelings, while simultaneously hurting and titillating the male targets.

---

38 Boxer and Cortés-Conde (1997), 279.
39 See Boxer and Cortés-Conde (1997), 279.
40 See Schieffelin (1986), 166.
41 See Kotthoff (2006), 15.
42 See Kotthoff (2006), which applies to the whole paragraph above and the ensuing five.

In teasing, more often than not, basic gender behaviours and boundaries are clearly drawn. Older children and teenagers habitually tease each other for having or not having a boyfriend or a girlfriend. In girls' cliques, the chief topic of conversation is, statistically, male-female relationships—including matters pertaining to sexuality and physical allure. Usually, teasing is a staple of such groups, whereby one girl teases another, e.g., by imitating her demeanours before boys whom she is trying to impress. Other participants can then join in and outspread the teasing act.

When boys are discussed, for the most part, they are not idealised. Rather, they are claimed to be sexually incompetent and/or naïve. In these humorous discussions, potent emotions such as jealousy and lust can be conveyed, confronted, and, to some extent, managed through the teasing acts. At the same time, rivalries over potential mates can be playfully staged so that existing friendships do not come under actual threat. After all, we often tease those whom we know well and whom we like.[43]

Nevertheless, due to its conspicuously cruel undercurrent, whether predominantly sadistic or callous, teasing can be experienced as genuinely threatening and life-disabling. This holds especially true in the beginning of romantic relationships and, quite obviously, among total strangers. Later on, instead, teasing can become an indication of the stability of the same relationship or of special friendship. Specifically, in making fun of one's own partner before an audience, references are typically made to shared group knowledge and particularly to a shared history of known interactions between the two romantically involved individuals.

Making fun of others, in this way, takes for granted a close relationship and reaffirms implicitly the closeness of said relationship. Thus even uninvolved jokers, who happen to perceive a romantic relationship as being strong and stable, frequently suspend with daily rules of politeness and propriety, and initiate teasing acts of their own. Teasing, however, is never entirely removed from the outright abuse of another person, and any mistake or miscalculation can easily transform the former into the latter. What one regards as harmless teasing, another may judge as being harmful bullying instead.[44]

---

[43] We expect most readers to have had direct experience of this sort of teasing among friends, relatives, and lovers.
[44] See Olweus (1993), Arnarsson *et al.* (2020), and Inchley *et al.* (2020).

3.1.3 Cruel Humour in Wartime

War is perhaps the most plentiful source of cruel humour.[45] Its survivors will often use sardonic humour to describe their brushes with death or their own incredible suffering. In parallel, the perpetrators of blatantly cruel actions will resort to noxious humour when describing their odious wartime experiences. The merger of comedy into tragedy or light into darkness can be grasped most potently on such occasions.

In wartime, laughter and ridicule play an important part in ensuring submission and self-sacrifice, both by isolating dissidents and by maintaining a clear mental distinction between 'us' and 'them'.[46] Normally, these ends are achieved by utilising the most derogatory stereotypes and humiliating depictions. Under the obvious pressures of wartime mobilisation, "humour" is used to "discredit both external and internal enemies, criticising hypocrites, pacifists, shirkers, profiteers, saboteurs, deserters, and outsiders".[47] (On the flip side, wartime governments must be mindful that the weapons of laughter and ridicule, in a context of heightened fears and arduous sacrifices, can be turned against them, sometimes with devastating effect.)[48]

Ridicule can thus be used in a potent way to censure any contravention of expected and/or established norms, especially by threatening potential and/or actual offenders with exclusion from the group: "ridicule relies on the menace of ostracism. Humans are not simply 'laughing animals', but are laughed at, with laughter a social activity".[49] Most of us would rather be subjected to direct hateful comments than to this kind of laughter. The "sanction of ridicule is based both on the threat of exclusion and the withdrawal of social approbation, menacing in-

---

[45] See Hewitson (2012), which applies to the whole sub-subsection at issue.
[46] Luigi Weber (2021) identified and discussed this logic of opposition in the lyrical glorification of warfare conducted by the fascist poet Filippo Tommaso Marinetti in the early 20th century, especially *qua* juxtaposition between 'male' and 'female' elements, as well as 'sadistic' and 'masochistic' ones.
[47] Hewitson (2012), 217.
[48] Ridicule can obstruct the most comprehensive and careful mobilisations against the most serious and most pernicious threats. Satirical social-media memes discrediting the scientific community during the Covid-19 pandemic or the ongoing global warming can thus infiltrate the minds of millions and lead to veritably "stupid" choices, i.e., in the 'technical' sense of Cipolla's (2011, 36; emphasis added) "golden … third law" of human "stupidity": "*A stupid person is a person who causes losses to another person or to a group of persons while himself deriving no gain and even possibly incurring losses.*"
[49] Hewitson (2012), 230.

dividuals' self-esteem and even their sense of identity".[50] Consistently, cruel jokes are used by authorities and social superiors
(1) to pressure young men into volunteering for service,
(2) to prevent them from deserting, as well as
(3) to manipulate the behaviour of the civilian population that has been left behind.[51]

As the incongruity theory demands, an effective sense of humour relies on our ability to make a psychological shift from the real and obvious to the playful and counterfactual, thereby transcending the 'here' and the 'now', to some extent. This means that humour always refers to what *is* as well as to what *is not*. Often, it does so in the most oblique ways, hence opening risky interpersonal avenues before us. As the contemporary British historian Mark Hewitson points out, humour is "notoriously unpredictable" and unnerving.[52] It can result in both laughter and sorrow, i.e., inclusion and exclusion.[53]

Inasmuch as the meanings of jokes and jests, at least partly, originate from the unconscious domain of the human psyche, they are often difficult to decipher: "They both subvert and reinforce norms by demonstrating that such norms exist and by showing how they can be transgressed."[54] As emphasised by Bergson himself, they provide us with means to anaesthetise our hearts. Hence, insofar as wars make sane people tremble, feats of humour, including cruel ones, can provide much-needed relief, even if only temporarily and, more often than not, at someone else's expense.[55]

---

[50] Hewitson (2012), 230.
[51] Hewitson (2012), 230.
[52] Hewitson (2012), 231.
[53] As noted, the term "unlaughter" is the brainchild of Billig (2005), who so-christened the audience's cruel refusal of laughing at the jokes or rejoinders of a cruelly-targeted person, as also discussed by Harvey (1999).
[54] Hewitson (2012), 230.
[55] This is a topic that we address in detail in *H&C3*.

3.2 More Views on Cruel Humour

> There is no character, howsoever good and fine, but it can be destroyed by ridicule, howsoever poor and witless.
> — Mark Twain[56]

3.2.1 Harry Harlow

Harlow embraced the superiority view of humour, which he saw as a means to elevate or maintain the self-image of the joker who always forms it in comparison with others. Therefore, the act of degrading others can be an effective, if not indolent, means for improving one's own status:

> Since it is far simpler to say derogatory things about others than it is to raise one's own status; by some incredibly brilliant bon mot, most humour lies in the physical or social degradation of others. Actually, even the ideal or playful humour often carries with it some direct or implied derogation.[57]

Harlow explained the relief theory in a similar manner, pointing to the role of anxiety, which is caused by the impending possibility of our personal inadequacies being publicly revealed, thereby carrying with it a grave threat to our *ego* due both to feelings of individual helplessness and the possibility of social degradation.[58] Certainly, our general levels of personal anxiety may be dissimilar, fluctuate over time, and involve very different triggers. However, according to Harlow, their common psychological basis is the fear of what other people may think of us.[59]

Crucially for our present investigation, Harlow saw cruelty as an essential component of most, if not all, "humour" proper. Indeed, six out of his eight categories of "humour" proper—"brutality", "physical degradation", "verbal degradation", "vulgar or sexual jokes", "social-group jokes", and "children's jokes"—involve some form of painful degradation of others, whether physical, mental, or both.[60] We touched upon these notions in the previous two chapters, and we also deal with them in both *H&C1* and *H&C3*, but we must now give the most detailed description of these six categories. As will become apparent, five of them contain explicitly derogatory and offensive jokes.

---

56 Twain (1894), 15.
57 Harlow (1969), 226.
58 See Harlow (1969), 226.
59 See Harlow (1969), 226.
60 See Harlow (1969), 229.

It is also important to restate our concluding observation from *H&C1*, i.e., that in outlining the remaining two categories of "humour" proper, which are the seemingly benign ones of "transitional abstract wit" and "the ideal or abstract comic", Harlow's empirical research failed to come up with any convincing examples, leaving us with the notion that no form of humour is victim-less.[61]

3.2.1.1 Brutality

The most primitive form of humour, according to Harlow, is sheer brutality, whereby the victim's degradation is brought about through his/her anxiety, anguish, and/or agony. The most blatant examples of such an ilk of cruel humour can be found in stories of Nazi officers in charge of concentration camps or of guards serving in them who enjoyed the greatest variety of acts of terror and torture.[62] Patent reminders of this kind of humour abound in verbal jokes.

To illustrate his point, Harlow gave an example of an American gangland story from the depression-ridden days of the 1930s:

> Let me tell you what happened last night. The old man came up to me and he said: "Sonny, you know I'm getting on to 70 and I'm starting to wonder where I'm going".
> "You don't need to worry about that, Dad", I said, "I know exactly where you're going". And with that I let him have all six slugs of the .38 right in the gut.[63]

Many people with a fully developed moral conscience may find it difficult to see anything akin to "humour" proper in this form, but then again: "Humour grades into callous cruelty, and what is amusing and what is cruel is determined by particular people or social classes and at particular times and within particular situations."[64] Even the most violent massacres and torments have been considered laughable—by *some* people and on *some* occasions. Harlow maintained—and we tend to agree—that a comprehensive theory of humour cannot be formulated without taking this fact into due consideration: "After all, there is a narrow boundary between sarcasm and sadism, between bantering and bestiality."[65]

---

61 Harlow (1969), 237–238.
62 See Harlow (1969), 237–238.
63 Harlow (1969), 237.
64 Harlow (1969), 238.
65 Harlow (1969), 230. Harlow's use of "callous cruelty" and "sadism" is not as binary as in the taxonomies by Hallie or Regan that we outlined in Chapter 1 and *H&C1*.

3.2.1.2 Physical Degradation

Slightly less 'primitive' than sheer brutality is the form of humour that involves physical degradation, e.g., pie-in-the-face throwing, snowballing, and dunking. Clowns rely extensively on this form of humour, and so have children's cartoons.[66] Harlow himself, having extensive experience in observing the behaviour of apes and monkeys, gave ample examples of such behaviours among caged chimpanzees, who develop the habit of filling their mouths with water, waiting for a keeper or an innocent bystander to come within range, and then drenching him/her.[67]

Occasionally, these animals even develop techniques for throwing dirt and/or excrements with amazing precision.[68] These manoeuvres are characteristically directed against humans who, according to Harlow, "have high ego status to an ape"; but they sometimes apply to other apes, who frequently engage in cruder forms of intra-species slapstick.[69] Following these encounters, the throwing chimpanzees and the unscathed members of the animal audience jump up and down, clap their hands, and emit sounds that can be sensibly interpreted as roars of laughter.[70]

Physical degradation can be accomplished symbolically as well, i.e., by aggression against property and objects rather than people. It may involve throwing toilet paper at a house ("teepeeing"), swapping street signs, spraying graffiti, grabbing a hat off someone's head, etc. This form of commonplace and aggressive humour often involves passive spectators who are aware of what is about to take place and derive pleasure from it. How this audience reacts, however, depends on the perpetrator, the victim, the audience's mood, and countless other factors, most of which operate tacitly.

This scenario is most telling of human nature, both at a general level and at the level of each specific member of the audience. As Harlow argued at length:

> Such comical situations are annual events at the University of Wisconsin near Bascom Hall. Bascom Hall rests on the top of a steep hill with two nearly perpendicular walks running down to the main street below. On winter days when the walks are coated with 'glare' ice, the male students frequently wait at the bottom of the hill to observe the inevitable. If an expensively dressed or overdressed sorority sister rolls over and over from one end of the hill to another, this precious, precipitous 'pratfall' is regarded as a very funny display. If a more modestly clad co-ed becomes a victim of the same down-fall, the event is regarded as mildly amusing. If an injured, crippled, or over-aged lass or lady loses her footing the result is not regarded as being a comical event. Thus, a single situation, the observation of a uniform

---

66 See Harlow (1969), 230.
67 Given their behavioural and genetic proximity to humans, we write "who" instead of "which".
68 See Harlow (1969), 230.
69 Harlow (1969), 231.
70 See Harlow (1969), 231.

act, can range from the delightful to the distressing. This represents a quantification of the humour of physical degradation. The lasses who lived in the social seclusion of their sacrosanct sorority society fell farther socially than the modestly clad co-eds and far farther than the females with physical handicaps. This is a situation involving physical degradation in which the humour is not mere physical degradation but is as well a prestige plunge of social significance. Fortunately this plunge, physical and social, does not permanently change the physical state of the victim but is humorous in that it shrinks the symbolic social gap between the females descending to the bottom of the hill and the masculine monsters already entrenched below. Human suffering can be amusing at an acceptable social level as long as the observer is not responsible for the event or accident. By using this mechanism, in many situations we achieve guile without guilt.[71]

The quite literal toppling of the powerful described in Harlow's example is a repetition of a theme that has been touched upon by almost all humour scholars. However, there are some particularly strong Freudian elements to it as well, which make it stand out in comparison. The young hormone-filled "masculine monsters" are eagerly waiting for the young maidens to fall, ignoring all but the prettiest and the most well-to-do, and thereby hard-to-get. On the page where the quoted passage is found, there is a cartoon displaying a falling co-ed, clad according to the times, in a dress that gets pulled up to her waist—which has no doubt fuelled the imagination of the plausibly libidinous crowd waiting at the end of the slope. The introduction of a sexual element in physical degradation is both common and important, at least from a psychological perspective, and particularly from a Freudian one.[72]

3.2.1.3 Verbal Degradation

Pranks and pantomimes aside, most humour is verbal. As Harlow stated so eloquently:

> It is easy to think of man as composed of his brain and brawn, but his psychological being is both created and clothed in a fabric of language. Thus, man's being is both wrapped in words and wounded by them. Consequently, to rephrase a childish chant: "Sticks and stones may break your bones, but words will never hurt you"[73]

---

[71] Harlow (1969), 231–232, which applies to the concluding paragraph too.
[72] As noted in Chapter 1, much Western culture was often far too prudish to directly tackle the sexual sphere as openly as Freud did. More on sexual matters and their import for humour and cruelty is said in *H&C3*.
[73] Harlow (1969), 232.

As we saw in Chapter 2, much, if not most, verbal humour is offensive. It is aimed at delivering hurtful messages, separating those who are 'in' and those who are not, hence exposing the proverbial Achille's heel of the targeted person/s, preferably in a lasting or irredeemable manner.[74] Harlow offered the dignified example of Oscar Wilde who, despite his acumen, could not save himself from becoming the butt of many a joke. Specifically, Wilde was known to be a great wit, but also tended to unconscionably plagiarise other people's jokes. The story is that he once heard a witty remark by the artist James Abbott McNeill Whistler, who was not only revered for his paintings, but also his clever way with words. On hearing Whistler's dazzling comment, Wilde remarked: "I wish I had said that myself". "Don't worry, don't worry", replied Whistler, "you will".[75]

This anecdote highlights two characteristics of nominal "humour" in the form of wit that Harlow was especially attuned to.[76]
(1) It involves the humiliation of someone who has a higher social status; and,
(2) it illustrates the importance of incongruity as well as of the speed of delivery. As Harlow put it:

> There is no time to marshal ego defences against the verbal lightning, whereas the ponderously prepared and propounded verbal assaults offer the recipient maximal opportunity to devise his defences and conceive his counter-strategy. Verbal degradation as humour is particularly facilitated when those dethroned achieved their lofty status through deviant devices that were less than totally honourable.[77]

Verbal degradation boosts the *ego* of the joker in two ways. It both raises his/her status by lowering that of his victim and lets him/her revel in the cleverness of the remark/s directed at the victim. As Harlow quipped: it "smacks simultaneously of dignity and degradation and is both two-faced and two-faceted".[78]

No human trait or individual is safe from the grasps of verbal degradation, which can attack both our virtues and our vices, fame or fault, power or poverty, strength and weakness.[79] As Freud himself noted on this point, this great adaptability of verbal degradation means that all those inner workings that we commonly repress, due to their sexual or violent nature, find potent and palatable ways to

---

[74] See Harlow (1969), 232.
[75] Harlow (1969), 232–233.
[76] As we discussed in *H&C1*, many 18th-century scholars contrasted "humour" with the term "wit" as two distinct forms of comicality. However, over the following two centuries, the former term appears to have phagocytised the latter.
[77] Harlow (1969), 233.
[78] Harlow (1969), 233.
[79] Harlow (1969), 233–234.

express themselves *qua* spoken or written humour.[80] Revealingly, Harlow himself borrowed a joke from Freud to illustrate this point. It tells of an aristocrat who, while visiting his peasants, sees a man in the crowd that bears a remarkable resemblance to himself. The aristocrat asks the man: "Was your mother at one time in service in the Palace?" The man immediately replies: "No, your Highness, but my father was".[81]

3.2.1.4 Vulgar or Sexual Jokes

Depending on our internalised levels of prudery and decorum, Freud's joke about the nobleman can, quite obviously, be classified as vulgar or sexual, which means that Harlow allowed for unclear boundaries in his classification—and indeed maintained that they are in no sense neatly separable.[82] Jokes of a sexual nature are often derogatory, after all, but that is not always clearly the case. As Harlow wrote: "The verbally vindictive refers more to the facts of sex than the acts of sex."[83]

This joke itself, although being sexual in nature, is also quite tame or even sanctified. There is not a hint of rudeness to be found in it, at least as far as the common American standards of prudence and propriety were concerned in Harlow's day—and they certainly were quite prudish, compared to, say, the humour of medieval Vikings or early-Renaissance comedians *à la* Rabelais.[84] As to how this joke should be best classified today, we leave it to each reader to pass judgement. While some of us may share Harlow's older standards, other readers may be less tolerant.

Harlow also maintained that "[s]exual and vulgar jokes represent two different categories but frequently these categories are far from separate. Possibly, the sexual relates more to propinquity and the vulgar more to propriety, but there are certainly no hard and fast distinctions between the two."[85] Among them, cruel jokes abound. Thus, Harlow used the example of a tale of an American scout during the Indian wars who caught up with a wagon train that had been sacked and burned by the Indians. To his surprise, the scout found a beautiful

---

80 See Chapter 1 and *H&C1*.
81 The original formulation is found in Freud (1960), loc 1060.
82 See Harlow (1969), 234.
83 Harlow (1969), 234.
84 The mutability of such standards contains a deeper cruelty of its own insofar as real people, in the course of their life, may find themselves applying principles of prudence and propriety that are not viable, either because of the times or social context, and therefore cause unwanted offences, self-debasements, lawsuits, etc.
85 Harlow (1969), 234.

young woman who had managed to stay alive, although she had been visibly beaten, stripped naked, and repeatedly raped. As the scout listens to her horrid story, he starts loosening his belt and says: "Lady, this just isn't going to be your day".[86]

Harlow agreed wholeheartedly with Freud, and with the noted Freudian Jacob Levine, on the notion that sexuality and aggression are the main topics of humour because they are the main sources of psychic tension, suppression, and repression.[87] It is true that nationality, social class, age, gender, religious belief, and/or culture at large can condition our reactions to humour. It is also true, as both Harlow and the Freudian Levine contended, that humour's basic themes are universal —essentially, aggression and sexuality. As Schopenhauer had already remarked in his metaphysical works, sex is, in particular, the fundamental drive in all human societies, which would cease to exist without it.[88]

Insofar as our sense of humour is formed on an individual basis, i.e., through the development of our own specific personality, our reactions to these basic themes may, can, and will differ. But nearly all of us are likely to remain able, nevertheless, to recognise humour *as* humour, even when it is very cruel. Therefore, many readers are likely to be disgusted or offended by Harlow's brief yarn about the American scout and the young woman, considering it vulgar and insufferably misogynistic. Still, most of us will also acknowledge the fact that, with its admixture of aggression and sexuality, it is patently a joke, and not, say, a political statement or an ethical injunction.[89]

3.2.1.5 Social-Group Jokes

Harlow's analysis of cultural or ethnic humour is itself solidly Freudian, both in his theoretical approach as well as in his choice of topics. Like Freud, Harlow emphasised the multiple forms, motives, and mechanisms within which this category of humour can operate. Four of them are prominent in his account.

(1) To begin, Harlow gave a very good example of how social-group competition can be achieved through simple humorous degradation.[90] It is the story of the Jewish and Episcopal heavens:

> An Episcopalian bishop mentioned that he had dreamed the night before of Jewish heaven and told his story at the request of a Jewish rabbi.

---

[86] Harlow (1969), 234.
[87] See Harlow (1969), 234.
[88] See Chapter 1 and *H&C1*.
[89] As noted in Chapter 2, there may be jests that are seen only as insults or attacks.
[90] See Harlow (1969), 235.

"It reminded me", he said, "of the tenement quarters of New York with old buildings packed side by side and women talking together on their back porches as they washed out the dirty clothes and hung the clean ones on the lines running from one building to another. In the front of the houses out in the streets were endless groups of boys and girls, some in ragged and dirty clothes, playing, shouting and rushing about".

"This is an odd coincidence", said the rabbi. "I too had a dream last night, but I dreamed I was in Episcopalian heaven".

"And what was it like?" asked the bishop.

"It was beautiful;" said the rabbi. "There was row after row of beautiful houses, all ornate, clean and immaculate. And between these rows of beautiful homes there were broad streets with stately trees on both sides, and parkways running down the middle".

"Yes, yes", said the bishop excitedly, "tell me more. What about the people?"

"Oh", replied the rabbi, "there weren't any people".[91]

Jokes or humorous remarks that are made about a cultural or an ethnic group by someone from the outside are often thinly veiled derisions or hostile acts.[92] However, when they are made by someone from inside the group, the techniques tend to be more varied and the derisory or hostile element may not be at play therein, or at least not as perceptibly.[93]

(2) As we saw in Chapter 2, there is also greater leeway given to insiders in the use of words and choice of topics. Hence, today's African Americans can use terms about their own race that would be frowned upon if they came out of the mouths of other human beings who, more or less sympathetically, are 'pigeonholed' into distinct ethnic categories (e. g., 'White', 'Jew', 'Kraut'). Similarly, gay comedians can use stereotypical images in their delivery that would not be considered funny when used by their heterosexual peers, whose enjoyment of such jokes must be parasitic.

As Harlow noted: "The jokes they tell are socially acceptable because the humorist himself is a member of a minority group and serves as a social shield against guile or guilt for both communicator and audience."[94] An essentially racist or homophobic joke, told by an insider, gives the outsiders a chance to indulge in their guilty pleasures.[95]

(3) There is also a third mechanism which may be at work in these jokes, since they can "express in hidden form the indomitable spirit of the persecuted popula-

---

91 Harlow (1969), 235.
92 Harlow (1969), 235.
93 See Harlow (1969), 235.
94 See Harlow (1969), 235.
95 As noted in Chapter 2, this in/out logic may be playing a role in making minority comedians so popular.

tion or even their capability to overcome in spite of fearful odds".[96] In other words, cruel humour can be used as a means of self-derision and, in unison, as a self-defence mechanism.[97] Notably, when we publicly mock ourselves, we leave little room for others to have a stab at us. Every bad thing, so to speak, has already been said.[98]

(4) Harlow observed as well that social group jokes tend to be lazily constructed, e.g., these jokes have often the same exact theme and structure, whether they are aimed at the Irish, the Italians, the Icelanders, or people from certain areas or locations within specific regions, cities, towns, institutions, and/or even buildings.[99] As Harlow asked: "What happens when you cross a Polack with a gorilla?" (The reply being: "You get a retarded gorilla.")[100] Change "Polack" to any preferred target group (e.g., blondes, philosophers, policemen, Tories), and the same joke is going to be told, again and again, wherever you may live, i.e., as long as you hurt the people belonging to the group/s that, for some reason, should be targeted.[101]

3.2.1.6 Children's Jokes

Although Harlow stated that children's jokes "represent variations of verbal degradation", he gives no clear examples that would support such a claim.[102] One is even hard-pressed to see that their gags possess "innocent derogation".[103] For sure, there is an element of superiority to be found in juvenile "Why did the chicken cross the road?" one-liners. Specifically, they are questions
(1) that cannot be answered by using adult logic, and
(2) that are meant to leave the audience bewildered.

The junior joker may then experience genuine dominance over the normally unassailable adult, even if the latter will probably feel put down by them.[104]

Harlow also held that "[c]hildren's jokes are intriguing in the sense that all the known mechanisms of humour exist within their content, but they are not mech-

---

96 Harlow (1969), 236.
97 More on this point is going to be discussed in *H&C3*.
98 Or so would one hope. Cruelly, keen critics seem capable of concocting ever new lines of sore mockery.
99 See Harlow (1969), 236.
100 Harlow (1969), 236.
101 Based on our experience, we could add "Italian", "Icelander", "man", "middle-aged man" and "Catholic".
102 Harlow (1969), 229.
103 Harlow (1969), 237.
104 Exceptions are conceivable, of course, depending primarily on individual features.

anisms with direct malicious meaning".[105] Here, once again, we are at a loss, as is often the case with such mutable and variously interpretable ideas such as 'humour', 'cruelty', and 'cruel humour'. How can something be considered derogatory, but still have no effect on the audience and no malicious intent by the joker? Let us leave it at that. Enough cruelty has already been unearthed in "humour" proper thanks to Harlow's pioneering studies in human and animal psychology.

3.2.2 Social Identity Theory

Humour, including of the cruel sort, is a complex, multi-functional, strategic discourse that can have miscellaneous, sometimes ambiguous, and contradictory purposes.[106] It can serve to create unity and signal that a person belongs to a given group, but it may also function to mark social boundaries by excluding others. The ways in which cruel humour is communicated and why it is expressed are highly dependent on context and vary greatly between social groups. Furthermore, there exists a close link between the use of cruel humour and identity construction. Assorted groups often develop distinctive norms, mostly of a tacit nature, about what is considered to be the proper mode for using humour among their members.

In other words, tacit norms and implicit expectations about what kind of humour is appropriate, what is considered a taboo topic, who is allowed to make fun of whom and what, or perhaps how, and how humour is responded to, vary enormously and decidedly amongst groups. By adhering to given norms, which are normally unwritten and volatile, speakers indicate their membership and depict themselves as assimilated members of this or that particular group. These tacit norms of appropriate humour apply to racial, ethnic, religious, and/or other forms of cruel humour, which may be considered fitting in one group but highly inappropriate and offensive in another. The room for error is, under all such circumstances, vast—and the consequences for error can be devastating for people's reputation, social inclusion and, at times, physical wellbeing, or even survival.[107]

Current social identity theory revolves around issues of intergroup relations, i.e., how people come to see themselves as members of one group or category of people (i.e., the so-called "In" group) in comparison with another (i.e., the

---

[105] Harlow (1969), 237.
[106] See Wolfers, File, and Schnurr (2017), which applies to the whole paragraph above and the following one.
[107] See Chapter 2 and, especially, *H&C3*.

"Out" group), and the diverse social and psychological consequences of this sort of categorisation. For example, having a specific social identity means
(1) being at one with a particular group,
(2) being like others in the group, and
(3) seeing things from this group's perspective.[108]

Cruel intergroup jokes provide a useful vent for individuals to emphasise their group identity and make effective distinctions between "In" and "Out" groups.[109]

Gender is an obvious research area for examining intergroup dynamics, since the identification of gender begins even before birth.[110] According to social identity theory, people engage in these modes of intergroup differentiation because they want to feel good about their own group membership and, ultimately, themselves. Most studies to date have only used binary categorisations of gender, i.e., comparing males with females.

The general expectation from such binary comparisons has been that both genders would experience an upsurge in their self-esteem and/or the esteem linked with group membership after hearing cruel jokes about the opposite gender. Similarly, both genders should experience a reduction in collective self-esteem after absorbing jokes that exhibit cruelty towards their own group. A recent study by American psychologists Jessica Abrams and Amy Bippus crystallised this standard approach: "Individuals will rate disparaging jokes that target the opposite gender funnier than jokes about their own gender... Individuals will rate disparaging jokes about the opposite gender as more typical than jokes about their own gender."[111]

The empirical results, however, have not been as clear-cut as the social identity theory would suggest, at least *prima facie*. True, the two hypotheses stated in the preceding quote appear to be supported by the extant data for women, as a group, but the findings have not been statistically significant for men as a group.[112] Essentially, women found male-targeted jokes significantly funnier and more typical of men.

This discrepancy was tentatively explained by Abrams and Bippus that
(1) anti-outgroup humour, when it is delivered by a group of perceived lower social status, might serve as an important and creative way in which it can es-

---

108 See, e.g., Stets and Burke (2000).
109 Abrams and Bippus (2011), 193.
110 See Abrams and Bippus (2011), which applies to the whole subsection.
111 Abrams and Bippus (2011), 195.
112 See Abrams and Bippus (2011), 198.

tablish a positive distinctiveness from an outgroup of perceived higher status.[113]
(2) The same authors also maintained that women may have a keener awareness of the existing social hierarchy involving the two genders or, more to the point, of their perceived inferior status.[114]
(3) Moreover, the two scientists suggested that women's ratings of jokes about men could be seen as a socially creative method for distinguishing themselves positively from men. Thus, women's cruel humour reflected their combined desire to maintain a positive social identity and denigrate men, e.g., by suggesting that a conspicuous lack of intelligence is more typical of "them" than of "us".[115]
(4) In such a way, moreover, cruel humour would unify women as a 'better' group.[116]

3.2.3 Benign Violation Theory

The theory of benign violation states that humour is elicited when we experience some threat to our wellbeing, identity, or normative belief structure ("violation") that, in the next instance, shows itself to be safe and/or acceptable ("benign").[117] Physical attacks like tickling, play fighting, and slapstick are funny when they are not harmful. Likewise, verbal humour misuses language, but it is amusing because it simultaneously makes sense given an alternative linguistic or logical norm.[118] (Koestler's idea of 'bisociation' is thus also reiterated.)

3.2.3.1 A Popular Theory
The theory of benign violation has been used to study humour prompted by hardship or tragedy or, more specifically, to investigate the factors that can either increase or decrease humour born from negative experiences. The pivotal concept in this endeavour is "psychological distance", which is said to facilitate humour

---

[113] See Abrams and Bippus (2011), 198.
[114] Abrams and Bippus (2011), 198.
[115] Abrams and Bippus (2011), 198.
[116] It should be noted that gender is one among many group identities to which a person may subscribe. Which group identities are important to that person, also regarding cruel humour, depends on highly specific circumstances.
[117] McGraw, Williams, and Warren (2014), 566, which was discussed at length in *H&C1*.
[118] See McGraw, Williams, and Warren (2014), 566.

up to a point, although too much distance decreases it.[119] In other words, "distance reduces threat, helping transform tragedy (a violation) into comedy (a benign violation), but too much distance can make comedy seem tame and uninteresting (a benign situation)".[120]

There are different forms of such a "distance" that have been considered: temporal (now *versus* then), spatial (here *versus* there), social (self *versus* other), and hypothetical (real *versus* imagined).[121] Our intuitions suggest that the more psychological distance we have, the more appreciative we would tend to be towards cruel humour, e.g., a joke about a tragic occurrence.[122] After all, a common response by a stand-up comedian who realises that a cruel joke has 'tanked' is: "Too soon?"

Moreover, scientific studies have confirmed these intuitions. For instance, people find revolting things more humorous when they are apparently fake, seem further away in space or time, or afflict someone else.[123] As seen in Chapter 1, this is consistent with the conclusions reached by Hazlitt and Schopenhauer in the 19th century.

However, contrary to our intuitions, recent empirical studies have found that psychological distance tends to decrease humorous responses to mildly aversive situations.[124] Getting hit by a car might be a source of a very funny story if it occurred 5 years ago, but much less if it happened yesterday. Conversely, if we hear a story of somebody stubbing a toe, it would be more humorous if it occurred yesterday than if it happened 5 years ago.[125] Joking about a tragedy is therefore liable of failure, and the benign violation theory outlines the two ways in which a situation can fail to be grasped as humorous: if the situation described is either purely violating (e.g., being tickled by a creepy stranger), or purely benign (e.g., tickling oneself).[126]

Cruel humour, in other words, requires just the right amount of danger, i.e., not too much and not too little. When the distance in time, space, social proximity and/or plausibility has become so extended that the event provokes absolutely no palpable sense of danger, were it even a hurricane (e.g., "Sandy" in 2012), it also ceases to be funny.[127] The theory at issue can be used to explain why factors that decrease feelings of danger can heighten the humour associated with highly

---

[119] McGraw, Williams, and Warren (2014), 566.
[120] McGraw, Williams, and Warren (2014), 566.
[121] McGraw, Williams, and Warren (2014), 567.
[122] See McGraw, Williams, and Warren (2014), 567.
[123] See McGraw, Williams, and Warren (2014), 567.
[124] See McGraw, Williams, and Warren (2014), 567.
[125] See McGraw, Williams, and Warren (2014), 567.
[126] See McGraw, Williams, and Warren (2014), 567.
[127] McGraw, Williams, and Warren (2014), 566.

aversive events (e.g., crashing cars), but also reduce the humour associated with mildly aversive events (e.g., stubbing toes). There is, in short, "a sweet spot for humor—a time period in which tragedy is neither too close nor too far away to be humorous".[128]

3.2.3.2 Some Critical Remarks

Critical assessments of the theory of benign violation have recently emerged from the work of two Bergen-based social scientists, Leo Kant and Elisabeth Norman, who pointed to several limitations of the theory that are relevant to the issue of cruel humour.[129] One is that jokes and jests containing norm violations that in no way can be seen as benign can sometimes be perceived as funny (e.g., laughing at the guillotined heads rolling around). Another is the failure to account for the obvious differences in what people find funny in a given situation, not least a tragic one. Some may be able to laugh at their own impending demise; others may not.[130]

Kant and Norman maintained as well that good theories of humour need to explain *why* it is that people sometimes feel compelled to tell cruel jokes that others find most insulting or inappropriate. Easy does it, really; even if easy ain't funny. So, why taking such risks? Clearly, and at the very least, what is intended to be funny by the person telling the joke is not always perceived the same way by the audience and *vice versa*. This sort of mistake is perpetrated by even the seemingly intelligent and the emotionally sensitive. One does not need to be a misfit to be able to misfire miserably in society.[131]

Cruel humour's 'sweet spot' is likely a deeply subjective and mostly tacit matter, which also reflects a variety of deeply-embedded socio-cultural variables, the misunderstanding and/or misapplication of which can have dreadful consequences for all those individuals who happen to make a *faux pas*. Being a far cry from funny can be no fun at all, and it can make the failed clowns cry for real. As Kant and Norman explained:

> To the extent that a joke refers to a person or group of people, the social distance to the joke would directly correspond to the social distance to those involved, whether it was a specific person or a group. Even jokes that do not refer to specific people may still have contents that

---

128 McGraw, Williams, and Warren (2014), 567.
129 See Kant and Norman (2019), which applies to the whole paragraph above and the following one.
130 The examples are ours.
131 We expect all our readers to have been guilty of blunder, at least once in their life *qua* humorous persons.

are relevant to the social roles, social identities, attitudes, cultural practices, values, and norms of a joke-listener. The social distance to the joke would then depend on the person's commitment or dedication to each of these.[132]

Significantly, both men and women enjoy sexist jokes more when they are targeting the other gender.[133] As Kant and Norman insisted, in this context, the perceived social distance between the joker and the joke is critical, i.e., whether the joke teller is seen as distant from or close to its cruel content. For example, it would affect our appreciation of a cruel joke about a conspicuously obese person, for good or bad, if we knew that the joker was married to one.[134]

Power asymmetry is another such variable that is significant in this context. For one, cruel jokes of a lewd character, when they are told by bosses, are more likely to be interpreted as sexual harassment than when the same exact jokes are told by co-workers, even if no genuine in-depth assessment of anyone's intentions has been pursued, i.e., in an often-unseen, cruel irony in the absence of knowledge of those aims which the person making the joke meant to attain by it.[135]

Something similar applies to the tacit cultural norms of our families, workplaces, schools, and of broader society, all of which are said to be playing a role in answering the thorny question of when it is in/appropriate to laugh, especially vis-à-vis cruel humour.[136] It is worth keeping in mind, in fact, that cruel humour is always testing these boundaries, both on a cultural and on an individual level, lest it stops being cruel or even humorous. As comedians know very well, effective humour is, more often than not, 'edgy', 'transgressive', or 'daring'. When the joker and audience have different cultural backgrounds and/or presuppositions, the joke or jest may not be well received—if it is received at all as an act of commonplace humour and not as an insult or a threat.[137]

3.2.4 Cognitive and Affective Aspects of Cruel Humour

A rather tired witticism goes as follows: "I let my accountant do my taxes because it saves time. Last spring it saved me ten years!"[138] The first sentence elicits a pic-

---

[132] Kant and Norman (2019), 4.
[133] See Kant and Norman (2019), 4.
[134] See Kant and Norman (2019), 4. The reader may recall the case of Baroncelli and Dworkin from Chapter 2.
[135] See Kant and Norman (2019), 4–5.
[136] See Kant and Norman (2019), 7.
[137] See Kant and Norman (2019), 7. See also Chapter 2.
[138] Willinger *et al.* (2017), 160.

ture of a busy professional who needs an accountant to do his/her taxes, while the reader recalls his/her common and, perhaps, prejudicial knowledge about the relationships between businesspeople and their accountants. A crucial cognitive "reframing" is then believed to happen when we come to the word "years" in the second sentence, insofar as this word calls for a reinterpretation of the word "time" *qua* time in prison, thereby shifting of the initial conceptual frame labelled "busy professional" into the successive conceptual frame labelled "crooked businessman".[139] (This "reframing", which clearly recalls Koestler's "bisociation", is also referred to as "blending" in contemporary psychological studies.)[140]

The understanding and the delivery of commonplace humour, not least of the cruel kind, is highly sophisticated information processing, which relies on many factors for its success, such as retrieval from long-term memory, problem-solving ability, verbal skills, abstract reasoning, overall intelligence, semantic finesse, etc.[141] Due to the emotionally-charged component of cruel humour, any discussion about the information-processing aspect of it would be incomplete without some reference to the affective sphere.[142] Both common sense and scientific studies reveal that our appreciation of humour, particularly of a risky character such as the cruel variety, is influenced by our mood. In essence, being depressed or in a bad mood will diminish our capacity to create, perceive, and/or enjoy it.[143]

In a recent psychological study by the Austrian humour specialist Ulrike Willinger and her associates, three distinctive groups were identified in connection with the comprehension of and preference for cruel humour.[144] The group that showed the most preference and comprehension of this kind of humour were those who scored highest on the intelligence tests, had higher educational levels, and showed the least amount of mood disturbance and/or aggression. The other two groups showed moderate comprehension and preference for cruel humour, had average non-verbal and verbal intelligence, but differed in terms of mood disturbance and aggressiveness. Therefore, one group measured low on these two factors, while the other had higher scores.

These findings support many previous ones regarding the notion that humour-processing depends upon cognitive as well as emotional aspects. But they also suggest that appreciation of cruel humour seems to be a complex information-processing task that requires higher-than-average intelligence. And yet, the subjects

---

139 Willinger *et al.* (2017), 160.
140 Willinger *et al.* (2017), 160.
141 See Willinger *et al.* (2017), 160.
142 See Willinger *et al.* (2017), 161.
143 See Willinger *et al.* (2017), 161.
144 See Willinger *et al.* (2017), which applies to the whole paragraph above.

who scored highest in the tests for aggressiveness were also the likeliest to dislike cruel humour:

> [O]nly those subjects who have no aggressive feelings towards others as well as no mood disturbance such as dysphoric or depressive mood can afford or get away with the playful exposure in the course of black humour processing. Another hypothesis would be that aggressiveness as well as bad mood could lead to a reduced information-processing capacity with respect to cognitively demanding humorous contents.[145]

It is important not to go overboard in the philosophical interpretation of empirical studies such as this one. By itself, no strong association was found between cruel humour-processing and verbal as well as non-verbal intellectual abilities, whereas the experimental subjects who recorded higher verbal and non-verbal intelligence scores showed the highest values with respect to cruel-humour preference and comprehension. These results, *per se*, only confirm a well-established, more general association between people's intelligence scores and their capacity for humour-processing, which obviously extends to cruel humour too.[146]

3.3 Cruel Humour and the Self

> Un giorno, ûn guærso o se ne stava a vedde
> Zûgâ ûnn-a partïa baella de ballon,
> A-o primo zêugo (cösa da no credde)
> Ghe va ûnn-a ballonâ in te l'êuggio bon
> Ch' a l'inorbì, ma lê no se sciâtò,
> E disse: Bonn-a nêutte, e o se n'andò.
> —Martin Piaggio[147]

A quick Google search will show that cruel jokes are in plentiful supply. Tens of millions of results will come up, depending on the phrasing of the question. This is hardly surprising. Cruel humour is extremely popular. To wit:

---

145 Willinger *et al.* (2017), 165.
146 See e.g., Greengross and Miller (2011).
147 As cited in Ballerini (1923), 80. [*One day went a one-eyed man to watch / a tamburelli game that was top-notch / and in the first inning (incredible affair) / a ball hits him in the eye that's fair / and makes him blind, but he showed no dismay, / and said:* Good night, *and walked away*]. In many countries around the world, local languages or so-called "dialects" are taken to convey comic effects with more aptitude than the official national language. Italy is such a country (Piaggio's dialect being Genoese).

> At 11:39 a.m., Tuesday, January 28, 1986, 73 seconds after launch, the space shuttle Challenger exploded. All seven crew members, including the first "Teacher in Space", were killed. Shocked millions witnessed the tragedy on television. Profound national grief and depression followed, reminiscent of the nation's reaction to the assassination of President Kennedy. Also paralleling the earlier tragedy was the appearance, within hours, of jokes like the following:
> What does NASA stand for? Need Another Seven Astronauts.
> How many astronauts will fit in a Volkswagen? Eleven. Two in the front, two in the back, and seven in the ashtray.[148]

This nasty text, selected from a 1994 article by US-based psychologists Herzog and Bush, may sound surprisingly cruel to us. Still, it is also a token of what we have come to expect, given the studies and remarks on cruel humour that have been reported in this book. As Herzog and Bush themselves pointed out, jokes like these proliferate after horrendous tragedies.

In particular, the two social scientists categorised cruel jokes as follows:
(1) "General",
(2) "Death",
(3) "Dead Baby", and
(4) "Handicapped".[149]

These categories differed in average preference among the chosen cohort of respondents (i.e., the standard fodder for today's social sciences: undergraduate students), with the two death-related categories having the lowest rating and the handicap-related category the highest.[150] At the same time, the jokes that were the most preferred in this sample were those that were also considered the least vulgar, the most surprising, or that had the best fit, i.e., the interplay between the punchline and its premises.[151] Interestingly, a better sense of humour was found to be positively related with a preference for cruel jokes.[152]

A further study by Herzog and Karafa introduced a distinction between, on the one hand, "sick" and "cruel humour" (aka "non-sick tendentious") and, on the other, a third, more innocent form of jokes (i.e., "non-sick non-tendentious").[153] The researchers then proceeded to examine the preference for "sick jokes" (i.e., general, death, dead baby, and handicapped) compared to "non-sick jokes" (e.g., nonsense, social satire, philosophical, sexual-hostile, demeaning to people, ethnic,

---

[148] Herzog and Bush (1994), 323.
[149] Herzog and Bush (1994), 323.
[150] Herzog and Bush (1994), 323.
[151] Herzog and Bush (1994), 323.
[152] Herzog and Bush (1994), 323.
[153] Herzog and Karafa (1998), 291.

and scatological jokes), i.e., commonplace humour that might tap into very serious yet non-sinister and/or non-tragic subjects, which is what sick humour does instead in a marked and characteristic way.[154]

"Sick" and "non-sick non-tendentious" jokes were rated as lower in preference than "non-sick tendentious", i.e., "cruel" jokes.[155] The results confirmed their earlier study, insomuch as they found that a good sense of humour was positively correlated with preference for sick and cruel jokes, but not for non-tendentious jokes. (It should be also noted that males showed more appreciation for cruel jokes than females, but the genders did not differ in preference with respect to non-sick non-tendentious ones.) In short, it can be said that we do seem to like cruel humour or, at least, so do the undergraduates that Anglophone social scientists regularly employ (or exploit?) as viable representatives of the entire human race.[156]

3.3.1 Do We Prefer Cruel Humourists?

A closely related question to "Do we prefer cruel humour?" is "Do we prefer cruel humourists?" Studies of bullying have, for example, led some authors to posit that cruel humour is one mechanism by which relationally aggressive adolescents become popular with their peers.[157] These studies are based upon the premises of peer-relation theory and research, suggesting that humour at large is an important feature of social interactions and relationships during childhood and adolescence. During these stages, all humour, not just cruel humour, can help facilitate interactions regarding selecting new friends, communicating information (e.g., about sexuality, growing-up, and peer norms), strengthening older friendships, but also showing dislike for certain peers and/or establishing relative status within the social group.[158]

Mixing humour with aggression reveals an equally complicated picture. An early study by the influential American psychologists Kenneth Dodge and Joie Coie distinguished between "reactive" and "proactive" aggression and found that, while both were related to social rejection, proactively aggressive boys were also viewed as leaders and as having a praiseworthy sense of humour.[159] In the 2010s,

---

154 Herzog and Karafa (1998), 291.
155 Herzog and Karafa (1998), 291.
156 Our Preliminary Remarks warned the reader about our quaint sense of humour and attempts at it. Here is one.
157 See e.g., Bowker and Etkin (2014).
158 See e.g., Bowker and Etkin (2014).
159 Dodge and Coie (1987), 1146.

analogous studies revealed that youngsters would bully others online because it made them feel funny, popular, and powerful.[160]

Although most of the bullying was perpetrated among friends and many indicated feeling guilty afterwards, it also demonstrated the importance of cruel humour in gaining status within the adolescent peer groups.[161] The same results, moreover, tie in neatly with the discussion of the superiority theory of humour throughout this book. So prominent is the presence of cruel humour—ranging from malicious gossip to physical pranks—that some scientists posited the "maturity gap" hypothesis, i.e., that adolescents admire aggressive and assertive behaviour because it is considered authority- and adult-defying.[162]

3.3.2 Do We Like Being Cruel to Ourselves?

Another interesting question regarding the preference for cruel humour is whether or not we have a proclivity towards being the butt of such jokes and jests. Is it possible to revel in being verbally attacked, receiving brutally unconstructive criticism, and/or suffering willingly offensive comments based on one's character and/or physical appearance? Can we really be so masochistic?

This might seem like an outlandish idea at first glance, but, as pointed out by the US-based Anna Kasunic and Geoff Kaufman, so-called "roasting" has a long history in Western comedy.[163] It can be found in the works of ancient Greek playwrights and Shakespeare, for example.[164] In the 20th century, it became common practice among clubs and organisations to hold testimonial dinners dedicated to roasting.[165] The Friars Club, founded in 1904, is known for its ceremonial dinners filled with jabs and sarcastic humour.[166]

Today, this practice has been made especially popular on the Comedy Central television network, which has broadcast roasts of celebrities like singer Justin Bieber, actor James Franco, and even former US president Donald Trump.[167] Moreover, "roasting" has moved online, most notably among the 2,200,000+ subscribers to *r/RoastMe*, a humour-focussed sub-community of the online forum *reddit.-*

---

160 See Mishna *et al.* (2010), 362.
161 See Mishna *et al.* (2010), 362.
162 See e.g., Bowker and Etkin (2014), 1323.
163 Kasunic and Kaufman (2018), 161.
164 See Kasunic and Kaufman (2018), 161.
165 See Kasunic and Kaufman (2018), 161.
166 See Kasunic and Kaufman (2018), 161.
167 See Kasunic and Kaufman (2018), 161.

com.¹⁶⁸ On this platform, people willingly post photos of themselves, offering to be the target of jokes, lampoons, and nasty comments that are, by standard norms, extremely offensive, blatantly impolite, and/or politically incorrect. Within this sub-community, alternative norms would seem to have developed and become acceptable, under the guise of comedic banter.¹⁶⁹

Nevertheless, while the postings displayed in this online community deviate from conventional social, moral, and aesthetic standards, they can also adhere strongly to context-specific norms to achieve their goals.¹⁷⁰ These norms, moreover, can be stated explicitly on these sites and/or emerge implicitly through patterns of interactions (e.g., 'likes' or downvotes).¹⁷¹ Content consistent with the community's norms is rewarded, while deviations (even those consistent with broader societal norms) are censured.¹⁷² The general directive for members of the community is "comedy, not hate", but their responses often contain racism, sexism, verbal threats, body-shaming, and homophobia.¹⁷³

Contrary to traditional roasts, where the roasters and the audience are typically friends and colleagues of the roastee, the roasters on *r/RoastMe* are anonymous strangers. As Kasunic and Kaufman pointed out, it is this peculiar blend of anonymity-*cum*-exposition and subversive-behaviours-*cum*-fixed-norms that make this online medium a fascinating and instructive milieu of study.¹⁷⁴ For one, they found that the directive of "comedy, not hate" was taken very seriously by the registered members of the online community, but in a way that could be rephrased as "original comedy, not unoriginal hate".¹⁷⁵

The members placed greatest value on creative, unique, and genuinely funny content, i.e., to post unoriginal content was one of the highest *RoastMe* offenses:

> Taboo and offensive comments are perfectly acceptable within RoastMe; being unoriginal, however, falls outside the RoastMe norms and violates RoastMe values. One participant explains that roasts that encourage suicide are not off limits, but do violate the rules if they do so in a generic, uncreative way. He explains that such roasts are unacceptable, saying, "If it's in the generic rules, like 'Kill yourself', because this is against the rules—roasts like

---

168 See Kasunic and Kaufman (2019), 162.
169 Interestingly, given the impersonal online nature of *r/RoastMe*, these norms are often less tacit than normal.
170 See Allison, Bussey, and Sweller (2019).
171 See Allison, Bussey, and Sweller (2019).
172 See Allison, Bussey, and Sweller (2019).
173 See Kasunic and Kaufman (2019), 161.
174 See Kasunic and Kaufman (2019), 161.
175 Kasunic and Kaufman (2019), 165.

that I don't think are allowed anymore. Because it's just too flatout and generic; if it was more creative then it would be allowed".[176]

Participants in the study criticised actions that, usually, would be viewed positively in other contexts, but violated r/Roast Me values. Offering direct, encouraging support to a roastee by posting something like "I hope you're okay" was frowned upon, insofar as it messed with the desired process.[177] Similarly, flattery was deemed inappropriate.[178] Many of the participants interviewed saw r/RoastMe as an outlet, a safe and unique space, where they could release built-up frustrations and give voice to taboo thoughts that they felt unable to express elsewhere.[179] This last consideration fits well within the standard relief theory of humour and with the Jungian reflections about the psyche's shadow that were introduced in Chapter 1.

The benefits of being the recipient of such a tirade of anonymous online vitriol may be foreign to many of our readers. Some may find such a masochistic penchant denigrating, not only at an individual level, but also in terms of ethnic groups, religious creeds, genders, sexual orientations, political affiliations, and/or cultural traditions that they believe themselves to embody, represent, and/or defend at a public level. Willingly offering yourself up for this abuse, however, might be a signal that no matter what people can come up with, you can 'take' it.

Similarly, many people are in the habit of making demeaning jokes about themselves, possibly to appear funny, but also as a way of disarming potential jokers—as Seneca observed centuries ago.[180] The participants in the r/Roast Me community speak of "skin-thickening", or:

> It just makes life so much better because even when somebody now insults you in the real world, you can laugh at it. Even though everyone's trying to tear each other down, there's still a feeling you came out as ... almost a newer version of yourself. You have this newfound respect for yourself, and thicker skin.[181]

Since our self-image is highly dependent on how others perceive us, an alternative reason for subjecting oneself to such cruel feats of public humiliation could be to get a ruthlessly honest opinion from online abusers about one's own appearance.

---

176 Kasunic and Kaufman (2019), 165.
177 Kasunic and Kaufman (2019), 165.
178 See Kasunic and Kaufman (2019), 165.
179 See Kasunic and Kaufman (2019), 165.
180 See Chapter 1.
181 Kasunic and Kaufman (2019), 167.

Granted, even though the comments are purposely mean and brutal and the remarks might not even be truthful at all, this seems to be a rationale for some of the interviewed roastees, i.e., a key reason for posting their pictures online is to "find insights into themselves" from anonymous strangers and learning ways in which they might improve.[182] On their looks, primarily. As reported, various interviewees admit to having changed their hairstyle, make-up, and clothing as a result of the corrosive feedback that they endured online.[183] Amir's horizons of wisdom and self-acceptance by way of humorous aggression, which we discussed in Chapter 2, are clearly of a very different nature.[184]

3.3.3 Do We Even Like Ourselves?

Another thought-provoking line of questioning into why we may find cruel humour alluring comes from a recent study by the US-based psychologist Emma O'Connor and her associates.[185] In accordance with popular belief, they proposed that men scoring higher in precarious manhood beliefs (PMB) expressed greater amusement with sexist and anti-gay humour, but not other forms of cruel humour, in response to the challenge to reaffirm their masculinity.[186] The theory of precarious manhood theory suggests that men differ in the degree to which they hold PMB, i.e., they differ in sensitivity and responsiveness to masculinity threats. Among those men who score higher in PMB, threats to masculinity provoke greater gender-based anxiety.[187]

Men who score higher in PMB are more likely to respond in ways that defend and/or restore their threatened masculinity.[188] Insofar as women and gay men symbolise femininity, i.e., the antithesis of masculinity, expressing disdain and/or negative prejudice against these groups allows men with high PMB to distance themselves from what they see as emasculating traits. Humorous discrimination against women and gay men, not least by means of cruel humour, can therefore

---

[182] Kasunic and Kaufman (2019), 167.
[183] See Kasunic and Kaufman (2019), 167.
[184] As we indicated in that chapter, Amir's humorous path for self-acceptance is culturally sophisticated and inevitably selective, for not all human beings are equally equipped with the necessary patience, interest and skill.
[185] See O'Connor et al. (2017).
[186] See O'Connor et al. (2017), 567.
[187] See O'Connor et al. (2017), 568.
[188] See O'Connor et al. (2017), 568.

function as a way of protecting and reaffirming a fragile masculinity, which the insecure individuals are clearly struggling with and pained by.[189]

Unsurprisingly, O'Connor *et al.* found a significant positive relationship between PMB and amusement following a masculinity threat that was unique to cruel humour, primarily in the shape of sexist and homophobic jokes.[190] This did not emerge for other cruel jokes that were used as control, e.g., anti-Muslim and neutral humour.[191] Furthermore, the researchers found that, following a masculinity threat, men higher in PMB expressed amusement with sexist and anti-gay humour because they believed it would reaffirm their masculinity.[192]

3.3.4 "I'm Only Joking!"

Humour, when performed in public, is inevitably an exploration into the mind of the audience. The joker bends the rules of conversation and perceptions of reality, striving to lure the audience into a shared fantasy world. Or into an utterly and ultimately nonsensical one, as Deleuze and Kozintsev would suggest.[193] This is quite a task, made even more difficult when it is not just the faculty of reason that is being put to the test in the audience, but also their moral fibre or aesthetic sense, as *per* standard instances of cruel humour.

We have been flooded by reports of *gaffes* from people in the public arena, perhaps also within our own family and work environments. As Baroncelli's own work openly suggested, "racism" itself can be argued to be "a gaffe", whether only or on top of other negative connotations.[194] If a cruel joke falls flat and offends more than it amuses, the humiliated joker frequently latches on to a response that the contemporary American psychologist A. Michael Johnson aptly named the "I'm only joking" defence.[195] The *Urban Dictionary* contains a distinctive definition of this type of cruel joker – "Schrödinger's Douchebag", i.e., "[a] guy who says offensive things and decides whether he was joking based on the reaction of people around him".[196]

---

[189] See O'Connor *et al.* (2017), 568.
[190] See O'Connor *et al.* (2017), 567.
[191] See O'Connor *et al.* (2017), 567.
[192] See O'Connor *et al.* (2017), 567.
[193] See Chapter 1.
[194] Baroncelli (1996), title. Needless to say, his book explores the many ways in which racism can occur.
[195] Johnson (1990), 1051.
[196] Obviously, this definition is morally biased against the "I'm only joking" defence.

The 2022 Oscars presentation provides a brutal current example of this humour gone wrong when Chris Rock, the renowned American stand-up comedian and actor, lampooned the baldness of Oscar-winner Will Smith's wife, Jada Pinkett Smith, who suffers from a disease involving hair loss. It cost Rock a slap in the face and some obscenity-laden abuse from the aggrieved husband.[197]

On a more deliberate note which our discussion of Harvey's views anticipated in Chapter 2, empirical studies indicate that most of these jokers vehemently deny that their remarks reflect their true attitudes, whereas those whom they have offended insist that the opposite is the case.[198] According to Johnson's reasoning, this difference between the joker's and audience's perceptions can be explained by using the framework of bias in attribution, i. e., how we view our own motivations and those of others.[199] Under such premises, the feckless joker can be said to be fixated on situational variables, such as the resolve to amuse the audience, while the listeners are focussed on the joker and internal, attitudinal, motivational, and/or personality-related factors.[200] In other words, audience members are often only marginally aware of the joker's intention to make them laugh, and so are more likely to attribute the offensive content of the joke to the joker's mind and character, including his/her fondness for cruelty.[201]

For the attributional account to make sense, the "only joking" defence must be based on the jokers' truthful accounts. It is just as plausible that these jokers are lying to save themselves from embarrassment, prosecution, or worse. Studies from the 1970s suggested that this apologia is used when a joke evokes unintended negative responses.[202] The same studies also hypothesised that cruel joking provides people with a medium for expressing risky attitudes in a conventional social context.[203] In other words, this excuse gives the joker a backdoor through which s/he can escape if the audience responds negatively to a possibly daring consideration cast in humorous terms. Another study from that era argued that, in addition to managing social probing and self-disclosure, the option of "taking back" a joke allowed the joker to save face and retain his/her reputation.[204]

Johnson later tested these views on the "only joking" defence:

---

[197] The incident should be recent enough not to require a specific source.
[198] See Johnson (1990), 1051.
[199] See Johnson (1990), 1051.
[200] See Johnson (1990), 1051.
[201] See Johnson (1990), 1051.
[202] As reported in Johnson (1990), 1051.
[203] As reported in Johnson (1990), 1051.
[204] As reported in Johnson (1990), 1051.

Subjects were college students (92 men and 43 women) who participated for course credit. Each subject completed one of two versions of a brief questionnaire. These questionnaires varied in one respect. One, the "self-attribution" version, began with the question, "When you tell jokes which might be perceived as mocking, hostile, or insensitive to the feelings of members of specific groups (e.g., African Americans, women, Polacks, Catholics, etc.), the jokes are representative of your attitudes toward those groups". In the "other-attribution" version this question was modified to read, "When people tell jokes ... the jokes are representative of the teller's attitudes...". The question, "When people laugh at jokes like those described in the first item, their laughter reflects acceptance of or agreement with the attitude expressed by the jokes", appeared in both versions of the questionnaire. This question was included to determine whether the self vs other manipulation generally sensitized subjects to the relation of offensive humor and attitudes. Hence, it is referred to as the "other-amusement" question. Subjects rated these questions on seven-point Likert scales with the following descriptors attached to the scale values: never (1), rarely (2), occasionally (3), half of the time (4), often (5), usually (6), and always (7). Subjects also reported their sex. Questionnaires were completed privately and no identifying information was recorded.[205]

The results of the experiment suggested that 'misfiring' people were indeed inclined to believe that their own jokes did not usually reflect their attitudes, even when other people were offended.[206] As surprising as it may sound to some of our readers, especially in light of the cruel humour that has been covered in these pages, *jokers are often sincere when claiming that they were only joking.*

In contrast, people were inclined to attribute consistency of attitude to other individuals' cruel jokes about half of the time.[207] Somewhat unsurprisingly, we are much more forgiving when we must forgive ourselves. This is a tremendous gulf, typical of attribution bias, and no doubt a significant source of conflict between jokers and audiences. Life's cruel irony crosses this chasm too, while plunging people straight into it.[208]

Since jokers do not believe that their cruel jokes are congruent with their attitudes, this raises another important question, particularly for psychologists. Why do people tell cruel jokes if they do not reflect their attitudes? And, relatedly, why do they do so, when there can be considerable attendant risks? In his study, Johnson offered three explanations.[209]

(1) One is that people who are insensitive to others or poor at predicting other people's reactions would be more likely to create such unintended offense.

---

[205] Johnson (1990), 1052–1053.
[206] Johnson (1990), 1054.
[207] Johnson (1990), 1054.
[208] Once again, the hermeneutical divergences and challenges discussed in Chapter 2 have duly resurfaced.
[209] Johnson (1990), 1055, which applies to the whole paragraph above.

(2) Another is that these people regularly or occasionally misread social cues and tell cruel jokes with the expectation that these will be in line with their audiences' attitudes, if not with their own. Poor readers of social cues would therefore be more likely to make blunders and then claim honestly that they were only joking.
(3) Third, which is more Freudian in nature, such a line of joking represents an avenue for the expression of cruel motives that are too threatening, shocking, or embarrassing to express directly in public or even to acknowledge consciously in private. The "only joking" defence might therefore be a classical defence mechanism that prevents awareness of anxiety-producing motives, while simultaneously allowing their indirect and disguised expression.

Along a Jungian line of interpretation, especially as *per* our reflections in Chapters 1 and 2, we should add that cruel humour could be interpreted as an avenue for letting our shadow 'breathe', i.e., to strive towards a healthier psychic balance, and whether such a type of commonplace humour is directed at others or at oneself.[210]

3.3.5 The Cruelty of Self-Deprecation

Given the evidence presented thus far, it seems almost obvious that people enjoy seeing others ridiculed. We also find people who seem to enjoy ridiculing themselves.[211] These individuals deliberately exhibit, often in exaggerated and comical forms, their own weaknesses and vices together with scores of embarrassments, humiliations, pains, and setbacks that they may have encountered in real life or even fabricated altogether. Somehow, in more or less creative ways, they all can be humorously cruel to themselves, as also discussed in Chapter 2.

3.3.5.1 General Considerations
Apparently, many people view such humorous self-disparagement as beneficial. Moreover, according to much empirical research, many of us hold it as true that

---

[210] This fourth explanation is ours, not Johnson's. More on this point is said in *H&C3*.
[211] See Stocking and Zillmann (1976), 455–456, which applies to the paragraph above and the ensuing two. Interestingly, the Nordic humour specialist Lita Sander Lundquist (2020) claimed self-deprecating humour aka self-irony [*selvironi*] to be the main characteristic of Danish humour. Icelanders, for their part, would seem to prefer joking about the Danes rather than themselves, as far as we can assess from our Nordic vantage point.

people who acknowledge their own shortcomings and are willing to display them in a light-hearted manner have a genuine sense of humour. In prosaic conversations, this attitude is contrasted with that of people who cannot laugh at their own expense and take themselves far too seriously.[212]

It is commonly believed that people who can poke fun at themselves are more self-confident. In contrast to those individuals who dare not display their deficiencies, the former type of people is presumed to be strong enough to display their vulnerability. Many also seem to believe it funnier to see people poke fun at themselves than to ridicule others. One would therefore expect the person who disparages herself to be perceived more positively than the individual who belittles a friend or an enemy; the character of the self-disparager is usually evaluated as funnier than that of the person disparaging others.[213]

Nevertheless, making fun of yourself could be counter-intuitive, at least insofar as it runs against much traditional Western wisdom, both popular and learned, emphasising the importance of appearing in a positive light to others and oneself.[214] Despite its frequent use, comic self-flagellation has not received much attention, although it has featured in the writings of Freud, especially in his discussions about Jewish humour. Analogously, as we alluded to in our discussion of Harlow's study of humour, the use of self-deprecating humour could be seen as a defence mechanism. By constantly and publicly putting ourselves down in a comical way, we leave very little room for others to do the same. Self-deprecation is a way to disarm the enemy.[215]

3.3.5.2 Two Specific Studies

An interesting study of whether cruel humour is directed primarily towards the self or others was conducted in the 1970s by two American psychologists, S.H. Stocking and Dolf Zillmann, who employed the already-conventional compliant cohort of college undergraduates.[216] The researchers first created humorous stories

---

212 Finding the correct level of 'seriousness', whatever this idea actually becomes in lived reality, is hard.
213 At a deeper level, such expectations reveal significant features of the socio-cultural context at issue. For one, the so-called "mother of psychoanalysis", Karen Horney (1950, 106), had already commented on "humor" *qua* "last face-saving device", which "is used to take the sting out of an otherwise unbearable shame".
214 See Kim (2014), 82.
215 Following Deleuze's insights, which we tackled in Chapter 1, such a strategy could be dubbed "masochistic".
216 See Stocking and Zillmann (1976), 455–458, which applies to the paragraph above and the ensuing two.

involving a variety of situations in which a male college student attempted something, but screwed it up and made a fool of himself. Three different versions of the stories were created: self-disparaging, friend-disparaging, and enemy-disparaging. In the self-disparaging version, the blunderer was the student himself, i.e., he was told to make fun of himself. In the friend-disparaging version, he was a roommate whom the student liked very much. In the enemy-disparaging version, he was a roommate that the student hated. The participants were then asked to evaluate the perceived funniness of the stories.[217]

Contrary to widely held beliefs, Stocking and Zilmann found that humorous self-disparagement not only failed to enhance the disparager's self-worth, but also was decisively detrimental to it. Both male and female participants tended to perceive the self-disparager as less confident than the individual who disparaged a friend, and as less confident than the person who disparaged an enemy. Both sexes also saw the self-disparager as significantly less witty than the individual who disparaged either a friend or an enemy, and as significantly less intelligent than the individual who, ungallantly, put down a friend.

As the authors cited above noted, this does not mean that humorous self-disparagement is always detrimental. In certain situations, it can be beneficial. For example, when a humiliation cannot possibly be concealed, a little humorous self-disparagement may do minimal damage and may, in fact, serve to deflect or supersede disparagement by others. It is also conceivable that a moderate amount of humorous self-disparagement may enhance the appeal of a highly regarded individual by bringing him/her to a more 'human' level. However, the actual evidence from this study suggests that *humorous self-disparagement constitutes genuine self-debasement.*

An additional in-depth analysis of self-deprecation can be found in a recent article by the Korean humour specialist Myung-Hee Kim, who approached this issue from three different perspectives: dispositional, situational, and interactional.[218]

(1) From a psychological point of view, the dispositional angle is a clear favourite, for it describes self-mockery—however cruel this may be—*qua* stable and stabilising individual personality trait, which is implicitly cast against the largely ungraspable background of the tacit cultural norms that apply to each individual case. Under some circumstances, however, such an attitude may reinforce broader

---

[217] Whether there can exist any intrinsic funniness, it is a problem that we are not able to solve.
[218] Kim (2014), which applies to the rest of the subsection.

conditions of social subordination that cannot contribute to an individual's sense of self-worth and wellbeing, e.g., among members of oppressed minorities.[219]

(2) Self-deprecation can also be seen as situational:

> Personality and individual differences aside, most of us display humility or show self-deprecation in some situations but not in others. Situational factors such as the relative status of individuals, degrees of intimacy, presence or absence of evaluation concerns, prior interpersonal experience, and different social settings might affect the use of humility in some specific contexts. Many languages including Korean and Japanese have an honorific system built into the language to show respect to the addressee or to humble oneself. In these languages, the speakers should assess the situation constantly to determine whether they should use honorifics.[220]

(3) Last but not least, there is the interactional aspect to self-deprecation. Contrary to the dispositional view, self-deprecation can, under certain circumstances, be a method of achieving a variety of communicative goals, i.e., it is a way for the joker to 'level with' the audience and become of 'one mind' with them.[221] Once again, however, this attitude may be consistent with the reinforcement of wider structures of discrimination and subjugation, as also discussed in Chapter 2 in connection with Harvey's critical assessment of humour *qua* means of "civilized oppression", in which both the oppressor and the oppressed play their part.[222]

3.4 Humorous Oppression

The relations between gender, humour and cruelty make for an especially interesting topic, which our discussion of Harvey's views in Chapter 2 has already previewed. On such relations, the contemporary German linguist Helga Kotthoff wrote:

> In Western societies there are various signs of change in the gender politics of humor. The traditional incompatibility between displaying femininity and active, and, in particular, aggressive joking is declining. This does not mean that gender is no longer a relevant category for humorous activities, but rather that the relevance of gender differs from context to con-

---

[219] As noted in Chapter 2, Harvey (1999) also criticised the victims of cruel humour for their complicity in it.
[220] Kim (2014), 83.
[221] Kim (2014), 83.
[222] Harvey (1999), title.

text. The simplistic model of the actively joking man and the receptively smiling woman has lost ground.[223]

Throughout Western history, women were often the objects, but rarely the subjects, of recorded jokes. The prolonged lack of female representation in high comedy, mass-media comedy, scholarly exchanges, and reported everyday banter has been more than glaring. Until recently, female humourists were almost completely absent from literary anthologies, and so were female caricaturists and cartoonists from mainstream exhibitions and editorial outlets. Kotthoff, moreover, related this female absence to a more general marginalisation of humour inside high culture.

As discussed in Chapter 1, in the period from the Renaissance through the Enlightenment, the educated elites identified themselves as a polite and socially refined class capable of disciplining thoroughly their social bodies and ranking clearly their public values.[224] Among the latter there transpired a deep desire to control women's bodies, minds, and fates, which extended to rejecting laughter's grimaces as contrary to 'proper' femininity, which required women to be beautiful, modest, decent, and quiet. Similarly related to this marginalisation of female humour was norm-violation, which underlies, in all likelihood, all forms of commonplace humour, insofar as some norm-breaking duality must be established for most if not all forms of humour to occur, whether logical, semantic, ethical, aesthetic, phonetic, etc.

Humorous communication plays an important role in the production of normality and normativity. However, as Kotthoff argued, it is equally true that it can create unconventional perspectives, whence there may arise 'subversive' longings for independence, creative power, and the freedom to take part in the affairs of the world.[225] The West's long-lived patriarchy was never susceptible to giving such norm-defining powers over to women, who had to struggle for and eventually win these powers, to a noticeable extent, in the course of the 19th and, above all, the 20th century.[226]

---

[223] Kotthoff (2006), 4, which applies to the ensuing paragraph as well.
[224] Kotthoff (2006), 4, which applies to the whole paragraph above.
[225] Kotthoff (2006), 5, which applies to the whole paragraph above.
[226] This battle continues in our century in many parts of the world, especially in the Middle East. However, as far as today's Western societies are concerned, the noted American feminist thinker Laura Kipnis (2018, pars. 6–8) stated that, despite some patriarchal vestiges, "women have power aplenty" to the point of being able to "wreck a guy's career with a tweet!" In other words, they can use cruel humour to destroy a man's reputation and/or livelihood.

3.4.1 Gender and Hierarchies

Social scientists have long explored the power dynamics of humorous communication. As the German-born sociologist Rose Laub Coser observed in her 1960 paper, "Laughter Among Colleagues", anyone who makes other people laugh has control, however fleeting and minimal, of the social situation.[227] Through the use of humour, a person can redefine a situation and redirect people's attention to the point of affirming or re-affirming one's dominance in the hierarchical social structure—or of challenging the established one, as Kotthoff also suggested.[228]

Coser's seminal study revealed indirect relationships between humour and gender, although this was not her primary goal.[229] Her study, performed in the late 1950s by using tape recordings of 20 faculty meetings at an American university psychiatric clinic, is a trophy of empirical documentation on the use of humour in the Western workplace, i.e., a juicy locus for the study of status and gender. The declared aim of Coser's study, incidentally, was to determine the role of humour in reinforcing group cohesion and the efficient maintenance of pre-existing social structures.[230]

Based on her data, Coser concluded that people at the top of the hierarchical social structure are freer to define social situations as well as steer conversations, especially from the instrumental level to the affective realm of group entertainment. The act of taking the initiative and having a group of people withdraw their attention from the topic under discussion is a daring and, frequently, aggressive one. Coser, in a quintessentially Freudian mode of thinking, claimed that humour always carried with it some aggression, whether or not it was overtly directed against a manifest target.[231]

In their use of commonplace humour, Coser's senior medical staff frequently targeted their junior colleagues. They, in turn, aimed their humorous comments at patients or their relatives, as well as at themselves. In essence, social hierarchy

---

[227] As cited in Kotthoff (2006), 8, which applies to the whole paragraph above.
[228] How far the challenge can go and be effective in the broader social sphere is a big question mark. As we noted already in *H&C1*, no government has ever abdicated its power because of sheer political satire, popular jokes, pasquinades, TV parodies, etc. Revolutions, to effect change, need barricades and bayonets, more often than not.
[229] Kotthoff (2006), 8–9, which applies to the whole paragraph above and the ensuing four.
[230] Cast in 'neutral' socio-scientific language, Kotthoff (2006) suggested that Coser was critical of these structures.
[231] Freud's enduring influence loomed large in the American social sciences of the 1950s and 1960s.

was closely reflected in the frequency of the staff's humour as well as in its chosen targets. In Coser's study, a junior member never made a joke about a senior staff member. Similarly, women seldom told jokes, since any show of aggression, whether open or thinly disguised, would come across as a challenge directed at their male colleagues.[232]

Coser observed that some of the female professors had a sharp sense of humour, told good jokes, made comic remarks, and enjoyed persiflage in more informal situations. However, in the formal setting of a staff meeting, these women hardly ever expressed their sense of humour, insofar as the pertinent socio-cultural expectations called for them to be adequately passive. As a result, even women in high-status positions were often seen as lacking humour.

Kotthoff's take on Coser's study also suggests that traditional female forms of joking are at one's own cost, while the traditional male forms are at other people's expense. Both kinds, in the end, would tend to be disadvantageous for the women of professional status at the psychiatric clinic. One must therefore be cautious about generalising the results of Coser's studies. Women of working-class status or professional females in different educational settings may well have exhibited different trends and traits.

In the end, Coser's studies gave weight to the socialising potential of commonplace humour, including cruel humour. Interestingly, many of the jokes that were made at the staff meetings dealt with inconsistencies in personal values or cultural norms.[233] The senior staff actively used humour to defuse such potential and/or actual conflicts by showing, in a humorous manner, how easily they could be solved. This strategy, however, was not equally available to every member of the group.

Subordinates would thus elicit sympathy by expressing their own role in conflicts. On the contrary, male seniors would take on the parental role of moralist-in-disguise and offer professional advice *via* joke-telling and other humorous expressions—including abrasive ones, at times. Given its constitutive duality, Coser saw humour as particularly well-suited for these tasks of teaching and correction, insofar as it fused together criticism with support, and rejection with acceptance.

---

232 Ironically, in line with Deleuze's understanding of "humour" proper as masochism, humourlessness may have been the humorous way by which individuals in subordinate hierarchical standings got what they really wanted.
233 Kotthoff (2006), 10–11, which applies to the whole paragraph above and the ensuing one.

3.4.2 Gender and Sex

Sex is ever-present in garden-variety humour. Historically, a large share of sexually explicit jokes has made fun of women.[234] However, the gradual and substantial affirmation of women's rights in the West during the 20th century has already produced radical changes in the acceptable and accepted standards for practical and verbal jokes, at least in the public domain of many developed countries. All such changes have been studied by numerous social scientists, health specialists, and humanists, who have consistently recorded how, in Western countries, more and more jokes have come to be increasingly at the expense of male targets while women have also become more and more visible in the comic sphere.

As we saw in Chapter 1, sex was a dominant theme in Schopenhauer's and Freud's theories. We also saw that the latter thinker's analyses, while insightful, were heavily influenced by the misogynist spirit of his times. According to Freud, the origin of sexual jokes is a social situation in which a woman frustrates a man's sexual overtures. The woman, by her mere presence, arouses a male's sexual desire to begin with, but then leaves it unsatisfied, more often than not. The aroused male then resorts to a ribald joke as an outlet for his frustration towards the woman. In particular, by exploiting sexual jokes, Freud claimed that the joker teams up with his male listener/s against some present or absent woman, and by telling or listening to the joke, both males sublimate their frustrated sexual urges.

In her work, Kotthoff emphasised that Freud maintained that commonplace humour *qua* form of sexual aggression was foreign to women, making all his analyses of humorous conduct decidedly male-oriented.[235] Also, while Freud stressed the passive role of the female, his writings showed a clear understanding of the narrow line that existed between ordinary sexual humour, flirting, seduction, and harassment. Tellingly, even in the more egalitarian Western workplaces surveyed by Kotthoff and other contemporary social scientists, it regularly results that, for one, older workers cultivate more often a joking style towards younger colleagues that is brim-full with sexual allusions—after all, older colleagues do not normally engage in games of actual courtship. For another, it regularly transpires that male employees use sexual humour in their conversations with female ones more often than the other way around.[236]

When it comes to sexual humour, the boundaries between acceptable behaviour and outright harassment have, historically, been fluid. This has become crys-

---

[234] Kotthoff (2006), 16, which applies to the whole paragraph above.
[235] Kotthoff (2006), 16–17, which applies to the whole paragraph above and the ensuing two.
[236] Whether such trends are pure socio-cultural constructs or reveal underlying biological drives is not known.

tal-clear in the past few decades, when more and more women have publicly come forward and described their experiences of sexual violence. Sexual molestation, as reported, may plausibly be dressed up as commonplace humour, which thereby becomes cruel humour. However, the harasser can still try to take refuge in the notion that "it was not meant that way".

As to when exactly this sort of lewd humour becomes or may legitimately be interpreted as harassment, it is no simple matter to assess, and countless courts of law, ethical committees, and boards of directors have experienced this complexity first hand. Life's cruelty flourishes in grey areas. If anything, the transformation of lewd humour into harassment frequently ends up being something that corporate bosses, expert panels, and trained judges must evaluate in each specific circumstance, following complaints and accusations, trying to gauge people's inner motives and whatever may plausibly lie behind the inherently ambiguous character of humorous language.[237]

Sexual humour, however, even when cruelly presented, can have beneficial implications too. For young gay men, for example, it has been observed that having free-wheeling randy conversations with their friends is a crucial source of information about their own sexuality, and it is also a key vehicle for sharing sexual health norms, e.g., calling someone else a "slut" or a "whore" for having sex without condoms.[238] Seemingly cruel, dramatic, and judgemental language, when used in communication between young gay men, can also be an integral part of the interpersonal bonding that generates a reassuring sense of shared culture and connectedness, which even crude terms such as "faggot" or "bitch" can establish.[239] Used by a heterosexual stranger, though, these terms would be unflinchingly interpreted as cruel homophobic slurs, whatever the actual intentions may be.[240]

3.4.3 Here's a Funny Joke about Rape!

Stand-up comedy has been a very popular form of entertainment over many decades. The content and the style vary greatly between different artists, but, as we noted in Chapter 2, audiences have frequently shown a preference for those comedians who explore the boundaries between what is funny and what is cruel. Their style is often seen as 'edgy', implying that they are unstopped by

---

[237] See also Farrell (1993) on the cruelly ambiguous social aspects surrounding this thorny matter.
[238] McDavitt and Mutchler (2014), 464.
[239] McDavitt and Mutchler (2014), 486.
[240] See McDavitt and Mutchler (2014), 486.

fear of repercussion, willing to 'speak truth to power', and eager to take on 'the establishment', or even go against the 'sheep mentality' of the masses.[241] As fabled comedian Lenny Bruce quipped: "I'm not a comedian. And I'm not sick. The world is sick and I'm the doctor. I'm a surgeon with a scalpel for false values."[242]

This is, at least, the picture painted by these comedians, their agents and fans. Another line of interpretation, instead, would suggest that they are just trying to get a laugh by being mean. Perhaps there is some truth to this dismal assessment of their *modus operandi*. Indeed, 2012 was infamously called "Year of the Rape Joke" by the American website *The Daily Beast*.[243] This moniker was chosen because of a notorious scandal during a stand-up act by comedian Daniel Tosh at the "Hollywood Laugh Factory".

The exact details of the story remain unknown, but it is believed that Tosh declared something to the effect of, "Rape jokes are always funny." An outraged woman in the audience heckled the comedian and voiced her disagreement. Tosh responded, much to the amusement of his audience at the time: "Wouldn't it be funny if that girl got raped by like, 5 guys right now? Like right now? What if a bunch of guys just raped her?" The woman fled the establishment, but later described her experience on her the social media Tumblr: "Even if the actual scenario was unlikely to take place … the suggestion of it was violent enough and was meant to put me in my place." The scandal went viral, and defenders of the comedian found themselves far outnumbered by the furious attackers.

Tosh's gang-rape shocking *gaffe* is significantly different from the usual stand-up routines, which may touch on rape as a topic.[244] The target, in this case, was a real person, not some hypothetical or fictional individual conjured up by the comedian. Yet, despite this difference, this *faux pas* cannot be entirely separated from other stand-up experiences and can serve to flag the risks incurred by such jokes in comedy clubs, or elsewhere. We recall that the audience reportedly laughed at Tosh's repartee, indicating that they interpreted his aggressive words in a light way. Or, at least, that they enjoyed them.

This anecdote reveals, among other things, the powers of persuasion that rhetorically competent comics wield under the guise of commonplace humour in the rather unique circumstances of a theatrical performance. This power dynamic, however, cannot be isolated and severed *in toto* from our culture's heritage on aggression, roaring triumph, and regressive attitudes about rape: "laughing at a rape joke in a comedy club cannot be divorced from the broader social practice of

---

241 See "The Dark Psychology" (2014).
242 As cited in Weems (2014), ix–x.
243 Cox (2015), 963, which applies to the whole paragraph above and the ensuing one.
244 See Cox (2015), 971–972, which applies to the whole paragraph above and the following one.

downplaying a real-life survivor's experience of violation". In the aftermath, a still-intriguing question was raised by many pundits, including stand-up comedians, academic feminists, and social scientists: Can a rape joke ever be funny?

The Paris-based cultural theorist Lara Cox provided a detailed analysis of 21st-century rape jokes, which have a very long history, as we noted in the preceding chapters. She reviewed the variety as well as the consistencies that can be found in the comic works of well-established contemporary American comedians such as George Carlin and Louis C.K.[245]

(1) On the one hand, she recognised how the latter's posturing differs from Carlin's overt verbal aggressions and vitriolic tirades against assertive women and/or feminism, exhibiting a docile and sensitive masculinity that has had the opportunity to flourish with the rise and widespread affirmation of women's rights.

(2) On the other hand, inasmuch as rape persists as a topic that can be treated humorously, despite its patent cruelty in lived reality, both lines of comedy are shown to insist on trite clichés, e.g., raping old, ugly women as being less severe than raping beautiful, young ones, and women secretly wanting to be raped.[246]

(3) Plus, we should be aware of some well-known cultural vestiges of patriarchy in today's Western mentalities, as expressed in outright prejudice, of course, but also humorously: the inevitability of male triumph; women's oversensitivity; and the notoriously humourlessness of females, especially those who openly advocate feminism.[247]

3.4.4 Women's Own Cruel Humour

As we discussed in Chapter 2, the West's comic talent pool has diversified enormously over the past two decades, giving rise to a flurry of women-authored rape jokes.[248] In particular, Cox focussed on the comedic acts by the American Sarah Silverman, who has used commonplace humour, not least of the cruel sort, in order to highlight situational ironies involving rape victims and, concomitantly, the hypocrisy of a culture that views rape as a serious crime while laughing at it in certain settings: "We need more rape jokes ... Needless to say: rape, the most heinous crime imaginable. Seems it's a comic's dream, though, because ...

---

[245] See Cox (2015), 965–970, which applies to the whole paragraph above and the numbered list.
[246] See Murray S. Davis (1999, 245) on "clichés" proper as spent "engines" of imaginative insight.
[247] See also Streeten (2020) on the third trite cliché.
[248] See Cox (2015), 965 and 974–976, which applies to the first two paragraphs of the subsection.

the material is so dangerous and edgy... The truth is ... it's the safest area in comedy ... 'cause who's gonna complain ... about a rape joke? Rape victims? They don't even report rape!"

Insofar as Silverman was making light of rape and may thereby come across as comical rather than tragic, she put her audiences in what Michelle Bemiller and Rachel Zimmer Schneider—whom Cox duly quoted—dub a "double bind" affecting women and, we should add, rape victims at large.[249] When confronted with a rape joke, which is a patent token of cruel humour, audiences are left with two main options: laughing or expressing dismay. If a woman or a rape victim laughs, s/he can be deemed complicit in the humiliation of his/her own particular social group with whom s/he may identify powerfully, at least in public. If s/he does not laugh, s/he can be seen as a killjoy. In either case s/he is likely to be effectively subordinated in the specific pragmatic setting.[250]

Then again, the American English specialist and feminist activist Carol Ann Mitchell argued that a constructive purpose can be found for rape jokes, i.e., they should ease people's fear of being raped, women *in primis*.[251] As we debate in *H&C3*, this sentiment aligns with our conclusions on the dual function of cruel humour at large, which can devalue in the most terrifying ways, but also offer unexpected and perhaps puzzling consolation, especially under brutal circumstances.

Given the importance of humour in our lives, it comes as no surprise that comic attacks have taken on a ritualistic form in various cultures.[252] In a true 'Bergsonian' fashion, many societies allow or even encourage teasing at the expense of others to effectively pressure these "others" to conform, e.g., by publicly exposing their supposed deficiencies or condemning the abuses for which they are held responsible. While it is generally considered impolite in most societies to humiliate others openly and directly, indirect entertaining jabs enjoy more leeway, for they provide subtle ways for circumventing social rules of courtesy and moral conduct, while also eliciting arousal and, hopefully, pursue socially constructive aims.

As we further observed in Chapter 2, these attacks are hard for the target/s to respond to, since the humorous assault carries with it the convenient excuse that it

---

249 See Bemiller and Zimmer Schneider (2010).
250 Largely ignored in the extant literature, the cruel plight of male victims of rape should also be mentioned, instead, in this book.
251 She too is mentioned in the survey of pioneering 1970s studies that Cox (2015) covers in her work.
252 See Kotthoff (2006), 13–15, applicable to the subsection's remainder. See Carlson (1991) on high-brow cases.

should not be taken seriously—or not 'too' seriously at least, wherever this elusive and decisive tacit threshold may be found. Whether in the form of teasing, mocking, gossiping, parodying, or ridiculing, such attacks are highly gender-specific, as well as responsive to more individual features, such as personal taste, disposition, mood, and intelligence on sensitive topics—all of which can vary enormously depending on the involved individuals.[253]

However marginalised in the public sphere, women have engaged in all such forms of cruel humour in more private group settings, replicating many issues of hierarchy and identity-formation that were addressed in the previous pages. Age, status, ethnicity, religious affiliation, exterior look, quirks, and the infinite variety of factors that can facilitate disparagement and denigration have all had a role to play.[254]

In one of history's subtle ironies, the traditional social construction of Western femininity has regularly included and promoted gender-specific attributes such as maternal warmth, conjugal caring, unconditional love, pious compassion, polite neighbourliness, and active cooperation. Therefore, it comes as no surprise that many studies of joking conducted among Western women show that commonplace humour was used to display commonalities, enhance equality, and foster group ties, intimacy, and familiarity. Joking at one's own expense was also recorded as important, which reduced the threat of aggression and facilitated peer relations.

Whereas men were far more likely to use hostile humour, women appeared to enjoy the inherently absurd elements of jokes in a more pronounced way. Absurd humour, *prima facie*, threatens no one. With deeper scrutiny, however, it too can be a source of painful embarrassment insofar as some individuals may be unable to grasp such pleasantry, which causes them to be labelled, or to self-label, as "thick", "stupid", "simple", "dour", or "lacking a sense of humour". This matter is the topic of the next subsection.

3.4.5 Embarrassment

Every time people come together, they bring the baggage of their previously defined identities and familiarity with the roles they are expected to play in their so-

---

[253] The point above should remind the reader that, as argued decades ago by the American psychologist Lawrence Kohlberg (1984), *not all individuals develop a moral conscience*, whether fully or partially, as still widely acknowledged and studied in the social and medical sciences all over the world (see, e.g., Bidaki *et al.* 2022). Perhaps, our readers succeeded in this development. Perhaps not. They might even be narcissists or sociopaths.

[254] Social scientists can therefore amuse themselves by exploring all such social factors.

cial interactions, including gender-related ones. In the communication that ensues, individuals will negotiate, both implicitly and explicitly, the roles and the rules applicable to the particular encounter and to which all parties should adhere. In other words, obligations and expectations will be realised through communication, which typically mixes verbal and non-verbal cues.

Under normal circumstances, each person commits to and maintains throughout not only her own image, but also the image of other interactants. In civilised interaction, in particular, one is expected not to intentionally call into question another person's publicly presented role-identity, and all parties can assume that their own role-identities are safe from attack. In short, they agree on avoiding embarrassing each other. However, sometimes, people do intentionally violate this expectation. And awkwardness ensues, if not worse.

3.4.5.1 General Considerations

According to a contemporary American communication specialist, William F. Sharkey, "embarrassment" can be defined as:

> a short lived emotional/psychological response of social chagrin (i.e., anxiety or fear that is due to negative sanctioning or lower evaluations from others) or uneasiness that occurs as a result of a discrepancy between one's idealized role-identity and one's presented role-identity and the uncertainty that follows an incident.[255]

It is, put differently, a set of circumstances where norms of communication are disrupted.[256]

Ridicule and teasing are the most frequent ways through which people deliberately embarrass others.[257] Moreover, intentional discomfiture is typically employed for strategic purposes, i.e., to establish control. Unsurprisingly, as far as the empirical measurements can be said to depict reality in a faithful and reliable manner, it works.[258]

Feelings of embarrassment are most frequently experienced in situations involving certain predicaments, most likely arising from some unfortunate or inappropriate utterance or behaviour in front of an audience.[259] Such predicaments often result from a violation of tacitly assumed communicative norms.[260] For in-

---

255 Sharkey (1995), 16. See also Sharkey *et al.* (2001), 1262.
256 See Petronio and Dollar (1988), 21.
257 See Sharkey *et al.* (2001), 1262.
258 See Sharkey *et al.* (2001), 1262.
259 See Petronio and Dollar (1988), 21.
260 See Petronio and Dollar (1988), 21.

stance, the hapless individual will experience discomfort over a disgraced public image. Characteristically, this loss of face is accompanied by a loss of self-worth, which can be transient or long-term, depending on the situation.[261] In most social situations, embarrassment develops unintentionally and spontaneously in the tide of communicative interaction and is engendered by a lack of poise.[262]

Embarrassment has been recurrently analysed in keeping with notions such as "presentation of self" and "performance of role".[263] Almost as frequently, it has been noted that this phenomenon represents the figure that the individual 'cuts' while interacting with others. Embarrassment can occur whenever some central assumption in a transaction is unexpectedly and unqualifiedly discredited regarding at least one of those are taking part. In such situations, it is inevitable that such individuals' identity becomes degraded.

Whenever we interact with others, our self-concept is on stage. All the actors are expected to acknowledge and honour the self that is being presented by the others. If one's identity is discredited by another actor, it results in embarrassment. In this scenario, one is obstructed from continuing with the role and instead will need to take stock of the situation, redefine it, and map the largely tacit conditions for continuing, if possible. Needless, to say, life's cruelty arises also under such circumstances.

3.4.5.2 Specific Strategies

In contrast to unintentional embarrassment, there are situations where people go to the trouble of planning in order to discredit and embarrass others.[264] This can be achieved through diverse means. Commonplace humour looms large among them, e.g., *qua* practical jokes, teasing, satirical puncturing of false fronts, and, perhaps most blatantly, ludicrous public degradation.[265]

Hidden within the psyche of specific individuals, the motives stated by 'embarrassors' for intentionally embarrassing another are manifold, and many of them could actually lie beneath the initiator's own self-awareness. Some people claim to pursue such a line of agency in order to establish or maintain power, while others purport to aim at negatively sanctioning their targets' ridiculed behaviour. Others say that they aim at discrediting the targets' image or achieving self-satisfaction. And there are those who see embarrassing others as a benign way of show-

---

261 See Petronio and Dollar (1988), 21.
262 See Martin (1987), 279.
263 Martin (1987), 279. All claims made in the paragraph above are based on this study.
264 See Martin (1987), 279.
265 See Martin (1987), 279.

ing solidarity, e.g., to indicate friendship, include others, socialise or initiate others, or just have fun.[266]

In our century, Sharkey et al. provided a useful list of such reported reasons. We simplify and synthesise it below.[267]

(1) *Showing solidarity or facilitating socialisation*
    Description: Focus on the group as a goal, i.e., to entertain its members, show solidarity to them, or help people socialise. The 'embarrassor's' goals for himself/herself is to get a laugh, gain status, and be one of the crowd. But sometimes positive goals on behalf of the 'embarrassee' are sometimes also claimed, such as him/her being the center of attention, made to feel important, or even honoured.
    Examples: "We did it just for fun", "I was trying to give him a good laugh on his birthday", "he embarrassed me just for fun", "I was being initiated into the fraternity", "We're always embarrassing each other. It's all done with good humour", "It's how we initiate a person", "I wanted to make this a time she would never forget", "It was my birthday", "To surprise me".

(2) *Negatively sanctioning behaviours for either of two purposes*
    Description: (A) The stated purpose is to teach an individual a lesson and get him/her to follow rules through punishment, or (B) To keep people in their place by discrediting them, retaliating, and puncturing false fronts.
    Examples: (A) "I reprimanded my child so he wouldn't do the same thing again", "I wanted to get this person to take a closer look at the problem", "I didn't do what my father told me to do", "I need my workers to show up on time", "I wouldn't stop bugging him". (B) "We didn't want him to get the job", "She deserved it, she was asking for it for some time", "He was lying to every one for a year. I just wanted them to see who he really was".

(3) *Establishing and maintaining power*
    Description: To attain control over people and situations, and to get ahead.
    Examples: "I wanted the supervisors to see that I was best for the job", "I needed to have the final say", "She just wants to control me".

(4) *Self-satisfaction*
    Description: Eliciting a response from another person for the sole purpose of self-amusement.
    Examples: "Because I thought it was funny", "He just likes to embarrass me", "I just wanted to see her reaction", "I just like to embarrass my brother", "I wanted to see the person blush", "She likes to see others flounder", "I wanted to see how the person would handle it".

Sharkey and his colleagues found that, when asked about the goals listed above, embarrassors most frequently claimed to be using embarrassment to show moral-

---

[266] See Sharkey *et al.* (2001), 1262–1263 on all such claims about motives.
[267] Sharkey *et al.* (2001), 1270–1271.

ly praiseworthy solidarity.[268] This was followed by the equally ethical goal of negatively sanctioning another's behaviour. Sharkey argued that attribution theory may explain these results insofar as the embarrassors tended to disown any dispositional reasons for their actions and claimed to have only positive, self- and other-enhancing aims (e. g., solidarity) or, barring that, blamed external factors (e. g., the target's inappropriate behaviour).

Perhaps unsurprisingly, targets tended to have a rather different view of the embarrassors' intentions. They most often refused to take blame and put the responsibility solely on the shoulders of the perpetrators. In short, while the embarrassed people 'see' some cruelty in these humorous instances, those who initiate them are not so likely to 'see' it too; at least, not to the same degree.[269]

3.4.5.3 Specific Settings

When a romantic partner is causing embarrassment to his/her significant other, it will not only impact the embarrassed person, but also the quality of their relationship.[270] Surely, one such incident would not necessarily cause much trouble, but if these take place frequently, the embarrassments start becoming a problem, and they may even signal underlying ones of a more serious nature.[271] As relationships are often fraught with tacit struggles for power, the partners resort to mischievous methods to get the upper hand, humorous ones *in primis*.[272]

As Sandra Petronio and a team of fellow American psychologists discovered in the late 20th century, those on the receiving end of embarrassment in romantic relationships tend to think that their partners are doing so intentionally, i.e., to try to control the relationship, impress others at the target's expense, violate a tacit or explicit norm of the relationship, or retaliate.[273] Similar power dynamics frequently play out at the workplace and in schools where a majority of subordinates maintain that their superiors intentionally embarrass them, also *via* commonplace humour, in order to establish or maintain power.[274] Statistically, this claim was closely followed by the one according to which such embarrassments have as their goal the humorous superior's self-satisfaction.[275]

---

268 See Sharkey *et al.* (2001), 1263. All claims made in the paragraph above are based on this study.
269 Once again, we are reminded of the hermeneutical challenges discussed in Chapter 2.
270 See Petronio and Dollar (1988), 21–22.
271 See Petronio and Dollar (1988), 21–22.
272 See Petronio and Dollar (1988), 21–22.
273 See Petronio and Dollar (1988), 21–27.
274 See Sharkey *et al.* (2001), 1263, and Martin (1987), 279.
275 See Sharkey *et al.* (2001), 1263.

As W.B.W. Martin recorded in his influential studies about the US school environment, "[s]ome teachers try to destroy students" and "[t]here are a few [teachers] who make a student feel worthless, incapable of comprehending anything, and totally undermined".[276] Other students in the sample even stated that some teachers made fun of them from time to time, for no reason at all other than to have a good laugh, and thereby cause them embarrassment.[277] What is more, some of the surveyed students felt that the embarrassment that teachers caused them was intentional.[278]

Studies conducted among teachers themselves support this conclusion.[279] Definitely, certain teachers admit using deliberate embarrassment to control their classrooms, even if it means that their selected targets will suffer.[280] Thus, these teachers must operate an anaesthesia of the heart, inevitably, as a means to an end—or a means to a means. As we also know from personal experience, embarrassment is a harsh, scathing, mean, but highly effective means of instruction or, at least, as Bergson made clear, social control and socialisation.[281]

The costs can be high, however. Being so cruelly embarrassed by a teacher can have wide-ranging consequences for the student. Among others, it can lead to growing a dislike for educators in general, becoming angry, fearing teachers' actions in the future, developing negative self-concepts, hating school, and dropping out.[282]

3.4.6 Ridicule

Ridicule is one type of cruel humour that can cause severe embarrassment, whether it is directed at some behavioural aspect or physical feature of an individual. The use of ridicule is universal in our culture, where it permeates social media, movies, advertisements and TV shows, cutting across age groups, social classes, ethnic groups, and genders. However, it seems to be particularly aimed at teenagers, thereby ingraining within them that it is 'uncool', say, to wear certain clothes or display certain behaviours—in a very Bergsonian manner.

---

276 Martin (1987), 283.
277 See Martin (1987), 283.
278 See Martin (1987), 283.
279 See Martin (1987), 290–291.
280 See Martin (1987), 290–291.
281 See Chapter 1 and Martin (1987), 290–291.
282 See Martin (1987), 290–291.

3.4.6.1 General Considerations

A rich part of schoolyard and playground bullying, being ridiculed is one of the principal fears of many students.[283] All of us, probably, have experienced ridicule and/or fear of ridicule and can easily relate to the unpleasantness of being laughed at by others. That is something that we normally want to avoid, even to the extent of forgoing important social relationships.[284] According to many empirical studies, social phobia (i.e., the persistent fear of scrutiny and possible humiliation by others) is the most prevalent of all anxiety disorders.[285]

Ridicule can be a nuanced act at times. The tricky part of being on its receiving end is that retaliation is often inappropriate, self-defeating, and seen as a loathsome inability to take a joke, as Harvey repeatedly highlighted in her research.[286] The target that tries to reciprocate is attacked further as "oversensitive" and a "poor sport", which in practical terms means that ridiculing someone is usually socially acceptable or at least easily tolerated, for getting out of it is extremely complicated. The frequent lack of repercussions for the initiator, moreover, makes ridicule a very popular and powerful tool to gain control over others and 'put them in their place'. In the peer-status mayhem of teenage life, this form of cruel humour is therefore the most common weapon of choice.

Its popularity is retained in adulthood as well. However, with age and experience, the methods become more polished, considerably subtler, and therefore less apparent. While anyone hurling insults at another person will be seen as rude and hostile, an individual who teases and taunts someone else with great skill can be considered witty or clever.[287]

Keeping in mind Bergson (Chapter 1) and our discussion of Harvey's views (Chapter 2), it can be assumed that ridicule affects more persons than just its initiator and intended target, extending to the observers too, whether casual or not. Just as it would elicit embarrassment and conformity from its target, the observers of someone being ridiculed will be affected emotionally and, more often than not, behave accordingly. Seeing another person being ridiculed has a profound inhibitory effect, since it increases the likelihood of interpersonal rejection and moti-

---

[283] See Janes and Olson (2000), 474.
[284] See Janes and Olson (2000), 475
[285] See, e.g., Kasper (1998), S1–S3.
[286] See Janes and Olson (2000), 474–475. All claims made in the paragraph above, plus the following five, are based on this study, which offers a useful review of previous research in the same field.
[287] As a matter of professional experience, we witnessed workplace bullies using this kind humour.

vates people to act in ways that can avert similar exclusions. Seeing someone being ridiculed inclines us to conform to the norm.[288]

3.4.6.2 Specific Studies

A variety of studies have shown that ridicule can function as a powerful modifier of behaviour. For example, 6-year-old children who observed videos discouraging certain behaviours, in which puppet models were corrected using either ridicule, commands, or suggestions, were found to be more affected behaviourally when they watched a puppet being ridiculed than when the same puppet received commands or suggestions. Interestingly, though, this did not work on 4-year-olds, meaning that it is only by the age of six that children have become sufficiently socialised to realise the punitive power of derisive and, in all probability, commonplace humour.[289]

An interesting 21st-century set of studies conducted in Canada by Leslie M. Janes and James M. Olson examined the consequences of "jeer pressure" on observers, i.e., the effects of ridicule on people other than the target. They showed that participants who were provided examples of other people being ridiculed were inhibited by the experience and, consequently, more conforming in their own behaviour and more fearful of failure. These participants only observed other people being ridiculed on video, i.e., they were not *in situ*. That these inhibitory effects appeared in an environment that was not personally threatening to the participants demonstrates the overlearned social nature of human responses to ridicule.[290]

In these studies, it transpired as well that observing ridicule of others increases the odds of possible rejection relating to the observer's own behaviour. Presumably, the mere possibility of disapproval manifests as conformity because people want to avoid behaving in ways that cause them to stand out, thus making them potential targets of ridicule. Interestingly, some participants were made to observe a person making fun of their own failures, and these did not evoke similar reactions. This means, psychologically, that the abstract linguistic-conceptual content of the humorous remarks, *per se*, was not responsible for the results. Rather,

---

[288] Rather than using an explicit prohibition from the outside, cruel humour reinforces select internal inhibitions.
[289] These distinctions are statistical. Nothing drastic happens on the sixth birthday.
[290] "Overlearning" implies no negative trait. It simply indicates internalised abilities that are now second nature.

their socio-personal intention (i.e., "other-derogation" *versus* "self-derogation") was the key element.[291]

Even though there were strong inhibitory effects seen in the experiments, the authors claimed that they were subdued compared to what may be reasonably expected from real-life situations:

> Several features of the first experiment argue for a stronger effect of jeer pressure than was actually obtained. First, real-life other-ridicule is often quite caustic, whereas the ridicule in this experiment was fairly innocuous; many of the jokes were too absurd to be sincere (e.g., "He was so ugly as a child that his parents had to tie a porkchop around his neck to get the dog to play with him") and, therefore, may not have been regarded as abusive. Second, there were no laughing bystanders on the videotape, whereas real-life ridicule often involves an amused audience. Third, the target of the ridicule was not present, whereas in real-life ridicule, an embarrassed target is typically visible. If other-ridiculing humor has inhibiting effects because it makes salient to observers that they also could be rejected, factors such as innocuous jokes, no audience, and an absent target might weaken these effects.[292]

Janes and Olson added a somewhat pedantic yet penetrating caveat in their studies.[293] Their findings did not document unequivocally that cruel humour, *per se*, played a necessary role in the effects of other-ridicule. Inasmuch as they did not include in their experiments an insulting condition involving derogation without any humour whatsoever, it was impossible to disentangle the effects of sheer disparagement from humour in other-ridicule. Therefore, it cannot be discounted that similar results could be obtained if the speaker had simply reviled the target. Insults, perhaps, may be as effective of disparagement as cruel humour, or even better.

However, as the same authors pointed out, given that ridicule is socially far more acceptable or tolerable than insults, it is important to document the effects of ridicule as such, should they even parallel or be less effective than those of insults. Also, one would expect that, when observing someone being insulted, people would conform to conventional behaviour for the same reasons. The pivotal point, then, is that even when it is rendered more palatable by levity, the disguised cruel derogation of other-ridicule affects observers most effectively.[294]

---

[291] In short, the superiority theory of humour is receiving a 'boost', should it need one.
[292] Janes and Olson (2000), 478.
[293] See Janes and Olson (2000), 479. All claims made in the paragraph above are based on this page.
[294] How deep the affective cuts go and hurt cannot be measured with exactitude, but only grossly and indirectly.

3.4.7 Gelotophobia

Despite the commonly held view that we should all be able to 'take' a joke that is told at our own expense, reality offers multiple constraints.[295]

3.4.7.1 General Considerations
Most of us are sensitive to even the sheer possibility that someone might be laughing at us. Surely, our readers will be able to recall or, at least, conceive of a setting in which they happen to be seeing a group of people laughing loudly and simultaneously looking their way. This situation of uncertainty can be even worse than when somebody makes a cruel joke at our expense *and* to our face. But none of us would be able to suffer endless tirades of derogatory humour, and some have even a pathological fear of being ridiculed.

As we have shown repeatedly with multiple examples, cruel humour is frequently directed at those who are generally seen as 'weaker' than us, whether due to mental limitations, socio-economic disvalues, prevalent socio-cultural prejudices, and/or physical abnormalities.[296] Historically, psychiatric patients have even been put out for display in town squares and circuses, as well as hospitals and prisons, where the public could ogle their unfortunate fellow humans as a source of humorous leisure.

Through the work of good-doers, reformers, and activists, not least in the Age of Enlightenment that we briefly addressed in Chapter 1, the rights of such people —in the Western world at least—have been eventually recognised and, to some extent, enforced. This granted these unfortunate individuals additional, if not entirely new, personal freedom from open acts of degradation performed in public. Their neighbours must then rely on more private occasions to enjoy this type of commonplace, cruel humour.[297]

Our likely innate instinct for cruelty, whether it is realised through humour or not, seeks out the weak spots of those we wish to attack.[298] These dreary triggers are not all obvious.[299] Some can be physical, whereas others are embedded in our mind. They may include prominent bodily features, such as a large nose, big ears, a protruding gut, a non-alignment of the eyes, a bald head, etc. Or it can suffice that

---

[295] See Ruch and Proyer (2008), 47, which applies to the whole paragraph above.
[296] See Ruch and Proyer (2008), 48.
[297] The media, as we discussed in Chapter 2, are filled with examples of cruel epicaricacy and crueller mockery.
[298] As discussed in *H&C1*, Locke was one of few Western thinkers who did not believe in such an innate instinct.
[299] See Ruch and Proyer (2008), 48, which applies to the rest of the paragraph above.

the targets have some behavioural quirks, a stutter, a foreign accent, unusual mannerisms, or eccentric views about some issue. It is also possible that they deviate from the crucial 'norm' in terms of class, ethnicity, profession, country of origin, gender, or sexual orientation. (Depending on the context, one and the same trait can be 'normal' or 'eccentric'.) It therefore comes as no surprise that some individuals must put up with cruel humour on a daily basis.

3.4.7.2 Specific Studies

Whatever the reason, common sense would dictate that being relentlessly made fun of is bound to have psychological consequences, both short- and long-term.[300] Among other things, it could lead to obsessive concerns about being ridiculed. Empirical studies confirm this hypothesis.

The contemporary German psychotherapist Michael Titze employed a technical term for it: *Gelotophobia*.[301] According to Titze, "gelotophobia" is pathological fear of being viewed as a ridiculous object by others.[302] Behaviourally, this condition manifests itself in marked fear of exposing oneself to others, inasmuch as the afflicted person assumes that others are constantly scanning them for signs of ridiculousness. The symptoms differ in potency, but include various levels of paranoia, sensitivity to offense, and social isolation.

Given that all of us are liable to being made fun of by means of cruel humour, every one of us could become a potential "gelotophobe". Clinically, however, there must occur other concomitant symptoms for "gelotophobia" to be mentioned, if not diagnosed. Gelotophobes have, *inter alia*, not learned to appreciate laughter in a positive way, not learned to appreciate positively motivated smiling, and are fearful of either or both eventualities. Gelotophobes will also appear cold and humourless, lack joy and spontaneity, and exhibit nonspecific psychosomatic traits such as blushing easily, tension-induced headaches, frequent trembling, or dizziness. And we must add to this sorry list an array of recorded sleep problems.

It has been speculated that the causes of gelotophobia are to be found in traumatic experiences of excessive ridicule in childhood or adult life. Additionally, it is thought possible that failing infant-caretaker interaction could also lead to feelings of primary shame that are exhibited later in life, inducing gelotophobia. However, it is important to note that, albeit amply discussed in the extant clinical literature, gelotophobia has not yet been recognised by the editors of the DSM as an official

---

300 See Ruch and Proyer (2008), 49.
301 As stated in Ruch and Proyer (2008), 50.
302 See Ruch and Proyer (2008), 50–52, which is the source for all claims made in the sub-subsection's remainder.

disorder. Rather, it is often reduced to social phobia, with which it shares some conspicuous common features—most notably, social withdrawal.

In any case, gelotophobes should be said to experience life's cruelty even in the light and merry domains of commonplace humour, smiling, and laughing. They are, in other words, an extreme case in the detection of cruelty within people's humour and daily existence at large, as well as in confirming the decisive presence of a subjective element—i.e., a Polanyian "personal coefficient"—leading to the plausible connotation of certain behaviours as both "humorous" and "cruel".

3.4.8 Jeer Pressure

Given the preceding reflections about gelotophobia, we return briefly to the studies performed by Janes and Olson, who coined the term "jeer pressure". In particular, we should recall here two experiments aimed at examining observers of cruel mockery, i.e., the effect of ridicule on people who are other than the target.[303]

In these studies, it was inferred that ridicule would have an inhibitory effect on the observers' conduct, i.e., that witnessing ridicule would lead the observers to avoid any behaviour that could possibly make them become a possible target of ridicule. In this connection, this postulated inhibition may not necessarily be due to conscious decision-making. People often lack the insight to articulate the causes of their behaviour and might also be unwilling to admit to themselves and/or others that their actions are stifled by ridicule, or by fear of it.

The first experiment conducted by Janes and Olson contrasted the effects of observing others being ridiculed with two additional different types of humour: *self-ridicule* and *no-target:*

(1) In the *other-ridicule* condition, a sample of (what a surprise!) undergraduate students watched a male, amateur stand-up comedian telling jokes that ridiculed another person—another male, to be precise. The jokes were directed at this unseen person's physical appearance (e.g., "His acne was so bad as a teenager we used to call him 'pizza face'"), his lack of romantic success (e.g., "He tried to join a lonely hearts club but they said, 'Hey, we're not that desperate!'"), and various other physical and behavioural misfortunes.

(2) A *self-ridicule* condition was then used to test whether the humour would have a different effect if it was self-directed. The exact same jokes were used in this condition and recited in the same order by the same comedian as in the *other-*

---

[303] See Janes and Olson (2000), 472–482, which are the source for all claims and quotes in this subsection.

ridicule condition (e.g., "My acne was so bad as a teenager they used to call me 'pizza face'"). This condition provided a baseline assessment of the effects of the content of the jokes. Because *self-ridicule* does not represent true rejection, Janes and Olson expected that it would not have the same inhibiting effects as *other-ridicule*.

(3) A third group observed *no-target* humour (e.g., "What has two gills, scales, and warns us about the dangers of smoking? The Sturgeon General!") recited by the same comedian.[304] This condition had different jokes than the experimental conditions, but it provided nonetheless a methodologically useful baseline assessment of the general effects of the particular type of humour at hand.

The participants were randomly assigned to view either the *other-ridicule*, *self-ridicule*, or *no-target* humour videotapes. After that, participants rated their perceived enjoyment. The results demonstrated that observing the ridicule of others appeared to have inhibiting effects by increasing conformity and fear of failure. Watching *self-ridicule* did not produce the same effects as *other-ridicule*, which went also to show that it is not the abstract conceptual-linguistic content of the jokes *per se* that was responsible for the results, but rather their socially situated unfolding and, probably, the intentions assumed to be at play therein.

Three features of this experiment suggested that we would find an even stronger impact of jeer pressure in real life:

(1) We all know that, unlike this particular experiment, the ridicule of others under normal circumstances is often quite caustic, whereas the experiment presented fairly innocuous and/or unlikely examples (e.g., "He was so ugly as a child that his parents had to tie a porkchop around his neck to get the dog to play with him").
(2) As importantly, there were no laughing bystanders on the videotape in the experiment, whereas in real life ridicule often involves an amused audience, as also Harvey explicitly remarked upon.[305]
(3) The supposed target of the ridicule in the experiment was not present, whereas in real life, more often than not, an embarrassed target is visible.

To address these issues, Janes and Olson designed their second experiment. This time around, the ridicule on the videotape was made more caustic. Also, the target

---

[304] It can be argued that this kind of humour targets fictional, *ad hoc* 'butts' of the joke, e.g., said "sturgeon", or that the comedian makes him-/herself a target by being intentionally nonsensical, hence 'abnormal'. Or rather, that the victimised targets are those listeners who fail to 'get' the joke, if not the rules of language at large.

[305] See Chapter 2.

of the supposed ridicule, as well as a laughing bystander, were present on the videotape. This experiment replicated almost exactly the results of the first.

The two researchers also measured the presumed mediating mechanism underlying the effects of ridicule, i.e., fear of rejection. It was shown that seeing someone being ridiculed increased the awareness of rejection in the observer's mind. Heightened accessibility of rejection appeared to be the psychological mechanism that was influenced by *other-ridicule* and that, in turn, impacted the fear of failure.[306]

3.4.9 Cruel Humour and Race

Ridicule can often be rooted in negative racial or ethnic prejudice, which does not need humour to be expressed.[307]

3.4.9.1 General Considerations

Think, for instance, of sweeping generalisations taken as anthropological or sociological truths, e.g., "Jewish businessmen are untrustworthy", "Romanian workers are lazy", "Russians are warmongers" or "Italian men are pigs".[308] However, humour allows for proffering statements akin to the previous ones, yet in ways that do not come across as equally confrontational or offensive insofar as, quite often, they can be said to be "just a bit of fun".[309]

Jokes denigrating a person on grounds of their race or ethnicity abound; many researchers have argued that they operate like those involving gender.[310] Specifically, the construction and dissemination of cruel humour of this kind includes the same three social agents as other forms of disparagement:
(1) the joker, who is constructing and/or disseminating the offensive message;

---

[306] Contrary to the authors' expectations, neither study found that *other-ridicule* had any effect on the participants' creativity. Thus, Janes and Olson (2000) suggested that this lack of effect might be related to the experimental procedures, rather than to creativity being immune to "jeer pressure". If, for example, the participants had been asked to contribute ideas in a group setting, perhaps those who had observed *other-ridicule* would be less willing to volunteer highly divergent or unusual ideas, not least funny ones, for fear of failure and attendant ridicule.
[307] As we have already remarked, there exist positive prejudices too, e.g., "Germans are punctual".
[308] The commonplace admission that exceptions prove the role can make these claims rhetorically indestructible.
[309] See our reflections on this exculpatory line in Chapter 2. See also Baroncelli (1996).
[310] Trindade (2020), 2768, which applies to the first two paragraphs in the subsection.

(2) the subject, butt or target of the joke; and
(3) the audience, who should find the cruel exercise amusing.[311]

Like gendered prejudicial comments, racist and ethnic ones are often clad in a humorous cloak, so that they may be conveniently dismissed as "just jokes", while the offended parties can be criticised insofar as they "cannot take a joke". If jokers are challenged, they can always put up the "I was only joking" defence, which we have already encountered in this chapter; or else, in a common variation on the same theme: "You got me wrong."[312]

3.4.9.2 Specific Studies

A thought-provoking recent study by a team of educational experts, led by psychologist Jennifer Katz, investigated white undergraduate students' responses to different types of racist comments.[313] The participants were randomly assigned to read about a peer who denigrated Blacks' intelligence by either a humorous or a non-humorous statement. Compared to those in the non-humorous arm of the experiment, those in the humorous condition evaluated the speaker in a less negative way and, furthermore, were assertive in their response to his/her message. Crucially, those students who received the message as a joke tended to evaluate the speaker less negatively than did those in the non-humorous condition.

Words may be far less harmless than the joker typically claims, however.[314] The persistent use of disparagement humour directed at certain social groups reinforces negative stereotypes which, for one, pervade today's cybersphere. In yet another cruel irony of Western history, the internet has become an unrestrained site for the expression of rabid racism—a far cry from the egalitarian dreams of some of its earliest developers.

Another recent study by the US-based sociologists Green and Linders used focus groups to investigate how different audiences perceive stand-up comedy that makes use of aggressive references to race and ethnicity. The participants of each focus group watched a number of relevant videoclips and, afterwards, a group moderator encouraged them to discuss their reactions to what they had

---

[311] These three agents are but the corners of the classical rhetorical triangle, which we discussed in *H&C1*.
[312] As previously noted, this can be the case, at least in the eyes of the initiator of the humorous event.
[313] Katz *et al.* (2019), 341, which applies to the whole paragraph above.
[314] Trindade (2020), 2768, which applies to the whole paragraph above.

heard and seen.[315] The results were such that, regardless of their race, nearly all the participants laughed while watching the clips. Also, all participants were able to designate certain parts of the clips that they found especially funny, as well as parts that they did not find entertaining.

Two important contextual aspects emerged thereof:
(1) The social setting mattered—in terms of the racial/ethnic composition of the people involved and implicated, i.e., the joker, the target, and the audience.
(2) The physical/institutional setting of where the jokes were delivered mattered, i.e., whether it was at a comedy venue or not.

The question of whether, sociologically, it is acceptable to joke about race or ethnicity seems to be deeply entangled within the milieu of humour's actual expression. The race or ethnicity of the comedians in relation to the jokes s/he delivered also came into play. This did not simply mean that the offensiveness of jokes was linked to the joker being of a different race than the one being targeted. Rather, insofar as the effectiveness of a joke is often intertwined with its offensiveness, the audience must interpret whether a joke's presenter strives to be funny, offensive, or both. This requires a complex, tacit weighing of the interaction between the joke, the joker, and the audience.

The outcomes of that weighing differed palpably between Black and white American participants. We further summarise these results below:
(1) The white participants placed more emphasis on the race/ethnicity of the comedians than the Black participants did, who Green and Linders claimed to be more comfortable discussing racial or ethnic issues and were more interested in the comedians' ability to accurately speak to their experiences. While the Black participants tended to deemphasise the race of the joker, the white participants saw it as a direct indicator of the comedians' experiences with race-related issues, and consequently thought that white comedians were more likely to come across as offensive.
(2) Another aspect of racial humour is the tension between trite stereotypes and allegedly realistic depictions of racial and ethnic differences. As with offensiveness, Green and Linders pointed to complex and largely tacit decision-making processes in assessing whether the use of stereotypes enhances a joke's perceived cruelty or diminishes it. Inherently, stereotypes consist of a reduction of complex social realities and individual experiences into recognisable figures that, in turn, derive their effectiveness from this exaggerated simplic-

---

[315] Green and Linders (2016), 250–251, which applies to the whole paragraph above, plus the ensuing three.

ity—comic, yes, but also political, epistemic, moral, etc.[316] While both white and Black people used perceived truth-value as part of their evaluation of racial or ethnic jokes, their evaluations were based on quite different experiences. The Black participants associated stereotypical representations with their own experiences, whereas white participants were dependent on their knowledge of stereotypes to make sense of the representations.

(3) Green and Linders also examined the extent to which the offensive element of racial humour could be seen as useful or serve productive social purposes.[317] While all participants in the study claimed to be committed to racial equality, their understanding of the role of racial comedy was different. Some respondents, both white and Black, saw racial or ethnic comedy as being of little use in correcting extant misunderstandings—it was simply too touchy a subject to joke about.

Other researchers have recognised the sensitive nature of racial or ethnic relations, but still considered this kind of humour, including of the cruel type, as having the potential to initiate and/or facilitate genuine debates and/or counter misconceptions. For the white participants, the possible significance of humour was due to its capacity to make it easier to talk about sensitive matters and break down barriers. None of the Black participants thought about racial and ethnic comedy in these terms, however. Rather, many Black participants pointed to two different potential benefits: the educational aspect of exposing the enduring troubles to non-Black audiences, and humour's potential for mobilising Blacks against social and economic inequality.[318]

3.4.10 The Paradox of Duality

In Europe, Solveig Wolfers, Kieran A. File, and Stephanie Schnurr have recently exposed the use of racist humour in a male Under-19 football team in Germany.[319]

---

[316] See also Baroncelli (1996), chap. 9.
[317] Green and Linders (2016), 258, which applies to the whole paragraph above and the following one.
[318] Interestingly, Banjo *et al.* (2017, 623) report that, when exposed to racial slurs, both Black and white participants showed higher arousal and increased attention. Their findings suggest that the cruel sting of racism and discrimination may well persist in contemporary, allegedly tolerant, and multi-cultural Western societies.
[319] Wolfers, File, and Schnurr (2017), 83–85, which applies to the whole paragraph above, plus the ensuing two.

Football, as our readers might know, has long been a home for unashamed racism. Both spectators and players have repeatedly been observed uttering or chanting myriad offensive obscenities and engaging in gleeful activities that robustly combine racist malice with rhetorical whimsicality. High-profile campaigns such as "Kick it Out", "Show Racism the Red Card", and "No Room for Racism" have thus been invoked by the international football's governing bodies on numerous occasions, seeking to promote messages of religious tolerance, multiculturalism, and racial equality.

Cruel humour of this ilk may be used to not only highlight and strengthen membership in a particular group, but also underscore the perceived differences and boundaries between different groups. In their study, Wolfers and associates used audio recordings of interactions among the players situated on the side lines of the football pitch or sitting on the substitutes' bench—during, before, and after matches and training. Also, they conducted in-depth interviews with players and observed the team in their daily activities.

The researchers found that the athletes built solidarity with other team members using cruel humour, often teasing each another and employing racially or ethnically charged comments. It also became clear that the players fell into distinct subgroups, typically along racial lines, which affected the team's cohesiveness. This happened because the players emphasised the cultural, religious, racial, and/or ethnic identities of their teammates, chose pronouns reflecting an explicit "us-*versus*-them" dichotomy, and placed themselves and others in relation to larger collectives. Generic, discriminatory, and maliciously racist taunts were much in evidence.

These disruptive behaviours were counterbalanced by the fluid, mutable, and largely jovial construction of their remarks, including aggressive ones, laughing together frequently and repeatedly using the "we" pronoun.[320] This study showed that athletic affiliations do not supersede ethnic or racial identities in organised teams, but rather that ethnic and racial classifications are integral to their identities as individuals, athletes, and teammates. Cruel humour played an important role in this process, as it helped the players manoeuvre through this maze, and construct their identities.

This sports-focussed study reiterated the so-called "paradox of duality" that is inherent to all humour, including its cruel instances, for this protean human artefact can contribute to both unification and separation effects. Their careful investigations illustrate that humour, not least when cruel, can be a double-edged sword

---

[320] Wolfers, File, and Schnurr (2017), 92–94, which applies to the whole paragraph above and the ensuing one.

which may bond or divide the joker and the so-called "butt of the joke"—and confound the wider audience in the process. Wolfers' research team could not deny that the football team's members regularly used raw humour and exploited all kinds of offensive notions born of 'everyday racism', i.e., yet another form of institutionalised cruelty *à la* Hallie. However, even the most obnoxious stereotypes, used humorously, could sometimes help the observed group's members to communicate with one another in constructive ways.[321]

3.4.11 Are You In or Out?

Chris Rock, who found renewed infamy at the 2022 Oscars, has built a career on risqué humour that is centred on and often pokes fun at Black people in his native country. As the host of the 2016 Academy Awards, however, he made a joke about Asian people that was met with a wave of criticism, prompting an apology from the Academy.[322] As Michael Thai and his co-authors point out, this incident, and others like it, raise the question of why this sort of joke tanked so spectacularly. Their straightforward answer was that while the Black Chris Rock may have the space to make Black jokes, Asian jokes are off limits.

We recall that the Benign Violation Theory outlined here sees cruel humour as eliciting two concurrent and contradictory realisations: on the one hand, the disparaging social and moral violation whereby a target group is denigrated; on the other, the content is benign, devoid of true malice, and is intended for entertainment. A troubling duality, indeed. Given the delicate subject matter, the line between acceptable commonplace humour and insufferable mockery is murky and controversial. Certain social cues may be crucial in augmenting perceptions of benevolence and thereby tipping the balance in favour of acceptable humour.

Group membership functions decisively as such a cue, especially in socio-cultural contexts where this stratification is seen at many levels, e.g., bureaucratic and educational, or is reflected in economic stratification. Cruel humour is better received if the joker is from the group that is being targeted rather than from an outgroup. Unlike other references to incongruency in the creation of humour, it is congruency that plays a key role, i.e., between the assumed identity of the butt of the joke and of the joker him-/herself.

---

[321] These ways are addressed and discussed in more detail in *H&C3*.
[322] Thai, Borgella, and Sanchez (2019), 1, which applies to the first three paragraphs in the subsection.

In addition, the researchers drew attention to alternative explanations, i.e., that certain jokesters (e.g., gay men) are given more latitude to engage in this sort of humour by virtue of their minority status.[323] According to their data, and as anticipated in our Chapter 2, members of low-status groups have broader license to transgress accepted standards of morality or propriety, relative to members of high-status groups. Negative prejudice enacted humorously by minority comedians is considered more benign than if enacted by majority ones.

Similarly, members of minority groups were more easily forgiven for attributions of racism, homophobia, or bigotry and were protected from immediate negative character judgements. Consist with these results and the so-called "David and Goliath" principle, cruel humour directed at groups with higher status was regarded as more permissible than cruel humour directed towards low-status groups. Punching up, then, was seen as far less troubling than punching down, even if the more modest pugilistic activity could still cause punched people to come out with a bloody nose or a black eye, metaphorically speaking.[324]

3.4.12 Does Cruel Humour Make Us Cruel?

In the early 2000s, a team of social psychologists led by the American specialist Thomas E. Ford sought to explain why exposure to racist and sexist humour increases tolerance of discriminatory events for people who are already prejudiced towards a group, while empirical evidence shows that, for other, less prejudiced individuals, it has no such effects.[325] Their studies produced the following conclusions:
(1) Humour activates a conversational rule of levity that switches from our usually more serious mindset to one characterised by light-heartedness. Unless some internal or external cues suggest that it is inappropriate for the interpreter to do so, people are likely to grasp cruel humour humorously.
(2) By switching to a light-hearted mindset, the listener implicitly approves of the standard communicated by the feat of cruel humour at issue, tacitly stipulating that, in this context, there is no need to be dismissive and/or critical of the apparent discrimination directed at the targeted group.

---

323 Thai, Borgella, and Sanchez (2019), 2–8, which applies to the whole paragraph above and the ensuing one.
324 Critchley (2002a and b) bases the entire distinction between false and "true" humour on punching down or up.
325 Ford and Ferguson (2004), 81–83, which applies to the whole paragraph above.

(3) The listener uses expansively this emergent, tacit communicative norm and increases his/her tolerance of discrimination against the members of the disparaged group.
(4) A highly prejudiced person is more likely to be influenced by such lax norms and use them as a new, personal standard for behaviour. Consequently, these people are more likely to become crueller as a result of being exposed to cruel humour.[326]

An interesting twist to this line of thinking was provided by a later study performed by a team of American social psychologists led by Donald A. Saucier, who tested whether racist humour may influence expressions of negative prejudice, presaging that such prejudice is more or less socially acceptable.[327] To this end, they selected riddles that were disparaging, confrontational, or neutral, and examined their effects on ensuing prejudiced expressions.

Their results showed that disparagement humour encouraged subsequent expressions of prejudice, even in brief social interactions. Their study also showed that the scrutinised individuals often misinterpreted the subversive nature of confrontational humour. Instead of seeing it as challenging expressions of negative prejudice, they regarded it as the genuine artefact, i.e., more cruel humour. Thus, in yet another nasty irony revealed by the study of humour, jokes that may have been created to subvert and inhibit negative prejudice can reinforce such bias. As Hallie and Kekes also observed, the road to hell is routinely paved with the best of intentions.[328]

3.4.13 The Rebound Effect

We could plausibly explain cruel humour *via* the relief or release theory. A recent study on "the rebound effect", for example, clearly demonstrated that a release mechanism of sorts is a crucial element in this sort of humour.[329] This response is the ironic consequence of people striving to manage their negatively prejudiced thoughts, which return with even greater force and result in even more poisonous

---

[326] Something analogous was detected in a recent study by Kohut *et al.* (2021, 647) on the ever-elusive aetiological link between "pornography" and "sexual violence", insofar as they concluded that this was the case "only among men who are predisposed to sexual aggression". Cruel fiction can make cruel men crueller.
[327] Saucier *et al.* (2018), 105, which applies to the whole paragraph above and the ensuing one.
[328] See Chapter 1.
[329] Ford *et al.* (2017), 458.

expressions.[330] Increased restrictions on public expressions of negative prejudice, then, might have some very perplexing unintended consequences.[331]

The study that we cite is based on the earlier ground-breaking study by Harvard psychology professor Daniel Wegner, the father of contemporary thought-suppression research.[332] The original spark was, however, an observation made long before him by none less than Dostoevsky, whom we keep encountering in our research. To be exact, in his travel diaries, the great Russian writer observed: "Try to pose for yourself this task: not to think of a polar bear, and you will see that the cursed thing will come to mind every minute."[333]

Intrigued by this statement, Wegner decided to put it to a test, in two phases.

(1) Wegner devised an experiment where participants were asked to verbalise their stream of consciousness for 5 minutes whilst being asked not to think of a white bear.[334] If the thought of a white bear did enter their consciousness, then they were asked to ring a bell. Despite, or perhaps because of these instructions, the participants were found to have thought of a white bear more than once a minute, on average.

(2) Wegner asked the participants to try to think of a white bear. Interestingly, they thought of white bears even more often than a specially created comparison group, who had been told to think of white bears in the first phase as well. The results indicated that when people are asked to suppress a certain thought for a few minutes, the request causes the thought to rebound later in their minds with even more prominence.

In short, trying to tamp down unwanted thoughts leads one part of our mind to avoid it, whereas another part keeps checking on whether it is securely kept out. Ironically, the latter activity constantly refreshes the thought avoided by the former part of our mind. Similar results were also found in successive studies involving subjects who had been instructed to suppress prejudiced thoughts.[335]

These studies also indicated that, by relieving normative pressure to suppress negative prejudice that prejudiced people frequently experience in social settings, cruel humour attenuated their rebound effects.[336] Somehow, this type of humour

---

330 See Ford *et al.* (2017), 458.
331 See Ford *et al.* (2017), 458.
332 See American Psychological Association (2011).
333 American Psychological Association (2011), par. 1.
334 See American Psychological Association (2011), which applies to the rest of the paragraph above.
335 See Ford *et al.* (2017), 459.
336 See Ford *et al.* (2017), 461.

operated as a safety valve to expel or, at least, express their 'dark' thoughts and attitudes.[337]

3.5 Humour's Cruelty

In light of the empirical studies discussed in this chapter, we must offer a final set of observations before moving on. First of all, not all cruel jokes are blatantly cruel. Some may appear innocent. Yet even the seemingly untainted ones normally carry a sting. Consider the following example: *A man walks into a library and orders a hamburger. The librarian puts a finger to her lips and says, "But Sir, this is a library". The man apologises and whispers back, "I'd like a hamburger, please".* Funny, isn't it?

Now, imagine witnessing in person the exchange described in the joke. Think, in other words, of what would ensue, should we remove the frivolity and unreality that, as seen in Chapter 1, Kozintsev felt constituted the quintessence of all humour. Many might find the event described above somewhat disturbing. Either the man is teasing the piteous librarian or he has mental-health issues. Only harmless puns and abstract witticisms might be inoffensive under this perspective. But they also are typically not as funny as many ordinary instances of commonplace humour. Not least the cruel ones which we witness amply, e.g., in cartoons aimed at children, as discussed in Chapter 2.

Besides, as we remarked earlier, even seemingly harmless puns and abstract witticisms may entail victims, intentionally or not. Consider, say, all those belittled listeners who happen to fail to 'get' the joke and/or appreciate its supposed humour, which clearly 'works' for so many other people.[338] Whenever and wherever such an occurrence takes place, these listeners normally experience embarrassment.[339] They may even feel genuine shame and hateful resentment, whether di-

---

[337] See Ford *et al.* (2017), 466. See also our remarks about the Jungian notion of 'the shadow' in Chapter 1. Such a line of thinking is going to be developed further by us too, in *H&C3*.

[338] Whether these people laugh sincerely or out of courtesy and/or fear of exclusion, it is something hidden in the depths of their souls, as opaque as they may be to social scientists or laypersons.

[339] Perhaps this sort of embarrassment, which shows both affective and noetic awareness of the socio-cultural context, might be a better test for artificial consciousness, rather than merely 'getting' a joke, as argued in Gimbel, Presser and Mogianesi (2021). Despite our love for science fiction, we remain sceptical about the plausibility of any such phenomenon, given especially Polanyi's (1962c, 277) insightful and simple debunking of the Turing test: *a successful deception is not the genuine artefact, no matter how effective it may be.* Animals are, in our view, much likelier to be conscious in the way in which human beings are, for we too are, after all, animals, not thinking

rected at themselves or at their amused company, if not at both.[340] Gelotophobes are, in this respect, an extreme manifestation of a spectrum-like phenomenon.

There is also one particularly cruel joke that is being played on us as we pursue our research and write books such as this one. Our discussion about "humorous cruelty" (Chapter 2) and "cruel humour" (Chapter 3), is fraught with the same problems as our previous book about humour in general, especially as regards its conceptual-linguistic definition.[341] We conceded defeat, as shown by our lists of family resemblances in Chapter 1 in this volume. And we are not alone in this miserable state of total routing, for even some of the greatest minds in Western culture have struggled in vain with this task, which is not devoid of perplexing implications with regard to the persistence of cruelty in our societies, as signalled by Hallie's reflections on the paradoxes of cruelty (Chapter 1).[342]

There arises as well the thorny question of what is funny, laughable, or worthy of a smile, which can only be answered on a personal basis.[343] When we look at "cruel humour", then, the definitional issue becomes only more problematic. Inserting the concept of 'cruelty' does nothing to simplify the issue. Quite the opposite. As in the case of humour, the term "cruelty" is difficult to define. It too is understood, ultimately, at a *personal* level. Still, as Chapter 3's review of the scientific literature and our daily experiences show us, cruel humour remains a very common way of communicating and interacting, and it can have life-enabling consequences, both at a personal and at a societal level, while opening plenty of uneven and/or unpleasant avenues as well. In the following chapter, we reflect on some of them, however briefly.

---

machines. As clever as comparative artificial models may be, we should never push them far, whether they are based on hydraulic engineering, optics, mechanics, chemistry, electromagnetism or informatics. The risk, in fact, is the *dehumanisation* of the human being or the loss of 'soul', i.e., the animating principle that computers lack, however we may wish to conceptualise such a notion (e.g., the 'brain'). (See also Tallis 2011.)

340 Our view of humour may appear rather gloomy. Still, we must remind our readers that we are to explore some of humour's redeeming qualities in *H&C3*, i.e., *not* here.

341 This conceptual-linguistic issue implies the possibility of discounting claims of "cruelty" as well as "humour" by merely defining either or both in a convenient way which empties the claims' validity *ipso dicto*.

342 Sometimes people are aware of this paradox and proceed nevertheless. As the Hungarian ethnographer Herrmann Antal stated about the early 20th-century paternalistic policies of 'civilised' Europe targeting the Romani populations: "*a little cruelty must be done in the name of humanitarianism*" (as cited in Dunajeva 2022, 45; emphasis added). See also Stauber and Vago (2022) for a study of the Roma's tragic past and difficult present.

343 We write "personal" in the Polanyian sense of an individual making responsibly claims that s/he thinks of as having objective, universal validity, as explained and defended in *H&C1*, to which we must refer the reader.

4 Dangerous Liaisons

We are lived by powers we pretend to understand.
—W.H. Auden[1]

4.1 A Doubt

As we mentioned in Chapter 3, there is a contradiction inherent in cruel humour, which simultaneously demeans a target and tells that the attack should not be taken seriously or too seriously—wherever the mysterious criteria for the qualifying "too" may be located.[2] Were we to follow wholeheartedly and a tad creatively Kozintsev's lead, which emphasises the constitutive nonsensicality and singular, event-specific non-seriousness of all humour, then we may never be justified in taking offense. According to Kozintsev, in fact, humour comes into being because of a person's intentional and/or habitual misinterpretation of reality, whether it is obtained by way of a supposed work of art (e.g., a film) or a more prosaic piece of interpersonal communication (e.g., a remark). As he wrote: "If possessing or experiencing a sense implies the ability to perceive and adequately interpret certain stimuli, then it must be admitted that humor is merely a malfunction of this ability… In other words, this quality is completely intrinsic to the subject, whereas the role of the object is minimal."[3] So, insofar as there might be no genuine victim, are we really justified in talking of "cruel humour"?

At a deeper level of scrutiny, a plausible logical corollary of Kozintsev's stance is that cruel humour cannot truly exist, for its very being consists, ultimately, in the epistemic misapprehension of a specific person who, whether intentionally or unintentionally, does not distinguish between that which really is and that which, *really*, is not. The cruelty of humour is fundamentally *apparent*, in the demeaning sense of the term that philosophers have ascribed to it since Plato's day, inasmuch as humour is a momentary deferral of logical thinking, semantic precision, and conceptual aptness. It is, in other words, a gap in the fabric of being that we should better picture as defined by its own negative ontology than by trying to say what it is, for humour comes into play when nothing can be taken seriously, not even words and associated concepts.

---

[1] Auden (2010). "In Memory of Ernst Toller", verse 19.
[2] Determining the threshold of propriety is an eminent example of tacit abilities, as *per* our account of Polanyi's (1962c) phenomenology and epistemology, which we discussed at length in *H&C1*.
[3] Kozintsev (2010), 38.

As none less than Addison admitted, back in the 18th century, it is "much easier to describe what is not Humour, than what is".[4] There is an onto-logical foundation for this perplexing fact. Within humour, there is nothing but its negating, which plays out, moreover, *in foro interno*. As Kozintsev stated:

> Pretexts are infinitely diverse; the comic reflection is eager to fasten, like a parasite, on any serious relation so as to disable it and to allow our imagination to play with "representations of the understanding, by which nothing is thought". *Laughter is never directed against anyone.* In the outside world there exist only pretexts for it. The true and only cause for laughter is always in us. "What are you laughing at? You're laughing at yourselves!"[5]

Under this perspective, Harvey's victimised victims (Chapter 2) or Cox's outraged women (Chapter 3) would be accurately and appropriately described as "thin-skinned", "over-sensitive", and "humourless", for they ccould be said to fail to distinguish between fiction and reality or, even more dramatically, being and non-being. Similarly, if we keep following Kozintsev, the same individuals could be said to fail to realise that, when making use of humour, however aggressively, the degraded individual, if there must be one, is not the proverbial "butt of the joke", but the joker him-/herself:

> Laughing at such cases and momentarily "degrading" our fellow man to the level not even of an animal but of a thing, we degrade ourselves. Our thoughtless laughter is not an expression of superiority or schadenfreude, as Hobbes believed, nor is it social retribution for absent-mindedness, as Bergson supposed. Looking at the situation from the metalevel, we do not rise above it, nor do we look at it from God's point of view, which has never been known to us. On the contrary, we descend from the level of fully acculturated beings to the level where culture still seemed foreign to our ancestors.[6]

The joker, by engaging in humorous conduct, is *ipso facto* detaching him-/herself from genuine socio-cultural reality, and reducing him-/herself to the same level as a circus clown, if not to that of a lower primate:

> The quintessence of detachment from our collective self is circus clowning. In it the feeling of absurdity and unnaturalness of the condition in which man placed himself when he decided to set himself off from nature, attains its maximal reification, and the conflict between the actual actor and the inferior Other attains the *nec plus ultra*. The situation here is entirely different from that of a dramatic actor playing roles which may contrast with his self and yet be appropriate. The clown plays no role other than that of *Homo sapiens* playing a role which is inappropriate for him. The outlandish masks, grotesque outfits, absurd and useless

---

4 Addison (1711), editorial 35.
5 Kozintsev (2010), 51; emphasis added.
6 Kozintsev (2010), 58–59.

things which the clown carries around, the chronic failures that befall him at the slightest attempt to do or say something reasonable – all this cannot be considered anything but a self-parody of man as a cultural being.[7]

The many self-righteous, raging and/or resentful butts of the joke that we have encountered earlier in this volume, under Kozintsev's unusual and perchance inflammatory perspective, could then be argued to be terribly and miserably mistaken in several respects:

(1) Epistemically, for they take seriously that which is said in jest or as true that which is false—indeed, that which cannot be true or false, insofar as the link between language and reality is suspended and the standard canons of communication stop applying.

(2) Morally, for they fail in exercising patience, aloofness, imperturbability, critical discernment, etc. Albeit apparently shocking, Kozintsev's implicit denial of cruel humour by its reduction to the experiencing subject is but a mirror-like image of a well-known ethical point made by a number of philosophical schools in Hellenistic times, i. e., that the wise person ought to learn to ignore all that can cause her anxiety, tribulation, fear, or unease (e. g., Stoicism and Epicureanism).[8] Uncultured people may get mad at jokes. Wise individuals do not.

(3) Psychologically, for they impute cruel intentions to individuals whose motives may be unknown to the agents themselves, e. g., the cruel bully ridiculing you is in reality a crying baby reaching out to you, i. e., a silly clown of sorts, as Kozintsev effectively intimates. Moreover, as we saw in Chapter 3, the initiator of cruel humour often has a very different perspective on the jest than its target/s.

(4) Aesthetically, for they confuse a playful mode of expression and interaction with a non-playful one. Insofar as the link between language and reality has been suspended from normality and the standard canons of communication do not apply, cruel humour should be interpreted for what it is, i. e., something silly in the most profound and total manner, rather than for what it is not, i. e., something serious.

---

7 Kozintsev (2010), 59.
8 E. g., given how widely and patently anonymous internet comments have become the predictable outlet of countless people's repressed rage, aggressiveness, and frustration, it could be deemed wiser to *learn to ignore* these comments altogether, rather than pay any serious heed to them and, in the process, let this form of "everyday sadism" be effective (Buckels *et al.* 2019, 328; the American IT expert Mike Pennucci 2020, 36, wrote aptly of "digital" and "virtual cruelty"). Arguably, the same logic of virtuous indifference should apply to acerbic referees and unimaginative critics. Writers, artists, and academics would then lead more serene lives.

(5) Socially, for they bring themselves down to the same pathetic level as the jokester. In short, people who take offense fall from being level-headed down to the assholes' level. (Pardon our French, but the vertical drop would not be as expressive without the two juxtaposed references to body parts. Besides, why should a reference to the rectum upset us?)

Gut feelings, intuition, common sense, and a candid analysis of the extant scientific literature would all appear to thwart such surprising and flippant notions, which are, however, philosophically intriguing. (Or at least, they should capture the curious reader's attention.) This thwarting being the case inasmuch as we can 'see', almost daily, that cruel humour is regularly and effectively used to aggressively take charge of individuals, groups, or even whole societies, by means of, e.g., ruthless attacks disguised as jokes, playful stereotyping, and negative prejudices cast in funny words.

Perhaps, all this 'seeing' is but an illusion. Were this interpretation of Kozintsev correct, then all these victimised individuals, groups, and societies should simply stop taking offence. As a result, the cruel humourist's grasp and his/her piercing sting would disappear, almost magically, and on the spot.[9] Yet, millions of people have apparently been fooled in this manner—all of them, everywhere, all the time, and for as many generations as recorded history can trace back.[10] (Well, with the noted exception of the aloof sage and, perchance, small infants and hopeless morons.)[11] In the ordinary world of Peter and Paul, whether unwisely or not, Peter is silly enough to scorn Paul with taunts and jibes, and Paul is so silly as to care about Peter's scornful utterances. Philologically, numerous instances of mockery and offensive ridicule have been recorded in the founding texts of Western civilisation itself, e.g., the Bible's Old Testament or Homer's *Iliad* and *Odyssey*.[12]

In the end, we must concede that Kozintsev's possible annihilation of the grounds for taking genuine offense is logically conceivable and it certainly allows

---

9 Should the cruel jokester have truly cruel intentions, then s/he would stop joking and attack truly.

10 As to scholars themselves, the general thrust of the extant literature points in the direction of explaining why mocking slurs are offensive and their use ought to be avoided, rather than highlighting their inherent vacuity as Kozintsev (2010) did, and hence the relative ease with which we can come to ignore them (see, e.g., Metz 2021).

11 Did you get upset at our use of "moron"? There you are. That's *the* matter that is being discussed.

12 See, e.g., Colakis (1986) on the mocking and generally negative connotations of Homeric laughter.

for a joke or two. At the same time, we must also acknowledge that it is empirically improbable or, at a practical level, irrelevant *vis-à-vis* real people's most frequently recorded reactions.[13]

4.2 A Dance

Be that as it may, insofar as cruel humour is so amply recorded and discussed (see Chapter 3), we continue on the assumption that it exists in reality.[14] Should it not be so, we should disregard veritable mountains of empirical research dealing with humorous conduct that is variously dubbed "disparaging", "denigrating", "offensive", "oppressive", "aggressive", "violent", "sick", "black", "dark", etc. As seen throughout this book, a multitude of such cruel themes, trajectories, and examples show up repeatedly in both the Western humanities and the world's social sciences: the widespread occurrence of *Schadenfreude*; the close relationship between laughter and the feeling of triumph over another person that has been merrily defeated and, perhaps, taunted because of it; the use of humour to further victimise victims as dull and humourless; the passive sadistic cruelty of the eager spectator that even today's mass media exploit to an enormous extent; etc.

Analogously, we assume that no single and crisp definition of our titular terms can be credibly produced. The variety of recorded meanings of both "humour" and "cruelty" are just too glaring and gigantic to be ignored or underplayed in good conscience. Terms such as these must be taken on their terms. Besides, their multiplicity explains why, in this book, we have traversed so vast a conceptual and historical plateau which embraces patently diverse phenomena and interpretations thereof from so many different centuries and disciplines.

In our study, we have been crossing an ocean with myriad currents, waves, coastlines, and islands. Or, to use another allegory, it is as though we have been dancing around a ballroom, moving sinuously from one end to another and meeting the many, unique individuals that share legitimately, whether we like them or not, that public space with us. Some of these individuals, admittedly, look rather odd, even dangerous, when not pathological. One of them is a Russian anthropologist. Another was an Italian playwright. There are hundreds of different guests.

By this dance, we also see how cruel humour remains a form of entertainment and/or behaviour that some people gravitate towards, not only as jokers and audi-

---
[13] Perhaps the fact that most people react angrily supports the notion of 'wisdom' being elitist and hard to attain.
[14] We write "be that as it may" because we are not 100 percent certain that Kozintsev, however eccentric, is wrong.

ences but, somewhat surprisingly, as targets. Is this masochism, perhaps, as Deleuze's investigations might suggest? As we also discussed, the use of cruel humour starts at an early age, where it features largely in children teasing one another or, more rarely, the adults that they encounter. Most of us experienced that sort of allegedly playful attacks in our schooldays and probably took part in delivering them too.

Furthermore, this humorous activity is in no way limited to youth, but follows us throughout life in common and seemingly well-functioning relationships at home, among friends, and even in the workplace. All of this, despite the enormous risks that it implies for people's reputations and careers. When mixed with sexual or ethnic elements, for one, it can destroy the joker's employment and economic security. To boot, it can devastate the laughee's confidence and self-respect.

In all these situations, teasing can advance from its playful elements into full-blown bullying or, at least, it may be perceived and denounced as such, thus unleashing a cascade of further frictions, frustrations, and disfavours. Under more favourable circumstances, bullying can turn into mere teasing, or so it can be viewed by many. Ambiguities and grey areas abound. After all, the difference between teasing and bullying is not a qualitative one, but an almost quantitative one, which produces different life-disabling results.

These results depend ultimately on specific circumstances, orbiting around inevitably diverse degrees of individual sensitivity as well as variously well-established socio-cultural conventional praxes, e.g., sporting activities, ritually-permitted excessive alcohol consumption, carnivalesque festivals and behaviours, hen and stag nights, etc. Unsurprisingly and unsettlingly, the victims of humorous aggression that claim to have been bullied or insulted expose themselves to the additional victimisation whereby they are labelled "oversensitive" or "thin-skinned".

Sociology, psychology, evolutionary biology, and other sciences dealing with human behaviour see no major impediment in explaining what cruel jokes and jests do for the joker, the butt of the joke, and/or the audience. A sense of superiority and one of belonging to the 'in' group are, according to most researchers, an obvious result. Similarly, the detrimental effects on the target are regularly observed too, such as his/her/their reported and/or inferred feelings of exclusion, loneliness, and shame.

Rather patent is also the frequent amusement and participation of the initial observers, who might even shift their allegiances and turn the tables on the joker him-/herself, reproaching him/her for his/her obnoxious behaviour and launching into retaliatory measures that can range from an *ad hoc* rebuke to generalised ostracism within the community. As Harvey's work exemplifies, there may even emerge a line of academic writing and ethical thinking that aims at countering oppressive, cruel humour and making it vanish once and for all, or as far as possible.

Strangely enough, people seem to willingly gravitate towards being targets of such cruel jokes, which they may even utter themselves.[15] Perhaps, as was noted with regard to Seneca's writings, we offer ourselves up as targets and laugh at other people's caustic remarks about us in order to show them that we cannot be hurt.[16] Or, perchance, we have developed a taste for such a subordinate role which we grew accustomed to, say, as a younger sibling or a weaker member of our kindergarten's cohort, or because of some pathological failure in our development.[17]

It is under such seemingly unfavourable circumstances, as Deleuze would argue on the basis of Freudian psychoanalysis (and Sacher-Masoch's *Venus in Furs*), that we learned how to get what we want by formally submitting to someone else's authority and commands. Masochism, as Deleuze intimated, can be a successfully duplicitous way to obtain that which is said to be forbidden. Indeed, as Prince Myshkin's complex literary case shows, a tendency to make ourselves the butts of jokes, cruel ones included, may signal our inherent goodness and general lack of any inherent proclivity towards aggressive behaviour or cruel agency of any kind, including the humorous one.

Although cruel humour can be a veritably potent weapon in the hands of anyone that is sufficiently skilled in its use, it also pushes the ethical, epistemic, and aesthetic boundaries of its audience, sometimes over tolerable limits, hence resulting in a backlash against the joker, who is always taking a risk whenever deciding to engage in such humorous activities. Even a bully surrounded by like-minded bigots may step past the limits of acceptability when venting commonplace humour cruelly, whether *vis-à-vis* a partner-in-crime, an obscure observer, his/her surviving shreds of moral conscience, or an Almighty God—many Western thinkers having been believers in a cosmic order of some kind and a superior creative intelligence.[18]

It is, however, in the very nature of cruel humour, and therefore one of the main attractions for the joker, that s/he can backtrack and try to create some distance between him-/herself and the potentially hurtful messages that s/he conveyed. The "I was only joking" defence, as we discussed in Chapter 3, is tried and tested. Moreover, as we addressed in the same chapter, cruel humour can be a

---

15 See, e.g., Gubanov, Gubanov, and Rokotyanskaya (2018), 382.
16 See Gubanov, Gubanov, and Rokotyanskaya (2018), 382.
17 Masochism *qua* result of aberrant sexual development is the standard explanation in Freud's work, which we addressed in detail in *H&C1* and found unnecessary to reiterate in the present volume.
18 We do not intend to minimise or ridicule any of these options, which the reader may value as s/he deems right.

major factor with regard to our self-identity and social self-placement, insofar as we build all of this 'selfhood' on what people say about us, not least by means of cruel humour.

In a less threatening guise, joking also gives people a socially acceptable way to more effectively convey information than using prim and proper conversation. Cruel humour can be a very practical channel through which 'snapshots' about the world can be effectively transmitted.[19] The joker can, for sure, use humour in a gentler way, perhaps chiefly as an expedient means of communication, hence correcting something in our behaviour that s/he feels is impeding our proper behaviour.

As seen in Chapter 1, Shaftesbury, for one, championed such gentlemanly humour, which he nonetheless regarded as a weapon to be wielded with shrewdness and sagacity by the refined elite. Even among their type, for social correction to occur, some pushing and pulling must occur. And people resent being manipulated, even if it is supposedly being done for their own good. That is perhaps why, albeit omnipresent or even necessary, the term "rhetoric" has always been connoted in negative ways, even when not exclusively so or not even primarily.

Yet adhering to societal rules of conduct is, as Bergson emphasised in the contexts of laughter and comicality, important for our personal wellbeing and the functioning of the larger community in which we happen to find ourselves living, learning, and being active. But not all traditions in our civilisation are beneficial to all their members, or at least not equally so. There are countless examples of cruel humour being used to pressure individuals and/or groups into submission on the basis of gender, race, ethnicity, religious affiliation, mannerisms, and myriad other factors, which we addressed in the preceding chapter.

Based on the sheer frequency and volume of cruel humour, we cannot help but agree with Harlow's dismal point that, while there might be in theory a kinder way to express humour, in nearly all practical cases this strategy seems to require a tint of cruelty to function properly. Cruel humour is, in short, humour as such, the cruelty of which may not be grasped due to ingrained habit, institutional familiarity, intellectual inertia, and/or popular preconceptions.

Consistently, we are drawn also to Bergson's explanation of humour as a corrective tool, bringing individuals and groups to heel to the larger and more powerful societal forces. This becomes clear and compelling in times of war, when humour, including openly cruel forms of it, is used very aggressively both to demean the enemy and to ensure popular participation in the patriotic effort.

---

[19] We addressed this notion in detail in *H&C1*. See also Laranjeira *et al.* (2022).

Wars are also a massive facilitating factor for cruelty, probably second to none, as we commented earlier.

Another reason that cruelty is such a dominant theme surrounding humour is that it "serves to transform the tragic events of our life into abstract ideas".[20] By abstracting an idea from concrete unpleasant experiences, we can reduce its psychological trauma. As some philosophers (e.g., Amir) and psychologists (e.g., Ainslie) have argued, cruel humour functions as a defence mechanism that helps us cope with difficult emotional situations, stimuli, aggressions, and responses.[21] We dive into this issue in *H&C3*.

Let us recall Bergson's anaesthesia of the heart as central to our understanding of both humour and cruel humour. This clinical yet lyrical metaphor necessitates the silencing of compassion, sympathy, pity, friendliness, and the like, and the corresponding continuation or reinforcement of aggression, surprise, playfulness, disgust, hatred, sloth, languor, and other emotions which can arguably let a person tolerate life's trials and tribulations.[22] Amir's and Morreall's noteworthy defence of humour and the comic view of life could be said to consist of cultivating just such a 'change of heart', to help us steer emotional responses away from tragic or even sublime moods and, instead, direct them into wisely unassuming ones centring upon levity, lightness, and laughter.[23]

We now reflect upon some of the most important references and reasonings that we have encountered in our dance so far, as mirrored in this subsection. With these additional reflections about the mutually empowering links between humour and cruelty, we should then be able to provide further meaningful insights into their dangerous mutual liaisons in our lives.

4.3 A Tetralogy

> The motto "Where there's a will, there's a way" is the superstition of modern man. Yet. In order to sustain his creed, contemporary man pays the price in a remarkable lack of introspection. He is blind to the fact that, with all his rationality and efficiency, he is possessed

---

20 Gubanov, Gubanov, and Rokotyanskaya (2018), 382.
21 Gubanov, Gubanov, and Rokotyanskaya (2018), 382.
22 We derive the idea that our passions may differ in 'temperature' or intensity from Hume (1979).
23 The eminently affective character of levity and laughter has been repeatedly remarked upon, whether in the 18th- and 19th-century musings about "humour" proper as reflecting an underlying mood (see, e.g., Schopenhauer in Chapter 1), or in later assessments of laughter's affective roots (see, e.g., Heller 2005). Thus, while there may be a necessary intellectual ingredient to all commonplace humour, or even 'true' humour, no such duality would be grasped as being humorous without any emotional reaction.

by 'powers' that are beyond his control. His gods and demons have not disappeared at all; they have merely got new names. They keep him on the run with restlessness, vague apprehensions, psychological complications, an insatiable need for pills, alcohol; tobacco, food-and, above all, a large array of neuroses.
—Carl Gustav Jung[24]

Humour has been thoroughly dissected as a principally, if not exclusively, human phenomenon which, for the most part, is applied in a vast array of social interactions. Indeed, even when intrapersonal, humour reveals itself as an internalised version of interpersonal life. As such, humour has been repeatedly described as the weapon whereby sufficiently *compos-mentis* persons have been able to inflict a conspicuous number of psychological and/or social wounds to one another, others, and themselves. So frequent and so hurtful has been this assault that many commentators have wondered about humour's relationship to the deeper make-up of the human being, whether in terms of evolutionarily inherited animal propensities for murderous cruelty or deeply buried other- and self-destructive motivations.

Humour's compelling ability to reveal 'subterranean' domains has been so noticeable to some pundits—Deleuze *in primis*—that its connotation *qua* viable avenue for metaphysical speculation has been espoused. By affirming and articulating the reality of a so-called "true humour", Schopenhauer and Pirandello avowed the idea that certain subtler and inherently dual types of humour can disclose much more than either a cruel social game or the savage roots of human life—and point us towards a profound, sublime, possibly dramatic truth concerning the human condition which, at least in their writings, is far from amusing. It could even be said to be *cruel*.

We can therefore sketch a very simple matrix which comprises the tetralogy resulting from joining the two most significant *foci* of humour (i.e., ordinary human reality and its deeper metaphysical substratum) and the two main types of cruelty, *per* Hallie's classification thereof (i.e., the afflictions caused to us by nature and those caused by humans):

	Natural cruelties	Human cruelties
Human humour	(1) Pains and posturing	(2) Predators and politics
Metaphysical humour	(3) Senselessness	(4) Insignificance

---

[24] Jung (1964), 71. Infused with Jung's characteristic wit, which subtly exemplifies cruel humour, this passage encapsulates several key themes of the tragic yet insightful Freudian worldview embraced by Deleuze and other postmodern thinkers, whom we discuss further in this subsection, while hinting at theological considerations too.

(1) Crying at birth, infant challenges with basic physiological functions, childhood tantrums and dramas, heart-wrenching teenage romances, growing pains, middle-age crises, old-age indignities, terrible illnesses, various injuries, impeding deformities, scary delusions, the fear of death, and innumerable dismal accidents—what is there in a person's life that is not marred with some suffering, whether physical or mental?[25] And which kind of suffering is not laughed at, more or less sincerely, to keep life's pain's scorching flame just a little distant?

Commonplace humour and, to a weighty extent, 'true' humour itself suggest avenues and opportunities to mock our sorry challenges and conundrums, as though they were less grievous and less bothersome. Cultures fostering humour *vis-à-vis* life's inevitable sorrows cultivate a complex set of posturing techniques whereby we can seek distraction and, in line with much psychological evidence, a modicum of relief. Yet, behind all such humorous occasions, and their momentary mechanisms for release, it is equally never too arduous a task to identify some genuine trouble, obstacle, fear, frustration, and/or stinging memory.

'True' humourists are, according to most proponents of this notion (e.g., Schopenhauer, Pirandello, and Leacock), particularly attuned to this dual relationship, which combines the superficial comicality of a person and/or event with deeper personal crises. Commonplace humour, instead, stresses the former while caring little, if at all, about the latter, especially if jokes and jests are directed towards or *at* someone else whose happiness we care little about, or not at all. As Santayana pointedly remarked, something closely akin to cruelty is at play whenever we ridicule, mock, make fun of, tease, etc. others, as well as ourselves—which we do more rarely, according to him. If anything, Chapter 3's subsections on teasing, bullying, humiliating, and ridiculing supplied sufficient empirical corroboration for such a link.

It may be more difficult to see how sadistic or brutal cruelty occurs when humour is direct and mirror-like. In its expression as self-mockery, the humour at work, whether commonplace or 'true', would mean that a person is able to derive some pleasure in admitting, and poking fun at, her own mistakes. Doing so should yet be painful, insofar as one's own shortcomings are recognised.

Prima facie, the ambivalent titillation at play resembles more an act of masochistic self-denouement than a manifestation of cruelty, whether sadistic or merely

---

[25] Genovesi (1758, 8–9) claimed that, above all else, "death scares us: it is the greatest among the dreadful things ... and cruel anxieties", and "it is so by nature, such that no reason can extinguish it", for death implies the "ceasing of being there", i.e., the total annihilation of "consciousness" itself. Historically, the Epicureans and Buddhism famously tried to do away with this fear, which seems however to have largely withstood their onslaught. People, by and large, still fear death —at least insofar as this fear has been regularly and plainly recorded in the literature on sick, dark, black, and cruel humour surveyed in the present book (see, e.g., Vosmer 2022).

brutal. The self-inflicted pain could even be said to play a protective role. As with Seneca's reflections in ancient times, avoiding self-pity and initiating self-derision can prevent others from mocking the self-deriding person at will, allowing her to enjoy a higher degree of control over the social context in which her mistakes have occurred as well as over the ridiculing that ensues.

Lastly, insofar as a person's consciousness can be plausibly thought of as internally divided (e.g., the Church Father's recognition of the devil's voice *versus* God's voice within our conscience, or Freud's tripartition of the psyche into *ego*, *super-ego*, and *id*), it is possible for one part to be the perpetrator, the other the victim.[26] At times, in fact, we can be our own worst enemy and cruellest derider, who knows perfectly well which buttons to push, which strings to pull, and which itches not to scratch.

(2) Santayana's writings highlight an intuition shared by many other experts, i.e., the notion whereby the necessarily satirical component of all humour and, *a fortiori*, of all explicit mockeries and nasty pranks, reveals something about the nature of the humorous phenomenon itself at the anthropological level. Said otherwise, humorous interactions entail a modicum of sadistic cruelty, akin to the psycho-physical arousal of the beast of prey on a hunting expedition. Whether we like it or not, we are a kind of animal. Thus, beneath the levities and tomfooleries of commonplace humour, one does not have to dig too much or too hard to retrieve traces of predatory logic and its attendant aggressive behaviours.

This heritage runs through many of the evolutionary accounts of commonplace humour and/or laughter as a direct descendant of attacking, biting, murdering, feeding on, and, at some later stage, sheer teeth-baring in ritualised displays of aggression that became, at an even later stage, nominally "playful" and effectively non-lethal—unless erroneously performed and/or wrongly interpreted. When mistakes occur, the cruel beast that humour hints at may surge and make the fight real.

Additionally, as we highlighted before, these mistakes can occur on the receiving side, which mistakenly construes playful aggression as an authentic threat. Thus, in ordinary contexts, edgy or unusual jokes are sometimes read as direct insults or sexual harassments with their ensuing load of aggravation, offense, resentment, rebuking, suing, disciplining, policing, etc. Indeed, the horrors of misfiring and/or misinterpreted humour can be so many and varied that one is left wondering why people still attempt any repartee in contemporary Western societies.

---

26 Whether more benefit ensues from facing life's cruelties head-on or from making light of them is a case-by-case empirical issue, which is however consistent with the axiological principles established by LVOA.

And yet they do continue. Shaftesbury, Addison, Beattie, Hazlitt, Santayana again, as well as Schopenhauer and Pirandello—so many Western voices have borned testimony to the cruelties entailed by commonplace humour, which they aimed at superseding, at least in their published proclamations, by way of 'refinement' in the arts and in the social mores. They were not very successful in their aims. The persistence of cruelty blatantly colours the realm studied by most contemporary social scientists investigating how humorous agency can be used to hurt people and/or is so felt by the recipients (see especially Chapter 3).

In this connection, long before Hallie, Shaftesbury added, albeit somewhat timidly and indirectly, that there exists a cruelly responsive dimension of humour. Specifically, insofar as irony and nonsense are activated in response to cruel social restraints placed upon our freedom of opinion, association, and/or speech, the oppressed party can still reactively lash out at the oppressor. This is no peaceable tit-for-tat. Even in its most refined versions, as Shaftesbury's seminal study of humour acknowledged, it is a weapon in an armed duel. Or, as Cassirer wrote regarding Shaftesbury, shrewd "swordsman[ship]".[27]

Responsive cruelties, not least of a humorous kind, are also at play in the body politic as means of self-assertion and self-defence. They include cartoons, satires, clever rejoinders, blatant derision, public humiliations, bringing-down-a-peg-or-two witticisms, peppering speeches with caustic retorts and barbed ironies, etc. In a subtle recognition of the endless and, normally, low-intensity struggling that has been engulfing human societies since their dawn, humour is commonly said to "punch up" or "down". Which means that the art of boxing, doubtlessly a fight of sorts, is presumed to be a standard and legitimate form of social interaction, even if patently violent and, at times, lethal.

Bound by accepted rules, honoured tradition, and mutual recognition, 'pugilistic' exchanges continue today, among many others, as a matter of prosaic and common-sense cruelty within, between, and across all social classes. They exemplify, among other things, Hallie's institutionalised cruelty, i.e., one which we are so used to that we no longer acknowledge it as being "cruelty" proper at all. Still, our very language keeps reminding us of the sorely painful ingredient of much, if not all, such commonplace humour, i.e., the "salt" that Koestler thought was present in all humorous 'dishes'.[28] We can list: "scathing", "mordant", "biting", "stinging", "bruising", "wounding", "piercing", "cutting", "penetrating", "acerbic", "bitter", "sharp", "cold", and "burning".

---

27 Cassirer (1953), 169. We further explore these responsive strategies in *H&C3*. As to Cassirer, we tackled his understanding of the genesis and development of modern "humour" in *H&C1*.
28 The association of "humour" proper (aka "wit" or "spirit") with "salt" may be alchemical, if not even archetypal (see Jung 1960–1990, vol. 14, par. 324).

Mixing poetry with surgery, Bergson's metaphorical notion of an anaesthesia of the heart is a powerful confirmation of the persistence of the 'salty' element of cruelty in our humorous social exchanges. Tersely, it points towards a socially permitted and/or recommended game of interpersonal pains which are concomitantly reduced (i.e., the anaesthetised heart) and increased (i.e., the target of the humorous discharge). Moreover, Bergson's approach, which has been so influential in both the Western humanities and the world's social sciences, reminds us that brutal cruelty can be reasonably said to be always at play in "humour" proper, for we cannot let sympathy prevail over ridicule, lest we land into tragedy or elegy. (Thinkers as diverse as Beattie, Hazlitt, Santayana, and Pirandello have confirmed this point.)

Sadistic cruelty may be at play too, arguably building on top of the former, thus instituting and/or intensifying the insistence upon, and/or the enjoyment of, the satirical component of humour, without which humour would never function as a means of social correction and, intra-personally, self-correction. (Bergson did not focus on self-mockery which, however, we have seen to be a widespread phenomenon.) As Bergson argued, in ways that have later been corroborated by much socio-scientific research, social conformity is obtained *via* commonplace humour by either whipping someone into desirable action or forcing him/her into cessation of undesirable agency.[29] Without a cruel sting, active and/or passive compliance could not be attained—or at least, not as easily.

(3) Deleuze's so-called "art of the aesthetic" is the most abstract and, possibly, most unfunny conception of "humour" proper that we have encountered.[30] According to him, humour, by bringing about the annihilation of meaningful individuality and, ultimately, of any kind of logico-linguistic sense, is *eo ipso* a rare, perhaps unique, intellectual channel whereby we can glimpse the ultimate nature of being *qua* undefined totality in all of its virtual and actual possibilities of manifestation, past, present, or future. Indetermined in its constitutive potentiality, yet infinitely potent in its constructed actualisations, humour brings us into that borderland between sense and nonsense that Chesterton had already intuited in Lewis Carroll's famous novels, which tug at the fabric of reality, playing around the edges of in/effability:

> It is not children who ought to read the words of Lewis Carroll; they are far better employed making mud-pies; it is rather sages and grey-haired philosophers who ought to sit up all night reading *Alice in Wonderland* in order to study that darkest problem of metaphysics, the bor-

---

29 Baier (1993) retrieved both mechanisms for social correction in the philosophy of David Hume.
30 We suspect that only a small cohort of philosophically inclined minds would find Deleuze truly amusing.

derland between reason and unreason, and the nature of the most erratic of spiritual forces, humour, which eternally dances between the two.³¹

Nursery rhymes, puns, logical paradoxes, and seemingly innocent wordplays hide a cruelly disturbing truth about the fundamental limitations and astounding contingency of language as well as thought itself. In an unpleasant game of inevitably disappointed thinking and impassably inadequate self-expression, humour *qua* Deleuzian "art of the aesthetic" tells us that 'something' *is*, even if we may never be able to say what *it* is, for all ideas and attendant linguistic renditions lack a deep and multifarious fountainhead of possible determinations. Puny, limited, and meaning-*less*, our greatest feats of epistemic creativity are thus exploded from within, if not mercifully derided, by humour's capacity for showing the quintessential conventionality and eventual contradictoriness of our linguistic, imaginative, and reasoning tools.

Not even the abstract domains of nonsense, *mots d'esprit*, absurdism, and brilliant quips can be said to be unblemished, as far as philosophical attributions of this kind of cruelty are concerned. If Harlow thought that innocent humour was an academic fiction and several pundits suggested that its historical roots bore the mark of cruel competition among witty courtiers, Deleuze's metaphysical conception of 'humour' captures an even deeper cruelty at play: the intrinsic and insurmountable limits of human understanding. Kozintsev, for his part, plunged directly into the bottomless disintegration of all meanings that humour delivers like no other human instrument of semiotic annihilation.

Even Polanyi's tacit dimension underpinning all fully conscious agency could be interpreted as another dismal reminder of the limits of sense, were it not for his fiduciary embrace of the intrinsic validity of the Western cultural tradition that, for him, embraced modern science—he practiced as a world-famous physical chemist—and religion—he was a Jewish convert to the Christian faith.³² Thus, the ultimate impasse of our understanding and articulation is not construed by him as a savagely cruel source of ontological and existential senselessness, but as a milder form of spiritual teasing:

> [A]n eternal, never to be consummated hunch: a heuristic vision which is accepted for the sake of its unresolvable tension. It is like an obsession with a problem known to be insoluble, which yet follows, against reason, unswervingly, the heuristic command: "Look at the un-

---

31 Chesterton (1958), 26. In *H&C1*, we discussed in finer detail both Chesterton's fascinating statement and Deleuze's own great admiration for Lewis Carroll's oeuvre.
32 Polanyi (2009), title page. We documented Polanyi's life and work in in *H&C1*.

known!" Christianity sedulously fosters, and in a sense permanently satisfies, man's craving for mental dissatisfaction by offering him the comfort of a crucified God.[33]

We leave it to the reader to ponder this fiduciary embrace, which some of us might find overly timid or conservative, and measure it against the undifferentiated sense-shattering totality that is acknowledged by Deleuze and Kozintsev in their works about "humour" proper.[34] This is the sort of deliberation for which a leap of faith may be required. It inevitably places us before a cruelly daunting existential choice about which Kierkegaard, most distinctively, wrote numerous clever works.[35]

(4) As an activity requiring logico-linguistic competences, Deleuze's metaphysical humour is probably also an instantiation of the inevitably cruel process of socialisation to which all sufficiently healthy psyches must be subjected. (The insufficiently healthy ones must endure, for their part, cruelties such as institutionalisation, subjection to other people's will, and even expedient abortion.)

Essentially, as Freudian psychoanalysis and some of its philosophical devotees have opined, this process of socialisation consists in taking that which is felt yet formless in the human soul and forcing it into intellectual pigeonholes. These are the social strictures through which our drives, emotions, strives, and mental forces at large must traverse.[36] This life-enabling process requires more than a modicum of genuine suffering, as *per* the common experiences of learning and training. Moreover, not all individuals can cope with this challenge, the application of which invariably generates neuroses and, at times, psychoses.[37]

As we noted earlier, Deleuze made "humour" proper a metaphysical instrument capable of revealing, or attempting to reveal, the cruelly sense-shattering root of human interaction. In particular, he cast the Freudian and psychiatric phenomenon of masochism as the most telling expression of such a singular humour, i.e., *qua* crafty logic of factual law-breaking by adhering to the letter of the law

---

[33] Polanyi (1962c), 212.
[34] It may be useful to reflect on the fact that even a committed dialectical materialist such as Gramsci (1977, vol.1, 466–467, Q4, par. 41) thought that fundamental epistemological issues such as our "certainty" with regard to "the objective existence of reality" is not something pertaining to "science *qua* the most economic description of reality", but to "common sense", i.e., "the most widespread and deeply rooted ideology", whereby people derive their "conception of the world, a philosophy, not a scientific datum".
[35] As already stated, we addressed at length Kierkegaard's reflections in *H&C1*.
[36] We do not address here the issue of creativity, which is in any case parasitic upon these inherited structures.
[37] We tackled in *H&C1* the cruelty of socialisation as recognised and discussed by Deleuze, Guattari, and others.

and, concurrently, contradicting its spirit. All sacred principles, even the paramount injunctions by God, can be challenged and pulverised humorously, opening the path to paradoxical outcomes.

Even if his conception of 'humour' is peculiar and not very funny, Deleuze had company arguing that humour can be a window through which we can view a cruelly puzzling world. Kozintsev correlated insights into this process. Schopenhauer and Pirandello did it too with their declared "true humour" actually hiding the potential and/or the partial realisation of just such disquieting truths about the human condition, which is far from amusing. Schopenhauer, even Leacock, showed us that the humourist's art can grasp the inextricable and baffling combination of comicality and tragedy lying at the heart of human existence. Casting light on its countless paradoxes and contradictions, including the essential duality of our transient being-in-the-world, so-called "true humour" smiles melancholically at each one of us humans, whose loving mothers condemned to death by the very act of giving birth to them.[38]

Similarly, such a true humour cries smilingly at the fate awaiting all human creations and civilisations, from the lowliest to the most glorious: eventual superseding, thorough neglect, sad misunderstanding, probable mis-recollection, inevitable forgetfulness, and annihilation. What have the Picts of Scotland ever done for us? Behind the sublime humourist's joke, as *per* the exchange between Hamlet and Polonius, to which Schopenhauer referred in his account of true humour, there lies a sublime, chilling, and inherently cruel realisation of our weakness, aimlessness, and insignificance. The grand scheme of things grinds each of us into homogeneous dust.

In yet another cruel irony of the human condition, after all that was involved in gifting us the ability to think, human thought comes to comprehend the miserable contingency and all-cheapening finitude of itself, its longings, beliefs, conventions, and creations. Hence, of human thought too. We strain to comprehend the cruel irony lurking behind all those pains and efforts, to which our own imperfect books on "humour" and "cruelty" proper belong too—also as a frustratingly self-effacing moment of limited self-realisation. Perhaps inasmuch as the weightiest thinking can only produce results that are eventually bound to disappear into nothingness, those pains and efforts are actually *not* warranted.[39]

---

[38] As grim as this last sentence may sound, it is actually a poignant signal for why we distinguished in our tetralogy "senselessness" from "insignificance". Whereas the former refers chiefly to *logico-linguistic* meaninglessness, the latter points towards *ethico-existential* meaninglessness.

[39] Each reader must make this evaluation on the basis of his/her common sense or philosophy.

4.4 A Taxonomy

As we posited in our Chapter 2, life's flow cannot be predicted. Its comic or humorous interpretation cannot be prescribed or preferred *a priori*. If anything, the inscrutable chaos of existence can drown an innocent person in the same water with which another's thirst gets quenched. Some people's glass can be so empty that the only water left is just enough to jump into it with a stone tied to the neck. And even then, the attempt may sometimes fail because of a silly mistake. Indeed, silliness can easily mock us under the most serious and sombre circumstances. Alas, the stone is too large for the glass that has been jumped into.[40]

Some of us may laugh at such an absurd order of things, but the drowning person should not be asked or expected to do so. Not even if such an action were to make the drowning quicker—which it probably would, in yet another irony of the same absurd order in which we live, suffer, and die. As ironic as it may sound, taking humour seriously and thinking about it in light of philosophy's venerable and complex history leads to some sombre, if not gloomy, considerations about the human condition.

This is especially true if we also include, as is the case in our book, the paradoxical irreducibility of "cruelty" proper in numerous (all?) aspects of human existence, as powerfully expressed by Hallie's philosophy.[41] Such dispassionate considerations can be extended by self-training into seeing how the pathetic can regularly destroy the comical, if not even one's ability to enjoy comedies and all that which is risible. Poignantly, the study of humour can teach us *humourlessness*.

We invite the reader to think, for illustration's sake, of all the alcohol-related anecdotes, jokes, pranks, and comedies that exist. Frequently, we are moderately entertained by the absurd behaviour of persons who have imbibed too much laughing water. It can be something that we witness in an alley on a Saturday night, learn about from a friend's yarn, see by way of video footage, or watch amusedly as this life is being represented in Hollywood comedies, e.g., the 2009–2013 *Hangover* film trilogy. We largely disregard the damage to health, reputation, and relations due to the consumption of intoxicants. The comedic beats the pathetic, big time.[42] Therefore, we may simply have something to laugh about. Drunken people usually come across as entertaining or funnily pathetic.

---

40 Unsurprisingly, failed suicides have been a standard staple in slapstick comedy, e.g., 'Snub' Pollard's 1923 *Join the Circus* and Laurel and Hardy's 1939 *Flying Deuces*.
41 Outlined in Chapter 1, a more detailed account of his views was offered in *H&C1*.
42 An analogous case is that of "folly", i.e., mental illness, which "was the dominant element in popular comedy in the ancient world", where "one of its distinguishing features was the foottown", which was reprised in medieval times and lasted, "[f]or five hundred years [, as] Gotham in Not-

It does not take much, however, to bring oneself to reflect upon the devastation that alcohol can cause. This is especially true if the woes of alcoholism have been part of one's own family history, genes, community, social experience, etc.[43] Once our mind is so directed, the ludicrous aspects of alcohol's excessive consumption become far less glaring—all the way down to nil.[44] And once this sort of considered approach to humour become second nature, the ridiculousness of the world in which we live and struggle becomes barely tenable, if not even imperceptible.

Gorgias' old advice to rhetors—fighting seriousness with playfulness and playfulness with seriousness—continues to be relevant. If jokes can kill philosophical reflection and all that is serious, as Hazlitt noted in the 19th century, so can serious philosophical reflection kill all that is jocular.[45] Explaining a joke or a pun routinely destroys their comic effect. As Voltaire famously stated: "Humour when explain'd is no longer Humour."[46]

According to Morreall and Amir, critical reflection, once it is unleashed, reveals considerable murkiness in the allegedly lighter, brighter and wiser realm of humour. In effect, following insights into the nature of laughter and humour that are as old as philosophy itself, we have argued here that humour, whether it is thought to be 'false' or 'true', requires at least a pinch of brutal cruelty— when not even an additional one of sadism.[47]

Humour's intimate kinship with cruelty is therefore contradictory only *prima facie*. Indeed, according to the grapevine, humour is, at heart, friendly. But, as it should be clear by now, things are not that simple. The grapevine does not always bear fruit, and if it does, its fruits may be poisonous or rotten. As we have written in our previous chapters, cruelty lives within humour and, at times, prospers.

---

tinghamshire, England" (Esar 1954, 88 and 90). Successive variations have included: "the April fool ..., the absent-minded professor ... , the fool's query" and the attendant "answer ... in the spirit it deserves", i.e., "a form of irony which rhetoricians call asterism", plus the 20th-century "comic character[s] ... of little Audrey ... [and] the little moron" (Esar 1954, 93–100).

43 See, e.g., Lynge (1997).
44 The Anglophone champions of the so-called "dry" movements in the 19th- and early 20th century represented this humourless approach to alcohol consumption. See, e.g., Winskill (1892).
45 Outlined in Chapter 1, a more detailed account of his views was offered in *H&C1*.
46 Voltaire (1994), 108.
47 As Schopenhauer, Hazlitt, and Santayana had also observed, what we find funny in comedies or common jocularity, most of us could not bear happening to ourselves or people who are dear to us. Although we know of no statistics on this point, we would submit that it is probably easier to laugh at one's own misfortunes rather than at those of our loved ones, especially our children and grandchildren. Still, individuals can arguably differ in this respect too.

Such a conclusion may seem paradoxical. Yet if we think of Hallie's account of cruelty as paradoxical, we may grasp why such a paradox should be accepted as plausible, if not sensible. After all, we have already encountered exemplifications of two paradoxes of cruelty in line with Hallie's comprehensive taxonomy. We mean, to be exact, paradoxes number 1 (i.e., "wanting the best and doing the worst") and number 5 (i.e., "responsive cruelty").[48]

In a further feat of corroboration of the mutual support that humour and cruelty can provide, it is not overly complicated to find pertinent examples for the other 'Hallian' paradoxes as well. Let us tackle them below.

(1) As concerns paradox number 2 in Hallie's taxonomy, which pivots around cruel education aimed at avoiding worse cruelty, this pedagogy can certainly embrace humorous cruelty. We can list, for instance: making children realise their foolishness by using biting remarks; awakening logical thought and self-awareness by effective doses of sarcasm in the classroom; scaring an obstinate person by way of a nasty prank to teach her a lesson; or warning one's compatriots of the dangers lying ahead by means of scathing satire or caustic criticism. A mild jolt may be the way to avoid shocking behaviours.[49]

As there have long existed *in terrorem* literary techniques, so are *in iucundum terrorem* techniques possible too. Essentially, they would be a variation on the theme of self-correction, insofar as they pivot around the notion that we can, by way of cruel humour, propel its recipient's will, ingenuity, creativity, commitment, self-observation, self-awareness, self-criticism, etc. On the broader social scene, ridicule, humiliation, putting down, and the whole armoury of humorously cruel devices could then become useful rhetorical tools whereby to mount defences, attacks, and counterattacks against, say, silver-tongued orators and cunning demagogues.[50]

---

[48] In a further exemplification of both these paradoxes, Pareto (1935, vol. 4, par. 1799) claimed that "the dogmas of the humanitarian religion", born as a response to the cruel injustices of the *ancien régime* and aiming at 'obvious' collective goods such as "Progress ... and ... equality", could unleash "a servitude oftentimes more cruel than what used to be known as slavery". Family dismemberments, forced relocations, re/education programmes and much else testify to the plausibility of Pareto's claim, and cruel irony, whether in Canada, Greenland, Russia, or China.

[49] Teachers' and parents' mock threats and sardonic reproaches can be read as components of that "cruel alphabet" that Deleuze and Guattari (1987 and 2004) argued to be part and parcel of the process of socialisation. Amir (2001, 11) herself came close to realising this paradox in her study of Platonic love with regard to the parent-child relationship, which is as frustrating and conflictual as it is emotionally deep and rewarding.

[50] Shaftesbury (1999) and Cassirer (1953), for their part, purported a defensive use of humour which extends to humorous cruelty, e.g., to defeat ill-meaning and/or dangerous adversaries in

(2) Regarding Hallie's paradox number 3, which pertains to the aesthetic value of cruelty, there seems to be no doubt whatsoever that the *fascinosum* of cruelty extends to humorous cruelty too. Not only have there been plenty of historical cases in which laughter and cruelty have walked hand-in-hand, as exemplified by the bizarre theatrical executions of the Roman circuses.[51] In addition, there have been endless corroborations of the intertwined experiences *vis-à-vis* common forms of fun whereby someone is humiliated, ridiculed, abused, mistreated, and/or variously caused to suffer. Vicariously, we are regularly exposed to all sorts of sadistic thrills, whether portrayed on a stage or screen.[52] In this reality, the morally safer thrills of joyfully witnessing whatever 'justice' being done, sometimes in the most gruesome ways, is possibly the most obvious of such forms.[53]

Hallie's own examples of "sexual pleasure", higher "awareness", the liberation of sensual "imagination", and "masochistic pleasure" evoke more forms, insofar as laughter or, for the champions of so-called "true humour", an unresolved admixture of comicality and pathos can plausibly accompany many valued domains of human life. These include:

(2a) artistic creations (e.g., the long-trained and painstakingly rehearsed comedies put on stage by poorly paid artists, who "are productive masochists");[54]

(2b) erotic practices (e.g., a dominatrix ridiculing her sex slave; pointed jokes and sore pranks exchanged by romantic partners during or around sexual intercourse);[55]

(2c) quests for spiritual enlightenment (e.g., the Zen master's amused humiliation of the well-meaning disciple; the smiling Socratic self-awareness of

---

open discussions and public matters. We discuss the life-enabling uses of cruel humour and humorous cruelty in more detail in *H&C3*.

51 Ancient Roman cruelties loom large in our research. Yet *ancient empires at large had cruelties aplenty*. See, e.g., the royal burning of captives from poor and rural provinces in 13th- to 9th-century BC Assyria, where it was believed that such a this-worldly disposal would prevent the victims from entering the afterlife (Dewar 2021).

52 Fascination with cruel depictions is a time-honoured phenomenon, as was discussed by Hartwig (1986).

53 Portmann (2000, 129–144) devoted an entire chapter to "Punishment and Its Pleasure". As to recent examples, we can mention the cheerful faces of people attending the execution of Libya's former leader, Muammar Gaddafi, who was sodomised with a bayonet before being shot in the head (Chulov 2011).

54 A. Phillips (1998), 45.

55 "Ethics and survival should constitute the limits of erotic behaviour, not propriety or normality" (A. Phillips 1998, 53). Humour and sado-masochistic practices not only resemble each other in being transgressive and relieving but can also coexist, as *per* the last two examples in the main text.

the seasoned researcher launching into yet another project that will bring him/her lots of exhausting work and no enduring fame);[56] and
(2d) the heightening of our sensuous being (e. g., rolling in the cold snow after a hot sauna; coaching a classical-singing student into stretching to the very limits his/her phonic faculties by way of ludicrous yet exhausting vocal exercises).[57]

Sometimes, the fun is worth the pain that it involves, or so it would seem. Which and how this nominal "fun" can be conceived of varies a lot, though. As classical ballet dancers, mountaineers, kick-boxing athletes, and road cyclists might testify, it may be 'fun' enduring years of painful training, sweat, horrible smells, blood, and frequent setbacks. Perhaps what we seek is the intensity of the experience, rather than some more palatable yet superficial hedonic stimulation. As the feminist author Anita Phillips poetically remarked in her 1998 book, *A Defense of Masochism:* "But why would the rose ever have become such a compelling symbol of love if not for its cruelly piercing thorns?"[58] And less lyrically, but more accurately: "Any intense experience – sex, art, even fleeting, momentary perceptions like the effect of inhaling the scent of a flower – can lead to an overpowering, self-shattering emotion... But the feeling of intense arousal of any kind is also painful."[59]

(3) Paradox number 4 is the one that, in all likelihood, touches the most upon the delicate matter of whether pleasure-seeking humour or pain-sparing humourlessness should be prioritised. Whenever we choose to make fun of anyone, ourselves included, are we considering how deep, prolonged and/or socially meaningful is the stinging involved? In the absence of precise criteria and in the presence of generic maxims of good conduct, shall we err on the side of caution or on that of risk-taking?

These interrogatives point to a fundamental moral question about humour, not just blatantly cruel humour, that each person must answer under specific circumstances, i.e., whenever she is required to choose whether to try to be funny or not, knowing that her attempt might fail, and/or that it might succeed by making some-

---

[56] Again, Amir (2017, 167 f) came close to acknowledging this paradox when discussing the importance of continued "dissatisfaction" in the intellectual life of philosophers who can always undo established conclusions.
[57] This paradox implies a larger moral issue, i.e., *consent*. We do not deal with this thorny issue here.
[58] A. Phillips (1998), 38.
[59] A. Phillips (1998), 39.

one suffer—even if just a little.⁶⁰ In an ideal world, people would always try—and be able to—strike the right balance. The real world is not like that, however, even among supposed 'peers' *à la* Shaftsbury or Harvey, i.e., people of equal status— whether they exist in reality or not (as noted, following Baroncelli, we are sceptical about this possibility).

Thus, a certain amount of exposure to humorous cruelty might be desirable for the sake of, as the phrase goes, "toughening up" one's own character to the mundane reality of an imperfect universe that, unhappily, seems to be our regular dwelling place.⁶¹ Perhaps we should even invite this kind of cruelty, which may fortify us, also in light of our own idiosyncrasies and imperfections. As the Scottish theologian James A. Simpson noted at the end of the last century: "The capacity to laugh at oneself is a mark of inner security and maturity. Though acquiring that ability can be painful."⁶² A non-lethal dose of wilfully sought and accepted pain, in other words, could be a healthy option under more or less tacitly codified yet auspicious social circumstances. As Phillips argued: "to seal [oneself] off from external threat, to go for invulnerability ... while [it] protects you from the outside world ... does not allow a flow between interior and exterior, causing a kind of irritable stagnation and a loss of nerve".⁶³

Awareness of ugliness and resilience to pain in the world in which we find ourselves thrown and bound to live in may be a crucial skill.⁶⁴ This being the case, at least and as long as such ugliness and pain do not impair our effective functioning. So qualified, awareness of ugliness and resilience to pain are likely to be important character traits of a mature person, existentially speaking.⁶⁵ As to determining whether, which, and how effective functioning has been impaired

---

60 Harvey (1999, 65) claimed that we can be cruel not only as initiators, but also "complicit" laughingstock by playing along with a morally horrid social game *and*, despite the experienced horror, not complaining.

61 Toughening up one's character and changing the world around oneself to make it less onerous are not mutually exclusive strategies. Above all, both require effort. They too are, as such, facets of life's cruelty.

62 J. Simpson (1998), 26.

63 A. Philips (1998), 41, whose heroic and hedonic embrace of pain recalls Rosset's work, as well as Nietzsche's.

64 As the US feminist thinker Arnault (2003, 155) argued, today's "Americans cherish the idea that good eventually triumphs over evil", but lived reality tells another, much grimmer tale. Many cultures share this American, arguably Hollywood-fed, mistaken idea of justice's victory in this world which is burning as we write.

65 Emphasis on hard challenges in character education varies among pedagogists, but is never absent, whether in Western contexts (see, e.g., DeRoche and Williams 2001, chap. 2) or Eastern ones (see, e.g., Huda *et al.* 2020).

or facilitated, that is tricky business indeed. Cruelly, grey areas, doubts, disagreements, and simple mistakes are part of the picture too.

The surest critical threshold is located at the point where no life-enablement occurs. That is also where life-functions cease. Before that point, we will have to do our best based on our defective and incomplete abilities. Thus, one may even entertain the notion that much commonplace humour might have to be tolerated, though perhaps not proactively pursued, even when it targets "individual outsiders and excluded groups", if such a humour can then "shape a distinct understanding of the world, which is additional to representations by those who portray their marginality through the arts".[66]

Worldly wisdom and functional socialisation could then be said to also depend on possessing these two traits, which cannot but include all those times when the awareness of ugliness and the resilience to pain have come to us in a humorous package.[67] This is not to mean that hardcore brutes and/or sadistic jokesters are to be consciously raised and favoured.[68] Rather, we mean that individuals capable of engaging in, *at the very least*, a modicum of refined bantering *à la* Shaftesbury may be better suited and likelier to operate effectively in a variety of social settings compared to individuals who are not tempered in even this low-temperature fire. Without any such transformation, one can melt as the temperature rises, even modestly.[69]

4.5 A Theory

Our odds of finding joy in life might well depend on accepting these paradoxes and, as far as cruel humour is concerned, possessing the abilities highlighted by paradox number 4 in particular.[70] As also recalled by one of the most famous

---

[66] Clements (2020), 6. Let us note that Clements is no advocate of outright cruelty. Quite the reverse.
[67] The other side of the same coin would then be the willingness to risk being cruel by way of humour, for the sake of proper social interaction and self-expression, if not of cautious self-defence, i.e., as *responsive* cruelty.
[68] Like the self-declared "radical feminist author" John Stoltenberg (2021, pars. 1–3 and bio), we do not approve of the machoistic "Alpha Code" instructing boys to become "real men".
[69] This closing joke is meant to make our reader think about the common derogatory use of "snowflake".
[70] The importance of suffering—adequately faced and understood by the individual—for the development of a mature personality is discussed in Corbett (2015). Significantly, Corbett's (2015, 290) Jungian approach was informed by his father's experiences as a concentration-camp survivor and the author's own ordeal as an oncology patient: "Suffering makes the ego face what it has been

comic minds of our era, the Pythonesque cartoonist and filmmaker Terry Gilliam, a mixture of "humour" and "cruelty" can spur great "creativity".[71] The point was made while discussing the ritual "degradations" imposed by older college students onto younger ones in American "fraternit[ies]" and "English public schools", where "brutalisation" capable of "a certain deadening of feeling" was part of the well-established traditions for much of the 20th century: "If [brutalisation] is meted out with a sense of humour, and an awareness that this is just a gauntlet that has to be run as a prelude to some kind of social acceptance, then the cruelty of it can be a vehicle for creativity."[72]

This is certainly the case if we pay heed to the philosophical existentialism of Rosset and remain willing to listen to that protracted current of philosophical thought that—from Seneca to Rorty—has kept retrieving the unpleasant sting of cruelty in every manner of intrapersonal recesses and interpersonal transactions. Not least those whence it was believed to have been expunged once and for all or in which it was thought not to be employed, by virtue of ingrained levity and cheerfulness.[73]

More or less adamant or unhappy about such a dismal realisation, these eminent voices have also supported the puzzling conclusion that cruelty, albeit so deeply loathed and so frequently contested, is an inevitable, indispensable, integral, and insisting constituent of life, whether we look at it from the standpoint of each individual or from that of collective co-existence. Without the abilities pertaining to paradox number 4, then, no happiness in life could even begin to be explored, not to mention attained or appreciated.[74]

Consistently with this uninviting yet persuasive interpretation of human existence, Amir's notion of intrapersonal "self-mockery", i.e., "compassionate aggression", could arguably be extended to the many interactions in which we regularly

---

ignoring, strips the persona, and makes us pay attention to parts of ourselves that have never had a chance to live."
71 Gilliam (2015), 43.
72 Gilliam (2015), 42–43. Apart from its callow irony, a deeper issue is at stake as, i.e., what sort of 'toughness' may be necessary and/or even desirable in people's formative years so that a society may be able to produce, say, surgeons, medics, trade unionists, firefighters, police officers, soldiers, and, if needed, resistance fighters or revolutionaries. There is no easy answer, of course. But the question remains relevant.
73 The persistence of cruelty in allegedly 'civilised' life is dealt with in detail in *H&C1*.
74 As seen in Chapters 1 and 2, Rosset, like Morreall and Amir, presupposed that the search for joy, however imperfect and steeped in disappointment it may be, is a worthy endeavour. Leopardi and Schopenhauer disagreed with him, albeit both would maintain that our ability to laugh in the face of life's horror is a worthy skill.

engage under the rubric of "humour", if and when linguistically socialised.[75] Her notion would therefore morph into an aptly named, plausibly mild, and personally advantageous form of communally-accepted suffering which prepares us for the much harsher challenges that, inevitably, life throws at us.[76]

Mocking one another in ways that do not leave us disabled on the battlefield of life might be, *a fortiori*, more useful than opting for stern agelasm or misogelasm which—we must acknowledge—have been a legitimate part of the cultural choices that have been experimented with throughout humankind's long and diverse history.[77] Whilst preserving some of the cruelty characterising humour's primeval roots, the acceptance of such a modified "compassionate aggression" would concentrate on other attributes that became more pronounced and existentially more advantageous over the centuries.

From an evolutionary perspective, the possibility, if not outright probability, of such an existential advantage may be the very reason why "humor" is still with us *qua* "leading factor in human progress", as Leacock confidently wrote in the 1930s—also boasting that "kindliness" had become by then the very "essence" of humour's most refined artistic manifestations.[78] This is what, optimistically, he claimed to have happened in the course of human evolution.

We write "optimistically" because Leacock's writings conveniently underplay a number of sobering qualifications:
(1) Buried in the largely inscrutable soul of each moral agent, lingering cruel motives make the threshold between kindness (aka "kindliness") and cruelty difficult to pinpoint with exactitude.
(2) The laughingstock's response to an act of interpersonal compassionate aggression cannot be predicted with certainty. Communication, especially when humorous, casts its own shadow, i.e., plain yet rarely simple *misunderstanding*— hence also failing to laugh, taking offence, misconstruing the misunderstand-

---

[75] The criteria and thresholds for proper and/or sufficient linguistic socialisation can vary across time and place.
[76] Lives spent devoid of much suffering, including major adversity, are the rarest of exceptions, in our view.
[77] We write "mocking" because Amir (2019, 125) "promote[d]" "humour" *qua* "self-mocking ridicule". As to the terms *misogelasm* and *agelasm*, or their nominal and adjectival forms *misogelast/ic* and *agelast/ic*, they refer, respectively, to a condemnation of laughter and/or merriment and refusal to go in for it/them (see Billig 2005, 14, crediting the Victorian poet and novelist George Meredith with their coinage).
[78] Leacock (1938), preface.

ing itself, spreading negative opinions, distancing oneself, and/or over/reacting in a negative manner, including by means of responsive cruelty.[79]
(3) The targets' seeming 'prickliness' can mean real suffering for them and/or others, e.g., sympathetic friends, loving spouses, close relatives, empathic observers, etc.
(4) The standards and the levels of this seeming prickliness vary enormously across places and generations, thus reducing, redefining, redescribing, and/or reassessing over time the supposed 'refinement' of humour itself, whether commonplace or true.

As regards the last item, Leacock's historical fate as a respected and then neglected humourist is quite telling. In a cruel irony of Canadian history, his own intentionally progressive, kind, and humane prose which aimed at pursuing "true humour" proper has later been 'discovered' to have been unreflectingly and unbearably too 'sexist', 'patriarchal', 'racist', and 'colonial' to be considered 'really' kind and humane, i.e., to be 'really' refined.[80] He couldn't be that funny, could he? Perhaps he wasn't, *really*.[81]

Furthermore, however liable to anachronistic *post-mortem* moral judgements, even that very same noble and ennobling "humour" proper that Leacock pursued and praised, can actually turn or revert into something nastier. As Leacock admitted: "Those who try to make people laugh, necessarily get afraid that they may not see the point and won't laugh, or won't laugh enough. Hence the tendency to make the point sharper and the angle of vision wider, to respond to the cruel demand, 'louder and funnier'."[82]

Cruelty, in other words, might well be capable of becoming kindness. But this transformation is neither always nor necessarily the case. Mistakes can and will be made, whenever encountering, enabling, expecting, and/or encouraging people

---

79 This phenomenon is discussed more extensively in *H&C3*. As to the line separating reaction from overreaction, it is far too context-dependant to permit establishing a clear rule or trenchant criterion. Risk is then added to risk. Error to error. And, conceivably, cruelty to cruelty.
80 See, e.g., Ritter (1986) and Nock (2007). Perhaps, in some decades' time, our own research will be condemned as immoral, unkind, and *passé* because of some sin or failing that we did not fully anticipate, e.g., adhering to logic, having eaten red meat, using English as our scholarly language, being monogamous, driving non-electric cars.
81 Beattie (1778, essay 2, 395) claimed that cultures' morphing in time is a crueller foe to comedy than tragedy. *A posteriori* denial of refinement is one aspect of this phenomenon. Inability to produce amusement is another.
82 Leacock (1938), chap. 3, sec. 3, par. 17.

to be funny.[83] People are fallible, as we know—hence we find also the "louder and funnier" instances upon which Leacock remarked.

The spontaneity and immediacy required for commonplace humour to arise and be effective adds the risks that are inevitably associated with any social activity that cannot be planned carefully, painstakingly, but rather largely improvised and chiefly predicated upon our lore of tacit abilities, which may simply not be up to the task. Making a witty remark at the drop of a hat, then, carries the danger of losing one's face with it, if unsuccessful. In Lewis Carroll's *Alice in Wonderland*, which is *inter alia* an eerie farcical mirror of real society's cruel aptitudes for unforgiving judgementalism and knee-jerk reactions, the swift response to a mistaken attempt at humour could be: "Off with his head!"[84]

What is more, some people may simply not care about making 'mistakes' of this unkind sort, which can be actively pursued by others instead. 'Progress' may matter to some individuals, particularly those who happen to be 'conscionable' or 'progressive', but it is not a concept that is inherently fated to universal victory. Nor is it destined for everlasting appreciation. As Chesterton cautioned his readers:

> [W]e must not count on the certainty even of comforts becoming more common or cruelties more rare; as if this were an inevitable social trend towards a sinless humanity; instead of being as it was a mood of man, and perhaps a better mood, possibly to be followed by a worse one. We must not hate humanity, or despise humanity, or refuse to help humanity; but we must not trust humanity.[85]

And Leacock stated:

> The original devil of malice was not so easily exorcized. It still survives. The development of humor was not always and exclusively of a refining character. One is tempted to think that perhaps the original source parted into two streams. In one direction flowed, clear and undefiled, the humor of human kindliness. In the other, the polluted waters of mockery and sarcasm, the "humor" that turned to the cruel sports of rough ages, the infliction of pain as a perverted source of pleasure, and even the rough horseplay, the practical jokes and the impish malice of the schoolboy. Here belongs 'sarcasm'—that scrapes the flesh of human feeling with a hoe—the sardonic laugh (by derivation a sort of rictus of the mouth from a poison weed), the sneer of the scoffer, and the snarl of the literary critic as opposed to the kindly

---

[83] See Polanyi's (1962c) understanding of "performances" in Chapter 2 and *per* our account in *H&C1*.
[84] Carroll (2008), chap. 7 *et passim*. Given that mistakes can be made by women too, then "Off with her head!" could also be heard. Equality cuts both ways. More on the cruelty suffered by unsuccessful humourists is discussed in *H&C3*. See also Kipnis (2017) on how unwelcome irony can be.
[85] Chesterton (2006), essay 2, part 2, par. 4.

tolerance of the humorist. Not even death, if we may believe the spiritualists, terminates the evil career of the practical joker. He survives as the thing called a "poltergeist" in German—or a something or other in English—a malicious noisy spirit, haunting for haunting's sake, and unfortunately beyond the grasp of the law.[86]

Aware of all these sorry limits and sardonic licences of humour, at least in some of its commonplace expressions, an externalised version of Amir's compassionate aggression can nonetheless be thought of as a plausible and, perchance, desirable element in human affairs, whether or not we will ever reduce, or seek to reduce in earnest, all commonplace humour to some ideal 'true' humour.[87] Civilisation can be uncivil, no matter how old it has grown to be, but it is civilisation nonetheless. Some progress would seem to have been made, after all. If not even warts and all.[88] We are no longer sinking clubs into each other's skulls as an ordinary laughing matter, are we?

Upon further reflection—and at the potential expense of the scholarly originality of all people involved—an externalised version of Amir's compassionate aggression might have long been in place in human civilisations, and to an massive extent.[89] Mild and customary, this arrangement would comprise all those civilised versions of the quasi-animal reality to which Morreall and today's evolutionary biopsychology refer as sheer monkey play among primates, including us.[90] For thou-

---

[86] Leacock (1938), chap. 1, sec. 5, par. 19.

[87] In his writings, Leacock ended up reiterating the emphasis on refined humour *versus* unrefined humour and pits nominal "true humour" *versus* all other (hence lower) forms of ridicule, despite the latter's higher empirical frequency and their Freudian and Bakhtinian psycho-social role *qua* cathectic safety valves. The search for refined forms of humour has been typical of the Anglophone tradition. Yet Leacock's terminology also points towards a geographically wider propensity of the Western philosophers of humour and cognate notions to focus on a predilect qualification that, somewhat magically, makes certain kinds of humour ontologically 'truer' than others.

[88] It is doubtful that all instances of commonplace humour should be credibly translated into Leacock's (1938, chap. 1, par. 5) "highest stage" of humour, which is akin to Amir's own "philosophic self-education" and the wise humour emerging thereof. As we have argued, this emancipatory path, whether desirable or not, is inevitably undemocratic. Moreover, it may fail to appeal to many people on account of causes that cannot be easily or effectively corrected, e.g., lack of imagination, unbeatable ignorance, petty egoism.

[89] Were originality to fall victim to our investigation, we would still have brought to the surface aspects of reality about which people rarely reflect or discuss. Besides, in Western philosophy, we have all been said to be nothing but Plato's footnotes. Genuine originality is, given this perspective, improbable.

[90] Additional relevant reflections on the ambiguous psychosocial mechanisms at play in this unkind kind of play were already presented in Chapter 3. Being part of our inherited biological propensities and childhood experiences, we become so used to this 'monkey business' that much com-

sands of years, despite the tragedies along the way, human beings have joked with one another with reasonable success, i.e., they have not been annihilated in the process. As cruel as it was, their humour was not fatal. And that is a positive result that we should not dismiss as a gift of history.

At the same time, as the existentialist and pessimist thinkers encountered in our book keep reminding us, all monkeys must suffer—not least any self-respecting higher primate or any clever, oddly naked, ape.[91] If Rosset and his many gloomy disciplinary companions were correct in their suggestions—and we believe that, by and large, they are—then having *some* fun in life implies accepting an indeterminate but positive cargo of cruelties too. These scholars would certainly also embrace the minimal painfulness of the very same monkey play studied by Morreall and said biopsychologists.

In a recent utilitarian rehearsal of Western pessimism, a professional ethicist concluded that the massive prevalence of pain over pleasure in a person's life makes bringing new life into this world morally unjustifiable.[92] Dealing with "humour" proper, instead, Eagleton rehearsed Rosset's existentialism: "There is cruelty and pain, then, but the world is to be affirmed in full knowledge of these facts... Comedy and fatalism are thus in collusion."[93] Once again, *we are cast between a rock and a hard place.* And we must choose which of the two we prefer. The human condition has a wicked sense of humour, if it has any at all.[94]

---

monplace humour mutates into an innocent textual phenomenon in the works of most proponents of the incongruity theory, whose analytical focus is so strongly placed on the incongruous message itself that the small amount of hierarchical interpersonal biting and the sore nipping accompanying it are either neglected or forgotten.

91 We are referring, by wordplay, to Morris (1967), the most successful work of zoology in the last century.

92 See Benatar (2006).

93 Eagleton (2019), 49–50.

94 This is how Amir (forthcoming) interpreted Rosset's "philosophy of laughter". First, even if the best comedy cannot but acknowledge, in one way or another, the inevitably cruel features of existence. We can still laugh at such features, hence experiencing some paradoxical, holiday-like, non-illusory pleasure, which consists in "the laughter of annihilation". Secondly, insofar as these cruel features include the tension between our tendency to seek a rational order behind everything, on the one hand, and the realisation that such an order is not in place, on the other hand, comicality can be said to be grounded in the ontology of the universe, for such a tension can be alternatively read as tragic as well as comical.

4.6 A Dictum

The paradoxicality of humorous cruelty is further exemplified by the oft-neglected reversal of a common phrase that we rehearsed in Chapter 1: "You've got to be cruel to be kind". Humour shows us how such a dictum can work in reverse: "You've got to be kind to be cruel".

Humour can be used as a seemingly light, playful, almost amicable instrument to not take seriously someone else or oneself. We can make a clever joke, display our wit, ridicule, and/or make light of anyone and anything, so as not to care about their plight or our own. Hazlitt's concerns about the frequent abuses of humour to pooh-pooh higher notions and/or better people pointed already in this direction. By turning serious matters into merrier ones, humour can cause us to neglect that which ought to be taken seriously.

While Morreall and Amir detected wisdom in such an ability, which can make the agony of existence and the world's many horrors a little less frightening, the intuitions that we can retrieve in Hazlitt's warnings suggest a different and far less accommodating notion. Specifically, the step taking us from not caring about someone's plight to not *having* to care about their condition is small. Repetition, habituation, and the seemingly consolation that smiling and/or laughing at tragedies entails can transform an occasional response into a persistent obduracy *vis-à-vis* the traumas, terrors, and troubling aspects of life.

No matter how many times we are told that *"is doesn't imply ought"*, that is how we appear to go about becoming and trying to remain moral persons, at least according to some noted thinkers.[95] After all, if we do not acquire habits of thought and action by repeated observation and agency, how else do we get them?[96]

Moreover, there can ensue major moral failures of imaginative empathy and genuine understanding. By reacting humorously to the tensions and contradictions that we encounter, a person can eventually lose her ability to put herself into someone else's shoes. Similarly, she can lose the ability to 'see' any good reasons why a different set of conditions and interactions should be advocated so that a super-individual standpoint for moral assessment and just conduct can be conceivably and competently constructed. Callousness, then, is facilitated, though with a smile.

---

[95] This moral quandary is too massive to deal within this volume. Hence, we limit ourselves to a hint.
[96] In a convoluted way, this is the conclusion reached by Dworkin (2011). LVOA points in the same direction.

It is therefore not altogether surprising to come across such a jovial brutality in workplaces and bureaucratic bodies, public as well as private. Whether active (e. g., a CEO joking about the union leaders' demands as nostalgic naïveté) or passive (e. g., the business pundits' amused approval of the CEO's conduct and implied agreement with him/her), humour feigns friendly politeness while pursuing effecting life-disablement. Under conditions of competition, political pressure, or any other paramount aim causing genuine emotional and/or imaginative engagements with other people or oneself to be discounted, humour can be most effective to belittle people without coming across as villainous.

If anything, as Harvey insisted, those who happen to complain about the humour itself can be easily victimised further as boors, troublemakers, and/or thin-skinned humourless people. If psychologically rewarding, their humiliation can even be sought after intentionally, moving past the point of callousness alone, and opening the gates to sadism. And still with a smile.

Hypothetically, as Harlow was willing to concede in theory but struggled so hard to retrieve in practice, there may be incongruities or dualities that show hardly any malice or hierarchical positioning. More often than not, quotidian humour evokes the superiority theory. Indeed, the more 'other' or 'alien' one is thought to be, the easier it is to turn him/her into a laughingstock and to be cruel to him/her, whether by means of elaborate satire, trite sexist and racist jokes, or clever pranks causing unease, fear, public denigration, self-doubt, self-loathing, and/or shame.[97] Thus, Schopenhauer's, Hazlitt's, and Santayana's critical observations cannot but highlight the issue of where the appropriate limits of compassion should be drawn for humour to continue to exist and, synchronously, be more or less immune from cruelty—insofar and inasmuch as cruelty is to be avoided.[98]

If we assume that cruelty ought to be shunned, we are bound to have qualms about humour, whether commonplace or 'true'. Humour, as we have already remarked, cannot happen without punching. The 'up' or 'down' of the blows, moreover, acquire their significance in connection with the wider social context in which the humour unfolds, i.e., *per* the general socio-ethical understanding of these two imaginary directions which have surfaced again and again in our research.[99] In and by itself, however, humour *punches*. That is to say, when humour

---

[97] Given the inevitable hierarchical role of humour at the perlocutionary level, it can be argued that the heralds of the incongruity theory focus so much on the message rather than on the speaker and/or audience that the audience becomes 'other' and 'alien' to the point of non-recognition and unintended moral blindness.
[98] Were we not concerned about cruelty's immorality, this issue would not arise.
[99] Further considerations on this matter will follow in *H&C3*.

is activated, it jabs primarily in the direction of its intended target, but also at whatever targets may also be reached by the fists that fly.[100]

Revealingly, a contemporary follower of Leacock's 'true' humour acknowledged implicitly the aggressive power inherent to this phenomenon when comparing it to an army's "light infantry" and juxtaposing it with "the artillery of fierce criticism".[101] Though it may not be a lethal blow on the head, humour's punching is no innocent caress either. Cannonballs are probably worse than bayonets, but bayonets cut deep nevertheless.

Upon closer logico-linguistic scrutiny, humour can actually be said to be punching down all the time, i.e., before striking in socio-ethical terms and, even more deeply, in terms of life disablement and/or enablement.[102] To be exact, if it is considered *in abstracto*, the initiator's humour cannot but establish an in-group from which the ridiculed target/s is/are excluded, together with all the people that the initiator excludes, e.g., those that are too 'slow', 'ignorant', 'dour' or 'dumb'.

As fleeting and as minimal as his/her interventions may be, the initiator thereby enjoys logico-linguistic power. This capability is the 'fuel' with which one is able to poke fun at the chosen target/s and/or dismiss *ab initio* some of his/her potential audience, whose emotional reactions are conveniently ignored. This would include their sense of belittlement, humiliation, exclusion, potential or actual targeting, unverified and unverifiable threat, etc.[103] Importantly, the experience of this vestigial power in times of great suffering, such as during genocide or among rape victims, is precisely why it has often been possible to use humour as a meaningful tool for resistance against victimisers, oppressors, invaders, patriarchs, and/or enemies of all kinds.[104]

Were the victims truly devoid of any power, no humour could take place at all —not even within the private domain of one's own psyche. Far from being another academic abstraction, numerous conditions of profound internalised powerlessness have been observed by psychologists working with victims of recurring

---

[100] Humour's punches can hit individuals, groups, and/or humankind at large, i.e., by way of misanthropic humour, which, despite its huge and cumbersome target, can be accomplished in subtle and nifty ways. See, e.g., Reinhart's (2020, 36 footnote) clever contrast between "the human species" and "cephalopods, paying close attention to their armpit-mouth-genitals and wry sense of wonderment, play, cruelty and humour".

[101] J. Simpson (1998), 28.

[102] See especially Chapter 2.

[103] For any jest to occur, some people must be left out and, possibly and plausibly, caused to suffer, in yet another reminder of the cruel fabric of reality highlighted by Western pessimists and existentialists.

[104] More is said on this point in *H&C3*.

abuse.[105] Humourlessness is among their most common symptoms. Also, one such example was poignantly portrayed in the final chapter of George Orwell's celebrated novel *1984*.[106] In it, an utterly abased Winston Smith is masterfully depicted; his prolonged and effective torturing by the cunning State agent O'Brien transformed him into a Big-Brother-loving and irreparably traumatised individual. At that plutonic point of violation and victimisation, Smith calmly awaits his execution; spiritlessly and incapable of hatred for his tormentors, vindictive rage, erotic desire, and, *à propos*, any sense of humour whatsoever.

4.7 A Dilemma

Given the apparent inevitability of cruelty in all acts of ridicule, if we opt for drawing a line, it is very likely that some cruelty will be allowed, sadistic and brutal, or merely brutal.[107] If we do not draw this line, then we have two opposite and probably academic options from which to choose.[108]
(1) At one end of the spectrum, we may allow anything to be fair game for levity, as exemplified through history by 'scandalous' humour poking fun at religion, racial divides, political injustices, sexual orientations, and/or existential anxieties.[109] Thoroughly secular and deeply liberal societies could be taken to be, at least *prima facie*, examples of such an option.[110]
(2) At the opposite end, we may decide to allow nothing to be fair game in the most 'Puritan' condemnation of humour in each of its manifestations.[111] No comedies. No clowns. No laughing in public spaces. No enthusiastic children

---

105 See, e.g., Bannister (2003), chap. 1–3.
106 Orwell (1961) had real roots: the Spanish Civil War and "communism under Stalin" (Wildemeersch 2013, 100).
107 As noted, knowing exactly and always which motives lie behind humour is probably impossible.
108 As we wrote "very likely" in the previous sentence, so do we write "probably" in this one. The semantic diversity of our titular terms, the dissonance of the reviewed conceptions, plus the opacity of human drives and purposes make us *humble*. Some readers will find this attitude frustrating, even cowardly. Others will agree. Again, in deciding whether to deem this approach frustrating or sensible, each reader is required to make a call under her own *personal* responsibility in line with the wisdom of Polanyi (1962c).
109 Monty Python's 1969–1973 *Flying Circus* TV series contains abundant examples of these forms of humour. Similarly, Westbrook and Chao (2020, 11) observe: "Comedians such as Rowan Atkinson and Ricky Gervais hold a virtually inhibition-free attitude that one should be unrestricted to joke about almost any subjects."
110 We write *"prima facie"* because no such societies exist in reality, as we will see in *H&C3*.
111 We tackle in *H&C3* how religious and cultural traditions have been sworn enemies of humour.

where adults may be present and rudely disturbed. Would such a world without humour be a good place to live in? Or would we be merely exchanging one form of cruelty for another?[112]

Were this puritanical option be chosen, we would be protecting everyone from uncompassionate as well as compassionate aggression by means of a ban on mirth, comedy, banter, etc. However uncouth, these activities have been a source of gratification throughout human history, if not before. And yet the popularity and near-universality of commonplace humour may not be a helpful or reliable guide if we are trying to determine that which is good and proper. As the British anti-cruelty campaigner Scott wrote: "Every reformative measure of any true value has resulted from the efforts of a minority and not in response to the wishes of the masses."[113]

Rather than being stuck in this paradox, a recognised middle path has been available for millennia and trodden relentlessly, namely sheltering some subject from risibility whilst keeping others available for target practice.[114] To this end, borders have been drawn regularly, for aeons. History is replete with such lines of demarcation, whether presented as religious injunctions, legal provisions, or variably unstable tacit norms of social etiquette and aesthetic taste.

Theoretically, drawing such a boundary is a distinct logical option which we can easily picture and entertain in our mind. Practically, however, it can be as thorny an enterprise as striking the right path in ever-changing courtship rituals, making politically correct lexical choices, trying to be brilliant participants at an exclusive dinner party, starting a conversation with a resentful partner, or sustaining an innocent verbal exchange with an antagonistic relative.[115] To put it mildly, it can be a bloody mess.[116]

We tread frequently on such an unsteady middle path whenever social circumstances call upon us to decide, sometimes in a split second, on whether to laugh at some unexpected event, join in some noisy group's amusements, or refuse

---

[112] The question is not purely rhetorical. We can easily conjure images of collective agelasm, if not misogelasm, such as the dourest communities of conservative Buddhists in Angkor or of Wee Frees in the Outer Hebrides.
[113] G. Scott (1996), 183.
[114] See, e.g., Gilhus (1997).
[115] We assume our readers will have had personal experience of at least some of these social settings.
[116] Yes, this is an attempt at humour, however quaint.

to do so—if not even chastise the amused gathering.[117] Collectively, there may be laws, written and unwritten, reflecting accepted standards that can vary enormously across countries, time, classes, ethnic communities, formal and informal contexts, levels of interpersonal familiarity, etc. As a result, we may find ourselves uttering remarks, and laughing with, *some* people which we would never utter in the company of *other* people, whose laughter we would find distasteful, crass, offensive, or inappropriate. This is hypocritical, perhaps. Or, as we explained in Chapter 2, it is an inevitable expression of our inner plurality.[118]

Moreover, as the Italian philosopher of language Carlo Penco observed: "it is well known that derogatory language is often used in groups or pairs as a joke or as a sign of confidence. (I may use derogatory language and you are not offended because you know that I don't mean it.)"[119] Where we are, with whom, what is going on, and when, are pivotal matters. As difficult as they can be to gauge with unerring ability and timeliness, social circumstances play a key role in making our attempts at humour more or less likely to be singled out for their alleged "cruelty", whether we acknowledge them to be so or not. And being accused of it, and then even chastised for it, are no laughing matters. More often than not, making a *faux pas* can be like stepping into the fire—*un pas dans le feu*.[120]

A flagrant *gaffe* or a grave fiasco can turn even the most revered socialite into a stigmatised rascal, especially in social milieus and/or social climates stoking up the fires of intolerance, moralism, dogmatism, dour seriousness, judgementalism, conformity, and their attendant general lack of charitability towards comedy, comicality, light-heartedness, and, of course, commonplace humour. Perchance, some of our readers have come across such milieus and climates, which are not merely hypothetical.[121]

Adapting hereby a tetralogy of cruel excess developed by the contemporary Brazilian jurist Paulo Barrozo—who himself derived it from Seneca's and Aquinas'

---

[117] We address in *H&C3* some of the ways in which humorous conduct is met with punitive cruelty.
[118] Each reader can decide which option is likelier. We ourselves are not sure about this matter.
[119] Penco (2017), sec. 2, par. 12. This essay is one of the very few extant English-language studies devoted to Baroncelli's philosophy.
[120] Today's numerous advocates of "humour" proper in all spheres of life tend regularly to underemphasise the life-disabling consequences that failed humour can have for its initiators and, in parallel, overestimate the power that heartfelt "apologies" and other forms of attempted atonement can attain (Cundall Jr. 2022, 98 *et passim*). The offended party, in point of fact, can retaliate in the cruellest, most unforgiving manner. They may even use these opportunities to unleash their sadism with impunity, for they were provided with a convenient *prima-facie* justification. And as we discuss in *H&C3*, failed humour can even cost the initiating person her very life.
[121] More on such milieus and climates is said in *H&C3*.

older conceptions of "cruelty" proper—we can conceive of four fundamental cases of cruel *faux pas* in humorous conduct.[122]

(1) "Agent-objective", i.e., a jest that is harsher than customary, e.g., throwing mud pies instead of rice at some newlyweds who are merrily walking out of the church.[123]
(2) "Agent-subjective", i.e., a harsher rendition of a customary jest, e.g., throwing merrily rice at the same couple, but with considerable projectile force.
(3) "Victim-subjective", i.e., a jest that is unbearable for its specific victim, e.g., throwing merrily rice at the same couple, one member of whom is allergic to skin contact with rice and other starch-rich edibles.
(4) "Victim-objective", i.e., a jest that violates human dignity, e.g., 'saluting' the couple walking out of the church with large posters portraying explicit sexual escapades involving either of them.

Whether we end up applying methodically abstract formulae and/or principles to highly specific circumstances or following our instincts and gut feelings, humour causes us to wander into a luscious forest that is, supposedly, full of mirth.[124] Yet the same luscious forest can also see careers, reputations, happiness, and/or subsistence harmed or ended precisely because of unsuccessful attempts at humour, which society's forces want to see duly reprimanded on some, but perhaps not all, occasions. Even when magnanimously given the benefit of the doubt, the failed humourist can still be treated ignominiously like a nowt.[125] What is more, paradoxically, chastising humour because of alleged "immorality" could be itself an example of "the self-deception and often the hypocrisy that seek to hide harm-doing under justifications". [126]

---

[122] See Barrozo (2008) and (2015, 1026 and 1031–1035), which we discussed in detail in *H&C1*.
[123] We assume our readers to be familiar with the mentioned festive tradition.
[124] In order to avoid compromising failures in our choice of jokes, three computer scientists—Hiroaki Yamane, Yusuke Mori, and Tatsuya Harada (2021, 6)—suggest that we should be selecting an item that satisfies "the following function: "$f_{p,n}(S_p(I)) \cap f_{CH}(S_{CH}(I)) \cap f_{FC}(S_{FC}(I)) \cap f_{LB}(S_{LB}(I)) \cap f_{AS}(S_{AS}(I)) \cap f_{PD}(S_{PD}(I))[,]$ where I is an item, $S_{k \in \{p,n,CH,FC,LB,AS,PD\}}()$ is a scoring function (i.e., applying softmax to the cell state), and $f()$ is a thresholding function that returns 1, when above/below the threshold $T_{upper,lower}$ Note that p, n, CH, FC, LB, AS, and PD represent positive, negative, Care-Harm, Fairness-Cheating, Loyalty-Betrayal, Authority-Subversion, and Purity-Degradation, respectively." Clearly, explicit programming is not the same activity as tacit performing.
[125] More on this point is said in *H&C3*.
[126] Hallie (1971), 248.

Trying to be funny is, at times, like juggling live hand grenades.[127] As both Morreall's and Amir's anti-tragic philosophical existentialisms testify—plus our own modest critique of it—a decision to commit ourselves to leading an intentionally humorous life can have deadly serious consequences.[128] As the scholars intimate, wisdom and the good life may depend on it. *Ex converso*, so do inanity and the bad life.

In the end, the more closely one looks at the phenomenon of humour, the more frequently s/he can spot traces of the blood whence it first acquired a medical meaning. "Sick humour" itself may well be the worthy nominal descendant of sick humours. And for all the sociability and sociality that "humour" proper is commonly meant to exhibit and enable, the sorry fate of those who fail at it is a sobering reminder of how societies can easily chew out and/or throw out their own members. It is true that it takes two to tango but—in keeping with the medical metaphor—the unsuccessful jokester is easily and swiftly left alone wading in the fango.[129]

4.8 A Debasement

The way in which jokes are received is itself no joke. As repeatedly discussed in this book, a mindless *faux pas* or a *gaffe* in the humorous context can have really serious consequences in a person's life, in spite of all the freedom of speech to which she may be entitled on constitutional and legal grounds. If and when people deviate from the tacitly established social norms, they can still be punished informally.[130]

---

[127] Instantiating further the paradoxical character of cruelty and its connection with the duality of humour, this juggling is actually a comic act performed by a character in Emir Kusturica's 1998 film comedy Црна мачка, бели мачор [*Black Cat, White Cat*], in which a hand grenade falls out of the character's hands and lands on a gaggle of geese, causing a booming, hilarious, deadly cloud of dust and feathers.
[128] Studying spontaneous verbal exchanges, Reichl and Kapogianni (2021, 1) speak of "risky ... trajectories".
[129] Contemporary British English uses "fango" to refer to mud from thermal springs used in the treatment of rheumatic diseases, but the original Italian term means simply "mud" in general. As to the quality of the couplet above, we are aware of its being a bit of a contrivance. Still, there were very few options available.
[130] Much more on these punishments is said in *H&C3*.

4.8.1 Chastisements

Perhaps the very fact that all these norms are ultimately mere conventions, even or especially when time-honoured, is the unspoken reason for why they are guarded with such a tenacity and, if needed, ferocity. Ostracism, debasement, and disparagement of the cruellest sort can be meted out within the community without barristers or magistrates getting involved—and without any consideration for the victim's dignity and wellbeing, no matter what his/her rights may be on paper.

These chastisements can plausibly be implicit means of justice. Or at least as plausibly, they can serve as avenues for explicit mean vendettas. Which of the two results is actually the case is a context-dependent matter that is bound to vary with each material juncture, the involved individuals, their cultural and legal communities, and an unspecifiable number of morally significant appurtenances, many of which are grasped only tacitly.[131] As it is for soups, beef, ice creams, sausages, crumpets, fruitcakes, muffins, blancmanges, and the proverbial pudding, whose crucial axiological proof comes with their edible apprehension, so it is, in an analogous sense, for our ethical evaluations, however ordinary and obvious they may often seem to be.[132] Ethics and aesthetics are close relatives, after all.[133]

Whenever we engage in these evaluations, the idiographically specific—indeed effectively unique—circumstances pertaining to each assessed case must be brought to bear on the general or universal principles guiding the agency of the persons involved in them (e.g., 'justice is good' and 'vendetta is bad'), as well as of the person/s passing the ethical judgement at issue (*ditto*).[134] Without an adequate understanding of precisely such more palpable circumstances, ethical judgements of this ilk are at risk of being unduly general, biased, too hasty, and/

---

[131] Passing moral and aesthetic judgements is an ultimately *personal* act (see Polanyi 1962c and Allen 2014). And as it should be clear by now, "personal" does not mean the same as "subjective" (see Chapters 1 and 2, as well as *H&C1*, which discusses in detail Polanyi's aptly-called "personal knowledge").

[132] Again, we are using "moral" and "ethical" as synonyms. As to "analogous", it is a reminder of the fact that *comparisons are made on the basis of shared predicates.* When some such predicates exist, analogy can occur.

[133] In the Western canon, Nietzsche is in/famous for making the origin of ethical values aesthetic in nature.

[134] See Allen (2014) for a precise and comprehensive account of the crucial ethical and logical 'steps' connecting the most abstract moral principles (e.g., 'the good') and maxims (e.g., "be good") with the unique sets of lived circumstances in which each and every im/moral act performed and/or judged by a person inevitably takes place.

or unfounded.[135] Judges, priests, psychiatrists, and parents are habitually required to pass such ethical judgements, and the skill that they may display in making convincing and/or constructive evaluations is, very often, a personal quality that receives much attention and appreciation within their broader societies and/or professional communities.[136]

Within this mundane yet complex evaluative context, *cruel humour* itself can easily and promptly resurface, also on the side of those who are condemning the *faux pas* or *gaffe*.[137] And in either case, whether provocative or responsive, humour's cruelty finds with uncanny constancy a target—aka a "butt", "game", "quarry", "prey", "bag", "pigeon, "goat", "mark", "foil" or "kill".[138] Commonplace humour and the most piercing insults can even become one and the same thing for some individuals and/or groups. Such unfortunate individuals' and/or groups' ordinary social designations are thus turned into both well-established terms of abuse *and* apt rhetorical tools whereby hilarity can be easily prompted in a great variety of settings, e.g., anecdotes, cartoons, parodies, satires, spoofs, one-liners, and comedies.

Concomitantly, a host of psycho-social categories and/or attendant mechanisms for exclusion, diminishment, degradation, and/or even outright exploitation are or can be triggered as easily. We can name, *inter alia:* someone's moniker within a certain family or group of people (e.g., debasing analogues of "you pulled a Monica", *per* the 1994–2004 American TV sitcom *Friends*); "teuchter" (i.e., a Highlander) and "sassenach" (i.e., an Englishman) in Scottish English; and "coatto" (i.e., a pleb or plebeian) [lit. "coerced"; from Lat. *cogĕre*, i.e., 'to force'] or "terrone" (i.e., 'southerner') [from *terra*, i.e., 'earth' or 'soil'] in contemporary Italian.[139]

---

135 We assume the reader to have come across tokens of such poor judgements in his/her life and, though maybe hard to admit publicly, produced some in his/her time, if not even in his/her mature years.

136 Sometimes, though, just individuals can be resented for, say, not going along with a crowd's vindictive mood, the contingent preferences of the alleged "best and brightest", or the unjust mores of the majority. Some canonical 'heroes' of Western civilisation were precisely such contrarians, e.g., Socrates, Jesus Christ, and Thomas More.

137 Bergson's socially situated conception of 'laughter' and 'comicality' comes to mind here (see Chapter 1 and *H&C1*).

138 *Nomen omen*. The language used to describe the aimed recipients of humour echoes invariably the cruel domains of warfare and hunting, for the most part.

139 As seen in Chapters 1 and 2, these socio-cultural aspects were pivotal for Harvey (1999), who worried about the 'normalisation' of cruel attitudes and praxes by way of humour. When such aspects are duly considered, the "benign violation theory" (Chapter 3) does seem inadequate. As to "detrusion", we use it here in its broader sense of 'pushing out' or 'down', for these are the cruel directions of, respectively, *othering* and *debasement*.

4.8.2 Sex

In keeping with the recurring insights into humour and sexuality offered by the likes of Schopenhauer, Freud or Harlow, we should also mention the ordinary yet frequently neglected example of sex workers.[140] In particular, we have in mind the forbidding circumstances when these workers have been driven into this line of employment by deprivation or violence, and/or who happen to continue exercising their profession because they "really needed the money" and had nothing else to rely upon, i.e., not even the hope of an alternative line of employment.[141]

Because of the uncharitable and puritanical social stigma that can still affect men and women employed in the sex industry (e.g., pornography), occupational opportunities can be horribly reduced *de facto*, even if they are not so *de jure*, and whether these opportunities belong to a working-class or a middle-class layer of socio-economic activity.[142] Although these persons may be more than qualified for their intended future jobs, they are often disqualified because of their 'indecent' past ones, which become the regular targets of cruel humour.[143]

---

[140] See Chapter 1 and *H&C1*.

[141] Davin (2017), 28. Sex workers who eagerly exercise their profession and/or take pride in it, not least on declaredly "feminist" grounds, are *not* the main focus here, e.g., Hartley (2018, title page *et passim*), Sullivan (2021), and Mastrantonio and Becker (2021). Still, these minoritarian cases are a reminder of the vast variety, inevitable intersectionality, and inherent complexity of all human motives and real lives. "Sex work", after all, is an umbrella-term covering different social domains and/or individual experiences. As Johnstone (2007) argued, "prostitution" itself covers many diverse realities, though we rightly focus, in both public debates and academic scholarship, on the most life-disabling ones, which clearly call for redressal. In its semantic plurality, "sex work" is thus akin to expressions such as "intellectual work" and "physical labour", which also embrace a huge plethora of singular, *personal* stories. More on these issues is discussed in *H&C3*.

[142] See, e.g., Voss (2012) and (2015), and Macleod (2021), who also consider the "stigma" from the consumer's perspective. The issues of pornography and Puritanism in allegedly "liberal" nations are addressed in more detail in *H&C3*. We write "socio-economic" to hint at the fact that no 'pure' economic realm exists, i.e., entirely dissociated from socio-cultural determinants and implications. "Working class" and "middle class" are not only a matter of income and/or labour skills under a capitalist regime, but they also tacitly entail connotations concerning respectability, schooling, lifestyle, marital prospects, taste, etc. (see, e.g., Kipnis 2006). As argued by McMurtry (2013b), capitalist economic structures free-ride on underlying socio-cultural and environmental systems which they: did not create themselves (e.g., language); frequently spoil (e.g., pollution); privatise for profit's sake (e.g., arable land); and resist paying for, even after damaging them (e.g., corporate tax evasion and tax avoidance).

[143] See, again, Voss (2015).

The occupational descriptors of these people, their typical cognates, their jobs' most conspicuous erotic characteristics, cynically expressible circumstances, and/or controversial ethical connotations can thus be found in all kinds of belittling, offensive, derogatory, and/or debasing expressions of commonplace hilarity, whether old or new, e. g., "son of a whore", "fluffer", "wanker", "slut", "poofter", "screamer", "tosser", and "trollop".[144] Cruel aims and humorous allusions to, say, onanism or orgasms can consequently lend each other a hand and make 'hitting' or 'hurting' a person and/or group both possible and probable while amusing others at the same time.[145]

Laughter is therefore initiated in a facile manner, normally without considering how the cruelty of humour is being combined with the cruelty of these workers' lived circumstances.[146] Somehow, Bergson's anaesthesia of the heart is accompanied by an anaesthesia of the smarts. And insult, as a well-known adagio recites, is thus added to injury.[147]

Initially, it may take a fair amount of creativity and repetition to get the job done, for not all members of the audience are likely to share the tacit background required for grasping easily and immediately the cruel humour at issue.[148] Later on, when such a tacit background is somehow present in the audience's minds, it may then take a single blow for the cruel humour at play to 'hit' or 'hurt' its target, whether s/he is a sex worker or, for that matter, anyone else who is believed to

---

[144] The libidinal roots of commonplace humour are tackled in further detail in *H&C3*. As to the chaotic constitutive character of *libido* itself, in line with Freud's understanding of it, it may not only be a threat to civil conduct, but also to oppressive socio-cultural structures, hence a potential "site of resistance" (Trimbull 2018, 522 *et passim*).

[145] Given humour's need for a 'butt' or 'target', as well as cruelty's having an 'aim', the physical notions of 'hitting' and 'hurting' someone are apropos here. Also, as remarked, humour is commonly said to "punch".

[146] Juvenile banter has often exemplified this crude humour, as also reported in Dickie (2003) and (2011).

[147] Humorous cruelty may well be added *intentionally* to known prior lived cruelty. We would then have a case of sadistic cruelty rather than brutal cruelty, in line with Regan's tetralogy of "cruelty" proper (Chapter 1).

[148] As seen in Chapter 2, Harvey (1999, title *et passim*) paid heed to the repetitive structures of humorous humiliation leading to "civilized oppression". As to whether sharing the necessary tacit background needed for understanding cruel humour entails being cruel, or whether this humour can be enjoyed innocently, they have been long and much debated issues in the expert literature about "humour" proper. See, e. g., Husband (1988). As argued in the previous chapters, we do suspect that a modicum of brutal cruelty is *de rigueur* whenever humour occurs, not to mention publicly acknowledged cruel humour as such. This brutality being different, however, from endorsing racist or sexist prejudices. It may be enough to simply 'switch off' one's affective reaction to them.

have been 'tainted' by the sexual domain, which so many cultures and so many individuals still have enormous difficulty in merely allowing for *qua* human conduct that is, say, purely natural, personally gratifying, aesthetically valuable, theologically acceptable, socially necessary, artistically presentable, and/or ethically commendable.[149]

Sometimes, sheer corporeality and/or the naked human body, whether in the flesh or in artistic depictions, are sufficient a cause for the greatest disquiet, and they can breed the most irrational and/or irate reactions.[150] Even if the blameworthy cruel *quid* of rape, sexual abuse, trafficking, and exploitation lies in these acts' and practices' cruel violence to the person, their sexual and carnal components cause nonetheless much shock and a deep-reaching unease, such that the sexually violated person receives stern condemnation too, whether openly or tacitly.[151] Perhaps, it is a case of deficiency in the adjudicating minds' vertical thinking. Certainly, for the affected victims, it is a cause of lateral sinking.[152]

No matter how pristine these allegedly 'tainted' persons' legal and ethical standing may be, their social one is condemned to wallow in the mud.[153] In line with John Stuart Mill's classic liberal intuitions about the actual limits and the most active enemies of individual freedom, public opinion is frequently a far

---

149 As concerns the difficult relationship of many cultural traditions with sexuality, more is said in *H&C3*. For the moment, let us just mention Hillman (1995) who contrasted repeatedly the sexually 'relaxed' and hedonistic world of ancient Greece with the much more 'prudish' and ascetic one of the Judeo-Christian West—also in its secular modern offshoots in the Anglophone world.
150 See, e.g., the covering of classical and Renaissance statues in Rome during an official visit of the Shia president of Iran (Abrams 2016) or the accusation of "sexism" concerning another Italian statue that, according to some angered commentators, was immodestly clothed (Santarpia 2021). More on censorship is discussed in *H&C3*.
151 See Hillman (1995), who reflected on the archetypal psychological forces involved in human sexuality and the illogicality and inhumanity that such forces can sometimes cause individuals and societies to face. As to the cruel realities of human trafficking and sex work, see, e.g., the 2022 documentary *Trafficking Survivors Testimonies* (2022) by the Catholic non-governmental organisation (NGO) Santa Marta Group.
152 We presume our reader to have grasped the implied parallel construction with so-called "lateral thinking".
153 See, e.g., "Monica Lewinsky" (2018, par. 12) on the "offensive and vulgar stigma" afflicting the titular person, who is reported to have stated that she had "'had a relationship with [US president Bill Clinton], a love affair', at a press conference", where "the[audience] only laugh[ed] at her", for they reduced their "love affair" to a single notorious act of fellatio, whence a dress stained with semen originated and, with it, a 'sex scandal' that entertained millions around the world, ruined Monica Lewinsky's (and, to a significant extent, Bill Clinton's) reputation, and caused considerable political bickering and institutional wrangling in the *fin-de-siècle* US. "Monica Lewinsky" (2018) is also a telling example of the global and callow character of much journalism on these 'torrid' matters.

more effective tyrant than public authority itself, and the former's subtler cruelty far more pervasive than the latter's heavy-handed one.[154] Whereas the latter comes burdened with cumbersome iron shackles and time-consuming paper trails, the former can operate swiftly, doggedly, and ubiquitously, e.g., by way of jibes and jokes.[155] The hangman's rope and antics are not needed to choke or snap another person's throat. A shrewd and sufficiently crude or lewd *flatus vocis* can accomplish *all* of that too, yet without having to break a sweat in the process.[156]

4.8.3 Liberty

Perhaps cruel cracks at large—whether sexual or not—should better be answered with clever retorts. Humour, as also seen in Chapter 3, can in fact be a way to preserve or, at least, to signal important spaces *of* and *for* individual freedom.[157] Thus, a committed liberal such as Baroncelli did like recalling and making use of a streetwise quip that he had overheard from an elderly anarchist shoemaker whom he happened to meet as a child in the working-class neighbourhood of 1950s Savona

---

[154] See Mill (2001). We discuss all these issues in more detail in *H&C3*. For the moment, we expect our readers to have sufficient knowledge of Mill's 1859 *opus magnum*, i.e., *On Liberty*, as to be able to grasp our meaning.

[155] 'Tainted' sex therapists can become comedic fodder too. See, e.g., Barbara Streisand's character in the *Fockers* film series (2004–2010), the titles of which are themselves a token of oblique humour about the sexual act.

[156] Grasping the contrast between the hangman's role in suffocating a person and cruel humour's ability to do 'the same' requires operating an imaginative leap *from* the physical context of the former metaphor and *into* the social one of the latter. We assume our readers to be able to tacitly 'get' this requirement and, also tacitly, the overall meaning of the previous three sentences, in line with Polanyi's reflections on tacit knowing (Chapter 2).

[157] In a 'responsive' humorous way, some Anglophone sex workers created the derisive acronym "SWERF" ("Sex Worker Exclusionary Radical Feminist") to label those self-declared "radical feminists" who oppose sex work *qua* possible, legitimate, and dignified choice for a responsible person to make (see "Angry Whores Anarcho Brigade" 2019). While poverty, coercion, trafficking, and abuse have been historically recorded as lying behind prostitution for centuries (see., e.g., Sanger 2013), sometimes even in socio-scientifically dubious ways (see, e.g., Chaumont 2014), it is neither logically nor empirically possible to discount notable exceptions to this dismal logic, especially but not even exclusively in the parallel realm of pornography, which has its own unique characteristics, medical needs, and peculiar socio-psychological background (see, e.g., Chapkis 2018, Hartley 2018, and McElroy 1997). LVOA can help in distinguishing and assessing the different cases as comprehensively life-enabling or disabling.

(northern Italy). It recited: *"it is better to have the police in the house than the neighbours at the door"*.[158]

This quip was, quite obviously, a comic hyperbole. Yet, for those who wish to ponder upon the old anarchist's wisecrack a little more seriously, it was also a concise parable.[159] Let us explain it most briefly.

Civil society, which so many Western intellectuals have been commending on countless occasions, might actually be a *crueller* enemy of personal liberty than the as-frequently maligned civil government, i.e., 'the State', whose coercive power the liberal institutions of the West were originally developed and directed against—to say nothing of the anarchists' political theories and violent fights.[160] Within liberal societies, acquiescent silent majorities and/or aggressive vocal minorities can conspire, often together with the extant economic forces, in the oppression of members, subcommunities, and/or even large swaths of their populations, despite all formal claims, charters, covenants, codes, and institutions that keep on talking overtly and unequivocally of "equality", "freedom", "dignity", "choice", "respect", and "opportunity".

The tacit discursive mantra that is at play in negating in actual practice people's formal rights is fairly straightforward, even if it implies distinct steps or strata. *In nuce*, some people are and will be 'superior', no matter what. Others, instead, are and will be 'inferior', whatever their nation's constitutional texts may spout.[161] And once this imbalance is believed to be the case by enough people, and/or by people of enough clout, humour can flourish, especially, though not exclusively, in its nastiest varieties.[162] After all, as seen in this book, superiority is one

---

158 Baroncelli (2009), 77; emphasis added.
159 We assume our readers to know the difference between these two rhetorical figures.
160 See, e.g., Shklar (1984) and (1989) on the history and aims of "liberalism of fear", which we briefly addressed in Chapter 1. Concerning the recurrent commendation of civil society, see, e.g., Maloney and Van Deth (2010). As for useful sources on anarchism, which have been historically responsible of much responsive cruelty, see Kinna (2012), part 4. Needless to say, the anarchists' critical stance with regard to the State has typically been much harsher than the liberals' one. While the latter seized control of the old aristocratic societies against which they fought, the anarchists never really had an opportunity to be in command of any large human community.
161 Axiologically as well as ontologically, there is no credible basis for such hierarchical claims, especially when sweeping and cross-generational (see, e.g., Galbraith 1977, chap. 2 and 8, making fun of social Darwinism's pretensions about the capitalist scions' self-/perception as being 'better' or competitively 'fitter' than the rest of us). Socio-culturally, however, these claims can become the toughest fabric of our lived reality, as also signalled in our book by the recurrent scholarly preoccupation with the direction of humour's assumed 'punching', i.e., 'upwards' or 'downwards', rather than, say, with humour's inherent brutal and/or sadistic cruelty (see Chapter 2).
162 This nasty humour does not have to be verbally vulgar or tawdry *per se*. Very *hurtful things can be uttered by way of witty, refined expressions*, which display rhetorical poise as much as in-

of the standard bases and/or explanations of humour itself, especially in its commonplace forms.[163] That it may survive or even prosper within liberal settings is, as a result, no great wonder, as also critically argued by Kekes and candidly admitted by Rorty.[164]

The explicit activity of keeping the social inferiors down, not least by means of cruel humour, is also likely to achieve the goal of proving further their inferiority. The butt of a joke is always implicitly and tacitly situated in a subordinate position, at least for the duration and the effect of the comic attack.[165] Not to mention other 'convenient' goals too, e.g., having a reliable supply of cheap labour, conditioning the inferior ones into thinking of themselves self-disparagingly, and/or reaffirming once more the elite's presumed superiority.[166] This alleged superiority being such that, ironically, it needs repeated buttressing by mocking, debasing, and/or jeering at the social inferiors. [167]

Not even the material improvement of some of these social inferiors can be enough to break the mould of so hierarchically stratified a society.[168] Expensive jewellery and fancy cars do not truly change the perceived status of those who parade them around with great effort and insistence, whether in their neighbourhood, in music videos, on YouTube, or *via* other social-media platforms. You may keep up with Joneses and perhaps with the Kardashians too, but you will never be able to match the Windsors.[169]

---

genious cruelty. In point of fact, they can add to the inherent insult the humiliating indication of the target's class and/or intellectual inferiority. After all, as Gruner (1997, chap. 2) suggested, humour is rooted in *homo sapiens*' competitive spirit.

163 See Chapter 1.

164 See Chapter 1 and *H&C1. H&C3* focuses on the cruel ironies of the liberals' ideals of 'free speech' and 'free markets'.

165 Occasionally, an upward, 'superior' position can be comical, e.g., two academics being 'lost in the clouds'.

166 Hallie's "institutional cruelty", which we discussed in Chapter 1 and *H&C1*, clearly applies to this case.

167 We saw in Chapter 1 how pronounced hierarchical class elements have been part and parcel of the modern meaning of "humour" proper since its inception in Shaftesbury's Albion.

168 This resilience does not imply that no other positive goal can be attained this way, e.g., increased tranquillity.

169 We are referring to the British Royal family, whose House was named, until 1917, Saxe-Coburg-Gotha. British aristocracy is, however, only one possible form of social hierarchy. Given the right circumstances, other hierarchies can be established and enforced, also by means of cruel humour, that have little or nothing to do with the *ancien régime:* 'cool' kids *versus* 'losers' in primary schools; enlightened 'reformers' *versus* uncouth 'rednecks'; groups deserving compassion *versus* groups deserving condemnation. Some hierarchies are rooted in money, others in physical endowments, others still in ideological or cultural values. See, e.g., Pareto (1968, 38–39) addressing, *inter*

The actual and/or on-credit purchase of piles upon piles of so-called "Veblen goods" can be insufficient, when not counterproductive, in order to redress a person's or a group's supposed inferiority, i.e., if an adequate amount of disapproving social opinion works against her/their advancement.[170] As the 20th-century Marxist thinker Herbert Marcuse wrote back in 1969, under unjust "rules of the game" there can exist "false and immoral comforts" signalling a "cruel affluence".[171] We are, after all, symbolic creatures through and through. It is primarily by way of symbolic intangible cages, then, that we imprison and get imprisoned—yet another cruel irony to be encountered in our research.[172]

In summary, the State can be said to be, at least in liberal societies, a less present and far less active foe than our own parents, siblings, spouses, friends, relatives, colleagues, acquaintances, neighbours, pundits of reference, employers, customers, casual observers, and/or quidnuncs, as regards making us do what we do not want to do and/or not do what we want to do.[173] *We* humans, individually, may well have all kinds of doubts about who or what sort of person we are, what exactly we need in this life (and/or in the next one), and which lifestyles should be thought of as truly 'decent', 'deviant', 'progressive', 'patriarchal', 'honourable', 'oppressive', 'licentious', 'liberating', 'humorous', or 'cruel'. (For sure, the authors of the present book have got plenty of such doubts.)[174] Nevertheless, so many of

---

alia, the influences of "humanitarian[ism]" and "feminism" in improving the social standing of "prostitute[s]". Albeit compassionate, Pareto (1968, 46) was ambivalent about such influences, which signalled for him the weakening of the "bourgeois" elites and the parallel dangerous empowerment of revolutionary "socialism".

170 Also known as "positional goods", Veblen goods are luxury items the demand for which increases as their price increases, inasmuch as these goods signal that their owners belong—or believe to belong—to the elite, e.g., penthouse apartments in New York, Ferraris and Lamborghinis, Rolex wristwatches, etc. Galbraith's (1977) insight runs deeper, however, for there can be hierarchies among the very rich that are not based on purchasing power and/or emulative ostentation, but on, say, ancestry, 'blue blood', taste, 'breeding' and/or 'race'. LVOA, on its part, reminds us of the fact that economic 'goods' can be bad for personal, collective, and/or eco-systemic life.

171 Marcuse (1969), 6.

172 See, e.g., Galbraith (1977, chap. 2) on 'new money' and 'old money' families under capitalist regimes.

173 Our own unconscious can be such a foe when understood *qua* Freudian *super-ego* (see Chapter 1). As the famous British psychoanalyst and child psychologist Melanie Klein (1987, 73) wrote: "The more cruel the super-ego the more terrifying will be the father as a castrator" (see also Klein 1948). Furthermore, we do not imply that the State is necessarily evil, i.e., a gaoler, robber, or warmonger. The State can equally be a healer, teacher, or satyagrahi. LVOA cuts through the received political dichotomies and distinguishes between a good and bad State, as well as a good and bad civil society, market economy, planned economy, etc.

174 As stated, *epistemic humility* informs our research.

these other people—parents, siblings, spouses, etc.—do not seem to have as many doubts about us, if any at all.[175]

Even if *they* are not us, these other people are frequently cocksure about who and what *we* are, what we need, and the paths which we are to tread or ought to tread.[176] Not even our few hard-won certainties can be adequate a defence against these embodied instantiations of social opinion.[177] *We* may know for sure that we are not pigeons, and yet *they* have at hand neat pigeonholes into which we are to be squeezed.[178] *We* may know for sure that we cannot fly; yet, *they* shall keep pushing us off one and the same steep cliff. The fall may be terrifying and the landing hurtful, yet we will go on enduring them, again and again, as though we were characters in a slapstick comedy or a cartoon.[179] Moreover, if we disagree with these cocksure people or deviate from their expectations about us, they can make their presence felt in all sorts of pressuring ways, including the potent tool of cruel humour.[180]

Surreptitiously, then, these people's conceit can easily become our lived reality —or a sizeable part of it—for *they* and *their* influence can be neither escaped nor avoided to an adequate degree.[181] *Their* assumptions, presumptions, prejudices, preconceptions, habits of thought, generalisations, and simplifications are the bricks of the edifice inside which we are allowed to move, if just a little.[182]

---

175 Were it not clear, "we" refers here to hypothetical individuals, not to this book's authors alone or in particular.
176 We expect our readers to have encountered such people and circumstances.
177 Ironically, we cannot deny *a priori* the possibility that, on occasion, *another person may know better* than us who we are, what we want, what we need, what we ought to be like, etc. Indeed, we cannot even deny it *a posteriori*, given the times when our parents or spouses were proven right *ex post*. (We suspect that some of our readers may be honest enough about themselves as to be capable of admitting, at least *in foro interno*, that they too were proven wrong about themselves by some relative or associate.) Yet this irony is not the main thrust of the paragraph above. It is just a qualification and reminder of how chaotic and uncertain our lives tend to be.
178 We presume our readers to have grasped the metaphorical character of the stated avian noun and lodgings. The same character applies to the two ensuing sentences in the paragraph above.
179 The cruelly Sisyphean fate of Wile E. Coyote, a famous member of the *Looney Tunes* family, springs to mind in this connection, as well as the sense of pity or outright "sympathy" that it evokes (Laine 2009, title *et passim*).
180 This theme is central in many works by Pirandello, whom we tackled in Chapter 1 and *H&C1*.
181 Eventually, not even Robinson Crusoe lived alone. (We assume our reader to know Daniel Defoe's 1719 novel.)
182 At times, extra room for manoeuvring and asserting oneself is conquered by people in inner, hidden, and/or duplicitous ways, e.g., by intensifying their interior psychic plurality or leading double lives. This phenomenon is particularly pronounced in the sexual sphere, which is also one of the most thoroughly policed and socio-culturally repressed. In any case, "people shouldn't

4.8.4 Responsibility

Normally, *their* convenient rules of thumb become the thumb under which our individual liberty is squashed and, to a significant extent, quashed. Our options in life, very self-perception, structures of habituation, and social acceptability are definitely *not* things that we can manipulate at will.[183] It is almost the opposite, in point of fact, despite the undeniable concomitant endurance of a modicum of individual responsibility which, ironically, becomes all the more personally precious and potentially pernicious.[184]

(1) On the one hand, exercising our minimal *quid* of personal responsibility means asserting our own individuality and making our life truly our own.
(2) On the other hand, our doing so in perceived defiance of general conformity and, whether by error or by intent, our crossing one of the many invisible lines tacitly drawn by our social controllers can backfire most spectacularly, including whenever the crossing at issue results from a 'mere' attempt at "humour" proper.[185]

In the end, this limited room for reframing our circumstances is no laughing matter—or, at best, a matter calling for a smirking, sad, and sardonic kind of laughter.[186]

As seen in Chapter 2, Harvey focussed on large-scale cross- and intergenerational forms of conversational debasement and concealed discrimination, not least by way of cruel humour, targeting people because of their race, class, caste, sexual life, and/or gender. Notwithstanding the frequent use of such a humour, the sufferings that these forms of debasement and discrimination entail

---

be envisaged as monolithic blocks of unchanging ideas, values or emotions." (Berhendt 2020, 172; emphases removed).

183 See, e.g., Maes (2019) on the cultural pressures facilitating women's eventual adoption of standards of sexiness that they are not truly comfortable with, including pressures emanating from the aesthetic realm of pornography.

184 We do not deny *in toto* the existence of personal freedom. We simply emphasise its cruel constrictions.

185 As tackled in *H&C3*, failed humour can expose a person to cruel physical and psychological retaliations.

186 As discussed in Chapter 2, the alternative between a tragic or a comic view of life persists under conditions of lifelong or cross-generational hardship. While Harvey stopped laughing, Morreall and Amir continued, thinking of humour as a helpful coping mechanism and, in essence, something better than rage, despair, or indifference.

are the stuff of tragedy and, tragically, history too.[187] However, on a smaller and more quotidian scale, real persons' wellbeing and lives can also be ruined, perhaps almost as thoroughly, by other people's insistent ostracising and/or bullying, not least *via* cruel humour too because of the most diverse, superficial, vague, unempirical and/or bizarre motives: ugliness, quirks, red hair, albinism, speech impairments, the fact that they are rumoured of making others feel "uncomfortable" or giving them the "creeps", irregular inflections, body odour, or the rather unscientific claim that they jinx things or bring ill-luck.[188] Being known or notorious for some failed, ill-received humour, funnily enough, can be one such intellectually peculiar yet interpersonally prosaic motive too.[189]

In academe's ivory towers, post-Hume theorists have been taught not to infer 'ought' from 'is'.[190] In the common world's cobbled streets and brick-lined factories, pre-posthumous individuals are taught not to think of 'can', even if the extant laws utter "may".[191] Suffering informal oppression, despite the acknowledgment of formal liberty, is, in essence, just one cruel irony among many.[192] Double standards, contradictions, hypocrisies, and even genuinely baffling paradoxes abound in all such prosaic settings, i.e., the daily lives of the near-totality of humankind.[193]

---

[187] An additional, *twofold cruel irony* is associated with these forms of discrimination. On the one hand, the members of the oppressive group may avoid talking about the ongoing discrimination, not even as a laughing matter (i.e., they engage in thorough self-censorship). On the other hand, the members of the oppressed group may be prevented from challenging the status quo, not even by means of commonplace humour. As an Indian comedian recently stated: "If we were Dalit stand-up comics going from village to village talking against the Brahmins, we would have been shot or killed or been under arrest" (Gursimran Khamba as cited in Ganguly 2020, 52).

[188] These mechanisms for exclusion and humiliation are very effective within small and tight-knitted communities: villages, neighbourhoods, offices, school cohorts, civil-society associations, etc. Countless comedic works have been based upon such diverse, superficial, and bizarre motives, whether cast as their trite yet efficacious comic continuation (e.g., Samuel L. Jackson's lisping character in Matthew Vaughn's 2014 action comedy *Kingsman: The Secret Service*) or as compassionate reflections about them (e.g., Pirandello 1911 and 1917, i.e., a novella and the one-act play based upon it, which was later adapted for the silver screen in a 1954 movie starring Totò, who was the leading comic actor in Italian cinema between the 1940s and the 1960s).

[189] Once again, this topic is discussed more extensively in *H&C3*.

[190] We argue against this notion in *H&C3*.

[191] We write "pre-posthumous" not only to establish a humorous parallel with "post-Hume", but also to hint at the traditional Christian notion that real freedom and *beatitudo* will be enjoyed *post mortem*. Were such a notion true, we should not have to worry much about owning "Veblen goods" and flashy trinkets, for we ought to have different priorities (see, e.g., Kierkegaard, as mentioned in Chapter 2 and discussed extensively in *H&C1*).

[192] By now, the reader must have gathered how frequently and variously does cruelty colour human existence.

[193] See especially our account of Hallie (1969) in Chapter 1 and *H&C1*.

And if the worrying picture of the human condition outlined by the likes of, say, Sade or Freud is correct, we are all pretty much screwed anyway from the very start.[194] Tellingly, the maverick 20th-century Austrian physician, psychoanalyst and experimenter Wilhelm Reich, who spent his life trying in vain to find a balance between the two opposite poles of neurosis-inducing social control and chaos-prone sexual energy, stated: "if the child is born a 'wild, cruel, asocial animal', then there is no end in sight for the emotional plague".[195]

4.9 A Dichotomy

As regards the roots and attitudes on "humour" proper that we have encountered in previous chapters, two cultural traditions (or subcurrents) emerge from the shifting emphases which Shaftesbury and many 18th-century British gentlemen would have thought of as expressing the ideal 'refinement'—hence as 'propriety', 'courtesy', 'political correctness', 'ethical awareness', *et similia*.[196] In particular, these cultural traditions (or subcurrents) can be said to differ notedly in their attendant willingness to tolerate or not tolerate any lack thereof, whether partial, total, casual, regular, or else. Good manners matter, especially if they can turn into bad means or mean matters.

---

194 *We expect the reader to be able to grasp the implicit humour of this concluding remark, whether s/he finds it in good taste or not.* Perchance, in keeping with the considerations about class and social strata offered in the present subsection, such a type of humour may have come across as too lowbrow and/or lowbred, at least *prima facie*. Were this the actual case, the present subsection would be further corroborated in its chief claims. Once again, in fact, deeply rooted hierarchical assumptions about social propriety and aesthetic standards would tacitly inform people's grasp of and direct their instinctive reactions to the material that they read, prior to any aloof refection. (See also our account of Polanyi's "tacit knowing" in Chapter 2 and, above all, *H&C1*.)

195 Reich (1967), 65. Reich (1953, 41; emphasis added) became in/famous because of his outspoken Marxist views, his unorthodox experiments, and for promoting the liberation of the human psyche from sexual repression by unashamed promiscuity and artificially augmented orgasms, insofar as he believed that "*cruelty*" is "born from frustration of the primary need for love and gratification of love in the mating embrace". Wherever he went, his views were met with hostility, more often than not. Significantly, Reich's books and diaries were burned by the German Nazis in the 1930s and the US courts of law in the 1950s. More on his work and worries is said in *H&C3*.

196 The semantic areas covered by each term overlap conspicuously and make them here *de facto* synonyms.

4.9.1 Two Subcurrents

Our conclusions on this issue are in line with Morreall's own juxtaposition of the cheerful Franciscan view of life, on the one hand, and stern Puritanism, on the other. Therefore, we offer here only a synoptic account which makes use of artfully simplified ideal types.[197] By so doing, we hope to deliver insight into the cruel veins pervading and colouring the phenomenon of humour, while also being a little facetious.[198] This last account, then, is no sophisticated treatise or argument. Just some brief humorous thoughts.[199] Besides, some of these views are explored and expanded upon more scholastically in *H&C3*.

(1) The first old Western tradition, or subcurrent, of humour is open to all comic registers, but only if one is successful enough in using it. Boisterous Roman comedies, Rabelaisian artistry, carnivalesque folklore, unbarred raillery, unforgiving stand-up comedy, and shameless roasting sessions would seem to instantiate, more or less adequately, this cultural tradition (or subcurrent), in different times and places. In line with this practice, if you are sufficiently funny, you can survive unscathed, even if your humour is cruel. Indeed, if you are very good at it, your reputation and/or income may actually be enhanced (e.g., professed 'jokesters' in politics such as Berlusconi and Boris Johnson, or merciless comedians such as John Cleese and Ricky Gervais).

A general sense of acceptance of human frailties and foibles, and of self-acceptance, animates this comic tradition, which also acknowledges our propensity to sinfulness and offers incentives to correct others and/or ourselves, also by means of biting humour. Certain individuals and/or groups are thus frequently singled out as targets, insofar as certain 'sins' and/or 'sinful' tendencies are commonly associated with them (e.g., young women, old men, shopkeepers, lawyers). Still, given that all kinds of comic registers can be deployed, there are opportunities aplenty for mocking people of all social classes. Hence, those who start the mocking can get a taste of their medicine in return, though not necessarily by the original butts of the joke who may belong to lower-status groups and communities. Rather, peers or social superiors will launch the rejoinders.

Insofar as social classes are concerned, cruel humour signals 'who is what', at least superficially. By observing whether a person is able or not to play with all the available comic registers and deploy them adroitly, especially the risky ones, her

---

[197] See Bakhtin's works on popular laughter and the voluminous literature about him.
[198] We kept these lighter remarks till the very end to counterbalance the gloom of the preceding ones.
[199] We have indeed remarked on the improbability of originality, but there is no reason to be hopelessly redundant.

class profile can be quickly gauged, if summarily and even erroneously at times. In essence, if you can do it or come across as being able to do it, you are likely to be believed to belong to a better group. If, instead, you can toy with few registers only, especially of the crass order, or create that poor impression, you are probably going to be tacitly classified as a 'redneck' or an unworthy spawn of the 'great unwashed'.

It is a crude and imperfect system of detection. No doubt. Yet it is one that is nonetheless part and parcel of our own lived experiences. After all, people's personal data and bank accounts are not always easy to access. Therefore, we must rely on other clues to figure out from which social stratum they come. Heuristics and rules of thumb, as imperfect as they may be, are a necessary fact of life.

Moreover, those who fail to play effectively with the various registers are likely to be found guilty of a *brutta figura*, i.e., losing face in a variously blameworthy manner, primarily aesthetic. Inevitably, these individuals come across as socially inept and, consequently, deserving of some apt censoring action, which can certainly include ridicule and, in the public sphere, extend to political caricature, satirical lambasting, and/or salacious lampooning. Ideally, these individuals should be mounted on a donkey and hit with rotting vegetables and excrements—an ancient penal practice in some parts of Europe.

Not stones or arrows, however. Words, however hurtful, are never equated to real and truly damaging weapons. Thus, hurtful words have better chances of survival, meaning that diffuse cruelties and diffuse carnivals characterise those societies and/or social milieus where such traditions happen to be most pronounced (e.g., Baroncelli's 1990s Italy or today's Western working-class establishments).

(2) There also exists an equally venerable Western tradition or subcurrent that aims at entrenching the circulation of few selected comic registers and excluding the others. No matter how funny one can be, there are themes and targets that ought to be left outside the realm of humorous agency. We could cite here: ethico-philosophical reflections on comic propriety in ancient times; early-medieval instructions to Christian monks and nuns about smiles and mirth; Puritan condemnations of earthly merriments; and recent moralising campaigns against outrageous comic films, risqué internet productions, irreverent cartoons, over-the-top violent videogames, and edgy streaming shows. All these attempts at dampening, directing, or deleting commonplace humour and other uncouth feats of creativity instantiate, more or less blatantly, the cultural tradition (or subcurrent) at issue in different times and places, whether we happen to be in agreement with each and every instance of it, some of them, or none at all.[200]

---

200 *The agreement at issue is far too context-dependent and ultimately personal to be assessed here*

Albeit not the only one, "selection" is a word that well describes this tradition which aims at fostering moral perfection and/or self-perfection above anything else. These goals are paramount, even if their pursuit means making humour secondary and/or irrelevant while reducing all other values to a moral one (e. g., aesthetic, historic, biological). 'Spotlessness' is the main aim, whether cast in religious or secular terms (e. g., "virtue" and "cultural sensitivity"). The incentives ensuring due correction can therefore be very strong. Humour, quite often, is considered inadequate to express all the disappointment, moral horror, disgust, and/or hatred for that which and those who make imperfection such a sore and enduring sight.[201]

The harshness and hurdles faced in the quest of moral perfection mean that only a select few ever make it. The leading Puritans called themselves "the Perfect", and they were a minority. Logically, social distinctions are bound to be sharp and stark, for only an elite of refined spirits can truly succeed in mastering those registers that, while permitting episodic humorous relief, are also immune to falling into any disreputable *faux pas*. Those who fail ought to incur the sternest reprobation, for their failure is ultimately moral in nature and, *a fortiori*, highly offensive. This breach also marks the difference between the perfect few and the imperfect many.

In the political sphere, correctness becomes of the utmost importance. Ideally, the public figures that fail in their adherence to the supreme principles of refinement should be quartered by horses and their body parts used as a warning to society at large—another well-known historic penal practice in many parts of Europe. As exemplified by the heated debates about the heretics' theological propositions in earlier times or those about politically incorrect ones today, words are equated to real weapons, and the most severe reprimands may ensue for their misuse. Unemployment, if lucky; political and/or social death, if hapless.[202]

Insofar as no psychic reality, whether individual or collective, can subsist without a modicum of relaxing laughter, special settings are established and managed to allow for occasional release. Public executions are probably the most notorious, as Harlow observed (see, e. g., Afghanistan under the Taliban). Yet concentrated cruelty conducive to laughter can also be experienced and exploited in collective

---

in a trenchant and universally compelling way. LVOA, however, can help us determine in principle which options are good and bad. Also, a number of cruel objections to merriment are going to be tackled and discussed in *H&C3*.

201 Ironically, humour's inadequacy in these contexts is an elusive matter of degree and tone, for "humour" proper is said to share much ground, both evolutionarily and behaviourally, with "disgust" (Jajszczok 2022, title *et passim*; see also W. Miller 1997).

202 We address this issue in further detail in *H&C3*.

campaigns against individuals, groups, and/or organisations that are regarded as unworthy of social esteem and therefore to be mocked rabidly and at will (see, e.g., our century's "male tears" Anglophone mugs mocking the discomforts voiced by purportedly privileged middle-aged white men). Also, *ad hoc* dedicated carnivals can be permitted so that the stringent moral rules of society can be loosened, whether under the excuse of acceptable intoxication (e.g., weekend binge-drinking sessions) or in the guise of promoting some high moral principle (e.g., uproarious gay-pride parades being a noble paragon of egalitarianism and social acceptance).[203]

These two traditions coexist and intermingle in today's Western societies, when they do not clash against each other. Neither is intrinsically bound to persist and/or prevail in the future. Historically, prominent faiths and fads have swung wildly in waves and splutters. As of the 20th century, for one, the cultural trends and preoccupations of the West's hegemonic power, i.e., the US, have frequently become those of Europe, analogously to the way in which those of the Italian intelligentsia of the 14th and 15th century became the leading cultural trends in much of educated Europe in the 16th and 17th centuries.[204]

To illustrate, we might choose how a contemporary teenage daughter may reply to her mother, who had the audacity of stating: "You've put on weight!" Among a typical Canadian middle-class family in, say, Ontario, the retort could be: "Mom, don't you dare! You can't say that kind of stuff anymore!" In a southern-Italian family of comparable wealth, education, and status, the rejoinder would probably come along the lines of: "Yes, and good sense too, unlike some people I know…".[205]

4.9.2 Two Cooks

On a parallel anecdotal course, we could also muse on an experience that we both have had as professional academics who cook most family meals.[206] We touched on this matter in *H&C1* when explaining how, in our complex nervous system, the distinction between the emotional and cognitive levels is not as clear-cut

---

[203] No Islamophobia, misandry, misanthropy or homophobia is implied by the chosen examples.
[204] This historical case was tackled in detail in *H&C1* in connection with Cassirer's studies about "humour" proper.
[205] Before the reader goes into a fit, let us repeat that this is a mere anecdote aimed at spurring reflection. Also, no anti-Canadian sentiment, fat-shaming or anti-Italian sentiment is implied by the chosen examples.
[206] Once again, reader beware! This is an anecdote aimed at spurring reflection.

as one might suppose *prima facie*, and these two levels frequently overlap. Thus, if we accidentally put our fingers on a hot burner, we remove them instantly, without thought.

From a Darwinian perspective, having to contemplate each reflex would surely come at life-threatening cost for the individual. However, if seconds after having removed a baked lasagne from the oven, I realise that the casserole is burning my hand through the oven mitts, I still opt for pain—all the way to the dining room table, also mindful of my fancy hardwood floor. In short, even the most basic reflexes can be overridden. Much brain function is devoted to inhibiting rather than initiating action. What happens, though, when we fail to hang on, despite trying?

Should a restaurant's sous-chef or cook happen to drop such a scorching casserole, the master chef or the manager could well announce: "You're fired!", while assigning the task of preparing another casserole to someone else. This attitude corresponds to the second Western tradition or subcurrent highlighted above, which we have characterised as nominally "Puritanical" or implicitly 'Canadian' (with the likely exception of Quebec).[207]

A different attitude would be reflected and played out in the opposite context, which we have roughly yet conveniently designated as "southern Italian" or "working class". In this latter setting, the master-chef or the owner of the restaurant would mock and even insult the sous-chef or cook who wasted a lasagne casserole. The boss may even call his/her subordinate an "idiot" in front of everyone else. But s/he would also order the same sous-chef or cook to prepare another dish. We believe the second scenario is more compassionate, despite the stinging humiliation that it involves. However, another individual with a different disposition might prefer the first one. Two options are on the table here. It may be yet another uncomfortable dilemma unearthed by our research.

The wisdom of these anecdotes—if we may use such a dignified term for these roughly sketched and very mundane examples—is that Western societies and members thereof can choose their humorous cruelty to a meaningful extent. They may champion a gentler world of sensitive individuals who opt for prudent silence, polite wit, and/or harmless chitchat. Or they may contribute to a ruder one, comprising unthinking and offensive individuals, as well as those who would rather engage in vigorous verbal swordsmanship, piercing wit, and/or barbed banter. Either way, also because of the multiple inequalities and injustices that these societies tolerate, cruelty persists.

---

[207] The remark on Quebec is a sample of our quaint sense of humour, not a deep ethnographic point.

In the former, more passive world, people's impolite thoughts are not given much of a way out and tend to fester inside their psyche, except for occasional celebrations allowing potent and concentrated discharges. In the latter, more aggressive world, people's impolite thoughts are given a quotidian way out, i.e., *via* humorous avenues, unless they are deemed truly excessive, even under lax circumstances which do not demand carnivals or similar celebrations. In either case, moreover, each person must be aware of additional factors that can make the use of humour, patently cruel or not, permissible and palatable, and of its failure to be either lightly or cruelly reprimanded.

4.9.3 Two Options

Humour's frustrating dilemmas and dramas reflect deeper ones. In human communication at large, in fact, different approaches and formulations are likely to resonate more or less un/inspiring to different personality types and/or individual persons, who may be well-read, university-educated, highly intelligent, and yet capable of disagreeing most vocally on all sorts of important subjects. With rare exceptions, entire academic disciplines and departments are thus divided, both externally and internally, on what counts or should count ideally as 'real' or 'true' knowledge, 'proper' research, the 'correct' method, and/or 'deep' or 'clear' understanding—as though there should be always just one such pathway rather than several, i.e., despite the contrary example that their own history provides.

Eventually, in one of the many cruel ironies affecting the world of scholarship and science, someone's deepest and fundamental insights become another's demented and farcical inanities; the former's revered master, the latter's ridiculed mystifier; one's substantial, concrete, and emotive immediateness, the superstitious, circumstantial, and illogical undependability of another; the lived experience of a traditional culture or old sage, the lacklustre evidence of a tarnished cult or odd screwball; and the most careful reasoning presented by one, the convoluted rambling perceived by the other. And yet, Puritans, pornographers, hermits, exhibitionists, extremists, empiricists, occultists, mystics, masochists, materialists, and moderates are, in spite of all their differences and disagreements, *people*—who yet spend much of their lives, as it were, in parallel universes, i.e., with limited, little or no chance of fruitful cross-communication.

What is more, living in a world in which contradictory traditions and social subcurrents pervade our lives, often painfully so, adds scorn to injury, for one is frequently left wondering about which social sphere s/he is currently in and, *a fortiori*, which open and, above all, *tacit* rules apply to it, and whether s/he has the correct grasp of them or not, if any at all.[208] Thus, we find ourselves pondering anxiously whether we should laugh or not, or make others laugh or not. Concomitantly, life's cruelty can almost be heard laughing at us in its subtle and exquisite way. It may be true that the unexamined life is not worth living. However, the thoroughly examined one is a sizable headache.[209]

---

[208] Tacit knowing is murky by definition; hence, the actual degree of a person's command of it is frequently revealed *via negativa*, i.e., by way of blunders which, as seen, can compromise careers, reputations, relationships, or even survival (as noted before, we discuss the assassination of comedians and cartoonists in *H&C3*). Shaun Miller (2022, 263) recently developed an analogous assessment of the sexual domain and the thorny issue of "consent" in particular, given that "[m]ost sexual initiations happen non-verbally" and the involved persons must then go "searching for clues and giving clues to see if it is ok to proceed, slow down, or stop". Eerily, humour and sex, which are both commonly associated with fun and joy, can be settings where errors cause traumas and tragedies. (More on the many and deep relations between these two settings is said in *H&C3*.)
[209] We expect the reader to have caught the indirect reference to Socratic wisdom.

Bibliography

"Angry Whores Anarcho Brigades Action Against Swerf / Terf NGO Offices" (2019). *Anarchistnews.org*, https://anarchistnews.org/content/angry-whores-anarcho-brigade-action-against-swerf-terf-ngo-offices [Accessed 20/08/2022].

"Bufera su Pio e Amedeo per le frasi su omosessuali, ebrei, neri: 'Il politically correct ha rotto'" (2021). *La Repubblica*, https://www.repubblica.it/spettacoli/tv-radio/2021/05/01/news/bufera_su_pio_e_amedeo_per_le_frasi_su_omosessuali_ebrei_neri_il_web_e_la_poitica_insorgono-298960541/?ref=RHTP-BH-I297139005-P3-S3-T1 [Accessed 21/02/2022].

"Frisky Benny Hill-style Fun Run Cancelled after Branded as 'Sexist'" (2017). *ITV News*, https://www.itv.com/news/wales/2017-07-27/frisky-benny-hill-style-fun-run-cancelled-after-branded-as-sexist/ [Accessed 21/02/2022].

"It Is Difficult to Get a Man to Understand Something When His Salary Depends upon His Not Understanding It" (2017). *Quote Investigator*, https://quoteinvestigator.com/2017/11/30/salary/#r+17380+1+2 [Accessed 25/10/2022].

"Marine Gets Beat Down Trying to Stop Bullies" (2013). *ABC News*, https://www.youtube.com/watch?v=txdTlBlHd_8 [Accessed 29/04/2022].

"Monica Lewinsky" (2018). *Woman Forum Daily*, https://woman.forumdaily.com/en/monika-levinski-kak-slozhilas-zhizn-samoj-unizhennoj-zhenshhiny-ameriki/ [Accessed 19/08/2022].

"On Eve of World Cup, FIFA Chief Accuses Qatar's Critics of Hypocrisy" (2022). *Dawn*, https://www.dawn.com/news/1721896 [Accessed 29/11/2022].

"Sun Yang: Eight-Year Ban for Chinese Olympic Champion" (2020). *BBC News*, https://www.bbc.com/sport/swimming/51670931 [Accessed 21/04/2022].

"The Dark Psychology of Being a Good Comedian" (2014). *The Atlantic*, https://www.theatlantic.com/health/archive/2014/02/the-dark-psychology-of-being-a-good-comedian/284104/ [Accessed 26/11/2021].

Abrahamson, Maria (2004). "Alcohol in Courtship Contexts: Focus-Group Interviews with Young Swedish Women". *Contemporary Drug Problems*, 31(1): 3–29.

Abrams, Amah-Rose (2016). "Italy Covers Up Nude Statues to Protect Business Meeting with Iran". *Artnet News*, https://news.artnet.com/art-world/italian-authorities-cover-up-nude-statues-for-iranian-president-414764 [Accessed 21/09/2022].

Abrams, Jessica R., and Bippus, Amy (2011). "An Intergroup Investigation of Disparaging Humor". *Journal of Language and Social Psychology*, 30(2): 193–201.

Adams, Guy B., Balfour, Danny L. and Reed, George E. (2006). "Abu Ghraib, Administrative Evil, and Moral Inversion: The Value of 'Putting Cruelty First'". *PAR*, 66(5): 680–693.

Addison, Joseph *et al.* (1891). *The Spectator. A New Edition* (ed. Henry Morley). London: George Routledge, https://onlinebooks.library.upenn.edu/webbin/gutbook/lookup?num=12030 [Accessed 01/05/2022].

Adler, Alfred (1921) [1912]. *The Neurotic Constitution* (trans. Bernard Glueck and John E. Lind). New York: Moffat, Yard, https://archive.org/details/dli.ernet.214523 [Accessed 01/03/2023].

Adler, Alfred (1930). *The Education of Children*. London: George Allen & Unwind, https://archive.org/details/in.ernet.dli.2015.190464 [Accessed 01/03/2023].

Adriaensen, Brigitte (2015). "Cultural Representations of Contemporary Mexican Drug Culture: Dark Humour and Irony in Relation to the Abject". *European Journal of Humour Research*, 3(2/3): 62–79.

Aesop (2002). *Aesopica* (trans. Laura Gibbs), http://www.mythfolklore.net/aesopica/index.htm [Accessed 27/09/2022].

Aguiar de Sousa, Luís (2022). "Cruelty, Bad Conscience, and the Sovereign Individual in Nietzsche's *Genealogy of Morality*". In Aguiar de Sousa, Luís and Stellino, Paolo (Eds.), *Violence and Nihilism*, 65–88. Berlin: De Gruyter.

Ahmed, Sara, and Bonis, Oristelle (2012). "Feminist Killjoys (and Other Willful Subjects)". *Cahiers du Genre*, 53(2): 77–98.

Ahroni, Ron (2020). "Detachment of Empathy: A Common Denominator for Two Theories of Humour". *The European Journal of Humour Research*, 8(1): 55–67.

Ainslie, George (2006). "Cruelty May Be a Self-Control Device against Sympathy". *Behavioral and Brain Sciences*, 29(3): 224–225.

Airaksinen, Timo (1995). *The Philosophy of the Marquis de Sade*. London: Routledge.

Alkiviadou, Natalie (2022). "Ain't That Funny? A Jurisprudential Analysis of Humour in Europe and the U.S.". *The European Journal of Humour Research*, 10(1): 50–61.

Allen, R.T. (2014). *Ethics as Scales of Forms*. Newcastle-upon-Tyne: Cambridge Scholars.

Allen, Valerie (2007). *On Farting. Language and Laughter in the Middle Ages*. New York: Palgrave Macmillan.

Allison, Kimberley R., Bussey, Kay and Sweller, Naomi (2019). "'I'm Going to Hell for Laughing at This': Norms, Humour, and the Neutralisation of Aggression in Online Communities". *Proceedings of the ACM on Human-Computer Interaction*, art. 152: 1–25.

Ambadiang, Théophile (2018). "Entre convivencia y disidencia: algunas observaciones sobre prácticas y discursos en torno al humor y la ironía en el contexto africano". *Actio Nova*, 2: 142–167.

American Psychological Association (2011). "Supressing the 'White Bears'". *Monitor on Psychology*, 42(9), http://www.apa.org/monitor/2011/10/unwanted-thoughts [Accessed 29/04/2022].

Amir, Lydia B. (1996). "Kierkegaard and the Traditions of the Comic in Philosophy". *Kierkegaard Studies Yearbook*, 1: 377–402.

Amir, Lydia B. (2001). "Plato's Theory of Love: Rationality as Passion". *Practical Philosophy*, 4(3): 6–14.

Amir, Lydia B. (2013). "Philosophy's Attitude towards the Comic. A Re-Evaluation". *The European Journal of Humour Research*, 1(1): 6–21.

Amir, Lydia B. (2014). *Humor and the Good Life in Modern Philosophy: Shaftesbury, Hamann, Kierkegaard*. Albany: State University of New York.

Amir, Lydia B. (2015). "The Tragic Sense of the Good Life". In Weiss, Michael Noah (Ed.), *The Socratic Handbook*, 97–128. Zurich: Lit.

Amir, Lydia B. (2017). *Rethinking Philosophers' Responsibility*. Newcastle-upon-Tyne: Cambridge Scholars.

Amir, Lydia B. (2019). *Philosophy, Humor, and the Human Condition. Taking Ridicule Seriously*. Cham: Palgrave Macmillan.

Amir, Lydia B. (forthcoming). *The Legacy of Nietzsche's Philosophy of Laughter: Bataille, Deleuze, Rosset*. New York: Routledge.

Andrew, Edward G. (1995). *The Genealogy of Values: The Aesthetic Economy of Nietzsche and Proust*. Lanham: Rowman & Littlefield.

Anscombe, Gertrude Elizabeth Margret (1963) [1957]. *Intention*, 2nd ed. Cambridge, MA: Harvard UP.

Aquinas, Thomas (1920) [ca. 1265]. *Summa Theologica* (trans. Fathers of the English Dominican Province), 2nd ed. Oxford: English Dominican Province.

Arab, Reza, and Milner Davis, Jessica (2022). "Humour and Belonging: A Thematic Review". *The European Journal of Humour Research*, 10(2): 1–13.

Arendt, Hannah (1985) [1958]. *The Origins of Totalitarianism*, 2nd ed. London: Harvest.
Aristotle (1933) [4th c. BC]. *Aristoteles in 23 Volumes*, vol. 23 (trans. W. H. Fyfe). Cambridge, MA: Harvard UP.
Armstrong, Gary, and Young, Malcom (2000). "Fanatical Football Chants: Creating and Controlling the Carnival". In *Football Culture: Local Contests, Global Visions* (ed. Gerry P.T. Finn and Richard Giulianotti), 173–211. London: Frank Cass.
Arnarsson, Ársæll Már (2016). *Síðustu ár sálarinnar*. Reykjavik: Háskólaútgáfan.
Arnarsson, Ársæll Már and Bjarnason, Þóroddur (2018). "The Problem with Low Prevalence of Bullying". *International Journal of Environmental Research and Public Health*, 15(7): 1535, doi:10.3390/ijerph15071535 [Accessed 21/09/2021].
Arnarsson Ársæll Már et al. (2015). "Suicidal Risk and Sexual Orientation in Adolescence: A Population-Based Study in Iceland". *Scandinavian Journal of Public Health*, 43: 497–505.
Arnarsson, Ársæll Már et al. (2020). "Cyberbullying and Traditional Bullying among Nordic Adolescents and Their Impact on Life Satisfaction". *Scandinavian Journal of Public Health*, 48(5): 502–510.
Arnault, Lynne S. (2003). "Cruelty, Horror, and the Will to Redemption". *Hypatia*, 18(2): 155–188.
Arróniz Parra, Santiago, and Padilla Cruz, Manuel (2022). "Joke Identification, Comprehension and Appreciation by Spanish Intermediate ESL Learners: An Exploratory Study". *The European Journal of Humour Research*, 10(1): 108–133.
Artaud, Antonin (1958) [1938]. *The Theatre and Its Double* (trans. Mary C. Richards). New York: Grove.
Arvanitakis, James, Fredriksson, Martin and Schillings, Sonja (2017). "Bellamy's Rage and Beer's Conscience: Pirate Methodologies and the Contemporary University". *Culture Unbound*, 9(3): 260–276.
Aschheim, Steven E. (1994). *The Nietzsche Legacy in Germany: 1890–1990*. Berkeley: University of California.
Ateneo (1990). *Schiavi e servi* (trans. Annalisa Paradiso and Jacques Daléchamps). Palermo: Sellerio.
Athanasiadou, Angeliki, and Colston, Herbert L. (Eds.) (2020). *The Diversity of Irony*. Berlin: De Gruyter.
Attenborough, Frederick (2014). "Jokes, Pranks, Blondes and Banter: Recontextualising Sexism in the British Print Press". *Journal of Gender Studies*, 23(2): 137–154.
Atwood, Margaret (2006) [1990]. "A Double-Bladed Knife: Subversive Laughter in Two Stories by Thomas King". In *Curious Pursuits: Occasional Writing*, 131–141. London: Virago.
Auden, W.H. (2010) [1939]. "In Memory of Ernst Toller", https://matthewsalomon.wordpress.com/2010/12/01/w-h-auden-in-memory-of-ernst-toller/ [Accessed 09/07/2022].
Austin, John Langshaw (1962). *How to Do Things with Words: The William James Lectures Delivered at Harvard University in 1955* (ed. J.O. Urmson). London: Oxford UP.
Avaliani, Sergi (2018). *The Philosophy of Pseudoabsolute*. Hauppauge, NY: Nova Science.
Avgerinou, Vassiliki, and Glakomatos, Stefanos G. (2011). "The Effect of Hooliganism on Greek Football Demand". In Jewell, R.T. (Ed.), *Violence and Aggression in Sporting Contests*, 155–174. Cham: Springer.
Ayer, A.J. (1987). "Sources of Intolerance". In Mendus, Susan and Edwards, David (Eds.), *On Toleration*, 83–100. Oxford: Clarendon.
Bachelard, Gaston (1933). *Les intuitions atomistiques. (Essai de classification)*. Paris: Boivin.
Bachelard, Gaston (1937). *L'expérience de l'espace dans la physique contemporaine*. Paris: Félix Alcan.
Bachelard, Gaston (1948). *La terre et les rêveries de la volonté*. Paris: José Corti.
Bachelard, Gaston (1961). *La flamme d'une chandelle*. Paris: PUF.

Bachelard, Gaston (1963) [1950]. *La dialectique de la durée*. Paris: PUF.
Bachelard, Gaston (1965) [1951]. *L'activité rationaliste de la physique contemporaine*, 2nd ed. Paris: PUF.
Bachelard, Gaston (1972) [1951]. *Le matérialisme rationnel*, 3rd ed. Paris: PUF.
Bachelard, Gaston (1982) [1941]. *La terre et les rêveries du repos*. Paris: José Corti.
Bachelard, Gaston (1983) [1942]. *L'eau et les rêves. Essai sur l'imagination de la matière*. Paris: José Corti.
Bachelard, Gaston (1990) [1943]. *L'air ey les songes. Essai sur l'imagination du movement*. Paris: José Corti.
Bachelard, Gaston (1992) [1934]. *La psychanalyse du feu*. Paris: Gallimard.
Bachelard, Gaston (2013) [1932]. *Intuition of the Instant* (trans. Eileen Rizo-Patron). Evanston.: Northwestern UP.
Baier, Annette C. (1993). "Moralism and Cruelty: Reflections on Hume and Kant". *Ethics*, 103(3): 436–457.
Bakewell, Sarah (2010). *How to Live: Or a Life of Montaigne in One Question and Twenty Attempts at an Answer*. London: Chatto & Windus.
Bakhtin, Mikhail (1976). "The Art of the Word and the Culture of Folk Humor (Rabelais and Gogol)". *Soviet Studies in Literature*, 12(2): 27–39.
Bakhtin, Mikhail (2014) [1940s]. "Bakhtin on Shakespeare: Excerpt from 'Additions and Changes to Rabelais'". *PMLA*, 129(3): 522–537.
Bakker, Hans (1995). "The Life World, Grief and Individual Uniqueness: 'Social Definition' in Dilthey, Windelband, Rickert, Weber, Simmel and Schutz". *Sociologische Gids*, 95(3): 187–212.
Baldini, Paolo, and Abatantuono, Diego (2021). "Non ho mai visto Milano triste. Abitavo nel palazzo di Gianni Rivera". *Corriere della Sera*, https://www.corriere.it/sette/incontri/21_agosto_13/diego-abatantuono-non-ho-mai-visto-milano-triste-abitavo-palazzo-gianni-rivera-4b2dc29a-f75e-11eb-83a2-ddb3d15a828f.shtml [Accessed 21/04/2022].
Banjo, Omotayo O. *et al.* (2017). "Experiencing Racial Humor with Outgroups: A Psychophysiological Examination of Co-Viewing Effects". *Media Psychology*, 20(4): 607–631.
Bannister, Anne (2003). *Creative Therapies with Traumatized Children*. London: Jessica Kingsley.
Baquie, Susan (2013). "How Does the Co-Existence of Humour and Violence in Contemporary Visual Art Indicate the Presence of Attributes of Janus?" PhD. Queensland College of Art.
Baraz, Daniel (2003). *Medieval Cruelty: Changing Perceptions, Late Antiquity to the Early Modern Period*. Ithaca: Cornell UP.
Barden, Garrett and Baruchello, Giorgio (2019). *Why Believe? Approaches to Religion*. Akureyri: University of Akureyri.
Bardon, Adrian (2005). "The Philosophy of Humor". In Charney, Maurice (Ed.), *Comedy. A Geographic and Historical Guide*, vol. 2, 462–476. Westport, CT: Praeger.
Barnes, Colin (1991). *Disabled People in Britain and Discrimination*. London: Hurst.
Baroncelli, Flavio (1996). *Il razzismo è una gaffe. Eccessi e virtù del "politically correct"*. Rome: Donzelli.
Baroncelli, Flavio (2001). "Le quattro indegnità dei liberali irresoluti". *Teoria politica*, 17(3): 23–47.
Baroncelli, Flavio (2009). *Mi manda Platone*. Genoa: il melangolo.
Baroncelli, Flavio (2011). *Alfabeto. Con scritti e testimonianze sull'autore* (ed Giovanna Carrara). Novara: Interlinea.
Barrozo, Paulo D. (2008). "Punishing Cruelly: Punishment, Cruelty, and Mercy". *Criminal Law and Philosophy*, 2: 67–84.
Barrozo, Paulo D. (2015). "Cruelty in Criminal Law: Four Conceptions". *Criminal Law Bulletin*, 51(5): 1025–1073.

Barthes, Roland (1970). "L'ancienne rhétorique. Aide-mémoire". *Communications*, (16): 172–223.
Bartsch, Shadi, and Schiesaro, Alessandro (Eds.) (2015). *The Cambridge Companion to Seneca*. New York: Cambridge UP.
Baruchello, Giorgio (2010). "Western Philosophy and the Life-Ground". In McMurtry, John (Ed.), *Philosophy and World Problems*, vol. 3, 1–79. Paris and Oxford: Encyclopedia of Life Support Systems.
Baruchello, Giorgio (2017). *Philosophy of Cruelty. Collected Philosophical Essays*. Gatineau: Northwest Passage Books.
Baruchello, Giorgio (2018a). *The Business of Life and Death, Volume One: Values and Economies*. Gatineau: Northwest Passage Books.
Baruchello, Giorgio (2018b). *The Business of Life and Death, Volume Two: Politics, Law, and Society*. Gatineau: Northwest Passage Books.
Baruchello, Giorgio, and Arnarsson, Ársæll Már (2023). *Humour and Cruelty 1: A Philosophical and Psychological Exploration*. Berlin: De Gruyter.
Baruchello, Giorgio, and Hamblet, Wendy C. (2004). "What is Cruelty?" *Appraisal*, 5(1): 33–38 and 56.
Bataille, George (1962) [1957]. *Death and Sensuality. A Study of Eroticism and the Taboo* (trans. Mary Dalwood). New York: Walker.
Bataille, George (1967) [1949]. *La part maudite*. Paris: Les Éditions de Minuit.
Bataille, George (1997) [1947–1991]. *The Bataille Reader* (ed. Fred Botting and Scott Wilson). Oxford: Blackwell.
Baudelaire, Charles (1988) [1857–1864]. "Le joueur généraux". *Le Spleen de Paris. Petits Poèmes en prose*. Paris: Club du livre.
Baumeister, Roy F. (1996). *Evil: Inside Human Violence and Cruelty*. New York: Freeman.
Baumeister, Roy F., and Campbell, W. Keith (1999). "The Intrinsic Appeal of Evil: Sadism, Sensational Thrills, and Threatened Egotism". *Personality and Social Psychology Review*, 3(3): 210–221.
Baxter, D.G. (1989). "Robert Burns and the Politics of the French Revolution". *Scottish Tradition. International Review of Scottish Studies*, 15: 55–69.
Bayless, Martha (2020). "Medieval Jokes in Serious Contexts: Speaking Humour to Power". In Derrin, Daniel and Burrows, Hannah (Eds.), *The Palgrave Handbook of Humour*, 257–274. Cham: Palgrave Macmillan.
Beattie, James (1778) [1777]. *On Poetry and Music, As They Affect the Minds; On Laughter, and Ludicrous Composition; On the Utility of Classical Learning*. Edinburgh: William Creech, https://archive.org/details/essaysonpoetrymu00beat [Accessed 01/05/2022].
Beaumont, Roger (1990). "Thinking the Unspeakable: On Cruelty in Small Wars". *Small Wars and Insurgencies*, 1(1): 54–73.
Beccaria, Cesare (1880) [1764]. *Crimes and Punishments* (trans. James Anson Farrer). London: Chatto & Windus, https://www.gutenberg.org/files/58700/58700-h/58700-h.htm [Accessed 01/05/2022].
Becker, Kenneth L. (2001). *Unlikely Companions: C.G. Jung on the Spiritual Exercises of Ignatius of Loyola*. Leominster: Gracewing.
Bell, Nancy (2015). *We Are Not Amused. Failed Humor in Interaction*. Berlin: De Gruyter.
Bell, P.A. (1978). "Affective State, Attraction, and Affiliation". *Personality and Social Psychology Bulletin*, 4: 616–619.
Bemiller, Michelle and Zimmer Schneider, Rachel (2010). "It's not just a joke". *Sociological Spectrum*, 30(4): 459–479.
Benatar, David (2006). *Better Never to Have Been: The Harm of Coming into Existence*. Oxford: Oxford UP.

Bengsson, Jan Olof (2006). *The Worldview of Personalism: Origins and Development.* Oxford: Oxford UP.
Bennets, Marc (2018). "Russia Pulls 'Despicable' Death of Stalin from Cinemas". *The Guardian,* https://www.theguardian.com/world/2018/jan/23/russia-urged-to-delay-death-of-stalin-release-until-summer [Accessed 21/04/2022].
Bentham, Jeremy (1817). *A Table of the Springs of Action.* London: Hunter, https://archive.org/details/b28738196 [Accessed 28/02/2023].
Bentham, Jeremy (1864) [1802]. *Theory of Legislation* (trans. R. Hildreth). London: Trübner, https://archive.org/details/in.ernet.dli.2015.218134/page/n3/mode/2up [Accessed 01/03/2023].
Bentley, Joseph (1967). "Satire and the Rhetoric of Sadism". *The Centennial Review,* 11(3): 387–404.
Berger, Peter L. (1969). *A Rumour of Angels: Modern Society and the Rediscovery of the Supernatural.* New York: Doubleday.
Bergson, Henri (1911). *Laughter: An Essay on the Meaning of the Comic* (trans. Cloudesley Brereton and Fred Rothwell). New York: Macmillan, https://archive.org/details/laughteressayonm1911berg [Accessed 03/03/2023].
Bergson, Henri (1960) [1889]. *Time and Free Will. An Essay on the Immediate Data of Consciousness* (trans. F.L. Pogson). New York: Harper & Bros.
Berhendt, Marc (2020). "The Moral Case for Sexbots". *Paladyn, Journal of Behavioural Robots,* (11): 171–190.
Berlant, Lauren (2010). "Cruel Optimism". In Gregg, Melissa and Seigworth, Gregory J. (Eds.), *The Affect Theory Reader,* 93–117. Durham: Duke UP.
Beveridge, William (1945). "4th April 1945 Letter to Arthur Freud", https://mobile.twitter.com/abenanav/status/1537048189957726208/photo/1 [Accessed 08/07/2022].
Bidaki, Reza et al. (2022). "The Moral Development Based on Kohlberg's Theory among Medical Students". *Journal of Social Behavior and Community Health,* 6(1): 802–809.
Bierce, Ambrose (2000) [1911]. *The Unabridged Devil's Dictionary* (ed. David E. Shultz and S.T. Joshi). London: University of Georgia Press.
Billig, Michael (2005). *Laughter and Ridicule. Towards a Social Critique of Humour.* London: Sage.
Bitani, Farahd (2014). *L'ultimo lenzuolo bianco.* Rimini: Guaraldi.
Black, Carolyn (1983). "Obvious Knowledge". *Synthese,* 56: 474–385.
Blake, Emily, and Gannon, Theresa (2008). "Social Perception Deficits, Cognitive Distortions, and Empathy Deficits in Sex Offenders". *Trauma, Violence & Abuse,* 9: 34–55.
Bochenek, Michael, and Brown, A. Widney (2001). *Hatred in the Hallways: Violence and Discrimination against Lesbian, Gay, Bisexual, and Transgender Students in U.S. Schools.* New York: Human Rights Watch.
Bodin, Jean (1955) [1576]. *Six Books of the Commonwealth* (trans. M.J. Tooley). Oxford: Blackwell.
Bodin, Jean (2001) [1580]. *On the Demon-Mania of Witches* (trans. Randy A. Scott). Toronto: Centre for Reformation and Renaissance Studies.
Boldizzoni, Francesco (2011). *The Poverty of Clio: Resurrecting Economic History.* Princeton: Princeton UP.
Borisov, E.M. (1986). "Argentina: Generals in the Dock". *Soviet Law and Government,* 25(3): 53–62.
Borloz, Sophie-Valentine (2017). "Du 'gaz de paradis des poëtes anglais' au 'sourire de force'. Sur les traces du gaz hilarant dans la littérature du XIXe siècle (France et Angleterre)". In Caraion, Marta and Danguy, Laurence (Eds.), *Le rire: forms et fonctions du comique,* https://www.fabula.org/colloques/document4559.php [Accessed 21/09/2021].

Boryslawski, Rafael (2020). "The Monsters that Laugh Back: Humour as a Rhetorical Apophasis in Medieval Monstrology". In Derrin, Daniel and Burrows, Hannah (Eds.), *The Palgrave Handbook of Humour*, 239–256. Cham: Palgrave Macmillan.
Bouquet, Brigitte, and Riffault, Jacques (2010). "L'humour dans les diverses formes du rire". *La vie sociale*, 2(2): 13–22.
Bowker, Julie C., and Etkin, Rebecca G. (2014). "Does Humor Explain Why Relationally Aggressive Adolescents are Popular?" *Journal of Youth and Adolescence*, 43: 1322–1332.
Bowman, Sam (2017). "In Defence of Neoliberalism". *Policy*, 33(3): 35–40.
Boxer, Diana, and Cortés-Conde, Florencia (1997). "From Bonding to Biting: Conversational Joking and Identity Display". *Journal of Pragmatics*, 27: 275–294.
Boyers, Robert, Bernstein, Maxine and Sontag, Susan (2015–2016) [1975]. "Women, The Arts, and The Politics of Culture: An Interview with Susan Sontag". *Salmagundi*, 188–189: 240–262.
Brecht, Bertolt (1939). *Life of Galileo*, http://www.socialiststories.com/en/writers/Brecht-Bertolt/Life-of-Galileo-Bertolt-Brecht.pdf [Accessed 04/11/2022].
Bremmer, Jan, and Roodenburg, Herman (Eds.) (1997). *A Cultural History of Humour: From Antiquity to the Present Day*. Cambridge: Polity.
Bridges, Robert (2014). "The Transience of DSM Categories", https://www.academia.edu/35095219/The_Transience_of_DSM_Categories [Accessed 21/09/2021].
Brodersen, Elizabeth, and Glock, Michael (Eds.) (2017). *Jungian Perspectives on Rebirth and Renewal. Phoenix Rising*. London: Routledge.
Brody, Morris W. (1950). "The Meaning of Laughter". *The Psychoanalytic Quarterly*, 19(2): 192–201.
Brown, Sarah *et al.* (2012). "General and Victim–Specific Empathy: Associations with Actuarial Risk, Treatment Outcome, and Sexual Recidivism". *Sex Abuse*, 24(5): 411–430.
Bruno, Giordano (1985) [1585]. *De gli eroici furori*. In *Dialoghi italiani, nuovamente ristampati con note da Giovanni Gentile* (ed. Giovanni Aquilecchia), 3rd ed., 927–1178. Florence: Sansoni.
Brzozowska, Dorota, and Chłopicki, Władysław (Eds.) (2012). *Polish Humour. Humour and Culture 2*. Krakow: Tertium.
Buccola, Gaetano Roberto (2019). *L'azione malata. Male universale e Bene individuale. Psicoanalisi del terrorismo*. Palermo: Carlo Saladino.
Buckels, Erin E. *et al.* (2019). "Internet Trolling and Everyday Sadism: Parallel Effects on Pain Perception and Judgment". *Journal of Personality*, 87: 328–340.
Buckels, Erin E., Jones, Daniel N. and Paulhus, Delroy L. (2013). "Behavioural Confirmation of Everyday Sadism". *Psychological Science*, 24(11): 2201–2209.
Buckley, F.H. (2003). *The Morality of Laughter*. Ann Arbor: University of Michigan.
Budson, Andrew E. *et al.* (2022). "Consciousness as a Memory System". *Cognitive and Behavioral Neurology*, 00(00) [sic], https://journals.lww.com/cogbehavneurol/Fulltext/9900/Consciousness_as_a_Memory_System.19.aspx [Accessed 29/10/2022].
Buijzen, Moniek, and Valkenburg, Patti M. (2004). "Developing a Typology of Humor in Audio-visual Media". *Media Psychology*, 6(2): 147–167.
Bülte, Tobias (2018). "Politisches Denken jenseits von Begründung und Fatalismus: Überlegungen zu einer erweiterten Lesart Judith Shklars". *ZPTh – Zeitschrift für Politische Theorie*, 9(2): 193–208.
Burbank, Victoria K. (1994). *Fighting Women: Anger and Aggression in Aboriginal Australia*. Berkeley: University of California.
Burke, Kenneth (1969). *A Rhetoric of Motives*. Berkeley: California UP.
Burns, Robert (1993) [1795]. *The Complete Illustrated Poems, Songs and Ballads* (ed. Samuel Carr). London: Chancellor.

Bursztyka, Przemyslaw (2019). "Culture and Its Irreducible Pluralities". *Eidos. A Journal for Philosophy of Culture*, 4(10): 1 – 4.
Busch, R.L. (1987). *Humor in the Major Novels of F.M. Dostoevsky*. Columbus: Slavica.
Butler, Judith (1994). "Bodies that Matter". In Burke, Carolyn, Schor, Naomi, and Whitford, Margaret (Eds.), *Engaging with Irigaray. Feminist Philosophy and Modern European Thought*, 141 – 174. New York: Columbia UP.
Calandra, Denis (1974). "Karl Valentin and Bertolt Brecht". *The Drama Review*, 18(1): 86 – 98.
Calder, Louise (2011). *Cruelty and Sentimentality: Greek Attitudes to Animals, 600 – 300 BC*. London: Archaeopress.
Campanario, Juan Miguel (2010). "The Parallelism between Scientists' and Students' Resistance to New Scientific Ideas". *International Journal of Science Education*, 24(10): 1095 – 1110.
Campillo, Antonio (2017). "Violencia, justicia y perdón". *Bajo Palabra*, 15: 85 – 98.
Canby, Vincent (1976). "Screen: 'My Friends', Italian Comedy: 4 Middle-Aged Men in the Provinces Outrageous Practical Jokes in a Parable". *The New York Times*, https://www.nytimes.com/1976/07/19/archives/screen-my-friends-italian-comedy4-middleaged-men-in-the-provinces.html [Accessed 12/09/2022].
Čapaitė, Rūta (2003). "The Everyday Life of Grand Duke Vytautas of Lithuania According to Contemporary Correspondence". *Lithuanian Historical Studies*, 8(1): 1 – 26.
Carlson, Susan (1991). *Women and Comedy. Rewriting the British Theatrical Tradition*. Ann Arbor: Michigan UP.
Carlyle, Thomas (1835) [1827]. "Jean Paul Friedrich Richter". In Cross, Maurice (Ed.), *Selections from the Edinburgh Review*, 2: 448 – 459. Paris: Baudry's European Library, https://books.google.bj/books?id=aD5BAAAAYAAJ [Accessed 12/12/2022].
Carlyle, Thomas (1850). *Latter-Day Pamphlets*. London: Chapman and Hall.
Carlyle, Thomas (1853). *Occasional Discourse on the N[*****] Question*. London: Thomas Bosworth, https://books.google.is/books?hl=en&lr=&id=IqLAyFjEh_4C&oi=fnd&pg=PA1&dq=thomas+carlyle+slavery&ots=cva8mfeyrw&sig=uHYOpF4_NHhPukI-SwQPQwdqWB0&redir_esc=y#v=onepage&q=thomas%20carlyle%20slavery&f=false [Accessed 13/01/2023].
Carmack, Betty J. (1997). "Balancing Engagement and Detachment in Caregiving". *Image: The Journal of Nursing Scholarship*, 29(2): 139 – 43.
Carmon, Irin (2016). "Donald Trump's Worst Offense? Mocking Disabled Reporter, Poll Finds". *NBC News*, https://www.nbcnews.com/politics/2016-election/trump-s-worst-offense-mocking-disabled-reporter-poll-finds-n627736 [Accessed 21/09/2021].
Carr, David, Arthur, James and Kristjánsson, Kristján (Eds.) (2017). *Varieties of Virtue Ethics*. London: Palgrave Macmillan.
Carroll, Lewis (2008) [1865]. *Alice's Adventures in Wonderland*. Jessup: The Millennium Fulcrum Edition, https://www.gutenberg.org/cache/epub/11/pg11-images.html [Accessed 15/11/2022].
Carroll, Noël (1990). *The Philosophy of Horror: Or, Paradoxes of the Heart*. New York: Routledge.
Carroll, Noël (1999). "Horror and Humor". *The Journal of Aesthetics and Art Criticism*, 57(2): 145 – 160.
Carroll, Noël (2014). *Humour. A Very Short Introduction*. Oxford: Oxford UP.
Carse, Alisa L. (2005). "The Moral Contours of Empathy". *Ethical Theory and Moral Practice*, 8: 169 – 195.
Carter, Angela (1991). *Wise Children*. New York: Farrar, Straus & Giroux.
Cartwright, David E. (2010). *Arthur Schopenhauer. A Biography*. Cambridge: Cambridge UP.
Casado da Rocha, Antonio (2005). "How Cruel is Disease?" *Appraisal*, 5(3): 141 – 143.

Casey, Terrence (2016). "In Defense of Neoliberalism", https://www.psa.ac.uk/sites/default/files/conference/papers/2016/Casey-In%20Defense%20of%20Neoliberalism%20(PSA%202016)_1.pdf [Accessed 12/10/2022].
Cassirer, Ernst (1953) [1932]. *The Platonic Renaissance in England* (trans. James P. Pettergrove). Edinburgh: Thomas Nelson.
Cassirer, Ernst (1980) [1923 – 1929]. *The Philosophy of Symbolic Forms* (trans. Ralph Manheim). New Haven: Yale UP.
Castiglioni, Arturo (2019) [1927]. *A History of Medicine.* London: Routledge.
Castoriadis, Cornelius (2005). *Figures of the Thinkable, Including Passion and Knowledge* (trans. Anonymously). N.d.a.: Costis.org–Lightning Archive, https://www.notbored.org/FTPK.pdf [Accessed 11/11/2021].
Cavell, Stanley (2003). "Foreword". In Felman, Shoshana, *The Scandal of the Speaking Body. Don Juan with J.L. Austin, or Seduction in Two Languages* (trans. Catherine Porter). Stanford: Stanford UP.
Cazamian, Louis (1930). *The Development of English Humour.* New York: MacMillan.
Cerniglia, Luca *et al.* (2019). "Intersections and Divergences Between Empathizing and Mentalizing: Development, Recent Advancements by Neuroimaging and the Future of Animal Modeling". *Frontiers in Behavioral Neuroscience,* 13: 212.
Césaire, Aimé (1972) [1955]. *Discourse on Colonialism* (trans. Joan Pinkham). New York: Monthly Review.
Chakrabarti, Arindam (1992). "On Knowing by Being Told". *Philosophy East and West,* 42(3): 421 – 439.
Chambers, E.S., Bridge, M.W. and Jones, D.A. (2009). "Carbohydrate Sensing in the Human Mouth: Effects on Exercise Performance and Brain Activity". *Journal of Physiology,* 587(8): 1779 – 1794.
Changoiwala, Puja (2016). *The Front Page Murders: Inside the Serial Killings that Shocked India.* London: Hachette.
Chapkis, Wendy (2018). "Performing Without a Net? Safer-Sex in Porn". *Faculty and Staff Scholarship,* 11, https://digitalcommons.usm.maine.edu/usm-faculty-and-staff-scholarship/11 [Accessed 28/11/2021].
Chaumont, Jean-Michel (2000). "Du culte des héros à la concurrence des victims". *Criminologie,* 33(1): 167 – 183.
Chaumont, Jean-Michel (2014) [2012]. "The Activist, the Ideologist and the Researcher. On 'Guesstimates' and Trafficking in Women" (trans. Markus Meckl). *Nordicum-Mediterraneum. Icelandic E-Journal of Nordic and Mediterranean Studies,* 9(1), https://nome.unak.is/wordpress/09-1/c66-interviews-memoirs-and-other-contributions/the-activist-the-ideologist-and-the-researcher-on-guesstimates-and-trafficking-in-women-2/ [Accessed 27/09/2022].
Chesler, Phyllis (2002a). "Women Are Nurturing? How About Cruel, Especially to One Another". *New York Times,* http://www.nytimes.com/2002/08/24/arts/24QNA.html [Accessed 21/09/2021].
Chesler, Phyllis (2002b). *Woman's Inhumanity to Woman.* New York: Thunder's Mouth/Nation Books.
Chesterton, G.K. (1911). *Appreciations and Criticisms of the Works of Charles Dickens.* London: Dent, http://www.gkc.org.uk/gkc/books/22362-h/22362-h.htm [Accessed 01/03/2023].
Chesterton, G.K. (1919) [1905]. *Heretics,* 12th ed. New York: John Lane, http://www.gkc.org.uk/gkc/books/heret12.txt [Accessed 02/10/2022].
Chesterton, G.K. (1929 – 1973) [1929 – 1938]. "Humour". In Garvin, J.L. *et al.* (Eds.), *Encyclopaedia Britannica,* 14th ed. Chicago: Encyclopaedia Britannica, https://nonsenselit.com/g-k-chesterton-humour-1938/ [Accessed 19/04/2022].
Chesterton, G.K. (1932). *Sidelights on New London and Newer York and Other Essays.* London: Sheed & Ward, http://www.gkc.org.uk/gkc/books/Sidelights_All.html [Accessed 01/03/2023].

Chesterton, G.K. (1958) [1909]. *Lunacy and Letters* (ed. Dorothy Collins). New York: Sheed & Ward, http://www.gkc.org.uk/gkc/books/Lunacy_and_Letters.txt [Accessed 01/03/2023].

Chesterton, G.K. (1997) [1925]. *The Everlasting Man*. Leicester: De Montfort University, http://www.gkc.org.uk/gkc/books/everlasting_man.pdf [Accessed 19/02/2022].

Chesterton, G.K. (2000) [1922]. "The Eclipse of Liberty". In *Eugenics and Other Evils*, part II, chap. VI. Leicester: De Montfort, http://www.gkc.org.uk/gkc/books/Eugenics.txt [Accessed 19/02/2022].

Chesterton, G.K. (2004) [1915]. *The Appetite of Tyranny. Including Letters to an Old Garibaldian*. Fairbanks: Project Gutenberg Literary Archive Foundation, http://www.gkc.org.uk/gkc/books/11605-8.txt [Accessed 19/02/2022].

Chesterton, G.K. (2006) [1935]. *The Well and the Shallows*. San Francisco, CA: Ignatius, http://www.gkc.org.uk/gkc/books/Well_And_Shallows.html [Accessed 01/03/2023].

Chesterton, G.K. (2008) [1912]. "The Divine Detective". In *A Miscellany of Men*, essay #34. Fairbanks: Project Gutenberg Literary Archive Foundation, http://www.gkc.org.uk/gkc/books/misc.html [Accessed 19/02/2022].

Cholbi, Michael J. (2000). "Kant and the Irrationality of Suicide". *History of Philosophy Quarterly*, 17(2): 159–176.

Christie, Nils (2017) [1996]. *Crime Control as Industry. Towards Gulags, Western Style?* London: Routledge.

Chulov, Martin (2011). "Gadafy's Killers Will Be Tried, Claims NTC". *The Irish Times*, https://www.irishtimes.com/news/gadafy-s-killers-will-be-tried-claims-ntc-1.632918 [Accessed 19/02/2022].

Cioran, Emil (1970) [1964]. *The Fall into Time* (trans. Richard Howard). Chicago: Quadrangle.

Cioran, Emil (2011) [1973]. *The Trouble with Being Born* (trans. Richard Howard). New York: Seaver Books.

Cipolla, Carlo M. (1988) [1973 & 1976]. *Allegro ma non troppo*. Bologna: Il Mulino.

Cipolla, Carlo M. (2011) [1976]. *The Basic Laws of Human Stupidity*. Bologna: il Mulino.

Clardy, Jesse V., and Clardy, Betty S. (1980). *The Superfluous Man in Russian Letters*. Washington: UP of America.

Clark, Camilla, and Warren, Jason (2016). "Humour in Dementia Studies is Not a Laughing Matter". *Nursing Standard*, 30(21): 32.

Clarke, Alan, Moran-Ellis, Jo and Sleney, Judith (2002). "Attitudes to Date Rape and Relationship Rape: A Qualitative Study". *Research Report 2* by Sentencing Advisory Panel of the English Court of Appeal.

Clarke, John R. (2007). *Looking at Laughter. Humor, Power, and Transgression in Roman Visual Culture, 100 B.C.–A.D. 250*. Berkeley: University of California.

Cleese, John (1968). "How to Irritate People". London: David Paradine Productions, https://www.youtube.com/watch?v=RxcQgpPxzgg [Accessed 19/02/2022].

Clements, Paul (2020). *The Outsider, Art and Humour*. New York: Routledge.

Cobain, Ian (2012). *Cruel Britannia: A Secret History of Torture*. London: Portobello Books.

Coetser, Yolandi M. (2020). "We Acknowledge that We Reside On…: Canadian Land Acknowledgments and South African Land Reform". In Masitera, Erasmus (Ed.), *Philosophical Perspectives on Land Reform in Southern Africa*, 121–143. Cham: Palgrave Macmillan.

Cohen, Dara Kay (2013). "Female Combatants and the Perpetration of Violence: Wartime Rape in the Sierra Leone Civil War". *World Politics*, 65(3): 383–415.

Cohen, Douglas and Strayer, Janet (1996). "Empathy in conduct-disordered and comparison youth". *Developmental Psychology*, 32(6): 988–998.

Colakis, Marianthe (1986). "The Laughter of the Suitors on 'Odyssey'". *The Classical World*, 79(3): 137–141.

Collins, Randall (1974). "Three Faces of Cruelty: Towards a Comparative Sociology of Violence". *Theory and Society*, 1(4): 415–440.

Colman, Ian *et al.* (2014). "Cartoons Kill: Casualties in Animated Recreational Theatre in an Objective Observational New Study of Kids' Introduction to Loss of Life". *British Medical Journal*, 349, doi: 10.1136/bmj.g7184 [Accessed 19/02/2022].

Constantinescu Mihaela-Viorica, Stanca, Măda and Răzvan, Săftoiu (Eds.) (2020). *Romanian Humour. Humour and Culture 5*. Krakow: Tertium.

Contrera, Malena, and Torres, Leonardo (2017). "Imaginário e contágio psíquico". *Intexto*, 40: 11–22.

Conze, Edward (1980) [1958]. *A Short History of Buddhism*. London: Allen & Unwin.

Cope, Theo A. (2006). *Fear of Jung: The Complex Doctrine and Emotional Science*. London: Karnac.

Corbett, Lionel (2015). *The Soul in Anguish: Psychotherapeutic Approaches to Suffering*. Asheville: Chiron.

Ćorović, Emir (2022). "Aggravated Murder in a Cruel Manner". *Crimen*, 13(1): 28–47.

Cosenza, Giovanna (2016). "Umberto Eco su Internet e i media digitali: Un anticipatore lungimirante, altro che apocalittico". *Dis.Amb.Iguando*, https://giovannacosenza.wordpress.com/2016/12/12/umberto-eco-su-internet-e-i-media-digitali-un-anticipatore-lungimirante-altro-che-apocalittico/ [Accessed 06/10/2022].

Cotte, Jérôme (2018). "L'humour éthique: Deleuze, Adorno, Derrida". PhD. University of Montreal.

Cowan, Mary L. *et al.* (2016). "It's the Way He Tells Them (and Who is Listening): Men's Dominance is Positively Correlated with Their Preference for Jokes told by Dominant-Sounding Men". *Evolution and Human Behavior*, 37(2): 97–104.

Cox, Lara (2015). "Standing Up against the Rape Joke: Irony and Its Vicissitudes". *Signs: Journal of Women in Culture and Society*, 40(4): 963–984.

Cristaudo, Wayne (2021). Book review of *Why Believe? Approaches to Religion*, by Garrett Barden and Giorgio Baruchello. *The European Legacy*, 26(5): 554–556.

Critchley, Simon (2000). "De l'humour". *Les papiers du Collège International de Philosophie*, 52: 1–53.

Critchley, Simon (2002a). "Did You Hear the One About the Philosopher Writing a Book on Humour?" *Richmond Journal of Philosophy*, 2: 40–45.

Critchley, Simon (2002b). *On Humour*. London: Routledge.

Cumbow, Robert C. (2008). *The Films of Sergio Leone*. Lanham: The Scarecrow.

Cundall Jr., Michael K. (2022). *The Humor Hack: Using Humor to Feel Better, Increase Resilience, and (Yes) Enjoy Your Work*. Eugene: Resource.

D'Agostino, Fred (2008). "Original Position". In Zalta, Edward N. (Ed.), *Stanford Encyclopedia of Philosophy*. Stanford: Stanford University, https://plato.stanford.edu/entries/original-position/ [Accessed 19/02/2022].

D'Amico, Masolino (2008). *La commedia all'italiana. Il cinema comico in Italia dal 1945 al 1975*. Milan: il Saggiatore.

D'Cruze, Neil *et al.* (2011). "Dancing Bears in India: A Sloth Bear Status Report". *Ursus*, 22(2): 99–105.

Daniel, Drew (2022). *The Joy of the Worm. Suicide and Pleasure in Early Modern English Literature*. Chicago: University of Chicago.

Darley, J.M., and Aronson, E. (1966). "Self-Evaluation vs. Direct Anxiety Reduction as Determinants of the Fear-Affiliation Relationship". *Journal of Experimental Social Psychology*, 2 (Supplement 1): 66–79.

Darnton, Robert (1984). *The Great Cat Massacre and Other Episodes in French Cultural History.* New York: Basic Books.
Darwin, Charles (1872). *The Expression of the Emotions in Man and Animals.* New York: D. Appleton.
Davenport, Manuel M. (1976). "An Existential Philosophy of Humor". *Southwestern Journal of Philosophy,* 7(1): 169–176.
Davetian, Benet (2009). *Civility. A Cultural History.* Toronto: University of Toronto.
Davin, Julie E. (2017). "'We Control It on Our End, and Now It's Up to You'–Exploitation, Empowerment, and Ethical Portrayals of the Pornography Industry". *Student Publications,* 543, https://cupola.gettysburg.edu/student_scholarship/543/ [Accessed 28/11/2021].
Davis, Murray S. (1993). *What's so Funny? The Comic Conception of Culture and Society.* Chicago: Chicago UP.
Davis, Murray S. (1999). "Aphorisms and Clichés: The Generation and Dissipation of Conceptual Charisma". *Annual Review of Sociology,* 25: 245–269.
Day, Michael (2015). *Being Berlusconi: The Rise and Fall from* Cosa Nostra *to* Bunga Bunga. London: St. Martin's.
Deen, Phillip (2020). "Was Dave Chappelle Morally Obliged to Leave Comedy? On the Limits of Consequentialism". In Amir, Lydia (Ed.), *Philosophy of Humor Yearbook,* 1: 135–152. Berlin: De Gruyter.
DeGrazia, David (1997). "Great Apes, Dolphins, and the Concept of Personhood". *The Southern Journal of Philosophy,* 35(3): 301–320.
Deleuze, Gilles (1970). *Spinoza: Philosophie pratique.* Paris: Presses universitaires de France.
Deleuze, Gilles (1988) [1966]. *Bergsonism* (trans. Hugh Tomlinson and Barbara Habberjam). New York: Zone Books.
Deleuze, Gilles (1989) [1967]. *Masochism* (trans. Jean McNeil). New York: Zone Books.
Deleuze, Gilles (1990) [1969]. *The Logic of Sense* (trans. Mark Lester and Charles Stivale). New York: Columbia UP
Deleuze, Gilles (1994) [1968]. *Difference and Repetition* (trans. Paul Patton). New York: Columbia UP.
Deleuze, Gilles, and Guattari, Félix (1983) [1975]. "What Is a Minor Literature?" (ed. And trans. Robert Brinkley). *Mississippi Review,* 11(3): 13–33.
Deleuze, Gilles, and Guattari, Félix (1987) [1980]. *A Thousand Plateaus: Capitalism and Schizophrenia* (trans. Brian Massumi). Minneapolis: Minnesota UP.
Deleuze, Gilles and Guattari, Félix (2004) [1972]. *Anti-Oedipus* (trans. Robert Hurley, Mark Seem and Helen R. Lane). London: Continuum.
Dell'Utri, Massimo (2016). "Putnam's Conception of Truth". *European Journal of Analytic Philosophy,* 12(2): 5–22.
Demont, François (2017). "Morale et humour chez Emil Cioran". *Le rire: forms et fonctions du comique,* https://www.fabula.org/colloques/document4565.php [Accessed 21/09/2021].
Dennett, Daniel C. (1984). *Elbow Room: The Varieties of Free Will worth Wanting.* Cambridge, MA: MIT.
Dennett, Daniel C. (1991). *Consciousness Explained.* London: Penguin.
DeRoche, Edward F., and Williams, Mary M. (2001). *Educating Hearts and Minds. A Comprehensive Character Education Framework,* 2nd ed. Thousand Oaks: Corwin.
Dewar, Ben (2021). "The Burning of Captives in the Assyrian Royal Inscriptions, and Early Neo-Assyrian Conceptions of the Other". *Studia Orientalia Electronica,* 9(2): 67–81.
DiCarlo, Christopher (2011). *How to Become a Really Good Pain in the Ass.* Amherst: Prometheus.
Dickie, Simon (2003). "Hilarity and Pitilessness in the Mid-Eighteenth Century: English Jestbook Humor". *Eighteenth-Century Studies,* 37(1): 1–22.

Dickie, Simon (2011). *Cruelty and Laughter. Forgotten Comic Literature and the Unsentimental Eighteenth Century*. Chicago: Chicago UP.
Diderot, Denis (1883) [1773]. *The Paradox of Acting* (trans. Walter Harries Pollock). London: Chatto & Windus, https://ia802606.us.archive.org/22/items/cu31924027175961/cu31924027175961.pdf [Accessed 11/02/2022].
Dillard, J. Amy (2011–2012). "Madness Alone Punishes the Madman: The Search for Moral Dignity in the Court's Competency Doctrine as Applied in Capital Cases". *Tennessee Law Review*, 79: 461–556.
Dodge, K.A., and Coie, J.D. (1987). "Social-Information-Processing Factors in Reactive and Proactive Aggression in Children's Peer Groups". *Journal of Personality and Social Psychology*, 53(6): 1146–1158.
Domino, George (1976). "Compensatory Aspects of Dreams: An Empirical Test of Jung's Theory". *Journal of Personality and Social Psychology*, 34(4): 658–662.
Dong, Wei (2022). *The Cultural Politics of Affect and Emotion. A Case Study of Chinese Reality TV*. Berlin: De Gruyter.
Dostoyevsky, Fyodor M. (1900) [1880]. *The Brothers Karamazov* (trans. Constance Garnett). New York: Modern Library, https://archive.org/details/fyodor-dostoyevskyfyodor-dostoyevsky [Accessed 01/03/2023].
Dostoyevsky, Fyodor M. (2014) [1875]. *A Raw Youth* (trans. Constance Garnett). Sydney: Project Gutenberg Australia, https://gutenberg.net.au/ebooks01/0100161h.html [Accessed 06/10/2022].
Dostoyevsky, Fyodor M. (2018) [1880]. *The Brothers Karamazov* (trans. Constance Garnett). Copenhagen: Suzeteo.
Douglas, Mary (1968). "The Social Control of Cognition: Some Factors in Joke Perception". *Man*, 3(3): 361–376.
Du Toit, David, and Whaley, Buck (2021). "Another Bloody Clean-Up: The Experiences of Trauma Cleaners in South Africa". *The Thinker*, 89: 95–103.
Dumas, Felicia (2020). "Les discours religieux orthodoxe et l'humour. Les pères spirituels et les fols-en-Christ". *Anadiss*, 30(2): 65–74.
Dunajeva, Jekatyerina (2022). *Constructing Identities over Time. "Bad Gypsies" and "Good Roma" in Russia and Hungary*. Budapest: Central European UP.
Dundes Alan, and Hauschild, Thomas (1988). "Auschwitz Jokes". In Powell, C., and Paton, G.E.C (Eds.), *Humour in Society*, 56–66. London: Palgrave Macmillan.
Dunner, Pini (2018). "Makers of History Who are Made by History". *Rabbi Pini Dunner*, https://rabbidunner.com/makers-of-history-who-are-made-by-history/ [Accessed 04/09/2022].
Dutta, Debaleena (2010). "Bearing the Burden of Native Experience: A Stylistic Analysis of Chinua Achebe's *Arrow of God*". *Rupkatha Journal on Interdisciplinary Studies in Humanities*, 2(2): 162–172.
Dworkin, Gerald (2020). "Laughing Matter". In Amir, Lydia (Ed.), *Philosophy of Humor Yearbook*, 1: 237–247. Berlin: De Gruyter.
Dworkin, Ronald (2011). *Justice for Hedgehogs*. Cambridge, MA: Belknap.
Eagleton, Terry (2019). *Humour*. New Haven: Yale UP.
Earle, John, Moran, Cahal and Ward-Perkins, Zach (2016). *The Econocracy: The Perils of Leaving Economics to the Experts*. Manchester: Manchester UP.
Eco, Umberto (1980). *Il Nome della Rosa*. Sonzogno: Fabbri-Bompiani.
Eco, Umberto (1983) [1981]. "Il comico e la regola". In *Sette anni di desiderio*, 253–261. Milan: Bompiani.

Eco, Umberto (1985). "Pirandello *ridens*". In *Sugli specchi e altri saggi*, 261–270. Milan: Bompiani.

Ehrstine, Glenn (2000). "Of Peasants, Women, and Bears: Political Agency and the Demise of Carnival Transgression in Bernese Reformation Drama". *The Sixteenth Century Journal*, 31(3): 675–697.

Elgadi, Mohamed (2018). "Torture in an Historical Context: Notes from Sudan". In Moore, Alexandra S., and Swanson, Elizabeth (Eds.), *Witnessing Torture. Perspectives of Torture Survivors and Human Rights Workers*, 21–35. London: Palgrave.

Ellenbogen, Glenn C. (1996) [1980–1996]. *More Oral Sadism and the Vegetarian Personality. Readings From the* Journal of Polymorphous Perversity. New York: Brunner/Mazel.

Ellis, Anthony (2009). *Old Age, Masculinity, and Early Modern Drama. Comic Elders on the Italian and Shakespearean Stage.* London: Routledge.

Elpidorou, Andreas (2015). "Affectivity in Heidegger I: Moods and Emotions in *Being and Time*". *Philosophy Compass*, 10(10): 661–671.

Emerson, Ralph Waldo (1841). "Self-Reliance", https://math.dartmouth.edu/~doyle/docs/self/self.pdf [Accessed 28/11/2021].

Enders, Jody (1999). *The Medieval Theater of Cruelty. Rhetoric, Memory, Violence.* Ithaca: Cornell UP.

Engle, Nate, and Helgatte, Stéphane (2018). "What Cannot be Measured Still Must be Managed". *The World Bank IBRD-IDA*, http://documents.worldbank.org/curated/en/211841526474954836/What-cannot-be-measured-still-must-be-managed [Accessed 24/09/2022].

Esar, Evan (1954) [1952]. *The Humor of Humor. The Art and Techniques of Popular Comedy Illustrated by Comic Sayings, Funny Stories & Jocular Traditions Through the Centuries.* London: Phoenix.

Esar, Evan (1961). *Humorous English: A Guide to Comic Usage, Jocular Speech and Writing, and Witty Grammar.* New York: Horizon.

Evans, C. Stephen (1987). "Kierkegaard's View of Humor: Must Christians Always be Solemn?" *Faith and Philosophy: Journal of the Society of Christian Philosophers*, 4(2): 176–186.

Fairfield, Paul (2000). *Moral Selfhood in the Liberal Tradition: The Politics of Individuality.* Toronto: University of Toronto.

Faktorovich, Anna (2020). "Sexual Sadism in Art Pre/Post-de Sade". Book review of *The Marquis de Sade and the Avant-Garde*, by Alyce Mahon. *Pennsylvania Literary Journal*, 12(1): 149–151.

Falkner, Thomas M., and De Luce, Judith (1989). *Old Age in Greek and Latin Literature.* Albany: SUNY.

Faris, Robert, and Tucker, Liann (2022). "Status Motivation, Network Stability, and Instrumental Cruelty". In Donoghue, Christopher (Ed.), *The Sociology of Bullying. Power, Status, and Aggression among Adolescents*, 120–138. New York: New York UP.

Farrell, Warren (1993). *The Myth of Male Power. Why Men and the Disposable Sex.* New York: Simon & Schuster.

Favazza, Armando R. (2011) [1987]. *Bodies Under Siege: Self-Mutilation, Nonsuicidal Self-Injury, and Body Modification in Culture and Psychiatry*, 3rd ed. Baltimore: Johns Hopkins UP.

Faye, Emmanuel (2001). "Dieu Trompeur, Mauvais Génie et Origine de l'Erreur selon Descartes et Suarez". *Revue Philosophique de la France et de l'Etranger*, 126(1): 61–72.

Feinberg, Leonard (1978). *The Secret of Humor.* Amsterdam: Rodopi.

Feldman, Martha (2015). *The Castrato: Reflections on Natures and Kinds.* Oakland: University of California.

Fernyhough, Charles (2017). *The Voices Within: The History and Science of How We Talk to Ourselves.* London: Profile Books.

Ferrero Cándenas, Inés (2007). "*Una violeta de más*, de Francisco Tario: crueldad, humor y praxis". *Revista Valenciana*, 2(4): 161–175.

Figueroa-Dorrego, Jorge, and Larkin-Galiñanes, Cristina (Eds.) (2009). *A Source Book of Literary and Philosophical Writings about Humour and Laughter.* Lewiston: Edwin Mellen.

Fine, Gary Alan, and Corte, Ugo (2022). "Dark Fun: The Cruelties of Hedonic Communities". *Sociological Forum*, 37(1): 70–90.

Fisher, Seymor and Fisher, Rhoda Lee (1981). *Pretend the World Is Funny and Forever: A Psychological Analysis of Comedians, Clowns, and Actors.* Hillsdale, NJ: Lawrence Erlbaum Associates.

Fiske, Alan Page, and Shakti Rai, Tage (2015). *Virtuous Violence: Hurting and Killing to Create, Sustain, End, and Honor Social Relationships.* Cambridge: Cambridge UP.

Fiske, John (2011) [1989]. *Reading the Popular*, 2nd ed. London: Routledge.

Fleming, Gerald (1966). "Attitudes to Modern Language Teaching Aids". *Audio-Visual Language Journal*, 3(3): 1–7.

Florêncio, João (2020). *Bareback Porn, Porous Masculinities, Queer Futures. The Ethics of Becoming-Pig.* London: Routledge.

Floris, Giacomo (2020). "Two Concerns About the Rejection of Social Cruelty as the Basis of Moral Equality". *European Journal of Political Theory*, 19(3): 408–416.

Forabosco, Giovannantonio, Ruch, Willibald and Nucera, Pietro (2009). "The Fear of Being Laughed at Among Psychiatric Patients". *Humor*, 22(1–2): 233–251.

Ford, Thomas E. *et al.* (2017). "Putting the Brakes on Prejudice Rebound Effects: An Ironic Effect of Disparagement Humor". *The Journal of Social Psychology*, 157(4): 458–473.

Ford, Thomas E., and Ferguson, Mark A. (2004). "Social Consequences of Disparagement Humor: A Prejudiced Norm Theory". *Personality and Social Psychology Review*, 8(1): 79–94.

Fox, Angelia (2017). "Wikileaks Many Publishing Awards FYI". *Medium*, https://medium.com/@Angel Fox1/wikileaks-many-publishing-awards-fyi-2aa8c67ec631 [Accessed 28/11/2021].

Frater, Jamie (2010). *The Ultimate Book of Top 10 Lists. A Mind-Boggling Collection of Fun, Fascinating and Bizarre Facts on Movies, Music, Sports, Crime, Celebrities, History, Trivia and More.* Berkeley: Ulysses.

Frede, Dorothea (2012). "The *Endoxon* Mystique: What *Endoxa* Are and What They Are Not". *Oxford Studies in Ancient Philosophy*, 43: 184–215.

Freeborn, R. (1989). Book review of *Humor in the Major Novels of F.M. Dostoevsky*, by R.L. Busch. *Slavonic and East European Review*, 67(1): 123–125.

Freese, Barbara (2020). *Industrial-Strength Denial. Eight Stories of Corporations Defending the Indefensible, from the Slave Trade to Climate Change.* Oakland: University of California.

Frege, Gottlob (1892). "Über Sinn und Bedeutung". *Zeitschrift für Philosophie und philosophische Kritik*, 100(1): 25–50, ttps://www.philosophie.uni-konstanz.de/typo3temp/secure_downloads/67505/0/c99ff447dfc9c50553da291d1a1dfdbb95eb983d/Frege_Sinn_Bedeutung.pdf [Accessed 01/05/2022].

Frege, Gottlob (1956) [1919]. "The Thought: A Logical Inquiry" (trans. M.P. Geach and M. Black). *Mind*, 65(259): 289–311.

Freschi, Francesco (1843). *Storia della medicina. In aggiunta, e continuazione a quella di Curzio Sprengel.* Florence: Speranza.

Freud, Sigmund (1928) [1927]. "Humour" (trans. J. Riviere). *The International Journal of Psychoanalysis*, 9: 1–6.

Freud, Sigmund (1957) [1915]. "Instincts and Their Vicissitudes". In *The Standard Edition of the Complete Psychological Works of Sigmund Freud: Volume 14, 1914–1916* (ed. James Strachey), 109–140. London: Hogarth.

Freud, Sigmund (1960) [1905]. *Jokes and their Relation to the Unconscious* (trans. James Strachey). New York: Norton. Kindle.

Friedman, Sam (2011). "The Cultural Currency of a 'Good' Sense of Humour: British Comedy and New Forms of Distinction". *The British Journal of Sociology*, 62(2): 347–370.
Fromm, Erich (1961). *May Man Prevail? An Inquiry into the Facts and Fictions of Foreign Policy*. Garden City, NY: Doubleday.
Fromm, Erich (1972) [1956]. *The Art of Loving*. London: Bantam.
Fry, William (2010) [1963]. *Sweet Madness. A Study of Humor*. New York: Routledge.
Fullilove, M.T. (2002). "Social and Economic Causes of Depression". *The Journal of Gender-Specific Medicine*, 5(2): 38–41.
Gadamer, Hans-Georg (1996) [1993]. *The Enigma of Health. The Art of Healing in a Scientific Age* (trans. Jason Gaiger and Nicholas Walker). Oxford: Polity.
Gadd, David et al. (2002). *Domestic Abuse against Men in Scotland*. Edinburgh: Scottish Executive.
Gagné, Maud (1970). "Divorce and Mental Cruelty". *Les Cahiers de Droit*, 11(3): 510–528.
Galbraith, James K. (2009). "Who Are These Economists, Anyway?" *Thought & Action* (special Fall issue): 85–97.
Galbraith, John Kenneth (1977). *The Age of Uncertainty*. London: BBC.
Galbraith, John Kenneth (1991) [1987]. *A History of Economics. The Past as Present*. London: Penguin.
Galbraith, John Kenneth (2004). *The Economics of Innocent Fraud: Truth for Our Time*. Boston: Houghton Mifflin.
Galbraith, John Kenneth (2007) [1967]. *The New Industrial State*. Princeton: Princeton UP.
Gamester, William (2017). "The Diversity of Truth. A Case Study in Pluralistic Metasemantics". PhD. University of Leeds.
Gane, Nicholas (2005). "Max Weber as Social Theorist. 'Class, Status, Party'". *European Journal of Social Theory*, 8(2): 211–226.
Ganguly, Shreyashi (2020). "Laughing About Caste. An Analysis of How Caste Considerations Find Representation in the Genre of English Stand-Up Comedy on the Internet in India". *Connections: A Journal of Language, Media and Culture*, 1(1): 43–54.
Garcia, Raquel (2014). "Conscious Political Incorrectness: A Legitimate Discourse in Mexican Narrative, Theater, and Stand-up Comedy". PhD. University of California, Davis.
Garrett, Aaron (2005). "Adam Smith über den Zufall als moralisches Problem". In Fricke, Christel, and Schütt (Eds.), *Adam Smith als Moralphilosoph*, 160–177. Berlin: De Gruyter.
Gasparri, Luca et al. (2022). "Notions of Arbitrariness". *Mind and Language*, https://onlinelibrary.wiley.com/doi/pdf/10.1111/mila.12443 [Accessed 08/12/2022].
Gatrell, V.A.C. (1996). *The Hanging Tree: Execution and the English People 1770–1868*. Oxford: Oxford UP.
Geertz, Clifford (1973). *The Interpretation of Cultures*. New York: Basic Books.
Genovesi, Antonio (1758). *Meditazioni filosofiche*. Naples: Simoniana, https://archive.org/details/bub_gb_4rRDPlpsDtMC [Accessed 01/03/2023].
Genovesi, Antonio (1824) [1768]. *Lezioni di economia civile. Part 1*, 2nd ed. In *Opere scelte*, 1–390. Milan: Classici Italiani, https://archive.org/details/bub_gb_VPTbL9medRYC [Accessed 01/03/2023].
Genovesi, Antonio (1825) [1765]. *Lezioni di commercio o sia d'economia civile*, vol. 2, 1st ed. Milan: Classici Italiani, https://archive.org/details/bub_gb_TPLAgUv9U4kC [Accessed 01/03/2023].
Gentile, Douglas A. (2013). "Catharsis and Media Violence: A Conceptual Analysis". *Societies*, 3: 491–510.
Gess, Nicola (2022) [2013]. *Primitive Thinking. Figuring Alterity in German Modernity* (trans. Erik Butler and Susan Solomon). Berlin: De Gruyter.
Gibson, James J. (1986) [1979]. *The Ecological Approach to Visual Perception*. New York: Psychology.

Gifford, G. Edmund (1962). Book review of *Emotion*, by James Hillman. *Psychosomatic Medicine*, 24(6): 615.

Gilhus, Ingvild Sælid (1997). *Laughing Gods, Weeping Virgins. Laughter in the History of Religion.* London: Routledge.

Gilyazova, Olga S., Zamoshchanskii, Ivan I. and Zamoshchanskaya, A.N. (2020). "A Liberal Arts and Sciences Education at the Russian Higher School: Concepts, Formats, Benefits and Limitations". *Perspectives of Science and Education*, 46(4): 10–22.

Gimbel, Presser, and Mogianesi (2021). "Dad Jokes, D.A.D. Jokes, and the Ghost Test for Artificial Consciousness". *Science and Philosophy*, 9(1): 73–89.

Gimbel, Steven (2017). *Isn't That Clever? A Philosophical Account of Humor and Comedy*. London: Routledge.

Gimbel, Steven, Chandra, Rushil and Zhan, Jingwei (2020). "Woke Comedy vs. Pride Comedy: Kondabolu, Peters, and the Ethics of Performed Indian Accents". In Amir, Lydia (Ed.), *Philosophy of Humor Yearbook*, 1: 211–219. Berlin: De Gruyter.

Gini, Al, and Singer, Abraham (2020). "Why'd You Have to Choose Us? On Jews and Their Jokes". In Amir, Lydia (Ed.), *Philosophy of Humor Yearbook*, 1: 17–31. Berlin: De Gruyter.

Glazko, Galina *et al.* (2005). "Eighty Percent of Proteins are Different between Humans and Chimpanzees". *Gene*, 346: 215–219.

Global Society (2021), 35(1) (special issue on humour and global politics).

Gnad, Peter J. (2012). *Bin in Afghanistan*. Berlin: epubli.

Goddard, Cliff, and Lambert, David (2022). "Laughter, Bonding and Biological Evolution". *The European Journal of Humour Research*, 10(2): 14–28.

Goetzmann, William N. (2017). *Money Changes Everything. How Finance Made Civilization Possible.* Princeton: Princeton UP.

Goldberg, Brenda (1999). "A Genealogy of the Ridiculous: From 'Humours' to Humour". *Outlines. Critical Social Studies*, 1: 59–71.

Goldstein, Donna M. (2013). *Laughter Out of Place: Race, Class, Violence, and Sexuality in a Rio Shantytown*. Berkeley: University of California.

Gollob, Harry F., and Levine, Jacob (1967). "Distraction as a Factor in the Enjoyment of Aggressive Humor". *Journal of Personality and Social Psychology*, 5(3): 368–372.

Graham, Stephen (2017). "The X Factor and Reality Television: Beyond Good and Evil". *Popular Music*, 36(1): 6–20.

Gramsci, Anotnio (1977) [1929–1935]. *Quaderni del carcere* (ed. Valentino Gerratana), 4 vols. Milan: Einaudi.

Granek-Catarivas, M. *et al.* (2005). "Use of Humour in Primary Care: Different Perceptions among Patients and Physicians". *Postgraduate Medical Journal*, 81(952): 126–130.

Granitsas, Dean Anthony (2020). "All Laughter Is Nervous: An Anxiety-Based Understanding of Incongruous Humor". *Humor*, 33(4): 625–643.

Graves, Alexander Jackson (2016). "'Destroy Me!': The Rape Fantasy as Transformation in a Japanese Male-Male Pornographic Video Game Series". MA. University of Maryland.

Green, Aaryn, L. and Linders, Annulla (2016). "The Impact of Comedy on Racial and Ethnic Discourse". *Sociological Inquiry*, 86: 241–269.

Greengross, Gill, and Miller, Geoffrey (2011). "Humor Ability Reveals Intelligence, Predicts Mating Success, and Is Higher in Males". *Intelligence*, 39(4): 188–192.

Greitemeyer, Tobias (2015). "Everyday Sadism Predicts Violent Video Game Preferences". *Personality and Individual Preferences*, 75: 19–23.

Grignard, Christopher (2009). "Our Hometown: A Canadian Gay Male Theatre Project". PhD. University of Alberta.
Griswold, Robert L. (1986). "The Evolution of the Doctrine of Mental Cruelty in Victorian American Divorce, 1790–1900". *Journal of Social History*, 20(1): 127–148.
Groos, Karl (1913) [1899]. *The Play of Man* (trans. Elizabeth A. Baldwin). New York: D. Appleton, https://www.gutenberg.org/files/58411/58411-h/58411-h.htm [Accessed 01/03/2023].
Grotius, Hugo (2005) [1625]. *The Rights of War and Peace* (trans. Jean Barbeyrac). Indianapolis: Liberty Fund.
Gruner, Charles R. (1997). *The Game of Humor: A Comprehensive Theory of Why We Laugh.* London: Routledge.
Grzybowski, Przemysław Paweł (2020). *The Laughter of Life and Death: Personal Stories of the Occupation, Ghettos and Concentration Camps to Educate and Remember.* Bydgoszcz: Wydawnictwo UKW.
Gubanov, Nikolay N., Gubanov, Nikolay I. and Rokotyanskaya, Ludmila (2018). "Factors of Black Humor Popularity". *Proceedings of the International Conference on Contemporary Education, Social Sciences and Ecological Studies*, 283(11): 379–383.
Gül, Fatih Cem *et al.* (2022). "Plasma and Aqueous Levels of Alarin and Adipsin in Patients with and without Diabetic Retinopathy". *BMC Ophtalmology*, 22(1), https://doi.org/10.1186/s12886-022-02403-0 [Accessed 04/09/2022].
Gümüsel, Günseli (2019). "A Comparative Analysis on Ancient Religions of the Middle East". In Sönmez, Sinan *et al.* (Eds.), *New Horizons in Social, Human and Administrative Sciences*, 147–174. Ankara: Gece.
Hacking, Ian (1999). *The Social Construction of What?* Harvard: Harvard UP.
Hague, Richard (2019–2020). "Scalpeen". *Appalachian Heritage*, 47/48(4–1): 29–36.
Hallevy, Gabriel (2015). *The Matrix of Insanity in Modern Criminal Law.* Cham: Springer.
Hallie, Philip P. (1954). "Camus and the Literature of Revolt". *College English*, 16(1): 25–32 and 83.
Hallie, Philip P. (1966). *The Scar of Montaigne. An Essay in Personal Philosophy.* Middletown: Wesleyan University.
Hallie, Philip P. (1969). *The Paradox of Cruelty.* Middletown: Wesleyan University.
Hallie, Philip P. (1970). "Sadean and Institutional Cruelty". In Korten, F.F., Cook, S.W. and Lacey, J.I. (Eds.), *Psychology and the Problems of Society*, 295–303. Washington: American Psychological Association.
Hallie, Philip P. (1971). "Justification and Rebellion". In Sanford, Nevitt, and Comstock, Craig (Eds.), *Sanctions for Evil. Sources of Social Destructiveness*, 247–263. Boston: Beacon.
Hallie, Philip P. (1972). "Prisoners, Twaddlers, and the Fire Chief". Book review of *Struggle for Justice: A Report on Crime* for the American Friends Service Committee. *The American Scholar*, 41(4): 674–677.
Hallie, Philip P. (1977). "The Ethics of Montaigne's *De la cruauté*". In La Charité, R. (Ed.), *Oh un amy! Essays on Montaigne in Honor of Donald M. Frame*, 156–171. Lexington: French Forum.
Hallie, Philip P. (1979). Book review of *Philosophy and Phenomenology of the Body*, by Michel Henry. *International Studies in Philosophy*, 11: 231–232.
Hallie, Philip P. (1985a). "From Cruelty to Goodness". In Sommers, C. (Ed.), *Vice and Virtue in Everyday Life*, 9–24. San Diego: Harcourt College.
Hallie, Philip P. (1985b) [1979]. *Lest Innocent Blood Be Shed: The Story of the Village of Le Chambon, and How Goodness Happened There.* New York: Harper & Row.

Hallie, Philip P. (1985c). "The Evil That Men Think—And Do". Book review of *Wickedness: A Philosophical Essay*, by Mary Midgley, *Ordinary Vices*, by Judith Shklar, and *Immorality*, by Ronald D. Milo. *Hastings Center Report*, 15(6): 42–45.
Hallie, Philip P. (1988). "Cruelty: The Empirical Evil". In Woodruff, Paul, and Wilmer, Harry A. (Eds.), *Facing Evil: Confronting the Dreadful Power behind Genocide, Terrorism, and Cruelty*, 119–129. Chicago: Open Court.
Hallie, Philip P. (1992). "Cruelty". In Becker, Lawrence C. (Ed.), *Encyclopaedia of Ethics*, 229–231. New York: Garland.
Hallie, Philip P. (1993). *Rescue & Goodness: Reflections on the Holocaust*. Washington: United States Holocaust Memorial Museum.
Hallie, Philip P. (1997) [1989]. "A New Kind of Rescue". In Michalczyk, John J. (Ed.), *Resisters, Rescuers, and Refugees: Historical and Ethical Issues*, 234–238. Kansas City: Sheed & Ward.
Halsall, Guy (Ed.) (2002). *Humour, History and Politics in Late Antiquity and the Early Middle Ages*. Cambridge: Cambridge UP.
Hand, Richard J. (2005). "Aesthetics of Cruelty: Traditional Japanese Theatre and the Horror Film". In McRoy, Jay (Ed.), *Japanese Horror Cinema*, 18–28. Edinburgh: Edinburgh UP.
Harakchiyska, Tsvetelina, and Borisova, Tanya (2020). "The Place of Humour Competence in Foreign Language Teaching and Learning". *Proceedings of ICERI2020 Conference*, 771–777.
Häring, Norbert, and Douglas, Niall (2012). *Economists and the Powerful: Convenient Theories, Distorted Facts, Ample Rewards*. London: Anthem.
Harlow, Harry (1969). "The Anatomy of Humour". *Impact of Science on Society*, 19(3): 225–240.
Hartle, Ann (2003). *Michel de Montaigne: Accidental Philosopher*. Cambridge: Cambridge UP.
Hartley, David (1801) [1749]. *Observations on Man, His Frame, His Duty, and His Expectations. In Two Parts*. Warrington: J. Johnson, https://archive.org/details/dli.granth.71827 [Accessed 01/05/2022].
Hartley, Nina (2018) [1994]. "Confessions of a Feminist Porno Star". In Jaggar, Alison M. (Ed.), *Living with Contradictions*, 176–178. New York: Routledge.
Hartwig, Helmut (1986). *Die Grausamkeit der Bilder: Horror und Faszination in alten und neuen Medien*. Weinheim: Quadriga.
Harvey, Jean (1999). *Civilized Oppression*. Lanham: Rowman & Littlefield.
Haslam, S. Alexander *et al.* (2019). "Rethinking the Nature of Cruelty: The Role of Identity Leadership in the Stanford Prison Experiment". *American Psychologist*, 74(7): 809–822.
Haugh, Michael (2017). "Teasing". In Attardo, Salvatore (Ed.), *Handbook of Language and Humour*, 204–218. London: Routledge.
Hazlitt, William (1845) [1819]. *Lectures on the English Comic Writers*. New York: Wiley & Putnam, https://archive.org/details/lecturesonengli01unkngoog [Accessed 01/05/2022].
Hazlitt, William (1912) [1830]. "On Prejudice". In *Sketches and Essays*, 56–60. Oxford: H. Frowde.
Healy, Margaret (2001). *Fictions of Disease in Early Modern England. Bodies, Plagues and Politics*. Houndmills: Plagrave Macmillan.
Heller, Agnes (2005). *Immortal Comedy: The Comic Phenomenon in Art, Literature, and Life*. Lanham: Lexington Books.
Helman, David H. (1988). *Analogical Reasoning. Perspectives of Artificial Intelligence, Cognitive Science, and Philosophy*. Amsterdam: Kluwer.
Henderson, Jeffrey (1991). *The Maculate Muse: Obscene Language in Attic Comedy*. Oxford: Oxford UP.
Hereniko, Vilsoni (2000). "Indigenous Knowledge and Academic Imperialism". In Borofsky, Robert (Ed.), *Remembrance of Pacific Pasts. An Invitation to Remake History*, 78–91. Honolulu: University of Hawaii.

Herzog, Thomas R., and Bush, Beverly A. (1994). "The Prediction of Preference for Sick Humor". *Humor*, 7(4): 323–340.

Herzog, Thomas R., and Karafa, Joseph A. (1998). "Preferences for Sick versus Nonsick Humor". *Humor*, 11(3): 291–312.

Hewitson, Mark (2012). "Black Humour: Caricature in Wartime". *Oxford German Studies*, 41(2): 213–235.

Hillman, James (1962) [1960]. *Emotion. A Comprehensive Phenomenology of Theories and Their Meanings for Therapy*. London: Routledge & Kegan Paul.

Hillman, James (1975). *Re-visioning Psychology*. New York: Harper & Row.

Hillman, James (1995). "Pink Madness or Why Does Aphrodite Drive Men Crazy with Pornography?" *Spring*, 57(1): 37–67.

Hillman, James (1996). *The Soul's Code. In Search of Character and Calling*. New York: Ballantine. Electronic version.

Hillman, James (1999). *The Force of Character – And the Lasting Life*. New York: Ballantine. Electronic version.

Hillman, James, and Ventura, Michael (1992). "We've Had a Hundred Years of Psychotherapy and the World's Getting Worse", http://michaelventura.org/wp-content/uploads/2013/11/from-We%E2%80%99ve-Had-a-Hundred-Years-of-Psychotherapy-and-the-World%E2%80%99s-Getting-Worse.pdf [Accessed 04/06/2022].

Hobbes, Thomas (1985) [1651]. *Leviathan*. London: Penguin Classics.

Hobbes, Thomas (n.d.a) [1651]. *De Cive*. London: R. Royston, http://www.public-library.uk/ebooks/27/57.pdf [Accessed 21/02/2022].

Hollinrake, Roger (2015) [1982]. *Nietzsche, Wagner, and the Philosophy of Pessimism*. London: Routledge.

Hongladarom, Soraj (2013). "Language, Reality, Emptiness and Laughter". *Prajna Vihara*, 14(1–2): 236–256.

Horkheimer, Max, and Adorno, Theodor W. (2002) [1944]. *Dialectic of Enlightenment. Philosophical Fragments* (trans. Edmund Jephcott). Stanford: Stanford UP.

Horney, Karen (1950). *Neurosis and Human Growth*. In *The Collected Works of Karen Horney*, vol. 11. New York: Norton.

Hotson, Gary Vincent (2000). "An Empirical Investigation of Jung's Dream Theory. A Test of Compensatory vs. Parallel Dreaming". MA. University of Manitoba.

Hoy, Mikita (1994). "Joyful Mayhem: Bakhtin, Football Songs, and the Carnivalesque". *Text and Performance Quarterly*, 14(4): 289–304.

Huda, Miftachul et al. (2020). "Understanding *Istifadah* (Utilizing Time and Chance) for Personality Development in Islamic Education". In Huda, Miftachul et al. (Eds.), *Global Perspectives on Teaching and Learning Paths in Islamic Education*, 268–288. Hershey, PA: IGI Global.

Huemer, Anna (2022). *Effeminate Rulers, Brave Soldiers? "Foreign" Masculinities in Selected Travelogues of Habsburg Diplomats in the Ottoman Empire*. Berlin: De Gruyter.

Hughes, Geoffrey (2010). *Political Correctness: A History of Semantics and Culture*. Chichester: John Wiley & Sons.

Hugo, Victor (2002) [1869]. *L'homme qui rit*. Paris: Gallimard.

Hume, David (1979) [1739]. *A Treatise of Human Nature*. Oxford: Oxford UP.

Humphrey, Chris (2001). *The Politics of Carnival: Festive Misrule in Medieval England*. Manchester: Manchester UP.

Hunt, Alan (1999). *Governing Morals: A Social History of Moral Regulation*. Cambridge: Cambridge UP.

Hurley, Matthew. M. et al. (2011). *Inside Jokes: Using Humor to Reverse-Engineer the Mind*. Cambridge, MA: MIT.

Hurley, Michael D. (2012). *G.K. Chesterton*. Liverpool: Liverpool UP.

Husband, Charles (1988). "Racist Humour and Racist Ideology in British Television, or I Laughed till You Cried". In Powell, C., and Paton, G.E.C. (Eds.), *Humour in Society*, 149–178. London: Palgrave Macmillan.

Hutchens, John K. (1963) [1933]. "Introduction". In James Thurber, *My Life and Hard Times*, 1–8. New York: Bantam Books.

Hutcheson, Francis (1973) [1725]. "Reflections upon Laughter". Reprinted as the Appendix to *An Inquiry Concerning Beauty, Order, Harmony, Design*, 102–119. The Hague: Martin Nijhoff.

Hutcheson, Francis (2007) [1747]. *A Short Introduction to Moral Philosophy*. Indianapolis: Liberty Fund.

Hyers, Conrad (1996). *The Spirituality of Comedy. Comic Heroism in a Tragic World*. New Brunswick: Transaction.

Inchley, Jo et al. (2020). *Spotlight on Adolescent Health and Well-Being: Findings from the 2017/18 Health Behaviour in School-Aged Children (HBSC) Survey in Europe and Canada. Volume 1: Key Findings*. Copenhagen: World Health Organization.

Infante, Dominic A., and Rancer, Andrew S. (1982). "A Conceptualization and Measure of Argumentativeness". *Journal of Personality Assessment*, 46(1): 72–80.

Ireland-Delfs, Thomas (2020). "Punching Up–Punching Down: Humor as a Tool of Subversion in the *Íslendingasögur*". MA. University of Iceland.

Irigaray, Luce (2002) [1985]. *To Speak Is Never Neutral* (trans. Gail Schwab). New York: Routledge.

Isenberg, Nancy (2017). *White Trash. The 400-Year Untold History of Class in America*. New York: Penguin.

Israel, Laura, Konieczny, Lars and Ferstl, Evelyn C. (2022). "Cognitive and Affective Aspects of Verbal Humor: A Visual-World Eye-Tracking Study". *Frontiers in Communication*, 6, https://doi.org/10.3389/fcomm.2021.758173 [Accessed 05/09/2022].

Izbicki, Thomas M. (1981). *Protector of the Faith: Cardinal Johannes de Turrecremata and the Defense of the Institutional Church*. Washington: Catholic University of America.

Jacobs, Struan (1997–1998). "Michael Polanyi and Spontaneous Order, 1941–51". *Tradition and Discovery: The Polanyi Society Periodical*, 24(2): 14–27.

Jajszczok, Justyna (2022). "Hideous or Hilarious? The Fine Line between Disgust and Humour". *The European Journal of Humour Research*, 10(1): 29–36.

James, William (1912) [1896]. *The Will to Believe and Other Essays in Popular Philosophy*, 15th ed. New York: Longmans, Green, https://archive.org/details/willtobelieveoth00jam [Accessed 01/03/2023].

Janes, Leslie M. and Olson, James M. (2000). "Jeer Pressure: The Behavioral Effects of Observing Ridicule of Others". *Personality and Social Psychology Bulletin*, 26(4): 474–485.

Jauregui, Eduardo S. (1998). "Situating Laughter: Amusement, Laughter, and Humour in Everyday Life". PhD. European University Institute.

Jenkins, Abigail (2022). "Large Bodies on Small Screens: Fat Representation in Contemporary American and British Television". PhD. University of Glasgow.

Jewell, R. Todd, (Ed.) (2012). *Violence and Aggression in Sporting Contests*. New York: Springer.

Johnson, A. Michael (1990). "The 'Only Joking' Defense: Attribution Bias or Impression Management?" *Psychological Reports*, 67(3): 1051–1056.

Johnstone, Rachael Lorna (2007). "Exploring the Concepts: Prostitution, Gender Equality, Respect and Modern Societies". Paper presented on 8 June 2007 at the International Conference

"Prostitution, Gender Equality, Respect and Modern Societies / Fara Vændi og Virðing Saman í Jafnréttisþjóðfélagi". Grand Hotel, Reykjavík.

Johnstone, Rachael Lorna (2010). Critical notice of *Eguale rispetto*, edited by Ian Carter, Anna Galeotti and Valeria Ottonelli. *Nordicum-Mediterraneum. Icelandic E-journal of Nordic and Mediterranean Studies*, 5(1), https://nome.unak.is/wordpress/05-1/critical-notice/ottonelli/ [Accessed 21/02/2022].

Johnstone, Rachael Lorna (2022). "The Greenland Reconciliation Commission: One More Step towards Independence?" *Nordicum-Mediterraneum. Icelandic E-Journal of Nordic and Mediterranean Studies*, 17(2), https://nome.unak.is/wordpress/volume-17-no-2-2022/the-greenland-reconciliation-commission-one-more-step-towards-independence/ [Accessed 13/09/2022].

Jonas, Hans (1984) [1979]. *The Imperative of Responsibility. In Search for an Ethics for the Technological Age*. Chicago: University of Chicago.

Jones, Steve (2013). "The Lexicon of Offence: The Meanings of Torture, Porn, and 'Torture Porn'". In Attwood, Feona et al. (Eds.), *Controversial Images*, 186–200. Cham: Springer.

Jouanna, Jacques (2012). *Greek Medicine from Hippocrates to Galen*. Leiden: Brill.

Jung, Carl Gustav (1958a) [1957]. *The Undiscovered Self* (trans. R.F.C. Hull). Boston: Little, Brown.

Jung, Carl Gustav (1958b). "The Zurich Tapes (1958 audio recordings)", https://www.youtube.com/watch?v=bzcT5hRfu5A&ab_channel=Marie-LouisevonFranz [Accessed 24/11/2022].

Jung, Carl Gustav (1960–1990). *Collected Writings* (ed. Herbert Read, Michael Fordham and Gerhard Adler; trans. R.F.C. Hull), 20 volumes, 2nd ed. Princeton: Bollingen/Princeton UP.

Jung, Carl Gustav (1964). *Man and His Symbols*. New York: Dell.

Jung, Carl Gustav (2009) [1915–1930]. *The Red Book. Liber Novus* (ed. Sonu Shamdasani; trans. Mark Kyburs, John Peck and Sonu Shamdasani). New York: Norton.

Kaiser, K.J. (2002). "Twenty-first Century Stocks and Pillory: Perp Walks as Pretrial Punishment". *Iowa Law Review*, 88(5): 1205–1241.

Kalman, Jason (2011). "Heckling the Divine: Woody Allen, the Book of Job, and Jewish Theology after the Holocaust". In Greenspoon, Leonard Jay (Ed.), *Jews and Humor*, 175–194. West Lafayette: Purdue UP.

Kant, Leo, and Norman, Elisabeth (2019). "You Must Be Joking! Benign Violations, Power Asymmetry, and Humor in a Broader Social Context". *Frontiers in Psychology*, 10: 1–10.

Kanu, Ikechuwuku Anthony (2017). "Igwebuike as a Wholistic Response to the Problem of Evil and Human Suffering". *IGWEBUIKE: An African Journal of Arts and Humanities*, 3(2): 63–75.

Kasper, Siegfried (1998). "Social Phobia: The Nature of the Disorder". *Journal of Affective Disorders*, 50 (Supplement 1): S3-S9.

Kasunic, Anna, and Kaufman, Geoff (2018). "'At Least the Pizzas You Make Are Hot': Norms, Values, and Abrasive Humor on the Subreddit r/RoastMe". *Proceedings of the Twelfth International AAAI Conference on Web and Social Media*, 161–170.

Katz, Bruce F. (1993). "A Neural Resolution of the Incongruity-resolution and Incongruity Theories of Humour". *Connection Science*, 5(1): 59–75.

Katz, Jennifer et al. (2019). "Just Joking? White College Students' Responses to Different Types of Racist Comments". *Journal of Diversity in Higher Education*, 12(4): 341–350.

Kaufmann, Eric (2021). "Academic Freedom in Crisis: Punishment, Political Discrimination, and Self-Censorship". *Center for the Study of Partisanship and Ideology*, report No. 2, https://cspicenter.org/wp-content/uploads/2021/03/AcademicFreedom.pdf [Accessed 20/10/2022].

Kazeem, Fayemi Ademola (2009). "Recent Trends and Future Prospects in Epistemology–A Review of John Kekes". *Philosophical Papers and Reviews*, 1(4): 52–58.

Keen, Steve (2001). *Debunking Economics. The Naked Emperor of the Social Sciences*. London: Zed.

Keirsey, David (1998). *Please Understand Me II: Temperament, Character, Intelligence*. San Diego: Prometheus Nemesis.
Keirsey, David (2010). *Personology*. San Diego: Prometheus Nemesis.
Keirsey, David, and Bates, Marylin (1984) [1978]. *Please Understand Me: Character and Temperament Types*. San Diego: Prometheus Nemesis.
Kekes, John (1996). "Cruelty and Liberalism". *Ethics*, 106(4): 834–844.
Kekes, John (1997). *Against Liberalism*. Ithaca, New York: Cornell UP.
Kennedy, Andrew K. (1989). *Samuel Beckett*. Cambridge: Cambridge UP.
Kenny, Kate (2009). "'The Performative Surprise': Parody, Documentary and Critique". *Culture and Organization*, 15(2): 221–235.
Kenny, Robert Wade (2008). "The Glamour of Motives: Applications of Kenneth Burke within the Sociological Field". *KB Journal*, 4(2), http://kbjournal.org/kenny [Accessed 12/09/2022].
Keynes, John Maynard (2008) [1936]. *The General Theory of Employment, Interest, and Money*. Zurich: ISN-ETH.
Kiblansky, Raymond, Panofsky, Erwin, and Saxl, Fritz (1964). *Saturn and Melancholy: Studies in the History of Natural Philosophy, Religion, and Art*. London: Nelson.
Kierkegaard, Søren A. (2009) [1864]. *Concluding Unscientific Postscript* (trans. Alastair Hannay). Cambridge: Cambridge UP.
Kiernan, Ben (2007). *Blood and Soil: A World History of Genocide and Extermination from Sparta to Darfur*. New Haven: Yale UP.
Kim, Myung-Hee (2014). "Why Self-Deprecating? Achieving 'Oneness' in Conversation". *Journal of Pragmatics*, 69: 82–98.
Kinna, Ruth (Ed.) (2012). *The Continuum Companion to Anarchism*. London: Continuum.
Kinsman Dean, Ruth A. (2007). "Expressing Sensibilities: Healing Functions of Humour in Palliative Care". In Warren, Bernie (Ed.), *Suffering the Slings and Arrows of Outrageous Fortune*, 191–206. Leiden: Brill.
Kipnis, Laura (2006). "How to Look at Pornography". In Lehman, Peter (Ed.), *Pornography. Film and Culture*, 118–129. New Brunswick: Rutgers.
Kipnis, Laura (2017). *Unwanted Advances: Sexual Paranoia Comes to Campus*. New York: Harper.
Kipnis, Laura (2018). "A Man Lost His Job to a Rape Joke. Are You Cheering?" *The Guardian*, https://www.theguardian.com/commentisfree/2018/dec/22/rape-joke-metoo-movement-career-repercussions [Accessed 21/02/2022].
Kirk, Richard M. (1983). "Political Terrorism and the Size of Government: A Positive Institutional Analysis of Violent Political Activity". *Public Choice*, 40(1): 41–52.
Klar, Elisabeth (2013). "Tentacles, Lolitas, and Pencil Strokes. The Parodist Body in European and Japanese Erotic Comics". In Berndt, Jacqueline, and Kümmerling-Meibauer, Bettina (Eds.), *Manga's Cultural Crossroads*, 121–142. London: Routledge.
Klein, Melanie (1948) *Contributions to Psycho-Analysis 1921–1945*. London: Hogarth.
Klein, Melanie (1987) [1928]. "Early Stages of the Oedipus Conflict". In *The Selected Melanie Klein* (ed. Juliet Mitchell), 69–83. New York: The Free Press.
Klepec, Peter (2021). "Sadizem, Schadenfreude in krutost". *Filozofski vestnik*, 42(3): 155–201.
Koestler, Arthur (1964). *The Act of Creation*. London: Hutchinson.
Kohlberg, Lawrence (1984). *Essays on Moral Development. Vol. 2. The Psychology of Moral Development: The Nature and Validity of Moral Stages*. San Francisco: Harper & Row.

Kohut, Taylor et al. (2021). "Testing the Confluence Model of the Association Between Pornography Use and Male Sexual Aggression: A Longitudinal Assessment in Two Independent Adolescent Samples from Croatia". *Archives of Sexual Behavior*, 50: 647–665.

Konner, Melvin (2022). "Is History the Same as Evolution? No. Is it Independent of Evolution? Certainly Not". *Human History as Natural History*, 20(1), https://doi.org/10.1177/14747049211069137 [Accessed 04/09/2022].

Kors, Alan Charles, and Peters, Edward (2001). *Witchcraft in Europe 400–1700. A Documental History*, 2nd ed. Philadelphia: University of Pennsylvania.

Kotthoff, Helga (2006). "Gender and Humor: The State of the Art". *Journal of Pragmatics*, 38(1): 4–25.

Kozintsev, Alexander (2010). *The Mirror of Laughter* (trans. Richard P. Martin). New Brunswick: Transaction Publishers.

Kramer, Chris A. (2020). "Subversive Humor as Art and the Art of Subversive Humor". In Amir, Lydia (Ed.), *Philosophy of Humor Yearbook*, 1: 153–179. Berlin: De Gruyter.

Krebs, Andreas (2010). "Producing the Whitestream: Micropolitics and the Persistence of Colonialism in Canada". PhD. University of Ottawa.

Krichtafovitch, Igor (2006) [2005]. *Humor Theory: Formula of Laughter* (trans. Anna Tonkonogui). Denver: Outskirts.

Krikmann, Arvo (2006). "Contemporary Linguistic Theories of Humour". *Folklore*, 33: 27–58.

Kuhn, Thomas (1970) [1962]. *The Structure of Scientific Revolutions*. Chicago: Chicago UP.

Kuiper, Nicholas A., and Martin, Rod A. (1998). "Is Sense of Humor a Positive Personality Characteristic?" In Ruch, Willibald (Ed.), *The Sense of Humor. Explorations of a Personality Characteristic*, 159–178. Berlin: De Gruyter.

Kuipers, Giselinde (2008). "The Sociology of Humor". In Raskin, Victor (Ed.), *The Primer of Humor Research*, 361–398. Berlin: De Gruyter.

Kurz, Heinz D. (2008). "Ricardian Vice". In Darity, William A. Jr. (Ed.), *International Encyclopedia of the Social Sciences*, 2nd ed., 241–243. Detroit: Macmillan Reference.

Laffranchi, Andrea, and Guccini, Francesco (2021). "Francesco Guccini il più amato dai teenager 'Io, un cialtrone di 80 anni'". *Corriere della Sera*, https://www.corriere.it/sette/incontri/21_gennaio_15/francesco-guccini-piu-amato-teenager-io-cialtrone-80-anni-0d5de25e-575b-11eb-8f51-2cbbf1c2346f.shtml [Accessed 21/02/2022].

Laine, Timo (2009). "Sympathy for the Coyote", http://s3.amazonaws.com/arena-attachments/1866949/6ab03c559405cf8b2131162466cd4aa3.pdf?1520627908 [Accessed 21/09/2021].

Laitinen, Arto (2017). "Hegel and Respect for Persons". In Giorgini, Giovanni, and Irrera, Elena (Eds.), *The Roots of Respect. A Historic-Philosophical Itinerary*, 171–186. Berlin: De Gruyter.

Landert, Daniela (2021). "The Spontaneous Co-creation of Comedy: Humour in Improvised Theatrical Fiction". *Journal of Pragmatics*, 173: 68–87.

Laranjeira, Carlos et al. (2022). "'Keeping the Light On': A Qualitative Study on Hope Perceptions at the End of Life in Portuguese Family Dyads". *International Journal of Environmental Research and Public Health*, 19(3): https://doi.org/10.3390/ijerph19031561 [Accessed 05/09/2022].

Lazebna, Olena et al. (2022). "O humor na perspectiva linguística". *Revista entre línguas*, 8(1), https://doi.org/10.29051/el.v8iesp.1.16925 [Accessed 05/09/2022].

Leacock, Stephen (1913). "Making a Magazine (The Dream of a Contributor)". In *Behind the Beyond. And Other Contributions to Human Knowledge*, 167–181. London: John Lane, The Bodley Head, https://www.gutenberg.org/ebooks/23449 [Accessed 22/12/2022].

Leacock, Stephen (1914). *Adventurers of the Far North. A Chronicle of the Frozen Seas.* Toronto: Glasgow, Brook, https://www.fadedpage.com/showbook.php?pid=20131201 [Accessed 01/03/2023].

Leacock, Stephen (1935). *Humor: Its Theory and Technique.* London: The Bodley Head, https://www.fadedpage.com/showbook.php?pid=20160929 [Accessed 22/12/2022].

Leacock, Stephen (1938). *Humor and Humanity: An Introduction to the Study of Humor.* New York: Henry Holt, https://www.fadedpage.com/showbook.php?pid=20160617 [Accessed 22/12/2022].

Leacock, Stephen (1942). *Our Heritage of Liberty.* London: The Bodley Head, https://www.fadedpage.com/showbook.php?pid=201410A3 [Accessed 22/12/2022].

Leacock, Stephen (2001–2009) [1914]. *Arcadian Adventures with the Idle Rich.* Fairbanks: Project Gutenberg Literary Archive Foundation, http://www.gutenberg.org/files/4020/4020-h/4020-h.htm [Accessed 21/02/2022].

Leacock, Stephen (2009) [1922]. "Have the English any Sense of Humour?" *My Discovery of England*, chap. 10. Fairbanks: Project Gutenberg Literary Archive Foundation, http://www.gutenberg.org/files/3532/3532-h/3532-h.htm [Accessed 21/02/2022].

Leacock, Stephen (2018) [1916]. "Humour as I See It". In *Further Foolishness. Sketches and Satires on the Follies of the Day*, chap. 17. Fairbanks: Project Gutenberg Literary Archive Foundation, http://www.gutenberg.org/files/11504/11504-h/11504-h.htm [Accessed 21/02/2022].

Lecky, William E.H. (1890) [1865]. *History of European Morals from Augustus to Charlemagne*, 3rd ed. London: Longmans and Green, https://www.gutenberg.org/files/39273/39273-pdf.pdf [Accessed 19/02/2022].

Lederer, Thomas (2006). "Fools and Saints: Derision and Regenerative Laughter and the Late Medieval and Early Modern Hagiographic Imagination". *Comitatus: A Journal of Medieval and Renaissance Studies*, 37: 111–146.

Lejeune, Denis (2012). *The Radical Use of Chance in 20th Century Art.* Leiden: Brill.

Lemm, Vanessa (2009). *Nietzsche's Animal Philosophy: Culture, Politics and the Animality of the Human Being.* New York: Fordham UP.

Lengauer, Erwin (2020). "Tom Regan's Philosophy of Animal Rights: Subjects-of-a-Life in the Context of Discussions of Intrinsic and Inherent Worth". *Problemos*, 97: 87–98.

Leopardi, Giacomo (1982) [1845]. *Pensieri.* Milan: Adelphi.

Leopardi, Giacomo (n.d.a.) [1835]. *Operette morali.* Milan: Einaudi, http://www.letteraturaitaliana.net/pdf/Volume_8/t345.pdf [Accessed 21/09/2021].

Leopardi, Giacomo (n.d.a.) [1898]. *Zibaldone di pensieri.* Milan: Einaudi, http://www.letteraturaitaliana.net/pdf/Volume_8/t226.pdf [Accessed 21/09/2021].

Lesser, Simon O. (1958). "Saint and Sinner–Dostoevsky's 'Idiot'". *Modern Fiction Studies*, 4(3): 211–224.

Lev-Ari, Shiri and McKay, Ryan (2022). "The Sound of Swearing: Are There Universal Patterns in Profanity?" *Psychonomic Bulletin and Review*, https://doi.org/10.3758/s13423-022-02202-0 [Accessed 12/12/2022].

Levene, Mark, and Roberts, Penny (Eds.) (1999). *The Massacre in History.* Oxford: Berghahn Books.

Levi, Primo (2018) [1947]. *Se questo è un uomo.* Milan: Einaudi.

Lévitt, Albert (1922–1923). "Extent and Function of the Doctrine of *Mens Rea*". *Illinois Law Review*, 17(117): 578–583.

Levy, Neil (2011). *Hard Luck: How Luck Undermines Free Will and Moral Responsibility.* Oxford: Oxford UP.

Lewis, Hywel (1982). *The Elusive Self.* London: Macmillan.

Lewis, Peter B. (2005). "Schopenhauer's Laughter". *The Monist*, 88(1): 36–51.
Lippitt, John (1992). "Nietzsche, Zarathustra and the Status of Laughter". *British Journal of Aesthetics*, 32(1): 39–49.
Litovkina, Anna T. (2015). "Anti-Proverbs". In Hrisztova-Gotthardt, Hrisztalina, and Varga, Melita Aleksa (Eds.), *Introduction to Paremiology. A Comprehensive Guide to Proverb Studies*, 326–352. Berlin: De Gruyter.
Litovkina, Anna T. *et al.* (Eds.) (2012). *Hungarian Humour. Humour and Culture 3*. Krakow: Tertium.
Litovkina, Anna T., Daczi, Margit, and Barta, Péter (Eds.) (2010). *Linguistic Shots at Humour. Humour and Cruelty 1*. Krakow: Tertium.
Litz, Brett T. *et al.* (2022). "Defining and Assessing the Syndrome of Moral Injury: Initial Findings of the Moral Injury Outcome Scale Consortium". *Frontiers in Psychiatry*, 13, https://doi.org/10.3389/fpsyt.2022.923928 [Accessed 04/09/2022].
Livy (Titus Livius) (1898) [ca. 15 BC]. *The History of Rome* (ed. W. Weissenborn and H.J. Müller). Leipzig: Teubner.
Llanera, Tracy (2017). "Ethnocentrism: Lessons from Richard Rorty to Randy David". *Philippine Sociological Review*, 65: 133–149.
Locke, John (1824) [1693]. *Some Thoughts Concerning Education*. In *The Works of John Locke in Nine Volumes*, 12th ed., vol. 8: 1–210. London: Rivington, https://oll.libertyfund.org/title/locke-the-works-of-john-locke-in-nine-volumes [Accessed 01/05/2022].
Lockyer, Sharon (2015). "From Comedy Targets to Comedy-Makers: Disability and Comedy in Live Performance". *Disability and Society*, 30(9): 1397–1412.
Lockyer, Sharon, and Pickering, Michael (Eds.) (2005). *Beyond a Joke. The Limits of Humour*. London: Palgrave Macmillan.
Lodge, David (1984). *Small World: An Academic Romance*. London: Secker & Warburg.
Lodi, Dario (2019). "Le Rivelazioni di Carlo M. Cipolla". *Homolaicus*, https://www.homolaicus.com/letteratura/cipolla.htm [Accessed 19/02/2022].
Lopez, Alan (2004). "Deleuze with Carroll. Schizophrenia and Simulacrum and the Philosophy of Lewis Carroll's Nonsense". *Angelaki*, 9(3): 101–120.
Lough, Thomas S. (1962). Book review of *Emotion*, by James Hillman. *American Journal of Sociology*, 67(6): 720–721.
Löwith, Karl (1997) [1978]. *Nietzsche's Philosophy of the Eternal Recurrence of the Same* (trans. J. Harvey Lomax). Berkeley: University of California.
Lukošienė, Mykolė (2016). "Boring Soviet Humor: The Artificiality of International Women's Day and an Imitation of Criticism". *Darbai ir dienos*, 65: 163–194.
Lundquist, Lita Sander (2020). *Humorsocialisering: Hvorfor er danskerne (ikke) så sjove (som de selv tror)?* Frederiksberg: Samfundslitteratur.
Luo, Simon Sihang (2021). "The Liberalism of Fear in China: Hu Ping and the Uses of Fear and Memory in Contemporary Chinese Liberalism". *Global Intellectual History*, https://doi.org/10.1080/23801883.2021.1977674 [Accessed 13/12/2022].
Lynch, Gerald (1988). *Stephen Leacock. Humour and Humanity*. Kingston and Montreal: McGill-Queen UP.
Lynge, Inge (1997). "Mental Disorders in Greenland". *Meddelelser om Grønland, Man and Society*, 21: 1–76.
Lyttle, Jim (2002). "The Ethics of Humour: Preliminary Thoughts". *Congress of the Social Sciences and Humanities*, http://www.jimlyttle.com/PDF/Learneds.pdf [Accessed 19/02/2022].

Macdonald, Graham (2005–2018). "Alfred Jules Ayer". In Zalta, Edward N. (Ed.), *Stanford Encyclopedia of Philosophy*. Stanford: Stanford University, https://plato.stanford.edu/entries/ayer/ [Accessed 29/04/2022].

Machiavelli, Niccolò (1908) [1515]. *The Prince* (trans. W.K. Marriott). London: J.M. Dent https://onlinebooks.library.upenn.edu/webbin/gutbook/lookup?num=1232 [Accessed 02/05/2022].

Mackenzie, Suzie (2000). "Finding Fact from Fiction". *The Guardian*, https://www.theguardian.com/books/2000/may/27/fiction.features [Accessed 04/05/2022].

MacKinnon, Catharine A. (1993). *Only Words*. Cambridge, MA: Harvard UP.

Macleod, P.J. (2021). "Influences on Ethical Decision-Making Among Porn Consumers: The Role of Stigma". *Journal of Consumer Culture*, 21(2): 381–404.

Maddison, Stephen (2013). "'It's Gonna Hurt a Little Bit. But That's Okay–It Makes My Cock Feel Good': Max Hardcore and the Myth of Pleasure". In Attwood, Feona, Campbell Vincent and Hunter, I.Q. (Eds.), *Controversial Images*, 170–185. London: Palgrave Macmillan.

Madigan, Edward (2013). "'Sticking to a Hateful Task': Resilience, Humour, and British Understandings of Combatant Courage, 1914–1918". *War in History*, 20(1): 76–98.

Maes, Hans (2019). *What is Sexy? Een oefening in feministische filosofie*. Antwerp: Vrijdag.

Maes, Hans, and Levinson, Jerrold (Eds.) (2012). *Art and Pornography: Philosophical Essays*. Oxford: Oxford UP.

Mahapatra, Mehak (2022). "Cauldron of Defining 'Cruelty' in Indian Family Laws". *Supremo Amicos*, 28: 322–330.

Maia Neto, José, Paganini, Gianni and Laursen, Christian (Eds.) (2009). *Skepticism in the Modern Age. Building on the Work of Richard Popkin*. Leiden: Brill.

Mairs, Nancy (1986). "On Being a Cripple". In *Plaintext*, 9–20. Tucson: University of Arizona.

Malaspina, Ermanno (2022). "From 'Zero Tolerance' to 'Turn the Other Cheek' and Back: Lucius Annaeus Seneca and the Graeco-Roman Roots of a Modern Transcultural Dilemma". In Balbo, Andrea, Ahn, Jaewon and Kim, Kihoon (Eds.), *Empire and Politics in the Eastern and Western Civilizations*, 191–210. Berlin: De Gruyter.

Maloney, William A., and Van Deth, Jan W. (2010). *Civil Society and Activism in Europe. Contextualizing Engagement and Political Orientations*. London: Routledge.

Mandeville, Bernard (1989) [1714]. *The Fable of the Bees*. London: Penguin.

Marcuse, Herbert (1969). *An Essay on Liberation*. London: Allen Lane.

Marcuse, Herbert (1970) [1964]. *One-Dimensional Man: Studies in the Ideology of Advanced Industrial Society*. Boston: Beacon.

Marcuse, Herbert (1972). *Counterrevolution and Revolt*. Boston: Beacon.

Marett, Robert Ranulph (1932). *Faith, Hope, and Charity in Primitive Religion*. New York: The Macmillan Company, https://www.giffordlectures.org/lectures/faith-hope-and-charity-primitive-religion [Accessed 01/03/2023].

Marfo, Charles Ofosu *et al.* (2022). "'By June, Everyone Would Have Died': Historicising Humour during the Covid-19 Pandemic in Ghana". *Modern Africa*, 9(2): 57–81.

Marinho Oliveira, Alexandra (2021). "Politics of Images: From the Brechtian Experience to Contemporary Arts". In Škrobánková, Klára, and Satková, Naďa (Eds.), *Politics and Community Engagement in Doctoral Theatre Research*, 46–52. Brno: Janáček Academy of Performing Arts.

Marinoff, Lou (2020). "Last Laughs and Dead Ends: How to Get Death's Goat, or Let's Put the 'Yin' back in Dying". In Amir, Lyida (Ed.), *Philosophy of Humor Yearbook*, 1: 195–209. Berlin: De Gruyter.

Marlin-Bennett, Renée, and Jackson, Susan T. (2022). "DIY Cruelty: The Global Political Micro-Practices of Hateful Memes". *Global Studies Quarterly*, 2: 1–11.

Marmysz, John (2003). *Laughing at Nothing: Humor as a Response to Nihilism*. Albany: SUNY.

Marra, Meredith (2022). "Laughing Along? Negotiating Belonging as a Workplace Newcomer". *The European Journal of Humour Research*, 10(2): 135–151.

Marshall, William L. et al. (1995). "Empathy in Sex Offenders". *Clinical Psychology Review*, 15: 99–113.

Marston, Kendra (2018). *Postfeminist Whiteness. Problematising Melancholic Burden in Contemporary Hollywood*. Edinburgh: Edinburgh UP.

Martchev, Milen, and Schnickel, Jacob (2022). "Humor in the Language Classroom: Teaching English in Japan". *National Institute of Informatics*, (n.d.a.): 33–50, https://jissen.repo.nii.ac.jp/?action=repository_action_common_download&item_id=2364&item_no=1&attribute_id=22&file_no=1 [Accessed 15/12/2022].

Martin, W.B.W. (1987). "Students' Perceptions of Causes and Consequences of Embarrassment in the School". *Canadian Journal of Education*, 12: 277–293.

Martinez, Rafael (1994). "Il significato epistemologico del caso Galileo: due diverse concezioni della scienza". *Acta Philosophica*, 3(1): 45–74.

Marwick, Alice E., and Caplan, Robyn (2018). "Drinking Male Tears: Language, the Manosphere, and Network Harassment". *Feminist Media Studies* 18(4): 543–559.

Mascall, Eric Lionel (1971). *The Openness of Being: Natural Theology Today*. London: Darton, Longman & Todd.

Mastrantonio, Luca, and Becker, Emma (2021). "Ho lavorato in due case: racconto una prostituzione onesta", https://www.corriere.it/sette/attualita/21_ottobre_02/emma-becker-ho-lavorato-due-case-racconto-prostituzione-onesta-a3695f2e-1f9e-11ec-b908-b44816b61f2f.shtml [Accessed 19/08/2022].

Matsumoto, David, and Willingham, Bob (2006). "The Thrill of Victory and the Agony of Defeat: Spontaneous Expressions of Medal Winners of the 2004 Athens Olympic games". *Journal of Personality and Social Psychology*, 91(3): 568–581.

Matthews, Dylan (2018). "Donald Trump, the Family Separation Crisis, and the Triumph of Cruelty". *Vox*, https://www.vox.com/2017/1/28/14425354/donald-trump-cruelty [Accessed 05/09/2022].

Mattio, Eduardo (2008). "Del Bazar a la Familia: Una aproximación crítica a las 'idealizaciones' politicas rortyanas". *Areté*, 20(2): 233–258.

Mayes, G. Randolph (2009). "Naturalizing Cruelty". *Biology and Philosophy*, 24(1): 21–34.

Mazières, Frédéric (2015). "Humour pervers, prison et écriture. Une analyse psychobiographhique de l'oeuvre romanesque du marquis de Sade". PhD. Sorbonne.

McCann, Damian (2011). "What Does Violence Tell Us About Gay Male Couple Relationships?" PhD. University of East London.

McCann, Pol D., Plummer, Dave and Minichiello, Victor (2010). "Being the Butt of the Joke: Homophobic Humour, Male Identity, and Its Connection to Emotional and Physical Violence for Men". *Health Sociology Review*, 19(4): 505–521.

McCartney, Donal (1994). *W.E.H. Lecky: Historian and Politician, 1838–1903*. Dublin: Lilliput.

McCoy, Alfred W. (2006). *A Question of Torture: CIA Interrogation, from the Cold War to the War on Terror*. New York: Henry Holt.

McCoy, Charles A., and Scarborough, Roscoe C. (2014). "Watching 'Bad' Television: Ironic Consumption, Camp, and Guilty Pleasures". *Poetics*, 47: 41–59.

McDavitt, Bryce, and Mutchler, Matt G. (2014). "'Dude, You're Such a Slut!' Barriers and Facilitators of Sexual Communication Among Young Gay Men and Their Best Friends". *Journal of Adolescent Research*, 29(4): 464–498.

McDonald, Paul (2012). *Philosophy of Humour.* Tirril: Humanities.

McDougall, William (1926). *An Introduction to Social Psychology.* Boston: John W. Luce.

McElroy, Wendy (1997). "A Feminist Defense of Pornography". *Free Inquiry,* 17(4), https://secularhumanism.org/1997/09/a-feminist-defense-of-pornography/ [Accessed 28/11/2021].

McGraw, Peter, Williams, Lawrence E. and Warren, Caleb (2014). "The Rise and Fall of Humor". *Social Psychological and Personality Science*, 5: 566–572.

McIntosh, William D. et al. (2003). "What's So Funny about a Poke in the Eye? The Prevalence of Violence in Comedy Films and Its Relation to Social and Economic Threat in the United States, 1951–2000". *Mass Communication and Society*, 6(4): 345–360.

McKee, Alan et al. (2020). "An Interdisciplinary Definition of Pornography: Results from a Global Delphi Panel". *Archives of Sexual Behavior*, 49: 1085–1091.

McMurtry, John (1971). "Kill'em! Crush'em! Eat'em Raw!" *Maclean's*, Oct. issue: 42 and 58.

McMurtry, John (1998). *Unequal Freedoms. The Global Market as an Ethical System.* Toronto: Garamond.

McMurtry, John (1999). *The Cancer Stage of Capitalism*, 1st ed. London: Pluto.

McMurtry, John (2002). *Value Wars: The Global Market Versus the Life Economy.* London: Pluto.

McMurtry, John (2013a). "Competition". In Becker, L.C., and Becker, C.B. (Eds.), *Encyclopedia of Ethics*, 277–280. New York: Routledge.

McMurtry, John (2013b). *The Cancer Stage of Capitalism: From Crisis to Cure*, 2nd ed. London: Pluto.

McMurtry, John (Ed.) (2011). *Philosophy and World Problems, Volumes 1–3.* Paris & Oxford: EOLSS.

Meckl, Markus (2016). "Latvia's Vanished National Heroes". *The European Legacy*, 21(4): 408–418.

Mees, Hayden L. (1966). "Sadistic Fantasies Modified by Aversive Conditioning and Substitution: A Case Study". *Behaviour Research and Therapy*, 4(4): 317–320.

Melville, Herman (2008–2017) [1851]. *Moby Dick; or The Whale.* Fairbanks: Project Gutenberg Literary Archive Foundation, https://www.gutenberg.org/ebooks/2701 [Accessed 29/04/2022].

Metz, Thaddeus (2021). "Exactly Why Are Slurs Wrong?" *Daimon*, 84: 13–29.

Meyer, John C. (2000). "Humour as a Double-Edged Sword: Four Functions of Humor in Communication". *Communication Theory*, 10(3): 310–331.

Meyers, Christopher (2004). "Cruel Choices: Autonomy and Critical Care Decision-Making". *Bioethics*, 18(2): 104–119.

Meyers, Jeffrey (2012). "Kafka's Dark Laughter". *The Antioch Review*, 70(4): 760–768.

Midgley, Julia (2011). "From Atrocities of War to a Skateboarding Cockatoo". *Senses & Sensibility in the Right Place–Proceedings of the 6th UNIDCOM/IADE International Conference*, http://reportager.uwe.ac.uk/mempics/jmidgley/Atrocities%20to%20Cockatoos.pdf [Accessed 05/09/2022].

Miguel, Edward, Saiegh, Sebastián M. and Satyanath, Shanker (2008). "National Cultures and Soccer Violence". *National Bureau of Economic Research*, Working Paper 13968, doi: 10.3386/w13968 [Accessed 29/04/2022].

Milgram, Stanley (1963). "Behavioral Study of Obedience". *Journal of Abnormal and Social Psychology*, 67(4): 371–378.

Mill, John Stuart (2001) [1859]. *On Liberty.* Kitchener: Batoche.

Miller, Christian (2018). *The Character Gap.* New York: Oxford UP.

Miller, Geoffrey (2000). *The Mating Mind.* New York: Anchor Books.

Miller, James (1990). "Carnivals of Atrocity: Foucault, Nietzsche, Cruelty". *Political Theory*, 18(3): 470–491.
Miller, Paul A., and Eisenberg, Nancy (1988). "The Relation of Empathy to Aggressive and Antisocial Behaviour". *Psychological Bulletin*, 103: 324–344.
Miller, Shaun (2022). "Sexual Autonomy and Sexual Consent". In Boonin, David (Ed.), *The Palgrave Handbook of Sexual Ethics*, 240–270. Cham: Palgrave Macmillan.
Miller, William Ian (1997). *The Anatomy of Disgust*. Cambridge, MA: Harvard UP.
Mingers, John (2008). "Management Knowledge and Knowledge Management: Realism and Forms of Truth". *Knowledge Management Research and Practice*, 6(1): 62–76.
Mini, Piero V. (1974). *Philosophy and Economics: The Origins and Development of Economic Theory*. Gainesville: UP of Florida.
Mireault, Gina C., and Reddy, Vasudevi (2016). *Humor in Infants. Developmental and Psychological Perspectives*. Cham: Springer.
Mishna, F. et al. (2010). "Cyber Bullying Behaviors among Middle and High School Students". *American Journal of Orthopsychiatry*, 80(3): 362–374.
Mogg, Ken (2005). "Hitchcock, Alfred". In *Senses of Cinema: Great Directors*, 36, http://www.sensesofcinema.com/2005/great-directors/hitchcock/ [Accessed 07/09/2022].
Moher, Andrew A. (2003–2004). "The Lesser of Two Evils? An Argument for Judicially Sanctioned Torture in a Post-9/11 World". *Thomas Jefferson Law Review*, 26: 469–489.
Montaigne, Michel de (1877) [1595]. *Essays* (trans. Charles Cotton). London: Reeves & Turne, https://www.gutenberg.org/files/3600/3600-h/3600-h.htm [Accessed 19/02/2022].
Montaigne, Michel de (2018) [1595]. *Les essais*. Chicago: The Montaigne Project.
Montale, Eugenio (2012) [1925]. "Spesso il male di vivere ho incontrato". In Santagata, Marco et al. (Eds.), *Testi, Autori, Generi*, 521. Bari: Laterza.
Montesquieu (2001) [1748]. *The Spirit of the Laws* (trans. Thomas Nugent). Kitchener: Batoche.
Montessori, Maria (1913) [1910]. *Pedagogical Anthropology* (trans. Frederic Taber Cooper). New York: Frederick A. Stokes, https://archive.org/details/pedagogicalanthr00montuoft [Accessed 01/03/2023].
Montessori, Maria (1971) [1932–1939]. *Peace and Education*, 5th ed. Adyar: Theosophical Publishing House.
Montessori, Maria (2009) [1914]. *Dr. Montessori's Own Handbook*. New York: Frederick A. Stokes, https://www.gutenberg.org/files/29635/29635-h/29635-h.htm [Accessed 05/11/2022].
Moore, Jr., Barrington (1969) [1965]. "Tolerance and the Scientific Outlook". In Wolff, Robert Paul, Moore, Jr., Barrington, and Marcuse, Herbert, *A Critique of Pure Tolerance*, 53–80. Boston: Beacon.
Mornati, Fiorenzo (2020). *Vilfredo Pareto: An Intellectual Biography: III. From Liberty to Science (1898–1923)*. Cham: Palgrave Macmillan.
Morreall, John (1983). *Taking Laughter Seriously*. Albany: State University of New York.
Morreall, John (Ed.) (1987). *The Philosophy of Laughter and Humor*. Albany: State University of New York.
Morreall, John (1998). "The Comic and Tragic Visions of Life". *Humor*, 11(4): 333–355.
Morreall, John (1999). *Comedy, Tragedy, and Religion*. Albany: State University of New York.
Morreall, John (2008). "Philosophy and Religion". In Raskin, Victor (Ed.), *The Primer of Humor Research*, 211–242. Berlin: De Gruyter.
Morreall, John (2013). Review of *The Mirror of Laughter* by Alexander Kozintsev. *Humor*, 26(1), 191–196.

Morreall, John (2016). "Philosophy of Humor". In Zalta, Edward N. (Ed.), *Stanford Encyclopedia of Philosophy*. Stanford: Stanford University, https://plato.stanford.edu/entries/humor/ [Accessed 21/02/2022].

Morreall, John (2020a). "Foreword: Philosophy of Humor—Not a Joke Any More". In Amir, Lydia (Ed.), *Philosophy of Humor Yearbook*, 1: xiii–xviii. Berlin: De Gruyter.

Morreall, John (2020b). "It's a Funny Thing, Humor". In Amir, Lydia (Ed.), *Philosophy of Humor Yearbook*, 1: 33–48. Berlin: De Gruyter.

Morris, Desmond (1967). *The Naked Ape: A Zoologist's Study of the Human Animal*. London: Jonathan Cape.

Moser, Keith (2022). "The 'Beautiful Abyss' of Human Cruelty, Anthropogenic Violence, and Other-Than-Human Friendship in Yamen Manaï's *Bel Abîme*". *Humanities*, 11(4), https://doi.org/10.3390/h11040094 [Accessed 04/09/2022].

Müller-Funk, Wolfgang (2022). Crudelitas. *Zwölf Kapitel einer Diskursgeschichte der Grausamkeit*. Berlin: Matthes & Seitz.

Mulligan, Kevin, and Correia, Fabrice (2021). "Facts". In Zalta, Edward N. (Ed.), *The Stanford Encyclopedia of Philosophy*, https://plato.stanford.edu/archives/win2021/entries/facts/ [Accessed 6/12/2022].

Murodova, Muqadas Ikromovna (2022). "Satire: Its Nature and Methods". *Science and Education* 3(1): 735–741.

Musek, Janek (2017). *The General Factor of Personality*. London: Academic.

Müth, Robert (1959). "L'idea della religione romana". Studi romani 7: 390–404.

Myler, Stephen F. (2017). "Playing the Victim–A Psychological Perspective". *Psychology and Behavioral Science*, 3(1), doi: 10.19080/PBSIJ.2017.03.555601 [Accessed 13/01/2023].

Nagel, Thomas (1979). *Mortal Questions*. Cambridge: Cambridge UP.

Nardin, Terry (2001). *The Philosophy of Michael Oakeshott*. University Park: Pennsylvania State UP.

Nell, Victor (2006). "Cruelty and the Psychology of History". *Behavioral and Brain Sciences*, 29(3): 211–257.

Newall, Michael (2012). "An Aesthetics of Transgressive Pornography". In Maes, Hans R.V., and Levinson, Jerrold (Eds.), *Art and Pornography: Philosophical Essays*, 206–228. Oxford: Oxford UP.

Niebylski, Dianna C. (2004). *Humoring Resistance. Laughter and the Excessive Body in Latin American Women's Fiction*. Albany: State University of New York.

Nietzsche, Friedrich (1911a) [1871]. "The Greek State. Preface to an Unwritten Book". In *The Complete Works of Friedrich Nietzsche, 13 vols.* (trans. Oscar Levy), vol. 2: 1–18. New York: MacMillan, https://www.gutenberg.org/files/51548/51548-h/51548-h.htm [Accessed 10/01/2022].

Nietzsche, Friedrich (1911b) [1883–1891]. *Thus Spake Zarathustra* (trans. Thomas Common). Edinburgh: T.N. Foulis, https://www.gutenberg.org/files/1998/1998-h/1998-h.htm [Accessed 11/01/2022].

Nietzsche, Friedrich (1997) [1881]. *Daybreak* (trans. R.J. Hollingdale). Cambridge: Cambridge UP.

Nietzsche, Friedrich (2002) [1886]. *Beyond Good and Evil* (trans. Judith Norman). Cambridge: Cambridge UP.

Nietzsche, Friedrich (2004) [1888 and 1895]. *Ecce Homo and The Antichrist* (trans. Thomas Wayne). New York: Algora.

Nilsen, Don L.F., and Nilsen, Alleen Pace (n.d.a.). "The History of the International Society for Humor Studies", https://www.researchgate.net/profile/Don_Nilsen/publication/291292764_Newsletter/links/56e9846d08ae3a5b48cc6bd7/Newsletter [Accessed 21/09/2021].

Nissan, Ephraim (2012). "A Tentative Evaluation of the Spread of Humour Studies Among Journals in Other Domains". *Israeli Journal of Humor Research*, 1(1): 107–184.

Nock, David A. (2007). "Stephen Leacock: The Not-So-Funny Story of His Evolutionary Ethnology and Canada's First Peoples". In Darnell, Regna, and Gleach, Frederic W. (Eds.), *Histories of Anthropology Annual*, 3: 51–69. Lincoln: University of Nebraska.

Noel, Jana (1999). "On the Varieties of *Phronesis*". *Educational Philosophy and Theory*, 31(3): 273–289.

Noonan, Gerald (1988). "Canadian Duality and the Colonization of Humour". *College English*, 50(8): 912–919.

Noonan, Jeff (2006). *Democratic Society and Human Needs*. Ottawa and Montreal: McGill-Queens UP.

Noonan, Jeff (2022). *Embodied Humanism. Toward Solidarity and Sensuous Enjoyment*. Lanham: Lexington.

Novic, Elisa (2020). "Remedies". In Francioni, Francesco, and Vrddoljak, Ana Filipa (Eds.), *The Oxford Handbook of International Cultural Heritage Law*, 642–663. Oxford: Oxford UP.

Nugent, Michael (2022). "Ambivalent Laughter: The Key to Preserving Playtime". *The European Journal of Humour Research*, 10(1): 37–49.

O'Connor, Emma C. et al. (2017). "Restoring Threatened Masculinity: The Appeal of Sexist and Anti-Gay Humor". *Sex Roles*, 77, 567–580.

O'Neill, Patrick (1983). "The Comedy of Entropy: The Contexts of Black Humour". *Canadian Review of Comparative Literature*, 10(2): 145–166.

Oakeshott, Michael (2004) [1923–1981]. *What Is History? And Other Essays* (ed. Luke O'Sullivan). Exeter: Imprint Academic.

Ochoa, Tyler Trent, and Newman Jones, Christine (1997). "Defiling the Dead: Necrophilia and the Law". *Whittier Law Review*, 18(3): 539–578.

Ofshe, Richard, and Watters, Ethan (1994). *Making Monsters. False Memories, Psychotherapy, and Sexual Hysteria*. Berkeley: University of California.

Oldham, Gabriella (1996). *Keaton's Silent Shorts: Beyond the Laughter*. Carbondale: Southern Illinois UP.

Olin, Lauren (2020). "The Comic Stance". In Amir, Lyida (Ed.), *Philosophy of Humor Yearbook*, 1: 49–71. Berlin: De Gruyter.

Oloskey Mills, Judith (1974). "Gogol's 'Overcoat': The Pathetic Passages Reconsidered". *Transactions and Proceedings of the Modern Language Association of America*, 89(5): 1106–1111.

Olson, Gary (2015). *Empathy Imperiled. Capitalism, Culture and the Brain*. Cham: Springer.

Olweus, Dan (1993). *Understanding Children's Worlds. Bullying at School: What We Know and What We Can Do*. Malden, MA: Blackwell Publishing.

Olweus, Dan (1999). *Bullying Prevention Program*. Boulder: University of Colorado.

Oppliger, Patrice A., and Shouse, Eric (Eds.) (2019). *The Dark Side of Stand-Up Comedy*. Cham: Palgrave Macmillan.

Orrell, David (2017). *Economyths: 11 Ways That Economics Gets It Wrong*, 2nd ed. London: Icon.

Ortega y Gasset, José (1946) [1930]. *Mission of the University*. London: Kegan Paul.

Orwell, George (1961) [1949]. *1984*. New York: Signet Classics.

Oster, Shai (1998). "Shoah Business. Humour and the 'Second Generation'". *Jewish Quarterly*, 45(3): 13–18.

Ottinger, Didier (2004). "The Circus of Cruelty: A Portrait of the Contemporary Clown as Sisyphus". In Cari, Jean (Ed.), *The Great Parade: Portrait of the Artist as Clown*, 35–45. New Haven: Yale UP.

Pack, Rachael L. (2018). "The Duty to Survive Well: Neoliberal Governance, Temporality and Breast Cancer Survivorship Discourse". PhD. University of Western Ontario.

Palmer, Jerry (1994). *Taking Humour Seriously*. London: Routledge.
Panzacchi, Enrico (1897) [1896]. "La musica". In *La vita italiana durante la Rivoluzione francese e l'Impero*, 3: 509–540. Milan: Treves.
Pareto, Vilfredo (1902–1903). *Les systèmes socialistes*. Paris: V. Giard & E. Brière.
Pareto, Vilfredo (1914). *Il mito virtuista e la letteratura immorale*, 2nd ed. Rome: Lux.
Pareto, Vilfredo (1935) [1916]. *The Mind and Society* (trans. Andrew Bongiorno and Arthur Livingston). New York: Harcourt, Brace.
Pareto, Vilfredo (1968) [1900]. *The Rise and Fall of the Elites: An Application of Theoretical Sociology* (trans. Hans L. Zetterberg). Totowa, NJ: Bedminster.
Parker, Ian (Ed.) (2015). *Handbook of Critical Psychology*. London: Routledge.
Part, Kai *et al.* (2011). "Gender Differences in Factors Associated with Sexual Intercourse among Estonian Adolescents". *Scandinavian Journal of Public Health*, 39: 389–395.
Pascal, Blaise (1993) [1670]. *Pensieri* (trans. Marco Magni). Milan: Rusconi.
Payer, Cheryl (1974). *The Debt Trap: The International Monetary Fund and the Third World*. New York: Monthly Review.
Pearson, Geoff (2012). *An Ethnography of English Football Fans. Cans, Cops and Carnivals*. Manchester: Manchester UP.
Penco, Carlo (2017). "Prejudice and Presupposition in Offensive Language". *Nordicum-Mediterraneum: Icelandic E-Journal of Nordic and Mediterranean Studies*, https://nome.unak.is/wordpress/volume-12-no-3-2017/conference-proceeding-volume-12-no-3-2017/prejudice-presupposition-offensive-language/ [Accessed 21/10/2022].
Pennucci, Mike (2020). "Trolling in Cyberspace". *Journal of Information System Security*, 16(1): 33–45.
Peretti, Luca, and Reizen, Karen T. (Eds.) (2019). *Pier Paolo Pasolini, Framed and Unframed: A Thinker for the Twenty-First Century*. New York: Bloomsbury.
Perlmutter, Daniel D. (2002). "On Incongruities and Logical Inconsistencies in Humor: The Delicate Balance". *Humor*, 15: 155–168.
Petronio, S., C. Olson and N. Dollar (1988). "Privacy Issues in Relational Embarrassment: Impact on Relational Quality and Communication Satisfaction". *Communications Research Reports*, 6(1): 21–27.
Pettit, Harry (2019). "The Cruelty of Hope: Emotional Cultures of Precarity in Neoliberal Cairo". *EPD: Society and Space*, 37(4): 722–739.
Pezzuto, Sophie (2019). "From Porn Performer to Porntropreneur: Online Entrepeneurship, Social Media Branding, and Selfhood in Contemporary Trans Pornography". *About Gender*, 8(16): 30–60.
Phillips, Anita (1998). *A Defence of Masochism*. London: Faber & Faber.
Phillips, John (2014). "Sade". *French Studies*, 68(4): 526–533.
Phillips, Susan E. (2007). *Transforming Talk: The Problem with Gossip in Late Medieval English*. University Park: Pennsylvania State UP.
Philpott, Simon (2005). "A Controversy of Faces: Images from Bali and Abu Ghraib". *Journal for Cultural Research*, 9(3): 227–244.
Piaggio, Martin (1923) [1846]. "Bonn-a nêutte dæta a tempo". In Ballerini, Esuperanzo (Ed.), *Umorismo Paesano*, 80–81. Turin: Alberto Giani.
Piaia, Gregorio (2011). "What Point is there in Studying the History of Philosophy Today?" *Maynooth Philosophical Papers*, 6: 67–73.
Pietrini, Sandra (2010). "Medieval Entertainers and the Memory of Ancient Theatre". *Revue internationale de philosophie*, 252(2): 149–176.

Pinto Guargati, Juan Felipe (2022). "Narrativas del Humor en Instagram: Rasgos culturales de memes en elm arco de la emergencia sanitaria Covid 19 en Colombia". Degree thesis. Universidad Santo Tomás.
Pirandello, Luigi (1920) [1908]. *L'umorismo. Saggio*, 2nd ed. Florence: Luigi Battistelli.
Pirandello, Luigi (1974). *On Humor* (trans. Antonio Iuliano and Daniel P. Testa). Chapel Hill: North Carolina UP.
Pirandello, Luigi (1986) [1904]. *Il fu Mattia Pascal*. Milan: Mondadori.
Pirandello, Luigi (1987) [1915]. "La Trappola". In *Novelle per un anno*, 329–332. Milan: Club degli Editori, https://www.bibliotecassredentore.it/wp-content/uploads/2020/11/PirandelloNovelleParte Prima.pdf [Accessed 11/10/2022].
Pirandello. Luigi (1911 and 1917), "La patente", https://ifr.uni.wroc.pl/sites/default/files/pirandello_tes tiit_la_patente_novella_e_commedia_0.pdf [Accessed 09/09/2022].
Platov, Ilya (2012). "Barbare et infidèle. L'image de l'ennemi turc dans la guerre de 1876–1878 en Russie à travers la presse, les brochures de propaganda, les corrispondances et les mémoires". *Cahiers balkaniques*, 36–37: 293–320.
Plester, Barbara, Bentley, Tim and Brewer, Emily (2022). "'It only hurts when I laugh'". *The European Journal of Humour Research*, 10(2): 116–134.
Polanyi, Michael (1948). "Planning and Spontaneous Order". *The Manchester School of Economic and Social Studies*, 16: 237–268.
Polanyi, Michael (1962a). "History and Hope: An Analysis of Our Age". *McEnerney Lectures*, https://youtu.be/5FT-NxvE7NQ [Accessed 21/09/2021].
Polanyi, Michael (1962b). "The Unaccountable Element in Science". *Philosophy Today*, 6(3): 171–182.
Polanyi, Michael (1962c) [1958]. *Personal Knowledge: Towards a Post-Critical Philosophy*. Reprint. London: Routledge.
Polanyi, Michael (1969a). *Knowing and Being: Essays*. London: Routledge & Kegan Paul.
Polanyi, Michael (1969b) [1959]. *The Study of Man*. Chicago: Chicago UP.
Polanyi, Michael (2009) [1966]. *The Tacit Dimension*. London: Routledge.
Polanyi, Michael and Prosch, Harry (1975). *Meaning*. Chicago: Chicago UP.
Portmann, John (2000). *When Bad Things Happen to Other People*. New York: Routledge.
Potter, W.J., and Warren, R. (1998). "Humor as Camouflage of Televised Violence". *Journal of Communication*, 48(2): 40–57.
Poulos, Christopher N. (2021). "Walking with/through a Savage History". *Journal of Autoethnography*, 2(1): 78–82.
Powell, Chris, and Paton, George E.C. (Eds.) (1988). *Humour in Society. Resistance and Control*. London: Palgrave Macmillan.
Pratama, Dendi, Gunarti, Winny and Akbar, Taufiq (2017). "Understanding Visual Novel as Artwork of Visual Communication Design". *Mudra. Journal of Art and Culture*, 32(3): https://doi.org/10.31091/mudra.v32i3.177 [Accessed 21/09/2021].
Prigent, Yves (2003). *La cruauté ordinaire : où est le mal?* Paris: DDB.
Prince, Stephen, and Hensley, Wayne E. (1992). "The Kuleshov Effect: Recreating the Classic Experiment". *Cinema Journal*, 31(2): 59–75.
Pritchard, Erin (2022). "'Get Down on Your Knees': Representing the Seven Dwarfs in the Pantomime". *Disability Studies Quarterly*, 42(1), https://doi.org/10.18061/dsq.v42i1.7576 [Accessed 05/09/2022].

Prosperi, Valentina (2015). "The Reception of Lucretius' Second Proem: The Topos that Never Was". *Lingue antiche e modern*, 4, http://all.uniud.it/lam/lamrep/2015/LAM_4_2015_Prosperi.pdf [Accessed 21/09/2021].
Provine, Robert R. (1996). "Laughter". *American Scientist*, 84(1): 38–45.
Provine, Robert R. (2016). "Laughter as a Scientific Problem: An Adventure in Sidewalk Neuroscience". *The Journal of Comparative Neurology*, 524(8): 1532–1539.
Pushkin, Alexander S. (1916) [1830]. "The Coffin-Maker". In *The Prose Tales* (trans. T. Keane). London: G. Bell and Sons, https://americanliterature.com/author/alexsander-pushkin/short-story/the-coffin-maker [Accessed 21/09/2021].
Quine, William V.O. (1963) [1953]. *From a Logical Point of View*, 2nd ed. New York: Harper & Row.
Quintilian (1920) [1st century AD]. *Institutio oratoria* (trans. Harold E. Butler.). London: William Heinemann, http://www.perseus.tufts.edu/hopper/searchresults?q=quintilian [Accessed 22/10/2022].
Ralkovski, Mark (Ed.) (2021). *Dave Chappelle and Philosophy. When Keeping It Wrong Gets Real*. Chicago: Open Universe.
Ramadhan, Febi (2019). "The Conspicuous Face of Punishment: Spectatorship and Public Governance in Public Caning in Aceh, Indonesia". Arryman Fellowship Paper, https://www.edgs.northwestern.edu/documents/working-papers/febi-r.-ramadhan_arryman-paper_final-draft.pdf [Accessed 21/09/2021].
Rand, Ayn (1964) [1961]. *The Virtue of Selfishness. A New Concept of Egoism*. New York: Signet.
Rand, Ayn (1997). *Journals of Ayn Rand* (ed. David Harriman). New York: Penguin.
Raphael, D.D. (Ed.) (1991). *British Moralists 1650–1800*, 2 vols. Indianapolis: Hackett.
Rapp, Albert (1951). *The Origins of Wit and Humor*. New York: Dutton.
Raskin, Victor (1979). "Semantic Mechanisms of Humor". *Proceedings of the Fifth Annual Meeting of the Berkeley Linguistics Society*, 325–335.
Rasmussen, Claire (2015). "Pleasure, Pain, and Place. Ag-gag, Crush Videos, and Animal Bodies on Display". In Gillespie, Kathryn, and Collard, Rosemary-Claire (Eds.), *Critical Animal Geographies. Politics, Intersections and Hierarchies in a Multispecies World*, 54–69. London: Routledge.
Raudino, Giuseppe (2003–2008). "Umberto Eco e il comico: gli scritti teorici e I giochi linguistici", https://www.academia.edu/36512863/Umberto_Eco_e_il_comico_gli_scritti_teorici_e_i_giochi_linguistici [Accessed 21/09/2021].
Redwine, Jr., James D. (1961). "Beyond Psychology: The Moral Basis of Jonson's Theory of Humour Characterization". *ELH*, 28(4): 316–334.
Regan, Tom (1983). *The Case for Animal Rights*. Berkeley: California UP.
Reich, Wilhelm (1953). *The Murder of Christ*. New York: Simon & Schuster.
Reich, Wilhelm (1967). *Reich Speaks of Freud* (ed. Mary Higgins and Chester M. Raphael and trans. Therese Pol). New York: Farrar, Straus and Giroux.
Reich, Wilhelm (1976) [1933]. *Character Analysis* (trans. Vincent R. Carfagno), 3rd ed. New York: Pocket.
Reichl, Isabella, and Kapogianni, Eleni (2021). "A Delicate Balance. Irony in the Negotiation of Refusals". *Journal of Language Aggression and Conflict*, 8(1), doi: 10.1075/jlac.00050.rei [Accessed 21/04/2022].
Reinhart, Martin (2020). "Know Your Name: A Short History of Occidental Knowledge Systems since the Renaissance". In Golding, Johnny, Reinhart, Martin and Paganelli, Mattia (Eds.), *Data Loam. Sometimes Hard, Usually Soft. The Future of Knowledge Systems*, 11–37. Berlin: De Gruyter.

Reiter, Wolfgang L. (2007). "In Memoriam. Ludwig Boltzmann: A Life of Passion". *Physics in Perspective*, 9: 357–374.

Renan, Ernest (1992) [1882]. *What is a Nation?* (trans. Ethan Rundell). Paris: Presses Pocket, https://www.academia.edu/33769892/What_is_a_Nation [Accessed 07/11/2022].

Renner, Karen J. (2013). "Evil Children in Film and Literature". In Renner, Karen J. (Ed.), *The 'Evil Child' in Literature, Film and Popular Culture*, 1–27. London: Routledge.

Richman, Joseph (1995). "The Lifesaving Function of Humor with the Depressed and Suicidal Elderly". *The Gerontologist*, 35(2): 271–275.

Ringrose, Jessica, and Renold, Emma (2010). "Normative Cruelties and Gender Deviants: The Performative Effects of Bully Discourses for Girls and Boys in School". *British Educational Research Journal*, 36(4): 573–596.

Ritter, Erika (1986). "Leacock and Leahen: The Feminine Influence on Stephen Leacock". In Staines, David (Ed.), *Stephen Leacock: A Reappraisal*, 11–16. Ottawa: University of Ottawa.

Robbins, Lionel (1935). *An Essay on the Nature and Significance of Economic Science*, 2nd ed. London: Macmillan.

Roberts, Alan (2019). *A Philosophy of Humour*. Cham: Palgrave Macmillan.

Roberts, Marc (2006). "Gilles Deleuze: Psychiatry, Subjectivity, and the Passive Synthesis of Time". *Nursing Philosophy*, 7(4): 191–204.

Robinson, Jonny (2019). "On Being Cruel to a Chair". *Analysis*, 79(1): 83–91.

Rocci, Carlotta (2021). "Allevatori irrompono alla presentazione di un libro per bambini sui lupi e minacciano l'autore". *La Repubblica*, https://torino.repubblica.it/cronaca/2021/08/14/news/allevatori_irrompono_alla_presentazione_di_un_libro_per_bambini_sui_lupi_e_minacciano_l_autore_un_provocatore_lupista_-314004995/?ref=RHTP-BH-I304495303-P3-S7-T1 [Accessed 21/04/2022].

Rodrigues, Suzana B., and Collinson, David L. (1995). "'Having Fun'? Humour as Resistance in Brazil". *Organization Studies* 16(5): 739–768.

Rogers, Ben (1999). *A.J. Ayer. A Life*. New York: Grove.

Rolfe, Mark (2022). "The Idea of National Humour and Americanisation in Australia and Britain". *The European Journal of Humour Research*, 10(2): 51–73.

Rolston, III, Holmes (1982). "The Irreversibly Comatose: Respect for the Subhuman in Human Life". *The Journal of Medicine and Philosophy*, 7: 337–354.

Ronson, Jon (2015). "How One Stupid Tweet Blew Up Justine Sacco's Life". *The New York Times Magazine*, https://www.nytimes.com/2015/02/15/magazine/how-one-stupid-tweet-ruined-justine-saccos-life.html [Accessed 21/04/2022].

Rorty, Richard (1984) [1983]. "Solidarity or Objectivity?" *Nanzan Review of American Studies*, 6: 1–18.

Rorty, Richard (1989). *Contingency, Irony, and Solidarity*. Cambridge, MA: Cambridge UP.

Rorty, Richard (2000) [1996]. "Religious Faith, Intellectual Responsibility and Romance". In *Philosophy and Social Hope*, 148–167. London: Penguin.

Rorty, Richard (2001). "The Decline of Redemptive Truth and the Rise of a Literary Culture". *The John M. Olin Center for Inquiry into the Theory and Practice of Democracy*. Chicago: Chicago UP, http://olincenter.uchicago.edu/pdf/rorty.pdf [Accessed 21/09/2021].

Roscigno, Vincent J., Lopez, Steven H. and Hodson, Randy (2009). "Supervisory Bullying, Status Inequalities and Organizational Context". *Social Forces*, 87(3): 1561–1589.

Rose, J. Coplen (2013). "Class Movements in the New South Africa: Post-Colonial Politics, Neocolonialism, and Mimicry in Pieter-Dirk Uys's *MacBeki A Farce to be Reckoned With*". *Modern Languages and Literatures Annual Graduate Conference*, 7, https://ir.lib.uwo.ca/mllgradconference/2013Conference/MLL2013/7 [Accessed 07/09/2022].

Rosen, Frederick (1990). "Majorities and Minorities: A Classical Utilitarian View". *Nomos* 32: 24–43.
Rosenblatt, Helena (2018). *The Lost History of Liberalism. From Ancient Rome to the Twenty-First Century*. Princeton: Princeton UP.
Rosset, Clément (1968). *Schopenhauer*. Paris: PUF.
Rosset, Clément (1991). *Principes de sagesse et de folie*. Paris: Minuit.
Rosset, Clément (1993) [1983–1988]. *Joyful Cruelty* (trans. David F. Bell). Oxford: Oxford UP.
Rousseau, Jean-Jacques (1997) [1755]. "Discourse on the Origin and Foundation of Inequality among Mankind. In The Discourses, and Other Early Political Writings" (trans. Victor Gourevitch), 111–222. Cambridge: Cambridge UP.
Ruch, Willibald, and Proyer, René T. (2008) "The Fear of Being Laughed At: Individual and Group Differences in Gelotophobia". *Humor*, 21(1): 47–67.
Ruch, Willibald *et al.* (Eds.) (2019). *Humor and Laughter, Play.fulness and Cheerfulness: Upsides and Downsides to a Life of Lightness*. Lausanne: Frontiers.
Rudorff, Raymond (1968). *Monsters: Studies in Ferocity*. London: Neville Spearman.
Ruiz Scaperlanda, Maria (2017). *Edith Stein: The Life and Legacy of St. Teresa Benedicta of the Cross*. Nashua: Sophia Institute.
Russalkow, Wladimir (1894). *Grausamkeit und Verbrechen im sexuellen Leben. Historisch-psychologische Studien*. Budapest: Minerva.
Russell, Bertrand (1965) [1952]. *Dictionary of Mind, Matter and Morals* (ed. Lester E. Denonn). New York: Philosophical Library.
Russell, Bertrand (1968) [1942]. "The Art of Rational Conjecture". In *The Art of Philosophizing, and Other Essays*, 1–36. New York: Philosophical Library.
Russell, Bertrand (2016) [1962]. 22 January 1962 letter to Sir Oswald Mosley, https://lettersofnote.com/2016/02/02/every-ounce-of-my-energy/ [Accessed 24/08/2022].
Ryle, Gilbert (1971). "The Thinking of Thoughts: What is 'Le Penseur' doing?" In *Collected Papers: Vol. 2. Collected Essays 1929–1968*, 480–496. London: Hutchinson.
Sade (1999) [1801]. *Histoire de Juliette ou les prospérités du vice*. In Selva, T., and Franval, J. (Eds.), *Oeuvres du Marquis de Sade*. N.d.a.: Sade-ecrivain, http://www.sade-ecrivain.com/juliette/juliette.htm [Accessed 17/05/2001].
Sade (2010) [1795]. *La philosophie dans le boudoir*. Chicoutimi: University of Quebec, http://classiques.uqac.ca/classiques/sade_marquis_de/sade_philo_dans_le_boudoir/sade_philo_dans_le_boudoir.html [Accessed 19/02/2022].
Saint John, Graham (2004). "Counter-Tribes, Global Protest and Carnivals of Reclamation". *Peace Review*, 16: 421–428.
Šajkovic, Miriam Taylor (1962). *Dostoevskij's Redeeming Image of Man*. Philadelphia: University of Pennsylvania.
Salmi, Hannu (2011). *Historical Comedy on Screen. Subverting History with Humour*. Bristol: Intellect.
Samson, Andrea C. *et al.* (2016). "Eliciting Positive, Negative and Mixed Emotional States: A Film Library for Affective Scientists". *Cognition and Emotion*, 30(5): 827–856.
Sandström, Niklas (2015). "Deathbed Selfie". MA. Aalto University.
Sanger (2013) [1858]. *The History of Prostitution: Its Extent, Causes, and Effects throughout the World*. New York: Harper, https://www.gutenberg.org/files/41873/41873-h/41873-h.htm [Accessed 27/08/2022].
Santarpia, Valentina (2021). "Spigolatrice di Sapri, la statua e le polemiche: 'È sessista'". *Corriere della Sera*, https://www.corriere.it/cronache/21_settembre_27/spigolatrice-sapri-nuova-statua-polemiche-sessista-d8188c34-1f64-11ec-b908-b44816b61f2f.shtml [Accessed 21/09/2022].

Santayana, George (1896). *The Sense of Beauty. Being the Outlines of Aesthetic Theory.* New York: C. Scribner's Sons, https://www.gutenberg.org/ebooks/26842 [Accessed 01/05/2022].
Santayana, George (1922). *Soliloquies in England and Later Soliloquies.* New York: Scribner's Sons, https://archive.org/details/soliloquicopytwo00santrich [Accessed 01/03/2023].
Santoro-Brienza, Liberato (2004). "On Laughter, Comicality, Humour". *Literature and Aesthetics*, 14(1): 71–87.
Sardegna Sotterranea (2017). "Tuvixeddu: Attorno alla necropolis, senzatetto e disperati", http://www.sardegnasotterranea.org/tuvixeddu-attorno-alla-necropoli-senzatetto-disperati/ [Accessed 29/09/2022].
Saucier, Donald A. *et al.* (2018). "'What Do You Call a Black Guy Who Flies a Plane?': The Effects and Understanding of Disparagement and Confrontational Racial Humor" *Humor*, 31(1): 105–128.
Sbattella, Fabio, and Molteni, Marzia Molteni (2008). *L'umorismo in emergenza.* Milan: Università Cattolica.
Scheler, Max (1915). *Abhandlungen und Aufsätze.* Leipzig: Weissen Bücher, https://archive.org/details/abhandlungenund00schegoog [Accessed 01/03/2023].
Scheler, Max (1921). *Vom Ewigen im Menschen. Erster Band: Religiöse Erneuerung.* Leipzig: Der Neue Geist, https://archive.org/details/vomewigenimmensc00sche [Accessed 01/03/2023].
Schieffelin, Bambi, B. (1986). "Teasing and Shaming in Kaluli Children's Interactions". In Schieffelin, Bambi B., and Ochs, Elinor (Eds.), *Language socialization across cultures*, 165–181. Cambridge: Cambridge UP.
Schlefer, Jonathan (2012). *The Assumptions Economists Make.* Cambridge, MA: Belknap.
Schoonbaert, Dirk, and Roelants, Gilbert (1996). "Citation Analysis for Measuring the Value of Scientific Publications: Quality Assessment Tool or Comedy of Errors?" *Tropical Medicine and International Health*, 1(6): 739–752.
Schopenhauer, Arthur (1896) [1851]. *The Art of Controversy. And Other Posthumous Papers* (trans. Thomas Bailey Saunders). London: Swan Sonnenschein.
Schopenhauer, Arthur (1897) [1851]. *Essays of Schopenhauer* (trans. Mrs. Rudolf Dircks). London: Walter Scott, https://archive.org/details/essaysofschodirc00schouoft [Accessed 01/03/2023].
Schopenhauer, Arthur (1903) [1840]. *The Basis of Morality* (trans. Arthur Brodrick Bullock). London: Swan Sonnenschein, https://archive.org/details/dli.ernet.470323 [Accessed 01/03/2023].
Schopenhauer, Arthur (1909) [1859]. *The World as Will and Idea*, 3 vols., 3rd ed. (trans. R.B. Haldane and J. Kemp). London: Kegan Paul, https://www.gutenberg.org/files/38427/38427-h/38427-h.html [Accessed 19/02/2022].
Schopenhauer, Arthur (1957) [1851]. *On Human Nature. Essays Partly Posthumous in Ethics and Politics* (trans. Thomas Bailey Saunders). London: George Allen & Unwind.
Schopenhauer, Arthur (1974) [1851]. *Parerga and Paralipomena: Short Philosophical Essays*, 2 vols. (trans. E.F.J. Payne). Oxford: Clarendon.
Schopenhauer, Arthur (2004) [1851]. *The Essays of Arthur Schopenhauer: The Wisdom of Life* (trans. Thomas Bailey Saunders). Salt Lake City: Project Gutenberg, https://www.gutenberg.org/ebooks/10741 [Accessed 28/10/2022].
Schuster, Aaron (2016). *The Trouble with Pleasure. Deleuze and Psychoanalysis.* Cambridge, MA: MIT.
Sclavi, Marianella (2008). "The Role of Play and Humor in Creative Conflict Management". *Negotiation Journal*, 24(2): 157–180.
Scott, George Riley (1996) [1960]. *History of Corporal Punishment.* London: Senate.
Scott, Tricia (2007). "Expression of Humour by Emergency Personnel Involved in Sudden Deathwork". *Mortality*, 12(4): 350–364.

Screech, Michael A. (2000). *Montaigne and Melancholy. The Wisdom of the* Essays. Lanham: Rowman & Littlefield.
Seabright, Paul (2012). *The War of the Sexes: How Conflict and Cooperation Shaped Men and Women from Prehistory to the Present*. Princeton: Princeton UP.
Seizer, Susan (2011). "On the Uses of Obscenity in Live Stand-Up Comedy". *Anthropological Quarterly*, 84(1): 209–234.
Seneca (1900) [56 AD]. *De clementia* (ed. Carl Hosius), http://www.thelatinlibrary.com/sen/sen.clem.shtml [Accessed 04/01/2022].
Serrano de Barrios, Nathaly (2020). "Tecnologías de Información Libre en la Gestión de las Políticas Públicas". In Yovera Reyes, Mario Jose (Ed.), *Desde la Voz de los Interesados. Políticas Públicas y Educación*, 170–184. San Felipe: UNEY.
Severgnini, Beppe (2021). "La destra, la sinistra e la mancanza di umorismo". *CorriereTV*, https://video.corriere.it/cronaca/fotosintesi-beppe-severgnini/destra-sinistra-mancanza-umorismo/1a0ae58e-1d16-11ec-a854-dd0bdfda3385 [Accessed 04/01/2022].
Shaftesbury (1732) [1709]. "*Sensus communis*, an essay on the freedom of wit and humour in a letter to a friend". In *Characteristics of Men, Manners, Opinions, Times*, 5th ed., 59–150. London: Egbert Sanger, https://babel.hathitrust.org/cgi/pt?id=uc2.ark:/13960/t8nc5vm4x&view=1up&seq=361 [Accessed 01/05/2022].
Shaftesbury (1999) [1711]. "A Letter Concerning Enthusiasm to Lord ****". In *Characteristics of Men, Manners, Opinions, Times*, 4–28. Cambridge: Cambridge UP.
Shapiro, Michael J. (1993). "Eighteenth Century Intimations of Modernity. Adam Smith and the Marquis de Sade". *Political Theory*, 21(2): 273–293.
Sharkey, William F. (1995). "Intentional Embarrassment: The Issue of 'Trust'". Paper presented at the Sixty-Fifth Annual Conference of the Western States Communication Association, Portland, OR.
Sharkey, William F. *et al.* (2001). "Intentional Embarrassment: A Look at Embarrassors' and Targets' Perspectives". *Personality and Individual Differences*, 31(8): 1261–1272.
Shatner, William (2022). "William Shatner: My Trip to Space Filled Me With 'Overwhelming Sadness'". *Variety*, https://variety.com/2022/tv/news/william-shatner-space-boldly-go-excerpt-1235395113/ [Accessed 10/10/2022].
Shaw, Beau (2015). "Nietzsche, Humor and Masochism". *Israeli Journal for Humor Research*, 4(2): 31–50.
Shearmur, Jeremy (1992). "In Defense of Neoliberalism". *Journal of Democracy*, 3(3): 75–81.
Sheridan, Peter (2007). "Mr Spock, Captain Kirk and a Bitter 40-year Battle". *Express*, https://www.express.co.uk/expressyourself/11182/Mr-Spock-Captain-Kirk-and-a-bitter-40-year-battle [Accessed 4/01/2022].
Shestov, Leo (1920) [1905]. *All Things Are Possible* (trans. S.S. Koteliansky). London: Martin Secker, https://www.gutenberg.org/ebooks/57369 [Accessed 19/02/2022].
Shildrick, Tracy (2018). *Poverty Propaganda: Exploring the Myths*. Bristol: Policy.
Shilikhina, Ksenia (2017). "Metapragmatic Markers of the *Bona Fide* and *Non-bona Fide* Modes of Communication". In Chlopicki, Wladyslaw, and Brzozowska, Dorota (Eds.), *Humorous Discourse*, 107–130. Berlin: De Gruyter.
Shipka, Daniel G. (2007). "Perverse Titillation: A History of European Exploitation Films 1960–1980". PhD. University of Florida.
Shklar, Judith (1984). *Ordinary Vices*. Oxford: Belknap.
Shklar, Judith (1989). "The Liberalism of Fear". In Rosenbaum, Nancy (Ed.), *Liberalism and the Moral Life*, 21–38. Cambridge, MA: Harvard UP.

Shook, John R. (2022). Book review of *Pragmatic Realism, Religious Truth, and Antitheodicy* by Sami Pihlström. *SATS*, https://doi.org/10.1515/sats-2022-0011 [Accessed 06/09/2022].
Sibony, Daniel (2009). "Les senses de l'humour". *Le journal des psychologues*, 269(6): 30–35.
Sills, Liz (2020). "The Evolution of the Funny: American Folk Hunmor and Gimbel's Cleverness Theory". In Amir, Lydia (Ed.), *Philosophy of Humor Yearbook*, 1: 73–96. Berlin: De Gruyter.
Silvestri, Paolo and Walraevens, Benoît (2022). "The Wealth of Humans: Core, Periphery and Frontiers of Humanomics". *Journal of Economic Methodology*, doi: 10.1080/1350178X.2022.2160003 [Accessed 13/01/2023].
Simon, Robert L. (1999). "A Review of *Against Liberalism*, by John Kekes". *The Journal of Value Inquiry*, 33: 109–117.
Simpson, E., (Ed.) (2008). *Witnesses to the Scaffold. English Literary Figures as Observers of Public Executions: Pierce Egan, Thackeray, Dickens, Alexander Smith, G.A. Sala, Orwell*. Lambertville: The True Bill.
Simpson, James A. (1998). *The Laugh Shall be First*. Edinburgh: Saint Andrew.
Singer, Marcus G. (2004). "The Concept of Evil". *Philosophy*, 79(308): 185–214.
Skegg, Keren (2005). "Self-Harm". *The Lancet*, 366(9495): 1471–1483.
Skey, Michael (2006). "'Carnivals of Surplus Emotions?' Towards an Understanding of the Significance of Ecstatic Nationalism in a Globalising World". *Studies in Ethnicity and Nationalism*, 6(2): 143–161.
Skúlason, Páll (2006). "Keynote Address: Questions of Technology". In Jónsson, Örn D., and Huijbens, Edward H. (Eds.), *Technology in Society/Society in Technology*, 3–11. Reykjavík: Iceland UP.
Skúlason, Skúli (2022). Intervention at the concluding panel discussion of the conference University for Democracy / Háskóli í þágu lýðræðis, University of Akureyri, Iceland, 11 November 2022, https://eu01web.zoom.us/j/66077913260 [Accessed 11/11/2022].
Skutsch, Carl (Ed.) (2005). *Encyclopedia of the World's Minorities*, 3 vols. New York: Routledge.
Slama, Paul (2022). "Nietzsche's Don Quixote between Zarathustra and Christ: Laughter, Ressentiment, and Transcendental Pain". *Nietzsche-Studien*, 51(1): 218–250.
Slavkova, Iveta (2022). "Camille Bryen Avant-Gardist/Abhumanist: A Reappraisal of an Artist Who Called Himself the 'Best-Known of the Unknown'". *Arts*, 11(2), https://doi.org/10.3390/arts11020043 [Accessed 04/09/2022].
Slucki, David, Finder, Gabriel N., and Patt, Avinoam (Eds.) (2020). *Laughter After: Humour and the Holocaust*. Detroit: Wayne State UP.
Smith, Adam (1904) [1776]. *An Inquiry into the Nature and Causes of the Wealth of Nations*. London: Methuen, https://oll.libertyfund.org/title/smith-an-inquiry-into-the-nature-and-causes-of-the-wealth-of-nations-cannan-ed-in-2-vols [Accessed 19/02/2022].
Smith, Daniel W. (2006). "Axiomatics and Problematics as Two Modes of Formalisation: Deleuze's Epistemology of Mathematics". In Duffy, Simon B. (Ed.), *Virtual Mathematics: The Logic of Difference*, 145–168. Manchester: Clinamen.
Smith, Dennis (2014). "Coping with the Threat of Humiliation: Contrasting Responses to the Eurozone Crisis in Greece and Ireland". In Petropoulos, Nikos, and Tsobanoglou, George O. (Eds.), *The Debt Crisis in the Eurozone: Social Impacts*, 84–108. Newcastle-upon-Tyne: Cambridge Scholars.
Smith, Matthew N. (2017). "Intentions: Past, Present, Future". *Philosophical Explorations. An International Journal for the Philosophy of Mind and Action*, 20(suppl. 2): 1–12.

Smith, Ryan (2022). "Adele's 'I Love Being a Woman' BRIT Awards Speech Sparks Transphobia Debate". *Newsweek*, https://www.newsweek.com/adeles-i-love-being-woman-brit-awards-speech-sparks-transphobia-debate-1677505 [Accessed 29/04/2022].
Smith, Vernon L., and Wilson, Bart J. (2019). *Humanomics. Moral Sentiments and the Wealth of Nations for the Twenty-first Century.* Cambridge: Cambridge UP.
Snelson, Jay Stuart (1993). "The Ideological Immune System: Resistance to New Ideas in Science". *Skeptic*, 1(4): 44–55.
Sover, Arie (2021). *Jewish Humor. An Outcome of Historical Experience, Survival and Wisdom.* Newcastle-upon-Tyne: Cambridge Scholars.
Sover, Arie (Ed.) (2018). *The Languages of Humour: Verbal, Visual, and Physical Humour.* London: Bloomsbury Academic.
Speier, Hans (1941). "The Social Types of War". *American Journal of Sociology*, 46(4): 445–454.
Spink, Kathryn (1997). *Mother Teresa: A Complete Authorized Biography.* San Francisco: Harper.
Spinoza, Baruch (1985) [1677]. *Ethics.* In *The Collected Works* (trans. Edwin Curley), 1: 408–620. Princeton: Princeton UP.
Spivack, Charlotte (2002). "Mirth and Mockery: The Devil's Way". In Hüsken, Wim, Schoell, Konrad and Søndergaard, Leif (Eds.), *Farce and Farcical Elements*, 59–70. Leiden: Brill.
Springer, Simon, and Gahman, Levi (2016). *Fuck Neoliberalism… And Then Some!* London: Active Distribution.
St. Clare, Kameron Johnston (2018). "Linguistic Disarmament: On How Hate Speech Functions, the Way Hate Words Can Be Reclaimed, and Why We Must Pursue Their Reclamation". *Linguistic and Philosophical Investigations*, 17: 79–109.
Stannard, Matthew B. (2004). "Beheading Video Seen as War Tactic". *San Francisco Chronicle*, https://www.sfgate.com/news/article/Beheading-video-seen-as-war-tactic-Experts-say-2759744.php [Accessed 29/04/2022].
Star Trek: Deep Space Nine (1999). "Episode Guide. Episodes 001–176", http://orma.iasfbo.inaf.it:7007/~mauro/TV/PDF/ENDED/STDS9.pdf [Accessed 19/09/2022].
Staub, Ervin (1999). "The Roots of Evil: Social Conditions, Culture, Personality, and Basic Human Needs". *Personality and Social Psychology Review*, 3(3): 179–192.
Stauber, Roni, and Vago, Raphael (Eds.) (2022). *The Roma. A Minority in Europe. Historical, Political and Social Perspectives.* Budapest: Central European UP.
Steele, Brent J. (2021). "A Catharsis for Anxieties: Insights from Goffman on the Politics of Humour". *Global Politics*, 35(1): 102–116.
Steggle, Matthew (2007). *Laughing and Weeping in Early Modern Theatres.* London: Ashgate.
Stein, Edith (1989) [1917]. *On the Problem of Empathy.* In *Collected Works* (trans. Waltraut Stein), vol. 3, 1–119. Washington: Institute of Carmelite Studies.
Stein, Susan I. (2000). "Humor, Hostility and the Psychodynamics of Satire". *Literature and Psychology*, 46(4): 26–41.
Stets, Jan E., and Burke, Peter J. (2000). "Identity Theory and Social Identity Theory". *Social Psychology Quarterly*, 63(3): 224–37.
Stocking, S. H., and Zillmann, D. (1976). "Effects of Humorous Disparagement of Self, Friend, and Enemy". *Psychological Reports*, 39(2): 455–461.
Stoddart, Helen (2000). *Rings of Desire: Circus History and Representation.* Manchester: Manchester UP.
Stoltenberg, John (2021). "Why Human Oppression Happens". *Mother Pelican. A Journal of Solidarity and Sustainability*, 17(1), http://www.pelicanweb.org/solisustv17n01page23.html [Accessed 29/04/2022].

Stoneman, Ethan, and Packer, Joseph (2020). "Reel Cruelty: Voyeurism and Extra-Juridical Punishment in True-Crime Documentaries". *Crime, Media, Culture: An International Journal*, 17(3): 305–326.

Stopes, Marie Carmichael (1920). *Radiant Motherhood. A Book for Those Who are Creating the Future*. London: G.P. Putnam's Sons, https://archive.org/details/radiantmotherhoo00stopuoft [Accessed 01/03/2023].

Storey, Robert (2003). "Humor and Sexual Selection". *Human Nature*, 14(4): 319–336.

Stott, Andrew (2005) [2004]. *Comedy*, 2nd ed. London: Routledge.

Straume, Ingerid, and Baruchello, Giorgio (Eds.) (2013). *Creation, Rationality and Autonomy: Essays on Cornelius Castoriadis*. Aarhus: Nordic Summer UP.

Streeten, Nicola (2020). *UK Feminist Cartoon and Comics. A Critical Survey*. Cham: Palgrave Macmillan.

Struiksma, Marjin E. *et al.* (2022). "Do People Get Used to Insulting Language?" *Frontiers in Communication*, 7, https://doi.org/10.3389/fcomm.2022.910023 [Accessed 16/09/2022].

Sullivan, Corrinne T. (2021). "Pussy Power: A Contemporaneous View of Indigenous Women and Their Role in Sex Work". *Genealogy*, 5(65), https://doi.org/10.3390/genealogy5030065 [Accessed 25/11/2021].

Sustersic, Federica (2015). "Stripping Humanity: Dehumanisation of Victims and Perpetrators in Gross Human Rights Violations Tested in the Bosnian Case". *International Journal on Rule of Law, Transitional Justice and Human Rights*, 6: 177–189.

Sutcliffe, Robert (2019). "'I'm Heartbroken at Losing My Job' for Sharing Billy Connolly Joke, Says Asda Till Worker". *Yorkshire Live*, https://www.examinerlive.co.uk/news/west-yorkshire-news/im-heartbroken-losing-job-sharing-16474726 [Accessed 26/11/2021].

Swabey, Marie Collins (1958). "The Comic as Nonsense, Sadism, or Incongruity". *The Journal of Philosophy*, 55(19): 819–833.

Swabey, Marie Collins (1961). *Comic Laughter: A Philosophical Essay*. New Haven: Yale UP.

Széll, Anita Andrea (2022). "Die kommunikative Funktion von Tiermetaphern als Erzeuger des Humors in den deutschen Übersetzungen einiger Poirot-Romane". *Journal of Languages for Specific Purposes*, 1(9): 139–155.

Tabensky, Pedro Alexis (2009). "Tragic Joyfulness". In Bortolotti, Lisa (Ed.), *Philosophy and Happiness*, 38–53. London: Macmillan.

Tacey, David (2011). "The Challenge of Teaching Jung in the University". In Bulkeley, Kelly, and Weldon, Clodagh (Eds.), *Teaching Jung*, 13–28. Oxford. Oxford UP.

Taels, Johan (2011). "Humour as Practical Wisdom". In Geybels, Hans, and Van Herck, Walter (Eds.), *Humour and Religion: Challenges and Ambiguities*, 22–34. London: Bloomsbury.

Takase, Fumiko (1983–1984). "The Function of Disguise in Ben Jonson's Comedies". *Ronshu*, 30: 1–14.

Tallis, Raymond (2011). *Aping Mankind: Neuromania, Darwinitis and the Misrepresentation of Humanity*. Stocksfield: Acumen.

Taparelli, Luigi (1851). *Saggio teoretico di diritto naturale appoggiato sul fatto*, 2nd ed. Livorno: V. Mansi.

Tapley, Robin (2013). "On Morreall: A Failure to Distinguish Between Play and Humor". *Journal of Value Inquiry*, 47: 147–162.

Tarachow, Sidney (1949). "Remarks on the Comic Process and Beauty". *The Psychoanalytic Quarterly*, 18(2): 215–226.

Taras, Raymond (2015). "Hurricanes as Mediatized Disasters: Latin American Framing of the US Response to Katrina". *The Minnesota Review*, 84: 69–82.

Taylor, Alfred Edward (1932). *The Faith of a Moralist*. London: Macmillan, https://www.giffordlectures.org/lecturers/alfred-edward-taylor [Accessed 03/03/2022].

Taylor, Charles (2017). "Converging Roads Around Dilemmas of Modernity". In Lowney II, Charles W. (Ed.), *Charles Taylor, Michael Polanyi and the Critique of Modernity. Pluralist and Emergentist Directions*, 15–26. Cham: Palgrave Macmillan.

Téllez, Freddy, and Rosset, Clément (1999). "Díalogo con Clément Rosset". *Ideas y Valores*, 110: 127–132.

Tennyson, Lord Alfred (1850). *In Memoriam*. London: Edward Moxon, https://archive.org/details/inmemoriam00tennrich/page/n13/mode/2up?q=types [Accessed 02/11/2022].

Tettamanzi, Andrea G.B., and da Costa Pereira, Célia (2014). "Testing Carlo Cipolla's Laws of Human Stupidity with Agent-Based Modelling". *HAL Archives ouvertes*, https://hal.archives-ouvertes.fr/hal-01085988 [Accessed 26/11/2021].

Thai, Michael, Borgella, Alex M. and Sanchez, Melanie S. (2019). "It's Only Funny if We Say it: Disparagement Humor is Better Received If It Originates from a Member of the Group Being Disparaged". *Journal of Experimental Social Psychology*, 85(103838): 1–10.

Thatcher, David S. (2016). "Eagle and Serpent in Zarathustra". *Nietzsche-Studien*, 6(1): 240–260.

Thomas, Leah, and Egan, Vincent (2022). "Subclinical Sadism: Examining Temperamental Predispositions and Emotional Processing". *Personality and Individual Differences*, 196, https://doi.org/10.1016/j.paid.2022.111756 [Accessed 15/12/2022].

Times Leader (2015). "'Ben & Cherry's' Porn Movie Withdrawn after Suit". https://www.timesleader.com/archive/46807/stories-27ben-26amp3b-cherry27s27-porn-movie-withdrawn-after-suit204193 [Accessed 26/11/2021].

Todaro, Joseph, and Miller, J. Mitchell (2014). "Beccaria, Cesare". In Miller, J. Mitchell (Ed.), *The Encyclopedia of Theoretical Criminology*, 1: 43–45. Chichester: Wiley Blackwell.

Tofighian, Omid *et al.* (2022). "Performances as Intersectional Resistance: Power, Polyphony and Process of Abolition". *Humanities*, 11(1), https://doi.org/10.3390/h11010028 [Accessed 04/09/2022].

Tolstoy, Lev N. (1900). *The Slavery of Our Time* (trans. Aylmer Maude). Maldon: Free Age, https://ia904509.us.archive.org/11/items/slaveryourtimes00tolsiala/slaveryourtimes00tolsiala.pdf [Accessed 11/06/2022].

Tosun, Sümeyra, Faghihi, Nafiseh, and Vaid, Jyotsna (2018). "Is an Ideal Sense of Humor Gendered? A Cross-National Study". *Frontiers in Psychology*, 9, article 199, DOI: 10.3389/fpsyg.2018.00199 [Accessed 13/12/2022].

Tourneur, N. (1927). "The Palio at Siena". *The Irish Monthly*, 55(654): 659–662.

Trahair, Lisa (2005). "Figural Vision: Freud, Lyotard and Early Cinematic Comedy". *Screen*, 46(2): 175–193.

Trimbull, Robert (2018). "Freud Beyond Foucault: Thinking Pleasure as a Site of Resistance". *Journal of Speculative Philosophy*, 32(3): 522–532.

Trindade, Luiz Valério P. (2020). "Disparagement Humour and Gendered Racism on Social Media in Brazil". *Ethnic and Racial Studies*, 43(15): 2766–2784.

Tripković, Boško (2018). *The Metaethics of Constitutional Adjudication*. Oxford: Oxford UP.

Tritle, Lawrence (2015). "Laughter in Battle". In Heckel, Waldemar, Müller, Sabine and Wrightson, Graham (Eds.), *The Many Faces of War in the Ancient World*, 117–134. Newcastle-upon-Tyne: Cambridge Scholars Publishing.

Trivers, Robert (2000). "The Elements of a Scientific Theory of Self-Deception". *Annals of the New York Academy of Sciences*, 907(1): 114–131.

Troncon, Renato (2017). "Dentro lo Humor: Lo spazio cognitivo del comico". *I castelli di Yale online*, 5(2): 339–365.

Turvey, Malcom (2021). "Jacques Tati and the Philosophy of the Sight Gag". In Amir, Lydia (Ed.), *Philosophy of Humor Yearbook*, 2: 27–44. Berlin: De Gruyter.

Twain, Mark (1894). *The Tragedy of Pudd'nhead Wilson*. Hartford, CT: American Publishing, https://archive.org/details/tragedypuddnhea00twaigoog [Accessed 01/03/2023].

Twain, Mark (1924). *Mark Twain's Autobiography*. New York: Harper & Bros, https://gutenberg.net.au/ebooks02/0200561h.html [Accessed 29/04/2022].

Ujhelyi, Adrienn, Almosdi, Flora, and Fodor, Alexandra (2022). "Would You Pass the Turing Test? Influencing Factors of the Turing Decision". *Psychological Topics*, 31(1): 185–202.

United Nations Department of Peacekeeping Operations (2010). "Review of the Sexual Violence Elements of the Judgments of the International Criminal Tribunal for the Former Yugoslavia, the International Criminal Tribunal for Rwanda, and the Special Court for Sierra Leone in the Light of Security Council Resolution 1820". New York: United Nations.

Utz, Arthur F. (1994). *Wirtschaftsethik*. Bonn: Scientia humana institut.

Vaihingen, Hans (1935) [1916]. *The Philosophy of 'As If'. A System of the Theoretical, Practical and Religious Fictions of Mankind* (trans. C.K. Ogden), 2nd ed. London: Kegan Paul, Trench, Trubner.

Vajda, Zoltán (2009). "Limited Expectations: Thomas Jefferson on the Moral Sentiments of Blacks and Race Relations". In Vajda, Zoltán (Ed.), *Within and Without Culture. Essays in Honor of Bálint Rozsnyai*, 277–286. Szeged: Jate.

Van Campen, Crétien (1997), "Early Abstract Art and Experimental Gestalt Psychology". *Leonardo*, 30(2): 133–136.

Van Lunteren, Frans, and Hollestelle, Marijn J. (2013). "Paul Ehrenfest and the Dilemmas of Modernity". *Isis*, 104: 504–536.

Van Overveldt, Lotus (2020). "Wonka, Witches, and Wormy Spaghetti. Transgressive Humour in Roald Dahl's Novels for Children". MA. Radboud University.

Vasey, George (1877) [1874]. *The Philosophy of Laughter and Smiling*, 2nd ed. London: J. Burns, https://books.google.is/books?id=g6jnKnyyJS0C&printsec=frontcover&redir_esc=y#v=onepage&q&f=false [Accessed 13/07/2023].

Veblen, Thorstein (1899). "The Preconception of Economic Science". *Quarterly Journal of Economics*, 13: 121–150.

Veblen, Thorstein (1904). *The Theory of Business Enterprise*. New York: Charles Scribner.

Veblen, Thorstein (1918) [1914]. *The Instinct of Workmanship and the State of the Industrial Arts*. New York: Huebsch, https://archive.org/details/cu31924055828622 [Accessed 01/03/2023].

Veblen, Thorstein (1924) [1899]. *The Theory of the Leisure Class; An Economic Study of Institutions*. London: George Allen & Unwin, https://archive.org/details/in.ernet.dli.2015.59315 [Accessed 01/07/2022].

Vélez, Iván (2020). *Torquemada. El gran inquisidor*. Madrid: La esfera.

Veneziano, Fabrizio (2008). "'These Wasps Behave Just Like Those Men Who...': Irony and Optimism in Baroncelli's Writings". *Nordicum-Mediterraneum. Icelandic E-journal of Nordic and Mediterranean Studies*, 3(1), https://skemman.is/bitstream/1946/1542/3/Veneziano.pdf [Accessed 29/04/2022].

Verberckmoes, Johan (1999). *Laughter, Jestbooks and Society in the Spanish Netherlands*. London: Palgrave Macmillan.

Verga, Giovanni (1881) [1880]. "La Lupa". In *Vita dei campi*, 141–152. Milan: Treves.

Veterinaria Italiana (2012). "*In memoriam*. Stuart Kenneth Hargreaves, DVM, 1946–2012", 48(3): 341–343.
Vickery, Kenneth P. (1974). "'Herrenvolk' Democracy and Egalitarianism in South Africa and the U.S. South". *Comparative Studies in Society and History*, 16(3): 309–328.
Vico, Giambattista (1948) [1744]. *The New Science*, (trans. Thomas Goddard Bergin and Max Harold Fisch). Ithaca: Cornell UP.
Villaggio, Paolo (2018) [1975]. "Intervista inedita alla televisione svizzera", https://www.youtube.com/watch?v=sv8oiLC4hSs&ab_channel=884C25 [Accessed 24/10/2022].
Voltaire (1912) [1755]. *On Toleration and Other Essays* (trans. Joseph McCabe). New York: G.P. Putnam's Sons.
Voltaire (1918) [1759]. *Candide* (trans. Philip Littell). New York: Boni & Liverlight, https://www.gutenberg.org/files/19942/19942-h/19942-h.htm [Accessed 19/02/2022].
Voltaire (1994) [1733]. *Letters concerning the English Nation.* London: Penguin.
Von Kraft-Ebing, Richard (1892) [1886]. *Psychopathia Sexualis* (trans. Charles G. Chaddock). London: F.A. Davis.
Von Manen, Max (2016) [2014]. *Phenomenology of Practice. Meaning-Giving Methods in Phenomenological Research and Writing.* London: Routledge.
Von Mises, Ludwig (1960) [1933]. *Epistemological Problems in Economics.* Princeton: D. Van Nostrand.
Von Mises, Ludwig (1998) [1949]. *Human Action. A Treatise on Economics*, 4th ed. Auburn, AL: Mises Institute.
Von Sacher-Masoch, Leopold (1989) [1870]. *Venus in Furs.* In Deleuze, Gilles, *Masochism*, 143–271. New York: Zone Books.
Vosmer, Susanne (2022). "The Matrices of Black Humor and Death". *The Israeli Journal of Humor Research*, 11(2): 6–28.
Voss, Georgina (2012). "'Treating It as a Normal Business': Researching the Pornography Industry". *Sexualities*, 15(3–4): 391–410.
Voss, Georgina (2015). *Stigma and the Shaping of the Pornography Industry.* London: Routledge.
Wallace, J.D. (1976). "Pulling the Plug: Who Decides?" *Canadian Medical Association Journal*, 114(1): 57.
Waller, William, and Robertson, Linda R. (1990). "Why Johnny (Ph.D., Economics) Can't Read: A Rhetorical Analysis of Thorstein Veblen and a Response to Donald McCloskey's *Rhetoric of Economics*". *Journal of Economic Issues*, 24(4): 1027–1044.
Walsh, David (2020). *The Priority of the Person: Political, Philosophical, and Historical Discoveries.* Notre Dame: Notre Dame UP.
Waterman, Stanley (1998). "Carnivals for Elites? The Cultural Politics of Arts Festivals". *Progress in Human Geography*, 22(1): 54–74.
Watkins, Devin (2020). "Pope at Angelus: Gossip 'A Plague More Awful than Covid-19'". *Vatican News*, https://www.vaticannews.va/en/pope/news/2020-09/pope-francis-angelus-fraternal-correction-healthy-habit.html [Accessed 29/04/2022].
Watt Smith, Tiffany (2018). *Schadenfreude: The Joy of Another's Misfortune.* London: Profile Books.
Weaver, Simon (2011). "Liquid Racism and the Ambiguity of Ali G". *European Journal of Cultural Studies*, 14(3): 249–264.
Weber, Karl J. (1840) [1838]. *Demokrit oder hinterlassene Papiere.* Leipzig: Phillip Reclam.
Weber, Luigi (2021). "La guerra sadica e la guerra dinamica di F.T. Marinetti tra '8 anime in una bomba' e 'L'alcova d'acciaio'". *Finzioni*, 1(2): 69–82.
Weems, Scott (2014). *Ha! The Science of When We Laugh and Why.* New York: Basic Books.

Weidenbaum, Jonathan (2020). "To Laugh in a Pluralistic Universe: William James and the Philosophy of Humor". In Amir, Lyida (Ed.), *Philosophy of Humor Yearbook*, 1: 117–133. Berlin: De Gruyter.

Welch, Michael (2022). *The Bastille Effect. Transforming Sites of Political Imprisonment*. Oakland: University of California.

Westbrook, Vivienne, and Chao, Shun-liang (Eds.) (2020). *Humour in the Arts: New Perspectives*. London: Routledge.

Westerink, Herman (2012). *The Heart of Man's Destiny: Lacanian Psychoanalysis and Early Reformation Thought*. London: Routledge.

Wicks, Robert (2008). "Nietzsche's 'Yes' to Life and the Apollonian Neutrality of Existence". *Nietzsche-Studien*, 34(1): 100–123.

Wiedemann, Thomas (2005) [1981]. *Greek and Roman Slavery*. London: Routledge.

Wilde, Oscar (1894). "The Sphinx". *The Victorian Web*, https://victorianweb.org/authors/wilde/sphinx.html [Accessed 12/12/2022].

Wilde, Oscar (1913) [1905]. *De Profundis*. London: Methuen, https://www.gutenberg.org/files/921/921-h/921-h.htm [Accessed 23/09/2022].

Wilde, Oscar (1994) [1890]. *The Picture of Dorian Gray*. Salt Lake City: Project Gutenberg Literary Archive Foundation, https://www.gutenberg.org/files/174/174-h/174-h.htm [Accessed 15/12/2022].

Wilde, Oscar (1995) [1895]. *The Illustrated Letters of Oscar Wilde* (ed. Juliet Gardiner). London: Batsford.

Wildemeersch, Marc (2013). *George Orwell's Commander in Spain: The Enigma of Georges Kopp*. London: Thames River.

Wilke, Sabine, and Cox, Geoffrey (1999). "The Sexual Woman and Her Struggle for Subjectivity: Cruel Women in Sade, Sacher-Masoch, and Treut". In *Women in German Yearbook: Feminist Studies in German Literature and Culture*, 14, 245–260.

Williams, Bernard (1981). *Moral Luck*. Cambridge: Cambridge UP.

Willinger, Ulrike et al. (2017). "Cognitive and Emotional Demands of Black Humour Processing: The Role of Intelligence, Aggressiveness and Mood". *Cognitive Processing*, 18: 159–167.

Wills, Thomas Ashby (1981). "Downward Comparison Principles in Social Psychology". *Psychological Bulletin*, 90(2): 245–271.

Wilson, Glenn D., and Cox, David N. (1983). "Personality of Paedophile Club Members". *Personality and Individual Differences*, 4(3): 323–329.

Wilson, Jacqueline Z. et al. (Eds.) (2017). *The Palgrave Handbook of Prison Tourism*. London: Palgrave Macmillan.

Winskill, P.T. (1892). *The Temperance Movement and Its Workers. A Record of Social, Moral, Religious, and Political Progress*, 2 vols. London: Blackie & Son.

Wittgenstein, Ludwig (1953). *Philosophical Investigations* (trans. G.E.M. Anscombe). London: Macmillan.

Wittgenstein, Ludwig (1989) [1921]. *Tractatus logico-philosophicus*. Milan: Einaudi.

Wolfers, Solvejg, File, Kieran A. and Schnurr, Stephanie (2017). "'Just Because He's Black': Identity Construction and Racial Humour in a German U-19 Football Team". *Journal of Pragmatics*, 112: 83–96.

Wollstonecraft, Mary (1988) [1792]. *A Vindication of the Rights of Woman*. New York: Norton.

Woodard, Roger (Ed.) (2009). *The Cambridge Companion to Greek Mythology*. Cambridge: Cambridge UP.

World Health Organization (2014). *Global Status Report on Violence Prevention 2014*. Geneva: WHO.

Wray, Matt, and Newitz, Annalee (Eds.) (1997). *White Trash. Race and Class in America.* New York: Routledge.
Wright, Drew M. (2017). "The Impossible Thought of Georges Bataille: A Consciousness That Laughs and Cries". MA. Georgia State University.
Wright, Lawrence (2008). "Ecological Thinking: Schopenhauer, J.M. Coetzee and Who We Are in the World". In Wyljie, Dan (Ed.), *Toxic Beginning? Identity and Ecology in Southern Africa*, 24–42. Newcastle-upon-Tyne: Cambridge Scholars.
Yamane, Hiroaki, Mori, Yusuke and Harada, Tatsuya (2021). "Humor Meets Morality: Joke Generation Based on Moral Judgement". *Information Processing and Management*, 58: 1–15.
Yu, Xiaoyang (2020). "Our Universe Is a Superdeterministic State Machine Built of Elementary Particles; Strong Electric Currents in the Human Neural Network Cause the Illusion of Free Will". *OSF Preprints*, doi:10.31219/osf.io/xh4r9 [Accessed 12/10/2022].
Zagaria, Andrea, Andò, Agata and Zennaro, Alessandro (2020). "Psychology: A Giant with Feet of Clay". *Integrative Psychological and Behavioral Science*, 54: 521–562.
Zahedi, Ramin (2015). "On Digital Philosophy (Discrete Physics) and the Cellular Automaton: A Prefect Mathematical Deterministic Structure for Reality–As a Huge Computer Simulation". *Citeseer*, arXiv:1501.01373v2 [Accessed 12/10/2022].
Zeigler-Hill, Virgil, and Marcus, David K. (Eds.) (2016). *The Dark Side of Personality. Science and Practice in Social, Personality, and Clinical Psychology.* Washington: American Psychological Association.
Zimbaldi, Diane (2012). "The Frida Kahlo Self-Portraits: The Objectification of Self as a Symbol and Statement". MA. Montclair State University.
Žižek, Slavoj (2012). "On the Desert of Post-ideology". *TIFF Originals*, https://www.youtube.com/watch?v=kugiufHh800 [Accessed 03/05/2022].
Žmolek, Michael Andrew (2019). "The Dark World of Reverend Malthus". *Proceedings of the European Studies Conference*. Omaha: University of Nebraska, https://www.unomaha.edu/college-of-arts-and-sciences/european-studies-conference/esc-proceedings/index.php#zeronineteen [Accessed 21/02/2022].

Index

Abraham 85, 86
absurd 26f., 45, 49, 62, 77, 84, 85f., 171f., 277, 304, 305, 358, 375, 388, 391
Addison, Joseph 12, 45, 48f., 50, 67f., 74f., 165f., 239, 247, 293, 375, 386
aggression, aggressiveness 5f., 13, 15f., 46f., 47f., 52, 58, 59, 61, 65, 70–72, 77, 84f., 91, 92, 99, 109f., 110, 126, 130f., 138f., 143, 165, 184f., 185f., 188, 192, 203, 207–209, 216, 272, 277f., 278, 281, 282, 289, 305, 314, 318, 327, 330, 331, 334, 341, 343–345, 347, 348, 350, 364, 367, 370f., 375–382, 385, 398, 399, 402, 406, 408, 418, 430
Ainslie, George 139, 141, 143, 155, 382
Amir, Lydia 28, 29f., 38f., 66f., 137f., 152f., 154f., 169, 170f., 181f., 184f., 201, 219–221, 238, 240f., 244f., 268–283, 285–288, 293f., 296, 298, 299f., 334, 382, 392, 393f., 395f., 398, 399f., 402–404, 411, 422f.
anaesthesia of the heart 66, 71, 204–207, 209, 210, 213–216, 218, 219, 227, 233, 355, 382, 387, 415
anger 74, 143, 147, 152, 205, 212f., 238, 264
anthropology, anthropologist 14f., 15f., 56, 81f., 119f., 125, 129f., 130f., 173f., 224f., 229f., 258, 363, 378f., 385
Aquinas, Thomas 33, 37, 95–97, 99, 129f., 138f., 144, 170f., 266f., 409
Aristophanes 68
Aristotle 3, 37, 57, 181f., 266f.
Arnarsson, Ársæll 90f., 91f., 149f., 309f.
Artaud, Antonin 114–116
asceticism 288

Bakhtin, Mikhail 42f., 178f., 179f., 203f., 216, 402f., 425f.
Baroncelli, Flavio 29, 43f., 173f., 186, 187f., 214f., 215, 222–224, 228, 230–232, 241f., 257, 326f., 335, 363f., 366f., 396, 409f., 417, 418f., 426
Barthes, Roland 206f., 246f.
Baruchello 19f., 20f., 39f., 46f., 150f., 168f., 220f., 236f.

Bataille, Georges 116f., 123f., 170, 184f., 223, 246f., 279–281
Beattie, James 44, 45, 48f., 74f., 164f., 204, 386, 387, 400f.
Beccaria, Cesare 98, 99, 110f., 117
Benign Violation Theory 57f., 202f., 323–326, 368, 413f.Berger, Peter 84
Bergson, Henri 38, 49f., 52, 53, 65–67, 70, 71, 73, 74, 78–81, 84, 173, 204–207, 227, 237, 238, 304, 311, 349, 355, 356, 375, 381, 382, 387, 413f., 415
Bierce, Ambrose 172f.
Billig, Michael 57f., 166f., 201f., 311f., 399f.
Bruno, Giordano 162f., 190f.
bullying 58, 90–94, 109, 131, 310, 330, 331, 356, 376, 379, 380, 384, 423

carnival, carnivalesque 42, 147, 157, 178–180, 203, 216, 229, 234f., 262, 379, 425, 426, 428, 430
Carroll, Lewis, 209, 226f., 387f., 388f,.401
Carroll, Noël 60, 164,
Cassirer, Ernst 22f., 33, 79f., 179f., 266f., 386, 393f., 428f.
Cervantes, Miguel de 68, 237f., 273
Chesterton, Gilbert K. 4f., 12f., 29, 38, 61f., 81f., 104, 121f., 154, 155f., 190, 192f., 208, 233f., 240f., 241f., 243–245, 247, 255f., 286f., 38, 401
Cioran, Emil 114, 231, 267f., 268f.
Collins, Randall 157f.
Commedia dell'Arte 172
Congreve, William 38, 44
Critchley, Simon 12f., 76f., 175f., 278f., 369f.

Darwin, Charles 6, 15f., 63–67, 70, 88, 92, 96f., 119f., 120f., 122, 174, 183, 209, 220f., 244f., 245f., 287, 418f., 429
Deleuze, Gilles 4f., 31f., 32f., 78–86, 151f., 229f., 233f., 234f., 281f., 335, 339f., 344f., 379, 380, 383, 387–390, 393f.
Democritus 181f.
Dennett, Daniel 181f., 275f.

denotation 78, 79f., 80, 81
Descartes, René 14, 15, 16f., 37, 123f.
Dickens, Charles 172f., 208
Diderot, Denis 158
Don Quixote 48, 68, 208, 237f.
Dostoyevsky, Fyodor 42f., 90, 119f., 123f., 141–143, 146, 147, 172f., 241, 268, 282f., 288f.

Eagleton, Terry 55f., 60, 403
Eco, Umberto 12f., 30, 86f., 227f., 294f.
ego 70, 75, 76, 85, 107, 140, 142, 151, 154, 175f., 228, 229, 262, 265, 284, 312, 314, 316, 385, 397f., 420f.
Esar, Evan 38, 157f., 208f., 284f., 392
existentialism 19f., 70, 114, 148f., 230, 268f., 270f., 273, 277–282, 287, 288, 290, 293, 388–390, 398, 403, 406f., 411

fanaticism 125, 127, 129f., 189
Figueroa-Dorrego, Jorge 38f., 44f., 47f., 51f.
Foucault, Michel 84f.
Freud, Sigmund 6–8, 26f., 49, 57, 61, 70–78, 81, 84, 96f., 120, 140f., 144, 154f., 164, 165, 173f., 175f., 178, 180, 193f., 216, 219, 223, 227, 256, 259, 263, 264, 266, 272, 305, 315–318, 338, 339, 343, 345, 380, 383f., 385, 389, 402f., 414, 415f., 420f., 424

Galbraith, John Kenneth 14f., 23f., 149f., 196f., 221f., 418f., 420f.
Galen, Aelius 26f., 37f., 39, 40, 41, 146, 288
gender 47f., 57, 71, 84f., 91, 92, 162f., 177f., 201, 212f., 255, 263, 302f., 307, 308, 309, 318, 322, 323, 326, 330, 333, 334, 341, 343–346, 350, 351, 355, 360, 363, 364, 381, 422
genocide 104, 130f., 133, 174, 406
Gruner, Charles 157f., 204, 205f., 419f.
Guattari, Félix 31f., 78, 229f., 389f., 393f.

Hallie, Philip P. 9f., 10f., 90f., 107–112, 125, 132, 134–137, 155–157, 169, 171f., 181f., 186–189, 193, 197, 200f., 210, 216f., 222, 239, 249f., 252, 258, 260, 279, 296f., 303, 313f., 368, 370, 373, 383, 386, 391, 393, 394, 410f., 419f., 423f.

Harlow, Harry 37, 53, 57, 58, 157, 301f., 312–321, 339, 381, 388, 405, 414, 427
Hartley, David 48f., 247f., 414f., 417f.
Harvey, Jean 13f., 28f., 46, 47f., 122f., 166f., 168f., 169, 173, 176, 177f., 194f., 198–201, 220f., 224–226, 233, 239f., 252, 253, 255f., 258, 291–293, 299, 303, 311f., 336, 341, 356, 362, 375, 379, 396, 405, 413f., 415f., 422
Hazlitt, William 44–46, 48–50, 52, 74f., 131f., 184f., 204, 219, 232f., 239, 281, 293, 294, 324, 386, 387, 392, 404, 405
Hegel, Georg W.F. 15f., 110, 273, 276f., 278f.
Hippocrates 39, 40, 146
Hitler, Adolf 109f., 125, 127, 129, 130
Hobbes, Thomas 15f., 37, 57, 99, 131, 375
Hugo, Victor 37, 238f.
Hume, David 99, 179f., 257, 282, 382f., 387f., 423
Hutcheson, Francis 96–98, 117, 179f.

incongruity theory 47, 48, 56, 59, 60, 62, 63f., 68, 76, 84, 89, 96, 207, 209, 239, 244f., 263, 266, 273f.,278f., 298f., 304, 311, 316, 403f., 406f.
irony 5f., 7, 15f., 18, 21, 23f., 24, 28f., 34f., 37f., 42, 45f., 50, 52, 57f., 68, 69, 85, 95f., 109f., 144, 147, 171f., 174f., 181, 188, 194, 195, 199, 215, 236, 237f., 273, 274, 277f. 283–289, 338f., 348f., 350, 370, 386, 390–393, 398f., 401f., 421f., 423, 430

Jews, Jewish 13f., 31, 57, 75f., 109, 124f., 126, 192, 195f., 221f., 258, 260f., 304, 319, 339, 363, 388
Jonson, Ben 41, 270f.
Jung, Carl Gustav 7f., 9f., 22f., 26f., 28, 33, 40f., 49f., 80f., 96f., 102f., 107f., 114, 123, 139–144, 154, 164, 196f., 197, 218, 228–230, 232, 242, 279., 289f., 298, 333, 338, 372f., 383, 386f., 397f.

Kant, Immanuel 33, 37, 43f., 76f., 124f., 181f., 216f., 286
Kekes, John 25, 104, 105, 370, 419
Kierkegaard, Søren 12f., 15f., 26f., 38, 123f., 272, 280, 281f., 389, 423f.

Koestler, Arthur   76–78, 88, 323, 327, 386
Kozintsev, Alexander   25, 78, 81–84, 146, 147, 194f., 240f., 265f., 283, 284f., 293f., 299, 335, 372, 374–378, 388–390

Larkin-Galiñanes, Christina   38f., 44f., 47f., 51f., 57f., 76f.
Leacock, Stephen   12, 29, 38, 74, 100f., 167, 168, 181, 183, 184, 193f., 197f., 208f., 223, 242, 243f., 277f., 292, 384, 390, 399–402, 406
Lecky, William E.H.   101, 102, 130, 157
Leibniz, Gottfried Wilhelm   80f.
Leopardi, Giacomo   116f., 178f., 220f., 283, 284, 290, 398f.
libido   71, 72, 130f., 143, 144, 153f., 172, 260f., 315, 359, 415f.
Locke, John   42, 97, 144, 359f.
Lucretius, Titus   33, 170, 299

Machiavelli, Niccolò   112, 113, 120, 158, 226f., 258
masochism   21f., 34f., 35, 73f., 84–86, 99, 103, 111, 128f., 143, 151, 180, 220f., 228, 270, 310f., 331, 333, 3399f., 344f., 379, 380, 384, 389, 394, 395, 430
McDougall, William   61f., 234f., 289f.
McMurtry, John   6f., 15f., 85f., 127f., 167f., 184f., 227f., 291f., 414f.
melancholia, melancholy   13, 50, 68, 212f., 274, 276, 297, 390
Milgram, Stanley   10
Mill, John Stuart   15f., 195f., 417.
Montaigne, Michel de   14f., 26, 33, 95–98, 101, 104, 109, 116f., 117f., 120f., 129f., 138f., 139, 144, 158, 160f., 181f., 223, 230, 274, 281–283, 294
Monty Python   22, 281, 4007f.
Morreall, John   30, 37, 38f., 57, 59f., 82f., 169, 197f., 270–272, 275–279, 283, 286, 288f., 292–294, 296, 299f., 301, 382, 392, 398f., 402–404, 411, 422f., 425
Mother Nature   121, 133, 154

narcissism   75, 80f., 142, 158, 350f.
Nell, Victor   134, 137–138, 155, 157f., 161
Nero, Claudius   94, 99, 109f., 202

neurosis, neurotic   14f., 73, 96f., 140f., 227f., 264, 424
Nietzsche, Friedrich   6f., 15f., 33, 96f., 120–124, 128, 137, 141, 155., 156, 164, 165f., 178f., 181f., 184f., 185, 214, 219, 237f., 274, 280f., 281f., 284–289, 295, 296, 298, 396f., 412f.
Noonan, Jeff   19f., 153f., 227f.

Orwell, George   407
othering, the Other   413

Pareto, Vilfredo   2f., 14f., 33, 145f., 186f., 189f., 190f., 393f., 419f., 420f.
Pascal, Blaise   33, 81, 123f., 281f., 287f.
phenomenology   4f., 12f., 24, 60f., 195, 196f., 234f., 297, 374f.
Phillips, Anita   119f., 141f., 161f., 220f., 227f., 394–396
Pirandello, Luigi   12, 29, 38, 46f., 67–70, 74f., 81, 168, 169, 208f., 237–240, 250f., 252f., 267, 273, 274f., 276, 278f., 286f., 306, 383, 384, 386, 387, 390, 421f., 423f.
Plato   9, 26f., 33, 37, 57, 181, 224, 229f., 285, 374, 393f., 402f.
Polanyi, Michael   4f., 6f., 7f., 12f., 13f., 19f., 24–27, 33f., 56f., 62f., 78f., 87, 123–127, 129, 132f., 146f., 150f., 169f., 196f., 197f., 225f., 226f., 232f., 234–236, 242f., 243f., 245f., 246f., 249, 250, 252, 256f., 266f., 300, 360, 372f., 373f., 374f., 388, 389f., 401f., 407f., 412f., 417f., 424f.
polysemy   1f., 11f., 24, 52f., 67, 87, 114f., 132, 150f. 153f., 187f.
predation   137
psychoanalysis   6f., 7f., 76, 78, 96f., 111f., 154f., 187f.
Puritanism, Puritan   145f., 288, 293, 294, 407, 408, 414f., 425–427, 429, 430

Rand, Ayn   96f., 119, 129f., 295, 296
Raskin, Victor   47f., 86–88
Rawls, John   15f., 275
Regan, Tom   105–107, 109, 134, 157f., 169, 194, 202, 210, 239, 313f., 415f.

484 — Index

relief theory 14f., 56, 61–65, 74, 89, 146, 147, 234f., 259, 280, 293f., 305, 311, 312, 333, 370, 384

Renaissance 40, 57, 113f., 179f., 293f., 317, 342, 416f.

rhetoric 14f., 22f., 32f., 43, 52f., 68, 69, 79f., 145, 204–206, 215f., 217f., 223, 246, 255, 257, 347, 364f., 381, 392f., 393, 413, 418f.

Rorty, Richard 7f., 12f., 102–105, 132, 213f., 269f., 270f., 275, 398, 419

Rosset, Clément 113–115, 148f., 269f., 281f., 288f., 290, 299f., 396f., 398, 403

Rousseau, Jean-Jacques 15f., 124

Russell, Bertrand 136f., 185f., 232

Sade, Marquis de 15f., 26, 96f., 99f., 115–119, 121, 122, 129f., 137, 141, 156, 158f., 182, 185, 214, 268f., 286, 290, 424

sadism 26f., 71f., 84, 98, 99, 113, 115, 116, 117f., 136, 152, 157f., 158f., 162f., 180, 182, 185, 186, 188, 194, 195, 202, 207–211, 239, 296, 313, 376f., 392, 405, 409f.

Santayana, George 45, 46, 74f., 114, 204, 207, 219f., 239, 267, 384–387, 392f., 405

satirical 46, 69

Schadenfreude 82, 170, 375

Schopenhauer, Arthur 12, 15f., 22f., 23, 47–51, 59, 74f., 89, 113, 117f., 121f., 131f., 162f., 168, 219, 237–240, 285f., 286f., 290, 298, 318, 324, 345, 382–384, 386, 390, 392f., 398f., 405, 414

Seneca, Lucius 23, 26, 94–97, 99, 117f., 128f., 138f., 139, 144, 158, 181f., 333, 380, 385, 398, 409

Shaftesbury, Anthony 42, 43, 48, 51, 61, 66f., 116, 179, 181f., 216, 218, 234f., 266f., 381, 386, 393f., 397, 419f., 424

Shakespeare, William 238, 239, 331

Shklar, Judith 93f., 94, 101–104, 132, 134, 157f., 418f.

Skegg, Keren 135–136Smith, Adam 14f., 15f., 33, 110, 189f., 226f., 230f., 295f.

Socrates 9, 68, 233f.

Spectator 45f., 67f., 247

Spencer, Herbert 6, 61, 244f.

Spinoza, Baruch 15f., 80f., 300f.

Staub, Ervin 133–136

superiority theory 56, 57, 62, 89, 157f., 166, 197, 198, 205, 206f., 209, 222, 239, 240, 245f., 266, 273f., 276f., 304, 312, 320, 331, 358f., 375, 379, 405, 418, 419

tacit knowing, tacit knowledge 78f., 246f., 249, 417f., 424f., 430f.

theatre 22f., 54, 68, 114, 116, 158f., 177, 179, 212f., 226f., 246f., 268, 298, 299

tickling 66, 209, 278, 323, 324

Tolstoy, Lev 15f., 162f.

true humour 12, 45f., 50, 51, 67–69, 74f., 88, 164f., 169, 181, 201f., 208f., 228f., 237–240, 243, 250f., 263, 267, 275f.,276, 285, 291, 295, 369f., 382f., 383, 384, 390, 394, 400, 402, 405, 406

Veblen, Thorstein 14f., 21f., 29, 123f., 128f., 159, 254f., 420, 423f.

Vico, Giambattista 15f., 22f., 33, 123f.

Voltaire 37, 123, 125, 213f., 392

von Sacher-Masoch, Leopold 99f., 380

Wittgenstein, Ludwig 3f., 11f., 15f., 33, 149, 267f., 268f., 296

www.ingramcontent.com/pod-product-compliance
Lightning Source LLC
Chambersburg PA
CBHW061923220426
43662CB00012B/1784